Second Edition

■

The
Psychology
of
Aging

Theory, Research, and Interventions

Second Edition

■

The Psychology of Aging

Theory, Research, and Interventions

Janet K. Belsky

Brooks/Cole Publishing Company
Pacific Grove, California

For David and Thomas

Brooks/Cole Publishing Company
A Division of Wadsworth, Inc.

Printed in the United States of America
10   9   8   7   6   5   4   3   2   1

Library of Congress Cataloging-in-Publication Data

Belsky, Janet, [date]
    The psychology of aging : theory, research, and interventions / Janet K.
Belsky. — 2nd ed.
        p.   cm.
    Includes bibliographies and index.
    ISBN 0-534-12114-4
    1. Aging—Psychological aspects.   2. Aged—Psychology.   3. Aged–
–Mental health services.   I. Title.
    [DNLM: 1. Aged—psychology.   2. Aging.   3. Mental Disorders—in
old age.   WT 150 B452p]
    BF724.55.A35B44   1990
    155.67—dc20
    DNLM/DLC
    for Library of Congress   89-9990
                                                                   CIP

Sponsoring Editors: *Philip L. Curson and Vicki Knight*
Editorial Assistants: *Amy Mayfield and Heather Riedl*
Production Coordinator: *Fiorella Ljunggren*
Production: *Bookman Productions*
Manuscript Editor: *Betty Berenson*
Permissions Editor: *Carline Haga*
Interior and Cover Design: *Lisa Berman*
Art Coordinator: *Bookman Productions*
Interior Illustration: *John Foster*
Photo Research: *Bookman Productions*
Typesetting: *Harrison Typesetting, Inc.*
Cover Printing: *Phoenix Color Corporation*
Printing and Binding: *Arcata Graphics/Fairfield*

(Credits continue on p. 385)

Preface

☐

I wrote the first edition of this book to fill a gap. In the early 1980s there were no gerontology texts on the market that were psychologically oriented, that comprehensively examined both aging research and practice, and that were also clearly aimed at students new to the field. Today, in 1989, *The Psychology of Aging: Theory, Research, and Interventions* (Second Edition) does have a few competitors. However, it is still unique—the only textbook available that provides a full picture of the far-ranging contributions of both academic and applied psychology to later life.

My goal is not only to give a balanced overview of the *whole* field but to show how psychological research translates into practice. So, as in the first edition, each chapter begins with an in-depth discussion of the academic research, followed by an extensive intervention section illustrating clinical applications of the research findings. Another unique feature that links research to practice is my use of clinical vignettes. To make the abstract content of the psychology of aging come alive in an immediate, concrete way for students, the information in each chapter (except the first) is illustrated by an extended introductory clinical case. This vignette is then referred to repeatedly throughout the chapter, vividly demonstrating the impact of the scientific findings on older adults.

Interesting students in gerontology remains my primary aim. That's why I have used an informal writing style, avoided technical jargon, and clearly spelled out concepts. At the same time, I have tried to write a book that is well grounded scientifically, treats readers as equals, and addresses readers at various levels of expertise. Rather than just list results, I carefully describe the procedures, biases, and limitations of the major studies. Whenever possible, I evaluate the accuracy of theories and explore the actual research evidence that substantiates a given intervention. I hope this book not only offers students a full portrait of what we know but also provides them with the tools and critical framework to question and evaluate future theory, research, and practice in the psychology of aging.

Finally, readers familiar with my earlier book will recognize that this edition of *The Psychology of Aging* has the same carefully planned structure as the first. It is divided into six parts: Basic Concepts, Physical Processes, Cognition, Personality, Psychopathology, and Death and Dying. To provide continuity between chapters, I follow the characters in each vignette throughout the chapters that make up each given part. In this edition, too, I use the first chapter to raise issues and highlight questions that are explored in the rest of the book.

However, because so much change has occurred in both the psychology of aging and my writing during these intervening years, this second edition is more than an updated version of the first. It is a totally rewritten book. Today a shift in research priorities begun in the early 1980s is fully in place. Psychologists are less likely to focus on abstract theoretical questions and more likely to study topics with immediate, pressing applications to daily life. The standard laboratory investigations of cognition, memory, and reaction time are less in vogue. Researchers who still work in these traditional areas of psychology now typically try to redesign their studies to reflect "real life." At the same time there has been an explosion of interest in practical topics that had been relatively unprobed six years ago, such as grappling with the challenges of disability and health care or exploring caregiving and family relationships.

A second major new development concerns high-quality longitudinal studies. Since the first edition of *The Psychology of Aging* was published, the findings of the landmark Baltimore Longitudinal Study have become genuinely available, transforming our understanding not just of physical aging but of important research topics for psychologists such as personality consistency (or change) and the ways people cope with stress. Other studies have enriched our knowledge of issues as different as the course of retirement and widowhood, what predicts marital happiness, how families cope with caregiving, and the behavioral trajectory of Alzheimer's disease. Much of the book had to be rewritten simply to reflect these new trends.

For example, because of the astonishing explosion of information, I could no longer lump normal aging, prevention, disability, and health care together in one chapter as I did in the first edition of the text. So, in this edition, Chapter 2 deals with normal aging and prevention alone. A new chapter in the section on Physical Processes, entitled Disability and Health Care (Chapter 4), explores functional impairments, the growth of geriatric medicine, community services for dealing with the frail elderly, and nursing home care. Part 4, Personality, also has a much needed new chapter: in Chapter 8, The Family, I describe the research on late-life marriages, adult children and elderly parents, caregiving, and grandparenthood. Other sections have been expanded dramatically—for example, the discussion of personality, widowhood and retirement, and Alzheimer's disease.

Practice as a writer also forced me to undertake a renovation of a different type. During the years between these two editions, I wrote an omnibus guide to aging for older people. This experience taught me to describe the literature in an informal and personal way and also gave me a much more comfortable grasp of both academic and applied gerontology. As I became more relaxed and confident as a writer and a gerontologist, I came to feel strongly that this second edition could be more clearly written, scientifically precise, as well as more interesting and readable. So, I decided to rewrite practically every sentence of the book.

This second edition, however, is far from being just the product of my ideas alone. My choice of topics and the revisions I made were profoundly influenced by the suggestions of the reviewers I was privileged to have: Victor Cicirelli of Purdue University, William Haley of the University of Alabama in Birmingham, Clara Pratt of Oregon State University, J. Thomas Puglisi of the University of North Carolina, Jon Nussbaum of the University of Oklahoma, Walter Smith of the Weston School of Theology, and William Stone of the University of Virginia. I was also lucky to be working with an outstanding group of professionals at Brooks/Cole: Phil Curson, Psychology Editor, Fiorella Ljunggren, Production Services Manager, and Lisa Berman, Designer. The contributions of Rosaleen Bertolino of Bookman Productions and Betty Berenson, my diligent and long-suffering copy editor, are much appreciated. Finally, there is one constant that has remained amid this long catalogue of differences between then and now. This book, like the first, would not have been written without the support and encouragement of my husband, David, my fellow traveler through life.

Janet K. Belsky

Contents

☐

Part 1   Basic Concepts   1

Chapter 1   Stereotypes, Realities:
The Psychological Study of
Later Life   2

Stereotypes, Realities   3
   Demographic Realities   5
   Personal Realities   10
The Psychological Framework   12
   Emphasis on Age Irrelevance:
     Psychoanalytic Theory and Behaviorism   13
   Emphasis on Positive Change:
     Jung's and Erikson's Theories   22
   Emphasis on Many Perspectives:
     The Life-Span Developmental View   24
Developmental Research Methods   25
   Cross-Sectional Studies   26
   Longitudinal Studies   28
The Basic Themes in the Following Chapters   33
Key Terms   34
Recommended Readings   34

Part 2   Physical Processes   35

Chapter 2   The Aging Body   36

Biological Theories of Aging   40
   Random-Damage Theories of Aging   43
   Programmed-Aging Theories   44
Extending Our Maximum Life Span   45
Normal Aging   46
   The Findings of the Baltimore Study   46
   How Normal Aging Affects Us   48
   Selected Aging Changes   48

Chronic Disease   51
   Chronic Disease versus Functional Disability   51
Lifestyle, Aging, and Longevity   53
   The Impact of Good Health Practices   55
   The Impact of Stress   56
   The Impact of Life Changes   57
   The Impact of Autonomy and Control   59
Interventions   60
   Modifying Type A Behavior   61
   Eradicating Incontinence   62
Key Terms   63
Recommended Readings   63

Chapter 3   Sensing and Responding to the Environment   64

Our Senses   67
   Our Windows on the World: Vision   68
   Our Bridge to Others: Hearing   74
Taste and Smell   80
Motor Performance   81
   Age Changes in Response Speed   82
   The Source of Age Changes in Response Speed   83
Interventions   86
   Designing Housing for the Elderly   87
   Adapting Private Homes for the Elderly   89
Key Terms   90
Recommended Readings   90

Chapter 4   Disability and Health Care   91

The Disability Trajectory   93
The Medical Profession and Older Adults   95
   How Physicians Treat Their Older Patients   95
   How Older Patients Treat Their Physicians   98
Community Alternatives to Nursing Homes   99
   Home Care   101
   Day Centers and Programs   103
   Respite Care   103
   Specialized Services   105
Nursing Home Care   105
   The Institutions   107
   The Residents   109

Interventions 113
Key Terms 114
Recommended Readings 114

Part 3 Cognition 115

Chapter 5 Intelligence and the IQ Test 116

The Measure 119
Age Changes on the WAIS and Other IQ Tests 121
Conclusions and an Important Interpretation 123
The Impact of Nonintellectual Influences on
Age Declines 127
    Differences in Education 127
    Differences in Test-Taking Strategy 128
Illness, Death, and IQ 131
    The Complicated Link between IQ Losses and
        Illness 131
    The Fascinating Link between IQ Losses and Death 133
Questioning the Underpinning: The Validity of
the IQ Test 135
Interventions 136
    Designing an Age-Relevant Intelligence Test 136
    Improving Performance on Current Tests 140
Key Terms 141
Recommended Readings 141

Chapter 6 Cognitive Processes: Memory and Creativity 142

Memory 145
    The Basic Framework for Understanding Memory 146
    The Older Person's Problem with Memory 147
    What Helps or Hinders Memory in Later Life? 149
    Making the Translation from Laboratory to Life 150
    Interventions 153
Creative Achievements 156
    The First Findings and the Debate They Caused 157
    Creativity in the Arts 159
    Creativity in the Sciences 162
Key Terms 166
Recommended Readings 166

Part 4   Personality   167

Chapter 7   Internal Aspects of the Person   168

The Historical Framework   171
   The Kansas City Studies: Emphasis on Change   171
   Conclusions, Criticisms, and Controversy   173
   Disengagement Theory: The Idea and the Debate   176
Present Research   178
   The Baltimore Study: Personality Stability   178
   Conclusions, Criticisms, and Controversy   180
   Maturity, Regression, or a Different Way of
     Handling Stress?   182
The Conclusions: Change and Consistency   184
Sexuality   186
   Age Changes in Sexual Response   187
   Sexual Interest and Activity   189
   Factors Affecting Sexuality in Later Life   191
   Illness and Sexual Function   193
   Interventions   194
Key Terms   195
Recommended Readings   195

Chapter 8   The Family   196

Older Married Couples   199
   The Marital-Quality Studies   199
   Elderly New Lovers and New Marrieds   204
Adult Children/Elderly Parents   207
   Quantity Does Not Mean Quality   209
   Caring for an Ill Parent   210
   Interventions   212
Grandparents   214
   Grandparenting Styles   216
   Interventions   219
Key Terms   220
Recommended Readings   220

Chapter 9   External Changes: Retirement and Widowhood   221

Retirement   223
   The Early Retirement Norm   224
   The Retirement Decision   225

The Consequences of Retirement   230
Interventions   235
Widowhood   237
Bereavement   239
Life as a Widowed Person   246
Interventions   249
Key Terms   251
Recommended Readings   251

Part 5   Psychopathology   253

Chapter 10   Mental Disorders 1: Description, Diagnosis, Assessment   254

Epidemiology of Later-Life Mental Disorders   257
Purposes of Epidemiological Studies   257
Problems in Measuring Psychological Disorders   257
Psychological Problems in Old Age   258
Dementia   260
Symptoms of Dementia   260
The Prevalence of Dementia   262
Alzheimer's Disease   263
Multi-Infarct Dementia   267
Personality Changes and Dementia   268
The Strains and Stresses of Caregiving   270
Accurately Distinguishing Dementia from Delirium and
    Depression   271
Depression   273
Symptoms and Prevalence of Depression   274
Categories and Causes of Depression   275
The Worse Consequence of Depression—Suicide   279
Assessment   281
The Diagnostic Question   282
Assessment Strategies for Dementia   284
Recommendations   285
Key Terms   286
Recommended Readings   286

Chapter 11   Mental Disorders 2: Treatment   287

The Older Person and the Mental Health System   290
The Older Person's Contribution to Poor Care   292

The Mental Health Provider's Contribution to Poor
Care   295
Psychotherapy   296
Psychoanalytic Psychotherapy   297
Behavior Therapy   302
Group Therapy   307
Marital and Family Therapy   309
Chemotherapy   311
Antipsychotic Drugs   312
Antidepressant Drugs   313
Antianxiety Drugs   313
Psychotropic Drugs and the Older Person   314
Treatments for Dementia   315
Environmental Treatments   315
Biological Treatments   318
Treating the Second Casualty: Families   319
Key Terms   320
Recommended Readings   320

Part 6   Death and Dying   323

Chapter 12   At the End of Life   324

Death as an Abstract Idea   327
The Thought of Death   327
The Fear of Death   328
Illness and Ego Integrity: Two Factors that May Influence
the Intensity of Death Anxiety   330
The Experience of Dying   332
The Person's Experience   332
The Health Care System   336
Interventions   339
Hospice Care   340
Humanizing Hospital Care   343
Helping the Dying Person by Psychotherapy   345
Key Terms   346
Recommended Readings   346

References   347

Name Index   369

Subject Index   379

Part 1

Basic
Concepts

Chapter 1

□

Stereotypes, Realities: The Psychological Study of Later Life

□

Stereotypes, Realities
- Demographic Realities
  - Personal Realities

The Psychological Framework
- Emphasis on Age Irrelevance: Psychoanalytic Theory and Behaviorism
  - Emphasis on Positive Change: Jung's and Erikson's Theories
  - Emphasis on Many Perspectives: The Life-Span Developmental View

Developmental Research Methods
- Cross-Sectional Studies
- Longitudinal Studies

The Basic Themes in the Following Chapters

Key Terms

Recommended Readings

O̶lder people think and move slowly. They do not think as well as they used to or as creatively. They are bound to themselves and their past and can no longer change or grow. They can learn neither well nor swiftly, and even if they could, they would not wish to. Tied to their personal traditions and growing conservatism, they dislike innovations and are not disposed to favor new ideas. Not only can they not move forward, they often move backward. They enter a second childhood, often caught in increasing egocentricity and demanding more from their environment than they are willing to give to it. They become irritable and cantankerous, yet shallow and enfeebled. They live in their past. They are aimless and wandering of mind, reminiscing and garrulous. Indeed, they are studies in decline, pictures of mental and physical failure. They have lost and cannot replace friends, spouse, job, status, power, influence, income. They are often stricken by diseases that restrict their movement, their enjoyment of food, the pleasures of well-being. Sexual interest and activity decline. The body shrinks; so does the flow of blood to the brain, which does not utilize oxygen or sugar at the same rate as formerly. Feeble, uninteresting, they await death, a burden to society, to family, and to themselves. (A description of the stereotype of old age adapted from Butler, 1974.)

■

STEREOTYPES, REALITIES

If you, too, bring these thoughts to the psychology of aging (a field also called **geropsychology** or **gerontological psychology**), you are not alone. Surveys show that Americans view old age as the worst time of life (Bennett & Eckman, 1973). People also share a well-developed conception about the specific characteristics labeled "old" (Rodin & Langer, 1980). Negative ideas, like those so starkly spelled out above, are also held by many health care workers who regularly work with older adults (Leiderman & Grisso, 1985; Solomon & Vickers, 1979).

True, wisdom is one positive attribute that has been associated with old age since ancient times. But the assumption that aging equals incompetence also has a history that goes back at least to ancient Greece. Despite the media's effort to dispel this view with images of active and productive older adults, it prevails. Unless their behavior proves otherwise, older people are still seen as basically less competent (Avolio & Barrett, 1987), less intelligent, and more physically frail (Lachman & McArthur, 1986) than young adults. The fact that perceptions such as these have appeared in so many cultures, offers disturbing hints that to some extent they are built-in to our nature as human beings. At a very young age, children describe old people as dependent, unattractive, and weak. In far-flung areas of the globe—the Aleutian Islands, Paraguay, Australia—children view the elderly with distaste (Jantz, Seefeldt, Galper, & Serock, 1976; Miller, Blalock, & Ginsberg, 1984–1985). While people over age 65 do see themselves in a less negative light, they too view "old people" negatively (Milligan, Powell, Harley, & Furchtgott, 1985) and are even vehement in their aversion to traits attributed to their life-stage (Rodin & Langer, 1980).

The children questioned in one of these studies reacted with horror to the thought of being old. Most were convinced they would never reach that un-desired state. Their responses (for example, "Oh no, not me. I'm not getting old") have a sad echo at the opposite end of the life span. Older people are reluctant to attribute old age to themselves, too.

People cling to a self-definition of being middle-aged long after the chronolog-ical clock suggests a reassessment. In a study of people aged 60 and over (Bultena & Powers, 1978), when respondents were asked whether they thought of them-selves as middle-aged, elderly, or old, 75% checked the first choice, only 10% the last. When the same subjects were interviewed 10 years later—now all aged 70 or more—their answers had changed, but not as much as we might expect. One-third still called themselves "middle-aged." Only one-fourth felt they de-served the label "old."

Even over age 80, far from everyone accepts the label "old." In one survey, one-fourth of the men and one-fifth of the women over this age said that the word simply did not apply to them. As one respondent in this large national survey puzzled, "The calendar tells me I'm old, but I still feel middle-aged" (Shanas, 1984).

A moment's reflection suggests one reason for these answers. It may be simply too difficult for people to face up to the reality that they have the negative qualities associated with old age. But another possibility was revealed in the study when researchers returned to question subjects a decade later (Bultena & Powers, 1978). People who had shifted their identity to "old" over the 10 years attributed their changed self-definition to negative events, particularly declining health. Those who still saw themselves as middle-aged could not see any sim-ilarity between themselves and the stereotype of the frail, incompetent elderly.

So it may well be that people who view themselves as middle-aged are right. They do not deserve the term *old*. But if even by age 80 a significant minority of Americans do not fit the characteristics we call "typical" of old age, then the negative stereotype does not fit the vast majority of older adults. Rather than older people being out of touch with reality, we may be oblivious to the truth about them. We may be guilty of a prejudice similar to racism or sexism: **ageism,** or negatively stereotyping people over age 65.

Without denying that ageism still affects our treatment of the elderly and governs our thoughts about growing old, there is encouraging evidence that the rigid stereotypes we have about older people do seem to be breaking down. At the same time as we "know" the generalizations, we freely admit that they do not apply to many older adults. We are more likely to give older people credit for good performance, to assume that when they do something well, it is due to inherent ability, not pure luck (Lachman & McArthur, 1986). In fact, rather than just view being old in an unidimensional negative way, today we seem to have a confusing welter of ideas about old age. For instance, when Daniel Schmidt and Susan Boland (1986) asked college students to list as many traits as possible stereotypically linked with being old, they got a hodgepodge of responses. Older people were seen as frail and incompetent but also as resilient and tough. They were labeled as quarrelsome and set in their ways, but were also viewed as generous, loving, and wise. This suggests that while we still think of older people in traditional ways, these ideas have been supplemented by new perceptions. The strange outcome is a set of firmly held *contradictory* thoughts about what older people are like.

So reality may finally be permeating the stereotype. Older people defy easy generalizations. Many are active, involved, and competent; some are ill and frail. Some are at the height of their powers; others, the embodiment of decline. The words "golden years" sometimes genuinely fit this life-stage; at other times they are a cruel parody. More than at any era before, today diversity and individual differences are the hallmark of aging. This diversity is a theme we will be returning to repeatedly in the chapters to come.

Perhaps our best introduction to the tremendous variability that characterizes the landscape of aging is by a bird's-eye glimpse of the territory we will be probing in the following pages: a demographic portrait of older people.

Demographic Realities

Demography, the study of populations, gives us a snapshot of the terrain of old age. It also illustrates why probing this landscape is such an imperative task: The elderly among us are now an army. The most significant demographic trend in our century is the phenomenal increase in the ranks of older adults. (The statistics in this section are from the U.S. Senate Special Committee on Aging, 1984, 1987.)

In 1900 only 1 out of every 25 Americans was elderly. By 1986 there was a radical shift: 1 in 8 people had passed age 65, the arbitrary entry point of old age. The actual number of older adults had increased almost tenfold: from 3.1 million to 29.2 million.

As Figure 1-1 shows and Figure 1-2 suggests, understanding late life will become increasingly crucial as this demographic shift becomes even more pronounced in the next decades. By the year 2010, 1 out of 7 Americans will be elderly. By 2030, the ranks of the elderly will swell to 1 in 5. This accelerated increase is due mainly to the bulge in the population called the postwar baby boom. (After the Second World War, actually from about 1946 to 1964, the birth rate soared.) Because the baby-boom generation will gradually turn 65 over the next few decades, we will become a genuinely top-heavy society, one in which more than half of all Americans will have passed their 40th birthday (see Figure 1-2).

Two influences are responsible for the phenomenon called "the aging of America." After the baby boom, in the late 1960s and 1970s, the birth rate dropped, causing the proportion of older people to rise. Also—and far more

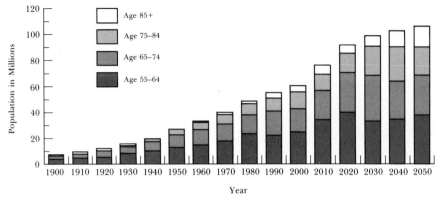

Figure 1-1. Population aged 55 and older, 1900–2050.
Source: U.S. Senate Special Committee on Aging, 1987.

important—during this century life expectancy jumped to an unparalleled extent. A U.S. baby born in 1900 could expect to live only to age 48; that person's great-grandchild, born in 1984, could expect to survive an extra quarter century, to age 74. During these brief eight decades, life expectancy has increased by more than a generation.

Life expectancy statistics also reveal the two most important facts about the landscape of late life—it is mainly female, and, increasingly, it contains more and more of the very old. The social consequences of each demographic fact are great.

The first phenomenon, many more older women than men, is illustrated in Figure 1-3. Not only do Whites outlive people of other races, but now women, no matter what their ethnic group, outlive men. While in recent years, due in part to declining mortality from that disproportionally male killer, heart disease, this male/female disparity has been narrowing a bit, the gender differences in life expectancy are still pronounced today. In 1985, for instance, women could expect to outlive men their age by a full 7 years.

This differential translates into startling comparisons, particularly at life's uppermost rungs: In 1986 in the age group 65–69, for every 100 women there were 83 men; at age 75–79 there were only 64 men. Over age 85 the ratio was even more lopsided: 100 to 40.

So the reality is that most married women will become widows. Most widows will not remarry. And, because there is also a trend away from living with children, older women now and in the future will probably live alone (see Chapters 8 and 9).

While a variety of factors—from greater vulnerability to accidents, to living a less healthful lifestyle, to a propensity to die from heart disease and stroke—may converge to explain the gender difference in life expectancy, the second important fact, more people of advanced old age, has a simpler cause. Earlier in this century dramatic gains in life expectancy occurred among the young and middle-aged. Since the 1950s our strides have been primarily toward extending

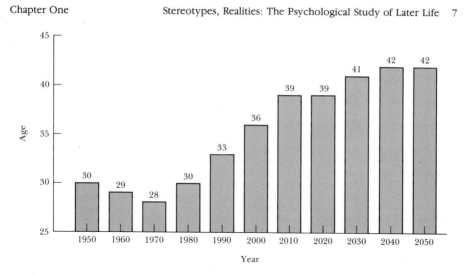

Figure 1-2. Estimates and projections of the median age of the U.S. population.
Source: U.S. Senate Special Committee on Aging, 1987.

longevity in the later years. For instance, Americans who reached their 65th birthdays in 1985 could expect on average to live another 16.8 years. From a brief interlude before death in 1900, senior citizenhood has grown to a distinct era of life.

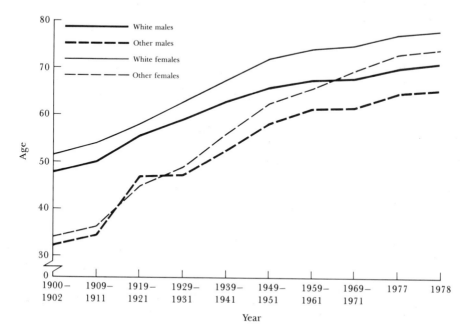

Figure 1-3. Life expectancy at birth, 1900–1978.
Source: The White House Conference on Aging, 1981.

This evolution of senior citizenhood as a genuine life-stage has resulted from a difference in the pattern of disease control. During the first half of this century, cures were developed for many acute or infectious diseases (such as diphtheria). These illnesses killed the young and old alike, so their eradication allowed most people to live past youth. Since that time we have become better able to limit (but not cure) diseases that tend to strike in later life. People reaching 60 or 65 now live on for years because of inroads in the mortality rate from these late-life illnesses called **chronic diseases** (heart disease, cancer, stroke) (Rosenwaike & Dolinsky, 1987).

In part this decline in mortality can be traced to medical advances such as improved medications and better surgical techniques. However, a good deal of the credit seems to belong to us. Lifestyle changes such as the new emphasis on fitness and taking care of our health have correlated in a remarkable way with the recent increase in later-life life expectancy. As we will see in the next chapter, exercising, eating the right foods, being concerned with our health earlier on really do seem to help stave off the onset and slow the advance of chronic disease.

The elongation of senior citizenhood means that unparalleled numbers of Americans are now living to their 9th, 10th, or even 11th decades of life. Not only are people over 85 one of the fastest growing segments of the population, as Figure 1-4 clearly shows, but we can expect the ranks of our oldest-old to dramatically increase in future years. In fact, by 2030 the current 1% of all Americans over 85 is expected to reach more than 5%.

One great boon is that four-generation families are now common. Many people in their 60s (and even 70s) will have the pleasure of having a parent still living. But there is a problem along with this wonderful news. While we have added time to the end of the life span, we have not necessarily given these family patriarchs (or, more likely, matriarchs) a high-quality life. The increase in the numbers of people living to their 80s and 90s means more sick elderly and so an expanding need for medical and nursing care. In fact, by about the 9th decade of life the chance of being physically disabled by illness increases dramatically. In part because of this higher probability, gerontologists often find it useful to make a distinction between two chronological subgroups of older adults: the **young-old** and the **old-old.** The young-old, arbitrarily defined as people aged 65 to 75, are typically free from disabling illnesses. The old-old, those in their late 70s and beyond, seem to be in a different class. Since they are more likely to have physical and mental disabilities, they are more prone to fit our traditional stereotype of the frail, dependent older adult.

Further facts about the landscape of later life, though, suggest we should be cautious in making additional generalizations. Despite some variability, older people are found in all 50 states in much the same distribution as the young. As we might predict, they do reside in higher numbers in Florida—in 1984, 17.6% of all Floridians were over age 65. But in most other states the frequency is within 2 points or so of the 13% we would expect. Furthermore, the vast majority of elderly Americans live in their own homes. Only 5% of the over-65 population live in nursing homes. Though the differential is narrowing, the elderly do have

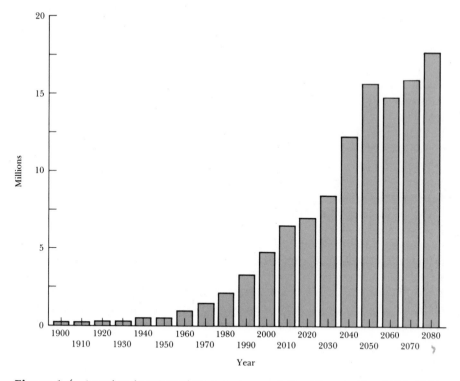

Figure 1-4. Actual and projected increase in population 85 and older, 1900–2080. *Source: U.S. Senate Special Committee on Aging, 1987.*

fewer years of education: in 1986 about one-half were high school graduates, compared to three-fourths of Americans aged 25–65. They also are less well off financially—in that same year the median income of an "elderly" family was $19,932 versus $32,368 for a family head under 65. However, here, too, diversity and not uniformity seems to be the rule. The elderly are represented on all rungs of the economic and educational ladder.

Minority Aging: Some Predictable Exceptions. The demographic facts about minority aging in the United States have many themes in common with those just discussed: a dramatic growth in the elderly population, women outliving men, and a marked increase in the numbers of old-old. However, the statistics about elderly minorities—especially Blacks and Hispanics—offer a depressingly predictable counterpoint to those for Whites. (Because of Whites' higher life expectancy, lower fertility rates, and the recent influx of young non-White immigrants, the elderly population is disproportionately White.) Blacks or Hispanics who do reach age 65 are much more likely than Whites to live in poverty: In 1986 the poverty rate of elderly Blacks (31%) was nearly triple and that of elderly Hispanics (22.5%) was more than double that for elderly Whites (10.8%). There are also predictable differences in education and geographic distribution: In 1986 fewer than one in five elderly members of minorities had completed high school; half of all elderly Whites had. Elderly minority members are more likely to live in industrial states in large cities within poverty areas or, if they are Black, are disproportionately concentrated in the South.

In other words, just as it does at every life-stage, race and ethnic group is a powerful determinant of the quality of life in old age. The socioeconomic disadvantages so apparent earlier on are just as limiting for minorities in life's last stage. That is why gerontologist Jacquelyne Jackson coined the evocative phrase **double jeopardy** to describe the limitations imposed by being minority and old (see Jackson, 1985).

Recently, though, Jackson has cautioned against lumping all minorities according to any single phrase (Jackson, 1985). For instance, the experience of elderly Asian-Americans and elderly American Blacks may be as different from one another as they are from elderly Mayflower descendants. However, the phrase "double jeopardy" is likely to fit many more Americans than ever in the decades to come. Because of their higher birth rates (and life expectancy gains), during the first half of the 21st century the fraction of the elderly population that is Black and Hispanic is expected to swell dramatically—to almost 30%. So, unless their economic status can be changed earlier in their lives, the ranks of older Americans will become more heavily composed of disadvantaged minorities, and the inevitable result will be more people who will fit at least the economic stereotype of later life—poor and old.

Personal Realities

Statistics, however, provide only an external snapshot. They may usefully be supplemented by a more experiential view. What are the current problems older Americans face? What are their satisfactions and what are their major concerns?

Luckily we have this information from a nationwide survey of older adults. In 1981 the National Council on the Aging, a voluntary organization, commissioned Louis Harris to conduct a comprehensive survey on aging in the United States. The public at large was questioned; so was a representative sample of older Americans. Like a similar Harris poll conducted 7 years before, this survey was an in-depth exploration of attitudes, perceptions, feelings, and facts. Here are a few highlights of the poll (Harris & Associates, 1981).

Americans of all ages, including the elderly, viewed economic concerns— "inflation, high cost of living, high prices"—as the greatest problem facing older adults today. But despite this shared perception that financial concerns rank first in importance to the elderly as a group, only two in five older adults polled actually admitted that lack of money was a significant problem in their own lives. In fact, the Harris elderly were less likely to report being bothered by insufficient income than the younger adults (in Chapter 9 we will explore some possible reasons for this surprising finding).

The survey also revealed misperceptions of the extent of problems facing the elderly in several other areas. For instance, a substantial majority of the younger Harris respondents rated "fear of crime" and "loneliness" as very serious problems for most elderly, but only a minority of the older adults cited these as serious problems for themselves. However, the percentage of older people listing fear of crime as very important in their lives was substantial (25%) and slightly higher than that of the younger adults (20%). This greater fear may actually be adaptive. Perhaps because older people are more fearful, they are more cautious to avoid high-risk situations. The surprising statistic is that the elderly are *less* likely than younger Americans to be the victims of violent crime (Janson & Ryder, 1983).

Economic anxiety and fear of crime are pressing problems for Americans of all ages. But one difficulty clearly is more important to people over age 65: poor health. In the poll 21% of the elderly said their health was "a very serious problem," compared with 8% of the respondents aged 18 to 54. The older people polled cited the high cost of care as the most difficult aspect of being ill and in need of medical services. (Chapter 4 discusses why cost is such a *critical* health care issue in old age.) The elderly were also troubled by the lack of transportation to and from doctors or medical facilities. Only 5% listed quality of care as an important concern.

It comes as no surprise that health is a more salient problem for Americans over age 65. But a final highlight of the Harris survey flies in the face of another firmly held assumption—that compared to any other age, old age is the unhappiest time of life. Responses of the elderly to a life satisfaction questionnaire yielded surprising evidence contradicting this widespread view. As Table 1-1 shows, the elderly rejected the idea that, for them personally, the present is the least desirable time. They did not agree that their lives were dreary or monotonous, or that at their time of life the past becomes dominant and interests erode. This cross section of older Americans reported being satisfied both with who they were in the past and who they were now. A full half said they were just as happy in this supposedly "worst" life-stage as they were earlier on.

These responses do need to be qualified. Overall, life satisfaction scores in the 1981 Harris survey were lower than in the poll taken 7 years earlier. Moreover, because older people in America tend to have a bias against complaining (as we will see in the chapters to come), we may assume these answers are skewed on the positive side. Finally, not all people over age 65 share this uplifting view of their present life. Life satisfaction varies greatly from person to person. People in poor health are more likely to have low morale (Larson, 1978). Also, Blacks and Hispanics are another category of the elderly whose later years are more in keeping with the gloomy view. Still the Harris results are testimony against the rigid stereotype. A full one-third of the elderly respondents refer to their older years as their best years.

In summary, the demographic statistics show that we cannot categorize the older population in rigid, unidimensional terms. The Harris poll demonstrates that for many Americans old age is far from a period of unremitting gloom. These facts offer a valuable first approach to reality. However, they do not address our ingrained negative stereotypes. Those beliefs largely concern behavior, so it is only by examining behavior in older adults that we can really determine their accuracy. The purpose of the psychological study of later life is to provide this understanding.

THE PSYCHOLOGICAL FRAMEWORK

At an accelerating pace since the end of the Second World War (Riegel, 1977) psychology, the study of behavior, has been turning its attention to the elderly (see Figure 1-5). Psychologists now study the physical reality of aging, focusing on the behavioral aspects of physiological change. They are exploring in depth how aging affects memory, thinking, and intelligence. They scrutinize personality, family relationships, and the impact of important age-related events such as retirement and widowhood. They examine mental disorders—their characteristics, causes, and possible cures. They are also studying death, the inevitable end of old age. The following chapters systematically examine psychological theory, research, and practice in each of these essential areas. I hope that by

TABLE 1-1. Responses of persons aged 65 and older to positive and negative life satisfaction statements.

	Percentage Agreeing	Percentage Disagreeing	Percentage Not Sure
Positive statements			
As I look back on my life, I am fairly well satisfied	87	11	2
Compared to other people my age, I make a good appearance	84	7	8
I've gotten pretty much what I expected out of life	81	14	5
The things I do are as interesting to me as they ever were	69	27	4
As I grow older, things seem better than I thought they would be	53	38	9
I have gotten more of the breaks in life than most people I know	62	31	6
I would not change my past life even if I could	64	29	6
I expect some interesting and pleasant things to happen to me in the future	62	28	11
I am just as happy as when I was younger	48	48	4
I have made plans for things I'll be doing a month or year from now	49	47	4
These are the best years of my life	33	60	7
Negative statements			
I feel old and somewhat tired	45	51	3
My life could be happier than it is now	55	40	5
In spite of what some people say, the lot of the average person is getting worse, not better	48	39	13
When I think back over my life, I didn't get most of the important things I wanted	36	59	4
This is the dreariest time of my life	27	70	3
Most of the things I do are boring or monotonous	21	76	3
Compared to other people, I get down in the dumps too often	18	78	5

Source: Harris & Associates, 1981.

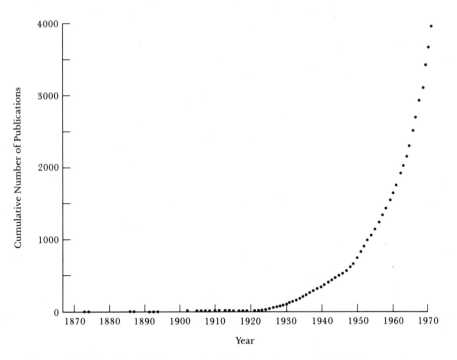

Figure 1-5. One hundred years of publications in psychological gerontology.
Source: Riegel, 1977.

reading them, you will come to appreciate the contributions that those of us who scientifically study individual behavior are continuing to provide about the reality of the aging process and older adults.

Many psychologically oriented theories have been applied in an attempt to understand aging. These often quite circumscribed theories run the gamut from models of how memory operates to attempts to account for the emotional reactions to the painful event of losing a spouse. Amid this diversity, though, a few theories stand out. And although many research techniques are used in gerontology, of particular importance are the main ones used to assess developmental change. In the chapters to come, the theoretical perspectives and research strategies described in the next sections will be mentioned time and time again.

Emphasis on Age Irrelevance: Psychoanalytic Theory and Behaviorism

Behaviorism and psychoanalytic theory are the two most influential approaches to human behavior. It should come as no surprise, then, that these theories are often applied to understanding the behavior of older adults. However, since they are general accounts of how human beings operate, neither of these important theories has specific concepts describing late life. The same general principles governing psychological functioning at any age are also applied to old age.

(What follows are highly attenuated descriptions, "bare bones" outlines of these sophisticated approaches to human behavior, which highlight just how different the behavioral and psychoanalytic perspectives on aging have traditionally been.)

Behaviorism.   Behaviorism (or learning theory) has been the premier theoretical system that has shaped modern psychology. To its originators, a single axiom captured the essence of their revolutionary world view—the environment determines human actions. To understand behavior, we should look to the rewards a person is exposed to in the outside world.

Traditionally, behaviorists have forcefully argued against the importance of biology. Our actions are changeable, not determined by our genes or immutable givens at birth. Behaviorists have concentrated on what could be directly measured, preferring actions to feelings, needs, and fantasies. (Box 1-1 describes, on the other hand, how radically these original tenets have been changed by the emergence of a new approach—**cognitive learning theory**—which focuses on these unobservable thoughts.) They deemphasized the past: The key to changing behavior lies not so much in exploring a person's history but in rearranging his or her current life. In their view, a small handful of mechanisms explain how we act. Responses are either acquired directly, through classical or operant conditioning, or indirectly, through modeling (observational learning).

Classical conditioning, the most primitive type of learning, involves involuntary responses, actions, or physiological reactions outside conscious control. Here the response elicited by one stimulus is paired with another. After a number of pairings or in many cases even one association, a connection is formed and the response is now elicited by the new stimulus alone.

Classical conditioning explains why we salivate when we smell a steak sizzling on the grill. It accounts for that happy feeling that (it is hoped) wells up when as elderly alumni we once again set foot on the campus where we spent those wonderful college years. In actual practice, however, behaviorists most often invoke this type of learning to explain the presence of "unreasonable" negative emotional reactions—for instance, the intense fear of leaving her house 75-year-old Mrs. Smith develops after falling at the corner of Main and Vine. According to the simplified model, falling, a stimulus evoking the response of fear, occurred in conjunction with being at Main and Vine. Because of this pairing, the initially neutral stimulus of being at that corner was classically conditioned to fear.

But why does the fall at Main and Vine evolve into the fear of going out at all? To answer this question, the behaviorist might use another important concept, **generalization.** Generalization refers to the fact that once a response is learned in one situation it tends to spread to others along a dimension of similarity. So, in our example, fear learned in connection with Main and Vine generalized to all streets and then to setting foot outside the house. Furthermore, we might even expect Mrs. Smith to feel a twinge of fear when walking around in her house.

The experience of the fall may also involve the second major type of learning,

BOX 1-1
Behaviorism Comes of Age

A mere generation ago many behaviorists rigidly adhered to the principles described in the text—downplaying the importance of biology and priding themselves on studying only responses that could be externally measured and quantified. They firmly believed that genetic predispositions were relatively unimportant, that internal processes (feelings and thoughts), because they were not observable and verifiable, could have no place in a genuinely scientific study of human beings.

Today the behaviorist who feels this way is on the fringe. Few behaviorists argue against the idea that our biological makeup can powerfully shape what we learn. Biological predispositions (and biological interventions) are often actively taken into account in devising treatment plans. Most important, the idea that only observable actions are important has been completely abandoned over the past 20 years. Thoughts, feelings, and fantasies are now fully legitimate. Changing these "inner" feelings is seen by a whole school of therapists as the key to psychological change. This 180-degree shift in orientation—called **cognitive learning theory**—perhaps more than any other, forms the true centerpiece of behaviorism's coming of age (Mahoney, 1977).

The many psychologists who call themselves cognitive behaviorists have not abandoned the other tenets of learning theory. They still believe that behavior must be scrutinized in a rigorous, scientific way. However, instead of accepting the idea that only external actions are important, they focus on charting, measuring, and changing a person's ideas about the world. According to cognitive behaviorists, understanding the way we think about the environment is more important than understanding the objective characteristics of the environment itself. Human learning is not just a function of a mechanical linking of external stimulus and overt response. It is also a product of our cognitions—of how we feel and what we believe. And just as our thinking affects how we act, the reverse may be equally true. How we actually behave can produce marked cognitive change.

☐

operant conditioning, if it then causes avoidance, that is, Mrs. Smith's refusing to set foot out of the door. While physiological or involuntary reactions can be operantly conditioned, too, in general, operant (or instrumental) conditioning is the major mechanism behaviorists have used to explain our conscious or voluntary actions. Here the principle is simple. Actions that are rewarded, or **rein-**

forced, will tend to recur. Those that are not reinforced will **extinguish** (that is, disappear). In the example, relief from fear would be a potent reinforcer and maintain Mrs. Smith's response of never venturing out.

Traditionally, behaviorists have viewed operant conditioning, with its simple explanatory principle of direct reinforcement, as possibly accounting for all voluntary behavior. It can explain responses as varied as a physically able nursing home resident's refusing to walk or an elderly mathematician's working long hours in her field after her retirement.

Because of the prevalence with which operant conditioning has been used to understand the actions of older adults, it is important to look at this type of learning in slightly more detail. For instance, what do we need to know about reinforcement when using the operant approach? Several essentials can be illustrated by using the two very different responses just described.

First, although some rewards, such as money or praise, tend to be reinforcing for most people, often what constitutes a reinforcer is variable and person-specific. Each of us has his or her hierarchy of reinforcement, those events ranked from least to most important in motivating us. In the case of the nursing home resident, attention from the staff is likely to be high on that list, as this attention is what seems to be motivating his refusal to walk. On the scientist's hierarchy, the same reinforcer may not appear at all. For the scientist the reward seems to be the possibility of making an important discovery. But still we cannot be sure. The nursing home occupant might refuse to walk because this allows him to avoid a disliked resident whose room is down the hall or because of an altruistic desire to keep a sick roommate company. The scientist's work might have a far from lofty cause; she might be avoiding the boredom of household responsibilities, or perhaps avoiding a disliked spouse. So a second principle about reinforcement is that the reinforcer can best be determined only by a quite objective criterion—an event is a reinforcer if it increases the probability of the preceding behavior.

Finally, the frequency or schedule with which reinforcement is delivered has a crucial impact. Different schedules of reinforcement, such as being rewarded after every response, at predictable intervals, or at unpredictable intervals, produce profoundly variable patterns of behavior.

For instance, if the actions of the nursing home resident and mathematician were resistant to extinction (that is, continued for a long time in the absence of a current reward), we would expect a variable-ratio reinforcement schedule to be the cause. This is a quite common pattern in daily living. Rewards come at unpredictable intervals, and so people learn persistence, the idea that if they keep responding they will eventually get what they want. We would imagine that the nursing home staff sometimes coaxed or pleaded with the resident to try to walk, then let him use a wheelchair when a nurse was particularly rushed. We would envision the mathematician as understanding the hit-or-miss quality of scientific discovery. This would teach her a lesson of a superficially different type: only sometimes do ideas have merit, and only sometimes does hard work result in tangible rewards.

Actually, when used in conjunction with the concept of generalization, this most prevalent reinforcement schedule helps us understand the gerontological finding that personality traits such as "dependency" or "the tendency to work hard" can be quite stable from youth to old age (see Chapter 7). Not only may behavior that is periodically reinforced tend to persist over months or even years, it may generalize to the different life circumstances old age can bring—explaining why though now she needs help cooking and dressing, a woman refuses to give up her independence and move in with her daughter; making sense of why, despite being retired and finally able to relax, an older man frantically fills his day with appointments just as he did during his working years.

So, as we explore the "facts" about behavioral consistency in the following chapters, keep in mind the concepts of variable reinforcement and generalization. In addition, the concepts of nonreinforcement and extinction may partly explain many instances of late-life behavioral change—losses as different as IQ decrements after a person experiences a heart attack (see Chapter 5), or hearing impairment (see Chapter 3), or because society no longer sees her as sexually attractive, why an older woman's sexual feelings tend to erode (see Chapter 7). But a behaviorist would be remiss in looking only to direct reinforcement in explaining these or any other examples of late-life behavior because there is another way the responses of any older person might also be learned—by *modeling*.

In **modeling,** responses are learned by observation, by imitating what others do. People tend to imitate behaviors they see being reinforced. Other factors, such as the similarity of the model to the learner, may make this type of imitative learning more likely to occur. For instance, in our examples, Mrs. Smith may have developed her fear of leaving the house after learning that an elderly neighbor, just like herself, broke her hip and had to enter a nursing home after falling on the street. The mathematician may have learned to work long hours by observing the behavior of an admired colleague and seeing the many false leads for every genuine breakthrough made by this eminent man. The attention the staff gives to the nursing home resident's bedridden roommate may really be producing the resident's refusal to walk. If he acts incapable he can have this important reinforcer, too.

So behaviorists have looked to events occurring directly to the person, and to exposure to models to understand older people. As described in Box 1-2, they have used this same perspective in engineering behavioral change. Throughout this book, we will see how the principles just described are employed to treat specific problems, promote functioning, and improve the quality of life in old age.

Before turning from this very brief description, I must emphasize a crucial final fact about the laws of learning and the behavioral perspective on late life. The principles of learning are neutral and universal. The same mechanisms explain actions praised as good, derided as bad, or labeled as "typical" of later life. For instance, a nonbehaviorist might view Mrs. Smith or the nursing home resident quite negatively—as "neurotic" people. The mathematician, on the other hand, might be admired for her devotion to her field and her strength of character. And someone else viewing the actions of these older people might

BOX 1-2
A Behavioral Treatment to Promote Walking

The hypothetical example of our nursing home resident is not unusual. Often in institutions, older people do develop incompetent, incapable behaviors such as using a wheelchair when they are physically able to walk. Excessive dependency may be encouraged or reinforced by staff members too harried or rushed to give disabled older residents the extra time they need to negotiate independently. In nursing homes there are plenty of opportunities to model incapable behaviors.

To illustrate the power of operant techniques in reversing excessive helplessness, L. M. MacDonald and A. K. Butler (1974) decided to attack the very behavior we have been discussing—that is, to get two physically capable nursing home residents to walk when they insisted on using wheelchairs. On the surface, it seemed a formidable goal. Both residents had been urged again and again for several months by both staff members and their families to walk, with no success.

First, as is standard in the behavioral approach, the researchers observed the behavior as it normally occurred. They watched the typical procedure the nursing home staff followed: accompanying the residents and talking with them as they were transported by wheelchair to the dining room located on a different floor. This conversation, the researchers decided, would be the reinforcer made contingent on walking alone.

Then the researchers instituted the treatment phase. Each day they told the subjects to walk to the dining room and leaned over to help each older person stand. If the person did stand up, she was praised and offered conversation. If she refused, she got stony silence in transit to the meal. This simple strategy quickly produced a marked change— both older women walked to the dining room.

To illustrate that the new competent behavior could just as easily be reversed, MacDonald and Butler then used the same strategy to (temporarily) reinstitute the original response. Now the person was praised and talked to only if she rode to the dining room. Walking was met with silence. Needless to say, within a few days each resident was once again acting incompetent. Reinforcement, the simple mechanism producing learning, had had its inevitable effect.

□

make another seemingly logical inference: The first two older adults' actions could be seen as the excessive caution or obstinacy of old age; the mathematician's as the wisdom advancing years bring.

But behaviorists bring a totally different perspective to traits, actions, and attributes that we tend to view as characterological, either as a fixed part of person or—more central to our discussion—as natural or intrinsic to late life. Whereas others nod knowingly about "the wise older scientist," the "typically stubborn" nursing home resident, or the "predictably too cautious" older person afraid to go out, behaviorists see responses shaped by the universal laws of learning. There are no attributes inherent in people or aging. If it appears that there is a fixed ("wise," "cautious," or "obstinate") elderly way to behave, it is because older people tend to be exposed to similar environments and to have similar behaviors reinforced.

This nonevaluative approach is quite different from the perspective our second major psychological framework—psychoanalytic theory—brings to understanding later life and older adults.

Psychoanalytic Theory.   The principles that have formed the basis of modern learning theory are succinct, simple, and easily spelled out. This economy of precepts does not apply to the psychoanalytic approach. Psychoanalytic theory is a diverse amalgam of ideas—a system that has been added to, modified, and amended from its very inception.

This means that people who subscribe to this rich theory of human behavior may disagree radically on specifics. However, they do share some basic beliefs. They believe that what happens in childhood is important to psychological health. Typically, they believe that personality is basically formed at a quite early age (5 or earlier) and then remains relatively stable throughout life. They think that personality has a definite structure. It has conscious and unconscious aspects. The deepest layer of personality, the unconscious, is a very important determinant of human behavior.

In addition to having conscious and unconscious components, personality also has three parts: the id, the ego, and the superego. The id is present at birth. It is the mass of instincts, wishes, and needs we have when we enter the world. The ego and superego evolve during early childhood. The ego, the largely conscious, reality-oriented part of the personality, is formed when children realize that their needs cannot be immediately satisfied. Gratification must yield to the requirements of the outside world. Ego functions involve logic, reasoning, thinking, and planning; in other words, getting what we want in an ordered, realistic way. The superego develops next. It is the moral arm of the personality, the unconscious internalization of parental and societal prohibitions, norms, and ideals.

In sum, during the first crucial 5 years of life, we learn to conform to the requirements of being a human being. Desires must be adapted to reality. Sometimes they must be abandoned altogether in order to live a moral, ethical life.

According to this theory, our parents are responsible for the adequacy of these accommodations and so for our lifelong mental health. If they are empathic and sensitive during these crucial early childhood years, we will develop a strong ego that will enable us to weather and adapt to all the crises of living, including those of late life. If our parents are insensitive or for some other reason their caretaking ability is impaired, our ego formation will not be optimal and we will be prone to the eruption of the unconscious, likely to develop problems when encountering the stresses of old age. (As is true of behaviorists, today's psychoanalytic theorists are much less rigid about these ideas. They often grant that genetic predispositions can play a significant role in mental disorders, are less likely to blame parents alone, and even admit that events after early childhood can cause basic personality change.)

Thus, according to the traditional theory, stressful events endemic in late life—becoming ill, being widowed, retiring—are tests of psychological functioning. These stresses strain the capacity of the ego to adapt. It is here, if our childhood experiences have not been ideal, that we are most likely to use defense mechanisms to cope and to develop psychological problems.

So, for traditional psychoanalysts, the way a person behaves in old age is consistent with a lifelong behavioral pattern, or personality style (Berezin, 1972). Late life is a time of external stress and therefore much potential psychological disturbance. To understand behavior we must look beneath the surface: What unconscious needs, fantasies, and wishes are motivating the person's surface response? We can more clearly understand this very different perspective on old age by exploring briefly the way that an ultratraditional psychoanalyst might view the behavior of the three older people described in the last section.

The psychoanalyst would see Mrs. Smith's fear of leaving her house and the nursing home resident's refusal to walk as symptoms arising out of an unconscious wish. For instance, in Mrs. Smith's case, the analyst might hypothesize that the fall stimulated a powerful childhood yearning to be taken care of, a desire so foreign to the older woman's self-image as an independent adult that she cannot consciously admit it. Not going out of her house would be an ideal psychological solution—one that both permits the true desire to remain unconscious and also satisfies it by having Mrs. Smith's children take care of her shopping and outside chores. For the nursing home resident, the wish might be the need to punish a rejecting parent, a lifelong desire that becomes activated in any situation where other people are in control. In this case, the stress of being institutionalized plus the similarity of the nursing home environment to the dependent one of early life would be seen as evoking an "acting out" symptom of this type.

In both instances, however, our very traditional psychoanalyst would feel that these hypotheses can be confirmed only by examining each person's childhood. In the specific events, experiences, and themes of those long-distant earliest years would lie the key to these pathological symptoms.

Our cases also illustrate the scenario that, according to this model of human behavior, produces psychological symptoms at any age. A highly stressful event in the present—here falling in the street and entering a nursing home—taxes the ability of the adult part of the personality, the ego, to remain firmly in control. Because of deficiencies in childhood experiences, ego formation has not been ideal. So the unconscious desire wins. The sign of its victory over the reality-oriented part of personality is the symptom or psychological problem itself. Furthermore, firmly believing that each personality is stable or fixed, our psychoanalyst would predict that similar episodes probably punctuated each older person's past. Earlier life stresses would have had the same tendency to provoke a psychological disorder. In fact, they would have produced symptoms having an identical meaning to those being observed now.

Our psychoanalyst would bring the same perspective to understanding the third older person, the dedicated mathematician: Her pattern of hard work would also have its roots in a particular set of long-unconscious childhood needs. However, because her behavior seems appropriate and mature, this analyst might put her in a different category than the two other older people: "Although once again we could only know for certain by thoroughly investigating her childhood, the scientist's actions do imply an ego in full control, the psychoanalytic criterion of genuine mental health."

Each Theory's Importance in the Psychology of Aging.

Behaviorism is by far the dominant theoretical framework psychologists have used for understanding late life, clearly outranking the psychoanalytic point of view. Especially in recent decades, the tenets of psychoanalytic theory have been widely criticized; the utility of classical psychoanalytic techniques for curing emotional problems assailed. At the same time as these criticisms have taken their toll, behaviorism's new and less rigid cognitive approach (see Box 1-1) has helped gain converts to learning theory. The simple fact is that more practicing psychologists than ever are interested in behavioral techniques. But numbers only partially explain why behaviorism historically has had such unusual appeal to gerontologists. Its popularity lies in its philosophy, which becomes apparent when we look at the very different implications the two theories have for older adults.

Behaviorism is optimistic. Behaviorism's environmental explanation is a refreshing antidote to the negativism of conventional thinking about old age (Hoyer, 1973; Labouvie, 1973). Aging does not have to lead to irreversible decline. Older people are not doomed to behave in preordained, deficient ways. Not only can behavior be changed, it can be modified quite easily. In addition, because history, or time spent acting in a certain way, is irrelevant to the ease with which a person can change, older adults are not at a disadvantage. They are as capable of modifying their behavior as the young.

Behaviorism is broad in scope. The principles of learning account not just for the category of responses called personality but for any human activity. So the theory can be used to understand and help the older person in every area of life.

Psychoanalytic theory has neither of these virtues. It focuses only on personality and psychological problems. Moreover, if anything, its tenets have tended to contribute to, rather than dispel, the negativism about old age: The beginning phase of life, not its end, is seen as crucial. This is the period on which we should focus our attention. Behavior is fixed from childhood. It is particularly difficult to change when cemented in over many years. Old age is a season of loss, the most difficult time of life.

These fundamental differences in optimism, in acceptance of the elderly as worthy of study, and in the ability to study the older person in a comprehensive way have led to a natural self-selection. Psychologists interested in the elderly often have an affinity for the learning theory approach; those who follow the learning theory approach are more likely to be interested in the elderly.

However, we cannot discount the impact of psychoanalytic theory. Many gerontologists do use this important theory to understand older adults. Their research and clinical insights have provided us with important information about personality stability and change in our middle and later years, about how people adapt to crises such as the loss of a spouse or approaching death, and about psychological problems that tend to be more prevalent among older adults. (These contributions will be apparent in the last half of this book.) Also, the negativism and neglect inherent in the traditional Freudian model have been vigorously opposed by the growing number of psychoanalytically oriented practitioners who treat the elderly today. Moreover, other theories with roots within the psychoanalytic tradition present a very different picture of life's last stages. According to Carl Jung and Erik Erikson, later life is a time of evolution. It is a period of often positive personality change.

Emphasis on Positive Change: Jung's and Erikson's Theories

Jung and Erikson have redressed Freud's neglect of adulthood by developing concepts about personality that take old age into account. Jung's theory is an explicit rebuke to traditional psychoanalytic theory. Jung considers the last half of life to be more interesting and more important than the first. Erikson's beliefs are less extreme. But though he doesn't see later life as inherently "better" he still thinks of it as a period to which attention should be paid.

Jung's Basic Concepts.   Jung's positive ideas about late life are intrinsic to his well-developed theory of what motivates human beings (see Mattoon, 1981). Once Freud's enthusiastic protégé, Jung abandoned the psychoanalytic movement in 1912 and set up his own very different psychoanalytic school. Jung's disagreement with Freud centered on his mentor's idea that all psychological development takes place by the age of 5. Jung violently opposed this retrospective (past-oriented) approach to life: Who we are as adults cannot *simply* be a reflection of infantile needs; the present and future are centrally important too. As a natural outgrowth of this prospective (future-oriented) view of human nature, Jung was especially interested in exploring psychological growth during the second half of life.

Jung hypothesized that midlife (age 40 or so) is an important emotional turning point. In fact we can trace the origin of the now familiar concept of the "midlife crisis" to Jung's ideas about adult development. He begins his discussion with the time of life from puberty to about the mid-30s. During this period, which he calls youth but we would call young adulthood, our life thrust is to establish ourselves. We are energetic, passionate, self-absorbed—concerned with satisfying our sexuality, obsessed with carving out our niche in the world. In our late 30s physical and sexual energy begin to wane. We are now settled. We know the shape of our capacities, the contours of what we can do. We either are successful or perhaps beginning to make peace with the idea of not setting the world on flame. So a kind of turning inward naturally occurs. Introspection and contemplation become ascendant. Relationships, understanding the meaning of life, and giving to others become our predominant concerns.

Jung believes that negotiating this transition is hazardous. Many people are unable to relinquish "the psychology of the youthful phase" and continue this orientation into middle and later life. They stagnate, becoming vain, unhappy, and rigid. However, if development proceeds in an ideal way, a pinnacle is reached. We can be transformed into a spiritual being.

Jung believes that this reorientation completes us psychologically. We can accept and integrate all the facets of our personality, even ones that we had previously denied. Thus, a natural outgrowth of this midlife change is less differentiation between the sexes. Men become more tolerant of the previously repressed feminine component of their personality. Women give more play to their deemphasized masculine side.

Jung also believes that this transition has a major function. It occurs in order to prepare us for impending death, an event he views not as the low point but as the culmination of life. This same assumption about the purpose of personality change in our later years, shorn of Jung's mystical elevation of death into an ultimate good, is shared by our second psychoanalytic observer of old age, Erik Erikson.

Erikson's Basic Concepts.   Erikson's hypotheses about late-life psychological development, unlike Jung's, are not embedded in a theory that stresses the inherent value of the future compared with the earlier years. According to Erikson, there are eight critical turning points or steps of development we go through from birth to old age, each tied to a particular chronological period of life. The past is still critically important. A person cannot master the issue of a later stage unless, on balance, the developmental crises of the previous ones have been traversed. The developmental crisis of life's eighth stage is **ego integrity** versus despair. Here is how Erikson describes the late-life pinnacle of ego integrity:

> It is a post-narcissistic love of human ego—not of the self—as an experience which conveys some world order and spiritual sense. . . . It is the acceptance of one's one and only life cycle as something that had to be and that, by necessity, permitted of no substitutions. . . . It is a comradeship with the ordering ways of distant times and different pursuits . . . [but] the possessor of integrity is ready to defend the dignity of his own life style against all physical and economic threats. . . . Ego integrity, therefore, implies an emotional integration which permits participation by followership as well as acceptance of the responsibilities of leadership [1963, pp. 268–269].

So Erikson describes the developmental goal of old age in a very similar way as Jung did. As is true of Jung's ideally integrated spiritual person, the person who has reached ego integrity has transcended egotism and self-interest to fully accept his or her place in the scheme of life. For Erikson, however, achieving this inner balance and harmony depends on a specific process: being able to accept one's past.

According to Erikson, the person who has achieved ego integrity is able to accept death. A quite different fate befalls the older adult wracked with regret about past mistakes made, dreams unfulfilled. Frustrated and bitter because it is too late to make amends for the years poorly spent, this older person is desperately afraid of dying. In Erikson's evocative words, the emotion that haunts this individual's final days is despair.

Each Theory's Importance in the Psychology of Aging.   In contrast to Jung's theory, Erikson's ideas about later life are widely known, cited, and accepted by many gerontologists, particularly clinicians who provide direct services to the elderly. Erikson's ideas are much easier to comprehend than Jung's arcane, more philosophical and theological (rather than psychological) ruminations about personality. Erikson describes the concept of integrity versus despair simply and succinctly within a few pages of one book (1963; see also Recommended Readings). Most important, he does not basically depart from the mainstream psychoanalytic framework used for understanding people of any age.

But despite their widespread acceptance as truth, there have been surprisingly few attempts to evaluate the accuracy of Erikson's ideas. Is Erikson right that the critical task of old age is to make peace with our past? Is he correct in saying that reaching ego integrity enables a person to accept death? And how do Jung's more esoteric views fare in the real world when we examine how personality actually changes in the later part of life? These are some questions that we will explore in later chapters when we examine the research bearing on Jung's and Erikson's ideas.

Emphasis on Many Perspectives: The Life-Span Developmental View

Our discussion reveals that a major theme in the psychology of aging concerns change. Three opposing points of view have been offered about development in later life. The first, epitomized by the quotation at the beginning of this chapter (and also strongly implied in traditional psychoanalytic theory) is the widespread idea that aging equals decline. The second, which we can see both in behaviorism and also in the traditional psychoanalytic point of view, is that older people are basically no different than the young. That is, there is no change inherent to age. Finally, there is the alternative just mentioned. There may be change for the better, evolution in later life.

The final psychological orientation we will discuss, the **life-span developmental approach** (Baltes, Reese, & Lipsett, 1980; Baltes & Willis, 1977) embraces each of these ideas. This approach to older people is actually not a defined theory or assumption about the direction of change. Instead, it is a prescription to be open-minded: Pluralism (a variety of points of view) is the best policy to follow in describing and explaining psychological functioning in later life.

Life-span developmentalists are interested in development from birth to death. They view development as a lifelong process. They are interested in describing its regularities and in spelling out the influences responsible for age-related change. But the underlying theme that shapes their writing is the necessity of adopting an eclectic, ecumenical, all-encompassing approach. Pluralism is important in every area of the psychology of aging. It is crucial in examining theories. Many models of development and theoretical world views are important in enriching our understanding of older adults. Pluralism is also essential in describing behavior in the real world. Change in late life is multidirectional. Different aspects of behavior change in diverse ways. In addition, individual people differ greatly from one another; so, too, their patterns of aging follow diverse, specific forms.

For instance, wisdom may increase as people age, while physical stamina generally declines. Activities such as reading may remain stable as we advance in years, while other interests, such as going to the theater, may change. Along each dimension people of a given age will vary greatly. And the way they develop over time in each aspect of psychological functioning may be quite different from the way many of their peers do.

The reasons or causes for age-related changes are also variable. For instance, while for one person a given transformation may be traced to a normative (or typical) age-related event such as physiological loss, for his neighbor the same change may have a more atypical cause, perhaps having to cope with an unexpected late-life trauma, the death of a child. This means that strategies to help improve behavior in the elderly should not be confined to one or a few techniques. A variety of approaches may be useful in enhancing the quality of life for a given older adult.

Actually, giving practical help is another aim of this eclectic world view. Life-span developmentalists want both to describe and explain and also to optimize psychological functioning during a person's later years.

DEVELOPMENTAL RESEARCH METHODS

Because psychologists are interested in all aspects of behavior in later life, the research techniques used in studying the aging process and older adults are extremely diverse—covering the gamut from rigorously controlled laboratory investigations conducted by the most confirmed experimentalist to impressionistic naturalistic observations a committed clinician might undertake. But amid the diversity that will be so apparent in the following pages, one type of research stands out. As noted, in gerontology we often want information about change. How do older people differ physiologically from the young? How does behavior during old age really change from behavior during other chronological periods of life? Or does behavior remain similar throughout life? Is it true that, as the stereotype says, aging brings mental decline? Or do some intellectual functions actually improve in the latter part of life? Is it accurate, as Erikson and Jung suggest, that new aspects of personality and different interests and concerns emerge as we advance in years? Or does personality remain stable? Are we essentially the same people at age 70 as at age 25? To answer these and the myriad other fascinating questions we have about development, special research methods are required. The two strategies most often used are cross-sectional and longitudinal studies.

Cross-Sectional Studies

Because cross-sectional research is infinitely easier to carry out, this approach is by far the strategy used most often to assess developmental change. In **cross-sectional studies** different age groups are compared at the same time on the variable the researcher is interested in, for example, muscle strength, maximum cardiac output, motor speed, mental health, attitudes toward military preparedness, or any of a multitude of choices. Often, before being tested, the groups are matched or made equal on important variables other than age that are likely to affect their scores. For example, if we were using the cross-sectional method to determine the accuracy of the stereotype that people become more politically conservative as they age, we would first pick equal numbers of young adults, middle-aged, and elderly people (for instance, thirty subjects aged 20–35, thirty aged 40–55, and thirty aged 65 +), taking care to match our groups for extraneous influences that might affect their scores (for example, social class, educational level, ethnic background). We then would administer a questionnaire assessing political attitudes and compare the scores of the three age groups. If there was in fact a statistically significant trend toward less liberal attitudes in successively older groups, we would conclude that our hypothesis was supported. As people grow older they do indeed develop more conservative views.

However, this easy conclusion would be wrong. Because we are not examining people over time, we cannot assume that these differences between age groups reflect changes that actually do occur as people advance in years. For instance, although a study carried out a generation ago might show that at older ages people are more conservative, today the same research might show a very different trend. Because of changes in the economy, the need to rebel against the older generation, or simply an age-related tendency to conform to the dominant political ethos, the youngest subjects might espouse the most conservative views. The most liberal attitudes might be held by the now middle-aged 1960s generation or by the oldest subjects, shaped and molded by the liberalism of the Roosevelt years.

This not unreasonable possibility points up an extremely serious problem with cross-sectional studies. They do offer us good information about **age differences,** but they do not accurately reveal **age changes.** In this research strategy, true changes that occur as we advance in years are confounded with differences due to an extraneous factor—being in a different birth group. In gerontology, differences between people born at different times are called *cohort differences*.

Cohort is a crucially important word in the psychology of aging. It is a term very similar to generation but it encompasses a less clearly specified time interval. **Cohort** refers to any group of people born within a specified short period. For instance, people born in 1920, in 1945, and in 1960 constitute distinct cohorts. Snapshots of them at the same age would reveal marked differences not just in appearance but in many aspects of psychological functioning. Variation is inevitable because each cohort is exposed to a unique set of cultural and societal experiences as it travels through life.

Not only do cohort factors contaminate the results of cross-sectional studies of attitudes, they are an important source of bias affecting the outcome of research exploring questions we think might be more immune. For instance, they powerfully affect the results of cross-sectional studies of physical performance and of investigations probing the relationship of intelligence or memory to advancing age. In each of these cases, at least in the past, this research method typically has yielded erroneously gloomy findings: more loss seems to occur as people grow old than really should occur.

As our discussion of the new fitness ethic and its impact on late-life life expectancy clearly implies, younger cohorts have been exposed to an environment promoting better health than those born earlier. The same has been true of the intellectual environment. As our demographic comparisons also show, younger cohorts, on the average, have many more years of schooling. Apart from age, these cohort differences in health and formal schooling give younger groups an inherent advantage; the old are handicapped by having been born at their particular historical time. The true extent of the physical or mental decline age *itself* brings is exaggerated to an unknown degree.

Cross-sectional studies also cannot answer other important questions we are likely to have about development: They cannot tell us whether aging patterns vary from person to person; or how consistent (or changeable) individuals are over time; they cannot give us insights about how what we do and what happens to us in earlier life affects how we feel and function in our later years. For example, given the cross-sectional finding that sexual activity declines with age, is there a subgroup that stays stable, or that actually becomes more interested in sex over the years? If we are very physically fit at 40, are we likely to maintain our relative standing compared to our peers in later life? Do young adults who are introspective or very fearful also have these personality traits in their later years? How do midlife activities such as exercising, regularly watching the nightly news, and not smoking relate to physical or intellectual capacities decades later? Do traumatic childhood events or an adulthood plagued by misfortunes predict an unhappy old age? While we can get answers of some sort to immensely relevant questions such as these by asking people to reminisce about their past, by far the best strategy is to be there on the scene to measure what is going on. This means using the all important *longitudinal* approach.

Longitudinal Studies

In **longitudinal studies** one or several cohorts are selected and then periodically tested, ideally using the same measures, over a number of years. This strategy provides a rich source of information about changes that occur with age in the group as a whole and in particular people in the sample. However, there also are some problems with this ambitious research technique.

First, conclusions based on longitudinal studies ideally should be restricted to the particular cohort(s) the researcher has chosen to study. Because each cohort is unique, it may show an idiosyncratic pattern of change as it ages. So our ability to make *universal* assumptions about aging from longitudinal studies is limited. We should, in good conscience, be cautious about generalizing about aging in the abstract on the basis of data from any single cohort.

There are also serious practical limitations involved in conducting this type of research. Longitudinal studies require a substantial investment of effort and time. The investigator or research team must remain committed to the study and be available to continue it over years or, as is often best in studying adults, over decades. The topic of the research and the measures used to gather information must not become obsolete over the intervening years. Subjects must be recruited who will agree to make the same demanding commitment. This sample must be searched out anew each time an evaluation is due. All of these problems become more acute the longer the study goes on. For this reason, longitudinal studies that span decades are few and far between; those covering several eras of life (such as from youth to old age) are very rare.

The difficulty with getting subjects to commit themselves to the study and return for subsequent tests is more than just a practical problem. It leads to perhaps the most important built-in bias in the longitudinal method. Because participating in a longitudinal study requires such a demanding commitment, subjects who volunteer for this type of investigation tend to be highly motivated and unusually responsible. They also are more likely to be personally involved in the questions the study is measuring. This means that the subjects in these studies tend to be an elite, high-functioning group, not representative of the cohort as a whole.

Furthermore, even among this self-selected sample, people inevitably do drop out as the study progresses. In later and later evaluations fewer and fewer of the initial subjects remain. But this attrition is not random either. The least able people are likely to leave. So those who stay to complete the study are an especially well-off subgroup, almost guaranteed to be unrepresentative of their age peers.

For instance, in gerontological research a major reason people give for dropping out of longitudinal studies is poor health (see Table 1-2). Subjects who do not complete the series of tests are often too ill or have died. Being ill, however, affects performance in aspects of behavior far afield from just physical skills. So, the healthiest subjects, those who remain in the study, are likely to be high functioning on a variety of indexes an investigator might choose. Findings based

TABLE 1-2. Panel attrition during the first four observations of the Duke study.

Observation	Dates	Subjects with Complete Records	Percentage of 256 Who Returned	Percentage of Nonreturnees			
				Died	Ill	Refused	Other
I	5/55–5/59	256	—	—	—	—	—
II	9/59–5/61	192 (10 added)	71	43	23	20	14
III	1/64–3/65	139 (1 added)	52	63	26	2	9
IV	10/66–7/67	110	41	68	18	1	13

Source: Busse, 1970.

on this group will almost certainly exaggerate the extent of any gains age brings, or minimize the losses that take place with advancing years.

So longitudinal studies have the opposite bias from cross-sectional research. They typically offer too optimistic a picture of our later years. This favoritism is exacerbated by another procedural necessity of the longitudinal method: It involves subjects repeatedly being given the same tests. As we know, the more often we take a test the better our performance is likely to be because experience and familiarity tend to lower our anxiety and increase our efficiency. This means that as they return for subsequent tests the participants in longitudinal studies have an increasing advantage: the beneficial effect of more and more practice.

Finally, even among the cohort being studied, the longitudinal method does not allow us to measure the effects of age in a pure or uncontaminated form. Here, too, pure age changes, those advancing years themselves produce, are subject to an important confounding influence: the many life conditions and environmental events that affect the rate of aging at a particular time. For example, because of a lung-cancer scare in a certain year, many people in the cohort we are following might give up smoking between two of our tests. Or, to use a compelling recent example, because of the eruption of panic over AIDS, at age 40 the sample whose lives we are tracing might abruptly report a dramatic decline in the frequency of intercourse. So lung capacity, which normally regularly declines, could one year mysteriously appear to improve; or sexual activities, which typically would remain quite stable at this age, could suddenly dip in a puzzling way. In both of these examples, events occurring around the time of the evaluation have obscured the "true" or "real" age changes that exist. This is why this type of bias is called **time-of-measurement effects.**

Luckily, several decades ago a preeminent gerontological researcher (Schaie, 1965) devised an ambitious research strategy designed to separate or partial out, true age changes from cohort and time-of-measurement effects. Werner Schaie's procedures, called **sequential strategies,** involve following *different* cohorts simultaneously over time and making a series of cross-sectional and longitudinal comparisons between the groups. As with longitudinal studies involving one cohort, Schaie's techniques require a good deal of effort. However, in some of the most rigorous research in adult development this sophisticated methodological procedure for assessing true age changes has been employed.

BOX 1-3
Beware of the Correlation/Causation Mistake

An **experiment** is the research tool used to study causes. Subjects are randomly assigned to different groups. Every factor is held constant except the one whose impact we want to assess. If the group exposed to the intervention or treatment does differ in the way we hypothesize, then we are able to firmly say that what went before caused the particular result.

As is true in every other area of psychology, making the statement "this antecedent has this consequence" is vitally important in the psychology of aging. But the experimental approach simply cannot be used to answer many of the most important questions about causes gerontologists have.

For example, we cannot conduct an experiment to test Erikson's hypothesis that reaching ego integrity enables a person to accept death—it would be very difficult to conduct an experiment to answer that vital question. Does exercising regularly throughout adulthood indeed promote a healthy old age? Unfortunately, we simply cannot easily manipulate these antecedents. So to determine the truth of these questions researchers typically measure preexisting differences in ego integrity or exercise and then relate them either to a consequence now (that is, low fear of death) or, as in the longitudinal approach, to some years in the future (that is, late-life health). In both instances, they use what is called a **correlational approach,** seeing how one variable relates to one or several others. If an association (or correlation) between the variables does exist, then a statement about a cause might be made: Regular exercise during youth and middle age does promote health in the later years. Reaching ego integrity indeed enables a person to be able to accept death.

Particularly when people are not familiar with research, this type of conclusion is often made. Sometimes it is accurate. However, as a closer look at our examples shows, assumptions about causes based on correlations can also be terribly wrong.

For instance, the relationship between exercising during adulthood and good late-life health might really be incidental, due to a more basic underlying cause: good genes. People less sickly, more biologically fit, might have more energy during adulthood and so be prone to exercise more. Their same genetic makeup might also produce a healthier old age. A general predisposition toward a calm and accepting approach to living might underlie both ego integrity (being at peace with one's past) and a low fear of death (being at peace with one's end). The association between the two qualities in older people might not really mean the first caused the last, as we at first assumed.

If we could control for every likely competing explanation (the alternatives just mentioned and others), then we could confidently make statements about causes by using a simple correlational approach. However, as quite often this cannot be done, keep in mind this caution: When examining this very prevalent research strategy in the following chapters, be wary. Although we often will be tempted to do so, make assumptions about possible causes with care.

□

Two Important Examples.   Despite their deficiencies, however, longitudinal studies are inherently superior to cross-sectional ones. For all its problems, there is simply no better way of genuinely understanding the aging process than to measure that process as it actually occurs in flesh-and-blood human beings. While cross-sectional studies can also give us valuable information, longitudinal investigations form the cornerstone of gerontology. Because of their unusual scope, two longitudinal studies in particular stand out as gerontological cornerstones: the Duke study and the Baltimore study.

The **Duke Longitudinal Study** (see Busse, 1970) was begun in the mid-1950s by a multidisciplinary team of researchers at Duke University. These early gerontological researchers set out to explore an almost uncharted area of inquiry at the time: the aging process in normal older adults. Their study was to be extremely comprehensive. Extensive medical, psychological, and sociological data were to be collected during each of a series of tests. Although mainly completed more than two decades ago, the Duke Longitudinal Study not only played a seminal role in the evolution of gerontology as a field, it remains our most important single source of information about what the years after age 65 are like.

The volunteers for this landmark investigation were residents of Durham, North Carolina, ranging in age from 60 to 90. They were chosen to reflect the age, sex, ethnic, and socioeconomic distribution of the older population in the area. None was institutionalized. All were required to spend 2 days at Duke University at regular intervals from the study's beginning until their death. The inducement was a series of free medical examinations and the satisfaction of contributing to a new field.

At the initial round of tests there were 256 participants with complete records, but, as always happens with longitudinal studies, at each evaluation that number regularly decreased (see Table 1-2). Examinations were repeated every 3 or 4 years until 1965, and every 2 years until 1972. Since then there have been various follow-ups on the subjects who survived. (A second, shorter-term Duke study conducted during the 1970s explored a more limited set of changes among a group of younger volunteers aged 45 to 65.)

An amazing 788 or so pieces of information about each subject were gathered at each test. Medical data included a complete history and an extensive physical examination. Particular attention was paid to the assessments of vision, hearing, and cardiovascular functioning. Doctors rated each person for overall health and degree of disability. Participants also rated themselves in these areas.

The volunteers were also examined neurologically. They were evaluated for current psychological disorders and questioned about psychological problems earlier in life. They were given an intelligence test and several comprehensive tests of personality. Their response speed was measured. A full social assessment was made. At each subsequent examination they were questioned about life satisfaction, work and retirement, sexual behavior, family relationships, level of activity, and activities engaged in both currently and in the past.

The outcome has been manifold and rich. The Duke study has given us valuable information about how older people function and behave in areas as different as hearing and vision, sexuality, cognition, and personality. It has offered insights on how older people adapt to changes such as retirement and widowhood and physical disability, how interests change or remain the same in old age, how well older people cope with stress.

However, despite all it has taught us, the researchers who conducted this intensive investigation of later life did not have the tools we have today—the more sophisticated ways of assessing physiological performance, the improved methods for assessing personality and thinking, the modern statistical procedures for assessing consistency and change. Furthermore, by limiting themselves to people in their 60s and older, at least in this first, most comprehensive Duke study, the research team left the wider picture—How do we change in the crucial decades before age 65?—just as shrouded in mystery as ever. The Baltimore Longitudinal Study, our nation's premier ongoing investigation of aging, is filling in the gaps.

The National Institute on Aging sponsored the **Baltimore Longitudinal Study,** which was begun in 1959. The study is in its fourth robust decade of existence today. Like the Duke study, this investigation is being carried out by a multidisciplinary team of researchers probing age changes in many areas of life. However, here the aim is even more ambitious because the lens is far wider than old age: it is to understand how people develop and change *throughout* adulthood. Subjects ranging in age from 20 to over 90 have been recruited. So far about 650 men and 350 women have volunteered. People who enter the study are asked to make an especially intense commitment. Depending on their age, they must return either every year or every 2 years to spend several days at the Gerontology Research Center in Baltimore ideally for the rest of their lives. At each visit a comprehensive medical history is taken. The most thorough medical examination is made. Hundreds of physical capacities are measured, from grip strength, to reaction time, to the amount of body fat, to how deeply a person can breathe. Participants are given tests of memory and learning. Their personalities and methods of coping with stress are regularly probed. Here, too, the payoff has been well worth the investment of effort and time. Particularly in the physical arena, the Baltimore study has not only mapped out totally uncharted territory but has contributed in the most basic practical way to enhancing the quality of life in our middle and later years (as will be described in the next chapter).

THE BASIC THEMES IN THE FOLLOWING CHAPTERS

In the chapters to come several themes will organize the discussion. Because they are the most comprehensive studies in the field, whenever possible, findings from the Duke and Baltimore studies will be highlighted. Because the lifespan developmental view stresses the need for a comprehensive approach to aging, this orientation is the guiding spirit I will follow in the succeeding pages. Most important, though, is the perspective I bring from being a clinical psychologist: Understanding the personal experience of aging is critical. It is essential to explore practical approaches for making that experience the best it can be.

To highlight the personal experience of aging, at the beginning of each chapter I have devised a case vignette tailored to the information in that chapter. While I hope these vignettes bring home the reality that our abstract gerontological concepts and research findings always apply to people (and make the content of each chapter more vivid and relevant), please remember that these clinical cases are not meant to embody universal reactions or even experiences typical of older adults. I cannot emphasize strongly enough that diversity and individual differences are the hallmarks of life after age 65—just as they are at any other stage of life.

To highlight strategies devoted to enriching the experience of old age, I have ended each chapter with examples of practical interventions that apply to the topics discussed. In reading through these attempts to provide concrete help, be cautious, too. Aging should not be thought of as a deficiency or pathological state in need of cure. Keep in mind that what has been done to enhance the quality of life in old age falls far short of what potentially is possible because until quite recently the elderly have been relatively neglected by both psychologists and others whose job it is to provide psychological services.

In addition to focusing on applications, a more academic orientation shapes my writing. Even more important than memorizing the findings is having the skills to assess the quality of the research that produced the results. So rather than just listing "the facts," in the following pages I will carefully *describe* studies—how they were conducted, the subjects that were recruited, the measures that were employed, and the biases inherent to a particular approach. Hopefully, you will emerge from this book both with an up-to-date understanding of what we know today and with the tools to critically evaluate future theory, research, and practice in this rapidly growing field.

Then, there is this final caution. Although occasionally I will present information about biological and social aspects of aging, this book is basically limited to the psychology of later life. But my special focus should not imply that gerontology is compartmentalized into isolated subspecialties. As I hope our look at the Duke and Baltimore studies demonstrates, researchers in a variety of disciplines often collaborate in studying older adults. We would see the same phenomenon by glancing through a gerontological journal or attending a meeting of the Gerontological Society, the national organization of researchers and clinicians whose professional interest is later life. Gerontology is a truly multidisciplinary field!

KEY TERMS

Geropsychology
Gerontological psychology
Ageism
Demography
Chronic disease
Young-old
Old-old
Double jeopardy
Cognitive learning theory
Classical conditioning
Generalization
Operant conditioning
Reinforced
Extinguish

Modeling
Ego integrity
Life-span developmental approach
Cross-sectional studies
Age differences, age changes
Cohort
Longitudinal studies
Time-of-measurement effects
Sequential strategies
Experiment
Correlational approach
Duke Longitudinal Study
Baltimore Longitudinal Study

RECOMMENDED READINGS

Birren, J. E., & Schaie, K. W. (Eds.). (1985). *Handbook of the psychology of aging* (2nd ed.). New York: Van Nostrand Reinhold. The second edition of this definitive compendium of research in the psychology of aging. Glance through the table of contents to get an overview of the diverse topics psychologists study. Difficult.

Erikson, E. H. (1963). *Childhood and society* (2nd ed.). New York: Norton. This book contains the chapter describing Erikson's eight stages of development. Moderately difficult.

Harris, L., & Associates. (1981). *Aging in the eighties: America in transition*. Washington, DC: National Council on the Aging. The book describing the Harris poll. Gives information on how older Americans feel about themselves, being "old," and their life circumstances.

Palmore, E. (Ed.). (1970). *Normal aging*. Durham, NC: Duke University Press.

Palmore, E. (Ed.). (1974). *Normal aging II*. Durham, NC: Duke University Press. Two-volume summary of the Duke findings. Moderately difficult.

Shock, N. W., Greulich, R. C., Andres, R., Arenberg, D., Costa, P. T., Lakatta, E. G., & Tobin, J. D. (Eds.). *Normal human aging: The Baltimore longitudinal study of aging*. (NIH Publication No. 84–2450). Washington, DC: U.S. Government Printing Office. "Midpoint" summary (as of 1984) of the Baltimore findings and published articles based on the study. Moderately difficult to difficult depending on the article.

U.S. Senate Special Committee on Aging. (1987). *Aging America: Trends and projections* (1987–88 ed.). Washington, DC: U.S. Dept. of Health and Human Services. The definitive source for demographic facts about older Americans, covering topics as diverse as income, work and retirement, geographic distribution, illness disability and the utilization of health care services, living arrangements, minority aging, and many more. Not difficult.

Part 2

■

Physical
Processes

Chapter 2

□

The Aging Body

□

Biological Theories of Aging
- Random-Damage Theories of Aging
  - Programmed-Aging Theories

Extending Our Maximum Life Span

Normal Aging
- The Findings of the Baltimore Study
  - How Normal Aging Affects Us
    - Selected Aging Changes

Chronic Disease
- Chronic Disease versus Functional Disability

Lifestyle, Aging, and Longevity
- The Impact of Good Health Practices
  - The Impact of Stress
  - The Impact of Life Changes
- The Impact of Autonomy and Control

Interventions
- Modifying Type A Behavior
- Eradicating Incontinence

Key Terms

Recommended Readings

Sam Kennedy, a youthful looking 65-year-old dentist, has finally gone back to work after his heart attack. Those endless days spent in the intensive care unit had been terrifying, but they came as no surprise. Both Sam's father and older brother had died of heart attacks in their late 50s. Because of this, for the past 5 years, Sam felt he was living on borrowed time. He never expected to make it past 60, much less past 65. He felt he was fated (but being a scientist he called it genetically programmed) to die prematurely, in the same abrupt way.

Lillian Kennedy teased her husband about being a workaholic, but her kidding had a serious undertone. She intuitively felt that the pressure Sam put himself under to work 60-hour weeks might have caused this heart attack as well as the milder one he had had 10 years earlier, at 55. After this first heart attack, Sam began to regularly exercise. He was proud of sticking to his program—waking up at 6 A.M. Monday, Wednesday, and Friday for a 2-mile jog. He was thrilled about his new trim body and often bragged that he felt younger physically now than he had in years. On the other hand, Dr. Berg's other recommendation at the time, "Don't work so hard," had fallen on deaf ears.

To Sam, dentistry is more than a job. It is the center of his life. He had built up his practice from nothing. Many of his patients had been coming for decades; some for more than 35 years. Sam simply could not give up those long-standing relationships, especially when he worried about the care that a younger, more inexperienced dentist might provide. It was hard to refuse new referrals, too, when he was still so skillful with his hands.

Sam took special pride in the fact that age had made so few inroads in his professional skill. Because dentistry demands such speedy and delicate manipulations, he had expected to reach his prime by his 30s and then helplessly witness his abilities slide downhill. However, the slight loss of dexterity he did notice by his 40s seemed more than compensated for by his breadth of experience. He was fond of saying he was better with his hands than many dentists half his age. But, there was one recent case he did not like to think about, a complicated root canal he had to refer to a younger man.

Unlike after his first heart attack, this time Sam could not go right back to work. He needed time to recuperate; and Dr. Berg predicted it would be at least a month before Sam could see any patients at all. Knowing her husband, Lillian was worried about the emotional effect this enforced vacation might have. Just last year Sam had cut short a month's European tour. He felt nervous being away from the office so long.

Unfortunately, Lillian's fears were justified. Instead of regaining his strength, Sam seemed at a physical standstill. Each cardiogram showed improvement. But Sam complained of feeling weak and exhausted. Some days he could barely get out of bed.

Lillian was sure the main cause was emotional. She could see how

Sam's anxiety about his heart was a constant preoccupation, how he focused on every ache in his chest. She noticed how carefully he moved and walked, how frightened he was about exerting himself in any way. She also blamed herself. It had been so easy to agree with Sam that he was too ill to take out the garbage or leave the house. Wasn't it she who had started this downslide by treating Sam as an invalid during the first week after he returned home? But self-blame did nothing to improve matters, so Lillian turned to Dr. Berg for help.

Dr. Berg was concerned, too. In fact, he said, because what was happening to Sam was so common psychologically after a heart attack, a few years ago he had hired a psychologist specializing in behavioral medicine to consult to his practice one day a week. When the nurse made an appointment with Dr. Smith for that Friday, Lillian felt a rush of relief. Now something would be done to get Sam back on the road to a productive life.

Dr. Smith asked Lillian to make a list of the things she did for Sam that she felt he could do on his own. They agreed that she should firmly but gently refuse to do these jobs and at the same time praise her husband for any attempts he made to stretch himself physically. Even though it was difficult, Lillian had to say she was "busy" when Sam asked her to make lunch or to pick him up from the corner store. Most important, they agreed that the best cure would lie in getting Sam back to work. But how could they accomplish this goal?

Lillian had a brainstorm. Perhaps she could convince Sam to see some especially needy patients by appealing to his sense of responsibility: "Mr. So and So needs that dental work so badly, but he is frightened to go to anyone else. If he doesn't have that surgery soon, the tooth will have to come out." Lillian felt sure that if her husband could just get to the office, the downward cycle could be broken: his spirits would rise and his energy would be rechanneled from his chest and gloomy thoughts of his imminent demise.

When Lillian left the session she was anxious. What if this plan was dangerous and actually increased Sam's risk of another heart attack? What if Sam really was incapable physically of living a more independent life? Luckily, though, she followed through. The results were almost immediate. The depressed, feeble stranger is fading. Lillian is getting her husband back!

■

As we have seen, many gerontologists disagree with the idea that age 65 should be the marker that signals our entry into old age. Although any specific age is arbitrary, they feel that if a marker should be picked, about age 80—the age dividing the young-old from the old-old—is a more appropriate one. As people reach their late 70s, the balance tips more from robust to frail. The prevalence of physical problems accelerates. For the first time, many people have limitations in their ability to negotiate daily life. Serious physical and intellectual impairments, while never typical, are much more common than before.

Our perceptions reflect this subtle shift. Suddenly, from taking health for granted, we marvel at the woman over age 80 whose mind is as sharp as ever. We sing the praises of the man who "at his age" still drives or swims a mile or plays golf.

From the biologist's point of view, however, aging begins much earlier, at a time of life when we still call ourselves young adults. In addition, in contrast to the psychological theories described earlier that view growing old in positive terms, a biological perspective on aging involves the unremitting negatives of the stereotypic view: aging equals loss. Biologists can sometimes even trace the beginnings of these losses to infancy. For instance, the development of **athero-sclerosis** (fatty deposits on our artery walls) is a reliable physical change that occurs as we advance in years. (We would expect that Sam Kennedy, for example, has considerable atherosclerosis, as these fatty deposits, when they totally clog an artery, are what cause most heart attacks in middle and later life.) However, the beginning signs of atherosclerosis have been found in infants and advanced signs of this condition were found in autopsies of many Vietnam War casualties in their 20s.

Most biological signs of aging, though, begin to set in soon after we reach adulthood, in our late 20s or early 30s (Tobin, 1977). A leading biologist (Strehler, 1962) has suggested that we use several criteria to decide whether a particular physical change qualifies as truly "intrinsic" or basic to aging: The change should be deleterious, making functioning worse. It should be progressive, gradually getting more pronounced as the years pass. It should be universal, affecting every member of our species to some degree.

The important fact about changes that are intrinsic to aging is their inev-itability. They cannot be eradicated unless we tamper with the biological process that causes us to age.

Scientists are still not sure how intrinsic to aging some changes that predict-ably occur in Western countries as people age really are. For instance, while all Americans can expect to develop atherosclerosis to some degree, in some nonindustrial societies, atherosclerosis is less pronounced or even possibly absent (Ostfeld, 1975). If there really are places in the world where people do not develop this life-threatening problem, it may not be intrinsic to our makeup as human beings and so may be preventable. So it is important to understand which physical changes are true aging signs because we may be able to control or eliminate those that are not.

On the other hand, even when a physical change is inherent to aging, the situation may not be hopeless. The *degree* to which the change develops can often—though not always—depend partly on us. So, in the event that atheroscle-rosis is indeed inherent to aging, by modifying our lifestyle (exercising and eating a low-fat diet) we may be able to slow the advance of this cause of heart attacks and strokes—our top late-life killers.

Another important fact about aging is that as we get older we are increasingly susceptible to disease. When physical changes experienced with advancing age occur to a moderate degree, they are called **normal aging,** but, as we will see more clearly later in this chapter, when these changes become pronounced or extreme they are labeled **chronic diseases.** Furthermore, even when a physiological change does not shade directly into a given chronic illness, it weakens us and so makes us more susceptible to a variety of diseases (Hayflick, 1987; Johnson, H. A., 1985). So the chance of developing many different types of diseases increases with age. In addition, older people are more likely to have multiple illnesses and to get certain characteristic illnesses—the chronic conditions inextricably linked to normal aging itself. Our vignette illustrates a typical example. Sam Kennedy's heart disease is closely tied to the normal deterioration in the heart and arteries that occurs as we age. In fact, in autopsies performed on the very old, it is common to find many pathological changes, illnesses that, even though not the actual cause of death, would have ended the person's life within a matter of weeks or months (Comfort, 1979).

Aging also has a fixed end. Even though there are reports of long-lived people (see Box 2-1), there is little substantiated evidence that any of us survives beyond about age 115. While scientists argue about whether this fixed limit beyond which none of us can live is totally rigid (Fries, 1986) or imperceptibly shifting up (Myers & Manton, 1984), everyone agrees that our **maximum life span** has not changed much for the past 100,000 years. What has changed dramatically is our **average life span,** or the time we can expect *on the average* to live.

Figure 2-1 illustrates how markedly average life expectancy has varied in different eras and societies. It also shows that in cultures where more and more of us survive to the upper reaches of our possible life span, the life expectancy curve looks increasingly boxlike. The ideal is a genuine rectangle. We would have cured all illnesses. All of us would fulfill our species-specific biological potential, living out the full number of years human beings potentially can.

Our maximum life span is long in comparison with most animals. Although rare species, such as the Galapagos tortoise, do outlive us, human beings survive much longer than any other mammal. The horse can live about 46 years, the goat 20, and the mouse only slightly more than 3 (Eichorn, 1979). While other physical indexes are correlated with mammalian longevity, too (for instance, basal metabolic rate and body temperature), Edwin Busse (1977) speculates that our comparatively large brain is responsible for our long life because a mammal's index of cephalization, or ratio of brain to body weight, is positively related to its life span. According to Busse, the survival advantage our large brain may confer is that more neurons can function as reserves to replace those we lose in the wear and tear of daily life.

BIOLOGICAL THEORIES OF AGING

Scientists interested in the biology of aging want to understand what causes the patterns just described—the typical characteristics of normal aging; the close

BOX 2-1
Long-Lived Populations—A Hoax or a Lesson for Us?

Despite the tremendous life expectancy progress we have made, we are still not fulfilling our biological potential. Few of us live to 90, much less to over a century. Many of us spend the final few years of life coping with disabilities, our lives restricted by chronic disease. This is why the discovery of extremely long-lived people is so tantalizing. If there really are places on earth where people often live past 100 and enjoy full, active lives until they die, we would be able to enhance our life span by natural means, without even searching for an aging clock.

Three remote, nonindustrialized communities are supposed to have an unusually high proportion of healthy active centenarians: a village in Ecuador, a principality in Pakistan, and the highlands of Georgia in the Soviet Caucasus. To explain why these people live so long, experts look not to genes but culture and environment.

After spending months in Soviet Georgia, anthropologist Sula Benet (1977) hypothesized that several environmental factors explained the longevity among these mountain people. The Georgians ate a low-fat, low-calorie diet made up mainly of fruits and grains; they were expected to do active outdoor work until an advanced age; and, rather than being devalued, in Georgia age brought respect. In fact, in this remote part of the world, living beyond a century was a badge of highest merit, a cause for great acclaim.

Keeping physically active, not eating fats, and being respected for being old may be life-enhancing. However, a more objective look at the older residents in these communities uncovers a disappointing fact: There is no evidence that they actually do outlive the rest of us (Medvedev, 1974)! When, for example, researchers (Mazess & Forman, 1979) examined birth and census records in Ecuador, information that was very difficult to obtain, they found that the long-lived people they interviewed typically inflated their ages by a decade or more. The records showed that none of the supposed centenarians in the village had really reached this advanced age. In these remote villages, the publicity and status attached to being very long lived (plus the lack of objective records) may make inflating one's age an overwhelming temptation. Adding those extra years may not even be a fully conscious action, because as adults our specific age becomes unimportant, and so from time to time we do "forget" how old we really are.

The practice of adding years to life may not just be confined to these remote villages. In nursing homes I have noticed residents embellishing on an already advanced age to impress listeners, just as a 15-year-old insists he is 18 or a 5-year-old brags that she is really 6 or 7. It seems as if only when we leave youth and approach our normal life expectancy is our age a liability. Once we reach our 80s or 90s, age once again becomes an achievement. It is transformed into a badge of a life well lived.

□

1	New Zealand, 1934–1938	6	U.S. (Whites), 1900–1902
2	U.S. (Whites), 1939–1941	7	Japan, 1926–1930
3	U.S. (Whites), 1929–1931	8	Mexico, 1930
4	England and Wales, 1930–1932	9	British India, 1921–1930
5	Italy, 1930–1932	10	Stone Age People

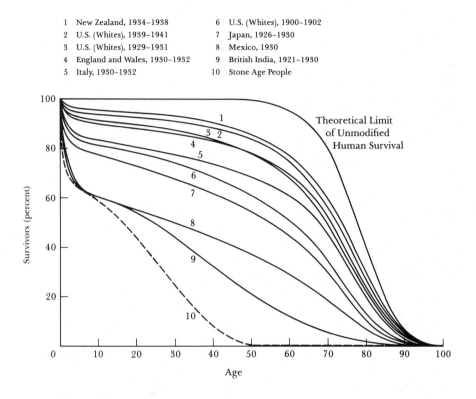

Figure 2-1. Historical and geographical differences in the human survival curve.
Source: Comfort, 1979.

association of advancing age with illness and particularly with certain types of chronic conditions; the maximum human life span and its relationship to that of other species (Brash & Hart, 1978). To be plausible, any hypothesis should explain or at least be compatible with as many of these facts about physical aging as possible. To delve into the numerous fascinating theories of why our body ages is well beyond the scope of this psychologically oriented book. (I urge readers who want to explore this topic to consult any of these excellent review articles: Busse, 1977; Busse & Blazer, 1980; Comfort, 1979; Hall, 1976; Martin, G., 1985; Shock, 1977.) However, I will briefly mention a few hypotheses, theories centering around changes in the basic units of our body—our cells.

Our body is composed of two constituents: *cells*, either able to divide or nondividing, and *intercellular connective tissue* whose main constituents are fibrous proteins called collagen and elastin. Most biologists assume that problems and processes within our cells are the root cause of aging and death. However, some argue that changes in the collagen-rich substance that surrounds our cells may be an important factor, too. As we grow old, the normally pliable collagen and elastin molecules form cross-links and so become stiffer. This loss of elasticity is partly responsible for benign signs of aging such as wrinkled skin. It also causes potentially life-threatening changes such as **arteriosclerosis** (the loss of elasticity of artery walls). Biologist Robert Kohn (1978, 1985) suggests that stiffened collagen and elastin may in itself be an important cause of aging and death because by making our tissues more rigid and less permeable, it impairs the passage of materials throughout our body and so may prevent needed nutrients from getting to our cells.

The different cellular hypotheses about why we age can be grouped into two categories: theories that postulate that aging and death occur because of randomly occurring cellular damage and theories that postulate that a specific preset biological program orchestrates and oversees the process (Marx, 1974a, b).

Random-Damage Theories of Aging

According to gerontologists who subscribe to **random-damage theories of aging,** accumulating mistakes in our cells' ability to produce proteins are the main cause of aging and death. Protein molecules are vital because they form the basis of all cellular reactions and functions. DNA, the genetic material in the nucleus of each cell, programs how our bodies develop and work by serving as the blueprint from which these molecules are produced. The DNA molecule must uncoil and coil again in the process of producing proteins. But in this repeated uncoiling and reconstituting, the DNA molecule tends to develop changes in its structure. These changes, called mutations, probably occur continuously in the course of our being exposed to environmental insults and the cells' work. Because they were responsible for our evolution from one-celled organisms, mutations are obviously not all bad. However, most are deleterious. If their harmful effects are important or widespread enough, they will cause so many defective proteins to be produced that the cell will die.

Our cells have repair mechanisms to correct these spontaneously occurring DNA mistakes, but as we age the DNA mistakes may become more frequent and the repair system itself may not work as efficiently. So, over time, unrepaired damage accelerates.

According to this scenario the physical changes we experience as we age are the visible signs of this accelerating DNA damage. As more DNA mistakes accumulate, more faulty proteins are produced and more of our cells malfunction and die. Eventually, enough cells or enough critically important ones are lost from our body to cause our death.

In interesting support of this theory, the maximum life span of a given mammal turns out to be related to the strength of its DNA-damage-control capacities when its cells are subjected to the deleterious effects of ionizing radiation in the laboratory (radiation causes the DNA molecule to mutate). Mice with a maximum life span of only 3.3 years have the most fragile DNA of any mammal. In contrast, we human beings have the most resilient DNA, and the longest life span.

Other biologists, who agree that aging and death are caused by random cellular damage, believe that the DNA mutation rate—at least outside of the laboratory—is too slow to cause the basic problem. They feel that the most important damage probably occurs further down in the system. Furthermore, they argue that the environmental substances that cause DNA to mutate, such as radiation, affect the genetic material of dividing cells the most, whereas impaired or destroyed postmitotic (nondividing) cells are responsible for the most dramatic symptoms of aging. Critically important parts of our body, such as our brain and spinal cord, are made up of postmitotic cells. Some gerontologists (Hall, 1976) point out that since changes in these structures are most likely to result in our death, an adequate theory of why we age should specifically account for what causes postmitotic cells to malfunction and die.

Programmed-Aging Theories

Random-damage theories of aging assume that there is no master plan that causes us to age and die. In contrast, there is another, equally reasonable idea: Old age, like growth, is specifically programmed and timed. Biologists who believe in **programmed-aging theories** have different ideas about where our "aging timer" is located, what sets it off, and what operates it. What they do agree on, though, is that the orderly, predictable quality of the physical changes we undergo as we advance in years suggests that the aging process must be orchestrated by a coordinated, overall plan. And the fact that each species has a fixed life span suggests that some sort of genetic programming must be involved in aging and death (Hayflick, 1987).

An aging and death "clock" set to go off at a certain time might be located in the DNA of each cell. Or the clock might be more centralized, placed in a system responsible for coordinating many bodily functions. If a centralized aging clock really does exist, two places in particular, because they have such a widespread influence on the body, seem especially likely places for it to reside: the hypothalamus and the immune system.

The Hypothalamus as an Aging Clock.   The **hypothalamus** is a tiny structure in the brain that has effects on the body far beyond its size. It is responsible for coordinating essential bodily functions, such as eating, sexual behavior, temperature regulation, and emotional expression. It has a key role in regulating physical growth, sexual development, and reproduction. This important structure is responsible for the death of at least one critical body system. By shutting off the production of estrogen at about age 50, it ushers in menopause and so ends a woman's capacity to conceive and bear a child (see Chapter 7). Its far-ranging effects on many other organs make it a good candidate to regulate many other manifestations of aging, too, harboring the clock or series of clocks that times our death (Comfort, 1979).

The Immune System as an Aging Clock.   Our **immune system,** spread out over our body tissues, has the crucial job of protecting us against foreign substances such as viruses or bacteria. In response to any alien substance, either a microorganism or incipient cancer (cancer cells are also foreign to our body's tissues), the immune system responds rapidly, producing differentiated "killer cells" and specialized molecules called antibodies tailored to kill the invader cells. The thymus, a gland involved in the intricate immune response, slowly disappears during adulthood. Biologist Roy L. Walford (1969) has suggested that this gland may be an aging pacemaker because its disappearance can signal a weakening of the immune system that has far-ranging effects.

A well-tuned immune system must make a delicate differentiation—recognize and get rid of foreign substances and at the same time spare our own cells. According to Walford, as our immune system weakens, deficiencies develop in both of these functions. Impairments in our aging immune system's ability to stave off foreign attack partly explains why older people are more susceptible to dying from infectious illnesses and also to getting cancer. Deficiencies in our immune system's ability to recognize our own cells may cause it to attack our own tissues—accelerating cell loss. This assult on our body's own cells, called an autoimmune response, may be partly responsible for a variety of age-related diseases, illnesses as different as diabetes and dementia. So, by looking at the type of damage a faulty immune system can wreak, we can explain many of the distinctive illnesses that befall us as we advance in years.

EXTENDING OUR MAXIMUM LIFE SPAN

If a weakened immune system is responsible for aging, we may discover ways to slow our aging rate by stimulating immune functions. If old age is programmed by a hypothalamic clock, ways of setting the timer back might be found. If random DNA damage is the cause of aging and death, we might develop substances that slow the mutation rate or strengthen the system involved in DNA repair. So research on the biological basis of aging can have a most profound practical impact: Instead of prolonging the lives of some of us to some extent, the most we can hope for by curing any *specific* disease, the inquiry into why we age might allow us to retard old age for everyone and lengthen our *maximum* life span.

Interestingly, one way of extending the maximum life span has been known for more than a half century: systematic calorie restriction. In a remarkable series of experiments begun in the late 1930s, researchers found that by underfeeding laboratory rats, it was possible to increase their maximum life span by as much as 60%. The key is an unusual type of underfeeding, what Walford (1983) has labeled "undernutrition without malnutrition." The animals are restricted to much less food, but given a diet that is nutritionally rich. They are simply allowed as few empty calories as possible.

It used to be thought that to be effective, undernutrition had to be started very early, from the time an animal was weaned. And the price of extending the life span was delayed puberty. True, the rats lived much longer, but the diet primarily lengthened the period of life before the onset of adult fertility. However, more recent studies suggest that mild caloric restriction begun as late as midlife can extend longevity, too, though the impact is much more modest than when this life extension strategy is begun early on. (For a much more complete description of the fascinating research on underfeeding, or information about another strategy, lowering body temperature, which has been shown to enhance longevity in cold-blooded animals, consult Schneider & Reed, 1985.)

I must emphasize that what affects some lower animals does not necessarily apply to us, and, best selling life extension books aside, there is no evidence that *any* diet can extend the maximum life span of human beings. We can only hope that the breakthrough that pushes up our maximum life span to, let's say, 130 and puts off the onset of aging until 85 is the blessing it should be, and not a double-edged sword—extending our time on earth at the price of diminishing our pleasure in life.

NORMAL AGING

While modifying the aging process at its root is not yet within our grasp, we do know more about that process than ever before. What is physical aging really like? What happens to our body as the years pass? The landmark Baltimore Longitudinal Study is unlocking this mystery.

The Findings of the Baltimore Study

As little as a quarter century ago, scientists knew little about how people normally changed physiologically as they grew older. Medical tests and treatments were based on young adult standards despite the fact that most people got diagnosed and treated medically in middle and late life. Doctors often knew that the bodies of their older patients were different, but they had to use the laboratory standards based on young people for testing or treating the 70-year-olds they saw. The dosages of drugs they gave to their older patients often seemed excessive. They had been calibrated on people in their 20s and 30s, when our body is at peak physiological shape.

The ongoing Baltimore study (see Chapter 1) has changed medical practice by giving us age norms for some important laboratory tests (Tobin & Andres, 1979). For example, diabetes used to be diagnosed indiscriminately when a person's blood sugar exceeded a certain fixed amount. However, this cutoff point had been established without considering that blood sugar might normally rise with age and that a similar elevation might not have the same pathological significance for the old as for the young. In fact, the researchers found that with the traditional standard, half their volunteers over age 60 were identified as diabetic even though only a minority had symptoms of the disease. Deciding that the standard, not older people, needed changing, they established different cutoff points, ones based on chronological age.

As we know, the main purpose of the Baltimore study is to chart how we change physiologically over the years. Two of its major insights are that variability is the hallmark of normal aging and that there are several distinct aging patterns.

Variability Is the Hallmark of Normal Aging.   The first major finding of the study is something we know just from observing how people the same age look and act: There are tremendous individual differences in aging rates. Some 60-year-olds seem physically more like 40; some 40-year-olds appear more like 65. These differences in outer appearance are mirrored on physiological tests. Abilities as different as lung function, grip strength, and sugar metabolism all vary widely among people the same age (Andres, 1979; Shock et al., 1984).

So, in physical functioning, as in every other arena of life, diversity and individual differences are essential when describing older people. While inevitably we must make generalizations about the aging process and older adults, we must keep in mind that any given person may be quite different from the norm.

Even when we look within the person, the study shows that making global generalizations is unwise. Our different tissues and body systems also vary in their aging rate (Tobin, 1977). Our clinical vignette is a good example. While Sam Kennedy's manual dexterity is much above average—perhaps as good as a typical 30-year-old's—his heart seems physiologically older than we would expect based on his calendar age.

But, even though aging *advances* differently, both between individuals and within ourselves, there are generalizations we can make. The process itself occurs in predictable ways.

The Different Aging Patterns.   Interestingly, the Baltimore study shows that rather than changing in a uniform way, there are several distinct aging trajectories (Shock et al., 1984). One is the pattern we expect: certain physiological functions decline in a regular, linear way over the years. However, other functions are quite stable, either staying relatively unchanged or only declining in the terminal phase of life.

In another quite common pattern, physiological loss does occur but only when a person develops an age-related illness. For instance, among the (unexpectedly) high number of Baltimore volunteers who showed subclinical signs of heart disease, the pumping capacity of the heart declined with age. But if a volunteer had no evidence of heart disease, his or her heart pumped as well at 70 as at 30. While it had been thought that a man's body generally produced less and less testosterone (the male sex hormone), the Baltimore researchers found declining testosterone levels only in their older subjects who were ill.

In yet another pattern, while loss does occur, built-in mechanisms compensate physiologically for the decline. The most fascinating example happens in the brain. As the years pass, individual neurons are continually lost; however, in response to this erosion, the cells that remain literally grow more robust, adding new dendrites and establishing new interconnections, helping preserve thinking and memory (see Chapter 6).

So the traditional view of aging as just irreversible loss is wrong. Stability characterizes aging, too. And even when the years do take a physical toll, our body is surprisingly resilient. We have the capacity to grow and adapt even in areas (such as our brain) where people once never believed growth after maturity could occur.

How Normal Aging Affects Us

Still, despite this upbeat information, we cannot get away from the fact that the dominant theme of aging is physiological decline. The losses that do take place—in the pumping capacity of our heart, in how deeply we can breathe, in the ability of our kidneys to filter wastes—affect how we function in a specific way. As we get older, our ability to perform at top capacity physically gradually declines. Luckily, most organ systems have an extra **reserve capacity**, so these internal changes are only noticeable when we must stretch ourselves to our physical limit, or if they have progressed so far that they interfere with daily life (Johnson, H. A., 1985).

For example, to an athlete, the small physical losses that happen early on are painfully apparent: At 30, most professional athletes know their playing days are limited. Most of us only start to think "my body isn't working as well" years later. In our 40s, it is harder to play a strenuous game of tennis. We don't bounce back as fast from an accident or illness. The physiological losses of normal aging only become a *daily* fact of life when they have progressed even further. In our 70s we may have to take our body into frequent account in planning our day. Normal aging has finally permeated normal life.

The concept of reserve capacity explains why older people are especially vulnerable in stressful situations of all kinds—running for the bus, undergoing surgery, leaving the house in the sweltering summer heat. Age-related physiological decrements cause special problems any time a high level of physical performance is needed, when coping depends on having the reserves to meet these challenges. For instance, while Sam Kennedy found that normally his dental skill seemed unimpaired by age, when a case demanded the highest level of physical performance, he had to refer the patient to a younger colleague.

Selected Aging Changes

So far we have considered physical aging in general terms. Now we turn to specific aging changes. Because of their intrinsic interest, I have chosen to focus on just two classic signs of aging, wrinkled skin and gray hair, and describe what causes these changes to appear. Because of their impact on older people's ability to be independent, we will also look briefly at two other nonfatal aging changes, those affecting our joints and bones. However, a reasonably complete description of how our body ages is well beyond the scope of this psychologically oriented book, so anyone interested in exploring this topic should consult the excellent book on physical aging (Whitbourne, 1985) recommended at the chapter's end.

Wrinkled skin, gray hair, and to a lesser extent stiffness and loss of mobility in joints and bones are reliable hallmarks of growing old. Interestingly, there is no research on how undergoing these changes, or any of the multiple alterations of physical aging, affects our self-concept or our world view. However, we do have this moving first-hand description from the writer Simone de Beauvoir (1972): "When I was forty I still could not believe it when I stood in front of the looking glass and said to myself 'I am forty'. . . . Old age is particularly difficult to assume because we have always regarded it as alien, a foreign species" (p. 283). Being 41 myself, I am convinced that the way aging changes our external image can have a profound impact on the way we think about ourselves. More than any other marker, I credit my gradually graying image as causing a shift in my perceptions. Today I no longer think of myself as a young woman. Now I *genuinely* know I am the age I am. Our first realization we are adults, not 18, may be just as startling: All of a sudden we look in the mirror and are shocked—or hopefully pleased—to see our first gray hair, the beginning of wrinkles around our mouth and eyes.

Graying of Hair.   Our hair loses color when the cells at the base of the hair follicle that produce pigment for each hair either die or just produce less and less pigment. Interestingly, the appearance of gray hair is actually a transitional phase in this process, the time when hairs that have not lost their pigmentation and nonpigmented hairs are interspersed. Eventually, as more and more hairs become nonpigmented, gray hair gradually appears lighter and eventually becomes totally white (Selmanowitz, Rizer, & Orentreich, 1977; Whitbourne, 1985).

Skin Changes.   The visible signs of age in our skin are creases, furrows, and sagging. These reliable signs of growing old, which occur in all of us to varying degrees, are caused by the damaging effect of time itself, as well as damage from an external source—in particular, exposure to the sun's rays.

Our skin begins to wrinkle about the same time that our hair starts to gray, in our 20s and 30s. Wrinkling begins in the areas that are used the most (Rossman, I., 1977); so people who are used to laughing may find their personality indelibly fixed in little lines around their mouth and eyes. Those used to frowning unfortunately suffer the same fate; their mood may be permanently imprinted on their face. So our skin is more than just an envelope covering our body. As we get older, it can also be the visible reflection of who we are inside.

Wrinkling is the end product of several changes. Over time, the outer, epidermal layer of our skin becomes thinner and more furrowed (cells are eroding faster than they can be replaced). Also, the main constituents of the skin's middle, or dermal, layer, collagen and elastin, form cross-links and lose their elasticity. As these molecules stiffen, our skin develops indelible creases. An age-related reduction in the activity of the oil glands compounds the problem, drying out our skin, making it rougher and more easily damaged by the wind and sun.

Changes in Joints and Bones.   The effects aging has on our joints and bones, like changes in our external appearance, remind us we are growing old. We are stiffer, less agile, more stooped. These skeletal changes, however, are especially important because of their impact on daily living. If severe or marked, they may significantly limit mobility and so make an older person unable to handle life independently. As with the alterations in appearance, these changes are progressive and affect all of us to some extent. However, they usually set in years (or decades) later than skin and hair changes and have their most important impact in old age.

Beginning at about age 40, the density of our bones begins to decrease. The bones become more porous, brittle, and fragile. The degree to which we are prone to this condition, called **osteoporosis,** in later life seems to be influenced by genetics as well as lifestyle (exercise and calcium and vitamin intake in our earlier years) (Adams, 1977; Whitbourne, 1985). Gender is important, too. Because women have more fragile and less dense bones to begin with and because the estrogen depletion that occurs at menopause seems to accelerate this skeletal change, the rate of bone loss may be as much as two times as high for women as for men (Whitbourne, 1985).

Even though in itself not life-threatening, osteoporosis is a major indirect cause of disability and death because when bones are porous, they are liable to be broken at the slightest fall. Unlike the "many cracks" that characterize young adult fractures, the brittle osteoporotic bone tends to break cleanly and completely. (A good analogy is the difference between what happens when we bend a green stem and a dry twig. The more pliable stem tends to develop fissures and not completely crack; the twig easily snaps in two.) This means that broken bones heal much less easily and completely in the elderly, with serious consequences. Because an older person may never fully recover from a fracture, it may signal a permanent loss of independence. If the person is unable to care for herself, she may even have to enter a nursing home. Some elderly people, frightened by this prospect, become overly cautious about avoiding a fall. This fear in itself may cause them to limit their lives. So the psychological impact of osteoporosis plus the physical disability it can cause make it a centrally important change that occurs with age.

The other most important change that takes place in the skeletal system involves the joint cartilage which cushions our bones. Throughout life our joints are subjected to pressure each time we move, run, or stretch. This continual wear and tear eventually causes the protective covering over the ends of the bones to erode, a condition called **osteoarthritis.** When serious, the resulting exposure of bone on bone at each joint causes pain, stiffness, and loss of mobility. Although all older people have this wearing away to some degree, only a minority have painful osteoarthritis. However, enough do to make this problem one of the most common chronic illnesses of old age (Kart, Metress, & Metress, 1978; U.S. Senate Special Committee on Aging, 1987).

Ironically, even though wear and tear actually are responsible for the problem, movement (that is, exercise) seems to offer the most promise of increasing joint flexibility and reducing pain. Exercise strengthens the muscles that support the joints, which puts less stress on the tendons and ligaments. It also may indirectly stimulate joint repair, by enhancing cardiovascular function and so enabling more blood to get to the joints (Whitbourne, 1985).

CHRONIC DISEASE

As you may have noticed, osteoporosis and osteoarthritis are perfect examples of normal age-related physiological changes that, when they occur to an extreme degree, are called chronic diseases. So, the main reason that chronic illnesses are increasingly common in older and older age groups, is that they are often part and parcel of normal aging. Normal aging changes tend to shade into chronic disease. This means that in our later years, the traditionally clear-cut distinctions between what is "normal" and what is "an illness" tend to blur or erode. While we may argue about where the cutoff point lies, it is sometimes a matter of semantics whether a given change is labeled "normal" or an "abnormal condition" or disease state (see Johnson, H. A., 1985; Ostfeld, 1975).

Chronic diseases, in contrast to acute or infectious diseases, have certain characteristics. They are long-term, progressive, and (at least currently) often not curable. While a few chronic illnesses are caused by outside invaders such as viruses (AIDS, for example), most have no identifiable external cause. They seem internally generated, produced by a breakdown within the body itself. The emphasis in dealing with these illnesses is on prevention and long-term management, not on a short-term intervention that will produce a dramatic cure (Kart, Metress, & Metress, 1978; see also Chapter 4). Figure 2-2 lists the top ten chronic diseases and their prevalence in middle-aged and older adults. As the figure illustrates, Sam Kennedy's heart condition is high on the list, affecting more than one out of every four people over age 65.

Although children and young adults also suffer from them, chronic diseases are essentially illnesses of middle and later life. Eighty-five percent of people over age 65 have at least one chronic illness. As we advance in years, chronic disease is a more and more frequent accompaniment of life.

Chronic illness is also by far our nation's major category of health problem, costing billions of dollars in doctor visits, in days off work, in home and nursing home care. A tremendous effort is expended on research to understand the causes of these devastating diseases.

Chronic Disease versus Functional Disability

Chronic illness influences the elderly in far-ranging ways. As we will see in later chapters, its presence is linked to intellectual loss, lessened sexual desire and activity, and depression and other emotional problems. Some of these negative effects were apparent in our vignette. Sam Kennedy's illness had a profound effect on the quality of his life.

However, a chronic problem, when mild, need have little impact on the person. Much more crucial in understanding its relevance to a given individual is to know another fact—whether the illness causes disability, that is, whether it prevents that person from freely negotiating in the world. Chronic illnesses only have this effect a minority of the time. For instance, though more than four out of five of all community dwelling older Americans reported suffering from chronic illness in 1986, only one in four said they were disabled by their condition to any

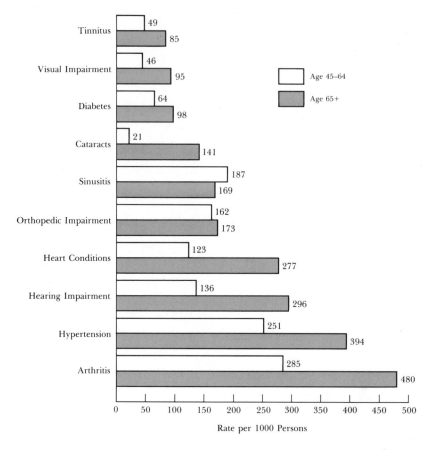

Figure 2-2. Morbidity from the top ten chronic conditions, 1986.
Source: U.S. Senate Special Committee on Aging, 1987.

significant degree. Only a very tiny percent—1.4%—were severely incapacitated, that is, totally bedridden by chronic disease (U.S. Senate Special Committee on Aging, 1987).

So, while they are closely linked, chronic disease is not the same thing as disability, and it is this latter behavioral measure of illness that may be most important in determining the quality of life in our later years (Rossman, I., 1978). Gerontologists call this crucial behavioral measure of illness in the elderly by a special name, **functional impairment.**

Functional impairment is so important an index of health in the elderly that gerontologists have developed a variety of ways of measuring it (see Bergner & Rothman, 1987). Some of the scales are quite broad, measuring functioning in many areas of life. Others are more narrow, designed to measure just how well a severely disabled person can perform the most basic life tasks (Katz, Ford, Moskowitz, Jackson, & Jaffee, 1963). The scale partially reproduced in Table 2-1, the Sickness Impact Profile (Bergner, Robb, Carter, & Gilson, 1981), is one of the most comprehensive. It assesses the person's ability to function in both physical and psychosocial arenas of life (covering sleep and rest, emotional behavior, body care and management, home maintenance, mobility, social interaction, ambulation, attention and concentration, communication, recreation and pastimes, eating, and work). However, it does leave out one piece of the puzzle—the life situation in which functioning takes place. This is important because the environment can either enhance the person's physical potential or exaggerate disabilities, producing impairment that does not need to be there. Gerontologists have a label to describe people who are functioning at a lower level than they need to be—**excess disabilities.**

Excess disabilities often develop because the person's life situation acts as a barrier to independent functioning. The barrier might be the actual physical environment. For example, Mrs. Chin's house is at the top of a steep hill and to get to the front door she must climb a set of steps. This means that though she has only minor trouble walking, she is housebound, unable to go out at all. Or, the barrier might be interpersonal. A well-meaning helper might produce excess disabilities by taking over jobs the person could do on his or her own. For instance, in part because Lillian Kennedy took over everything for her husband, he became an invalid.

As the vignette shows, it is easy for a loving person to inadvertently foster excess disabilities. It is natural to want to take over everything when we see a loved one struggling to dress, or cook, or walk. The temptation is just as compelling in less than loving environments such as nursing homes (see Chapter 4). Staff members often find it more convenient and much easier to dress or feed the disabled elderly in their care rather than waiting for them to dress or feed themselves. But these actions are doing the recipients a disservice. Excess disabilities can turn into true disabilities because inactivity weakens people, accelerating physiological decline. The very act of taking control and autonomy away from older people may in itself hasten disability and death. In addition, taking over deprives the person of the chance to live as productively as he or she can. So, when psychologists treat disabled older people, one goal they often have is to eradicate this waste of human potential. We will see many examples of this goal in operation throughout this book.

A recent study illustrates the considerable contribution "nondisease factors" make to disability and so underscores just how critical the psychologist's role can be in treating functional impairments in later life. When researchers (Summers, Haley, Reveile, & Alarcon, 1988) looked at a group of older people with osteoarthritis, they found that the actual severity of the illness as measured by rheumatologists' X-ray ratings of the affected joints was *not* highly correlated with scores on the Sickness Impact Profile. Instead, the person's psychological state—performance on tests of emotional coping, depression, and anxiety—was a much stronger predictor of how incapacitated he or she actually was.

LIFESTYLE, AGING, AND LONGEVITY

What we are born with (our genes and other influences fixed at birth) and what we are exposed to in the world in the course of our life are the twin factors

TABLE 2-1. Some items from the Sickness Impact Profile.

Dimension	Category	Items Describing Behavior Related to:	Selected Items
Independent	SR	Sleep and rest	I sit during much of the day. I sleep or nap during the day.
	E	Eating	I am eating no food at all, nutrition is taken through tubes or intravenous fluids. I am eating special or different food.
	W	Work	I am not working at all. I often act irritable toward my work associates.
	HM	Home management	I am not doing any of the mainte- nance or repair work around the house that I usually do. I am not doing heavy work around the house.
	RP	Recreation and pastimes	I am going out for entertainment less. I am not doing any of my usual physical recreation or activities.
Physical	A	Ambulation	I walk shorter distances or stop to rest often. I do not walk at all.
	M	Mobility	I stay within one room. I stay away from home only for brief periods of time.
	BCM	Body care and movement	I do not bathe myself at all, but am bathed by someone else. I am very clumsy in body movements.
Psychosocial	SI	Social interaction	I am doing fewer social activities with groups of people. I isolate myself as much as I can from the rest of the family.
	AB	Alertness behavior	I have difficulty reasoning and solving problems, for example, making plans, making decisions, learning new things. I sometimes behave as if I were confused or disoriented in place or time, for example, where I am, who is around, directions, what day it is.
	EB	Emotional behavior	I laugh or cry suddenly. I act irritable and impatient with myself, for example, talk badly about myself, swear at myself, blame myself for things that happen.
	C	Communication	I am having trouble writing or typing. I do not speak clearly when I am under stress.

Source: Bergner, Robb, Carter, & Gilson, 1981.

determining every aspect of who we are. They influence how we think and act, how we look physically and perform physiologically, and the rate at which we age and die.

For humans, however, it is difficult to tease out the precise contributions of inborn and environmental influences on aging and death. Being correlational, most studies that attempt to show a genetic contribution to aging neglect to rule out simultaneous environmental influences, and studies supposedly proving how the environment affects longevity often inadvertently fail to rule out inborn factors (Palmore, 1971b; Rose & Bell, 1971).

For instance, research showing that relatives have more similar life spans than unrelated people is often cited as evidence for the impact of heredity on how long we live. But this finding may have an environmental interpretation, too. Family members, having the same socialization experiences, may tend to develop similar health habits such as smoking or exercising. This similarity of habits, not genes, may be responsible for the more closely correlated deaths. So, with the caution that we can often make the same argument about the research demonstrating that the environment (or our lifestyle) influences longevity, we now look at just a few examples from the massive literature suggesting that living a healthful life slows up physical aging and increases longevity.

The Impact of Good Health Practices

That lifestyle can affect aging is strongly implied by the fact that in contrast to any previous time, today old age begins much closer to 80 than 65. As two authors in one recent book on the topic point out (Lesnoff-Caravaglia & Klys, 1987), this upward shift in the old age entry-point and the related rise in late-life expectancy is a relatively recent phenomenon, one that has coincided in a remarkable way with the emergence of the new emphasis on fitness and health the 1970s ushered in. **Prospective studies,** in which researchers follow thousands of subjects over the years, offer even more direct evidence that health practices affect longevity.

For instance, in one compelling example, 9,000 residents of Alameda County, California, have been followed since 1965 to trace the impact of lifestyle on illness and premature death. Researchers have found out that regularly following three simple health practices is highly correlated with longevity. The life expectancy at age 60 of the men in the study who did not smoke, exercised regularly, and kept their weight within normal bounds, was 82—a full 7 years longer than the men who followed none of these practices. Even at age 80 there was a significant longevity difference between the two groups—1.5 years (Kaplan, 1986).

The study also suggests that adhering to these simple health practices affects the quality of life, not just its length. The 60-year-old men who did not smoke, exercised, and were not overweight, were not only more likely to survive to 80, but were more likely to be healthy 80-year-olds.

Applying the impressive findings of this study to our vignette, the exercise program Sam Kennedy began after his first heart attack may really have been responsible for his outliving any other man in his family. But what about the

---

BOX 2-2
Exercise and Our Aging Rate

We might argue that because the relationship between good health habits and longevity in the Alameda study is correlational, we still have not shown beyond the shadow of a doubt that a more healthful lifestyle does affect aging and life expectancy. In order to prove this we need a *controlled* study where subjects are randomly assigned to a treatment or control group. Luckily, with regard to one health habit in the Alameda study—exercise—we do have this experimental proof.

In the genuinely experimental studies that have been done on the long-term effect of exercise on the heart, subjects typically begin a regular exercise program and then relevant physiological functions such as breathing capacity or heart rate are compared with the control group. Here is a typical example of a study of this type:

About 120 about-to-retire male volunteers aged 55 to 65 were randomly assigned to either a physical fitness training group or a control group (Cunningham, Rechnitzer, Howard, & Donner, 1987). The training program consisted of three group sessions of exercise per week for 1 year. (As with any good program, the intensity of the exercise was geared to the individual's particular health and physical capacities.) While on some indexes of cardiovascular aging, such as maximum heart rate, the training group was not significantly better than the control, the researchers did find marked differences between the two groups on one important index. At the end of the year, lung capacity was much greater in the subjects who had been systematically exercising than in those who had not. In other words, this study in common with many others suggests that while there are inroads of aging exercise cannot erase, it is able to improve some physiological functions that normally decline as the years pass (see Whitbourne, 1985).

□

---

advice he did not follow—to stop working so hard? Might putting himself under too much stress have contributed to his current heart attack?

The Impact of Stress

The idea that stress causes illness and hastens death has been a widespread popular belief since ancient times. However, it has only been during today's "era of the lifestyle" (Lesnoff-Caravaglia & Klys, 1987) that this idea has become accepted by the medical community, too. Doctors never totally discounted the idea that emotional stress could contribute to illness, but with a few notable exceptions they felt this was only true of a very limited category of diseases, those specifically defined as psychosomatic (ulcers and headaches, for instance). All other illnesses had purely physical causes.

In the past two decades, based on the contradictory evidence of studies such as those described below, physicians have been forced to abandon this view. A new field called **behavioral medicine** or **health psychology** (Schwartz & Weiss, 1977) has come of age.

Psychologists specializing in behavioral medicine do research on the psychological causes of illness and the psychological consequences of being ill. They explore the relationships between doctors and patients and among health care providers themselves. They use psychological interventions to get people to stick to good health habits or to treat a physical disease. While the birth of behavioral medicine was stimulated by the self-care revolt against high-tech medicine, one set of studies was especially important in providing impetus to this new field.

The Impact of Life Changes

In the mid-1960s two medical doctors, Thomas Holmes and Robert Rahe, decided to test a long-standing old wives' tale—that changes in life make people physically ill (Holmes & Rahe, 1967). They developed a life-events scale (the Social Readjustment Rating Scale) by having a large number of people rank a list of changes according to how great an upheaval each might represent. The scale includes both positive and negative events as the researchers felt that any change, good or bad, constitutes a stressor that may predispose us to getting sick.

Holmes and Rahe then tested the hypothesis that life changes are related to illness by using two techniques: (1) **retrospective reports,** asking ill subjects about the number of changes they had experienced in the 6 months prior to becoming sick, and (2) a prospective study, administering the scale to thousands of subjects and then looking at who later became ill (Rahe, 1974). Prospective studies, though more difficult to carry out, are methodologically superior to retrospective reports because, being longitudinal, they eliminate distortions from faulty memories.

The studies showed that people who had unusually high-change scores during a short period were indeed more likely to get sick. Depending on their particular physical vulnerabilities, they were more prone to illnesses as varied as cancer or a cold. However, the correlations between life change and illness are very small. So we cannot use the scale in a specific way to predict our chances of getting sick. We all vary widely in our capacity to adapt to change. In addition, despite each life event having a fixed ranking, we also probably differ in the extent to which individual changes are personally stressful. For example, while getting fired or becoming divorced might be a total shock and a terrible catastrophe to one person, to her neighbor these events might have a very different stress value, perhaps even coming as an expected relief.

Furthermore, contrary to Holmes and Rahe's original theory, positive life events may not be illness producing at all. When researchers questioned elderly residents of a public housing complex about their health and then compared their answers with the total number of changes versus the number of negative changes they had undergone, the *negative* events tally alone was correlated with self-reports of poor health. In other words, it really may be our new misfortunes, rather than our new blessings, that affect our physical well-being (Weinberger, Darnell, Martz, Hiner, Neill & Tierney, 1986).

The most compelling argument against the theory, however, is methodological. In demonstrating that life changes raise the risk of illness (as in the study above), researchers typically ask subjects to report on their health and then retrospectively on the changes they have experienced within the past 6 months. But wouldn't depressed people report both more illnesses and more negative life events? In other words, rather than having meaning, some gerontologists argue that the life-stress/illness link may really be an artifact, a function of the *general* worldview of the reporter (see Siegler & Costa, 1985).

A good way of testing if there is a genuine link between life changes and illness would be to look not at test scores but at what actually happens when people experience a high degree of change. Establishing the truth of the theory in this way is particularly important for gerontologists because in old age several events high on the scale are predictable happenings. In Chapter 9, as we look at the health consequences of two of these high-ranking events, retirement and widowhood, we will find that, luckily, these transitions (with the possible exception of widowerhood for men) do not seem to have the dire physical effects that Holmes and Rahe predict. However, another event listed lower on the scale has been linked to physical problems among older adults—moving to a new residence. In gerontology, the impact of moving on the elderly has been investigated so often it has been given a special name: the **relocation effect.**

The relocation effect was first discovered in a group of nursing home patients after their institution had closed. Researchers found a marked rise in the number of deaths during the first 3 months after these residents were relocated to another home (Aldrich & Mendkoff, 1963). Since then a variety of investigators have examined the impact of moves of varying types—from one community setting to another, from the community to a nursing home, and, as in the study above, from one institution to another.

A general pattern has emerged. Once again, contrary to what Holmes and Rahe predict, relocation in and of itself does not seem to have a negative impact on health. If a person is moving voluntarily and to a more suitable environment, it may actually be related to improvements in health and morale (Carp, 1968). However, older people are at risk of becoming ill when they move to a different, unfamiliar, less desirable setting, for instance, from their home to a nursing home rather than to another community setting. They are more prone to suffer negative physical effects when they are moved without adequate preparation. They are especially vulnerable when the decision is out of their control, when the person has not freely chosen to move (Moos & Lemke, 1985).

Actually, the ability to have control or exercise free choice in itself has important effects on the physical and mental well-being of the elderly. While gerontologists argue about the validity of life-stress/illness research, we have genuine experimental evidence that providing control to disabled older adults can be life-enhancing (Hofland, 1988).

The Impact of Autonomy and Control

In one dramatic experiment, Judith Rodin and Ellen Langer (1977) randomly assigned nursing home residents to two groups. The first listened to a lecture about the choices and opportunities for decision making that existed in the nursing home. They were encouraged to take on responsibilities such as planning their meals and caring for a plant in their room. The other listened to a "benign and caring" lecture, which, while just as positive, had a different message: "Let the staff take over your care."

Residents in the first group reported feeling happier, became more active and alert, and increased their involvement in activities. The effect was surprisingly long lasting, present at an 18-month follow-up. Most amazing, this simple control-enhancing communication had an impact on longevity, too. While over the 18-month period the death rate for the control group was about 25%, it was only 15% for the experimental group.

This compelling result led Rodin to investigate the health consequences of being in control in more depth (1986a, 1986b). She taught nursing home residents strategies to actively cope with their environment. Not only did the older people report less stress, once again the intervention had a physiological effect. The residents taught to take more active control over their lives had significant long-term reductions in corticosteroid levels, and, at an 18-month follow-up, significant improvements in health.

She also demonstrated that feeling more in control of the nursing home decision itself had physical consequences. Hospitalized older people destined for nursing homes were assigned to either an intervention group designed to increase their sense of having control over the decision or to a control group. One year later, the experimental group was more likely to have been discharged back to the community. Furthermore, of the variety of variables measured, next to initial health status, perceived control over the nursing home decision was the factor most strongly correlated with subsequent health. In other words, this encouraging study demonstrates that by making an involuntary move as voluntary as possible (that is, increasing a person's choices around an inevitable move), we may be able to lessen both the immediate physical effects of relocation and reduce the risk of illness for months to come!

In several reviews, gerontologists have summarized the growing body of research that suggests that increasing autonomy and decision-making powers among the elderly affects physical well-being (see *The Gerontologist,* June 1988; Rodin, 1986a, 1986b). But they urge caution, too. As with Rodin's studies, most of the research has been done with frail older people. Enhancing control may have much less physical impact among people not already made dependent by disabling chronic disease. Furthermore, as Rodin points out, people differ in the extent to which they *want* to have decision-making powers. Some are most comfortable letting others take over. They like to have the anxiety inherent in making choices removed. There are also times where having full control may be more anxiety-provoking than the reverse. For instance, how many older people would feel comfortable having absolute say over whether an ill spouse has the life-threatening operation the doctor recommends? But even if enhancing control is not a good thing for everyone, the impressive research on autonomy among the disabled suggests there is a real link between our emotions and how our body behaves.

INTERVENTIONS

Just as Rodin manipulated the sense of being in control, any environmental influence—from smoking to overstressing ourselves—that increases the risk of getting ill can be changed. However, changing even the simplest habits known to cause chronic disease can be difficult. The main reason is that illness-producing habits such as smoking are immediately reinforcing and so exert a naturally powerful pull. The prospect of punishment at an unknown future time often lacks the power in the present to stop us from practicing a lifestyle that shortens life.

The same applies to the research on life changes and autonomy. When faced with upheavals in our lives, how do we reduce their impact? How can we increase our sense of control when encountering the unavoidable restrictions life can bring? Professional help is often needed to put the insights about how the environment affects illness into practice.

Clinicians trained in behavioral medicine (most often psychologists, psychiatrists, and social workers) provide this help (see Davidson & Davidson, 1980). Using psychological principles, in particular, behavioral techniques, they train people to control their level of stress, usually by employing specific relaxation techniques; or sometimes, in the same way as Rodin did, by teaching strategies to actively cope with unpleasant events. They use psychological techniques to help deal with physical illnesses once they have developed, too. As in our vignette, this often means helping the older person function as independently as possible in the face of an unchanging chronic disease. However, it also may involve ameliorating or trying to cure physical conditions by using psychological strategies.

I have chosen interventions at opposite ends of the disability spectrum to illustrate how psychological techniques are being used to assist in the prevention and treatment of physical conditions. The first treatment is an example of a behavioral medicine intervention focused on prevention. Younger people are taught to change a behavior that increases the risk of premature heart disease. The second shows what can be done once a genuine problem has developed. It also illustrates how psychologists deal with a very different type of person— institutionalized older adults. (Once again I must stress that these are just two examples among literally thousands of published interventions in this flourishing young field.)

Modifying Type A Behavior

Type A behavior is a way of approaching life that has been shown to increase the risk of a person's dying from our nation's top killer—heart attack—in middle age. In the late 1950s, cardiologists Meyer Friedman and Ray Rosenman (1974) identified the characteristics of what they labeled the **Type A personality** and initiated a series of studies demonstrating that people with this personality trait did get more heart disease (Dembrowski, 1977). In contrast to calm, relaxed Type B people, Type As are competitive, short-tempered, achievement-oriented workaholics. They often put themselves under tremendous pressure, cramming more and more appointments into an overbooked schedule, working 25 hours a day. Sam Kennedy's tendency to compare his skill to dentists half his age, and to view professional success as everything, suggests he is a prime example of someone with this personality trait.

Reasoning that the underlying problem Type As have is an inability to relax, Ethel Roskies (1980) decided to treat this condition by training young type A men in relaxation techniques and systematically teaching them to relax in situations that normally aroused the Type A response.

Unfortunately, her first step in initiating this program, getting subjects to participate, was difficult. Like many other poor health practices, there are immediate reinforcements for continuing to behave in a Type A way. By making hard work important to succeeding professionally, society rewards people for having this personality trait. If the prospect of professional advancement or monetary gain is weighed against the possibility of a distant (though highly aversive) event like a heart attack, we can see why many Type A men might be reluctant to change their way of approaching life.

One strategy Roskies used to keep her subjects from dropping out was to treat them in groups. Once convinced to attend a session, subjects were enticed to continue by their very drive to compete and succeed. Group members complimented one another for attending sessions and learning to change their behavior. This aroused the competitive instincts of the men and so made it difficult for them *not* to follow through. Then, when they learned to relax, the new behavior became immediately reinforcing in itself. Rather than just being a strategy for possibly preventing a heart attack, the men found that far from inhibiting their ability to work, their new, less-stressed approach to life enhanced their productivity. They were more appreciated by their colleagues. Their creativity improved.

Subjects learned relaxation by practicing daily at home using taped instructions. When they had mastered the art of relaxing in this nonarousing situation, they implemented what they had learned at work, particularly in situations where Type A behavior would be most likely to occur. During a business meeting or when having a disagreement with a coworker, they specifically focused on relaxing when they felt their stress level begin to rise.

The program was a success. Type A behavior was replaced by Type B responses. While we would need a longitudinal study to assess its long-term effects, provided these young men do not revert back to their old behavior, we would expect that they would be less likely to develop and die from a heart attack.

Eradicating Incontinence

Incontinence in the elderly, in particular urinary incontinence because it is so much more common, has been called one of the most challenging problems in geriatric medicine. It is estimated that 5 to 15% of the elderly living at home suffer from this problem; it may affect more than 50% of the residents in nursing homes (as reported in Mitteness, 1987). To appreciate how important this condition has become we need turn no further than our TV set. Over the past few years advertisers are suddenly spending thousands of dollars on commercials advertising products to treat this previously "unmentionable" difficulty.

As we might imagine, incontinence can have marked psychological effects— impairing the older person's self-esteem and placing an emotional toll on family caregivers. In fact, more than any other problem, it is often the final indignity that prompts even the most devoted family to send an older relative to a nursing home (Milne, 1976; Noelker, 1987).

Incontinence is not a disease but a symptom that may have a variety of causes (Adams, 1977). One cause is mental impairment, either reversible or chronic (see Chapter 10); that is, a person who is confused or disoriented may be unaware of the physiological signal to urinate or defecate. Other conditions that may cause incontinence are any problem that limits mobility and so may prevent the person from physically getting to the toilet and illnesses directly affecting the organs involved in elimination (Adams, 1977). However, even when incontinence has a medical cause, behavioral interventions can work.

Richard Hussian (1981) instituted a behavior modification program to eliminate incontinence among 12 residents of a nursing home. He first observed these regressed incontinent older people for 2 weeks to establish a baseline of urinary "accidents." Then, during the next 2 weeks, he instructed the nursing staff to follow these rules:

1. Assist the resident to the toilet within 15 minutes of awakening in the morning. If the resident does not void, retoilet every half hour.
2. Offer the resident toileting every hour. Praise him or her if your offer is accepted, and then toilet immediately.
3. Praise the resident every time he or she voids. Inform the person if no voiding occurs.
4. If the resident does not void after 4 hours, toilet him or her every half hour.
5. Toilet within 15 minutes after an accident.
6. After every toileting, check for wetness of clothing 1 hour later. Praise the resident if he or she is dry; inform the resident if he or she is wet.

These instructions are designed to make continence inherently easier and also involve the systematic use of reinforcement and immediate feedback. Hussian's subjects were taken to the toilet at times they might logically need to urinate, were praised for continence, and were told when an accident occurred. As with any behavioral strategy, success depended on rigidly following a fixed procedure, and, at least during the 2-week intervention period, involved an unusual commitment from the staff. The payoff was worth it. The frequency of accidents was reduced from a baseline of 33 per day to an average of only 4. There was no relapse. A follow-up 2 weeks after the intervention revealed that only 2 of the 12 patients had had any accidents at all.

This example shows how just a brief environmental intervention can markedly improve even physical problems we tend to pass off as irreversible or "unchangeable" in old age. The next two chapters continue this theme, as we focus more directly on age-related disabilities and explore the often critical impact the environment has on promoting independence in later life.

KEY TERMS

Atherosclerosis
Normal aging
Chronic diseases
Maximum life span
Average life span
Arteriosclerosis
Random-damage theories of aging
Programmed-aging theories
Hypothalamus
Immune system
Reserve capacity

Osteoporosis
Osteoarthritis
Functional impairment
Excess disabilities
Prospective studies
Behavioral medicine or health
 psychology
Retrospective reports
Relocation effect
Type A personality

RECOMMENDED READINGS

Comfort, A. (1979). *The biology of senescence* (3rd ed.). New York: Elsiever/North Holland. Comprehensive examination of the biology of animal and human longevity and biological theories of aging. Difficult.

Kahn, R. L. (1977). Excess disabilities and the aged. In S. H. Zarit (Ed.), *Readings in aging and death: Contemporary perspectives*. New York: Harper & Row. The original article explaining the concept of excess disabilities. Not difficult.

Schneider, E. L., & Reed, D. (1985). Modulations of aging processes. In C. E. Finch & E. L. Schneider (Eds.), *Handbook of the biology of aging* (2nd ed.). New York: Van Nostrand Reinhold. Review of the literature of the various biological strategies that hold some promise of extending the maximum life span. Moderately difficult.

Shock, N. W., Greulich, R. C., Andres, R., Arenberg, D., Costa, P. T., Lakatta, E. G., & Tobin, J. D. (Eds.). (1984). *Normal human aging: The Baltimore longitudinal study of aging* (NIH Publication No. 84–2450). Washington, DC: U.S. Government Printing Office. Summary of the Baltimore findings and reprints of the journal articles summarizing the study as of 1984. Moderately difficult.

Whitbourne, S. (1985). *The aging body: Physiological changes and psychological consequences*. New York: Springer-Verlag. Catalogues the age changes that occur in each system of the body and explores the psychological consequences of these changes. Highly recommended. Moderately difficult.

Chapter 3

□

Sensing and Responding to the Environment

□

Our Senses
- Our Windows on the World: Vision
  - Our Bridge to Others: Hearing

Taste and Smell

Motor Performance
- Age Changes in Response Speed
- The Source of Age Changes in Response Speed

Interventions
- Designing Housing for the Elderly
- Adapting Private Homes for the Elderly

Key Terms

Recommended Readings

At 73, Sam Kennedy has still not had another heart attack. But recently he was forced to retire. It was not lack of stamina; he was able to be on his feet for those 8-hour days. The problem was speed and agility: he was just too slow to do an acceptable job. Often when taking an impression, the material would harden before he could extract it from the patient's mouth; even more embarrassing, sometimes it hardened before reaching a problem tooth. Good sense dictated it was time to retire. Besides, dealing with patients was a terrible strain because he found it so difficult to hear.

His hearing trouble had been obvious to everyone else for years. Sam seemed the last to know, even though he understood intellectually that poor hearing is an occupational hazard of dentistry because of the years spent next to the drill's whine. It was humiliating to feel frail and out of control, to continually have to ask: "Could you repeat that? I didn't quite catch what you said." Besides, the fault might not really be his. It could be the tendency everyone had to speak so softly or the awful increase in noise pollution in New York City. Hadn't noise forced the Kennedy family to change their brunch spot from a popular, crowded pancake house on Madison Avenue to an empty deli on Lexington?

Since 1979, the Kennedys, their daughter Jane, son-in-law Bill, and the grandchildren had had a happy tradition of assembling on the first Sunday of each month at the pancake house to talk and visit and gorge on homemade waffles with whipped cream and chocolate sauce. Now the scene of the gatherings was the deli, even though the syrup there was watered-down maple, the waffles as hard as rocks. Brunches at the pancake house had become shouting matches. While the food is much worse, family harmony is much better in a place where Sam has a chance of hearing the conversation.

The Sunday Sam suggested the switch, his family got upset, imagining he might be exaggerating his trouble hearing because he wanted to move the family's brunch place. Sam's daughter Jane was especially suspicious. Hadn't her father announced (too loudly as usual!) just a few minutes before that the chocolate sauce had deteriorated so much it now tasted bitter not sweet? Hadn't she noticed another difference in her father's hearing that seemed clearly premeditated—his selective trouble hearing *her?* Frankly, Jane felt offended by this. For some reason she was being tuned out. Rather than getting angry as was her typical response, Jane withdrew, focusing her attention on her mother during the family get-togethers. Distancing was simply a more comfortable way to act. Jane had come to dread conversations with her father, the headaches she got from straining to make herself understood.

Withdrawing did have an important benefit. For the first time since her teens, Jane and her mother began to confide in one another. When Jane opened up about Bill and the kids, her normally closemouthed mother responded with an anxiety of her own—her fear about her sight.

Lillian Kennedy had been happy when the ophthalmologist said her fuzzy vision had a treatable cause—cataracts. But then there was a letdown. Because she was over 70 and had diabetes, her seeing problems probably had a variety of causes, some untreatable. A cataract operation might not help much. Meanwhile, knowing her vision was failing all too often made Lillian want to cry. The sense of loss was especially intense when she attempted the activity that had always given her the most pleasure before, cooking.

Jane almost cried herself when she heard that her mother had given up gourmet French cooking. As Lillian explained, concocting those complex dishes was beyond her because the numbers on the stove, the measuring cup, and the food processor were too hard to see. The last straw was a humiliating dinner party when she had trouble seeing the color of a souffle in the window of the lit oven, took it out too soon, and totally ruined the main dish. She also turned down invitations to go to restaurants with friends. Seeing was hard enough during daylight; it was practically impossible in dim light.

Hearing this story made Jane realize she had to take action, so she asked a psychologist friend who worked with older people for advice. The friend suggested a commonsense idea: "Knowing your mother, can you think of ways of modifying the environment that would improve her life?" One place suddenly popped into Jane's mind—the kitchen.

Lillian Kennedy has begun inviting guests over for dinner again because of the actions her daughter took. Jane installed a high-intensity light in the oven, painted large numbers on the stove and any other utensil her mother might need, and replaced the fluorescent overhead kitchen light because of its intolerable glare. Jane even found a large-type nouvelle cuisine recipe book for the visually impaired. And, because of her talk with the psychologist, she learned something else. What looked like her father's lack of love was really lack of hearing. Jane's next plan is to use a similar environmental strategy to help Sam.

■

Basic to living is the ability to receive information about the environment. Just as crucial is the capacity to respond quickly to the information we do receive. Limitations in either of these capacities may have far-ranging effects. If severe enough or important enough, these limitations may make older people less independent, less able to competently negotiate life. They make the elderly feel vulnerable, out of control, less sure of themselves. They may make relationships more difficult and cut off pleasures as simple as enjoying a fragrant rose or a beautiful sunset. That is why this chapter is devoted to these changes—the alterations age brings to our senses and capacity to physically respond to our environment.

This means that this chapter, like the previous one, deals with negatives, things that go wrong in the latter part of life. But always keep in mind that, as with any age-related physical change, people vary greatly in the extent to which they suffer from the signs of deterioration described in the following pages. Genuine problems only become relatively common in advanced old age. Most people in their 60s and 70s have only minor losses in their senses, even in their ability to respond. Furthermore, there are always exceptional older adults whose capacities are superior to the average 40- or even 20-year-old.

There are also pitfalls in making comparisons between the elderly and younger adults in these important capacities. Tests measuring performance have a built-in bias against the old. We can see this clearly by looking at the standard vision or hearing test.

A person taking a hearing test is presented with a series of low-intensity tones and asked to raise a hand when a sound is heard. The well-known vision test involves identifying letters or numbers on a chart. Sensitivity or acuity on either measure is judged by the faintest stimulus that the person can perceive.

But older people tend to be more cautious than the young (Botwinick, 1966), not only in approaching these tests but in taking the more sophisticated tests of sensory acuity or response speed that psychological researchers use (Olsho, Harkins, & Lenhardt, 1985; Welford, 1977). When a man of 70 cannot quite make out a letter on an eye chart, his tendency is to err on the side of caution, deciding "I'd better not guess." When a psychologist measuring age differences in response speed tells an elderly woman to "push lever A as fast as you can when the green light comes on," she is likely to have a similar impulse. Younger subjects, being more prone to guess, are at an advantage. They may be judged as more capable in comparison with the elderly than they really are because their strategy maximizes the chance of doing well.

Finally, in reading the litany of losses that follows, keep this optimistic thought in mind. Some of the losses in vision, hearing, and motor performance that do take place with age may be modifiable. Studies strongly imply that our lifestyle (for example, being exposed to high levels of noise or leading a sedentary life) can accelerate sensory decline and even contribute to an inevitable age-related slowing of responses. So some of the problems some older adults have today might be escaped in part by future cohorts of elderly by being more health conscious and taking better care of their health.

OUR SENSES

The sensory information we get from the world comes from a rich variety of sources. We sense pressure, pain, heat, and cold through information provided from special nerve endings (receptors) in our skin. Sensory nerves in our muscles and joints inform us of the position of our limbs. A more poorly understood set of sensors feeds us information about the internal workings of our body. Losses in any of these functions can be important in an older person's life.

However, vision and hearing are our senses of first rank, those we worry most about losing, those most crucial in keeping us in contact with the outside world. As we might expect then, gerontologists have far more complete and detailed information about age changes in these two sensory systems than in any others. For these reasons, we will explore in depth how aging affects hearing and vision. However, we will also briefly look at taste and smell. While losses in these secondary senses do not have the dramatic consequences declining vision and hearing can produce, the research that has been done on age changes in taste and smell is especially fascinating. It also offers hints about how to preserve our enjoyment of one of life's great pleasures—the joy of eating—as long as we can.

Our Windows on the World: Vision

Some of the ways aging affects our sight are obvious. We notice in our mid-40s that we are having more trouble reading the newspaper or realize we need stronger glasses in order to make out the time on the clock across the street. However, our vision also changes in a variety of subtle, surprising, and unexpected ways as we grow old.

The most basic or all-encompassing seeing problem that increases in frequency in later life is poor **visual acuity.** A person with poor acuity cannot see things distinctly. Acuity is what the familiar eye chart tests.

Impaired acuity is only a major problem when it cannot be corrected by glasses or contact lenses. While we do not have national figures on just how much more prevalent minor uncorrectable problems of this type are, surveys show moderate or severe impairments in acuity are indeed much more common in old age. Of the estimated 1.4 million people in the United States unable to read newspaper print with conventional correction in 1977, almost two in three were over age 65. Of the more than 500,000 Americans suffering an even more extreme impairment, legal blindness, almost half were elderly (Botwinick, 1978). Furthermore, experts point out (Kline & Schieber, 1985) that, if anything, these figures probably err on the conservative side. So it is no wonder that we associate loss of sight with being old and that in one national poll blindness ranked second only to cancer as the most feared consequence of living to an advanced age (Cogan, 1979).

On the positive side, the statistics show that only a small minority of all older people suffer from even moderately impaired acuity. However, minor uncorrectable deficits in acuity do become quite common by the ninth decade of life. For instance, while three-fourths of the Duke Longitudinal Study volunteers in their 60s and more than half in their 70s had normal corrected vision in at least one eye, among those over age 80, only slightly more than one-third did (Anderson & Palmore, 1974).

Acuity declines slightly from early adulthood through the 50s and then falls increasingly rapidly after age 60 (Kline & Schieber, 1985). The Duke study, being longitudinal, was able to directly measure this accelerated drop. When volunteers' vision was tested twice, 10 years apart, the prevalence of poor visual acuity (corrected vision of 20/50 or worse in the better eye) increased by 13% among people first examined in their 60s. Among volunteers first tested in their 70s, the comparable 10-year rise in poor acuity was 32% (Anderson & Palmore, 1974).

Impaired acuity can hamper people in almost all of their activities. A second type of vision problem that occurs as we grow old has a more limited impact, though it is actually a more universal change. This is the familiar problem with near vision—a difficulty whose inextricable link to old age is reflected in its technical name, **presbyopia** ("old eyes"). Interestingly, this classic harbinger of growing old does not take place as abruptly as it seems to when people first tend to notice it in their 40s. The ability to focus sharply for near vision seems to lessen gradually beginning in childhood (Botwinick, 1978); it only grows severe and noticeable by middle age (Vaughan, Schmitz, & Fatt, 1979).

Presbyopia and poor visual acuity are straightforward problems. Other aging signs require careful attention to notice: Older people have special trouble seeing in dim light. They have problems in distinguishing colors, in particular those in the blue-green range. They tend to be more bothered by glare (being blinded by a direct beam of light); and have difficulty shifting focus quickly to objects at different distances. Their field of vision is narrower than a younger person's; they are not as able to see things at the periphery of their gaze (Colavita, 1978). Figure 3-1 illustrates the impact some of these difficulties have on an older person's ability to perceive the world.

These changes are caused by deterioration in the eye's structures and in the rest of the visual system. Often several types of deterioration in combination make a particular aspect of vision worse. This means, as was the case for Lillian Kennedy in the vignette, that even if a problem in one of the structures is treated, sometimes an older person's vision may not dramatically improve. Now we turn to a brief description of the structures involved in vision and how they change as we age. (As you read the following sections, refer to Figure 3-2.)

The Steps Involved in Seeing.   In order for us to see, light enters the eye through its outer cover, the cornea, passes through a clear, viscous fluid called the aqueous humor, and then through the iris, which can contract or expand to adjust the opening called the pupil. The light then travels through the lens behind the iris, and through a gel-like structure called the vitreous humor to reach the back of the eye, the retina. The retina, the eye's insulated back rim, is where the delicate visual receptors are located.

The major purpose of these structures is to filter and focus visual stimuli so the best possible image arrives at the receptors. The visual receptors, located on the retina, are the crucial link by which we make visual contact with the environment. Here light waves are transformed into the nervous impulses that are carried to the brain.

There are two types of visual receptors. The rods, concentrated at the periphery of the retina, are highly sensitive but only to gradations in brightness and are responsible for our seeing in dim light. The cones allow us to see in detail, are sensitive to color, and are located in the center of the retina. Impulses originating

Figure 3-1. Scenes simulating the vision of typical people in their 20s and in their late 70s or 80s. The upper panel illustrates increased susceptibility to glare; the lower, problems of acuity associated with poor contrast.
Source: Birren & Schaie, 1977.

in the rods and cones then travel to the brain via the neurons making up the optic nerve. They arrive at the part of the brain called the visual cortex.

Deterioration can occur anywhere along this pathway and affect our ability to see. And since our visual system does not function in a vacuum, aging in other parts of the brain may also affect how well an older adult perceives and processes visual stimuli (Ordy & Brizzee, 1979). Because the eye is the externally located, or **peripheral part of the visual system,** problems that occur here are called peripheral influences on vision. When the trouble is within the central nervous system, the person's difficulty is said to have a **central** cause. (Unless otherwise noted, the following information is taken from four reviews: Botwinick, 1978;

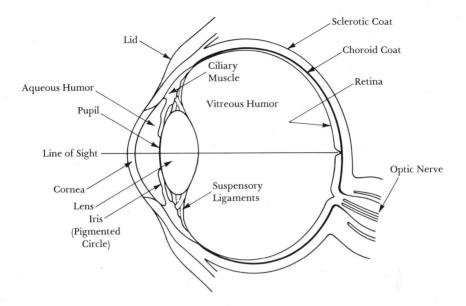

Figure 3-2. Anatomy of the human eye in cross-section.

Fozard, Wolf, Bell, McFarland, & Podolsky, 1977; Kline & Schieber, 1985; and Ordy & Brizzee, 1979.)

Age Changes in the Visual System.   Beginning at the eye's outer rim, several changes occur in the first structure we come to, the cornea, as we age. The most obvious is an opaque grayish band, the **arcus senilis,** which is so noticeable a feature of an older person's eyes. While sometimes seen as early as age 50, this band is typically not fully formed until the 60s. Its major negative result is to slightly reduce peripheral vision since the passage of light is affected by this opaque circle (Colavita, 1978).

Changes in the next major innermost structure, the iris and pupil, may reduce overall acuity. However, they cause the most difficulty in dim light, when we need as much light as possible to reach the retina. The iris is a pigmented (our eye color), circular structure with a hole, the pupil, in its center. In bright light the iris reflexively widens, causing the pupil to constrict. This reduces the amount of light reaching the sensitive retinal receptors and so prevents them from being damaged. In dim light the iris narrows and the pupil dilates, allowing as much light as possible to get to the rods and cones. This more rapid change, coupled with a gradual increase in the sensitivity of the rods, helps us see in the dark.

However, in later life the iris is less able to narrow. The consequence of this change is that older people have smaller pupils than the young in both dim and bright light, but the difference becomes more marked in darkness, when the pupil needs to be as large as possible to permit optimal vision (Birren, Casperson, & Botwinick, 1950). Having a smaller pupil means older people have a fixed internal dimmer. In bright light the dimming effect is not a big problem because

TABLE 3-1. The most common age-related eye diseases. (Cataracts are described in the text.)

Disease	Description
Glaucoma	A buildup of fluid within the aqueous humor (that results when the normally open passageway that lets the fluid circulate narrows or closes) causes increased pressure in the eye and ultimately permanently damages the retina or optic nerve. With early diagnosis, blindness can be prevented as special eye drops, medications, laser treatments, and sometimes surgery can help reopen the passage. Glaucoma is called "the sneak thief of vision" because it seldom produces early symptoms, so it is important to be regularly tested for this illness in middle and later life.
Senile macular degeneration	The neurons in the center part of the retina (called the macula) no longer function effectively. Symptoms may include blurred vision when reading, distortion or loss of center vision, and distortion of vertical lines. Early detection is important because sometimes laser surgery can improve vision.
Diabetic retinopathy	In this long-term complication of diabetes, the blood vessels that nourish the retina either leak fluid or grow into the eye itself and rupture, causing a serious loss of vision. Laser surgery can sometimes prevent blindness or severe vision loss.
Retinal detachment	The inner and outer areas of the retina separate. Detached retinas can often be surgically reattached with good or partial restoration of vision.

not much illumination needs to get in. But in darkness the impact can be dramatic, explaining why older people have particular trouble with night vision.

The dimming is far from minimal. It is estimated that changes in the pupil and iris, plus in the transparency of the lens, typically permit only about 30% as much light to reach the retina at age 60 as at age 20 (Saxon & Etten, 1978).

The lens actually changes in important discrete ways as we age. First as just mentioned, the normally clear lens gets more opaque. In the same way as looking through a dirty window makes it more difficult to see outside, this age-related clouding tends to impair overall visual acuity. It also makes older people more sensitive to glare because, as is also true when sunlight hits a dirty window, rays of light are scattered when they hit the lens. At the extreme of this age-related clouding is a totally blocked lens—a **cataract.**

Because no light can reach the retina when the lens is opaque, cataracts, when severe, cause blindness. However, they do not need to have this devastating effect. Unlike most other age-related illnesses, vision loss caused by cataracts is easily treated. The physician surgically removes the defective lens and either implants an artificial lens in its place or prescribes special contact lenses or glasses. (Unfortunately, as Table 3-1 shows, the other top-ranking illnesses causing vision limitations or blindness in older adults are nowhere near as curable.)

A second change in the lens' transparency affects color vision. Because the clouding that develops has a yellowish tinge, it produces a decrease in sensitivity to hues in the blue-green range, explaining why distinguishing between these colors is so hard for many older adults.

So far it seems as if the lens is merely a protective window. This is not true. This structure, which looks like a contact lens, has the important function of bringing objects at different distances into focus on the retina. It accomplishes this task by changing shape. When we view near objects, the lens bulges (curves outward). When we view distant objects, it flattens out and becomes elongated. This focusing ability deteriorates as we age in part because of a property of the lens itself. Throughout life our lens grows continuously, adding cells at its periphery without losing old cells. To make way for this growth, the older cells become compacted toward the center of the lens. Over time, this accumulation produces the loss of transparency discussed above. It also makes the lens too thick at the center to bend well. In addition, the ciliary muscle, which controls changes in the lens' shape, becomes less functional. The net effect is an overall reduction in flexibility, making shifting focus from near to far (and vice versa) more difficult. Because what is lost is the ability to curve, this explains why the inability to see close objects is such a distinctive age change.

While signs of deterioration in the retina (changes in the appearance of the retinal blood vessels and atrophy of the cells themselves) are apparent when the eyes of older adults are examined, experts argue about how important a contribution the retina makes to age-related vision changes. Does the decline in the number of cones contribute to losses in acuity and color discrimination, or can we lose many visual receptors without our ability to see being affected? (See Whitbourne, 1985, for a review of this issue.) What impact do changes in the retina (versus a more impenetrable lens or smaller pupil) have in impaired dark adaptation in later life? (See Kline & Schieber, 1985, for a review.) Dark adaptation, the gradual process that allows us to see much better in a dimly lit place, depends on chemical changes in the receptors. While the rate at which this process proceeds may not change too much with age, the level of sensitivity ultimately reached does. No matter how long a 70-year-old remains in the dark, she or he will not see nearly as well as the typical person of 25.

The same questions apply to the part of the visual system we cannot directly observe—the neurons comprising the optic nerve and the visual cortex. We gradually lose neurons as we age. How important is this erosion to vision in later life? Some experts point out that the more rapid decline in many visual functions that occurs after age 60 cannot be accounted for simply on the basis of deterioration in the peripheral structures of the eye. So, vision decrements in old age most likely also have a central nervous system cause.

Consequences of Visual Impairments. Despite this long list of negative changes, we must keep in mind that the *typical* older person does not have marked problems seeing. Furthermore, many elderly people may compensate for the minor losses they do experience by changing their behavior and so continue to live as fully. However, as the vignette suggests, more severe vision impairments may dramatically affect the quality of life in old age.

As in the vignette, do vision impairments in later life make people more isolated, depressed, or insecure? Do they affect cognition—impairing thinking and producing intellectual decline? While only longitudinal data can really answer these questions, studies comparing older people with very poor vision and those with normal vision on measures of personality and intellect offer some clues.

For example, Carl Eisdorfer (1970a, 1970b) used the Rorschach test, a widely used measure of psychopathology in clinical settings, to assess the mental health of Duke study volunteers with no vision deficit versus those with impaired sight. Contrary to his prediction, the performance of the two groups of volunteers was indistinguishable. On the other hand, when other Duke researchers (Anderson & Palmore, 1974) used different indexes—self-reports and social workers' ratings—they did find that volunteers with poor vision were functioning more poorly. They reported fewer involvements and activities; the social workers rated them as more isolated and less secure.

But notice the methodological flaw in this study. The social workers knew who had poor vision and who did not. Wouldn't they be predisposed to see more problems among the vision-impaired volunteers simply because we all assume (Han & Geha-Mitzel, 1979) that having this difficulty should produce isolation or insecurity? The next study, which set out to show that poor vision has a direct cognitive effect, has another type of methodological flaw, one typifying the difficulty of making conclusions from simple correlations.

When Loraine Snyder, Janine Pyrek, and Carroll Smith (1976) administered the mental status questionnaire, an oral test of simple cognitive abilities (see Chapter 10), to nursing home residents and found that those who were legally blind got significantly lower scores, they concluded that poor vision contributes to cognitive decline. However, the simple fact that the blind nursing home patients might have been generally less healthy could just as easily have accounted for their poorer test scores. Diabetes, for instance, produces a host of physical problems (impaired circulation, heart disease, stroke) that affect mental functioning, as well as being a leading cause of blindness. Wouldn't the legally blind group, being more likely to be diabetic, be more prone to suffer from these diseases, too? So, because these researchers did not control for overall health by matching groups on this relevant variable, their study does not tell us whether vision problems, in themselves, have any cognitive effect at all.

So, despite its intuitive appeal, we have no data that support the idea that old age limitations in vision—even when severe—have any effect on personality or intellect. However, this is not true of the toll the years take on our other sense of first rank, hearing.

Our Bridge to Others: Hearing

Although studies do conflict, we do have more solid evidence that age-related hearing problems affect the clarity of thinking and emotional well being. At first glance this seems puzzling because we tend to think of vision as our most important sense. However, while losing our sight cuts us off from the physical world, poor hearing wreaks damage in a more important realm of life. It prevents us from verbally communicating, and language is the bridge that connects us to other human beings (Saxon & Etten, 1978). So it is the interpersonal world we are deprived of when we lose our ability to hear. (Unless otherwise noted, the following information is from Corso, 1977; Maurer & Rupp, 1979; and Olsho, Harkins, & Lenhardt, 1985.)

Even more than poor sight, hearing impairments are the province of old age.

About four in five Americans with this problem are over age 45; more than half are 65 or beyond. In a national survey of late-life chronic conditions, poor hearing greatly outdistanced poor vision in prevalence—it was third in frequency; vision impairments ranked ninth (see Figure 2-2). To be aware that poor hearing is an old age problem we do not need the benefit of any statistics or even have to regularly talk to older adults. People over age 65 are 13 times as likely to wear the visible emblem of this deficit, a hearing aid, as is any other group.

On the other hand, only a minority of people over age 65 report this problem—for instance, less than one in three in the poll mentioned above (U.S. Senate Special Committee on Aging, 1987). Genuine deficits, those significantly hampering the ability to hear conversation, only strike a large percent of people in their late 70s. While these deficits are sometimes the end point of a steady loss beginning in midlife, other times they are not.

Cross-sectional studies suggest that our hearing begins to decline in our 30s (earlier for men than for women). Losses start accelerating by late middle age (Ordy, Brizzee, Beavers, & Medart, 1979). However, these are average figures, the degree of change revealed when different age groups are compared. When people are followed longitudinally, researchers find marked individual variability in the extent and pattern of decline. Some people do begin losing hearing in their 30s; others later (or earlier) on. For many the loss is more pronounced for high tones and slowly spreads to lower frequencies. Others do not show this typical age pattern of decline. Apart from different genetic vulnerabilities and the fact that there are distinct types of hearing diseases, one reason for this variation is that age-related hearing loss has a definite environmental cause—noise. People in noisy occupations (construction workers, rock musicians) lose hearing much earlier, sometimes having genuine handicaps by their 30s or even before. Prolonged exposure to the chronic low-level noise of simply living in a city also may contribute to age-related hearing difficulties. So, unfortunately, since noise pollution seems more endemic than ever, the prognosis seems grimmer for hearing than for many other problems of aging. At the same time that we are reducing the rate of other top-ranking chronic conditions (such as heart disease) by taking care of our health, poor hearing may be a more prevalent impairment in future surveys of older adults.

Even today the statistics on its prevalence probably err on the low side. Older people tend to be reluctant to admit that they have this particular difficulty. Poor hearing strikes at our vanity—it is so emblematic of being frail and old. The experience of not being able to hear can also easily be rationalized. "Other people are talking too softly. There is too much background noise." Furthermore, even experts have trouble agreeing on the level of impairment that constitutes a genuine handicap. One reason is that an older person's hearing can vary radically in different situations—depending on who is speaking and on the level of background noise. As in the vignette, a marked hearing problem in a crowded restaurant can almost disappear in a quiet place.

So, as is true of vision, age-related hearing losses have aspects that are surprising, that are not obvious at all. Poor hearing in later life is not, as we might think, an unvarying, all-or-none phenomenon.

People with old age hearing loss—**presbycusis**—have special difficulty distinguishing high-pitched tones; they have more problems hearing high-pitched voices (such as those of women or children), greater trouble hearing high-pitched sounds (such as consonants), or phrases (such as warnings) that even though loud are yelled in a high-pitched voice. They are much more bothered by background noise: the hum of traffic on the street, the drone of an air conditioner or fan. For them, the lower-pitched background noise tends to drown out conversation. Attention deficits compound the problem with noises of this type, as older people's reduced ability to filter out irrelevant stimuli makes it hard for them to concentrate totally on what they need to understand.

People with presbycusis also hear less well when someone speaks rapidly (Pickett, Bergman, & Levitt, 1979) or when they cannot see the speaker's face. The reason is that to compensate for their loss many hearing-impaired people read lips. When deprived of this added informational cue, they cannot piece together what is being said as well.

These selective difficulties can cause misunderstandings when people notice that sometimes the older adult can hear fairly well, other times practically not at all (Kart, Metress, & Metress, 1978; Rosenthal, 1978). As we saw in the vignette, the person may be accused of pretending not to hear, of turning hearing on or off deliberately. Friends and family may be prone to these suspicions because dealing with hearing problems is so frustrating. Suddenly we must struggle to achieve something we take for granted—a simple conversation.

Another problem, called **recruitment,** reinforces these negative ideas. A person suffering from this problem first cannot hear and then hears perfectly after a sound reaches a certain level of loudness. While only a minority of older people with presbycusis experience recruitment, when it is part of the person's deficit it can exasperate friends and relatives who are told to stop shouting just after being asked "Please repeat that. I can't hear what you said" (Oyer, Kapur, & Deal, 1976).

Just as is true of the eye, the ear is a complex structure made up of more externally located parts and receptors located within. The more external structures concentrate, filter, and focus sound, preparing it for transmission to the brain by the delicate receptors located in the inner ear. As we will see, however, unlike for vision, the cause of the characteristic late-life hearing deficit, presbycusis, is quite localized. (Refer to Figure 3-3 while reading the following sections.)

The Steps Involved in Hearing.   The first structure sound waves encounter on their way to the brain is the pinna, the apricot-shaped appendage we call our ear. After being collected by the pinna, the waves then travel along the ear canal (the external auditory meatus) to the eardrum (the tympanic membrane) where they cause vibrations that are transmitted to the next (now fully internal) part of the auditory system, the middle ear. The middle ear is a cavity containing three bones: the malleus, the incus, and the stapes. These bones amplify the vibrations and prepare them for transmission to the inner ear. It is in the inner ear that the actual hearing receptors, called hair cells, are located (see Figure 3-4).

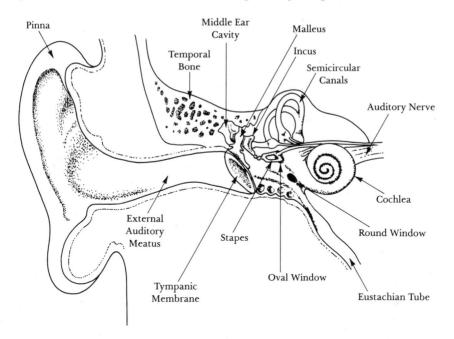

Figure 3-3. Anatomy of the human ear.

The part of the inner ear crucial to hearing is the cochlea. It is shaped like a coil and composed of three fluid-filled compartments. Vibrations arriving from the middle ear set up waves in these compartments and cause the basilar membrane,

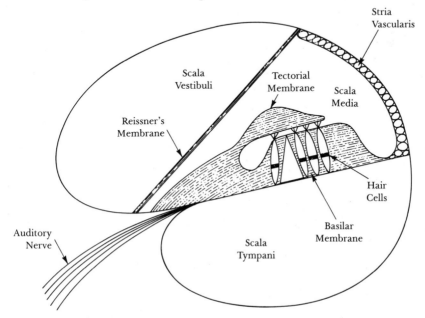

Figure 3-4. The human cochlea (cross section).

on which the hair cells sit, to bob up and down. The cells jiggle, shearing against the tectorial membrane located above. It is this bending or deformation that generates the impulses responsible for our experience of sound. Impulses set off in the hair cells then travel to the auditory cortex via the neurons of the auditory nerve.

The way we perceive the properties of a given sound—its pitch (highness or lowness), its volume (loudness or softness), and its timbre (complexity)—depends on the way the basilar membrane moves. Different sounds set up varying patterns of motion in the fluid-filled cochlea, which, in turn, cause different displacements of the basilar membrane. For each sound, a unique pattern of hair cells is stimulated to fire. It is through this complicated mechanism that we experience the jangle of a jack hammer, the stirring tones of a symphony.

Except for very low frequency tones, the location of the firing hair cells is important in discriminating pitch. Because of the physical properties of the basilar membrane, high-pitched tones cause maximal stimulation of the hair cells on the portion of the membrane at the base of the cochlea. Low-frequency tones stimulate hair cells toward the apex of the cochlea most. So our ability to hear high-pitched sounds depends on the firing of the hair cells at the base of the cochlea.

Age-Related Changes in the Auditory System.   In marked contrast to age-related vision losses, which are caused in large part by deterioration in the more external, image-focusing, structures of the eye, presbycusis is produced by changes in the inner ear—the part of the auditory system housing the actual hearing receptors.

While four types of inner ear deterioration produce presbycusis, a major cause is atrophy of the hair cells themselves. And it is the hair cells at the base of the cochlea (those coding high tones) that are most fragile, explaining the selective loss for these sounds. However, the central nervous system (deterioration of the neurons involved in hearing) may have a role, too, particularly in hearing deficits beginning in old age (Ordy et al., 1979). And, while they tend to have a more minor impact, the outer and middle ear may contribute to late-life hearing problems, too.

Outer or middle ear conditions that affect hearing may be as easily correctable as removing wax from the ear canal. Or, as is true for a middle ear illness called otosclerosis, they may require surgery to cure. When the main site of the trouble is in these outer parts of the auditory system, however, the person does not truly have presbycusis. Because what is impaired is the transmission or conduction of sound to the auditory receptors, the problem is called a **conductive hearing loss.**

Older people with a conductive hearing loss do not have special problems hearing high-pitched tones. Their difficulty is uniform and so less likely to be misinterpreted by loved ones because it is more similar to what we imagine a hearing difficulty should be. People with this type of hearing loss are also better off in another way: They are more apt to benefit by a device that magnifies all sounds equally, a hearing aid (see Box 3-1).

BOX 3-1
Hearing Aids: Getting Better All the Time

In the past, hearing aids were bulky boxes, obvious advertisements of old age. Furthermore, because they magnified all sounds equally, they were not very helpful for presbycusis, the characteristic late-life hearing loss. So, even if not bothered by the esthetics, many older people shunned a hearing aid. Better wear nothing than be victimized by the drone of background noise magnified much too much.

Today technology is transforming the way hearing aids look and sound (Leary, 1988). The newest devices fit into the ear canal and are almost invisible to the glance. The standard way of controlling the volume, via a control box wired to the aid, has also gone underground. A person can buy a remote-control credit-card-sized apparatus manipulated from a pocket, well out of sight.

More important, progress is being made at solving the problem of differentially magnifying higher pitched tones. Companies are experimenting with computerized hearing aids that monitor the pitch of sounds, selectively suppressing lower frequency noise and enhancing conversation sounds. These newer hearing aids are not for everyone. They are expensive and most appropriate for people whose impairments are not severe. But for the millions of elderly whose lives are limited by this debilitating chronic condition, these advances are good news indeed.

□

Consequences of Hearing Impairments.   Not hearing well increases our physical risk. Sound is a crucial way we learn of environmental dangers. But, as the vignette shows, the main toll this late-life problem takes is in the social realm. Loved ones may withdraw, defeated by the struggle to communicate; the older person may become uncommunicative rather than continually having to ask: "Please repeat what you just said." Another reaction might be to grow paranoid, reading betrayal into whispers half-heard (see Oyer et al., 1976).

Clinicians have long associated paranoid reactions with hearing problems that develop in later life. An isolated, hard-of-hearing elderly man may develop the idea that his neighbor is out to get him; a elderly widow may decide strangers on the street are whispering about her. No study suggests that hearing problems, in themselves, produce paranoia. However, in one interesting investigation, researchers (Cooper & Curry, 1976) did discover a higher-than-expected rate of poor hearing among hospitalized older patients diagnosed as paranoid. Furthermore, these paranoid older people tended to have had their hearing impairment for a long time. So deafness, particularly when it develops early, may predispose people who already have serious emotional problems to develop a paranoid reaction rather than another psychological disorder.

What about people who are not serously disturbed? While the research is contradictory (Thomas, Hunt, Garry, Hood, Goodwin, & Goodwin, 1983; see Whitbourne, 1985, for review), poor hearing has been linked to psychopathology even among normal older adults. For instance, in the same investigation where he found that Duke study volunteers with impaired vision were no worse off emotionally than those with normal sight, Eisdorfer also evaluated a group of hard-of-hearing volunteers (1970a, 1970b). These older people did show more signs of emotional disturbance, giving more constricted, rigid, and immature responses.

Hearing deficits have also been linked to that feared outcome—intellectual loss. When Samuel Granick, Mort Kleban, and Alfred Weiss (1976) gave an IQ test to two groups of older adults (one very healthy, the other with illnesses), they discovered that even people with relatively minor hearing impairments performed less well. This was especially true for the tests of verbal abilities. Here hearing problems were strongly correlated with lower scores (see also Thomas et al., 1983).

This study is particularly compelling because the researchers controlled for the relevant variable, health, and were testing subjects with small losses—problems that did not prevent them from hearing questions on the test. Are even subtle hearing difficulties physiologically associated with general central nervous system deterioration? Do they affect cognition because the hard-of-hearing person tends to withdraw from the world? Is it that they make people less attentive, less able to concentrate on information? Whatever the answer, this study underlines just how important this sense of supposedly second rank really is to how we function and behave.

TASTE AND SMELL

Because taste and smell work together to allow us to enjoy food, the inroads aging makes in these senses may make eating less pleasurable and so contribute to poor nutrition in some older adults. Smell is also an early warning system alerting us to hazards such as fire, so losses in this sense can make life less safe as well as limiting our joy in living (Engen, 1977).

Cross-sectional studies show that the elderly have less acute senses of taste and smell than younger adults do (Murphy, 1985; Schiffman, 1977, 1979; Schiffman & Pasternak, 1979). However, because these secondary senses are less critical than vision or hearing, we have little information about how taste and smell really change as the years advance. Does our sensitivity become less acute decade by decade, or decline primarily in old age? Are the cross-sectional age differences researchers typically find due to aging or illness, the fact that often sick older people are being compared with healthy young adults (Engen, 1977)? No matter why they occur, however, the differences when the young and the old are asked to use these senses are fascinating in themselves.

In the first of a series of studies on food sensitivity and preferences, Susan Schiffman (1977) blindfolded college students and elderly people and asked them to identify and rate the pleasantness of pureed foods after tasting them. Not only were the older people less able to identify the foods, they were more prone to rate them as bland tasting.

In her next study, Schiffman and a colleague (Schiffman & Pasternak, 1979) demonstrated that these altered perceptions were mainly due to impaired smell. The researchers asked subjects to discriminate between the odors of different foods compared in pairs, and then to rate what they smelled for pleasantness. Once again, the elderly were poorer at identifying most odors. However, their sensitivity varied from odor to odor. It was most acute for fruits, and so the older people gave fruit smells the highest marks for pleasantness.

This research shows that the reason for the frequent late-life complaint "food doesn't have as much taste as it used to" is not just nostalgia—believing that food was fresher or tastier in the good old days—but altered smell (Schiffman, 1979; see also Murphy, 1985). It also offers insights into why food preferences can change in apparently strange ways in old age. Older people may simply grow to prefer foods whose odors age impairs the least.

Altered smell sensitivity may also partly explain another common complaint older people have: "Food tastes bitter or sour." Foods such as chocolate and some vegetables tend to have a bitter taste that is masked by a highly pleasant odor. So when the sense of smell weakens, these foods may taste unpleasant (Schiffman, 1979).

For Schiffman, the logical next step was to try to improve the flavor of foods for her older subjects by amplifying the smell. She fortified pureed foods with artificial flavors and then had young and old people taste them and compare them for pleasantness with the same foods in their natural state. As she expected, the elderly gave the amplified foods the highest ratings. The college students ranked the adulterated foods lowest, complaining about their nauseating odor and overpowering taste.

This study clearly implies that amplified foods might be specially marketed to appeal to older consumers. However, since to some of us this tampering might have a sour taste from a health point of view, there may be a palatable way of enhancing the older person's enjoyment of food. One reason eating loses its appeal in later life is that dental problems (for example, ill-fitting dentures) make chewing difficult or painful. So by encouraging the elderly to see a dentist regularly and expanding Medicare to cover dental services, we might be able to improve the quality of old age in this important arena of life.

MOTOR PERFORMANCE

One of the first things we notice about the behavior of older people is the way they react. We are struck by their slowness, that they take so much *longer* to respond. This loss of response speed is not only one of the most observable signs of aging but one of the most well researched phenomena in the psychology of aging (Birren & Renner, 1977).

Responding quickly is essential to performing some very basic activities— crossing a street before the light changes, driving, avoiding getting hurt by stepping out of the way of environmental obstacles. Slow responding makes older people prone to accidents because it puts them out of sync with the pace modern life often demands.

Slowness also puts the older adult out of step with people. It can cause conflict because it is so discrepant from the rate at which the rest of us live. As we all notice when we find ourselves behind a slow older person at a supermarket checkout counter or behind an older driver going 40 in a 55-mile-per-hour zone, irritation automatically wells up. So the slowing age brings puts a damper on relationships and may be one reason our fast-paced, time-oriented society tends to have such negative prejudices toward the old.

Age Changes in Response Speed

When psychologists measure this slowing in the laboratory, they are looking at a major facet of what is called **psychomotor performance.** Psychomotor performance is simply our ability to quickly and accurately respond on tasks involving taking action. For instance, on one typical test of psychomotor performance a subject is handed a page of letters and told to "cross off all the As as fast as you can." In another, called a **reaction-time experiment,** the subject must make a predetermined response as quickly as possible when a signal appears: "Push button A as fast as you can when the green light comes on."

A predictable finding on tests of this type is more slowness: successively older-age groups perform less and less well (see Salthouse, 1985). In fact, age differences are so pervasive and reliable on psychomotor tasks that "slower responding" is one of the most certain predictions we can make about how our behavior as a young adult will change as the years pass (Birren & Renner, 1977; Welford, 1984).

However, the *magnitude* of the deficits depends on the task. Older people do more poorly on complex psychomotor tasks than on those demanding simple actions—performing more badly when aiming at a target than when a striking a table as fast as possible; doing much worse when asked to complete a sequence of steps rather than one. The main reason for these even exponential age declines in performance as the complexity of the task increases is that more complicated tasks require more thinking (Hale, Myerson, and Wagstaff, 1987). And it is "thinking time" versus "acting time" that slows most as we age.

Reaction-time studies illustrate that there are two phases involved in responding: mentally figuring out how to act and physically carrying out the action. In a simple reaction-time experiment subjects are told to do something (for instance, press a buzzer or tap a foot) as quickly as possible after a stimulus (usually a tone or light). In other reaction-time studies, subjects are confronted with two or more signals (for example, a green and a red light), each having a different appropriate response, and must tailor their action to the stimulus that appears. By measuring the time it takes from when a signal goes off to when subjects *begin* to lift a hand, researchers can isolate the time the mental or thinking phase takes. They then compare this figure with age differences in **movement time,** the actual time it takes to act. While older people do more poorly in both phases, the most pronounced age decrements typically occur in the first, or thinking phase (Hicks & Birren, 1970; Welford, 1977, 1984).

What happens during this internal phase, the period from when a signal to act occurs and the response begins? Researcher Alan Welford (1977) offers the following hypothesis. (See Figure 3-5 for a more comprehensive diagram.) First, information arriving from the sensory organs is fed to the brain. Here three discrete central nervous system (CNS) events logically take place: The information is perceived, then an action is decided on, then the response is programmed to be carried out. The end point is the action itself performed by the effectors— the voluntary muscles and the involuntary reactors of the autonomic nervous system.

According to Welford this set of steps probably takes place many times in the course of taking even the simplest actions:

> Performance hardly ever consists of a single run through the chain. . . . Even relatively simple actions such as picking up a glass or opening a door involve an iterative process in which an initial action . . . is followed by a series of smaller adjustments each of which depends for its precise form on the outcome of the one before. In other words data from the effector action and its results on the external world are fed back as part of the sensory input for the next run through the chain [pp. 450–451].

So what we think of as "responding"—the actual movements a person makes—is only the end point of a series of internal events. Now let's look at where in this chain the typical older person's problem probably lies.

The Source of Age Changes in Response Speed

Problems in the last step, taking action, may be crucial in explaining slowness in some older people (for example, those who suffer from arthritis or other diseases that greatly hamper movement). Problems at the beginning step, sensory input, could account for much of the slowness of others (for example, people whose hearing or vision difficulties made it a continual struggle to know whether the environment required taking action). However, since the reaction-time studies involve clear signals to respond and separate out the movement part of the chain, the marked age differences found here clearly suggest that the middle central nervous system steps are critical. In other words, as we age the main reason we react more slowly is that our central nervous system is less able to quickly process information (see Birren, 1974; Birren & Renner, 1977; Salthouse, 1985; Welford, 1969, 1984).

But if a slower-functioning central nervous system is the main problem, then we would not expect the older person's slowness to be just limited to physical responses. The elderly should be *generally* slower in all their actions—less quick

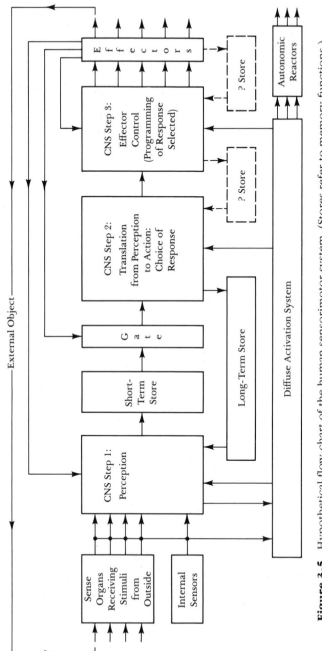

Figure 3-5. Hypothetical flow chart of the human sensorimotor system. (Stores refer to memory functions.)
Source: Welford, 1977.

BOX 3-2
Traffic Accidents and the Older Driver

Reacting quickly to unpredictable signals is essential to being a good driver. Seeing and hearing are just as critical. Age-related vision problems such as sensitivity to glare and impaired dark vision hinder night driving. To drive well under any conditions we need good visual acuity, adequate peripheral vision, and the ability to shift focus easily and well. Hearing is also important because sound gives information about the location of other vehicles. So we would expect driving to be much more dangerous for older people because of their difficulties with hearing, seeing, and response speed. Shouldn't the elderly have more accidents than any other age group (except perhaps teenage drivers)?

However, as Thomas Planek and Richard Fowler (1971) discovered in comparing middle-aged drivers (aged 50 to 64) with drivers over age 65, older people compensate for sensorimotor losses by avoiding high-risk driving situations. In this study, the elderly subjects reported driving less often at night, on expressways, during rush hour, and during winter than their younger counterparts.

Perhaps because they do take this greater care, elderly drivers do not have more accidents than younger adults. However, they do tend to be involved in accidents of certain types—the very ones we might imagine their particular difficulties would produce.

Elderly drivers are more prone to have accidents when they must make a rapid series of judgments and take decisive action, as when they have to change lanes (Planek & Fowler, 1971). They have a higher accident rate due to failing to notice or respond quickly enough to stop signs or traffic lights (McFarland, Tune, & Welford, 1964). In contrast, the most frequent accidents young drivers have are related to recklessness, not slowness or sensory loss—speeding, traveling on the wrong side of the road, operating faulty equipment (McFarland et al., 1964).

□

at remembering names or solving puzzles as well as opening doors (Birren, 1974). Unfortunately, this is true. While performance of verbal responses does not seem to fall off as dramatically as it does with genuinely physical actions (Jacewicz & Hartley, 1987; Salthouse, 1985), slow responding is indeed a pervasive fact of life in old age.

This generalization, though, should not lead us to overlook some important qualifiers: Slowness varies greatly from person to person; being quick is critical to performance only in some activities in life; age losses are most pronounced with complex tasks. So, before assuming deficiency in an older individual, we need to look carefully at the person and what he or she is being asked to do.

Consequences of Changes in Response Speed.   Our discussion explains why in the vignette Sam Kennedy had particular trouble with the components of his job involving speed. It also implies that if he could have eliminated those particular tasks he might have been able to put off retirement longer. The same can be said of any job—any time work requires a fast physical pace, it will be especially difficult for older employees. Laborers seem to intuitively understand the trouble an older body has with speed. Studies in factories show that older workers want, and are more often found in, jobs involving relatively heavy work (lifting, carrying). The reason is that this more strenuous type of work generally does not have to be done quickly. Speed-oriented jobs such as assembly line work present intense hardships for older employees (Welford, 1977).

But even on the assembly line, older laborers do not do as poorly as would be expected on the basis of laboratory tests. Any work involves well-practiced activities, and practice and experience seem to help compensate for the slowing that occurs with age (see Salthouse & Somberg, 1982, for a laboratory example). Selective attrition may be involved, too. Older workers whose performance does markedly decline may retire early, leaving only the relatively quick on the job. But who are these hardy older people? This leads us to an examination of the other variation in response speed mentioned earlier—its variability among people.

Individual Variability of Response Speed.   Older people who are physically active and athletic tend to have quicker reaction times (see Salthouse, 1985, for a review), outperforming the typical person their age and sometimes having reaction times comparable to young adults (Botwinick & Thompson, 1968; Spirduso, 1975).

Another individual difference correlated with reaction time is health, in particular, heart disease. In one study (Botwinick & Storandt, 1974), older people with cardiovascular problems had slower reaction times. In another, even that precursor of heart disease, Type A behavior, was correlated with slowness on a reaction-time test (Abrahams & Birren, 1973). A second category of illness associated with especially slow reaction times is disorders of the brain: strokes, brain tumors, Alzheimer's disease (Hicks & Birren, 1970).

INTERVENTIONS

The fact that athletic older people have quicker reaction times than other people their age highlights the fact that not all age-related slowness is preordained (Birren & Renner, 1977). Exercising, keeping physically fit, and taking care of our health may reduce the extent of the losses in response speed (and even in our senses) that are somewhat inevitable to growing old (Salthouse, 1985). Furthermore, since well-practiced skills seem to decline less, to preserve, for example, our ability to type 60 words per minute as long as possible, we need to keep on typing. As in so many other areas of life, exercise helps stave off age-related decline.

What about the older people for whom prevention or practice cannot work, those for whom slowness or sensory problems are an irreversible fact of life? Here the key is to rearrange the environment to minimize these disabilities that cannot be cured—the approach that helped so much in the vignette.

Environmental psychologist Powell Lawton (1970, 1975, 1985) has spelled out some principles underlying this **ecological** (or environment-oriented) **approach** to disabilities. Lawton first puts forth the following axiom: The more physically impaired the older person, the more crucial the influence of the outside world. People with disabilities are vulnerable to the environment in a way the rest of us are not, because we can perform competently in most settings in our society.

The vignette makes Lawton's point obvious. Compare the impact of being in the pancake house and in the deli on Sam Kennedy and his family. While the noise level of the two settings made a great difference to him, his family was equally at ease in both restaurants. Moreover, because restaurants would soon go out of business if their noise level made it impossible for most of their customers to hear, we would expect the Kennedy family to be comfortable in any restaurant in which they choose to eat. In other words, the environments we are exposed to in the course of living are typically tailored to fit or be congruent with our physical capacities. However, this fit applies to the dominant group in our society—people without disabilities. This brings us to Lawton's second axiom: To help people with physical impairments function too, we must redesign the world to fit their capacities. This strategy is called fostering **person/environment congruence** (Kahana, 1975).

According to Lawton, if the environment is too supportive it will encourage excess disabilities. In Chapter 2's vignette we saw an example in the interpersonal realm. Mrs. Kennedy tried to help her husband totally, and he began to function at a lower level than he was really capable of. But if the outside world is too complex or challenging, it will also promote incapacity, as we saw in this chapter's vignette. So the most appropriate environment is one that fits the person's capacities or, better yet, slightly exceeds them so the individual is challenged to function at his or her best.

These principles underlie an exciting new specialty—designing housing to fit the capacities of people with functional impairments. Here the idea is that the wider environment can serve the same purpose that glasses or a wheelchair do, as a constant support to compensate for an unchangeable condition. Devices that compensate for permanent impairments are called prostheses. Similarly, the specially planned housing and the suggestions for modifying private homes described below create what gerontologists call **prosthetic environments** (Lindsley, 1964; McClannahan, 1973).

Designing Housing for the Elderly

Over the past two decades there has been an explosion of interest in how architectural design can help maximize person/environment congruence. Work-

Figure 3-6. Atrium and dining room of the Captain Clarence Eldridge House.
Source: "Introduction: The Age of the Aging," 1981.

shops have been held, books written, and facilities planned and erected through the collaborative efforts of architects and gerontologists. This housing for the elderly serves a special goal. Through its physical design and the services it offers it aims to keep the older person with disabilities living as independently as possible for as long as possible. Here is a description of one housing project of this type (adapted from "Introduction: The Age of the Aging," 1981):

The Captain Clarence Eldridge House, in Hyannis, Massachusetts, was built to serve older people who need some help with daily life, but not the full array of services provided by a nursing home. To design the building, architects got advice from a variety of sources—managers of housing for the elderly, environmental researchers, and older people themselves. The facility was planned to promote physical independence and to also serve residents' psychological and social needs.

For example, the major public spaces, such as the dining room, are located around a central skylighted atrium (see Figure 3-6). This design admits the maximum amount of light as well as encouraging socialization. Residents are pulled to enter the communal room but can also observe what is going on in this public space before entering it. To enhance vision, bright colors and sharp contrasting hues have been used. Another striking feature is the lack of clutter, which encourages mobility.

This facility—an example of **congregate-care** housing—offers communal meals and other supportive services to its residents. However, it was also planned to foster as much independence as possible and with the need for privacy in mind. All residents have a private room with a kitchenette, so if they are able, they can do some cooking themselves.

Unfortunately, the careful use of design so evident here is not typical of housing for the elderly (Lawton, 1980). Much housing for the elderly, even though built for people with the impairments this chapter describes, was erected before gerontologists appreciated the impact design could have in promoting independence. Besides, it is expensive to build good housing. So even today some housing for older people may still have the flagrant flaws a survey revealed more than 20 years ago (Proppe, 1968): Facilities were poorly lit. They often had rooms approached by long corridors without benches where a frail older person could rest. They were noisy, with bare floors and walls that reflected sound rather than absorbing it. If anything, these residences for the elderly seemed designed to foster person/environment *incongruence*.

Adapting Private Homes for the Elderly

Most older people, even those with disabilities, do not live in special housing. They live in their own homes, often, as a nationwide poll commissioned by the American Association of Retired Persons revealed, in the same place where they have lived for decades (AARP, 1984). The vast majority of the several thousand respondents in this 1982 telephone survey owned their homes (80%). More than half had been living in the same place for at least 10 years. And 39% had lived in the same place for from 20 years to a lifetime.

From the standpoint of optimum functioning, one's home has a major advantage. It is a familiar setting for negotiating the tasks of life. There are the emotional advantages, too, and the security and the link to the past that a home lived in for decades provides (Lawton, 1985). However, visits to private homes where disabled people live show that the houses have often deteriorated because of their age and are poorly suited to their owners' new needs (Lawton, 1980, 1985). But simple modifications can foster person/environment congruence here, too.

To compensate for vision impairments the person's home should be well lit (Bozian & Clark, 1980). Overhead fixtures should be avoided, especially fluorescent bulbs shining down directly on a bare floor, as they magnify glare. Large numerals should be put on appliances and telephones (Huttman, 1977), and bright, contrasting colors should be used (Proppe, 1968; Schwartz, 1975). To prevent accidents caused by poor vision (or movement problems), furniture should be sparse (Schwartz, 1975), and there should be no raised floor areas (Huttman, 1977).

If the older home owner has a hearing problem, devices can be bought that amplify the sound of doorbells or telephones (Huttman, 1977). Double-paned windows and wall-to-wall carpeting also improve hearing, as they reduce the level of background noise.

To minimize losses of strength, doors should open automatically or be light enough to move easily (Lawton, 1975), shelves and storage places made easy to reach (Schwartz, 1975), and grab-bars should be installed in places like the bathtub where falling may occur (Huttman, 1977; McClannahan, 1973). Faucets should be easy to turn on and off; controls should be at the front of the stove (Huttman, 1977); and knobs on all appliances should not be too small or too smooth to be easily grasped.

With a bit of thought you could probably add to this list. You also might want to think of specific ways your neighborhood might be redesigned to make life easier for a disabled older resident. And it might be fun to list some ways of maximizing person/environment congruence in another essential area—your own behavior with older people who have the limitations this chapter describes.

KEY TERMS

Visual acuity
Presbyopia
Peripheral part of the visual system
Central part of the visual system
Arcus senilis
Cataract
Presbycusis
Recruitment

Conductive hearing loss
Psychomotor performance
Reaction-time experiment
Movement time
Ecological approach
Person/environment congruence
Prosthetic environments
Congregate care

RECOMMENDED READINGS

Birren, J. E., & Schaie, K. W. (Eds.). (1985). *Handbook of the psychology of aging* (2nd ed.). New York: Van Nostrand Reinhold. Chapters 12, "Vision and Aging"; 13, "Aging and the Auditory System"; 15, "Speed of Behavior and Its Implications for Cognition." Each of these chapters gives a comprehensive overview of the research in the area it covers. Difficult.

Lawton, M. P. (1975). *Planning and managing housing for the elderly.* New York: Wiley. Instructions on how best to plan housing for the elderly. Also summarizes research on housing for the elderly and life satisfaction in older people. Not difficult.

Welford, A. T. (1977). Motor performance. In J. E. Birren & K. W. Schaie (Eds.), *Handbook of the psychology of aging* (1st ed.). New York: Van Nostrand Reinhold. Comprehensive overview of the area. Difficult.

Chapter 4

□

Disability and Health Care

□

The Disability Trajectory

The Medical Profession and Older Adults
- How Physicians Treat Their Older Patients
- How Older Patients Treat Their Physicians

Community Alternatives to Nursing Homes
- Home Care
- Day Centers and Programs
- Respite Care
- Specialized Services

Nursing Home Care
- The Institutions
- The Residents

Interventions

Key Terms

Recommended Readings

Jane Kennedy began to notice the change in her mother two summers after Sam died of a massive heart attack. Lillian's "touch of arthritis" was now a genuine problem. Opening jars was painful. Sometimes it hurt her to open the cabinet doors. On bad days cooking even simple meals became an endurance test.

There were other signs that Lillian was going downhill physically. Even though Dr. Berg could not point to a specific illness, Lillian was tired and depleted. She took long naps in the afternoon. Getting up from chairs was a struggle; she could no longer walk to the store. Jane had to spend more and more time at her mother's house—doing the shopping and helping with the cooking and cleaning on Lillian's bad days. However, at least the 85-year-old woman still could live on her own. While managing was not easy, she could dress and bathe and get around.

That all changed on the snowy February day that Lillian fell down and broke her hip. As the weeks at Mercy Medical Center slid toward a month and walking was still impossible, the pressure to leave the hospital became intense. But where could Lillian go? The hospital social worker pointed out the obvious options: hiring a full-time attendant or having Lillian move in with Jane and her husband. But the choice she strongly recommended was a nursing home.

Jane knew she could not live with herself if she made this decision. What kind of child repays years of love and care by abandoning her mother to strangers in her time of need? Images of her well-loved childhood welled up, and Jane got almost physically ill at the thought of (in her words) "putting Mom away." Not only had she heard awful things about what went on beyond the walls of long-term care facilities, suppose Lillian got better, to the point where she could live on her own again? Once those institutional doors swung shut, Jane was terrified they might never swing open again. Better to reserve nursing home placement as the absolute last resort.

So, though they knew it would be a struggle, Jane and her husband took her mother in. Medicare paid for a physical therapist and nurse to visit twice a week. However, it did not cover the attendant Lillian needed while everyone was at work. While the expense was draining, Jane felt it was worth it for her peace of mind. But Lillian never did get much better. She continued to stay the same.

Jane might have been able to handle things if she had not gotten ill herself. In an ironic twist of fate, she stumbled running for the bus to work, came down hard, and fractured a bone. Dr. Berg said it might be months before she fully healed. At 60 she was not a young woman either. Rather than thinking about helping her mother, Jane needed to get some help for herself.

The last resort had clearly arrived. With the help of the hospital social worker and a local nursing home advocacy group, Jane got the names of the area's three best nursing homes. As she limped from visit to visit, she was pleasantly surprised. True, the residents who screamed or sat vacantly in the halls made her want to cry, but the facilities she visited were more appealing than she would have thought. She was especially impressed with a "teaching nursing home" committed to vigorous rehabilitation and humane ongoing care. The problem was the waiting list. Still, Jane felt that by putting her mother in the day program associated with this home and shifting the attendant's hours to evening, they might be able to hang on long enough until a bed opened up.

■

The path that leads to a nursing home begins with **functional impairment,** the difficulty in negotiating life that is the behavioral manifestation of chronic disease. Functional disabilities are what we really are referring to when we think of "old age"; they are at the core of our fears and terrors about growing old. So, even though a minority of all over-65-year-olds are disabled—as mentioned in Chapter 2, only about one in four elderly people report *any* problems negotiating life (U.S. Senate Special Committee on Aging, 1987; see also Table 4-1)—in this chapter we will look at this old age enemy in depth. How do functional impairments progress? What can be medically done about them? What community services are available to help older people who are having trouble walking, cooking, or getting around? And we will look at the place we automatically link with the most severe functional impairments of old age—nursing homes.

However, even though they aren't typical, the bad news is that impairments in the ability to function in basic ways do become increasingly more common at older ages. (Although as Table 4-1 shows, more than half of all people in their late 80s still report no trouble with basic personal care!) A study in which researchers (Osberg, McGinnis, DeJong, & Seward, 1987) looked at predictors of life satisfaction among a group of frail older adults underlines just how crucial these kinds of impairments are in determining the quality of life in old age. Compared to any other influence they examined—finances, social relationships, marital status—the extent of the person's functional impairment was the factor most closely correlated with morale. In other words, to paraphrase the old saying, in old age we don't have anything if we don't have the ability to take care of ourself.

THE DISABILITY TRAJECTORY

Our first step in understanding functional impairments is to get some information about the disability trajectory itself. Is the downward spiral described in the vignette predestined to occur? Once a person does develop minor disabilities, does the situation typically get worse and worse? The cross-sectional statistics in Table 4-1 only hint at an answer to this compelling question. Reliable answers depend on longitudinal research, studies actually tracing the fate of these impairments over time.

When Thomas Chirikos and Gilbert Nestel (1985) followed several thousand middle-aged men over a 15-year period from 1966 to 1981, they found that while the common pattern was toward greater loss, with more people reporting more problems as the years passed, specific disabilities also improved. For instance, more than 9% of the men who had problems stooping or kneeling in 1976 did not have the same trouble in 1981. More than 8% found that their difficulty in standing lessened. Although many men did develop new problems to replace those that had disappeared, this study also shows that functional impairments are sometimes less irreversible than we might think.

Even when people are over 65 and develop problems in negotiating life, they are not predestined to just decline. When Duke researchers (Palmore, Nowlin, & Wang, 1985) restudied several hundred volunteers who had been assessed 10 years earlier (all were now over age 72), on average they did find moderate losses in functioning. However, there was a good deal of variability. Some people had suffered dramatic physical declines. Others stayed relatively stable over the years. Once again, some were *more* independent physically than they had been a decade before.

The fact that disabilities are not always permanent was highlighted when 190 patients at risk of nursing home placement were assigned to an inpatient geriatric program offering vigorous rehabilitation (Liem, Chernoff, & Carter, 1986). Almost all improved. The number with partial or total independence increased from 87 to 173. The number able to walk on their own rose from 42 to 127. While I must stress that to be admitted to this unit, people had to be good candidates to profit from rehabilitation, this success rate not only shows that improvement is possible but that interventions to attack functional impairments may really be effective.

Attacking disabilities involves providing high-quality health care services—community alternatives to keep less severely disabled people out of institutions and rehabilitation-oriented nursing home care. It depends on people too, in

TABLE 4-1. The percent of elderly people reporting difficulty in one or more personal care activities, by age, 1984.

| Age | Total | Number of Personal Care Activities That Are Difficult | | | | |
		None	1	2	3	4–7
		Percent				
65 plus	100.0	77.3	9.2	4.7	2.8	5.9
65–74	100.0	82.9	7.8	3.7	1.9	3.7
65–69	100.0	85.3	6.8	3.1	1.5	3.2
70–74	100.0	79.9	9.1	4.4	2.4	4.2
75–84	100.0	72.2	11.2	5.4	3.7	7.4
75–79	100.0	75.9	10.8	4.3	3.3	5.7
80–84	100.0	65.6	12.1	7.4	4.6	10.4
85 plus	100.0	51.2	12.8	10.2	6.7	19.2

Source: U.S. Senate Special Committee on Aging, 1987.

TABLE 4-2. Number of physician contacts by age, 1986. (Excludes people in institutions.)

| Age Group | Contacts | | |
	Number (thousands)	Percent Distribution	Average Number per Person, per Year
All ages	1,272,191	100.0	5.4
Under 25	376,173	29.6	4.2
25–44	352,234	27.7	4.7
45–64	293,925	23.1	6.6
65 plus	249,858	19.6	9.1
65–74	137,737	10.8	8.1
75 plus	112,121	8.8	10.6

Source: U.S. Senate Special Committee on Aging, 1987.

particular the profession most responsible for shaping the health care older adults get. How well our nation succeeds in limiting the disabilities of old age depends on the way physicians deal with their older patients and the orientation they bring to the chronic impairments of later life. It depends on the consumers of medical care too, how older people utilize the health care system, how they view their own health and physical disabilities.

THE MEDICAL PROFESSION AND OLDER ADULTS

As Table 4-2 shows, older people are by far the heaviest consumers of physicians' services. This is especially true of the oldest old. While in 1986 younger adults (aged 25–44) saw a doctor an average 4.7 times, visits for people aged 75 and above were more than twice as high—10.6 (U.S. Senate Special Committee on Aging, 1987). It is ironic, then, that the orientation of traditional medicine is so ill suited to treating the chronic, disabling conditions that occur among these most frequent users of medical care.

How Physicians Treat Their Older Patients

According to the medical model, a doctor's job is to diagnose an underlying illness, make a medical intervention, and cause a dramatic cure. But what we know about illness in the elderly flies in the face of this approach. Older people suffer from *chronic* illnesses, diseases that cannot be cured. While single-shot, cure-oriented interventions can sometimes be effective with illnesses of this type (for instance, surgery to get rid of a tumor or to clean out clogged coronary arteries), in old age a curative approach is frequently ineffective with chronic disease. Ongoing management is required in dealing with these illnesses: regularly monitoring the problem, increasing the person's ability to function given an unchangeable diagnosis, an illness that never goes away (Kart, Metress, & Metress, 1978).

Effectively treating illness in old age requires that doctors widen their focus: from attacking disease to waging war against that equally important foe, disability (Libow, 1982; Williams, 1986). This may mean no longer focusing exclusively on life-threatening illnesses (cancer, heart disease) but seeing conditions that people do not die from are important, too. As we have seen in the last two chapters, while they lack the drama of being fatal, osteoporosis, hearing and vision problems, and arthritis markedly erode the quality of life in old age. For instance, of the four most prevalent disabling illnesses of the elderly in 1986—heart disease, hypertensive illness, hearing impairments, and arthritis (U.S. Senate Special Committee on Aging, 1987)—only the first two are a direct threat to life.

Attacking disability involves different diagnostic strategies. Because the presence of "heart disease" or "arthritis" on laboratory tests may be less important than how that diagnosis affects daily life, in evaluating older patients, doctors may have to incorporate measures of functional impairment into their battery of diagnostic tests (see Chapter 2).

Their treatments may also have to be changed. Attacking disability involves using techniques outside the doctor's traditional realm of expertise—exercise, physical therapy, nutrition, psychological help, changing the environment to facilitate getting around. So, to be helpful to their disabled older patients, physicians may have to work more collaboratively, consulting with social workers, dietitians, and physical therapists. They must view these lower-status health care professionals as having important contributions to make. This means giving up another cornerstone of the medical model—the doctor in absolute control (see Williams, 1986).

As we might imagine, this reorientation has been difficult for the medical profession. In fact, it is only within the past two decades that organized medicine in the United States has made a genuine effort to develop training programs that address the needs of older adults (Williams, 1986). As recently as 1976 a national survey revealed that only 15 of 96 medical schools polled offered separate courses on aging. Three years later, however, the figure had jumped to 81 (Kane, Solomon, Beck, Keeler, & Kane, 1981). It was not until 1987 that a licensing examination was developed for our nation's youngest medical specialty, **geriatric medicine.**

Doctors who specialize in geriatric medicine devote themselves to the medical problems of older adults. They know that in old age disease can present itself differently than earlier on; that, for example, the only symptom of a heart attack in an 80-year-old patient may be mental confusion or indigestion, not wrenching pain (Adams, 1977; Butler, 1978). They understand what is physically normal at age 80, so they are careful not to pass off treatable diseases as "normal aging" or read pathology into normal age changes. They are committed to treating disability and sharing their authority with other health care professionals. Sometimes they work in a totally multidisciplinary way, as part of a geriatric team at a hospital or clinic.

Do geriatric teams help stave off disabilities or improve the quality of life in old age? Four studies evaluating this new approach suggest yes. While in one study, being assigned to a geriatric team made no difference in subsequent health (Kerski, Drinka, Carnes, Golob, & Craig, 1987), in three others it had a positive impact. Compared to groups given standard medical care, elderly patients assigned to geriatric teams either had lower mortality, fewer hospitalizations and nursing home placements, or higher morale and functional health at a later point (Rubenstein, Josephson, Weiland, English, Sayre, & Kane, 1984; Yeo, Ingram, Skurnick, & Crapo, 1987; Zimmer, Groth-Juncker, & McCusker, 1985).

For instance, when Laurence Rubenstein and his colleagues (1984) randomly assigned frail elderly inpatients to either an innovative geriatric evaluation unit or a control unit given standard care, they found that after 1 year the people being treated by the geriatric team were better off on a host of indexes of health: They had fewer hospitalizations, less hospital days, and were less likely to be admitted to a nursing home. Their functional health was better; they had higher morale; they were *much* less likely to die. This heartening study offers a ringing endorsement of this new approach to improving the quality of life in old age.

Unfortunately, however, only a tiny minority of doctors specialize in geriatrics. Geriatric clinics or services serve an even more miniscule fraction of older adults. So to really understand how the medical profession is treating the elderly we need to look at the average private practitioner, the person who is not geriatrically trained. How do these typical physicians actually treat patients over age 65?

Older people frequently complain that, because they are over 65, doctors give them short shrift. Practicing gerontologists have also decried the fact that physicians generally neglect their older patients. Unfortunately, a study conducted by researchers at the Rand Corporation lends these personal observations scientific weight (Kane et al., 1981).

A random sample of physicians in private practice was asked to record the amount of time spent with each patient over a number of days. These figures were then looked at as a function of the person's age. The researchers predicted that because patients over age 65 were most likely to be seriously ill they would be given the most attention. Surely doctors would need to devote more effort to examining their elderly patients. They would have to spend more time explaining the more complicated treatments often needed to manage chronic disease. Instead, the reverse was true. Comparing people aged 45 to 54, 55 to 64, and over 65, the researchers found relative stability in the average time spent with the two middle-aged groups and a marked drop in time spent with the oldest group. This was true of office, hospital, and nursing home visits and of all seven medical specialties the researchers examined. Either because older patients are seen as hopeless cases or for some other reason, doctors do give them less attention.

The Rand Corporation study was done in the 1970s, when the effort to focus on the medical needs of the aged was in its beginning stages. However, a study done more than a decade later suggests that in some respects doctors still act differently with their patients over age 65 (Greene, Hoffman, Charon, & Adelman, 1987). By videotaping doctor/patient interviews of five randomly chosen private practice physicians, researchers found that with older patients, the doctors tended to focus on the person's physical symptoms alone. Conversations about the behavioral impact of an illness—whether the person was having trouble getting around, or was worried or depressed—more often took place with younger adults.

However, the patients as much as the physicians seemed to be to blame. During their visits, the older people tended to only bring up their dizziness, or pain, or blood pressure. Younger patients raised more questions related to functioning, focusing both on their symptoms and how their illness was affecting their life.

So, when the elderly are given less attention, they may be partly at fault. Being trained in the idea that the doctor is the ultimate authority, when they visit their physicians, they may be less aggressive in bringing up their concerns (Haug, 1981). Because they demand less, they get less. This brings us to the other side of the equation—the older patient.

How Older Patients Treat Their Physicians

In a 1975 national survey (see Shanas & Maddox, 1985), one out of every eight older Americans living in the community said that they needed a doctor but were not seeking medical care. One-third said the reason was lack of money. The other two-thirds gave explanations of a different kind. They did not believe that the problems they had were serious enough to need a doctor's attention. Furthermore, "at my age, what can a doctor do?" A more recent investigation of age-related differences in emergency room use had a similar theme. Unlike younger adults, people over age 65 did not use the emergency room for minor complaints—they were likely to arrive by ambulance in a medical crisis, to come only when they were seriously ill (Baum & Rubenstein, 1987). These studies suggest that rather than overusing doctors, if anything, the elderly err on the opposite side, not seeing a physician when they really should.

Sociologists who study older patient/physician relationships point out that the elderly also suffer from therapeutic nihilism. They may be just as prone to self-diagnose treatable conditions as old age as their physicians are (Haug, 1981; Shanas & Maddox, 1985). One reason seems to be that in later life our definition of being ill tends to shift. Aches, pains, and physical distress otherwise labeled as a disease that needs treatment are viewed as "normal" at age 70 or 85. In interesting support of this theory, while physician and patient assessments of health do correlate with one another, when disagreements occur, studies show that patients rate themselves as healthier than would be indicated on the basis of medical tests (Heyman & Jeffers, 1963; LaRue, Bank, Jarvik, & Hetland, 1979; Maddox & Douglass, 1973; Tissue, 1972). For this cohort of North American and Western European elderly, a cultural norm against complaining may contribute to this deemphasis of illness, too. For example, when older people in different countries are asked to evaluate their health, in the United States, England, and Denmark, over half rate it good. In Poland, Yugoslavia, and Israel, fewer than one-quarter make that claim. Since actual rates of illness and disability do not appreciably differ from country to country (see Shanas & Maddox, 1985), these variations seem to reflect very different norms. In Eastern Europe, health complaints in old age are tolerated and accepted. In the West they are seen as signs of weakness and discouraged.

But this traditional Western virtue of suffering in silence (Shanas, 1962) may really be a liability when it prevents people from "bothering" their doctor when they are genuinely ill. To use the health care system appropriately, this cohort of elderly people may have to be taught not to label aches and pains as "just old age." Furthermore, since some illnesses (such as a heart attack) may not announce their presence via intense symptoms in old age (Adams, 1977), older people may have to be educated to call their doctor at even subtle signs that their physical condition has changed. Just as crucial, the elderly and their families need education of a different kind—when disability strikes there are alternatives to nursing home care.

COMMUNITY ALTERNATIVES TO NURSING HOMES

When older people have trouble walking or moving or getting around, and families cannot care for them, the knee-jerk reaction is to consider a nursing home. But a nursing home may not be needed. As the studies evaluating outpatient geriatric team care imply, some nursing home residents do not absolutely need to be in an institution. They could live in the community if appropriate alternatives were available or if they took advantage of the alternatives that do exist. For instance, in one demonstration project people at risk of nursing home placement called a special triage number. Through the use of community resources, the team operating the project was able to keep 25 to 30% of these callers at home (Hodgson & Quinn, 1980).

As the vignette shows, the decision to put a loved one in a nursing home is frequently made at a time of crisis. The patient is in a hospital and must be discharged soon. Handling life at home is impossible. There is a mad scramble to find a nursing home bed. There is little time to explore other possibilities or even to select the best nursing home (Flint, 1982).

But people in a hospital are at their physical worst. The problems they have in the midst of a medical emergency may not be a good gauge of their physical capacities later on. As our longitudinal look at functional impairments shows, disabilities are not always irreversible. Even severe problems in negotiating life sometimes markedly improve. The fear is that putting people in nursing homes when they do not really need to be institutionalized actually makes recovery less likely, because being offered too much care fosters excess disabilities—promoting incapacity, not an independent life.

A comparison of patients who entered nursing homes with two other groups with similar disabilities receiving home care suggests that this fear may be realistic. After 3 months the patients getting care in the community made greater improvements in their ability to function, and their morale was higher than the people in nursing homes (Braun & Rose, 1987).

Inappropriate nursing home placement is also financially wasteful. Nursing home care is expensive, costing thousands of dollars a year. Medicare covers a

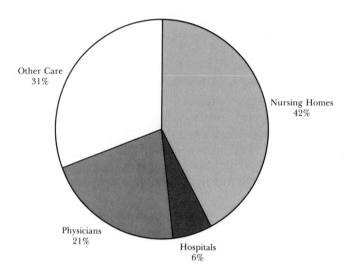

Figure 4-1. Where the out-of-pocket health care dollar for the elderly goes, 1984. *Source: U.S. Senate Special Committee on Aging, 1987.*

startling less than 2% of the cost (Rabin & Stockton, 1987). The tragedy of the Medicare system is that it covers only acute or curative care. Once care is labeled as custodial, chronic, or continual, Medicare will not pay.

Although nursing home insurance does exist, on a practical level it is unavailable to the vast majority of older adults. Not only is it costly, a mid-1980s review of 31 policies showed that qualifying for this type of insurance can be extremely hard. Companies often impose numerous eligibility restrictions—for instance, weeding out anyone with obvious disabilities or denying coverage if a person answers yes to any health related question. Policies have numerous "exceptions" or may provide very limited coverage for certain types of nursing home care (Weiner, Ehrenworth, & Spense, 1987). This means that older people with some means typically begin by paying the nursing home fees privately. In fact, as Figure 4-1 shows, among people over age 65, the highest fraction of out-of-pocket health care expenses goes not to doctors or hospitals but to nursing homes—42% of every health care dollar in 1984 (see also Rabin & Stockton, 1987). After some time in a nursing home, savings are depleted, and the person becomes eligible for Medicaid, the health care insurance system for the poor that does cover custodial care. So another anxiety is that once admitted to an institution, financial considerations keep people from leaving even when they physically can.

Is it true, as Jane Kennedy assumed in the vignette, that once in a nursing home, the chances of being discharged are very slim? The following study gives a (somewhat) reassuring answer to this widespread anxiety (Retsinas & Garrity, 1986). In tracing the pattern of discharges at a Rhode Island nursing home over 6 years, the researchers found that of the 419 residents who left the home (either by being discharged or by dying), 26% returned to the community, either to their own home or the home of a child. Interestingly, the patient's prognosis at entry turned out to be the best predictor of his or her eventual fate. Most people whom doctors expected should be able to return home did so. In other words, nursing homes are not just a final holding pattern before death. They are also places where people get the rehabilitation they need to live outside.

But even if placement can be temporary, that does not mean that nursing homes should be the only alternative to living totally on one's own. When people need only a minor or moderate amount of help in negotiating life, there should be intermediate-level services to prevent them from either choosing between no care or the intense care of a nursing home. Luckily, these community services exist. They are middle links in an effort to offer what is called a **continuum of care,** a spectrum of services tailored to the needs of people at all points on the disability continuum.

In Chapter 3 we looked at one intermediate-level service, congregate care housing. Now we will look at three aimed at keeping people in their own homes: home care, day care, and respite care.

In the following discussion keep these points in mind: (1) These services vary in their availability. (2) They in no way substitute for the primary support that keeps frail older people in the community—our nation's families (see Chapter 8).

Home Care

Home care is the most well known alternative to nursing home placement. It's an array of services involving everything from round-the-clock nursing to a few hours per week help with housekeeping (see Table 4-3). Because of advances in technology, today even people who genuinely need 24-hour skilled nursing home care can get services in their homes if they are able to participate in one of the few free demonstration projects for Medicaid recipients or are willing to foot the enormous bill privately. Generally speaking, however, home care, like any community service to prevent institutionalization, is most appropriate for people who have minor to moderate disabilities, have an involved family, or need short-term rehabilitative care.

A major impediment to utilizing home care (or any other community alternative to nursing homes) is cost. Just as Medicare only covers care defined as "rehabilitative" in a nursing home, this same condition applies to its paying for noninstitutional care. Unless the service is defined as medical or cure-oriented and a doctor certifies that the patient needs that type of care, Medicare will not pay. This means that while the services of a skilled nurse or physical therapist may be covered, as happened for Lillian Kennedy in the vignette, Medicare does not pay for the person most responsible for the older disabled person being able to function outside of an institution—the attendant or home health aide. While the custodial-care-oriented Medicaid system does cover the services of these workers, specifically how much care it pays for varies from state to state. So even though home care was developed in part to cut the financial burden of institutionalization, getting *ongoing* care of this type is expensive, too. It may only be a genuine alternative when a person needs minor help, is wealthy enough to pay

TABLE 4-3. Home care personnel, a partial services list.

Personnel	Services
Social workers	Provide counseling and find, coordinate, and supervise home care services.
Registered dietitians	Plan special diets to speed recovery from illness or to manage conditions such as diabetes.
Physical therapists	Use exercise, heat, light, water, and such to treat problems of movement.
Occupational therapists	Teach people how to function at their best with disabilities—for example, how to do housework from a wheelchair.
Nurses	RNs (registered nurses) provide skilled nursing care; LPNs (licensed practical nurses) offer simpler nursing services. The former are more highly trained and are needed mainly to treat complex medical conditions.
Homemaker/ home health aides	Usually the primary caretakers; may do cleaning, housekeeping, bathing, dressing, and other types of personal care. Their job title varies considerably, depending in part on the mix of help provided. For example, "homemaker" or "housekeeper" may be the title when the person mainly does cleaning; "home health aide" or "attendant" may be used when personal care is mainly involved.
Chore workers	Assist with services such as yardwork, home repair, or heavy cleaning.

Source: Adapted from National Home Caring Council, 1981.

privately for extensive help, or has an income limited enough to qualify for Medicaid.

The fact that government-funded home care may not serve the needs of chronically disabled people was underlined by a Canadian research report (Béland, 1986). The researcher noted that though the home care program in Quebec was set up to keep older people otherwise destined for a nursing home in their own homes, it was virtually incapable of performing this mission. Care was rarely available for more than 12 continuous weeks. On average, only 2 hours per week were provided to people in need. So rather than serving the genuinely disabled, the real clientele for this program were either people recuperating from an acute medical problem or those with very minor problems in negotiating life.

When home care services are freely available, do they prevent nursing home placement? An evaluation of five U.S. demonstration projects in which home care was offered free of charge to disabled older people suggests that the answer is yes only if the person is in imminent danger of going to a nursing home. In the four projects in which participants were randomly recruited from the ranks of disabled community-dwelling elderly, the programs did not reduce the rate of subsequent institutionalization (compared to control groups not in the project). But in the one where participants were identified and recruited at the actual point of applying to a nursing home, the program did result in lower nursing home use (Capitman, 1986). This is not to say that these projects did not improve the quality of life or enhance morale among the people they served or the families struggling with their care (see Chapters 8 and 10). It merely shows that removing the economic deterrent to home care may only be effective at putting off nursing home placement when people cannot handle life in the community using the systems that now exist.

Day Centers and Programs

While day care has become more widely available, this community service for the disabled is much less frequently used than home care, serving only an estimated 20,000 people as of 1982 (Rathbone-McCuan & Coward, 1986). In a **day program** the person goes to a center where treatment and social activities are offered. Day centers are usually open from 9:00 A.M. to 4:00 P.M. five days a week, though people may choose the number of hours or days they attend.

While there is a wide variety of day care programs, in general programs can be classified into two basic types: **Medically oriented day centers** provide active rehabilitation or are health care oriented. They are staffed by health care workers who see their mission as providing social stimulation and medical care. The main focus of **social day care** is nonmedical. While programs of this type may offer health-oriented programs, they are mainly set up to provide activities and socialization for isolated, disabled older adults.

Advocates of day care emphasize its advantages over home care. It offers a more stimulating environment than the older person might have, isolated at home. It may also be more cost effective and convenient than one-to-one care. It may lessen the risk of mistreatment because the older person is cared for in a social setting (see Belsky, 1988).

However, these virtues are offset by disadvantages. Day care does not offer the flexibility of home care. The hours are fixed; the centers are not open at night; and they cannot be used during an acute illness. Day programs also serve a limited group—people who fit the qualifications for the particular program. Furthermore, it may be more difficult to convince an older person to go to a day center than to have someone come to his or her home.

These liabilities suggest that day care, no matter how available it does become, may never have genuinely wide appeal. For instance, though a survey done in the early 1980s showed that the quality of day care centers set up at the time to serve Alzheimer's patients was excellent, the actual fraction of the eligible population who took advantage of this service was small (Mace & Rabins, 1984).

Respite Care

While home care and day care ease the burden on caregiving families, their primary purpose is to help the disabled older person cope. However, helping caregivers is the only goal of the newest community service to keep people out of institutions—**respite care.**

The person receiving respite care periodically enters an inpatient setting (a nursing home, group home, or hospital) or is looked after by a specially trained caregiver at home so family members get time off from ministering to their relative. Interestingly, though it is the least available of any community service, when caregivers of dementia patients were polled about what help they needed

BOX 4-1
The Continuing Care Retirement Community:
An Innovative Method of Insuring for Disability

Perhaps the cleverest approach to avoiding the financial catastrophe of nursing home care is the development of a new type of housing for the elderly: the **continuing care retirement community.** In contrast to traditional recreation-oriented retirement communities, the central focus of this type of retirement housing is care for disability. All continuing care communities offer nursing home care, though they differ in how extensive their coverage is. They also offer more services (housekeeping, meals, personal care) tailored to the needs of people at intermediate points on the disability continuum than traditional retirement housing does.

Unfortunately, however, there are some major drawbacks to this innovative method of insuring for disability (Branch, 1987). As is true of nursing home insurance, continuing care communities are expensive—requiring a large entry fee and substantial monthly payments. So, though not just for the wealthy, they are only an option for the comfortably middle class. They are also only open to people who are good health risks. Most continuing care communities require prospective applicants to pass a physical examination. Many stipulate that people must be under a certain age to even apply.

Even with this careful screening, living in this type of community does not necessarily ensure financial peace of mind. As its residents age and need health care, the community must continually attract enough healthy new people to balance out those who are ill. The cost of health care services may rise precipitously; or an unusually high percentage of the community may need long-term care. Actuarial statistics are used to compute a community's probable health care needs, leaving its residents vulnerable to deviations from the expected illness odds. If the health care costs of a community do go up too much, residents may have two unpleasant alternatives: a steep increase in their costs or bankruptcy. As of this writing (1989), there is no federal legislation to protect the life savings of people who invest in continuing care. A 1986 survey showed that less than half of the states had passed protective laws (Netting & Wilson, 1987). So despite its inherent appeal, this innovative way of financing long-term care is more fraught with pitfalls than might first appear.

□

the most, respite services ranked first (Caserta, Lund, Wright, & Redburn, 1987). This suggests that respite care may be extremely helpful when families are committed to taking care of a relative totally on their own but need a bit of periodic free time.

Specialized Services

A variety of more limited services also exist to keep people out of nursing homes: home-delivered meals, transportation, shopping assistance, home repair. One of the most innovative of these programs is the lifeline emergency response system developed by psychologist Andrew Dibner. Subscribers to this hospital-based service pay a small monthly charge to have their telephone hooked up to a central switchboard. Someone calls daily to check in. If there is no answer, a neighbor is contacted who comes by to check. The frail older person living alone has the comfort of knowing help will arrive soon in a medical emergency if he or she cannot reach the phone.

None of these services make nursing home care obsolete. Sometimes people genuinely need the type of care that can best be offered in a setting of this type; for example, when they are having ongoing serious trouble in negotiating and have no family or need a level of care family members cannot provide. In fact, rather than nursing homes becoming less important as alternatives such as home care and day care have mushroomed, the explosion of the old-old ensures that they will continue to be a familiar fixture of North American life. The rest of this chapter offers an overview of what this fixture of life is really like.

NURSING HOME CARE

Nursing home is the catchword for any inpatient setting that provides **long-term care;** shelter and services to frail older people in need of medical and personal care over an extended period. At any one time the nursing home population only comprises 5% of all people over age 65. However, this statistic is a gross underestimate of the degree to which long-term care actually touches the lives of older adults.

About 2 decades ago, Robert Kastenbaum and Sandra Candy (1973) pointed out that because it is cross sectional, the 5% figure says nothing about an older person's chances of actually going to a nursing home at some point in his or her life. They revealed what they called the "5% fallacy" by noting the place of death mentioned in Detroit newspaper obituaries of all people over age 65 during a year. Fully 24% of the deaths occurred in nursing homes, revealing that over age 65 the probability of *eventually* being in an institution is not tiny but an uncomfortably large one in four.

And one in four may be an underestimate, too. Kastenbaum and Candy only counted people who *died* in nursing homes, not those who were once residents and then died somewhere else. A longitudinal follow-up of older people who had died within 10 years after they were originally studied lends weight to this idea.

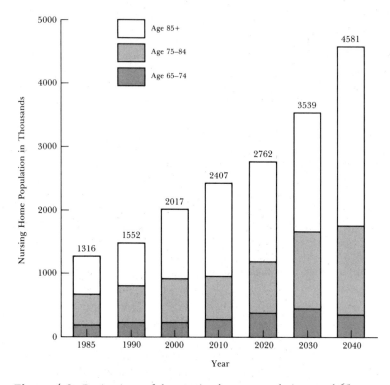

Figure 4-2. Projections of the nursing home population aged 65 years
and older by age group, 1985–2040.
Source: U.S. Senate Special Committee on Aging, 1987.

In tracing the lives of this group, the researchers (Vincente, Wiley, & Carrington, 1979) found that 39% had been in a nursing home at one point.

So, going to a nursing home is something older adults are right to fear. Recent estimates suggest that as many as half of all elderly women will eventually experience this life event (see U.S. Senate Special Committee on Aging, 1987). On any given day there are more than 1 million older Americans living in long-term care. The number of nursing home beds has increased dramatically over the past 3 decades (see Figure 4-2 for some future projections). In fact, there are now more beds of this type than medical surgical beds. The enormous cost of this expansion drains not just older people but society, too—most of the billion-dollar nursing home industry is financed by Medicaid (Rabin & Stockton, 1987).

Concomitant with this dramatic growth has come a storm of criticism about the abuses that go on within the walls of nursing homes. They are viewed as dumping grounds where people are left to languish unattended as they wait for death. They are thought to offer scandalously poor care—either neglecting their residents' valid needs for help or, at the opposite extreme, fostering excess disabilities by providing too much care. Nursing home life is thought to create psychological problems and hasten physical decline. Are these indictments totally accurate? To attempt an answer we need to look closely at the institutions themselves as a prelude to our main goal, understanding the residents they serve.

The Institutions

Types of Nursing Homes.   Nursing homes vary in every conceivable way. One may be much like a hospital, offering intensive medical services to seriously ill older people. Another may be more like a college dormitory, offering room, board, and personal care to less-disabled residents. Homes differ in size, staff/patient ratio, and philosophy. Their residents may vary, too. Although the law prohibits discrimination in admission, many nursing homes cater to the needs of a certain religious or ethnic group—serving familiar food, observing traditional holidays. Some freely accept people with Alzheimer's disease or those who are bedridden, others try to confine their occupants to people who are not severely physically or mentally impaired (Flint, 1982). But despite this diversity, nursing homes can be categorized in two ways: by the intensity of care they offer and by their mode of ownership. The first distinction is crucial. To get reimbursed by Medicaid (or Medicare), nursing homes must be classified as offering either skilled or intermediate care.

Skilled nursing care facilities provide the highest level of care, including round-the-clock nursing, physical and occupational therapy, social services, and recreation. **Health-related facilities (or intermediate-care facilities)** are for people who do not need the intensive care of a skilled facility but do need ongoing assistance in functioning. They offer less in the way of nursing and personal care. Because intermediate-care facilities do not provide intensive nursing services, Medicare never pays for intermediate care.

Many nursing homes offer both types of care. The advantage of a **multilevel facility** is that when a resident's physical needs change and a different level of care is needed, services can be gotten in the same place (though probably on a different floor or building).

The different ownership categories of nursing homes mirror hospitals. **Proprietary homes** are owned and run privately for a profit. **Voluntary homes** are operated by nonprofit organizations such as church groups. **Public homes** are city or state owned. Recently there has been a tremendous increase in the number of chain-owned proprietary homes. There is some concern that for-profit homes, because they are in the business to make money, deliver worse care. This brings us to another dimension differentiating long-term care institutions—quality.

Quality of Nursing Homes.   Anyone who visits several nursing homes will be struck by the variations in quality. Some facilities are beautifully designed, provide a rich array of services, and have staff members who seem committed to providing humane care. Others are at the opposite end of the spectrum, richly deserving the term snake pit.

One critical influence affecting the quality of a nursing home is the clientele it serves. Nursing homes catering to the more affluent elderly tend to look more physically appealing, have better services, and generally provide higher quality care (Kart & Manard, 1976; Kosberg, 1973, 1974). Affluent older people get better care for obvious economic reasons. There is also a less apparent reason they tend to be better served. Staff members at homes catering to well-off residents are more likely to come under public scrutiny because these relatively well-off older people are more likely to have friends and relatives who visit more frequently and complain if they see maltreatment or neglect (Barney, 1974). The fact that outside visitors help keep nursing homes accountable was suggested when researchers compared how much attention the staff at selected homes paid to different residents. Residents who got the most visits were given the most staff time (Gottesman & Bourestom, 1974).

Nursing home quality has been measured using indexes such as staff/patient ratio, number of services, or rankings of the attractiveness of the physical plant. Quality has been assessed via less objective dimensions, too—whether residents report being satisfied or how responsive or attentive the staff seems to be. While homes rich in objective resources also tend to rank higher on these more intangible indexes of quality (Kosberg, 1973), sometimes a nursing home will rank high on certain dimensions of quality and low on others.

In one national survey (Lemke & Moos, 1986), size was positively related to some indexes of institutional quality. Large homes tended to provide more security and offer residents a wider array of services. However, there was a trade-off. Smaller homes scored higher on staff/patient rapport. Interestingly, this study also suggested that there is some truth to the idea that the cost-cutting motive results in poorer care. On average, the nonprofit facilities the researchers evaluated got higher ratings on most dimensions of quality than the proprietary homes did. The nonprofit homes had more comfortable physical environments, lower staff/patient ratios, and more services. They also offered residents more autonomy and a higher level of control. This is crucial because of the extensive research that suggests that providing control and enhancing free choice can be crucial to health and well-being among frail older adults (see the discussion of Rodin's findings in Chapter 2).

While gerontologists almost unanimously agree that providing as much autonomy as possible to disabled older people is important (the whole June 1988 supplementary issue of the *Gerontologist* was devoted to this point), even the most humane institution necessarily limits choices in the most basic areas of life. Decisions we take for granted, such as where to live, when to get up, or what meals to prepare, are not an option to people living in long-term care facilities. While many restrictions on autonomy are the unavoidable price of being physically dependent and living in an institution, some go above and beyond what is necessary. A survey of admission agreements at 200 California nursing homes showed that residents were frequently asked to waive important rights as the price of entering—control over their finances, the chance to get grievances heard, the ability to make free decisions about their medical care (Ambrogli & Lenard, 1988). Many admission contracts were unreadable, omitted essential terms, or contained clauses that were against the law. Residents might be deprived of such critical freedoms as access to their medical records, the right to receive visitors of all ages at reasonable times, and the right to use the pharmacy of their choice.

While one impact of this alarming survey was that in 1987 the California legislature passed a model bill with strict guidelines regulating nursing home admission contracts in that state, as of this writing (1989) there is no federal law discouraging these practices. This study suggests that an implicit aim of many nursing homes may be to take control *away* from residents rather than to foster it.

Research on what goes on behind the walls of long-term care facilities is just as disturbing. Leonard Gottesman and Norman Bourestom (1974) selected a random sample of people at several Detroit area nursing homes and charted their behavior at regular intervals, at each observation noting what a resident was doing and the type of attention he or she was getting from the staff. More than half the residents were observed doing nothing at all (that is, staring into space). Only 7.5% of the time were they seen interacting with the staff members. Genuine nursing services went on even less frequently—only 2% of the time.

Unfortunately, this lack of attention seems predictable given the attitudes many nursing home personnel bring to their work. When Linda Noelker and Walter Poulshock (1984) explored the relationships among residents and staff members of a nursing home that prided itself on offering "personalized care in a familial atmosphere," they found little intimacy and widespread negative feelings toward the residents on the part of the staff. Distance, disengagement, and lack of respect characterized the residents' relationships with one another, too, though to a lesser degree. While the average length of time they had lived together was more than 3 years, less than half of these older people reported they felt close to another resident; their intimate relationships lay outside the nursing home.

These studies suggest that every grim idea we have about nursing homes is right. However, they apply to the situations that existed a decade (or two) ago. Because of continuing efforts to improve the quality of long-term care, the nursing home of the 1990s may really be a less malignant, more humane place. And even if conditions have not changed much, before we blame the nursing home industry for providing substandard care, we should look at the actual characteristics of the people that industry serves. It may be that the residents themselves partly shape the care they are given. Some of what nursing homes do may be unavoidable, perhaps even excusable, in view of the population that actually uses long-term care.

The Residents

Types of Nursing Home Residents.   Nursing home residents vary greatly in background, temperament, and almost every other characteristic that can differentiate people (Manton, Liu, & Cornelius, 1985). The characteristics of the "typical" resident will also differ depending on whether we choose to study people admitted to or discharged from nursing homes or use as our reference group those currently residing in long-term care facilities. When we choose, as is most common, to profile residents actually living in nursing homes, our portrait may be excessively negative. Those who stay a long time, the most disabled, may be overrepresented. So keep these cautions in mind when making generalizations about the nursing home population. Still, it is fair to make some general statements about this diverse group (see Brody, 1977; Gelfand & Olsen, 1979; Rabin & Stockton, 1987; U.S. Senate Special Committee on Aging, 1987).

As we might imagine, nursing home residents tend to be very old—almost half are over age 85. Because of gender differences in longevity and the fact that women are more likely than men to have illnesses that are disabling but not life threatening (for example, arthritis or osteoporosis), they are overwhelmingly female. They are also mainly white. (Minority members have a lower life expectancy, and unfortunately institutional care is not as freely available to nonwhites.) Since nursing home care is largely financed by Medicaid, currently at least, they are poor. Most important, they have physical problems that warrant institutional placement. In order to be admitted to a facility offering skilled or intermediate care, a person must be certified as having a level of disability compatible with care of either type.

Placement in a home, however, does not depend just on a person's physical capacities. It critically depends on the quality of his or her social supports, in particular the presence or absence of involved family members. A disproportionate number of unmarried elderly people (single, divorced, or widowed) live in institutions, and these single residents are significantly healthier than their married counterparts. As we will see in Chapter 8, a spouse is the first line of defense against institutionalization. Provided they are physically able, husbands and wives typically shoulder the burden of caregiving when a marital partner is having trouble functioning on his or her own. The second line of defense is children (usually daughters). So people with few (or no) immediate family members are overrepresented among the residents of nursing homes.

A study of the reasons prompting admission to an urban nursing home (Brody, 1977) highlights the critical function family members play in keeping older people out of institutions. While admission to the home was usually sought as a last resort after many physical and life stresses and when the person was in the hospital, not infrequently the last straw occurred when a caregiver had become unavailable—that is, the caregiving spouse, child, or child-in-law had become ill or died.

Personality and Psychopathology of Nursing Home Residents.
On almost any measure of mental health, people living in nursing homes rank as disturbed. Not only are the majority cognitively impaired, apathy, low self-esteem and depression are endemic among the residents of long-term care facilities. From our brief look at nursing homes, we might assume that this unfavorable psychological profile is caused by institutional life itself. Surely the conditions within these institutions would make even the most well adjusted person feel disengaged, demoralized, and depressed.

A more accurate assumption, however, is that people who have reached the point of applying to nursing homes are already psychologically disturbed. While the institution itself may not help matters any, emotional problems existed among the prospective residents before they entered the nursing home. Sheldon Tobin and Morton Lieberman discovered this was so during the first phase of a longitudinal study of adaptation to institutional life (Lieberman & Tobin, 1983; Tobin, S. S., 1980). When they interviewed and tested three groups of disabled older people (matched for marital status and degree of physical impairment)— nursing home residents, elderly who had applied for nursing home admission but were on a waiting list, and elderly who had not sought nursing home care— they found that the waiting list sample and the people already in the home had identical symptoms. Compared to the group not seeking institutional care, they were less emotionally responsive, cognitively intact, and had lower self-esteem.

Although people who apply to nursing homes may have poorer mental health for many reasons, Tobin and Lieberman suggest that to some extent the act of choosing institutionalization itself may have produced the high levels of psychopathology. Just as they did for Jane Kennedy in the vignette, nursing homes conjure up terribly negative images for older adults. To older people, applying for institutional placement may symbolize irrefutable evidence of incapacity and impending death (Tobin, S. S., 1980).

The Appropriate Nursing Home Resident.   However, despite the widespread belief that nursing home placement is the last way station before death, there are people who live on for decades within the walls of long-term care facilities. Some are happier and more content within a nursing home than outside. In one study, researchers (Sherwood, Glassman, Sherwood, & Morris, 1974) found that if a resident's life situation was quite difficult, placement resulted in a rise in morale. For the older people judged as genuinely needing an institution (those in poor health, with few financial resources, and living alone), nursing home life was a welcome relief, a haven from the anxiety of having to handle life in the community.

In addition to precarious life circumstances, personality seems to predict how well suited people are to living in a nursing home. Unfortunately, though, some not very appealing traits predict good adjustment to this way of life.

The main purpose of Tobin and Lieberman's study was to follow their elderly subjects as they entered and adjusted to nursing home life. Those who declined least mentally and physically (or improved) at the end of a year had a constellation of unpleasant traits. They tended to be aggressive and intrusive. They were likely to blame others rather than themselves. They were low in empathy and maintained a distrustful distance from other residents (Turner, Tobin, & Lieberman, 1972).

Given the depressing conditions of institutional life, these results should come as no surprise. Aggressive behavior may be the best response in a situation where resources are often limited. People who fight may be more likely to get more of what they need. Keeping emotionally distant from others and unresponsive to their suffering may be adaptive in places where people have such painful disabilities or are near death.

Luckily, however, one positive trait is associated with good adaptation to

BOX 4-2
Outsiders: A Route to Improving Nursing Homes

The studies showing that residents who get more visitors get more staff attention, suggest that one way of improving conditions in nursing homes would be to make what goes on within the institutional walls more open to public scrutiny. So one focus of the movement to improve long-term care has been to make nursing homes less set apart, more permeable to the community (Barney, 1974).

The University of Michigan–sponsored Community Council Project is one of these efforts (Barney, 1987). In this demonstration project a 6- to 12-person council (composed of local citizens, friends and relatives of residents, and residents themselves) was set up for each individual nursing home. Depending on the residents' needs, the council plans programs such as regular get-togethers, parties in the nursing home to which the community is invited, and lectures and seminars. Sometimes council members just mingle with the residents on regular visits to offer a listening ear. Sometimes the council's main function is to agitate for reforms within the home. The purpose of the project is to offer residents concrete services and at the same time help keep the staff accountable by making outsiders an integral part of the nursing home.

The principle that outsiders help protect against abuses and ensure high-quality institutional care also underlies these two more widely established advocacy programs.

In the nursing home ombudsman program, the residents of nursing homes are visited by a volunteer advocate, a trained person whose job is to listen to and mediate their complaints. Sometimes an ombudsman may aggressively push for reform. Or a given ombudsman may function as a caring listener, offering emotional support (Monk & Kaye, 1982).

The second type of program, an advocacy group, monitors what goes on in nursing homes in a more multifaceted way. In addition to serving as advocates for residents or perhaps employing a person to mediate complaints in area nursing homes, these organizations (composed of people interested in nursing home reform) often publish brochures on selecting a nursing home or offer counseling and guidance to family members on negotiating placement and finding high-quality long-term care. They also agitate for nursing home legislation—lobbying for tighter regulations on the nursing home industry and petitioning representatives to sponsor bills related to nursing home rights.

□

nursing homes—the ability to explore and think about feelings. Among Tobin and Lieberman's sample, subjects who scored high on a measure of experiencing (those most able to introspect, to focus on their inner life) had adjusted better at the end of the first year. It seems that being able to reflect on feelings (at least before entering a nursing home) may help enable people to better weather the indignities of institutional life.

INTERVENTIONS

As nursing homes proliferated, popular articles and books about abuses spotlighted the need for nursing home reform. The evolution of geriatric medicine, increased attention to the needs of frail older people, and studies of the type discussed in this chapter provided the professional impetus to make the 1980s a decade of change in long-term care. We already know a bit about one way nursing home care is evolving. There is now much more appreciation than ever before of the importance of giving residents as much control as possible over their lives. As a recent survey showed (Hegeman & Tobin, 1988), programs running the gamut from special services or enriched individual attention for residents with special problems, to vigorous rehabilitation, to intensive training to upgrade the skills of the staff are frequently available at top-quality nursing homes. Perhaps the most radical example of how different nursing homes can be today from the traditional custodial long-term care institution is epitomized by the evolution of a whole new institutional entity—the **teaching nursing home.**

The Jewish Institute for Geriatric Care on Long Island, New York, is one of our nation's longest established facilities offering this different model of long-term care. Even though it is linked physically (connected by a tunnel) and professionally with a major teaching hospital of the State University of New York Medical School, the institute is an autonomous entity with its own budget, administration, and physical plant. Its attending staff is comprised of the geriatric faculty at the medical school.

This nursing home belies many of the "facts" in this chapter about the conditions that exist in long-term care facilities. Rather than being left to languish unattended, here residents are given state-of-the-art treatment by multidisciplinary teams composed of geriatric fellows and interns. In addition to the personalized care offered by these teams, a full range of services is available from auxiliary geriatrically trained professionals (dentists, psychiatrists, and so on) depending on a person's needs.

Consonant with the principles of geriatric medicine, the emphasis at the institute is on enhancing functioning and improving the quality of life. While a full complement of services is offered to residents who cannot leave, whenever possible the emphasis is on vigorous rehabilitation and discharge to the community. For instance, over a representative 16-month period, more than half of the elderly residents admitted to a special inpatient rehabilitation unit at the facility were discharged to their homes (Adelman, Marron, Libow, & Neufeld, 1987). In addition to the inpatient units, there is a home care program and day hospital.

Teaching and training are primary goals. As they rotate through the institute, students in a variety of disciplines get supervised experience in geriatrics and emerge as specialists in this new field. According to Director Leslie Libow (1982), making nursing homes a focal point for geriatric education is the best way of ensuring humane, high-quality institutional care. Libow points out that hospitals only evolved from "pest houses" to their current position as the vital center link in the health care system once their mission was defined as teaching. He feels that when nursing homes become genuine places for learning, they, too, will no longer be seen just as houses of death and despair. In fact, nursing homes should rightfully be one hub of the expanding movement this chapter describes—the effort to improve health care for all disabled adults.

KEY TERMS

Functional impairment
Geriatric medicine
Continuum of care
Home care
Day program (medically oriented day
    centers; social day care)
Respite care
Continuing care retirement community
Long-term care

Skilled nursing care facilities
Health-related (or intermediate-care)
    facilities
Multilevel facilities
Proprietary homes
Voluntary homes
Public homes
Teaching nursing homes

RECOMMENDED READINGS

Autonomy and long-term care. (1988). *Gerontologist, 28* (June 1988). The whole issue is devoted to a discussion of autonomy and control among disabled older people. Some articles are speculative or philosophical. Others cover research on how autonomy is either enhanced or discouraged by institutions, society, the legal system, and older adults' families. Still others probe the feelings of older people themselves. Moderately difficult.

Hague, M. R. (1981). *Elderly patients and their doctors.* New York: Springer. Articles describe physician/patient relationships, how older people perceive their own health, health care in various settings, the principles of geriatric medicine. Not difficult.

Libow, L. (1982). Geriatric medicine and the nursing home: A mechanism for mutual excellence. *Gerontologist, 22,* 134–141. Lecture given by well-known specialist in geriatric medicine. Read for a discussion of the principles underlying this new approach to health care. Not difficult.

Rabin, D. L., & Stockton, P. (1987). *Long term care for the elderly: A factbook.* Oxford: Oxford University Press. Offers a wealth of statistics and facts about long-term care within and outside of institutions. Also has chapters covering disease and functional disabilities, family caregiving, and financing care. Not difficult.

Williams, T. F. (1985). Geriatrics: The fruition of the clinician reconsidered. *Gerontologist, 26,* 345–349. Another lecture by a leader in geriatric medicine spelling out the principles of this new specialty. Not difficult.

Part 3

Cognition

Chapter 5

□

Intelligence
and the IQ Test

□

The Measure

Age Changes on the WAIS and Other IQ Tests

Conclusions and an Important Interpretation

The Impact of Nonintellectual Influences on Age Declines
- Differences in Education
- Differences in Test-Taking Strategies

Illness, Death, and IQ
- The Complicated Link between IQ Losses and Illness
- The Fascinating Link between IQ Losses and Death

Questioning the Underpinning: The Validity of the IQ Test

Interventions
- Designing an Age-Relevant Intelligence Test
- Improving Performance on Current Tests

Key Terms

Recommended Readings

The third year after her husband died, Karen Johnson got the courage to seriously consider fulfilling a lifelong dream of getting a college degree. She had hobbies and interests; her precious family and friends. Still, something was lacking in her life, a gap that close relationships, volunteer work at the local nursing home, and the intensely pleasurable season ticket to the symphony had not been able to fill. Her reading was satisfying, but she yearned to discuss the books she read with other people. She also yearned to share the fruits of her lifelong passion, writing short stories. While she thanked God she had not been burdened with the problems young people faced growing up today, she also felt a twinge of envy. Now a college education was accepted, even expected. In her day it had been rare for a woman; in her family it had been out of the question.

But Karen was scared. Wouldn't she feel foolish and out of place as the only white-haired woman in class? Even more important, she was afraid of failure, terrified of simply not being able to do the work. After all, it had been a good 50 years since she had left school. Besides, everyone knows that as people get older, their intellect inevitably begins to go. If only there were some way of being reassured that she was capable, she would be at Westville State in a minute. She even noticed in last Sunday's paper that the college was offering tuition-free courses to anyone over 65.

The solution to her dilemma came from a surprising source: an experience with her 10-year-old grandson. Billy was doing poorly in school, and psychological testing was recommended. Her daughter asked Karen to go with her and the boy to the sessions to offer moral support. Karen noticed that the psychologist, who seemed competent and approachable, not only evaluated children but adults. The outcome could not have been better. Dr. Stagestad said there was no need to worry about Billy's inherent mental ability. He was more than capable of doing the work. Noticing the dramatic impact this pronouncement had on her distraught daughter, Karen knew what she had to do—make an appointment for psychological testing for herself!

So, two Tuesdays later, it was Karen who needed her daughter's presence for moral support, as the minutes inched toward what she half jokingly called "the hour of truth," her 1 o'clock appointment with Dr. Stagestad. Sitting in the waiting room, heart pounding, unable to focus on anything, Karen realized just how insecure she really was about her mental processes, the toll the years had taken on her quickness of mind. No matter how much she read or was complimented on her intellect, she knew she was no exception to the rule: as a person gets older, memory and reasoning ability inescapably erode.

Luckily, the psychologist understood this particular emotion older people routinely bring to testing, so she took special care to try to allay Karen's anxiety. Because Dr. Stagestad also knew the impact of fatigue on test performance by the elderly, she suggested that they make three rather than the customary two appointments to complete the evaluation. In this case Dr. Stagestad felt relieved that she was being asked to evaluate Karen's potential for performing well in an academic situation. In general, she felt uncomfortable giving the standard intelligence test to older people because she believed that it was inappropriate for measuring the skills involved in intellectual competence in the real world.

Dr. Stagestad planned to base her conclusions about Karen's abilities on how well she did on a single test, the revised Wechsler Adult Intelligence Scale, or WAIS-R. To allay Karen's fears, Dr. Stagestad gave Karen a preview of what was to come: In the first session she would be asked questions; in the second she would be manipulating materials. The different subparts of the test measured different types of skill. It was impossible to know the answer to every question. If Karen was unsure, it would pay to guess.

Still, knowing the scenario in advance did little to defuse Karen's fear. Even though the first few questions were almost foolishly easy, Karen was so agitated she could barely croak out a response.

Soon, though, her fear subsided; it was so clear she was doing well. True, the questions on each subtest got increasingly difficult, so she eventually knew that some of her guessed-at answers were wrong. However, she was gratified to see that her lifelong practice of keeping mentally active and interested in the world had paid off. Her reading and knowledge in a variety of areas were amazingly beneficial on several parts of the test.

Unfortunately, her pride evaporated early in the second session. Now the types of things she was being asked to do were totally foreign to her daily life. On this part of the test she had to perform tasks as ridiculous as putting together puzzles or arranging blocks. Had she known about this section, she kidded, she would have crammed in some on-the-job training, time in the playroom with her 4-year-old grandson.

She was also anxious about her response speed. As Karen explained, it was unfair to ask older people to work in this way—putting them under pressure to tackle unfamiliar tasks that had to be done within a certain time. She wondered aloud what this part of the test could possibly reveal about her thinking both in and outside of school. It helped only slightly when Dr. Stagestad told her that on this part of the test (as well as on the first) she was being compared only with people her own age.

Despite her qualms, the outcome was ideal. Dr. Stagestad said Karen would have no trouble mastering college work. She complimented her on her verbal ability. In verbal skills—which Dr. Stagestad took care to point out were most closely related to the ability to do well in school—not only was Karen far superior to the average person her age, she was even above the mean for the average 20-year-old.

When Karen asked timidly how she had done on the second part of the test, the psychologist said, "As well as the typical person your age." This was amazing in view of what she had felt was an abysmal showing.

Dr. Stagestad ended her comments by expressing one concern: the only thing that really might interfere with Karen's schoolwork was fear. She advised Karen to use the test results as a therapeutic tool. Whenever Karen found herself getting anxious about writing a paper or taking an exam, she should evoke the image of what she was being told now. There was no reason a woman of her intellectual abilities should not be doing superior work!

■

In the previous chapters I described a straightforward, undebatable fact. In spite of all the qualifications and individual variation, when we look at physical aging, loss of function is a dominant theme. The task of this chapter is much less neutral or clear-cut: to explore the delicate question of whether there are similar decrements in cognition with age. The idea that people get less intelligent as they get older is far from a dry, academic proposition. Intense debate has surrounded this most sensitive and far from settled topic.

Psychologists argue about every aspect of age changes in intelligence. They question the evidence itself, as different ways of collecting data produce different conclusions about the timing and extent of age declines in intelligence test scores. They debate its meaning: "What are the underlying reasons for the IQ losses that do exist?" Finally, for more than a decade they have been looking critically at the appropriateness of the measures themselves, questioning whether existing tests of intelligence are really doing an adequate job of tapping cognitive ability in middle-aged and elderly adults.

Perhaps our best introduction to these interlocking issues lies in examining the actual content of the test around which much of the controversy has swirled: the Wechsler Adult Intelligence Scale, or **WAIS** (Wechsler, 1955). There are many global or general measures of intelligence, but the WAIS (and now its successor, the WAIS-R) is almost certain to be the test given when an older person arrives at a psychologist's office for an evaluation. In addition, what this standard intelligence test revealed about age and IQ has provided the ammunition for the age/intelligence debate. (The updated WAIS, the WAIS-R [Wechsler, 1981] is, in most cases, virtually identical to the 1955 test.)

THE MEASURE

As the vignette illustrates, the WAIS consists of two parts, a verbal scale and a performance scale. Each scale is divided into subtests, each of which taps a specific verbal or nonverbal skill (see Table 5-1). Items on the subtests range from easy to increasingly more difficult. The verbal scale is given first.

If we closely examine the content of the subtests, we see that the two parts of the WAIS differ in another, less obvious way, than just requiring verbal versus nonverbal responses. The verbal subtests, in large part, measure a distinct type of intellectual ability—our store of knowledge. This focus on learned or "absorbed" knowledge is especially apparent in four of the six subtests: information, comprehension, arithmetic, and vocabulary. Here what is being tested is the person's knowledge of historical, literary, or biological facts; knowledge relating to competent functioning in the world; knowledge of mathematics; knowledge of the meaning of specific words.

In contrast, the performance subtests (with the possible exception of picture completion) have a different orientation. Here the tasks are relatively unfamiliar—to manipulate blocks, pictures, and puzzles. The object is to measure on-the-spot analytical skills, how well the person can master a new, never before encountered problem. In addition, speed is critically important. Not only are all the performance subtests timed, in contrast to just one verbal one, but on some a special premium (bonus points) is given for the quickest solution. Speed is really the only or major ability assessed on one performance scale in particular, digit symbol, where the person must transcribe quite easy symbols as fast as possible.

The vignette illustrates another important fact about the test. The IQ is not derived by simply adding the number of points accumulated but by comparing how people score *relative* to their age group. In other words, the actual, or in

TABLE 5-1. The WAIS subtests.

Scale	Description	Sample Simulated Item
Verbal scale		
1. Information	Fund of knowledge (literature, biology, and so on)	How many wings does a bird have?
2. Comprehension	Knowledge of appropriate behavior, of how to negotiate the environment	What is the advantage of keeping money in the bank?
3. Arithmetic	Arithmetic (time limit)	If two apples cost 15¢, what will a dozen apples cost?
4. Similarities	Verbal analogies (reasoning)	In what way are a saw and a hammer alike?
5. Digit span	Memory (repeat series of digits in same or reverse order)	Say these numbers right after me: 5-2-9-6-6-3.
6. Vocabulary	Word definitions	What does _____ mean?
Performance scale		
1. Digit symbol	Copy symbols (time limit)	
2. Picture completion	Pictures; subject asked to identify what is missing (time limit)	
3. Block design	Set of blocks with a different pattern on each side; subject asked to arrange them to conform to design on a card (time limit)	
4. Picture arrangement	Set of pictures; subject asked to arrange in correct sequence so they tell a coherent story (time limit)	
5. Object assembly	Puzzles; subject asked to put them together (each is an object, such as a hand; time limit)	

Source: Adapted from Wechsler, 1955.

TABLE 5-2. IQ equivalents of raw scores (items correct) at different ages.

Raw Score	Age Group and IQs*							
	20–24	25–34	35–44	45–54	55–64	65–69	70–74	75 +
90	151	153	157	164	169	173	179	185
60	112	114	118	125	130	133	140	146
30	73	74	79	86	91	94	101	107
1	35	37	41	48	53	56	63	69

* WAIS-R differences, while not as pronounced, are similar.

Source: Wechsler, 1955.

measurement terminology, "raw" score a person gets has a very different meaning if that individual is 20, 50, or 85. So, the WAIS is like any classroom test that is graded on a curve. A person's final score (or IQ) is based not on absolute performance but on his or her performance compared with others in a particular reference group. In this case, the reference group is special—people one's own age.

Unfortunately, however, as Table 5-2 shows with regard to the performance scale, older reference groups are less and less able. Reading across the table we can clearly see how in each successively older age group identical raw scores (correct items) translate into increasingly higher IQs. In fact, when we compare the oldest and youngest groups the difference is astonishingly marked. For instance, a raw score that for a 20-year-old means normal intelligence translates into "highly superior intelligence" at age 70. A raw score of 30, alarming enough to fall into the retarded range at age 24, is simply "average intelligence" in old age. As gerontologist Lissy Jarvik (1987) so starkly reminded the gerontological community in a recent lecture on the aging brain, we cannot escape the fact that by young adult standards the average older person ranks as mentally deficient!

But do these depressing findings also extend to the verbal scale? Is the dramatic age decline confined mainly to particular subtests? And what about the methodology used to derive these unvarnished "facts"? Would we see the same age loss if we looked at data other than the cross-sectional studies used to determine these norms? These questions bring us to the issue that provoked the first heated argument in the age/intelligence debate—the accuracy of the data—the actual timing and extent of age changes on the WAIS.

AGE CHANGES ON THE WAIS AND OTHER IQ TESTS

Figure 5-1 shows changes on the verbal and performance parts of the test separately for the age groups used to derive the WAIS norms and so answers our first question about the verbal versus performance parts of the test. There is indeed a very different pattern of loss on the two scales. After a peak in the early 20s, performance scores steadily decline in each older age group. In contrast, though there is also some age decline in the verbal IQ, the graph shows it is far

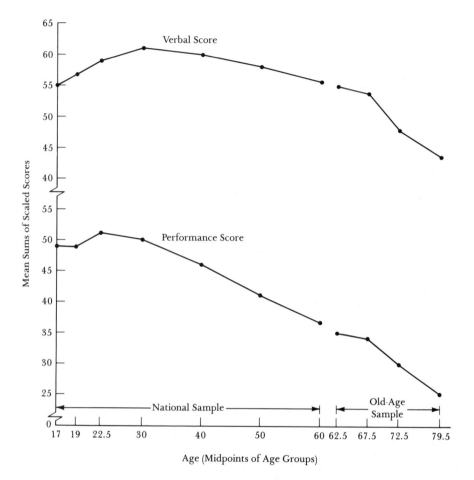

Figure 5-1. Verbal and performance scores as a function of age.
Source: Adapted from Doppelt & Wallace, 1955.

less marked. Verbal scores reach a peak somewhat later than performance scores and decline precipitously only in later life, in the 70s.

The psychologists who developed the norms for adults aged 64 and older (Doppelt & Wallace, 1955) also examined age differences on each of the verbal and performance subtests. What they found gives us a fuller picture of the specific types of cognitive skills that tend to either be relatively immune or sensitive to the inroads of age. Among the six verbal measures, similarities and digit span seem the most affected—they decreased the most. None of the four subtests described earlier as measuring stored knowledge showed much change. In contrast, a much more uniform pattern characterized the performance subtests: regular, steady, consistent losses on all the tests.

This decades-old finding has been repeatedly confirmed. For example, when Jack Botwinick (1967) summarized nine studies examining age differences on the various subtests of the WAIS and its related predecessor, he discovered an identical pattern in each case: little decline on the verbal measures; pronounced decrement on the performance scales. In fact, better performance on verbal subtests, and more rapid, regular decline beginning as early as the 20s on speeded tests tapping nonverbal skills has been found so consistently that in the gerontological literature it has been given a special name—**the classic aging pattern** (Botwinick, 1967, 1977).

No matter how much we emphasize that the verbal losses are relatively small, what I have said so far offers no cause for celebration about the relationship of intelligence and advancing age. If anything, these studies amply confirm Karen Johnson's bleakest fears about her intellectual abilities. However, these findings are all derived from *cross-sectional studies,* and by now we should be very suspicious of considering this source of data alone. We surely know too much about the pitfalls of inferring genuine age changes from simple differences between age groups to take these gloomy statistics as the final word. Do longitudinal studies also reveal this picture of unremitting decline? Do they, too, show the classic aging pattern?

As we might expect from knowing their contrasting bias, longitudinal studies do offer a much more positive view. In fact, through middle age, many actually show that people improve on the verbal part of the test (see reviews by Botwinick, 1977; Labouvie-Vief, 1985). However, even here the classic aging pattern emerges. While verbal scores may stay the same or increase, decline—though to a lesser degree—is still evident on nonverbal, timed tests.

Is there ever a time the classic aging pattern breaks down? Interestingly, because they explored age changes in a more differentiated way—among older adults themselves—the Duke researchers were able to clearly document that there is.

In a longitudinal investigation spanning 10 years, Carl Eisdorfer and Francis Wilkie (1973) administered the WAIS several times to two groups of Duke study volunteers: people initially in their 60s and those initially aged 70 to 79. Among the first (or young-old) group the classic aging pattern was apparent: a 2-point decrease on the performance scale, a 0.6-point loss on the verbal IQ. (Note how different this degree of loss is from the much sharper decline a cross-sectional study would be likely to show.) However, the findings for the volunteers initially in their 70s were totally different. In the old-old group, IQ losses at each evaluation were regular and pronounced; at the end of the 10 years losses averaged a full 7.3 points. Also, in these oldest subjects, the classic aging pattern had evaporated. Losses were nearly equal on the verbal and performance IQs. (Actually, in the cross-sectional research involving the oldest WAIS subjects we can also see this pattern. Notice how in Figure 5-1 the slope of the verbal curve changes after the late 60s, becoming almost identical to that of performance scores.)

CONCLUSIONS AND AN IMPORTANT INTERPRETATION

So, the truth about age changes in WAIS performance lies somewhere between the overly negative "facts" portrayed by cross-sectional studies and the overly

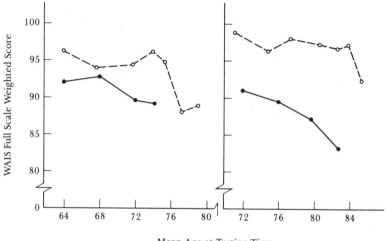

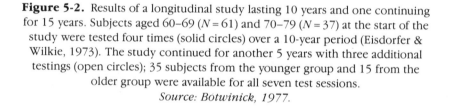

Mean Age at Testing Time

Figure 5-2. Results of a longitudinal study lasting 10 years and one continuing for 15 years. Subjects aged 60–69 (*N* = 61) and 70–79 (*N* = 37) at the start of the study were tested four times (solid circles) over a 10-year period (Eisdorfer & Wilkie, 1973). The study continued for another 5 years with three additional testings (open circles); 35 subjects from the younger group and 15 from the older group were available for all seven test sessions.
Source: Botwinick, 1977.

positive picture longitudinal studies convey. We know from Chapter 1 that cross-sectional studies are likely to overestimate true age losses in most arenas of life. In the next section, as we explore more fully the crucial impact of cohort factors on IQ scores, we will see why this bias has been especially pronounced in studies of cognition and age. We also know to be wary of data from longitudinal studies. They are just as likely to minimize the true extent of age declines.

We can see the positive bias inherent in the longitudinal method when we compare the curves in Figure 5-2. (This compelling example is from a review article by Botwinick, 1977.) The figure shows just how much the longitudinal requirement of using subjects who return for a *series* of testings changes a study's results. The lower curves show the results of the 10-year-long Duke study just described and the upper curves show an extension of this same research for an additional 5 years. That is, Eisdorfer and Wilkie not only followed their subjects for 10 years but then continued, examining the cognitive performance of the much smaller group of volunteers who were able to participate in three additional test sessions.

As we can see in Figure 5-2, not only is the 15-year group more capable in general, but if we examined just the performance of these Duke study volunteers we would reach a much more optimistic conclusion about age and IQ. Here no decline occurs until the late 70s, implying that our results from the 10-year group must be positively skewed, too. In other words, just as we cannot judge the economic character of New York City as a whole by strolling on the advantaged Upper East Side, in the longitudinal method we tend to study an elite, unrepresentative fraction of the cohort as a whole; so as a portrait of normal aging our data almost inevitably will err on the optimistic side.

However, despite their quantitative differences, it is remarkable just how qualitatively similar the variety of longitudinal and cross-sectional studies charting age and IQ relationships have been (see reviews by Botwinick, 1977; Labouvie-Vief, 1985). The classic aging pattern tends to be found until late in life (see also Jarvik, 1973). At some point this pattern yields to uniform decline. As researcher Gisela Labouvie-Vief (1985) has commented, these facts at least are not in question. We now look at the important attempt to integrate and make sense of the facts—an application of a two-factor theory of intelligence (Cattell, 1963) to fit development throughout life.

According to Jack Horn (1970), there are several distinct types of adult intelligence, of which two are most important. **Crystallized intelligence** reflects the extent to which a person has absorbed the content of the culture. It is the store of knowledge or information we have accumulated over time. Because it involves learned information, this is the cognitive ability that most of the verbal subtests of the WAIS seem mainly to be measuring (Horn, 1970). The second broad type of intelligence is more tied to biology—a central nervous system (CNS) at its physiological peak. **Fluid intelligence** reflects our on-the-spot reasoning ability, a skill not basically dependent on experience. This type of intelligence seems to be tapped more by the performance subtests.

Horn believes that these two types of intelligence follow a very different trajectory as we age:

> At first [fluid intelligence] and [crystallized intelligence] are indistinguishable . . . the accumulation of CNS injuries is masked by rapid (neurological) development in childhood, but in adulthood the effects become more obvious. Fluid intelligence, based upon this, thus shows a decline as soon as the development of CNS structures is exceeded by the rate of CNS breakdown [Horn, 1970, as quoted in Labouvie-Vief, 1985, p. 502].

So fluid intelligence, as is true of other abilities directly tied to physiology, reaches a peak in early adulthood and then regularly declines. On the other hand, because it reflects experience and learning, Horn hypothesizes that crystallized intelligence follows a quite different pattern in relation to age. This cognitive ability remains relatively stable or increases as the years pass because the rate at which we acquire or learn new information in the course of living balances out or exceeds the rate at which we forget. However, in old age, crystallized intelligence also falls off. The reason is that at a certain time of life the cumulative effect of losses—of job, of health, of relationships—cause disengagement from the culture (see Chapter 7), and so forgetting finally exceeds the rate at which knowledge is acquired.

There is other evidence that crystallized intelligence becomes quite similar in its pattern of deterioration to fluid intelligence in old age. When tests specifically tailored to measuring just these two aspects of intelligence in their pure form are

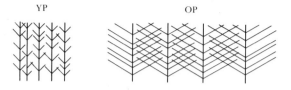

Figure 5-3. Schematic diagram of the neurons of a young person
and an elderly person.
Source: National Institute on Aging, 1983.

given to older adults, the clear differentiation between these skills does not exist. The elderly do not show the same independence between the two classes of ability that younger people do (Baltes, Cornelius, Spiro, Nesselroade, & Willis, 1980).

Horn's fluid/crystallized dichotomy is satisfying because it seems to fit so many real life phenomena. For instance, we can invoke this two-factor theory of intelligence to explain why in creative endeavors more dependent on mastering a body of knowledge or experience—philosophy, history, writing psychology textbooks(!)—people may reach their peak later in life than in professions where the essence of creativity involves using a medium (such as language) in totally novel ways or coming up with original solutions to isolated problems—writing poetry, making breakthroughs in mathematics or physics (see Chapter 6). The theory also seems to account for differences among other professions—explaining, for instance, why age is more of an enemy to an air traffic controller who must quickly analyze constantly changing information than to the CEO of an airline who by his 50s has finally accumulated the years of on-the-job experience to perform at his occupational peak (see also the discussion of information processing in Chapter 3). Even more compelling than these real life parallels are the new findings with regard to the plasticity of the brain itself. It turns out that there is a fascinating *neurological* analogue to the finding that crystallized intelligence tends to remain stable (or increase) until retirement age!

When Steven Buell and Paul Coleman (1979) compared the neurons of a group of subjects who had died at about age 80 with those who had died at about age 50 and with a group of people who had died of dementia (the average age of this group was about 75), they were astonished to find that the neurons of the normal elderly had much more extensive interconnections than those of the middle-aged people (see Figure 5-3). This finding of more neural branches suggests that we physiologically compensate for the brain cell erosion that occurs as we age by the cells that remain growing more robust. In other words, this heartening study offers a genuine biological foundation for why crystallized intelligence is relatively preserved as the years pass.

Even more fascinating, in a later study, Coleman (1986) found a neurological parallel to the finding that in later life an overall breakdown in this type of intelligence occurs. This time he actually measured dendrite growth in a section of the brain called the dentate gyrus in four groups: young adults, middle-aged people, old people (aged 70) and very old people (aged 90). From his calculations he estimated that on average we may "grow" 3 million millimeters of dendrites in middle and later life. The growth occurred in Coleman's middle-aged subjects and the 70-year-olds, but in the oldest group (the 90-year-olds) it had stopped. In other words, this may be the physiological reason for the rapid decline in verbal IQ scores in advanced old age!

So the fluid/crystallized distinction provides a neat explanation for the classic aging pattern and its breakdown in old age. It is supported by new neurological findings, and it makes sense of many phenomena in the real world. However, it far from wraps up our discussion of age and IQ. So far we have been viewing differences in test performance between the elderly and the young as though they were written in stone, exploring possible intrinsic or physiological reasons why the elderly do worse or better on certain parts of the IQ test. However, perhaps this premise is not quite correct. Rather than taking these differences in test *performance* as reflecting immutable differences in capacity, there may be important extraneous—nonintellectual—reasons why older people do worse on IQ tests.

THE IMPACT OF NONINTELLECTUAL INFLUENCES ON AGE DECLINES

We all know from our own experience that a poor test score does not necessarily mean we are incapable—for example, when excessive anxiety or a fever causes us to get a lower grade than we should on a crucially important exam. Now imagine that in addition to being more likely to be ill and more prone to develop paralyzing anxiety, you have either never taken an exam before or haven't taken one for 50 years, and you will understand the handicaps the elderly bring to intelligence tests. In other words, the 70-year-old and the 20-year-old are emphatically not equal on everything as well as years of life when they enter the test-taking situation. There are a variety of reasons *apart* from inherent ability why older people might get lower scores on intelligence tests.

Differences in Education

As we saw in Chapter 1 and the vignette, older cohorts, on the average, have fewer years of formal schooling. This simple lack of comparable education is one important factor apart from pure ability that almost certainly loads the test-taking dice in favor of the young (Baltes & Schaie, 1974; Granick & Friedman, 1973). Because many subtests on the WAIS verbal scale tap material directly learned in the classroom—vocabulary, mathematics, historical or literary knowledge—the test is not just measuring a person's aptitude for schooling, it is also measuring the quality of the schooling that has been received. So here we see how justified the outcry against the practice of labeling the IQ a measure of pure intellectual aptitude really is. The barest look at the questions shows why not just older people but anyone deficient in educational experiences (for example, minorities, the poor) is at a severe disadvantage in taking the test (for a more in-depth exploration of this issue, see Gould, 1981).

Not only is the average older person who enters the test-taking situation handicapped by less years of formal instruction, that person lacks an important other skill school confers—the knowledge of how to take examinations. The older person may not have taken a test for the past 50 years, the young adult (or even the middle-aged person) is likely to have had years of experience taking tests. So another bias against the old is simple differences in practice. The WAIS is likely to be a totally novel experience for most older adults.

Years of education is a bias that is particularly obvious in cross-sectional studies because of the clear differences in average years of schooling when we compare young and elderly cohorts. However, my point about test-taking experience implies that it also affects the outcome of longitudinal research. As with any skill, the further we get from the specific environment in which that skill was learned and practiced, the less adept our performance is likely to be. We would expect, then, that unless a person's job involved experience taking examinations or was dependent on using the academic-type content tapped by the verbal WAIS, that individual's score on the test might naturally decline as more and more years since formal schooling elapse.

An implication of this argument is that older people in occupations that most closely fit the demands of the WAIS might show the least decline on test scores compared to the young. There is indeed evidence that this is so. In one study comparing old and young professors, the typical cross-sectional finding was even reversed (Sward, 1945). Professors aged 60 to 80 surpassed their colleagues in their 30s on vocabulary and information tests. While we might argue that the professors in this study may have been intrinsically more able than the younger faculty members, an equally logical reason for their better performance is simple length of experience. The work of a professor involves skills very similar to the content of these particular tests (Horn, 1970).

So Karen Johnson in the vignette is probably right in attributing her good performance on the verbal part of the WAIS in part to having kept up her interest in intellectual activities. Experience with academic or education-related material and keeping intellectually "fit" really do seem to help a person, at least on some verbal subtests of the WAIS. (We will return to the critical issue of "exercising cognitive skills" on IQ in more depth at the end of the chapter.) But in the second area where schooling is an advantage, her behavior was more like the typical older person's—she approached the test poorly. Because of this, like many people her age, her score may not have reflected her genuine capacities.

Differences in Test-Taking Strategies

Karen Johnson's experience epitomizes one type of poor approach older people are prone to bring to intelligence tests. They tend to be intensely anxious. Studies have explored the impact of this factor plus two others on IQ scores: excessive caution and fatigue.

Clinicians have long noticed that older adults, more than younger people, are anxious in situations in which their intellect is being evaluated. About 15 years ago, Susan Whitbourne (1976) empirically demonstrated that these impressions

TABLE 5-3. Selected items from the modified anxiety achievement test
used by Whitbourne.

Debilitating subscale
1. Nervousness while being tested hinders me from doing well.
2. In a test situation in which I am doing poorly, my fear of a low score cuts down my efficiency.
3. The more important the testing situation, the less well I seem to do.
4. I find my mind goes blank at the beginning of any kind of test and it takes me a few minutes before I can function.

Facilitating subscale
1. I work most effectively under pressure, as when the task is very important.
2. When I enter some kind of test situation, nothing is able to distract me.
3. Nervousness while taking a test makes me do better.

Source: Whitbourne, 1976.

are accurate, revealing not only that older people are indeed more fearful when taking tests of memory and thinking but how much this greater fear hurts the elderly when their performance is being compared with the young. Whitbourne's study is particularly striking because her subjects were a group of far from typical elderly. They were a test-taking elite, educationally interested and experienced in taking examinations.

Being anxious during a test is not necessarily bad; because anxiety arouses us, it may actually help performance. So in looking at the impact of test anxiety, Whitbourne took care to measure the facilitating and debilitating types separately, using a scale devised for that purpose (see Table 5-3). Her main hypothesis was that *debilitating* fear would be more prevalent among her older sample than among young adults. She also checked on the idea that this type of anxiety would indeed impair performance by seeing whether it correlated with poorer scores. Her subjects were carefully matched for educational experience. The young adults were attending college; the elderly were involved in a continuing education program in which constant evaluations were part of the curriculum.

Using a memory test that involved instructions to remember as much as possible about the content of sentences, Whitbourne did find that the older group had more debilitating anxiety. And a high level of this type of anxiety did negatively affect performance. It was associated with lower scores. Moreover, it was obvious that the older people were excessively anxious just by observing their behavior. All the college students readily agreed to participate in the study, but more than one-quarter of the older people Whitbourne asked refused. Few of the young adults but many of the older subjects were visibly upset during the testing session. In fact, five of the older subjects were so anxious that they refused to complete the experiment.

The vignette and the earlier discussion of ageism clearly show the reason for this excessive fear. At the core of our old age stereotype is mental decline. So many elderly people, like Karen Johnson, enter testing situations doubly burdened. Their unfamiliarity with tests makes being tested inherently more anxiety provoking. Added to this is the ominous meaning a mental evaluation has in later life: "Now I will come face-to-face with the fact that my mind is not what it used to be."

Anxiety such as this can have a host of negative outcomes. As many of us know from bitter experience, it can cause us to block on any answer because when we focus on our fear we are unable to focus on what we need to know. Or, being a potent aversive stimulus, classically conditioned fear can cause total avoidance. As was true in Whitbourne's study, older people may simply run away, refuse to be tested at all. Or, if less excessive, anxiety may simply constrain older people and make them overly cautious. They may not want to risk answering a question unless they are absolutely sure. Because on the WAIS there is no penalty for wrong guesses, this strategy will minimize the chances of doing one's best.

The detrimental impact of caution in answering IQ-test items has been revealed in a study in which researchers gave pretest instructions either encouraging elderly subjects to guess or not (Birkhill & Schaie, 1975). The participants then took a five-part test of intelligence tailored to measure fluid and crystallized abilities in a pure form. The instructions encouraging guessing did help. Elderly subjects in the group urged to guess did significantly better on three of the scales than the comparison group told the opposite, that it was better to leave items they were not sure of blank. While this study does not demonstrate that older people do indeed adopt a too cautious response style on IQ tests, because we know from Chapter 3 that this is their bias on other tests, it seems reasonable that this is true. What the study does show in any case is how this predisposition not to guess tends to lower IQ scores.

So Dr. Stagestad was right in the vignette to take special pains to calm Karen Johnson and encourage her to guess. The psychologist's idea of having her complete the evaluation in three sessions rather than two was also wise. As the next study implies, fatigue is another ability-extraneous factor that may cause older people to get lower scores than they should on IQ tests.

Using the same five-part test of fluid and crystallized abilities, Carol Furry and Paul Baltes (1973) explored whether a tiring pretest treatment given to adolescents, middle-aged subjects, and older people might have different effects on subsequent scores. Half the subjects in each age group were asked to perform a routine letter-finding task for 20 minutes before taking the IQ test.

As the researchers hypothesized, the fatiguing intervention did have a more detrimental effect on the older subjects because it magnified cross-sectional age differences between the groups on several of the subtests.

Once again, this finding is important because of what it implies—a tendency to tire more easily may partly underlie age losses in IQ scores. Perhaps it is not reasonable to use exactly the same format for everyone when giving a long and demanding test such as the WAIS. Because a 70-year-old may not have the physical stamina of a 20-year-old, by taking care to make everything about the testing situation equal we may in fact be subtly stacking the deck against the old.

When we talk about older people being too anxious or prone to tire easily (or even being excessively cautious) to perform at their best on intelligence tests we are really referring to how these influences affect attention—the way they impair the ability to concentrate and focus on the test. But "attention" or focusing on a task that needs to be solved is not just irrelevant to intellectual ability. It is an important facet of intelligence in itself. How much do age-related deficits in the capacity to concentrate, focus, and attend *in themselves* contribute to the changes in fluid and crystallized abilities that occur as we age?

To explore this question, Lazar Stankov (1988) gave a variety of standard tests of intelligence and memory (including the WAIS) and different measures of attentional abilities to different-aged adults. The measures of attention tested capacities such as the person's ability to search for and pick out the correct item, flexibly shift focus to solve a problem, and filter out irrelevant information to get the correct response. Using sophisticated statistical analyses, Stankov demonstrated that declines in the "attentional factors" measured by these tests were indeed crucial in explaining age changes in fluid intelligence, and affected crystallized abilities, too. When he controlled for age changes in attention, the decline in fluid intelligence virtually disappeared; increases in crystallized intelligence became even greater in his older subjects by controlling for age-related decrements in the ability to attend.

So changes in the ability to concentrate and focus on problems also seem to play an important part in the changes that occur on the WAIS subtests with age. Now we turn to a discussion of an age-related influence that is almost predestined to destroy the ability to concentrate, the variable absolutely central to any discussion of intellectual loss in later life—health.

ILLNESS, DEATH, AND IQ

When ill health is temporary—when a person has the flu or a headache or another acute disease—we can genuinely label it as an ability-extraneous factor that, like anxiety, artificially depresses performance on IQ tests. But when an older person's test performance is affected by an illness that does not go away—a *chronic* disease—the reason for the loss is not irrelevant to ability. That person's reasoning and thinking powers are rendered permanently less acute by the ravages of the disease. However, even if it may indeed reflect a new, lower capacity, sickness is an important variable other than age itself that may account for the relationship between declining IQ and advancing years. Older cohorts may do more poorly on IQ tests not just because they are older but because they are more likely to be ill. The dramatic WAIS decline even longitudinal studies show among the old-old may not be due just to age, but that for the first time during these years chronic disease strikes almost everyone.

The Complicated Link between IQ Losses and Illness

The accelerated drop in IQ at the time of life when for the first time chronic illness is rampant—in the 70s—strongly implies that poor health is a variable explaining age changes in IQ. So does our discussion of the differing results of cross-sectional and longitudinal studies and of longitudinal research of varying lengths. We know from the earlier chapters that an important way subjects in longitudinal studies are special has to do with their health. Subjects often do not complete these studies because they are too ill or have died. So when we see little age loss in longitudinal studies and even more stability the longer the study goes on, we must suspect good health in the sample as a main cause. Conversely, illness seems a good explanation for IQ losses, as more and more decrement occurs as a function of age when we choose samples that are less and less physically select.

These comparisons, however, only offer indirect evidence that being ill is important in explaining the age differences in IQ scores. Striking and direct evidence for its deleterious effect comes from one of the earliest gerontological studies to explore the aging process in depth (Birren, Butler, Greenhouse, Sokoloff, & Yarrow, 1963). The purpose of this study was to examine aging apart from disease, so the investigators took care to recruit a healthy group of subjects. Forty-seven male volunteers aged 65 to 91 and rated as disease free on the basis of a medical exam participated in a 2-week series of tests.

However, during the course of this extensive evaluation, the researchers discovered that their carefully selected sample really was composed of two distinct groups. One group was indeed totally healthy, showing only the most benign aging changes (for example, osteoarthritis). The other, comprising somewhat fewer than half of the men, did have signs of subclinical illness. Even though at the time they had no overt symptoms, ten subjects, for instance, had changes suggestive of heart disease (we now know from Chapter 2's discussion of the Baltimore study's findings that subclinical signs of heart disease are indeed surprisingly prevalent in "healthy" men). This subgroup had higher blood pressure and other laboratory findings showing less than optimal health.

In the end, this unexpected finding of a less healthy subsample really was a bonus rather than a problem. It gave the researchers a chance to compare the two groups of elderly men with each other as well as with young adults. Undoubtedly, the most interesting comparisons occurred on the WAIS (Botwinick & Birren, 1963). The classic aging pattern was apparent for both samples. The two groups did relatively well on the verbal part of the test and had markedly lower scores compared to the young adults on the performance scale. However, there were fascinating differences in performance between the two elderly groups. The totally healthy men outperformed their counterparts on a full 10 of the 11 WAIS subtests. This consistent difference in performance, though admittedly correlational, seems to offer overwhelming evidence of the deleterious effect of even *slight* deviations from health on IQ scores.

If even subclinical signs of illness affect intelligence, we can only expect genuine chronic disease to have a more extreme impact. Perhaps our primary candidate to look at in this context is heart disease. This illness is such a prevalent accompaniment of aging. The discussion in Chapter 2 implies that impairments in the heart's capacity to circulate blood adequately may have both a direct physiological impact on mental functioning as well as affecting IQ indirectly by causing disability and so withdrawal from life (as happened with Sam Kennedy in Chapter 2's vignette).

Interestingly, however, the link between heart disease and lower IQ is not as automatic as we might think. When researchers (Thompson, Eisdorfer, & Estes, 1970) correlated medical signs and physician ratings of cardiovascular symptoms with WAIS scores among the male Duke study volunteers, at first they did find that disease-free subjects did better, particularly on the performance part of the test. However, after an added control, the relationship evaporated. The volunteers with heart disease were disproportionately Black and of lower socioeconomic status. Taking these variables into account, there were no IQ differences at all between the ill and healthy groups.

By definition this study excluded the severely ill, people who were too sick to return to be tested. So it may be that, beyond a certain point, heart disease does affect IQ. However, the lesson of this study is that we should be cautious in assuming intellectual loss is a predictable fate once a loved one develops even a chronic disease we might expect to affect thinking—a warning that applies doubly to abnormal findings on laboratory tests.

For instance, in an early study with the young-old Duke study volunteers, Francis Wilkie and Carl Eisdorfer (1973) found that slightly elevated blood pressure might actually protect against IQ loss in later life. When they followed their subjects for a decade (Eisdorfer, 1977) those with normal blood pressure had relatively stable IQ scores. Those whose readings were much too high did show the expected IQ declines. However, subjects whose blood pressure was only slightly higher than normal improved in performance over the 10 years!

Does this mean that slightly high blood pressure should not be treated in the elderly because it has cognitive benefits? To determine whether this widely believed implication of Eisdorfer and Wilkie's findings was indeed correct, Baltimore researchers tried to replicate the Duke results as well as explore blood pressure/intelligence relationships throughout adulthood in a more comprehensive way. Paul Costa and Nathan Shock (1984) categorized Baltimore volunteers from their 20s to their late 80s according to whether they had low, average, or high systolic or diastolic blood pressure and then related these readings to scores on the various subtests of another intelligence test (the Army Alpha) over time. Interestingly, in this study high blood pressure was *neither* good *nor* bad for cognitive performance. In fact, at no age did it have any relation to IQ at all!

This is not to say that severe untreated high blood pressure may not adversely affect intelligence (as well being life threatening) or deny the clear-cut evidence that a variety of late-life medical disorders as well as self-ratings of health (see Field, Schaie, & Leino, 1988) are associated with IQ declines in later life. Still, the lesson of this careful study is that, while perhaps not positive either, in old age we cannot assume that every physical problem or pathological condition causes cognitive loss.

The Fascinating Link between IQ Losses and Death

However, even if only *serious* medical problems cause IQ losses, we have a whole new avenue to pursue. Not only might we use the presence of disease to predict possible IQ declines, we might even do the opposite. Perhaps a sudden drop in IQ might be a clue to an otherwise undiagnosed disease. In other words, the WAIS might have a whole new purpose as an instrument for physical diagnosis—it might be used as a behavorial barometer to show that illness has struck. This behavorial-index-of-illness idea actually has a long history in gerontology.

The possibility that performance on the WAIS might be used as a clue to changes in a person's physical state first became evident in a longitudinal study of cognition done in Germany in the 1950s (Riegel & Riegel, 1972; Riegel, Riegel, & Meyer, 1967) when an accidential observation suggested a related idea was true—IQ performance might be a barometer of approaching death. In what began as a straightforward study charting age changes in cognition, Klaus Riegel and his colleagues administered a variety of tests including the WAIS three times at 5-year intervals to a large group of men and women aged 55 to 75. However, while analyzing the data, these observers noticed something unusual about the dropouts over the 15 years. Particularly for participants under age 65, people who died before completing the study had lower IQ scores than those who did not. Even more significant, subjects who died between the second and third evaluations showed an unusual decline in their scores from the first to the second examination. In other words, a sudden drop in IQ over and above what is "normal" seemed to predict impending death. The name the researchers coined for this finding was especially apt—the **terminal-drop phenomenon.**

In another early longitudinal study of cognition, exploring IQ changes in a sample of aging twins, Lissy Jarvik and her coworkers (Blum, Clark, & Jarvik, 1973; Jarvik & Falik, 1963) refined this idea. They, too, found evidence of terminal drop, but in their investigation the "death-predicting losses" were confined to the WAIS verbal scale. Because changes in three verbal scales in particular (similarities, digit span, and vocabulary) discriminated between the survivors and nonsurvivors in their sample, Jarvik and her colleagues developed a formula based on yearly perentage losses in these tests to predict closeness to death. Changes above a certain level they called "critical loss." Critical loss on two or more scales was an ominous harbinger of imminent demise.

I must emphasize that far from all studies agree that the phenomenon called terminal drop really exists. For instance, one carefully controlled investigation using the Duke volunteers failed to document any signs of it at all (Palmore & Cleveland, 1976). However, while her practice of charting "critical loss" using specific verbal subtests may not be valid, we do have more recent evidence confirming Jarvik's observations that sudden loss on the normally stable verbal WAIS may indeed be an ominous physical sign in later life.

When researchers (Cooney, Schaie, & Willis, 1988) looked at dropouts from Schaie's landmark Seattle longitudinal study (see Box 5-1), they found that while there were no general differences in overall IQ between those who dropped out and those who remained, this was not true of the tests tapping crystallized abilities (vocabulary, verbal fluency). Later-middle-aged people who subsequently dropped out due to illness had previously scored lowest on these measures; in old age unusually low scores on these specific tests were characteristic of those who subsequently died. In other words, perhaps because decline in this aspect of intelligence is not typical of normal aging, changes in *crystallized abilities* do indeed seem to be a cognitive barometer of disease.

The Baltimore study puts this finding about crystallized abilities into a larger framework. One of the fascinating findings of the study is that any sudden decline on a test measuring a normally stable function seems to signal disease. So this compelling Baltimore observation (Shock et al., 1984) suggests that in addition to tests of crystallized abilities other behavioral or medical measures might also be used to diagnose the presence of a serious physical problem (or impending death). A sudden drop in the verbal WAIS may indeed be just one barometer among many that indicates that what was normal aging has become genuine pathology.

QUESTIONING THE UNDERPINNING:
THE VALIDITY OF THE IQ TEST

So far we have been focusing on age changes on the WAIS, similar intelligence tests, and the trajectories that fluid and crystallized abilities follow as people grow old, become ill, and approach death. Now it is time to shift perspectives for yet a third time. Perhaps the very underpinning on which we have based our discussion is wrong. The abilities we have been talking about may not be all there is to intelligence. Worse yet, the WAIS and other measures may not be doing a good job of measuring the qualities that really constitute the essence of being intelligent in the real world.

As I mentioned earlier, for several decades the WAIS and related IQ tests have been under fire, declared unfair, or even banned (Bersoff, 1973). There is considerable justification for this public concern and action. The names these scales go by strongly imply that they measure something more than they actually do. In psychological language this controversy involves questions of **validity.** The WAIS and other standardized intelligence tests may not be accurately measuring what they purport to—an immutable ability or fixed attribute called "intelligence" (see Bersoff, 1973; McClelland, 1973). For instance, in our discussion of how years of schooling, or test-taking familiarity, or anxiety biases the test against older people, we saw clearly that the WAIS cannot be measuring just cognitive capacity in a pure form. Even the lesser assumption that the test accurately measures current intellectual performance has also been criticized. The compelling argument as applied to the elderly proceeds like this (see Birren, 1973; Charles, 1973; Schaie, 1977–1978, 1978).

All intelligence tests are limited, bound by the particular framework from which and reference group for whom they are constructed. There can be no transsituational or totally context-free IQ test, as any measure must refer to specific behaviors that are signs of intelligence in a particular setting. The earlier tests on which the WAIS is based were constructed to measure intellectual ability in a particular setting—school. For this reason, though the WAIS and related measures are better indexes of intelligence for children and adolescents, there are questions about their validity for middle-aged and older adults. Except in unusual cases such as Karen Johnson's, the main situation in which intelligence is called for during adulthood is not the classroom, as it is during youth.

For this reason, during the past decade some of the most prominent psychologists who study cognition and age (for example, Labouvie-Vief, 1985; Labouvie-Vief & Blanchard-Fields, 1986a and 1986b; Schaie, 1977–1978, 1978, 1980; Willis & Baltes, 1980) have become interested in devising new, more **age-relevant intelligence tests.** These measures, they argue, unlike existing tests of fluid and crystallized abilities, must have what they call **ecological validity.** By this phrase they mean the tests must be tailored to the actual life situations and skills appropriate to intelligence during adulthood.

INTERVENTIONS

So it is not surprising that attempts to develop an age-relevant IQ test form one centerpiece of intervention research in cognition and age. Side by side with these efforts is another thrust that is just as interesting but less revolutionary: to improve the performance of older people on tests of intelligence as traditionally defined.

Designing an Age-Relevant Intelligence Test

As we might imagine because of his vocal convictions about the inadequacy of current measures, K. Warner Schaie (see Box 5-1) has spearheaded the current drive to develop an age-relevant IQ test. His contribution is theoretical: to divide the life span into stages and devise a typology of skills that might be important to intelligence at these times of life (1977–1978; see Figure 5-4). During the first life-stage, childhood and adolescence, Schaie speculates that the essence of intelligence is ease of learning. Our primary aim is to acquire the content of the culture and the skills to be an independent adult. During the next part of life, young adulthood, cognitive competence means how well we can use what we have learned to achieve life goals. Schaie calls this the achieving stage. During our middle years, responsibility, good long-range decision making, and the ability to integrate complex relationships are the hallmarks of being intelligent. Finally, in old age, questions of "why should I know" achieve primary importance. Here, in what Schaie calls the reintegrative stage, personality and attitude are much more critical to cognition than ever before.

This typology clearly shows why the WAIS, with its focus on problem-solving skills, speed, and the mastery of school-related material, may not be a valid index of intelligence during adulthood. Especially during the second half of life we need tests of real world intelligence—measures that capture the wisdom, good sense, and balanced perspective on living that are the hallmarks of being intelligent in life. Furthermore, Schaie suggests that to capture this elusive quality a more concrete type of IQ test may be needed than the abstract WAIS, one

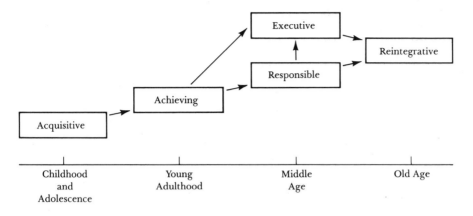

Figure 5-4. Schaie's stages of intelligence.
Source: Schaie, 1977–1978.

explicitly tied to the life situations people face that demand intelligent behavior (Schaie, 1977–1978; Scheidt & Schaie, 1978).

Drawing on Schaie's ideas, psychologist Gisela Labouvie-Vief has elaborated on the specific ways real world intelligence may differ from the abilities measured by standard intelligence tests (Labouvie-Vief, 1985; Labouvie-Vief & Blanchard-Fields, 1986a and 1986b): Real world intelligence does not involve picking out the correct answer to an abstract problem—which the WAIS and all other IQ tests ask us to do—but being able to think in a different mode. In school people who can solve abstract problems are the intelligent ones. But real world problems often have no clear-cut right or wrong answers. Making intelligent life decisions means being sensitive to the many perspectives involved in issues and integrating them to arrive at answers that are "wise" rather than formally correct. It also means knowing when to transcend rational logic in making decisions. People who have real world intelligence are socially smart. They have a gift for empathy, for being able to shift from abstract logic to the logic of the heart.

Recently, Gisela Labouvie-Vief and Fredda Blanchard-Fields (1986a and 1986b) have been experimenting with questions they hope might eventually constitute an age-relevant intelligence test. Their strategy is not to ask questions that have a rigid right or wrong answer but to pose life dilemmas and have people write paragraphs about how they would respond. These open-ended essays are then categorized as either more or less "intelligent." Here is an example:

> John is known to be a heavy drinker especially when he goes to parties. Mary, John's wife, warns him that if he gets drunk one more time she will leave him. John goes to an office party and comes home drunk. Does Mary leave him?

According to formal logic, the correct answer to this dilemma is a rigid yes: "Mary said she would leave, so, of course, she does." However, as we all know, this solution may not constitute the most intelligent response in the real world. Being life intelligent involves appreciating the pros and cons of this choice for Mary, for

BOX 5-1
The Baltes-Schaie/Horn-Donaldson Debate

I hope the discussion shows just how difficult it is to make simple declarative statements about intelligence and age. First, there are the far from positive facts, the discouraging findings of cross-sectional studies; then, their more positive counterweight, the picture longitudinal studies convey. Finally, there are the mitigating explanations: the impact of ability-extraneous influences on IQ test scores and the questions about the validity of the tests. So it is not surprising that even experts have differed sharply about what the research means. These professional disagreements erupted into public debate when the research on this emotion-laden topic appeared in the pages of the *American Psychologist.*

Alarmed by articles written by Paul Baltes and K. Warner Schaie (1974; Schaie, 1974) in the *American Psychologist* and *Psychology Today* that put the most positive cast on the findings, Jack Horn and his colleague (Horn & Donaldson, 1976) felt compelled to set the record right. Their rebuttal was followed by a rejoinder (Baltes & Schaie, 1976) that, in turn, evoked an irate response (Horn & Donaldson, 1977) and yet another attempt to set the record straight (Schaie & Baltes, 1977). This unique public clash, whose participants are the leading researchers in the field, puts in sharp focus the different interpretations that can be made from the "facts" about intelligence and age.

In their original articles, Baltes and Schaie strongly implied, based on the heartening findings of Schaie's Seattle Longitudinal Study, that the assumption of intellectual decline with age is a myth. In this landmark investigation of cognition—the first systematic methodological attempt to parcel out cohort factors from age declines—several hundred Seattle residents of different ages were tested three times over 14 years and sequential strategies were used to estimate the impact of "cohort" versus "age" on declining scores. Because differences between cohorts seemed to account for much of the test score losses, as Baltes and Schaie explained, this study definitely sets to rest the widespread idea that intelligence goes downhill as we age.

Horn and Donaldson (1976) strongly disagreed. They contended it is simply not true that no decline exists at all. Schaie's research itself revealed losses in a very important intellectual ability. Even the most optimistic reading of his data showed inescapable declines on tests measuring fluid abilities.

Baltes and Schaie countered by saying they had been misinterpreted. They had never meant to imply that no aspect of cognition falls off, merely that the assumption of *universal* decline is false. They pointed to the fact of large individual differences in stability and stressed the impact of ability-extraneous factors on the performance of older adults. Most important, they voiced misgivings about the validity of IQ tests—

the assumption that they measure intelligence in an adequate way. They concluded that a life-span developmental position should be crucial to any summary statement. Intellectual change as we age is multidirectional. It occurs in varying degrees in different individuals; it varies in a complex way across specific abilities.

Horn and Donaldson responded that this was a distortion, an attempt to obscure the fact that decline does clearly occur. They made another interesting point. By questioning the merits of the IQ test and by adopting the life-span perspective that everyone ages differently, Baltes and Schaie were really giving up; what they were really saying is that it is impossible to describe, measure, and generalize about intelligence in a scientific way.

The final reply (Schaie & Baltes, 1977) was brief: The assumption of universal decline is not only false, adopting it would have serious social consequences. Rather than assuming that the deficits that occur are irreversible, we should explore how cognitive losses in old age can be modified. This approach will have both theoretical and practical importance; it is more positive and humane.

A 1988 postscript to this mid-1970s debate shows just how much positions have softened now that the idea of universal cognitive decline as we age is widely known to be a myth. Today, Schaie is much more relaxed about making cognitive generalizations; he is even comfortable admitting that there is a time in life when loss is the dominant theme. In fact, according to his most recent Seattle analyses (Hertzog & Schaie, 1988), the picture is really quite straightforward: increases in general intelligence during young adulthood, stability during our middle years, and finally, beginning at about age 60, a shift to modest IQ declines.

□

the children, for John. A response that shows that the reader has taken these multiple interpersonal perspectives into consideration is rated as the optimally intelligent one.

How valid is this novel approach to measuring intelligence likely to be? Clues come from examining how people of different ages score on the questions Labouvie-Vief and Blanchard-Fields have devised. Based on the idea that life intelligence increases with experience, if this attempt to capture real world intelligence is indeed promising, we would expect that the age group most immersed in negotiating life's conflicting demands would get the highest scores. This seems to be the case. In their first tentative investigations the researchers have found that early adolescents score lowest; the peak scores are achieved by the very age group we expect to perform particularly well—people in their middle years.

Improving Performance on Current Tests

We know by now that our IQ score is really a composite—part inherent ability, part the variety of potentially changeable external, nonintellectual factors (anxiety, familiarity, education) that influence how we perform. We also know that ability-extraneous influences exert a particularly potent negative impact on test performance in later life. The implications of these facts is quite positive: There may be a good deal of plasticity in the IQ, particularly in old age. There may be considerable room for improving cognitive competence among the elderly.

Behaviorists would have taken this optimistic stance all along, as their whole orientation stresses looking first to the environment versus biology for the source of an older person's deficits. In fact, an operant perspective suggests that the simple concept of extinction accounts at least in part for cognitive losses in old age. The life situation of a retired person or someone restricted by functional impairments to looking at four walls may simply provide too little reinforcement for intellectual skills (Baltes & Labouvie, 1973; Labouvie-Vief, Hoyer, Baltes, & Baltes, 1974). So, as with any behavior that is not reinforced, thinking and reasoning inevitably erode.

This suggests that providing opportunities to "exercise cognitive skills" might be one antidote to age-related cognitive decline. Society should offer more avenues for older people to keep intellectually active and interested. The special educational and volunteer programs described in Chapter 9 in the discussion of retirement are interventions that fall into this category. Another approach is more specific and focused: directly train older people in the skills measured by the IQ test.

It seems logical that training might improve a person's IQ scores, provided we looked at scales measuring crystallized intelligence; but what about that most biologically based category of cognition? Can training improve fluid abilities, too? The studies clearly suggest the answer is yes. For instance, when researchers offered elderly subjects practice on one test measuring this facet of cognition, not only did their scores on that task improve but so did their performance on other tests of fluid abilities. Even more impressive, the beneficial effects of the training persisted. At a 6-month follow-up the elderly group given training still did significantly better than a comparison group of untutored older adults (Plemons, Willis, & Baltes, 1978).

Another, more recent study echoes this theme (Blackburn, Papalia-Finlay, Foye, & Serlin, 1988). Older people were assigned to either training at improving figural relations problem solving (a fluid test) or a control group. Because the researchers wanted to explore if certain types of training were more effective, they used two conditions. In one, participants were given formal instructions in how to solve the specific problems; in the other, they were given practice generating their own solutions and the chance to discuss the tasks with one another in a group. As in the earlier study, both groups performed better on a variety of tests of fluid abilities both at the time and to a lesser extent later on. However, self-generated group practice had more durable effects, as the gains this group made were maintained more over time.

Another study (Labouvie-Vief & Gonda, 1976) shows that simply practicing can result in improvement on other cognitive tasks, too. One group of elderly subjects was given specific training in monitoring their performance on a reasoning task by making statements such as "What do I have to do?" or "Think before I give up." A comparison group was just given experience on the test. The researchers then looked for improvement both on the training task itself and on another measure of reasoning. They found some provocative results. On an immediate test using the original measure, the subjects given specific training were superior both to the control group and the subjects who simply practiced. Overall, however, simple practice was more beneficial. The subjects in this group performed better than the other two groups both at a later testing on the original measure and at both testings on the transfer task. In other words, here, too, we see that performance on IQ type tests can be improved, in particular with training of an unexpected kind—pure (nondirected) practice itself.

The real point of these studies, however, is not so much to show a change in test scores, but to bring home a much more relevant to real life point—old age intellectual deficits are far from "inherent," "unmodifiable," or "incapable of being changed." Intellectual abilities can improve in later life, just as they can at any other life-stage.

KEY TERMS

WAIS	Terminal-drop phenomenon
Classic aging pattern	Validity
Crystallized intelligence	Age-relevant IQ tests
Fluid intelligence	Ecological validity

RECOMMENDED READINGS

Baltes, P. B., & Schaie, K. W. (1976). On the plasticity of intelligence in adulthood and old age. Where Horn and Donaldson fail. *American Psychologist, 31,*720–725.*

Horn, J. L., & Donaldson, G. (1976). On the myth of intellectual decline during adulthood. *American Psychologist, 31,* 701–719.*

Horn, J. L. & Donaldson, G. (1977) Faith is not enough: A response to the Baltes/Schaie claim that intelligence does not wane. *American Psychologist, 32,* 369–373.*

Labouvie-Vief, G. (1985). Intelligence and cognition. In J. E. Birren & K. W. Schaie (Eds.), *Handbook of the psychology of aging* (2nd ed.). New York: Van Nostrand Reinhold. Review of the literature on age and intelligence from the "optimistic" perpective of the researcher most immersed in developing an age-relevant IQ test. Moderately difficult.

Schaie, K. W., & Baltes, P. B. (1977). Some faith helps to see the forest: A final comment on the Horn and Donaldson myth of the Baltes/Schaie position on adult intelligence. *American Psychologist, 32,* 1118–1120.*

---

* The fascinating and at times acrimonious debate over how to view the facts about intelligence and age. Highly recommended. Not difficult.

Chapter 6

□

Cognitive Processes: Memory and Creativity

□

Memory
- The Basic Framework for Understanding Memory
  - The Older Person's Problem with Memory
  - What Helps or Hinders Memory in Later Life?
- Making the Translation from Laboratory to Life
  - Interventions

Creative Achievements
- The First Findings and the Debate They Caused
  - Creativity in the Arts
  - Creativity in the Sciences

Key Terms

Recommended Readings

Karen Johnson decided to enroll in two courses. She chose one in which she felt confident of doing well, creative writing, and another that she was far from sure of, introductory psychology. Psychology was intimidating because of the huge number of facts and concepts to be learned. Plus, Karen did not relish having her grade based on multiple-choice exams. No matter how glowing Dr. Stagestad's remarks had been, Karen could not help thinking: "I was only ranked exceptional compared with other people my age. In a room full of young adults, won't I still fall short?"

At least she could be sure about creative writing. The quality of her short stories did not seem to have deteriorated over the years. In fact, life experience seemed to lend them greater depth. She had no fears about being blocked. The urge to write was as strong today as it had been in her 20s. So was the outpouring of pages she regularly produced, which was remarkable because she had heard that creativity declines as a person ages.

Memory, though, was a different matter. Two weeks ago Karen had forgotten a hairdresser's appointment; even worse, this past month she had accidentally stood up a close friend for lunch. Just last Friday at the party her son had given to celebrate finishing his first novel she had been astonished at how she had forgotten the name of an occasional guest. But this negative train of thought had to stop. Karen had enough insight about herself to understand that these depressing preoccupations always happened those Sundays her (perhaps soon to be famous) boy forgot to call.

When David finally did call on Tuesday, he laughed off these concerns. He had some compliments to deliver relating to that very point. During the party several people had commented on Karen's marvelous memory—not only was it flattering that after meeting so many people she could remember them, it was a refreshing rebuke to those stereotypes about old age. At least two people not given to flattery at all, David's agent and the book reviewer at the *Times*, said that Karen's recall of names and faces put their memory to shame.

David was too polite to say what he was really thinking. His mother's complaints followed a predictable pattern. She got upset about her memory when she was really upset about other things. Now it was because she was feeling neglected; because he was so absorbed in his book he was paying less attention to her. David thought bitterly that his mother was focusing on an ailment of old age instead of admitting a more selfish emotion to herself. She was not totally happy now that he finally had a chance to become the next Stephen King. She half wished his success would not happen because it would leave him less time for her. Thank God, she would be kept busy with her new plan to go to college. And getting out in the world again would force her to do what he had urged her to do all along—get an appointment book like everyone else.

Actually, her semester in college did go a long way toward erasing Karen's preoccupations about her mental state, especially the praise from her creative writing professor and the "A" she got for outstanding work. This experience even gave her ammunition when David confided he was afraid he could not write a book as good as *The Evil Mist* ever again. Although she could not speak for everyone, her experience certainly showed that creative work could be produced at any age.

The only depressing event of the semester was that "C" in psychology—a grade that was particularly annoying because it was so undeserved. Each time after handing in a test, much of the information that Karen had blocked on out of anxiety had the annoying tendency to miraculously reappear. This led her to question a statement Professor Smith made in a lecture on memory in people her age. Citing studies in which elderly people had been asked to remember nonsense syllables, he said a marked decline in memory is typical, perhaps even universal, in later life.

■

In Chapter 5 we looked at the relationship between age and cognition in a general way—exploring how that global quality intelligence changes as we grow old. Now we turn to changes in some specific cognitive processes. The two abilities that I will focus on in the following pages, memory and creativity, differ to the greatest possible extent. However, our preconceptions about the fate of these aspects of thinking in later life share a common theme: When people get older, we assume that their memory gets worse. Since central to our sterotype of old age is the idea of greater rigidity, the implication is that people automatically become less creative as they reach their later years.

This chapter's discussion of memory is limited to normal older people. (Chapter 10 describes pathological disorders of memory such as Alzheimer's disease.) In contrast, I have chosen a very different approach in discussing age and creativity here. I am not confining myself to old age but exploring research on creative achievements throughout adulthood. Most important, my focus will be on the few studies that have been done on creativity in a very atypical group, the small fraction of people genuinely involved in producing unique, original work.

Ironically, then, while memory outranks every other subject as a core research area in the psychology of aging—for instance, a survey from 1960 to 1980 showed that articles on this topic comprised well over half of all the psychological entries in gerontological journals (Poon, 1985)—the discussion in the second half of this chapter is more specialized and out of the mainstream than any other in this book. I feel this imbalance is necessary because creativity and aging is a topic that should be covered. Unfortunately, however, we simply have very little research on how this important facet of thinking normally changes as people grow old.

MEMORY

More than any other problem, poor memory is the complaint that epitomizes old age. Even though we may be too sophisticated to assume that all older people are senile, we still assume that most elderly people have suffered some memory loss. As was true in the vignette, older people share this perception. Most, if asked, would probably say they are more forgetful than they used to be. Some, in just as telling a way, would brag "my memory is a good as ever."

The fact that poor memory is a salient component of our perceptions about being old was demonstrated in a compelling study: Judith Rodin and Ellen Langer (1980) filmed three actors aged 20, 50, and 70 reading the same speech. Scattered through the approximately 10-minute monologue were a few references to memory lapses (for example, I forgot my keys). People of different ages then watched the film of either the young, middle-aged, or older actor and were asked to write a paragraph about what the person was like. Those who saw the 70-year-old frequently described him as forgetful. No one who saw the middle-aged person or the young adult read the identical speech mentioned poor memory. Unfortunately, the older people who saw the film were just as likely as the younger viewers to see the 70-year-old as slipping mentally, and were even more likely to evaluate him in a negative way.

This is just one of several studies suggesting that we are primed to expect poor memory in older people. When someone is over 60, or 70, or 80, we interpret normal forgetting in an exaggerated, more ominous light. But what is the basis of this deficiency we naturally take for granted? Answers to this question have been vigorously pursued by psychologists in rigorous laboratory research.

Traditionally, laboratory investigations of learning and memory have had a certain format. A list of words, letters, or nonsense syllables is presented orally or visually to a group of elderly people and young adults. After a certain number of presentations, recall of these items is compared. Or, in a common variation on this procedure, called **paired-associate technique,** items are presented in pairs and then the subject is given one member of the pair and asked to remember the other. When the subject is asked to remember the items without any hints, the approach is called **free recall.** When hints are given, such as the first letter of the correct word, the technique is called **cued recall.** The third and easiest type of test is the **recognition** approach. As in multiple-choice tests, the subject must simply pick out the correct answer from a number of possibilities.

In general, these studies have shown ample reason for our prejudices about memory and age. The elderly almost always do significantly worse then the young (see Table 6-1). As we will explore in the discussion of pathological memory in Chapter 10, physiological changes in the part of the brain that

TABLE 6-1. A typical example illustrating the types of age differences in memory scores between old and young subjects.

Group		Mean Age (Years)	Mean Vocabulary Score (WAIS)		Recall (Mean No. Correct) Trial List	Recall (Percentage Correct) Trial List
Old	1	73.2	46.6	M	2.8	28
				SD	2.9	
	2	75.6	47.1	M	2.8	28
				SD	2.8	
	3	74.2	47.1	M	3.0	30
				SD	2.5	
	4	73.3	42.6	M	2.8	28
				SD	2.3	
	Mean	74.1	45.9		2.85	28.5
Young	1	16.1	52.6	M	7.2	72
				SD	2.2	
	2	16.2	48.9	M	7.2	72
				SD	2.3	
	3	15.9	50.6	M	7.2	72
				SD	2.5	
	4	16.2	49.3	M	7.1	71
				SD	2.5	
	Mean	16.1	50.3		7.18	71.8

Source: Adapted from Hulicka & Grossman, 1967.

encodes memory may in part underlie this poorer performance. However, variations in the tasks themselves also make a great difference in the degree of deficiency older people show. This brings us to a major purpose of the hundreds of publications devoted to memory and age. They have been carried out not so much to show that a deficiency exists but to explore the reasons for the problem: "In what aspects of remembering do older people have the most trouble?" "What is the source of the deficits older adults show?" (See Craik, 1977; Poon, 1985; Poon, Fozard, Cermak, Arenberg, & Thompson, 1980.) To understand this issue, we need a more general framework, a brief outline of the way the process of memory is typically conceptualized today.

The Basic Framework for Understanding Memory

According to the currently widely accepted information-processing model, memory is an active process involving *attention* and *rehearsal.* Information passes through three separate stages or stores on the way to becoming a memory (the description below comes from a review by Poon, 1985).

First, stimuli arriving from our senses are held briefly in a **sensory store** specific to that sense. For example, visual images enter a visual store (or *iconic* memory); the sounds we hear, an auditory store (or *echoic* memory). This first memory "bin" or store is simply a raw image, somewhat like a photocopy, which deteriorates quite rapidly—within ½ to 2 seconds. Individual features that we notice, however, are transformed into verbal information and enter the second store—**primary memory.**

Primary memory is best viewed as a kind of temporary holding place rather than a structured store. The information that can be kept here is limited to a handful of items. As more material enters this limited capacity space, other information is displaced or pushed out and lost. A compelling real life example of primary memory and its limitations happens when we get a phone number from information and immediately make the call. We know by experience that we can dial the seven-digit number without having to write it down and our memory will not fail us provided the phone rings. If we get a busy signal, though, and have to try again, mysteriously memory fades. The information has simply slipped out of this second memory stage.

To prevent this from happening, the solution, of course, is to rehearse the phone number—to "memorize" it. In the words of memory researchers, this means we must transfer the information from this holding area to the third and final store—**secondary memory.**

When we speak of memory, we are really talking about the contents of this last system. Secondary memory is the relatively permanent, large-capacity store that is the repository of our past. In order for us to genuinely be able to remember something (the phone number or anything else) the information in this large store must logically have undergone three steps: It must have been adequately learned, or been **encoded** in the first place; it must have been adequately **stored;** and, finally, it must be capable of being **retrieved,** or gotten out.

The Older Person's Problem with Memory

While studies differ as to whether older people have modest deficits in sensory and primary memory (see, for reviews, Craik, 1977; Poon, 1985; Smith, 1980), memory researchers do agree on one point: the *main* locus of age declines in memory lies not in problems in these first two systems. It resides in secondary memory. Where the arguments have been vigorous and protracted is in determining what facet or process involved in secondary memory is at fault. Are memory deficits in old age due mainly to an acquisition (encoding) problem, a storage problem, or a retrieval problem? (See Poon, 1985; Smith, 1980.) Or, in less technical terms, has the older person simply inadequately learned the material in the first place, improperly stored it, or is the problem mainly due to difficulties in getting the information out?

Our reasonable approach to answer this question would be to devise studies that eliminate a single memory process in particular and then to compare the performance of old and young subjects. If age differences are minimized or even significantly reduced on that type of test, then logically the older person's main problem would be with the step or process that was omitted. This, in fact, is a strategy that has implicated *retrieval*—getting stored information out of secondary memory—as at least part of the older person's difficulty.

Recognition tests (such as multiple-choice exams) and measures of cued recall (where the person is given hints such as the first letter of the word to be remembered) largely eliminate the retrieval step because the correct answer is either totally or partly made available and so does not have to be searched for and retrieved (Smith, 1980). Tests of this type, while easier for everyone, seem to help older people the most: performance differences between the young and old are less marked or even almost disappear when cues are used. So impaired retrieval must be the main source of the memory deficit often observed in late life.

But does this "evidence" really prove retrieval is the main problem? Many researchers answer no. In one study, researchers (Harkins, Chapman, & Eisdorfer, 1979) demonstrated that a better *guessing strategy,* not better memory itself, could be responsible for the relatively good performance by the elderly on recognition tests. When they specifically evaluated age differences in response strategy on a memory test of this type, they found that in this unusual case the elderly group spontaneously adopted a guessing strategy that resulted in better scores, making it simply appear that their memory was as good as the young adults'. So, according to these researchers, recognition memory may be just as impaired in older people as recall, or almost as much. Previous studies may have overlooked this by not taking age differences in test-taking approaches into account.

The primary criticism, though, of seeing the older person's problem as retrieval based on these findings is that the findings themselves do not actually prove retrieval is at fault. In fact, studies showing less age deficit when cues are given are just as compatible with the opposite interpretation—a problem localized in the acquisition stage. Let's follow this chain of reasoning carefully: Having a good strategy for organizing material so it can be remembered easily is a skill involved in acquisition or the first, encoding, memory stage. But if the older person is deficient in this arena, problems would show up mainly on free-recall tests when an answer must be produced literally out of the air. When recognition and cued-recall tests are used, there is less need for a good encoding technique because when external cues are provided, a person does not have to rely totally on his or her internal system of encoding material for easy access.

So the reason age differences are especially pronounced on free-recall tests may also be poor learning skills. Memory tests of this type are the ones that are most sensitive to differences in a person's initial encoding strategy (Smith, 1980).

This discussion offers insights into why pinpointing the nature of the problem older people have in remembering is so complicated. The retrieval stage is difficult or practically impossible to isolate from the stage of initial learning (Arenberg, 1980; Poon, 1985; Smith, 1980). Actually, rather than continuing to argue about *which* memory process is at fault, today many investigators would probably agree with this summary statement made by psychologist Leonard Poon: "Both retrieval and encoding deficits are implicated in the lower performance of older adults. . . . it is not likely that . . . deficits can be isolated to one stage or component but rather that deficits are widespread in the entire cognitive system" (1985, p. 443).

Even if we cannot identify learning or retrieval as definitively as fault, however, devising tests to show when age differences are more or less pronounced can tell us a great deal. What situations make remembering more difficult or easier for older people? What does this tell us about the specific problems the elderly have?

What Helps or Hinders Memory in Later Life?

In fact, one of the older person's problems is with encoding. As was suggested in the previous section, the elderly remember less well because they tend to use less efficient learning strategies. Irene Hulicka and Joel Grossman (1967) offered direct proof of this hypothesis in a classic study done more than 2 decades ago. The researchers first compared a young and an old group on the standard paired-associate learning task and found the typical result: the elderly did not do nearly as well. Then they questioned the two groups about the way they went about learning the items and found clear differences. The young people much more frequently reported using **mediators**—they formed a visual image including the words or linked the unrelated items by imagining them in a sentence.

This strategy helps. It is much easier to remember *tree* if when we are given the words *bat–tree* we imagine a bat sitting in a tree than if we simply memorize the unconnected words by rote. And, in fact, when the researchers gave their subjects special instructions about using mediators, the performance of both the young and the old improved. However, the older people were helped more, and so age differences in performance were reduced. Since this finding has been confirmed several times (see Poon, 1985), it is clear that inefficient memorization techniques are indeed one factor that accounts for the poorer laboratory performance of the old.

In addition to this poor internal style, external facets of the test situation also handicap the older adult. One crucial aspect of the situation is predictable from what we know about how older people perform on intelligence tests: when remembering demands speed, the elderly will perform poorly.

Once again, that being under time pressure hurts the elderly was first revealed in a decades old study involving paired associates. Robert Canestrari (1963) tested old and young people under three conditions. The first two demanded responding within a certain time. Subjects had to remember the correct word within either a 1 ½ -second or a 3-second interval. The last did not involve speed; subjects could take as long as they wanted to study the words and could also answer at their own pace. As we might expect, age differences were particularly marked under the first two conditions. When they had unlimited time to learn and remember, the elderly subjects did take longer. Their performance, though, was comparatively much better than before.

Another important facet of the situation is familiarity. Older people perform best when the memory task is as relevant as possible to their lives. (We will return to this very important point later on.) In fact, perhaps because having real life associations with these items put them at an advantage, in one study where the learning test involved age-relevant words (*retirement, widowhood*), older people even outperformed a group of young adults (as reported in Poon, 1985).

Each of these studies has theoretical importance; it helps us get to the root of the deficiency older adults have. But each also has clear practical implications.

To facilitate memory in later life, it might be helpful to teach the elderly either mnemonic techniques or strategies for making the material they need to remember as personally relevant as possible. To enhance recall we should make sure older adults are allowed as much time to remember (and learn) as they want.

Making the Translation from Laboratory to Life

Ideally, most research on memory and age should have these clear real life applications. We should be able to translate studies designed to probe abstract questions about memory in the psychological laboratory into a definite set of prescriptions for remedying the problems that older people have in the real world. Unfortunately, though, it is only within the past decade that linking academic research to practical action has become an important priority (Erikson, R. C., 1978; Erickson, R. C., Poon, & Walsh-Sweeney, 1980; Fozard & Popkin, 1978; Sinnott, 1986). Why has this obvious imperative priority been relatively neglected for so long?

Problems Inherent in the Academic Research.   One factor that has impeded the translation from research to practice is interprofessional disagreements, conflicting interpretations within the field itself about what the studies show (Poon, 1985; Poon et al., 1980). Researchers, as we saw earlier, not only disagree about whether the older person's problem lies in the encoding, storage, or retrieval phases of memory, some even dispute the utility of this basic scheme for viewing and understanding memory (Salthouse, 1980). This lack of consensus, not just about what the findings themselves reveal but about the whole way to view remembering, impedes action. Without a firm idea about how to even conceptualize what may be wrong, it is difficult to spell out a remedial plan.

Then there is the critical question of validity. Is performance on academic memory tests an adequate index of memory in real life? Memory tests have been criticized as not really valid for the same two reasons as IQ tests have been: nonintellectual influences (anxiety, fatigue, and so on) may underlie much of the poor performance of the old; laboratory memory tests may be too irrelevant to the real world.

One paramount nonintellectual influence is apparent in the vignette. Karen Johnson's memory was only poor during an artificial, highly stressful situation— taking an examination. In real life situations her ability to remember was actually remarkable. The point is that any situation in which memory is being formally evaluated is likely to be the poorest showcase for an older person's general ability. In addition to becoming excessively anxious or perhaps more prone to tire easily when memorizing a long list of items (Woodruff & Walsh, 1975), another property unique to memory studies may bias these tests against the old.

As I implied in my description of the types of memory tests, the traditional way experimental psychologists evaluate memory has been to make the information to be memorized as meaningless as possible. Subjects must memorize pairs of completely unrelated words; they must learn lists of nonsense syllables or random letters or numbers. The rationale is that only by ridding the stimuli to be remembered of any meaning can researchers truly determine that the situation is equal for everyone and so compare abilities in a pure, uncontaminated form. Ironically, however, this so called most fair approach may be unfair to the old.

This possibility was brought home to Irene Hulicka (1967) when she attempted to use the standard procedure with a group of elderly and young adults. Asking the groups to memorize a list of unrelated paired associates evoked strong resistance among the older subjects in particular. A full 80% refused to complete the study. Many gave as their reason: "I cannot participate in something that makes such little sense." Only when the requirement was changed to make the task more applicable to real life did the older group consent.

So Hulicka concluded that this very strategy of making the situation the same for everyone may actually be making the situation unequal for older adults. Older people are likely to be less motivated when the test content seems meaningless or irrelevant. Their poor performance on standard memory tests may not so much be due to a memory deficit as to a simple inability to become interested in the research. Moreover, memorizing nonsense syllables or unrelated words is something a person would never be asked to do outside the laboratory. There is a real question, then, about the validity of these laboratory studies because they have been specifically designed to be maximally removed from memory in real life (Hartley, Harker, & Walsh, 1980; Hunt, 1986).

There is reason for these concerns. As I mentioned earlier, when the items to be remembered are personally relevant, older people perform much better on memory tests (Poon, 1985; Poon et al., 1986). Furthermore, training on academic-type memory tasks does not translate into improvement on tests more similar to the requirements of the real world. In a study demonstrating this (cited in Erikson, R. C., et al., 1980), elderly subjects were first given practice memorizing paired associates. This training made it easier for them to memorize other lists of paired associates. However, there was no generalization to other, more common tasks such as remembering a grocery list. This disappointing lack of transfer suggests that the connection between the laboratory and performance outside is more tenuous than we have hoped.

To many researchers these depressing findings had a clear message—to really understand about how memory operates in later life, use tests that reflect the kinds of memory demands that older people actually face. So the new research trend is to use true-to-life memory tasks to explore how older people function (Poon, 1985; Sinnott, 1986): How well can the elderly fit names to faces, remember the location of objects in space? (See Sharps & Gollin, 1988.) How does the ability to recall the content of a conversation or remember the message of a paragraph differ in later life? (See Stine & Wingfield, 1988; Zelinski & Miura, 1988.) These are situations older people are exposed to in the course of living. And while the elderly often perform somewhat more poorly than young adults on these tests, too, they tend to do better than on the old-style memory tasks. Sometimes, as in the following study, they do just as well as the young:

Using the Baltimore volunteers, Jan Sinnott (1986) devised an ingenious naturalistic approach to testing age differences in everyday memory. She asked respondents from their 20s to their 80s to remember a list of different events that occurred during the 3 days of being tested at the Gerontology Research Laboratory. Some of the events that had to be recalled were salient and needed for action: "How do you get from your room to the testing room or the cafeteria?" "What are the hours that dinner is served?" Others were incidental and unimportant: "What materials were on the table while you were solving problems, tissues, pencils, what?" "How many problems were you asked to solve?"

On a test that examined recall for both types of events, the young volunteers did outperform the old, but *only* on the items measuring incidental (or irrelevant) events. For the truly relevant material—the information that had to be remembered in order to function during the 3 days—the memory of the older people was as good as that of the young.

This study is appealing because it gets to the heart of a major problem with making generalizations based on traditional memory studies. Even if in old age our memory system works less well in the abstract, this may not matter as much as we might think in real life. As Sinnott points out, one implication of her study is that older people flexibly compensate for age-related deficits in the ability to recall. In this case, they seem to narrow focus. Rather than remembering "more," they concentrate more on what they really need to remember and so—*when it counts*—their memory is relatively unimpaired.

Problems Inherent in the Differing Goals of Experimenter and Clinician.   So a main reason why laboratory studies are hard to translate into practice is that many factors other than decline in inherent ability determine how well an individual functions and remembers in the real world. In addition, the goal of much academic memory research—to isolate a deficit (for instance, in a system such as encoding) and make generalizations about "old age"—is alien to the way a practitioner operates (Hunt, 1986). People interested in determining the reasons for real life memory failures do not want to uncover abstract truths but to explore why a particular, idiosyncratic individual is having problems remembering. While they clearly can get clues about the older person they are trying to help from knowing the problems average older people have, their job is to uncover the unique configuration of reasons causing *that person's* trouble.

In fact, one general fact about memory in later life is the fact of individual variability (Erikson, R. C., 1978; Erikson, R. C., et al., 1980). Different people have different types of deficits, which, in turn, may have quite different causes. This is clearly illustrated in the vignette. Karen Johnson only had problems remembering in a special context—under the stress of taking an exam. That is, rather than being due to an encoding problem or a defect in intrinsic ability, her difficulty was caused by a noncognitive factor: text anxiety. So the key to treating Karen's problem would not be to enhance her memory but to reduce her anxiety. In addition, it would involve knowing that a misperception was at the root of her memory complaints—her tendency to label herself as having a poor memory when she was depressed.

Does this inability to accurately self-diagnose memory characterize other older people, too? Almost two decades ago, a compelling study suggested that Karen's tendency to read in memory problems when she is feeling unhappy is far from unusual. When memory complaints in older subjects were correlated with objective memory tests and depression, researchers discovered to their surprise that the perception of having a problem had little relation to a person's performance on memory tests. Instead, it was associated with depression. People who were depressed were likely to believe their memory was poor (Kahn, Zarit, Hilbert, & Niederehe, 1975). While not every study agrees that self-reports of memory problems have no basis in reality, the link between complaining about this stereotypic old age problem and the emotional disorder of depression has been reconfirmed repeatedly (see Niederehe, 1986, for a review). For instance, in a study done a decade later, subjects reporting a high degree of depressive symptomatology were much more likely to complain of forgetting than those with lower symptom levels or none (O'Hara, Hinrichs, Kohout, Wallace, & Lemke, 1986).

So complaints about memory problems in later life should not automatically be accepted at face value. They may be more diagnostic of an emotional problem than a difficulty in the cognitive realm. To complicate matters further, this same emotional problem—depression—rather than a lack of inherent ability, may cause cognitive deficits. As we will see in Chapter 10, one symptom of depression in the elderly is memory impairment, problems remembering so severe that they can even be mistaken for Alzheimer's disease.

Obviously, then, if our discussion of memory is limited to only its purely cognitive facets, it would leave out many reasons for forgetting in real life. The real world memory deficits a given older person may have may be due to depression, anxiety, lack of interest, anger, or any of the multiplicity of nonintellectual reasons that cause us to forget at any time of life.

Interventions

For this reason, experts (Erikson, R. C., et al., 1980; Fozard & Popkin, 1978; Poon, Fozard, & Treat, 1978; Poon et al., 1986) have suggested that in assessing an older person who complains of memory problems a thorough effort should be made to understand many dimensions of psychological functioning. Difficulties in specific facets of remembering, such as acquisition skills, should be measured. The person performing the evaluation should carefully define the particular situations in which memory problems occur. If possible, the tests used to assess memory should reflect real life. Only when the older person has been examined in this comprehensive way can the diagnostician best know how to intervene. Depending on the results of the evaluation, here are some treatments that might be used.

Training the Person.   If the person's main problem is deficient learning skills, then findings from the academic research can be directly applied. The laboratory studies of memory show that two approaches in particular can be effective: simple practice and special training.

A study by David Hultsch (1974) illustrates the value of simple practice in improving subsequent learning. Experience in memorizing lists reduced the time it took to learn subsequent lists. Because he wanted to show that age differences in memory are due partly to older people being out of practice, Hultsch hypothesized that the elderly would benefit the most from practicing. This was not true; practice helped the different age groups equally. However, though negative with regard to age differences, this finding is important with respect to offering actual help. To improve memory, we might simply give older people who need it regular memorization "assignments." As in so many areas of life, simple exercise enhances skills.

However, another route might be even more effective—directly teaching new, more helpful, learning strategies. This technique is called **cognitive skill training.** Cognitive skill training was used in the study described earlier in this chapter in which older people were taught to use mediators to enhance their ability to remember unrelated words.

Cognitive skill training has been used successfully in a variety of studies (Poon, Walsh-Sweeney, & Fozard, 1980; Treat, Poon, Fozard, & Popkin, 1978). In one heartening study (Treat & Reese, 1976) it actually erased performance differences between the young and the old. (Remember, though, we still do not know if in fact this training does generalize to real life.)

Here elderly and young adult subjects were assigned to one of three conditions. They were either given specific visual images that would link the paired associates they were to learn (for instance, for *tree–shoe* they were told to imagine a tree growing out of a shoe); instructed in using mediators but told to form their own images linking the words; or given no training (the control group).

Interestingly, though either type of instruction was helpful, when given as much time as they needed to answer, the elderly in the self-generated imagery group performed as well as the young. This finding reinforces the fact that, as is true in every cognitive situation, older people perform at their best when they are not under time pressure, when they can take as long as they want to respond. It also confirms the research showing that training in using mediators, especially just explaining the general principles underlying this mnemonic technique, is very effective in aiding memory in later life.

A training program involving instructions in using mediators as well as other mnemonic techniques (for example, see Belsky, 1988; West, 1985) might be used together with regular memory assignments. It also has been suggested that an optimal approach would be to conduct this training in groups (Treat et al., 1978). Groups would have the same benefit here as in the study using this approach to change Type A behavior (see Chapter 2). Members would reinforce one another for continuing to use the techniques. Groups also would offer an atmosphere of hope, in which change is viewed as possible. Perhaps most important, ongoing memory groups would ensure reinforcement for competent performance, reinforcement that we could not be sure the person's normal environment would provide. And, unfortunately, we have clear-cut evidence showing that—at least in some situations—lack of reinforcement for good memory may indeed contribute to the memory deficiencies observed in older adults (Kahn & Miller, 1978).

BOX 6-1
Memory Training and Memory Complaints

Since cognitive skill training improves memory, we would expect this objectively better performance to lessen an older person's fears. Seeing that their memory is so much better, older people who have undergone a training program of this type should have fewer memory complaints.

However, the discussion in the text suggests something quite different might be true, too. If memory complaints are more a function of depression than objective reality, the extent of improvement on memory tests should be unrelated to the magnitude of a person's concerns.

To examine which of these ideas might be correct, Steven Zarit, Kenneth Cole, and Rebecca Guider (1981) did a bit of dissembling: they assigned elderly subjects either to a memory training group or a current events discussion group and told people in both groups that the sessions would help improve memory. As expected, though, actual recall improved only for participants in the first group.

On the other hand, memory complaints were reduced equally after participation in either group—a finding that once again emphasizes that we should be somewhat skeptical about self-evaluations of memory in later life. But the study also demonstrates something else important—simply believing one is being helped may be enough to reduce a person's fears.

☐

Modifying the Environment.   In the same way as they demonstrated how our stereotypes make normal forgetting stand out as "a problem" in later life, Ellen Langer and Judith Rodin showed the environment was partly to blame for memory deficits in old age (Langer, Rodin, Beck, Weinman, & Spitzer, 1979). This time the scene of their research was a nursing home. The researchers reasoned that living in a nursing home would naturally cause memory to erode since in institutions remembering is not needed to function in daily life. To prove their point they set out to demonstrate that by making remembering important again to residents, they could reverse some of what looked like a purely age-related psychological deficit. (Notice how this study foreshadows the finding that when information is highly relevant to action, memory, at least among the nonfrail elderly, may be relatively unimpaired.)

First, the researchers approached residents individually four times during a 6-week period, engaging each person in a discussion for 30 to 40 minutes. There were two experimental conditions, one in which the interviewer revealed a good deal about herself and the other in which self-disclosure was low. At the end of each "conversation session," residents were instructed to think about current happenings in their life so they could discuss them during the next interview. The researchers hypothesized that the older people exposed to the high-disclosure manipulation would be more motivated to remember because having a genuinely personal conversation had to be a potent reinforcer for these attention-starved older adults.

They were right. This particular group of older people improved on subsequent memory tests. Nurses also rated the residents exposed to the high-disclosure conversations as being more aware and active. The low-disclosure interviews, on the other hand, had no impact. Subjects in this condition were no different than those in a control group.

Next, the researchers used a more concrete reinforcer, chips that could be cashed in for gifts. This time they visited residents nine times during a 3-week period, once again using two different experimental treatments. In the first, residents were reinforced for remembering facts such as the names of nurses on the floor or what they had eaten for breakfast. Residents in the second condition were also given the chips, but their reinforcement was not contingent on good performance.

Needless to say, contingent reinforcement produced better memory. Subjects in the first group had better recall, not just for the specific information they had been reinforced for remembering, but also for other facts about their current life.

As I stressed in discussing Rodin's research on autonomy in nursing homes (see Chapter 2), we must be cautious in applying these findings from the nursing home to noninstitutional life. Many of these residents had genuine memory disorders, problems of a different order of magnitude than the mild deficiencies we have been discussing. Furthermore, institutions are highly abnormal settings, one of the few environments in life where remembering is not critical to staying alive. However, the research demonstrating how exercising memory skills improves performance, how memory is better for information that is relevant to life, even the fact that gains in the content of what is remembered (that is, in crystallized intelligence) may occur at least until the retirement years, clearly imply that these nursing home investigations do have a wider point—being in a stimulating environment is important to keeping memory fine-tuned. Just as is true for physical abilities, an outside world that discourages the development of excess disabilities and promotes cognitive exercise is ideal.

Now we turn to the fascinating but specialized studies of creative achievements and age.

CREATIVE ACHIEVEMENTS

While memory researchers may argue about the exact nature of the problem, there is little controversy about fact that real decline often occurs. The same is true of at least one aspect of intelligence discussed in the previous chapter—no matter how heated the debate over the issue as a whole, there are few disagreements that fluid intelligence in particular does decline with advancing age. This consensus has unfortunate implications for the topic we are about to discuss. Doesn't fluid intelligence, the ability to arrive at an original solution to a problem, describe the very skills that are a core component of creativity? Doesn't this imply that in the same way as fluid abilities, creativity begins to decline beginning quite early in adulthood?

However, age must have a more complicated relationship to creativity because to make an original contribution in any field, fluid intelligence is far from all that is required. A person must be motivated and enthusiastic. It would help to have the physical stamina to put in long hours and the financial resources to make it possible to devote a good deal of time to one's work. It would be good not to be too emotionally sidetracked, not to be pulled by competing commitments to family, coworkers, or other interests.

Crystallized intelligence—knowledge and experience—is obviously important, too. In particular professions a long training period and extended practice honing creative skills are important requirements for performing at one's best. In some it is essential for a person to spend years learning what has already been done (Zuckerman & Merton, 1972). In some, even time living would be a critical plus, fields in which maturity and wisdom count heavily. Factors apart from the actual subject matter of the work are often crucial, too: how competitive a particular profession is, or the chance it offers people at different life-stages to do original work.

So, we cannot predict the time of life creativity flowers or fades simply by looking at the graph charting fluid intelligence and age. We have to consider many other influences as well, some intrinsic to the person's biological and psychological capacities at different stages of life, some a function of the type of creative work being done. In fact, because age/creativity relationships are likely to be so different for different fields, after describing the early studies of creativity and the controversy they caused, I will examine separately the two major areas in which people make creative contributions—the arts and sciences.

The First Findings and the Debate They Caused

A controversial book published in the early 1950s launched the scientific study of creativity and age. In *Age and Achievement* (1953), Harvey Lehman described the results of an impressive, exhaustive investigation he made into the peak period of creative achievement in a wide variety of fields (see for synopsis, Lehman, 1960). Lehman examined traditional scholarly areas and also non-academic ones such as athletics, typing, and chess. He studied the ages at which college presidents, heads of large corporations, and Supreme Court justices had occupied their jobs. He examined movie directors, foreign diplomats, and authors of notable church sermons.

What generated the most debate, though, were his findings about original work in the arts and sciences. The relationships he uncovered echoed the bleak cross-sectional findings that were currently all that was known about IQ and age. Young adulthood was the time of maximum creativity. After the 30s, the chances of producing a significant contribution rapidly declined. This negative picture was fairly consistent—it held across fields as different as poetry and physics. For instance, Lehman's analyses showed that chemists aged 40 to 45 produced only half as many significant contributions (per person) as those a decade younger. By age 60 to 65, production in this field declined to a mere 20% of what it had been in the early 30s, when creativity was at its peak. An even more striking loss was evident in the work of symphony composers. Here, by the early 50s, productivity had fallen to a mere 20% of the maximum (see Dennis, 1956).

As with the data on IQ and age, these gloomy statistics were immediately questioned. Lehman had arrived at his figures using a questionable strategy. He looked through several textbooks and histories in each field and copied down each work listed, then determined the age of the person who had made the contribution by looking up his or her birthdate and subtracting it from the date of the work. If the various histories he consulted tended to agree in listing the contribution, he included it in his calculations. Finally, he divided his age listings by the total number of creators in that field living at the time (Lehman, 1960).

Wayne Dennis, Lehman's primary critic, pointed out that this methodology has several weaknesses (Dennis, 1956, 1958, 1966). First, it does not consider that there may be a bias in the citations in the textbooks. Isn't it possible that a textbook writer, particularly in a scientific field, would list a person's youthful pioneering breakthrough rather than the equally creative work produced in subsequent years to validate it? Furthermore, there is a natural tendency in compiling a history to include early work at the expense of what has been done more recently because in both the arts and sciences a given production is only established as a "breakthrough" or "masterpiece" after it has stood the test of time. But this represents a subtle bias against the later work of the many people making creative contributions who are alive today. Their early, youthful work would be included in the history; their recent creative work, even if just as good, would not be there.

Second, there is a problem specifically for the sciences in judging age/creativity relationships from text citations. In every scientific field there has been a steady increase in competition. Over the years more and more people have entered the sciences and more and more works have been produced (see Table 6-2). This rapid growth rate means that in successive years an increasingly smaller percentage of the total works in a field can be listed as significant, which, in turn, means that each older scientist had an easier time getting his or her early contributions listed. The scientist's youthful work may be better. But it may also have been mentioned as significant because of what Dennis labeled competitive advantage, the smaller field of competitors itself.

However, to Dennis unquestionably the most serious shortcoming of *Age and Achievement* was that Lehman failed to take into account the very different life spans of creative people. If we die young we are obviously deprived of the chance to produce creative work when we are old. But Lehman included data for short-lived creative people in his analyses along with figures for those who did have the chance to produce masterpieces in old age, the long-lived. This clearly represents a built-in favoritism for the early decades. Only the fraction of

TABLE 6-2. Percentage of scientific publications cited in six sourcebooks, by decade of publication.

Decade	Number of Publications	Percentage Cited
1810–1819	13,085	0.2
1820–1829	20,866	0.1
1830–1839	29,608	0.1
1840–1849	43,125	0.1
1850–1859	43,325	0.1
1860–1869	80,421	0.05
1870–1879	106,001	0.06
1880–1889	178,390	0.03
1890–1899	198,038	0.02

Source: Adapted from Dennis, 1958.

geniuses who were long-lived had a chance to demonstrate that creative work can indeed be done later in life (Dennis, 1956; Riley & Foner, 1968).

To Dennis (1966) this suggested a simple corrective strategy—to give the later years their fair weight, one's analyses should be confined to creative people who have lived a full life span. So Dennis examined age/creativity relationships among a large group of artists and scientists all of whom had lived to age 79 or beyond. Furthermore, because of his qualms about using citations in textbooks, he decided to get the names of these people from simple listings of every published work in the field. However, this means his statistics represent something very different than Lehman's. They are much more a measure of pure output rather than the best creative work produced.

As Table 6-3 shows, just as Dennis predicted, his figures are a refreshing contrast to those compiled in *Age and Achievement*. For most professions, midlife, the 40s and 50s, was the most productive life era. The 60s were the most creative decade in two fields where we might expect wisdom to count the most, history and philosophy. In addition, rather than declining sharply, productivity gradually sloped off. In many fields it declined only slightly even at the oldest ages.

The table also shows an interesting pattern of variability in the three broad areas for creativity. In general, losses occur earlier in the arts than in the sciences. Creative output in the sciences falls off earlier than for history, philosophy, and other forms of scholarly research. It also reveals that, as we would suspect, the peak age for producing creative work differs markedly from field to field.

Who is correct, Dennis or Lehman? Why might age be an enemy to people in certain professions and a plus to those immersed in other types of creative work? To attempt to answer these questions, researchers have narrowed their focus, probing age/creativity relationships in more defined areas of life.

Creativity in the Arts

Psychologist Dean Keith Simonton (1975a, 1975b, 1977a, 1977b) has done the few studies that build on Lehman and Dennis's early investigations in that

TABLE 6-3. Production of creative works in selected fields in each decade of life by persons living to age 79 and above.

Field	Number of Persons	Number of Works	Percentage of Work Produced during Decade					
			20s	30s	40s	50s	60s	70s
History	46	615	3	19	19	22	24	20
Philosophy	42	225	3	17	20	18	22	20
Scholarship	43	326	6	17	21	21	16	19
Means			4	18	20	20	21	20
Biology	32	3456	5	22	24	19	17	13
Botany	49	1889	4	15	22	22	22	15
Chemistry	24	2120	11	21	24	19	12	13
Geology	40	2672	3	13	22	28	19	14
Invention	44	646	2	10	17	18	32	21
Mathematics	36	3104	8	20	20	18	19	15
Means			6	17	22	21	20	15
Architecture	44	1148	7	24	29	25	10	4
Chamber music	35	109	15	21	17	20	18	9
Drama	25	803	10	27	29	21	9	3
Libretta writing	38	164	8	21	30	22	15	4
Novel writing	32	494	5	19	18	28	23	7
Opera composition	176	476	8	30	31	16	10	5
Poetry	46	402	11	21	25	16	16	10
Means			9	23	26	21	14	6

Source: Adapted from Dennis, 1966.

important arena for creativity—the arts. As part of a systematic research program exploring factors that influence artistic productivity, Simonton turned to the critical variable of age.

Simonton (1975a) first looked at literature, poetry, imaginative prose (fiction), and informative prose (nonfiction), exploring age/creativity relationships in many historical eras and across a variety of cultures. He felt literature was an ideal medium for studying life-span changes in creativity in a relatively pure form because in this type of creative endeavor achievement is closely tied to a person's actual skills. Producing high-quality work in the sciences is more dependent on factors that are not simply a function of inherent giftedness—having access to laboratory facilities, getting grants, being at the appropriate career stage to concentrate on research.

Unlike Dennis, Simonton based his analyses on writers who died young and those who died at later ages, using a special technique he developed to control for differences in longevity. He felt uncomfortable confining his sample to people who lived a very full life span since only 15% of great writers have survived to age 80. He reasoned that this small fraction might be unrepresentative of the total group of literary geniuses in ways other than unusual longevity.

Luckily, examining age/creativity relationships in many settings and times offered a built-in control for competitive advantage. In literature, unlike the sciences, the number of people entering the field has not steadily increased. Simonton found instead a wavelike fluctuation; in particular cultures at certain historical times, the field becomes more crowded and then, after reaching a peak, the number of competitors gradually declines. So, by casting a broad net throughout history and exploring literary creativity in cultures apart from our own, conditions promoting youthful achievement would be automatically counterbalanced by situations when creativity was favored later on in life.

In his survey of several hundred of the best writers humanity has produced—names gathered from literary histories and anthologies—Simonton discovered fascinating differences among the three types of literature. Poets produced their best work when youngest—at a modal age in their late 30s. The peak age for producing fiction was somewhat older—the early 40s. Nonfiction peaked last—at age 50. After controlling for longevity and other variables, the differences between fiction and nonfiction shrank to an insignificant 2 years, but the tendency still remained for poets to reach their creative peak at a significantly younger age than prose writers.

This poetry/prose difference makes intuitive sense. Writing poetry is supposed to be an activity of youth. Actually we even associate this type of creativity more with the intense emotional storms of adolescence than with the 30s. Writing poetry involves the ability to play with language and rebel against conventions by using language in novel ways—also qualities we link with being young (Simonton, 1975a). Writing a book demands more sustained discipline. Writing a novel (or even, as in our vignette, a short story) seems more dependent on maturity, on the understanding of people and life gained at least in part through having lived. So for these two important creative activities, the fit of the art form with individual development does seem to explain why people reach their creative peak at different times of life.

Simonton made another interesting discovery. Among the very different cultures and historical eras he studied there was amazing uniformity. The peak ages for producing prose and poetry were the same in almost every culture and historical epoch, suggesting that environmental conditions or social norms have surprisingly little impact on at least these two major avenues for creative expression.

However, note an important discrepancy. In this study the peak period of literary creativity occurs much earlier than in Dennis's work. As we can see by looking at the statistics in Table 6-3, according to Dennis some nonfiction writers (those producing histories and other scholarly works) reach their creative prime in their 60s. The peak ages for novel writing and poetry are also about a decade older than Simonton suggests. Perhaps the reason is due to differences in what was being measured. Simonton measured high-quality work; Dennis, pure activity. If this is true, however, then the disturbing implication is that as a person ages, just as much work may be produced, but more *lower* quality work.

Lehman brought up this very point in order to account for the differences between his figures and Dennis's: Data based on the mere number of publications does not negate the fact that creativity falls off early on. While people may indeed continue to produce just as much as they grow older, the production of high-quality work still declines. Dennis (1966) disagreed, suggesting that it is only reasonable to assume that more work equals more high-quality work, too. Logically, the number of major works should be a constant proportion of the total produced. It was in part to determine which of these very different conceptions was correct that Simonton (1977a) undertook yet another study of creativity and age.

This time he examined ten of the most eminent composers of classical music, exploring a hypothesis that differed from both Dennis's *and* Lehman's: as these musical geniuses aged, the proportion of high-quality works, rather than decreasing or remaining stable, should rise. Because energy and motivation wane as we get older, Simonton reasoned that fewer and fewer works should be produced over time. But, because experience should bring enhanced competence, more of what these geniuses did produce should be of the highest caliber.

Examining the ratio of major works to total works during each 5-year period in the lives of these ten brilliant men, Simonton found that Dennis's hypothesis of stability, or a constant proportion, best fit the data. In addition, for this handful of world-class geniuses, the time of peak creativity was the early 30s. After a steep rise to that age, productivity (and the production of one's best work) sloped off, but only very gradually.

This encouraging finding mirrors Karen Johnson's experience, but on a much grander scale. For musical geniuses, growing old is far from the death knell of creativity. True, there are some losses after the 30s, but people are clearly able to produce highly creative work to the end of life.

Creativity in the Sciences

If continued creativity is characteristic of the most brilliant innovators in music, then this has implications for a widespread belief held about scientists. The prejudice is that particularly in the physical sciences and mathematics, the great breakthroughs are made by people at a remarkably young age. As far as making major contributions, even the 30s are sometimes seen as "over the hill"; the really important discoveries are made even earlier, by people at the threshold of adult life. To buttress this idea, people cite Newton and Einstein. Both geniuses formulated their ideas about the world while in their mid-20s.

Unfortunately, this stereotype may have especially malignant effects in science because here the support of the outside community can be crucial to producing high-quality work. If this point of view is widely accepted, wouldn't it be more difficult for older scientists to get good work published or, even more important, to get access to the facilities and financial support necessary to make scientific discoveries? This brings up the point alluded to earlier. In the sciences, in particular, forces *other* than pure ability influence a person's chances of making creative contributions at different times of life.

Fred Reif and Anselm Strauss (1965) spelled out one of these extraneous influences, an important force apart from inherent ability that they feel loads the dice against older scientists and so makes it appear that they are inherently less creative than the young—rapid scientific discovery. Particularly in the physical sciences, the exponential accumulation of knowledge makes what students learn during their training relatively obsolete soon after they leave school. True, a scientist may be up to date in the particular area that is the focus of his or her research. However, if that specialty goes out of fashion or the person's findings are eclipsed by later research, the scientist may be at a dead end.

At this point, Reif and Strauss say, the scientist has two alternatives—change specialties or go into nonresearch work. Taking the first route is much more difficult. It means reeducating oneself and competing with younger scientists who have enthusiasm and recent training in the new area. Besides, by this time there is usually a family to support and changing fields would mean taking a salary cut. Often the most reasonable alternative is to abandon research work and take a job in administration, public service, or private industry where the pressure to be creative is not as intense. As Reif and Strauss argue, even the most eminent scientists are prone to make this shift later in their careers. It is simply too difficult to refuse the lucrative and prestigious positions outside research that are offered to these high achievers as a very consequence of their early creative achievements.

A study exploring prestigious nonresearch leadership positions in the academic community implies that Reif and Strauss have a point (Shin & Putnam, 1982). There may be an impetus to leave research for administration in a scientist's older years. When the researchers looked at the average age at selection of university presidents and the heads of national professional organizations such as the American Psychological Association, they found that these high-status administrative posts are indeed usually occupied by people relatively late in their careers. The study, covering the years 1901–1975 with a sample of 12 of the most important universities and associations, showed that a kind of reverse ageism was clearly in force. The mean age at which university presidents were selected was 51; for the heads of scientific associations, the average age at appointment was even older, 57. Furthermore, this phenomenon has become more prevalent in recent years. When the researchers looked at their three successive 25-year periods separately, there was a clear trend toward older appointees over time, a tendency that could not be completely accounted for by age changes within the scientific community itself.

A second facet of this study is relevant to the idea that it is in the hard sciences and particularly those that are most mathematical that creativity flowers early. The investigators also examined the mean age at selection of a third, even more elite group, Nobel Prize winners. Recipients in physics, chemistry, and physiology or medicine, on the average, were in their early 50s—a full 10 years younger than those who received this highest honor in literature. Considering that it takes some time after a person makes a discovery to win the award, we would suspect that these scientists had done their groundbreaking work at a relatively young age.

There were also age differences depending on how rigorous the particular science was. Nobel Prize winners in physics tended to be a few years younger than those in chemistry. Recipients in chemistry were slightly younger than those in physiology or medicine. The age variation was small; however, it does fit in with the general belief that in the most mathematical or "hardest" sciences the breakthroughs are indeed made by the young.

Two sociologists (Zuckerman & Merton, 1972) spelled out the possible reasons why this might be so when they hypothesized that the codifiability of a particular science should have an impact on the peak time of life at which discoveries tend to be made. By **codifiability** these theorists meant something almost identical to scientific rigor—the extent of consensus about the truth among workers in the field, the degree to which knowledge in the profession is encompassed in a few succinct theories rather than a mass of descriptive facts. In highly codified fields, they reasoned, several factors conspire to favor creativity when people are young. The compact body of knowledge makes it easier to master the content of the field at an early age. This parsimony, as well as the high degree of consensus, also makes becoming outmoded a greater risk. Because more people are likely to be working on the same problem, an established person's research is more likely to be challenged. When this challenge is successful, unlike the situation in a looser discipline, what the researcher has done is immediately rendered passé, definitively labeled wrong.

So Shin and Putnam's findings for the Nobel Prize winners may be accurate because they make such good sense. But this implies that the gloomy predictions about *all* older scientists Lehman made decades earlier may be correct, too. We cannot assume that just because Lehman was wrong about older artists he was wrong about older scientists. Luckily, however, we do have evidence for the sciences that disproves the idea that creativity erodes early on. Stephen Cole's work is especially compelling because it involves the very people the stereotype could have harmed the most, typical working scientists, not the tiny handful of geniuses at the top of each field (Cole, S., 1979).

First, Cole used a cross-sectional approach, selecting a random sample of scientists of varying ages and examining their productivity (both total output and high-quality work) over a 5-year period. He chose disciplines within both the physical and social sciences because he also wanted to explore whether the codification hypothesis was true.

Using as his index of quality the number of times a paper was cited by other researchers (information published in the *Science Citation Index*) and automatically controlling for competitive advantage by focusing on a single 5 years, Cole discovered that age had a slight curvilinear relation to creativity. Productivity usually rose to a peak in the early 40s, leveled off or declined slightly to about age 50, and then dropped off quite slowly after that. Furthermore, as was true in Simonton's study of musical geniuses, the curves for total output and for high-quality work, though differing in steepness, were very similar. Contrary to what the codification hypothesis would predict, so were the shapes of the curves for professions varying greatly in scientific rigor.

Next, Cole used a longitudinal strategy and chose one particular field, mathematics. He decided to study mathematicians in particular because, as mentioned, in this field in particular creativity is supposed to peak very early on and then steadily decline.

Cole selected a random group of mathematicians who had received their Ph.D.s between 1947 and 1950 and followed their careers for the next quarter century, looking once again at both their total number of publications and their high-quality work (gleaned from the *Science Citation Index*). When he broke the

---

BOX 6-2
Inherent Talent versus Positive Reinforcement
and Scientific Creativity

The fact that there are stable differences in research productivity does not explain how these differences come about. One possibility is that strong publishers are simply the most talented. Another looks to the environment: scientists whose first efforts to publish are reinforced will be motivated to continue to work. Not only will they want to keep publishing, they will be given the best resources to make discoveries. People whose youthful efforts are not well received will get discouraged and slacken off. They will also not have the same access to research grants or lab facilities to continue to do high-quality research.

We could get one clue that reinforcement or "accumulative advantage" is indeed important if we found that individual publishing patterns became increasingly unequal as a given cohort of scientists aged. Though not ruling out the importance of inherent ability, this finding would suggest that the truism "success breeds success" applies in the scientific realm as in so many other realms of life.

In looking at a group of mathematicians, physicists, and chemists, Paul Allison and John Stewart (1974) found this very pattern over time. As the scientists aged, their output became more and unequal. Strong publishers became stronger; weaker ones produced less. In some cases, the less productive scientists eventually gave up and no longer published at all.

□

---

25 years into 5-year periods, he found a surprising and encouraging result. There was basically no change in the total level of scientific output over this period. Furthermore, the *Science Citation Index* of 1975 (the end of the 25-year period) showed that there was also basically no change in the production of high-quality work.

In sum, Cole's research offers powerful evidence of continued scientific creativity in the very field where youth is believed to count the most. And, if little age decline occurs among mathematicians, if we looked at the work of scientists in less rigorous disciplines, we might find an even more encouraging result— more scientific activity and better caliber work over the years.

So this is the answer to our major question about age and scientific creativity. However, we have neglected one that is more interesting to anyone doing creative work. Does high or low productivity tend to be a lifelong pattern? If a person is highly creative when young, how likely is she or he to continue being creative through later life? Looking at age groups in the aggregate cannot give us this information, but the methodology Cole used in studying mathematicians can.

Because his study was longitudinal, Cole could follow the publication patterns of individual mathematicians over the quarter century, looking for evidence of consistency or change. He first classified his sample into strong publishers, weak publishers, or nonpublishers based on their publication records during one 5-year period, then noted whether they maintained the same relative ranking during other periods. This simple procedure showed that stability was the rule. Rarely did a person shift more than one category; almost half of the sample never changed ranks at all.

A more recent study of research productivity among 1000 academic psychologists found a similar trend (Horner, Rushton, & Vernon, 1986). Although overall productivity did vary at different times of life, reaching its peak at about age 40 and then decreasing in the later years, how much an individual published was much more a function of his or her enduring characteristics than of age. People who started out as strong publishers continued to be prolific—even at age 55 to 64 producing more papers than their less productive peers did at their peak.

Does this striking evidence of consistency apply to other aspects of behavior over the years? Do other traits or qualities we have as young adults also endure as we travel through life? This is a central question we will explore in the next chapter as we turn from the cognitive realm to another important dimension of life—personality.

KEY TERMS

Paired-associate technique
Free recall
Cued recall
Recognition
Sensory store
Primary memory

Secondary memory
Encoding, storage, and retrieval phases
Mediators
Cognitive skill training
Codifiability of a field

RECOMMENDED READINGS

Cole, S. (1979). Age and scientific performance. *American Journal of Sociology, 84,* 264–272. Dispels the idea that scientific creativity wanes significantly with age. Moderately difficult.
Poon, L. W., et al. (Eds.). (1986). *Handbook for clinical memory assessment of older adults.* Washington, DC: American Psychological Association. A diverse set of technical articles covering the evaluation of memory in later life in clinical settings. Most articles deal with the usefulness of specific medical and psychological tests at diagnosing dementia; however, issues such as the impact of depression and noncognitive factors on assessment are also explored in depth. Difficult.
Poon, L. W., Fozard, J. L., Cermak, L. S., Arenberg, D., & Thompson, L. (Eds.). (1980). *New directions in memory and aging.* Hillsdale, NJ: Erlbaum. Diverse, highly technical collection of articles. One section shows the different perspectives that experts bring to understanding memory and aging. Another, how memory research can be translated into giving help. Difficult.

Part 4

■

Personality

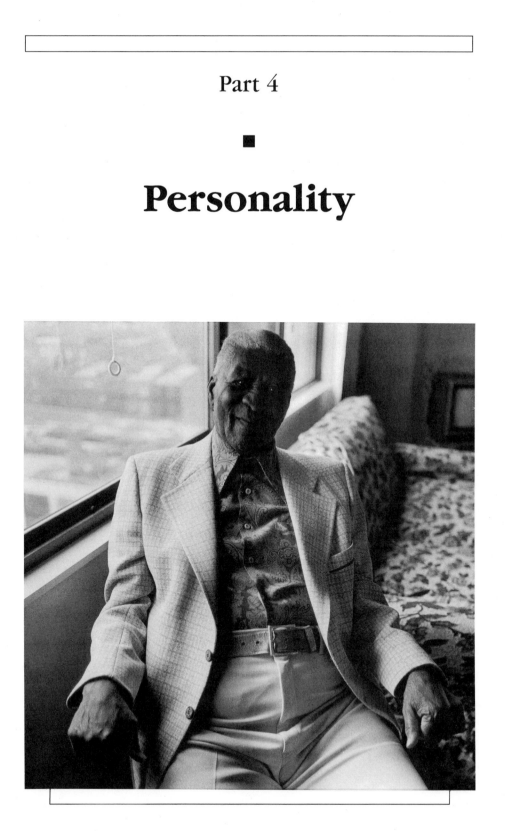

Chapter 7

□

Internal Aspects
of the Person

□

The Historical Framework
- The Kansas City Studies: Emphasis on Change
  - Conclusions, Criticisms, and Controversy
- Disengagement Theory: The Idea and the Debate

Present Research
- The Baltimore Study: Personality Stability
- Conclusions, Criticisms, and Controversy
- Maturity, Regression, or a Different Way of Handling Stress?

The Conclusions: Change and Consistency

Sexuality
- Age Changes in Sexual Response
  - Sexual Interest and Activity
- Factors Affecting Sexuality in Later Life
  - Illness and Sexual Function
    - Interventions

Key Terms

Recommended Readings

Within the past 5 years, José Fuentes, a 53-year-old factory supervisor, has noticed a change in priorities. He has lost the drive to achieve that always guided his life. Since his promotion he has a flood of paperwork. But instead of relishing Sundays spent working, he resents them. Wouldn't it be better to spend these precious years with his family rather than chasing the god of success?

This inner change is surprising. It seems so unlike himself. From an early age José accepted the fact that work was his number one priority, that he felt most alive competing to be the best. In rare moments spent in self-analysis, he attributes this compulsion to the effect the Great Depression had on his parents. He grew up listening to stories of his father desperately trying to find work, of his mother trying to stretch what food the family had. He still feels shame remembering being in the same position right after getting married—the frustrating weeks searching for a job, the humiliation of accepting money for himself and Teresa that his parents could not really afford to spare. What a relief it was to find a union job at Industrial Mills. At the time, he gladly gave up his dream of becoming a professional artist. It was so important never to be dependent again!

And José finds he's changing in other ways, too. He used to need to be the boss in the house. Now he routinely consults Teresa on decisions; sometimes, he feels lost without her advice. While it sometimes bothers him a bit to no longer be the tower of strength in the family, he cannot help seeing this new ability to bend as a sign of maturity. It certainly has led to a more interesting marriage and to a much better relationship with his children, Tomás and Rosa.

On the whole, José is satisfied with his new self. While he has lost his sense of power, certainty, and purpose, his zest in active combat, and the intense emotional ups and downs of his younger years, he feels he has gained a more balanced perspective on life. A perfect example happened last year when Tomás quit law school to become a playwright. Earlier, José would have been outraged. He would have screamed, yelled, argued, and perhaps stopped speaking to his son. Now he is able to accept Tomás's choice with a measure of calm. While he is just as convinced that his son is making a major mistake, he knows better than to cut off his nose to spite his face. No matter how much he wishes things were different, the price of having an enraged son or no son at all is not worth the self-satisfaction of having his say. Besides, Tomás has turned out well in really essential ways. He is a considerate, responsible, loving human being. And, from José's new, "older" perspective, he can appreciate the larger view. "Nothing is forever. One day my son will come to his senses and settle down!"

The reasons for his transformation puzzle him. Is it a point of view gained simply from having lived 53 years? Is it due to finally getting that longed for promotion or the shock of finding his two babies grown up?

Perhaps his father's death set the shift in motion from frantic over-achiever to mellow older man. Or it might be "hormones" or the subtle loss of physical stamina that he has been noticing lately. Or he might be preparing psychologically for retirement, even though he does not expect that event to occur for at least a decade.

Not only is it impossible for him to assign a cause for the change, he really can't tell how different he has become. José feels like a transformed man, but in his new, more accepting spirit he can also entertain the possibility that he has changed less than he thinks. This hit him strongly when he ran into a friend he had not seen since 1969. Over the years his childhood buddy had made a killing in real estate, moved away, and acquired a new wife. However, these external transformations seemed to have little internal effect. Carlos seemed to have the same mannerisms, the same interests, even the same problems. At the Blue Starr Tavern where they stopped to have a drink and catch up with each other, Carlos bitterly raged about his second wife in the same way he used to about the first. Thank God, José thought, he had learned more about living over the years. He could not help wondering, though, when Carlos had the nerve to say: "I'm surprised at how little life has softened your opinions or changed the way you treat Teresa and the kids. Isn't it time to begin to relax?"

■

Nowhere can we see more clearly that the pluralistic life-span developmental approach to aging reflects the complexities of life than in studying personality. In research examining how our values, interests, needs, and activities change as we grow old, we can find support for many of the theories described in Chapter 1. Most important, we find no one pattern fits aging. Some studies show we change dramatically; others suggest that stability is the dominant theme of adult life. Sometimes the grim "aging as decline" stereotype is borne out; other research suggests that as we age we are better able to handle life's ups and downs. As Freud (and the negative stereotype) assumes, are older people rigid, fearful, immature, less able to cope? Or, as Jung feels, do the years bring emotional growth, full maturity? Do the major events in adult life—marriage, becoming parents, making our way in the world—change us greatly? Or do they leave little imprint on who we are? Are we the same people at 80 as at 25? As we explore the research and controversies these compelling questions have provoked, we will see why conclusions about personality and aging are so elusive and come to fully appreciate just how true the words "we all age differently" are.

By focusing on change and stability in general, however, we are leaving out the specifics, the perceptions we all have about the concrete changes in personality age brings. Certainly one of the most upsetting of these fixed ideas is spelled out in the ageism quotation at the beginning of this book: as people grow old they become less and less sexual. So this chapter ends with an in-depth discussion of sexuality because this aspect of life is so important and because sexual loss is such a central, frightening component of our stereotype of old age.

THE HISTORICAL FRAMEWORK

The Kansas City Studies: Emphasis on Change

Research on personality and aging was definitively launched in the mid-1950s when a team of social scientists at the University of Chicago began a large-scale investigation of personality in middle and later life. In search of answers to that fascinating question of how our attitudes, emotions, and interests change as we age, the researchers chose a group of stereotypic Americans (white, middle-class men and women ranging in age from 40 to 90) living in a typical U.S. city (Kansas City, Missouri) and descended to plumb their subjects' attitudes and feelings, to examine the ways they lived.

Eventually more than 700 people participated in the Kansas City Studies of Adult Life. The first investigation, from which almost all the information on personality was gathered, was cross sectional. The second phase was a short (6-year) longitudinal study involving several rounds of testings (Cumming & Henry, 1961; Neugarten & Associates, 1964).

To measure personality, the research team gave their subjects a variety of tests: paper-and-pencil measures of attitudes and feelings, and, because they were psychoanalytically oriented, a projective test called the Thematic Apperception Test (TAT) that tapped less conscious processes. The researchers also probed their subjects' lifestyles, asking about activities, interests, how involved they were with people, how often they left the house.

The interviews and tests measuring more on-the-surface aspects of personality showed no systematic age differences, suggesting that the more conscious aspects of personality do not change in a predictable way as people age. The findings were very different, however, when the researchers looked at their measure of unconscious processes, the TAT.

The TAT is a popular test used to diagnose emotional problems in psycho-analytically oriented mental health settings. A series of pictures is shown and the patient is asked to tell a story about each scene. The theory is that the stories offer a kind of emotional X-ray, revealing the person's unconscious concerns, emotional conflicts, and worldview.

While clinical psychologists have no specific scoring system for using the TAT, the University of Chicago team used this well-known test in a unique way. They looked for *systematic* changes that characterized the stories of older versus younger subjects and then constructed rating scales to score the stories along these dimensions alone. Using this technique, they discovered that a transformation they labeled **interiority** was occurring. As people aged they seemed to lose interest in the outside world and become more preoccupied with themselves.

TABLE 7-1. A sample TAT card depicting a vigorous muscular figure, possibly nude, who could be going up or down a rope and responses illustrating the three different mastery styles.

Active Mastery	Passive Mastery	Magical Mastery
The hero demonstrates his strength usually in successful competition. However, the rope may break off at the moment of triumph, and the respondent may deride the hero as a show-off. The hero strives vigorously, sometimes zestfully, toward a self-determined productive goal.	The hero is immobilized by environmental forces that do not collaborate with his action or that block it—the rope is slack, the cliff is slippery. The hero is threatened by destructive external forces or forces turned against himself (suicidal) or he is out of control and a threat to others (homicidal). The hero climbs, though without much involvement. The hero lacks force. He is tired or ill. The hero plays on the rope or uses it to see something, to get food, and so on.	The hero is not erect. The rope is not a rope.

Source: Adapted from Gutmann, 1969.

This change was suggested by differences in the "ego energy" and "mastery style" of the stories the Kansas City subjects produced at successively older ages (40–49, 50–59, and 60–71).

Ego energy (Rosen & Neugarten, 1964) referred to a vigorous, passionate, energetic involvement in life as opposed to passivity. This dimension was measured by scoring stories according to how much action and feeling they contained, whether people not actually on the card were introduced, and whether a story contained conflict. The researchers found a steady decline in ego-energy ratings, implying that in their 50s people begin to pull back emotionally from the world.

The second dimension captured this retreat in a different way. This time David Gutmann (1964, 1969) categorized the stories according to what he called **mastery style** (see Table 7-1). When the main character succeeded (or viewed success as possible) because of his or her own competence, a story was rated as expressing *active mastery*. When the protagonist depended on luck or others to succeed, the story was rated as having a *passive mastery* theme. To Gutmann these two types of stories represented very different approaches to life. The person either felt powerful, able to meet challenges head on, or hung back from the world, feeling powerless to shape his or her fate.

The third style, *magical mastery,* showed an even more profound degree of withdrawal. Stories of this type ignored or misinterpreted the actual scene on the card, suggesting that the person had abandoned the real world in favor of fantasy.

And, in the same way as was found for ego energy, the stories of the two older groups contained more and more passive and magical mastery themes.

Based on these findings, the research team concluded that by their 50s people start to emotionally withdraw. Even though, as in the vignette, at this time of life they are often at the pinnacle of their careers, they lose interest in the outer world and become more preoccupied with the inner self. From a traditional psycho-analytic perspective, this emotional retreat looks like a sign of pathology. However, it may not have this meaning if we see it as a preparation for life's last stage (Gutmann, 1969). The research team felt interiority was positive and adaptive, an internal precursor enabling people to accept the role losses and limitations in activity old age inevitably brings.

Another change the University of Chicago team found was even more interesting because it was unexpected. When Bernice Neugarten and David Gutmann (1964) constructed a special TAT card picturing a young man, a young woman, an old man, and an old woman and asked the Kansas City respondents to tell a story involving all four figures, they found fascinating age differences in the way the older people were described. While the younger subjects (aged 40–54) described the old man and old woman according to standard gender stereotypes: he was dominant, she gentle and submissive, older respondents (aged 55–70) reversed the adjectives: the woman was portrayed as powerful and controlling, the man as passive, submissive, and sweet. So the researchers concluded that in later life the personality differences between the sexes blur or reverse: "Women . . . seem to become more tolerant of their own aggressive egocentric impulses; . . . men . . . of their own nurturant and affiliative impulses" (Neugarten & Gutmann, 1964, p. 89).

Conclusions, Criticisms, and Controversy

These findings support Jung's clinical hunches about personality change and age in an uncanny way. As described in Chapter 1, Jung hypothesized that people become psychologically more like the opposite sex in the latter part of life and also become less interested in success and mastery, though he describes interiority in a positive way, not as an erosion of power, but as an expansion to a higher level of development. Paradoxically, the negative aspect of the concept of interiority dovetails with Freud's ideas about aging, too. As people grow old they shrink back, become fragile and fearful, and retreat into fantasy.

The University of Chicago findings confirm our stereotypes. We expect people to withdraw and become self-absorbed in old age. While not as explicit in the stereotype, the idea that women become more masculine and men more feminine in later life is a surprisingly widespread perception, too. In gathering evidence for the validity of this sex-role shift, Gutmann (1977) examined myths and folktales from around the world. He found that the tough, cruel, aggressive old woman (that is, the witch) is a stock figure in children's fairy tales, as is the gentle, tenderhearted old man.

But, as times changed, researchers grew more sophisticated about methodology, psychoanalytic theory became less fashionable, and gerontologists raised more and more questions about the Kansas City results. Even by the early 1970s, the pre–women's movement ideas of the cohort doing the research began to seem dated. After the upheavals of the 1960s, would men and women ever still be described according to the rigid gender stereotypes offered by the Kansas City 40-year-olds? Psychologists increasingly disputed the theory underlying the TAT, that through telling stories about pictures people reveal a more elemental, "truer" self. They had become sensitive to the pitfalls of inferring age changes from cross-sectional studies, and of assuming universality from a sample limited to white, married, middle-class adults. Based on upsetting evidence that measures used to tap personality often do not measure the traits they are supposed to (see Campbell & Fiske, 1959; Fiske, 1971), they criticized the conceptual leaps the University of Chicago researchers had made from their data. Does the finding that older people tell more limited, less imaginative TAT stories really signify decreasing involvement in life, or does it simply reflect the fact that the elderly are more uncomfortable taking any test and so naturally produce more constricted responses on a measure of this type (see Chapters 5 and 6)? Couldn't the qualities labeled "ego energy" really just be indexes of verbal fluency or creativity, both of which might also decline by late middle age?

Most damaging were the subsequent studies. Often the Kansas City results could not be reproduced (see Neugarten, 1977). While some studies did support aspects of the research (Foley & Murphy, 1977; Gambria, 1979–1980; Lowenthal, Thurnher, Chiriboga, & Associates, 1975), others showed *no* hints that people change in either of these two ways as they age (Costa & McCrae, 1980). Furthermore, when a study suggested that these personality changes might actually take place, it was almost always a cross-sectional one (Neugarten, 1977), leaving the most damning criticism of this landmark investigation untouched—the University of Chicago researchers were really measuring cohort differences, not true age changes. So the findings of the Kansas City study gradually fell into disfavor, leaving only one member of the research team to argue the pro side of the debate.

Gutmann's cross-cultural research (1969, 1977) has convinced him that men and women do develop more traits of the opposite sex as they age. However, while he originally felt this change to be *intrinsic* to growing old, he now sees it as due to the environment—the different pressures we face as younger versus older adults.

According to Gutmann (1980, 1985) personality differences between the sexes are needed in first half of adulthood because of what he calls the **parental imperative.** In order to best rear children, nature has set up a division of labor that, despite the women's liberation movement, still usually takes place along traditional sex-role lines. The man mostly provides for the physical needs of the family and the woman handles the emotional sphere, taking care of the day-to-day child care, offering the stereotypical female qualities of understanding, patience, and selflessness. Once the children have left the nest, however, a kind of "return of the repressed" occurs. Women are able to express the masculine

---

BOX 7-1
The Environment and Waxing and Waning Sex Roles

Among the cross-sectional studies that support the idea that in later life personality differences between the sexes are less distinct is a study that bears out Gutmann's concept of the parental imperative yet extends his idea in an interesting way.

Researchers (Feldman, Biringen, & Nash, 1981) divided 800 men and women, not by age, but by the particular stage in the family life cycle they were in (for example, adolescent, married without children, grandparent) and probed their sex-role inclinations by a self-report personality test. The results supported Gutmann's TAT findings. The largest gender differences in personality existed in the parenting stage; the smallest in the empty nest stage of life. But, rather than just getting less and less pronounced in a unidirectional way, sex-role differences actually waxed and waned in different life-stages. In other words (if we are not just seeing cohort changes), this study suggests that supposedly biologically based differences in temperament may be more fluid, flexible, and determined by the environment than we think. And, in response to the shifting life circumstances we face as adults, we may either emphasize or downplay our "masculine" or "feminine" side.

□

---

qualities they have had to dampen down to ensure their children's development. Men are able to relax, giving more play to their nurturant, feminine side.

An exploratory study done by Gutmann and a colleague (Cooper and Gutmann, 1987) suggests that for women the waning of the "parental imperative" does correlate with more "masculine" character traits. When the researchers compared TAT mastery styles of two groups of mothers in their 40s, one in the "empty nest" phase of parenthood and one with children still in the house, they found, as they had predicted, that the stories of the empty nest women had more active (versus passive or magical) mastery themes. In interviews, too, the empty nest women were more prone to describe themselves as assertive and dominant than their counterparts actively immersed in raising a child.

Research on personality has moved far beyond the Kansas City studies (see Bengtson, Reedy, & Gordon, 1985, for a review). Few gerontologists, apart from David Gutmann, are still engrossed in arguing for the truth of the Kansas City results. But this landmark study is important because it stimulated so much debate, and in the process of trying to validate these first findings about change, personality and aging evolved into a mature field. The controversial theory that grew out of the Kansas City findings about lifestyle gave gerontology the same precious legacy.

Disengagement Theory: The Idea and the Debate

In studying the activities of the Kansas City subjects, the University of Chicago researchers found signs of withdrawal here too, shifts similar to the psychological transition to interiority but occurring about 10 years later.

Beginning by about the mid-60s, the number of roles people had, such as "mother" or "worker," decreased dramatically. Respondents spent more time alone each day, and they had fewer and fewer contacts with people per month. This reduction in external involvement, along with its internal, psychological harbinger, led two members of the research team to propose an idea that has provoked more anger, spawned more debate, and evoked more research than any other theory in social gerontology—**disengagement theory.**

According to Elaine Cumming and William Henry (1961), in old age a gradual process of disengagement occurs. People automatically distance themselves from society, they withdraw from the world. But, rather than being a sign of pathology, Cumming and Henry proposed that disengagement in our later years is universal, normal, and natural. In fact, it is the right way to age.

The reaction to this provocative idea was swift: Cumming and Henry's pronouncement must be disproved! If allowed to stand, disengagement theory seemed to put a scientific stamp of approval on ageist practices such as mandatory retirement—forcing people to withdraw from the mainstream of society at a certain age (Cath, 1979). Moreover, the idea that retiring to a rocking chair is appropriate in later life seemed totally false. Wouldn't people be damaged if they were encouraged to follow this advice, advised to step back emotionally from life? So an alternate idea about the right way to age was quickly proposed. In **activity theory,** the key to happiness in later life is to stay as involved in life as possible.

During the 1960s and early 1970s, as gerontologists feverishly tested the truth of these contrasting ideas, they learned a good deal about doing gerontological research, about activity and disengagement, and about the complex factors that are really related to happiness in later life.

Early on it became clear that deciding between the two theories was more complicated than had first appeared. For one thing, the activity/disengagement dimension was not unitary. For instance, in part because relatives tend to rally around when an older family member is in poor health, being involved with one's family turned out to be unrelated to the extent to which a person was involved in other areas of life (Carp, 1968; see also Chapter 8). Furthermore, quantitative measures of involvement, such as the number of contacts with other people per week, were being used to measure what was really an emotional phenomenon, the *feeling* of being disengaged or passionately involved in life. Most telling, while many studies did show a slight correlation between life satisfaction and keeping active, others did not (Lemon, Bengtson, & Peterson, 1972). The small positive relationship between activity and morale that was often found seemed due to a more basic, underlying variable: being in good health (Larson, R., 1978). So "keep as active as possible" was shown to be too simplistic a prescription for the ideal way to age. Some older people were best off being active; others were most content sitting on the sidelines of life.

Personality, as we might imagine, is central to whether one is satisfied being active or disengaged. This was suggested by a subsequent study done by the Chicago team using the Kansas City subjects. Bernice Neugarten, Robert Havinghurst, and Sheldon Tobin (1968) looked at activity and life satisfaction in relation to a person's basic personality style. Among the well adjusted or what they called "integrated" men and women, they found a mix of highly active and relatively inactive older people, all satisfied with life. Among the emotionally disturbed respondents, disengagement coupled with low morale was the rule. So happiness seemed a function, not so much of activity, but of personality. Disengagement could be a highly satisfying way of life for a well-adjusted person; it could be an acutely unhappy way of living for someone who was disturbed.

Looking at activity and disengagement in this context also showed the researchers something else important. Certain types of people were disproportionately active or disengaged. The Kansas City subjects classified as "armored-defended people" (people who were highly success oriented but who kept their feelings under rigid control) were likely to keep very active in later life. The type of person classified as "passive-dependent" tended to gratefully retire to a rocking chair. So it became clear that disengagement, far from being predestined or forced on people, was actually under their control. It was a way of living older adults either chose or rejected depending on what fit them emotionally.

This implies that we might find more truth to activity theory if we defined keeping active in a deeper, more qualitative way. Rather than just "doing many things" or "keeping very busy," our morale in later life (and at any age) may depend on finding activities that are *meaningful* to us. An introverted, philosophical person might find most meaning in life by reading and contemplating the world from a rocking chair. An outgoing, energetic person might only be content by keeping active in the objectively measured, obvious sense, filling each day with things to do.

A fascinating study of 33 retirement-aged men and women suggests that when we consider *meaningful* activities, the advice "keep active" is indeed more sound. Daniel Ogilvie (1987) asked his subjects to rank their identities, the life roles that were most important to them, in order (for example, (1) mother or father, (2) gardener, (3) choir member, (4) church member, (5) volunteer, and so on) and then questioned them about the extent to which each role brought out their "best" versus "worst self," the qualities they valued or disliked about themselves. He next asked them how much time they spent involved in each role and probed their morale. The relationships were strong and direct. People who spent the most time expressing their highest ranking identities were the most content human beings. In other words, by measuring activity in its qualitative, or emotionally felt sense, Ogilvie's study suggests that activity theory may indeed be right. Keeping involved in life in the way that fits us emotionally may be critically important in our later years.

Despite his small sample, Ogilvie's results are particularly striking because of the unusually high correlations he found. He uncovered much stronger associations between his two variables than researchers typically get between health and morale, the factor that, until this study, had been most highly related to life satisfaction in the elderly (see Larson, R., 1978). But, as with any correlation, his finding raises the question of causes. Do happy people see what they are doing as having meaning because they have a generally contented approach to life, or do meaningful activities *produce* happiness in old age? And if meaningful activities are the key to a fulfilling old age, why do some older adults flounder cut off from these roles? Is it fate or unfortunate events (widowhood, retirement, illness) that prevent people from enacting their most prized identities, or do people shape their own fate? Some of us cannot construct meaning amidst a sea of opportunities; others extract satisfying identities from the most impoverished outer life. According to the most prolific researcher probing personality and aging today, the answer is clear. Paul Costa believes events do not shape us—we shape the world to fit who we are.

PRESENT RESEARCH

The Baltimore Study: Personality Stability

As mentioned earlier, perhaps the most devastating criticism of the Kansas City results was that, being based on cross-sectional data, they might reflect cohort differences rather than true age changes. Unfortunately, cross-sectional findings are especially suspect in studying adult personality change, since different cohorts vary greatly in their feelings, attitudes, and approaches to the world. We can see this clearly by thinking of the cohorts reaching adulthood in the late 1950s, late 1960s, and late 1980s. Within just these few decades, young adults have flip-flopped from conservatism to rebellion and back to conservatism again! While as we age our outlook on life and worldview are also shaped by the particular historical moment in which we live, longitudinal studies have more of a chance of revealing transformations in personality that really may be related to growing old itself. In the 1950s we did not have these studies. Today, because of the Baltimore Longitudinal Study, we do.

As the director of the Section on Stress and Coping at the National Institute on Aging (NIA) and the coordinator of personality research for our nation's most important ongoing study of adult life, Costa has been in a unique position to measure how personality changes over decades by analyzing the Baltimore volunteers' scores on paper-and-pencil personality tests over the years. Many gerontologists believe that what he and his NIA colleagues have found signals the death knell of the University of Chicago ideas about change—**personality stability** is the hallmark of adult development. The best prediction about how the years will change us is that they will not (Costa & McCrae, 1980, 1984; Costa, McCrae, & Arenberg, 1980, 1983; McCrae & Costa, 1984).

Much of the evidence that Costa and his colleagues have found that shows that personality stays remarkably stable over adult life involves studies they have done of the the following three traits, which are broad dispositions the researchers believe (based on factor analytic techniques) underlie most of the more limited aspects of personality measured on standard tests:

1. **Neuroticism** is a general tendency toward maladjustment (that is, anxiety, hostility, depression, self-consciousness, emotional distress) rather than mental health. For instance, is the person stable and well adjusted or psychologically vulnerable, prone to break down?
2. **Extraversion** reflects interpersonal openness (that is, outgoingness, warmth, gregariousness, activity, assertion). For instance, is the person at ease and happy with others, enthusiastically engaged in life, or does he or she feel most comfortable living a more solitary, withdrawn life?
3. **Openness to experience** involves the willingness to take risks, to seek out new experiences or try new things. For instance, does the person love the unbeaten path, the newest thrill, or is she or he cautious, conservative, uneasy deviating from the tried and true?

According to Costa and his colleagues, measuring these basic dispositions longitudinally allows us to evaluate the truth of many theories and preconceptions about age-related personality change. For instance, if people regress, becoming infantile and emotionally unstable in old age, neuroticism scores should peak in later life. If the stereotype that age brings conservatism, caution, and rigidity is correct, then over the years there should be a linear decline in scores on openness to experience. And, if increasing interiority does categorize the aging process, extraversion scores should steadily decrease as people grow old. But none of these phenomena take place. The Baltimore volunteers' scores on each of these dimensions are roughly the same at every age.

But the Baltimore subjects are an elite group. Can we really expect their changes (or, in this case, nonchanges) to be representative of the population at large? It is one thing to say that among highly educated, relatively healthy, upper-middle-class people personality remains stable. What about among the less fortunate, those more likely to bear the brunt of the reversals of old age—the poor, the uneducated, the ill? To show that the Baltimore findings do have wider validity, Costa and his colleagues (Costa & McCrae, 1986; Costa, McCrae, Zonderman, Barabano, Lebowitz, & Larson, 1986) decided to demonstrate that the Baltimore subjects' scores on neuroticism, extraversion, and openness to experience at each age were similar to those of a more typical group of Americans.

So they got access to the subject pool from a national study involving almost *15,000 respondents*—the National Health and Nutrition Examination Survey, or NHANES—and gave this huge sample a short version of the same personality test they had used with the Baltimore volunteers. The mean scores of the two groups revealed only very minor differences, suggesting that the Baltimore results do

BOX 7-2
The Key to a Happy Old Age: Personality

It is common to yearn for those things that will bring happiness. We think if only we were richer, more beautiful, more physically fit, we would be absolutely content. But if health, wealth, and beauty really are the keys to happiness, why is the group most deficient in these attributes, older people, seemingly no less content than younger adults (see Chapter 1)? Why is it that objective assets—from socioeconomic status to contact with family, even to health—are not highly correlated with morale in old age? If what we have does not produce happiness, then the saying that happiness resides in us might very well be true.

Just as with the other traits he has studied, Costa's research (Costa & McCrae, 1984; Costa, Zonderman, McCrae, Cornoni-Huntley, Locke, & Barabano, 1987) suggests that happiness is an enduring aspect of our personality, that it is a quality relatively immune to the vicissitudes of life. Happy young people tend to be content and fulfilled in later life. The person who becomes the stereotypical cranky, miserable older person was probably a neurotic, unfulfilled young adult. But if the predisposition to be happy is indeed stable, is this wonderful quality something we carry around from birth? As the psychoanalysts believe, is a happy life outlook shaped during the crucial first 5 years of life? If we look at the world in shades of gray, are we fated for unfulfillment or can we ever change? Since even Costa points out that some people in his studies do change radically over the years, this suggests that the prognosis is not totally grim (see Shock et al., 1984). It is possible to triumph over the worst psychopathology and construct a happy, contented life.

□

indeed generalize to Americans at large. Furthermore, when the researchers looked cross sectionally at age differences in extraversion, openness, and neuroticism in this very different sample, they found that stability seemed to be the dominant theme here, too. While older age groups did have slightly lower scores on the three dimensions, the differences were very small indeed.

Conclusions, Criticisms, and Controversy

Should we take this research to mean that by early adulthood our personality is cast in stone? Costa himself cautions against this sweeping conclusion, stressing that his cross-sectional research simply shows that we do not change in a *predictable* or systematic way as the years pass. It does not imply that we never change at all. And, while his longitudinal investigations suggest we can see many characteristics of the potential 70-year-old in the youth of 25, the clarity of our crystal ball also varies greatly from person to person. There are always some people who do change a good deal as the years advance. Furthermore, he cautions that his findings only apply to these broad traits, not to other aspects of personality, such as the way we cope with upsetting events (as we will see in the next section). We also must remember that even if these *underlying* traits do stay stable, they may translate into very different surface behavior at different life-stages. For instance, a person who rates high in neuroticism might be phobic and anxiety-ridden at age 20, hostile and bitter at age 65. People open to experience might even appear to change totally from year to year, as they shift interests, jobs, and friends in pursuit of anything foreign, different, and untried (Costa, McCrae, & Arenberg, 1983).

Just as the Kansas City findings were questioned, Costa's conclusions have been criticised, too. Psychoanalytically oriented psychologists have argued that since Costa's studies were based on personality tests in which subjects are asked to check off whether a list of statements applies or does not apply to them, they may not capture more underlying changes that do occur. We might, as the University of Chicago team did, find genuine age transformations if we explored personality in a deeper, less on the surface way. Other critics have suggested that the type of self-report questionnaires the NIA researchers used, tests in which subjects have to answer "agree or disagree" to fixed questions, may inflate the extent of consistency because of the operation of what are called *response sets*. When people are repeatedly tested, they answer items in the same way because their *test-taking style* is fixed or stable—not their personality.

Actually, every personality test has limitations. Even when people are assessed at a single point in time, different measures of the same traits often do not relate to one another in a satisfactory way (Campbell & Fiske, 1959). A person rated as highly aggressive by his friends might not rank himself as aggressive on a self-report scale. Signs of aggression on the TAT might not appear in measures of behavior or on any other self-report test. So it comes as no surprise that in exploring personality over time contradictory results are the norm (see, for review, Bengtson, Reedy, & Gordon, 1985; Neugarten, 1977) and that the very few other longitudinal studies spanning large chunks of adult life offer very different impressions about how stable our personality is as adults.

For instance, by combining data from two large-scale investigations of child rearing begun in the 1930s, Norma Haan, Roger Millsap, and Elizabeth Hartka (1986) got information about personality from a core group of subjects at an amazing seven points during their *whole* life span: early childhood, late child-hood, early adolescence, late adolescence, early adulthood, middle adulthood, and old age. The personality test used in these studies, the California Q Sort, is very different from the self-report inventory the NIA researchers employed. Rather than responding in a fixed way to items, people who take this type of test structure their responses themselves. They are given a pile of statements and asked to sort the cards into categories that best describe themselves.

Interestingly, in this study change and stability were *both* dominant themes.

Some aspects of personality shifted dramatically over time; others stayed relatively constant. Some adjacent age spans were times of great change; others were more quiescent, producing many fewer transformations in the self.

Perhaps the most startling finding of this uniquely long longitudinal study was that childhood and adolescence turned out to be the periods of greatest stability. In direct contrast to what Freud predicts, adulthood was a time of greater internal change. The 15 years of early adulthood (from about age 17 to 33) were a time of especially intense flux. Perhaps because this period spans the transition from adolescent dependence to full adult maturity, subjects changed more radically over this time than at any other two points in the study.

To make sense of their remarkable finding that adulthood, not childhood, is the time of life when personality is most malleable, the researchers offered this interesting hypothesis: Changes in the outer fabric of life may tend to propel internal change. During childhood and adolescence the externals in our life tend to be relatively stable. We are usually being cared for in a protected environment, insulated from the tests adulthood brings—having to make our own way in the world. As adults (particularly in our 20s and early 30s) our life tends to change radically. Many of us marry, become parents, establish a career. At this age how we cope depends on us. So, if bumping up against life's challenges causes change, it makes sense that adulthood might be the time of most internal flux.

But does encountering life's ups and downs change us for the better? This brings us to a critical question: As people grow older, do they get more mature?

Maturity, Regression, or a Different Way of Handling Stress?

It is in that crucial aspect of our personality, our ability to cope with life, that growing old is supposed to bear real fruit. As in the vignette, most of us hope that our life experience will teach us emotional resilience, the ability to cope better with the setbacks and losses that are the price of being alive. But the studies discussed so far offer no hints that life experience does bring maturity. According to Costa, neuroticism is as common in middle and later life as at any other age. Gutmann's research on mastery styles has an even more depressing message. The age-related increase in passive and magical mastery responses suggests that as people grow older they cope in a *less* mature way, depending on other people, not themselves, to fight their battles and retreating into fantasy rather than actively dealing with challenges and threats.

Luckily, at least in handling some specific traumas, years of living do confer resilience. The most clear-cut example is the death of a spouse. A variety of studies (described in Chapter 9) suggest that older widowed people are less at risk of suffering prolonged, unremitting bereavement reactions than middle-aged or younger adults. Being older also seems to make a difference in how well we are able to accept the fact of having a life-threatening disease such as cancer (Ell, Mantell, & Hamovich, 1986) or handle impending death (see Chapter 12).

However, widowhood and serious illness are normal, or at least not unexpected, stresses in later life. And as Bernice Neugarten and Nancy Datan (1975) have argued, the stressful impact of any event is less intense when the change is **on time** (expected at that age) versus **off time** (not appropriate at that life-stage). Logically, widowhood or serious illness should be more difficult to accept when either interrupts us in our vigorous middle years than when it occurs at the "correct time," after a long life. So the fact that older people tolerate the *expected* losses of later life better than younger people does not answer the question of whether age brings emotional resilience. To really assess if this is so we need to examine the way people cope with stresses that are not age related, for instance, by seeing how older versus younger people react to *any* important challenge, threat, or loss. This is just the strategy Costa's NIA colleague, Robert McCrae, used with the Baltimore volunteers.

McCrae (1982) divided his respondents into three age groups (24–49, 50–64, and 65–81), questioned them about how they had handled the most important life stresses they had experienced within the past 6 months, and then looked at differences in the maturity of their coping styles. While many of the age differences he uncovered were not inherently more or less mature (see below), the older people were less prone to two regressive coping styles: They were less likely to report escaping into fantasy or exploding in anger when confronted with life's blows.

The Baltimore subjects are an advantaged group, the very type of people we might expect to handle stress in a more mature way as the years pass. Studies of more representative elderly have painted a less upbeat portrait, sometimes even supporting the stereotype that older people cope in a more immature way (Pearlin & Schooler, 1978; see Shenfeld, 1984–1985, for review). But McCrae's finding is not an isolated one either. In a more recent cross-sectional study comparing young adults, middle-aged, and elderly people, researchers (Irion & Blanchard-Fields, 1987) also found that the youngest group had more immature coping strategies (escape avoidance, hostile reactions, and self-blame). The middle-aged and elderly groups reported handling life in a more mature way.

Most studies suggest, however, that while there are distinct age differences in how people cope, it is hard to classify these different methods of handling stress as either more or less mature. Perhaps because the upsetting events we tend to face in our later years (illness, widowhood, and so on) are more unchangeable, older people tend to use more passive strategies, such as "I found new faith" or "I went on as if nothing had happened," in handling stress. Perhaps because the reversals of earlier life (getting fired or being rejected by a loved one) tend to be handled best by taking concrete action, younger people more frequently report actively trying to change the situation, such as "I stood my ground and fought for what I wanted" or "I made a plan and followed it" (Folkman, Lazarus, Pimley, & Novacek, 1987). And, perhaps because the intensity of our emotions may wane with age (Schultz, 1985), or, since these studies have all been cross sectional, due to the value this cohort of the elderly places on a stiff upper lip, older people more often report cutting off their feelings, preferring to "refuse to dwell on the problem" or to "think of something else" and not cry on a friend's shoulder or fly into a rage when faced with the reversals and disappointments of life (Felton & Revenson, 1987).

So, in this aspect of personality, who we are as adults is far from set in stone. Rather than approaching the different challenges we face as younger and older people in the same way, we seem to flexibly tailor our actions to fit the situation. Or, in the encouraging words of the Baltimore researchers, "Older men and women do not rigidly maintain habits of coping that, although appropriate in youth, have outlived their usefulness. Instead, as stresses change so do coping responses (Shock et al., 1984, p. 167).

THE CONCLUSIONS: CHANGE AND CONSISTENCY

I hope our discussion shows that there is no right answer to the question of whether we change or stay the same as the years pass. If we use self-report inventories measuring traits, we have to conclude that, in most important ways, we do not change much. When we use less structured personality tests or examine coping styles, more pronounced change seems to be the rule. Every study shows that some people react totally differently at age 70 than at age 25, and that others seem remarkably unchanged. For this reason it is appropriate to end this chapter by describing a longitudinal investigation that fully captures this diversity (Maas & Kuypers, 1975). The subjects in this study were the parents of the people followed from early childhood to later life (see Haan, Millsap, & Hartka, 1986). Both parents and children had been originally examined as part of two Depression-era investigations of child rearing. In the late 1960s Henry Maas and Joseph Kuypers (1975) unearthed this data and saw a unique opportunity. If they could retest these original parents, they could find out about how people change over a 40-year period, from their 30s to their 70s.

Because their study was not originally planned as longitudinal, Maas and Kuypers had to make inferences about similarity from different measures and were only able to find a fraction of the parents. So their findings are tenuous and speculative. Still, as well as serving as a model of the complexity that is the hallmark of research in this area, what they did discover helps us pull together some common themes of the confusing literature charting personality consistency and change.

Based on interviews, Maas and Kuypers grouped their subjects into several lifestyle and personality types (see Table 7-2). They then looked for early adult antecedents of these late-life patterns of living and personality styles. They found a good deal of continuity in lifestyles but only for fathers. For instance, the "hobbyist" men (those immersed in activities) had been active in outside projects during their young adult years, too. Those who were "unwell-disengaged" had been sickly in their early 30s.

In contrast, the mothers' lifestyles often shifted more radically in fascinating ways. For instance, mothers categorized as having "work-centered" lifestyles in their 70s, those who were enthusiastic and committed to a job, had often seemed depressed and apathetic as young adults. It was as if the role they had found themselves in during their 30s (that of full-time mother and housewife) had never fit their real talents or interests. When they were freed of this ill-fitting identity in

TABLE 7-2. Examples of two personality and three lifestyle types of parents.

Type	Characteristics
Personality (five total types of mothers; four of fathers)	
Mothers Person-oriented	Behaves in giving way; sympathetic or considerate; has warmth; is compassionate; arouses liking and acceptance.
Fearful-ordering	Basically submissive; favors conservative values; uncomfortable with uncertainty, complexity; basically anxious.
Fathers Person-oriented	Behaves in giving way; cheerful; dependable and responsible; straightforward, forthright, candid; productive, gets things done; submissive.
Active-competent	Interesting, arresting person; critical; skeptical, not easily impressed; rebellious and nonconforming; verbally fluent; masculine in style and manner.
Lifestyle (Six total types of mothers; four of fathers)	
Mothers Husband-centered	Life focused on husband and marriage.
Uncentered	Few interests; nonengagement with others in giving or receiving relationship; most not married.
Work-centered	Highly involved with and satisfied with work.
Fathers Family-centered	Life revolves around marriage, parenting, and grandparenting.
Hobbyist	Leisure-time interests and activities most important.
Unwell-disengaged	Ill, withdrawn; unsatisfied with life and marriage.

Source: Adapted from Maas & Kuypers, 1975.

later life, they could really blossom. In contrast, another group, called the "uncentered," who were unfocused, unhappy, and at loose ends in their 70s, had been happy as young housewives in their 30s. Unfortunately, they seemed unable to replace their family-centered identity with another satisfying one that fit their life situation 40 years later. In the present, as empty nest mothers and often widows, they were floundering.

Maas and Kuypers hypothesized that these gender differences in change were due to the fact that over the years the women's life situation had usually shifted much more radically than the men's. Other than retirement, few external upheavals occurred that might have forced these all still-married men to change their style of life. In contrast, marked changes in what the researchers called "contexts" often took place in the women's lives, alterations that forced them to live in a different way. In their later years some women had to go to work for the first time to make ends meet. All could no longer live lives focused on their families because their children were grown and often their husbands had died. So Maas and Kuypers concluded that shifts in the outer conditions of life are one important force that causes us to change as we age.

In contrast to these differences in lifestyle, personality consistency was more prevalent among the women than the men. This gender difference seemed to be due to the fact that consistency was most often found among the older people rated as emotionally disturbed, and unfortunately a greater number of the women than the men were typed in this way. In a provocative finding, while respondents who were well adjusted seemed quite dissimilar to who they had been as young adults, there were clear early adult antecedents for those categorized as most disturbed. Among these poorly functioning older people, emotional disturbance seemed to be a consistent pattern, one that was also present in youth.

If we combine the results of this interesting study with the others discussed in this chapter we can tentatively conclude that two influences seem important in shaping the extent to which we change as adults. If our life is stormy, full of external upheavals, we may be more prone to change as the years pass than if our life is calmer, free of wrenching events. Fluctuations in the external fabric of life seem to be an important force that promotes change. On the other hand, an internal influence—psychopathology—seems to foster consistency. Perhaps because emotional disturbance acts as a blinder, reducing our ability to learn from experience, even preventing us from seeing the real world, *highly* disturbed people seem much the same at age 80 as they did at age 25.

For the rest of us, the research suggests that two prescriptions may be important to having a happy, fulfilling old age—be reasonably healthy and well adjusted to begin with and find the late-life lifestyle that best expresses our inner self.

In the rest of this chapter we turn to sexuality, an area of life where normal physiological loss, society's expectations, life events, enduring predisposition, and interests all interact to produce both change and consistency as the years pass.

SEXUALITY

Since sexuality has both physiological and psychological facets, we might argue that it does not really fit into a chapter on personality change. But since it determines so many of our thoughts and actions, this important dimension of life permeates who we are in the most basic ways. Not only are there the thoughts and behaviors centered around having sexual relations, but there are the hours we spend dressing to look sexually attractive and the time devoted to flirting or fantasizing. For many of us the idea that we are sexually appealing is central to the way we think about ourselves. Much of the way we relate to the opposite sex has an underlying sexual theme.

But in our society all of these ways of behaving are expected to change at a certain age. Despite the media attention given to a few "elderly" sex symbols, we still equate youth with sexuality, age with the end of the sexual side of life. Women are shunned as unappealing sex partners as early as their 40s. Elderly men are expected to be impotent or not much interested in sex. Not only do we accept these stereotypes as true, we see them as appropriate. Even in our anti-Victorian age we still have some firmly held ideas that sexuality in late life is a sign of pathology or somehow disgusting.

That sexual loss is a frightening, central component of our old age stereotype becomes clear when we look at a good barometer of our attitudes and anxieties, the jokes we tell. Palmore (1971a) copied jokes about aging from different anthologies and sorted them according to subject. He discovered that jokes about old age often had a sexual theme. Many dealt with the waning potency of elderly men or surprising evidence of intact sexual prowess. Here is a typical example (Cumming & Henry, 1961, p. 18):

> An old man who had just married a 20-year-old woman went to his doctor for advice because he wanted to keep his bride happy. . . . The doctor advised him to get a young female companion for his wife as a roomer in their home. Three months later the doctor saw the old fellow again. "How's your wife?" the doctor inquired. "Fine, she's pregnant." "And your roomer?" "Well, she's pregnant, too!"

As we can see, the superficially positive theme of this joke masks a deeper negative message. The joke would not be funny if it were about a younger man. Its humor lies in its shock value—older men are simply not supposed to be this sexually active or capable.

The problem with this idea and the other prejudices we have about late-life sexuality, is that, as with any stereotype, they limit people to behaving in a certain way. Moreover, these fixed assumptions are self-fulfilling prophecies, to some extent producing the very behavior they predict. Wanting to have sex, acting on those feelings, and being able to perform physically once in a sexual situation are intimately dependent on how we feel about ourselves. If older people accept the idea that they are sexually unattractive or incapable, their interest, activity, and performance will be affected in the most negative way.

Keeping in mind that it is impossible to tease out the dampening impact of the pressure older people are under *not* to be sexual from the true losses that age brings, we now turn to research probing the last aspect of sexuality just mentioned—the ability to sexually perform.

Age Changes in Sexual Response

William Masters and Virginia Johnson (1966) were the first people to investigate the actual physiology of sexuality. Among the 700 people who agreed to have sexual intercourse in their laboratory and so furnish data for their landmark studies was a small group, 39 couples, in which at least one partner was over age 50. Masters and Johnson called these people their geriatric sample. However, only 20 of the men and 11 of the women were over age 60 and so really deserved this name.

In view of the strong prohibitions against older people having sex, we might expect that, while Masters and Johnson's younger volunteers would be atypical of the larger population, their "geriatric sample" would be a strikingly unusual group—much more sexually uninhibited than the average person their age. So their responses show us more about what is possible physiologically as we grow old rather than what is typical.

Among the older women, Masters and Johnson found several age changes in sexual responsiveness. Breast size did not increase during sexual arousal, as it does in the young. The sex flush (a pinkish rash that normally occurs during sexual excitement) was not as intense. Contraction of the rectal sphincter during orgasm, an indication of an intense sexual experience, rarely occurred.

In all women general changes in the reproductive system that take place after menopause indirectly affect sexual responsiveness. Menopause is ushered in when the body's production of the hormone estrogen, which regulates the menstrual cycle, falls off dramatically. While its most crucial effect is to end a woman's capacity to bear children, estrogen depletion also gradually changes the vagina and surrounding tissues.

During a woman's childbearing years, the walls of the vagina have thick, cushiony folds that expand easily to admit a penis or accommodate childbirth. After menopause, the vaginal walls gradually become thinner, smoother, and more fragile. The vagina shortens and its opening narrows. The size of the clitoris and labia decreases. There is a diminution in the amount of sexual lubrication. Masters and Johnson found it takes longer after arousal for lubrication to begin and that the fluid was not as copious as in younger women. The net effect of these changes is to limit sexual enjoyment since intercourse is more uncomfortable. Some women even stop having sex.

However, estrogen depletion has little effect on sexual *desire*. The male hormone testosterone, present in the female body, too, seems to regulate the intensity of the sex drive in both men and women. In fact, Masters and Johnson found that the clitoral response to sexual stimulation was virtually identical among older and younger women. This is important because the clitoris is thought to be the actual seat of sexual arousal. Also, the older women studied were just as capable of reaching orgasm as the younger group. On average, though, they did have fewer orgasmic contractions and less prolonged orgasms than the young volunteers.

Interestingly, these age differences did not apply to the three most sexually active older volunteers. Their orgasms were indistinguishable from those of the 20-year-olds, and their vaginal lubrication was also as copious and rapid. Perhaps these women were just an unusual physiological elite. Or, it may be that in the sexual area, too, exercise—that is, regular activity—helps stave off age-related decline and that some physiological losses supposedly inevitable to age are more reversible than we might imagine.

In sum, Masters and Johnson's findings about women were very upbeat. Age brings only relatively minor changes in sexual responsiveness. The researchers concluded with a brief but important statement: "There is no time limit drawn by advancing years to female sexuality" (Masters & Johnson, 1966, p. 247).

Unfortunately, their findings were much less encouraging for the opposite sex. Men did show marked physiological changes. Some were similar to the auxiliary signs of decline found in the women, a loss of the sex flush and fewer rectal-sphincter contractions at orgasm. However, others were quite central, affecting a man's actual capacity to have intercourse. For example, erections occurred less spontaneously and required more time and effort to develop. They also tended to be more fragile and were liable to be lost before ejaculation occurred. As the following study shows, these differences seem to be signs of an overall decline in the resilience of the erectile system (cited in Solnick, 1978).

Using a device attached to the penis, researchers monitored the erections of young men (aged 19–30) and older men (aged 48–65) as they watched an erotic

movie. Not only did the young group's erections occur an average (
fast, but the whole character of their responsiveness differed fr
men's. The young men tended to quickly develop and then pai
erection only to respond rapidly again when stimulated by anoi
contrast, the older men had erections much more gradually and v
rebound after a partial loss. Moreover, their erections never reacııcu ιιιc ....
imum sizes measured in the young volunteers.

Masters and Johnson found changes in the intensity of the orgasm itself. Older
men had less explosive ejaculations. If an older man maintained an erection over
a long period, ejaculation resulted in a seepage of seminal fluid rather than an
expulsion.

Penile detumescence after orgasm was more rapid. Rather than occurring in
two distinct stages as it did among the young, it happened all at once. Masters and
Johnson also charted the refractory period—the time after reaching orgasm
before another erection (or orgasm) can occur. In contrast to the younger men,
the older subjects could not redevelop an erection for 12 to 24 hours after a
previous ejaculation.

These losses, however, far from suggest older men are sexually incapable or
impotent (as will become clear in the next sections). In fact, because erections
can be maintained for longer periods before the pressure to ejaculate becomes
overwhelming, it has been suggested that, from a woman's point of view, age may
even make men better sexual partners (see Corby & Solnick, 1980). This evidence of slowed but not absent performance for older men, coupled with the
more encouraging physiological findings for older women, gives us a framework
for looking at studies probing the two other aspects of sexuality mentioned
earlier—how sexually interested and active are people in middle and later life?

Sexual Interest and Activity

Unfortunately, getting accurate information about sexual interest and activity is
difficult. Researchers must convince people to answer questions about this
normally most private topic. Those who do agree to discuss their sexual practices and feelings, as with Masters and Johnson's subjects, are almost certain to
be a more uninhibited fraction of their cohort. Furthermore, the temptation
to be less than truthful about this emotion-laden topic seems strong. Not only is
being open with strangers embarrassing, it can be upsetting to be totally honest
with oneself. These problems are magnified when a researcher is studying older
people (Botwinick, 1978). Here the prohibitions against discussing sex are most
ingrained and intense. We might expect even more pressure to minimize or
exaggerate the truth in order to try to dispel or conform to stereotypes about
how older people should behave. With these cautions in mind, let's turn to the
insights three large-scale studies that have probed this difficult topic have
revealed.

The only comprehensive national survey that has been done of sexuality in
later life was sponsored by a surprising organization, Consumers Union. In the
late 1970s every *Consumer Reports* subscriber over age 50 was sent a question-

naire covering sexual practices, feelings, and capacities. Because people were encouraged to write paragraphs about their personal experiences, the book describing this survey is the opposite of a dry statistical report: it is a compelling account of both the problems and the rich sexual potential that exists in later life (Brecher & Consumers Report Book Editors, 1985, see also Recommended Readings).

The CU survey exploded the idea that older people are asexual. A passionate sex life was flourishing among many respondents, including people in their 80s and 90s, golden anniversary couples, and even some respondents with daunting physical impediments to having intercourse. However, as a study of the sexual practices of "average older Americans," it has severe shortcomings. Not only are *Consumer Reports* subscribers as a whole quite liberal, those who spent the hours needed to fill out the questionnaires are probably an especially sexually liberated group. So to validate the results of this study, we need other investigations, those exploring the experience of more representative older adults. Ideally these studies should be longitudinal, so that rather than relying on the distortions memory can produce, we can directly measure how sexual feelings and behavior change over time. Luckily we have that research—the two Duke Longitudinal Studies and the Baltimore Longitudinal Study of Aging.

As part of a psychiatric interview, the Duke study volunteers were asked to estimate the frequency with which they had intercourse or, if they had stopped having sexual relations, to say when and explain why. They also were instructed to rate the intensity of their interest in sex and compare it with the strength of their feelings in the past. Since 1967 the Baltimore men have also been questioned about their sexual activities as they return over the years. By combining these studies with the CU data, we do get fairly reliable information about sexual practices and how they change in middle and later life (see Martin, 1981; Newman & Nichols, 1960; Pfeiffer, Verwoerdt, & Wang, 1968; Verwoerdt, Pfeiffer, & Wang, 1969).

The first way sexual interest and activity change is predictable. As both men and women age, all three studies show that both gradually decline. Interestingly, however, the Duke study suggests that the decade of the 70s may be a sexual watershed for men. About three-fourths of the Duke respondents in their 60s reported having sexual intercourse and an even higher proportion said they still had sexual feelings to a mild degree. In their 70s, however, most reported giving up intercourse. The number reporting a high or moderate sex drive also declined dramatically over these 10 years. By their 80s and 90s, about four-fifths of the men no longer engaged in intercourse. However, even at this advanced age, half said they still had sexual feelings to some extent.

Because their study was longitudinal, the Duke researchers could measure just how universal this pattern of decline is. Are all men really fated to become less sexual in later life? Looking at individual subjects over a 3-year period they discovered that sexual loss is far from inevitable. A full 20% of the elderly men actually reported *more* interest in sex and more frequent activity at least over this short period.

Is the decline that men normally experience a terrible psychological blow?

According to the Baltimore study, the answer is no. When the NIA researchers asked their older male volunteers if they would prefer having their youthful sexual vigor restored, only a minority, 33%, said yes. Among the 88 men (2 out of 5) aged 65 to 79 who reported being less than fully potent, only 10% were bothered enough by their problem to seek medical advice. So, if we can generalize from this upper-middle-class group of men, age-related sexual loss is far from the emotional tragedy for older men we expect it to be when we are young.

The studies reveal a second striking fact. At every comparable age, women report much less sexual interest and activity than men. In the Duke study, this male/female disparity, while always great, was astonishingly pronounced among people in their late 60s. Almost three in four of the men in this age group said they had sexual feelings; only one in five of the women did.

These differences may be due partly to response style. For cultural reasons we might expect males to exaggerate the presence of sexual feelings, females to underreport the extent. However, the fact that these gender differences were present and also marked among the more liberated CU women, suggests that they are valid. And, when we look at the different impact the environment has on sexuality among men and women, we can understand why they should exist.

Factors Affecting Sexuality in Later Life

Because some people stay sexually interested and active into their 90s while others give up sex at an early age, the Baltimore and Duke researchers decided to explore what factors predict these marked individual differences (Martin, 1981; Pfeiffer & Davis, 1972). Among the variety of variables they explored for both men and women, one stood out: People who reported being highly sexually active in the present said they were very sexually active in their youth. So, provided we can accept the validity of these retrospective reports, here, too, we see how continuity powerfully shapes our life. One key to predicting our sexual future lies in looking at our sexual present and past. Unfortunately, if we are female, the externals of our future are important, too—specifically, whether we have a partner.

The Duke researchers found that the only factor predicting continued sexual activity for women, other than age and past sexual enjoyment, was marital status. More than 40% of the married Duke women over 65 said they were sexually active. Only 4% of the large group of single and widowed Duke women said they were. In contrast, 82% of the elderly Duke men without a wife said they were still having intercourse—a figure even higher than that of the married volunteers!

So, even though their physiological capacities decline less, social factors conspire to make sexual loss a more predictable fact of life for women as they age. Not only are many middle-aged and elderly women widowed, but they are often barred from having sexual intercourse outside of marriage by the scarcity of available men and, at least for this cohort, an upbringing that stressed that extramarital sex was wrong. Just as important, they are limited by that important perception our society shares: older women are not desirable sexual partners. Specifically, we no longer see women as sexually attractive when they begin to show clear physical signs of age, usually in their 40s. For men, however, sexual desirability is more tied to power or status, so if anything, it increases after midlife. It is only when retirement signals that a man has lost this key to his attractiveness, or genuine physical frailty strikes, that our society begins to see older males as a poor sexual choice (Block, Davidson, & Grambs, 1981).

Aging women do compensate somewhat for the lack of a partner by increasing the frequency of masturbating (Brecher & Consumer Reports Book Editors, 1985; Christenson & Gagnon, 1965). However, another adaptation many may make is to simply lose interest in sex. So, as with any behavior that is not reinforced, sexual desire fades as women age.

Not only does a partner's absence play an important role in an older woman's sexuality, his presence does, too. When the Duke researchers (Pfeiffer et al., 1968) questioned eight elderly married couples in their study who had stopped having intercourse about their reasons for doing so, the couples' overwhelming response was that the man was the cause: six couples agreed that the husband was responsible; one couple blamed the wife; and the final couple disagreed, each taking responsibility.

Even for married couples who continue to have intercourse, the husband seems to set the sexual pattern and rate. When Cornelia Christenson and John Gagnon (1965) asked older married women to estimate how often they had intercourse and then looked at their answers in the context of whether their husbands were older, younger, or the same age, at every age the women with younger husbands reported having intercourse most frequently; those with older husbands, the least. We might argue that more sexually liberated women, those most inclined to be sexually active, are more likely to flout convention by choosing younger spouses. However, these results are more reasonably viewed in the simpler way: A women's sexual activity depends on her partner because— particularly in this cohort—the man is the one who tends to initiate sex. So, if a woman wants a highly active sex life, it may be better (at least in the abstract) for her to choose a younger mate.

This study also illustrates why at every age on the average women are less sexually active than men. Women usually marry, and so have their sexual activity dictated by older men (Newman & Nichols, 1960). And it helps us understand why in the Duke study the male/female disparity in sexuality was especially pronounced in the late 60s. The Duke study women in their late 60s probably often had husbands in their 70s, at the very age when sexual relations often stopped. But why were the 70s such a crucially important decade sexually for the Duke study men? This brings us to a second influence the researchers found was important to male sexuality, health.

In the Duke study, for men (but not women), both self-reports of good health and more objective indexes were correlated with continued sexual interest and activity. Because chronic diseases become especially prevalent in the 70s, illness may be the reason that many men in the study reported giving up sex during this decade. When we look at the reasons for male sexual dysfunction or impotence, we can see why illness has an especially profound effect on male sexuality.

Illness and Sexual Function

It is normal for a man to slow down sexuality as he ages but still be able to have intercourse. However, as our discussion of sexual activity clearly suggests, there is some truth to the stereotype. **Erectile dysfunction**—or the chronic inability to have an erection full enough for intercourse—does become a more common problem as men age. While psychological factors may be important, too, genuine physical reasons are often responsible. The normal age-related slowing down is compounded by medical problems that also inhibit the delicate erection mechanism.

An erection occurs when the intricate web of blood vessels and blood-containing chambers in the penis become engorged. The blood flow into and out of the penis is regulated by hormones, nerves, and tiny valves. A variety of age-related conditions may impair this process and so contribute to impotence: disorders affecting the blood vessels (arteriosclerosis, high blood pressure, diabetes); operations done in the pelvic area (bladder, prostate, or rectum surgery); injuries to the pelvic region and spine; diseases such as kidney ailments or multiple sclerosis.

Being ill may affect a man's sexual performance in a more circuitous way: the drugs given for a particular chronic illness may have sexual side effects. Medications taken for common late-life problems such as high blood pressure, arteriosclerosis, heart conditions, or depression often either affect a man's capacity to have an erection or inhibit desire.

Feeling sick can also have an indirect impact on sexuality, making any older person—either male or female—too tired, listless, or depressed to be interested in sex. There is the sometimes important element of fear, the idea that sexual excitement is "too taxing" and can lead to sudden death. This anxiety is especially common in connection with the top-ranking chronic illness among older men, heart disease.

When researchers questioned a group of people 11 months after each had a heart attack, most reported dramatically cutting down the frequency of intercourse (Bloch, Maeder, & Haissly, 1975). The researchers found that the major cause for the decrease was emotional, not physical. The person was either depressed, frightened of a relapse, or terrified of having another heart attack during sex.

The fear that intercourse causes a heart attack prevents people with a heart condition and their partners from fully enjoying sex (Corby & Solnick, 1980). However, though examples of this fate have captured our imagination, documented cases of people actually having heart attacks during intercourse are rare (Butler & Lewis, 1973). A general rule is that if a person with heart disease can comfortably climb a few flights of stairs or take a brisk walk around the block, he or she can safely resume having normal sex (Corby & Solnick, 1980).

Interventions

As the Baltimore study suggests, not all older people care about sexual loss or are interested in having a more active sex life. To decide that *every* older person should be interested in sex is just as limiting as to assume the opposite—that older people are asexual. However, because the barriers *against* being sexual in later life are especially intense, strategies to promote sexual fulfillment among older people have a special appeal. Since these barriers are both physical (mainly for men) and social (mainly for women) let's take a look at interventions to enhance sexuality in each category.

Enhancing Physiological Responsiveness.   While there are emotional reasons why older men are unable to get erections, in this age group the physical reasons loom large. However, tremendous advances have been made in treating even cases of impotence that have a clear medical cause. There are now erection-improving medications. If the problem is related to the blood vessels regulating blood flow into and out of the penis, surgery may help. Even when the person's condition cannot be cured or helped, there are solutions. Prosthetic devices can be surgically inserted in the penis to artificially produce an erection. These devices, called *penile implants,* allow men who are otherwise incapable to still be able to engage in intercourse.

None of these treatments are panaceas. They vary in effectiveness. They may produce unwanted complications. Still, depending on the cause of the man's problem, they may help a great deal.

Also, behavioral interventions can be surprisingly helpful at enhancing physiological responsiveness, too. In one study (Solnick, 1978), men aged 45 to 55 were given training in fantasizing with erotic stimuli. Half got immediate information about their erectile responses during the training sessions via a device attached to the penis; the other half did not get this direct feedback. At the end of the study both groups showed significant gains in the rapidity with which they achieved erections. They also reported increases in the average amount of time they spent having erotic daydreams and in their frequency of intercourse. Even though not statistically significant, the gains were especially pronounced for the men in the direct feedback group. So, even in the sexual arena of life, practice—or exercise—may be able to slow or reverse losses supposedly intrinsic to age!

Changing Society's Attitudes.   While it is important to educate everyone to have more tolerant attitudes toward sexuality among the elderly, a good place to start any reeducation program is with nurses. Nurses are often highly involved with older people. They have a good deal of control over expressions of sexuality in hospitalized or institutionalized older adults. The importance of offering this training—and making it more than intellectual—is evident in the following observations. In one study at a nursing home, researchers noticed that while the nursing staff expressed very positive feelings about the rights of older people to sexual expression, their actions spoke differently. When an elderly couple living at the home escaped and got a room at a motel, the nurses, agitated, immediately wanted to call the police to get them back (Wasow & Loeb, 1978).

To change this ingrained emotional response, one nurse (Monea, 1978) used an experiential teaching technique. She told her students to close their eyes and fantasize that they were a disabled older person. They were asked to imagine how the illness affected their sexuality and how caretakers would respond. Then, still with their eyes closed, they were given clay and told to sculpt it into an image reflecting their feelings. Next, they opened their eyes, wrote down a description of the sculpture, and chose partners for a 10-minute discussion of the experience. Finally, they met as a group to explore the feelings the exercise provoked. While no formal evaluation has been done of its effectiveness, learning experiences such as these—combined with the concrete facts discussed in this chapter—do seem to be making a dent in the deep-rooted feelings shared not just by health care workers but by many of us, that sexuality in old age is unnatural or wrong.

KEY TERMS

Interiority   Personality stability
Ego energy   Neuroticism
Mastery style   Extraversion
Parental imperative   Openness to experience
Disengagement theory   On-time or off-time events
Activity theory   Erectile dysfunction

RECOMMENDED READINGS

Brecher, E. M., & Consumer Reports Book Editors. (1985). *Love, sex, and aging*. Boston: Little Brown. Findings about sexuality (and love and marital happiness) enriched by general information on age changes in sexuality, concrete advice on treating sexual problems, and wonderful personal vignettes. A fascinating book! Not difficult.

Costa, P. T., & McCrae, R. R. (1984). Concurrent validation after 20 years: The implications of personality stability for its assessment. In N. W. Shock, R. G. Greulich, R. Andres, D. Arenberg, P. T. Costa, E. G. Lakatta, & J. D. Tobin (Eds.), *Normal human aging: The Baltimore longitudinal study of aging* (NIH Publication No. 84–2450). Washington, D.C.: U.S. Public Health Service. Article summarizing Costa's research on personality and his argument for stability. Moderately difficult.

Maas, H. & Kuypers, J. A. (1975). *From thirty to seventy: A forty-year study of adult life styles and personality*. San Francisco: Jossey-Bass. The study of personality consistency and change spanning 40 years. Interesting reading for case descriptions and methodology. Moderately difficult.

Neugarten, B. L., & Associates (Eds). (1964). *Personality in middle and late life*. New York: Atherton. The landmark Kansas City studies of personality. Includes a detailed account of the concept of interiority. Moderately difficult.

Chapter 8

□

The Family

□

Older Married Couples
- The Marital-Quality Studies
- Elderly New Lovers and New Marrieds

Adult Children/Elderly Parents
- Quantity Does Not Mean Quality
- Caring for an Ill Parent
- Interventions

Grandparents
- Grandparenting Styles
- Interventions

Key Terms

Recommended Readings

At age 84 Teresa Fuentes's father had a minor stroke. While he argued that he was perfectly capable of handling life on his own, his daughter knew otherwise. She had seen how he had aged on her last visit to Arizona. Could he still handle living all by himself? What about the future? Even a healthy man in his 80s needed a family close by. She determined to move him to Boston so she could monitor what was going on.

Teresa wanted her father to move into the spare room that had been her daughter Rosa's. But he was so resistant to giving up his independence she agreed to his moving into a small apartment around the corner from her house. After her father's second stroke she knew she had made the right choice. He could barely walk; he needed help dressing and bathing. She had to do his shopping and check up on him several times a day. Her brother did what he could, but she knew the responsibility was hers. That was the price of being the daughter in the family.

Teresa loved her father deeply. Still, caring for him was a strain. Rosa was going to law school. She had promised her daughter that she would take care of the children from 10 to 2 four days a week. She didn't want to let Rosa down to care for her father. And she enjoyed those hours she spent with Manuel and Marco so much. At 55 she was young enough to really be an active grandmother. Still, it was sometimes totally exhausting chasing those rambunctious twins around!

Her mixed emotions were upsetting. Why couldn't she feel better about her responsibility? Didn't it show a moral deficiency? She kept telling herself that her mother would have felt differently. Her parents had taken her grandmother in without a thought. But she could not help getting angry and resentful. When her father's illness made canceling a cruise she and José had looked forward to for months necessary, she silently fumed for days.

Caring for her father also took away from her time spent with José. Although José was nearing retirement, he still worked more than a 40-hour week. She had an awful premonition about his worsening emphysema that made their hours together too precious to waste. She was so lucky in her marriage—the highlight of her life. Rather than growing apart, especially since the children left the house, their marriage was stronger than ever before. They shared the same interests and life outlook and by now could finish one another's thoughts. After 32 years, Teresa's heart still burst with happiness when she heard José at the door.

Perhaps she should be content with her good fortune—her wonderful husband, her beautiful grandchildren, and that—as is normal today—she could be in her 50s and still have a parent alive. Yet she still felt pressured and overstressed. The other day she hated herself for thinking, "Life will be much easier when Dad passes away."

■

While we might think that Teresa Fuentes should be counting her blessings, the pressures she is facing deserve our sympathy, too. During this century, demographic changes have completely altered family life.

In 1900 most people did not survive past their 50s. If both sets of parents were alive at their wedding, a bride and groom felt blessed. Today, it is rare *not* to see grandparents walking down the aisle. Even great-grandparents may be there. Four-generation families are not uncommon. Even five generations are no longer the unheard-of phenomenon they used to be (Shanas, 1984).

In 1900 children and parents did not have to negotiate being adults together for more than a fraction of life. A person in his or her 40s had only a 10% chance of having two living parents. But by 1980 the time the generations shared adulthood had expanded dramatically: 40% of Americans in their late 50s had a mother or father alive. Even witnessing the 65th birthday of a child was no longer rare: In that same census, 10% of all people over age 65 had a child who was also over age 65 (Brody, 1985).

In 1900 the odds were only one in four that a newborn would have both sets of grandparents living. Being a grandparent meant delighting in young children, if a person was lucky enough to see the third generation born. But by 1976 luck became the norm. The chances of all four grandparents being alive at a grandchild's birth had climbed to almost two in three (Aizenberg & Treas, 1985).

This historic change in the family is mainly due to the upward shift in life expectancy, particularly among the very old (Rosenwaike & Dolinsky, 1987). Another factor is also involved. During most of this century, ages at childbearing have gradually declined. What was a 30-year separation between generations in the early 1900s is closer to 20 years today (Troll, 1971). This has caused an "acceleration of the generational wheels" (Hagestad, 1985), a compression in the time it takes succeeding generations to be formed. It is estimated today that about four generations are now conceived in about the same number of years that three were conceived before (Aizenberg & Treas, 1985).

These added generations have dramatically changed the age distribution of the family, tilting it toward people in middle and later life. The decline in fertility—from 4.2 children per family in 1900 to 1.7 in 1980—has accentuated this trend, making families "older" than ever before (Aizenberg & Treas, 1985). As the family ages, the job of raising children is still centrally important but it is no longer the sole function of family life. New concerns have emerged—negotiating the decades-long empty nest phase of marriage and taking care of a frail old-old parent for years.

Sociologist Ethel Shanas has used the label "pioneers" (1984) to describe today's four-generation families. Uncharted generational relationships must be negotiated; new roles must be carved out. How does a 65-year-old daughter relate to her 90-year-old mother? What is it like to be the grandmother of a 40-year-old corporation head? How does the sterotypical image of the frail elderly grandmother fit in with a transition that now typically occurs, as in the vignette, in the vigorous mid years of a woman's life?

In this chapter we will explore the research on three of these new relationships: late-life marital partner, adult child/aging parent, and grandparent.

Understand that, in addition to omitting other relationships such as siblings, this focus on dyads does not reflect the realities of family life in another way. As we saw in the vignette, living in a family means negotiating multiple relationships simultaneously, and a person's performance in one role (for example, wife or grandmother) affects her or his behavior in all the others (Cicirelli, 1983; Kuypers & Bengtson, 1983). So, in reading this chapter keep in mind that a family is a mosaic of relationships, that it's more than the sum of its parts.

Within the last decade there has been an explosion of interest in the aging family, making family relationships one of the most heavily probed new research areas in gerontology. However, as we see in this chapter, there still are real gaps in what we know. In part, the limitations I will point out in the following sections reflect the growing pains of a very new field (Mancini, 1984). As Shanas (1980) also points out, gerontologists who study the aging family are pioneers, too.

OLDER MARRIED COUPLES

The most important fact about marriage among the elderly is that it is primarily the territory of men. In 1986 slightly more than one in three women over age 65 had a living spouse. The figure for elderly men was three in four. Among the old-old, the gender disparity was even more pronounced: two out of three men over age 75 were married; only one in four women was (U.S. Senate Special Committee on Aging, 1984).

On the other hand, today marriage for women (and men) lasts an unprecedented length of time. For couples currently marrying at the average age (age 22 for women, 25 for men), provided they do not divorce, 64% can expect their marriage to last 40 years. If we combine the first usually childless years of marriage and the empty nest period, a full one-third of this time will be spent without children. In sharp contrast, in the late 1800s the empty nest phase of marital life lasted on average only a meager 1.6 years (all these statistics are from Aizenberg & Treas, 1985).

What is today's extended empty nest phase of marriage like? How does love and marital happiness change as the years pass? To answer these questions, two types of studies have typically been done. Either couples married different lengths of time have been interviewed, or researchers have compared marital satisfaction at different phases of the "family life cycle" (for example, after the birth of the first child, after the husband's retirement).

The Marital-Quality Studies

The results of the investigations have been frustrating. Depending on the study, any of the following different trajectories have characterized marital life (see, for reviews, Ade-Ridder & Brubaker, 1983; Cole, C. L., 1984).

The first pattern, one practically all the early research showed, bleakly confirms the old jokes. Happiness peaks at the honeymoon and over the years steadily declines. Familiarity, and the pressures of child rearing, leads to disenchantment. By the time a couple reaches their 50s, what was there has usually disintegrated. Furthermore, couples never recoup what they lost. They stay locked in unhappiness, and even grow further apart as their marriage enters the retirement years. For instance, in one typical example, researchers (Blood & Wolfe, 1960) questioned 909 Detroit wives married varying lengths of time. They found a steady decline in marital satisfaction, love, and companionship over the years. In another (Pineo, 1969), 1000 couples were interviewed at the 5-, 15-, and 20-year point. The grim result was the same: increasing disenchantment over time.

On the other hand, more recent studies suggest that marital happiness has a curvilinear shape. Satisfaction does dip after the children are born, but the low is followed by an upswing. While there is controversy about when happiness levels begin to rise (see Miller, B. C., 1976), many studies put the upturn around the empty nest point. According to this newer, more positive research, couples may regain some of what they once had when they are free from the pressures of bringing up children and have the luxury of focusing on one another again.

Is this curvilinear shape just a function of the children leaving the house? The Consumers Union survey of later-life sexuality, discussed in some depth in the last chapter, suggests not. When Edward Brecher and the Consumer Reports Book Editors (1985) looked at how marital happiness differed as a function of the number of years their over-age-50 respondents were wed, they found the same dip and rise. Happiness declined gradually, reached a low ebb after about 20 years of marriage, and then began to increase. Because this sample was primarily confined to people at the empty nest or child-free stage of marriage, the CU study suggests that the important factor involved in satisfaction may not be the wedge children can drive between a couple, but a marriage's simple length.

To complicate matters even further, a few studies fit neither the **continuous decline** nor this **curvilinear model** of marital life, either revealing that marriages are characterized by "continuity," essentially stable levels of marital satisfaction over the years (Traupmann & Hatfield, 1981), or that couples are happier during later life than at *any time before.*

What are the reasons for these glaring contradictions? Answers come from examining the methodology of the studies themselves.

Problems in the Marital-Quality Research.

Because conducting longitudinal research over long spans of adult life is so difficult, practially all the studies of marital quality have been cross sectional and so may be measuring differences in cohorts rather than how marriages really change over time. If older couples do report higher levels of satisfaction than middle-aged adults, is this because marital happiness is indeed greater in old age or because this cohort of older people is reluctant to admit psychological distress (see Chapters 1 and 4)? Is this result genuine or merely an artifact, due to the fact that older samples are skewed on the positive side, since unhappy marriages are more likely to end in divorce earlier on? Furthermore, inconsistent findings are predictable because researchers have measured the global, multifaceted concept "marital happiness" in diverse, even unrelated ways. If our index of marital happiness were based on romantic love, wouldn't our results be different than those of our colleagues who measured this variable by asking questions about loyalty, commitment, or companionship? Critics have also questioned the adequacy of the measures themselves. For example, is one commonly used question to tap conjugal happiness—"How frequently do you do things together?"—really a good index of that inner emotion, satisfaction with one's husband or wife (Schram, 1979)? And comparing age groups according to any set of standard measures has another built-in difficulty. The qualities that constitute good marriages themselves may change as the years pass and a couple ages.

For instance, in a study of the impact of illness on later-life marriages, one researcher found evidence that marital happiness may indeed be qualitatively different in later life. Colleen Johnson (1985b) interviewed 76 elderly couples after either the husband or wife had been discharged from a hospital, asking respondents about how happy they were in their marriage, the amount of conflict they had, how emotionally fulfilling their relationship was. Her results echo the newer uplifting research. In spite of undergoing this stress, most couples reported low levels of conflict. The majority said they were very satisfied with their marriage. However, examining these reports more closely, Johnson was struck by the unemotional, stoic way these happy marriages were described: "We've survived 55 years of it. Today they only last 2 or 3 years." "He's been a good provider and a good father." "Long ago I realized you can't change horses in midstream." True, these couples were contented, but would these same words be used to describe a good marriage at the honeymoon stage?

To Johnson, her study suggests that the criteria involved in having a good marriage are different as the years pass. Over time, we are cemented, not by the intensity of our passion, but by the length of our history—our backlog of shared ups and downs. "The fact of a marriage's mere survival connotes success."

Finally, the problems with incomparable or inadequate measures are compounded by using incomparable subjects—confounding life-stage with marital length; lumping the vigorous young-old with the frail old-old; studying marriage among the well-off and then generalizing the results to more "average" older adults (Aizenberg & Treas, 1985). To illustrate how our answers about whether older couples are happy depends on the samples we pick, consider these two recent studies of marital quality in later life:

Robert Atchley and Sheila Miller (1983) interviewed periodically from 1975 to 1981 an almost exclusively middle-class, college-educated, young-old group of older couples who were residents of a pleasant, crime-free, close-knit Ohio community. The researchers explored happiness levels and also looked at how similar in values, interests, and goals the long-married couples really were.

Their findings were extremely heartening. A high degree of conjugal happiness was typical. The couples were also amazingly alike—on a long list of goals and favorite activities giving *identical* answers about 80% of the time. People married the longest were the most similar, giving scientific weight to the cliché, "When they're together that long, they even begin to look alike." The researchers ended their paper with this comment: "It was a genuine pleasure to be around these couples. They accepted one another fully, were obviously devoted to one another, and were very much enjoying their lives together."

In marked contrast is a study of marital happiness among a much less elite group—a random nationwide sample of older adults (Depner & Ingersol-Dayton, 1985). Here respondents were not mainly middle class, nor well educated. They also were older on average than the couples Atchley and Miller interviewed. In fact, unlike other studies of late-life marital quality, these researchers did not lump all couples over 50 or 60 together as elderly. Because they wanted to examine how the aspect of quality they were interested in—supportiveness—varied as an older couple aged, they divided their subjects into three groups: age 50–64, 65–74, and over 75.

Unhappiness was the dominant theme. The older the couple, the less emotional support, respect, and health-related support husbands and wives reported giving and getting from one another. Rather than drawing closer to one another, this investigation suggests that at the end of their lives together, husbands and wives emotionally retreat.

So while marital happiness is alive and well among the socioeconomically advantaged, distance, disappointment, and isolation seem to blight many late-life marriages, too, especially among the less well off and the old-old. The truth, of course, is that marriages differ greatly, in old age and at any other age. Some older couples are happy; others are not. For many, the years bring disenchantment; for others, they may deepen love. For instance, in questioning 72 elderly couples, researchers (Swenson & Trahaug, 1985) found that while declining satisfaction was more typical, a fraction of their respondents reported feeling an increasing sense of commitment and love over the years. These people seemed to have the type of marriage described in the vignette, one reseachers (Cuber & Harroff, 1965) labeled several decades ago in a classic study of middle-aged, long-married couples as a **vital relationship:**

> The vital pair can be easily overlooked. . . . They do the same things, publically at least, and when talking . . . they say the same things—they are proud of their homes, love their children, gripe about their jobs. . . . But when we take a close, intimate look, the vital quality of the relationship becomes clear; the mates are intensely bound together psychologically in important life matters. Their sharing and togetherness are genuine. The relationship provides the life essence for both man and woman [quoted in Belsky, 1988, p. 93].

Keeping in mind that many marriages that are happy probably do not approach this blissful ideal, let's turn to a more comprehensive exploration of that relevant question: What influences affect an older couple's odds of marital happiness? The studies above suggest that objective parameters such as socioeconomic status and chronological age may be involved. Now we explore two other candidates, one a late-life event, the other ongoing and intrinsic—illness and personality.

Illness, Personality, and Marital Quality.   It seems reasonable that illness would be the most logical late-life event to erode marital happiness. It is hard to be giving when a person's energy is consumed by aches and pains; to feel loving when one's job shifts from life companion to nurse. In fact, when illness strikes an older couple, the burden of caregiving falls on the well spouse's shoulders, even when there are grown children around. Studies agree (Cantor, 1983; Johnson, C. L., 1983; Stoller, 1983) that when a husband or a wife is alive, sons and daughters don't really step in to help. Isn't a primary reason why marital supportiveness may be at its lowest ebb among the very old likely to be illness—illness makes people turn inward; causes disengagement from relationships; diminishes not just marital happiness, but pleasure in every area of life (Larson, R., 1978)?

In fact, when Atchley and Miller (1983) examined the impact of three life changes—retirement, moving (being a recent arrival in the town), and illness—on their Ohio couples, they discovered that illness was the only stress that had a significant effect. If a husband or wife became sick, the spouse's morale declined. Interestingly, the husbands were most affected; in a way they seemed more dependent on their marriage than their wives, because their life satisfaction was utterly dependent on having a healthy spouse.

However, while illness may erode a couple's joy with one another, Colleen Johnson's study suggests that it does surprisingly little to weaken the bond between husband and wife. When she questioned her socioeconomically diverse couples separately just after one had been discharged from a hospital, few said they had any major disagreements; most felt they could firmly rely on their spouse for emotional support. While it certainly is possible that over time caring for an ill spouse might rock a marriage (see Johnson, C. L. & Catalano, 1983), particularly if the illness is Alzheimer's disease (Zarit, Todd, & Zarit, 1986; see also Chapter 10), this study stands as a testament: In the midst of this tremendous stress even average older couples are surprisingly resilient, able to close ranks, and stay firmly committed to one another.

Other research supports Johnson's findings. Even when they are quite frail themselves, when a spouse needs caregiving, both *husbands* and wives are more prone to shoulder the job alone, are less likely to rely on home care or day care than a child would be. Furthermore, spouse caregivers take on the burden with a freer heart, reporting less ambivalence, conflict, and stress than caregiving daughters or sons (Cantor, 1983; Johnson, C. L., 1983; Johnson, C. L., & Catalano, 1983). We even have evidence that being thrust into this unaccustomed role can sometimes strengthen the marital bond. In a study in which husband and wife caregivers for Alzheimer's patients were compared (Fitting, Rabins, Lucas, & Eastham, 1986) one-quarter of the men said having to nurse their wife actually intensified their commitment to the marriage and increased their feelings of closeness and love. Colleen Johnson and Joseph Catalano use the evocative term *enmeshing* to describe this phenomenon (1983). As the spouse needs more caregiving, the couple reduces outside involvements, withdraws from friends and relatives, and turns inward to the marriage to satisfy all of their needs.

This is not to say that caring for a disabled spouse isn't stressful. For instance, in one study of wives of disabled older men, researchers labeled their caregiving subjects, the "hidden patients" (Fengler & Goodrich, 1979). However, the research shows that despite the personal toll it may cause, this cohort of elderly couples takes their vows of "in sickness and in health" extremely seriously.

So here, too, we see resilience where the stereotype would predict fragility; we find older people coping in a mature way in response to stressful events. We also see support for the continuity point of view. If stability is indeed an underlying theme of adult life, then stressful events such as illness should not affect the ongoing pattern of a marriage; at the most, they might further weaken unions already on shaky ground. In fact, the importance of "outer events" on a couple's relationship should pale before the impact of that overarching internal influence: personality. That is just what the most ambitious study of marital compatibility has shown (Kelly & Conley, 1987). This study, begun more than a half century ago by psychologist Lowell Kelly, is unique—the only one to trace the course of marriages from engagement to almost the golden anniversary year.

In the late 1930s, Kelly recruited 300 couples from engagement notices in the paper, gave them a variety of personality tests, and had friends rate their emotional stability. He and his colleagues then followed these couples over a 45-year period ending in 1980.

Over the years, 22 couples broke their engagements and 50 got divorced. Another group stayed unhappily married, together "by default." Of the five classes of variables the researchers examined—personality traits, early life history, attitudes about marriage, stressful life events during the marriage, and sexual history—these failed relationships were distinguished more by the psychopathology of their participants than by *anything* else. If a man's friends rated him as high in "neuroticism" at the time of his engagement, he was likely to have marital problems. A woman rated as "neurotic" was set up for an unhappy marriage or a future divorce.

Interestingly, whether a couple stayed together and was miserable or got divorced after years of marriage turned out to be a function of the *man's* personality. Neurotic men with low "impulse control" (that is, those who were prone to act out their misery) tended to engage in behavior (such as having affairs) that would force the end of an unhappy union. If a man was neurotic but high in impulse control, he did not act on his unhappiness and so the couple tended to stay married. So, in Depression-era marriages at least, the man holds sway over a union's fate—not only do his actions initiate a marriage, they terminate it.

In sum, while not negating the fact that age, illness, or socioeconomic status may also independently have some impact, this fascinating study resoundingly confirms Costa's idea that personality (more than any extrinsic influence) seems to shape our fate. For this cohort of older couples at least, the blame for an unhappy marriage is less likely to lie in life circumstances than within the self.

Elderly New Lovers and New Marrieds

So far we have been looking at the research on long-lasting marriages, at what happens many years later when people walk down the aisle at the typical time.

BOX 8-1
Golden Anniversary Households

The celebration of a half century of marriage is an accomplishment only attained by a small fraction of newlyweds—about 3%. While the curvilinear hypothesis of marital quality suggests that couples who attain this milestone should be unusually happy, we now know that marital happiness is likely to vary greatly even among this very select group. So, rather than just measuring happiness, one researcher decided to examine the actual *content* of the relationship—how they shared the daily chores of life—of golden anniversary couples. Sociologist Timothy Brubaker (1985) combed senior centers and newspaper announcements to find people married more than 50 years. Then he asked his respondents about the division of household tasks such as cooking, cleaning, and yardwork. Would these jobs be divided rigidly according to gender or would people married this long have evolved a more fluid arrangement in handling these concrete details of their shared life?

Interestingly, "masculine" tasks still were done exclusively by the husbands. They were responsible for the finances, repairs, work on the car. But in the traditionally feminine arena the rigid gender divisions had indeed broken down. Husbands shared the cooking, the cleaning, and the shopping. They might even take over most of the housework when their wife was ill. Did these husbands also help their wives more throughout the marriage, or was their involvement new, a product of being in their retirement years? Is this willingness to shoulder some of the burden of "women's work" at all related to the fact that these marriages endured for so long? Once again, answers to these tantalizing questions depend on doing that most ambitious type of research—longitudinal studies of marital life.

□

But what is love and marriage like when they strike in the autumn years? While the literature on this question is extremely sparse, two exploratory studies offer hints.

To chart the experience of love in late life, Kristine and Richard Bulcroft drew on the membership list of a twin cities (Minneapolis/Saint Paul) singles club to find a group of elderly lovers, people who were romantically involved but not married. They interviewed their respondents, whose ages ranged from 60 to 90, and compared their responses with those of college students in love (for a popular report of this study, see Bulcroft & O'Conner-Roden, 1986).

Being older did *not* dim the symptoms of romance. The older lovers felt the same heightened sense of reality, awkwardness, heart palpatations, intense excitement, and sweaty palms as did the 20-year-olds. Nor did it weaken the lure of the trappings of romantic love. Both young and elderly lovers enjoyed candlelit dinners, long walks, flowers, and candy.

However, there *were* differences. Among the older lovers, dating was more varied. In addition to traditional activities such as going to the movies or out for pizza, older couples might go camping or even fly to Hawaii for a weekend. The involvement was also faster-paced. People said that at their age there was not much time for playing the field. There were differences in the sexual area, too. The elderly lovers seemed to have more trouble deciding whether having sex was right. Although the rules today have changed, they grew up with a system of values that said that having extramarital intercourse is always wrong. However, in spite of their awkwardness, most decided to go ahead. Sexual involvement tended to develop early and was usually a vital part of the relationship. In fact, the majority of this very select sample reported that sex was *better* in later life (keep in mind the research in the last chapter suggesting that this, unfortunately, is not typical).

There was another critical difference. Few of the elderly lovers wanted the romance to end in marriage. The women were especially reluctant, reasoning that getting married was unnecessary. They did not have the push to make a family or a life together that young people have. They were also afraid that remarrying at their age would mean being saddled with the job of nurse. Many had cared for their husbands for months during his final illness. They did not relish the thought of added years spent as caregiver to a sick spouse (see the next chapter for some similar sentiments).

To find out what happens when people do remarry after age 65, researchers (Pieper, Petkovsek, & East, 1986) interviewed elderly couples married between 1 and 6 years. Surprisingly, these newlyweds (drawn randomly from Evansville, Indiana, city marriage records) were not younger, or more socioeconomically elite than the average over-65 resident of the city. However, they were dramatically different in health. As we might expect, older people who remarry late in life are much less likely to be ill than their contemporaries.

Some of these people remarried soon after being divorced or widowed. But many had lived for years before finding a new mate. The women were most surprised at the turn their lives had taken. Half said they had been sure they would never marry again.

Among the many reasons given for remarrying, companionship stood out. People married mainly in order to have someone to travel or to do things with; falling in love ranked a distant second.

These marriages were working out. The majority of the couples agreed they were *happier* in this marriage than the first. They felt their new marriage was better because now they were more mature. And marital happiness came easier at this time of life because the stresses of child rearing and establishing a career were past.

While truly testing the idea that second marriages in later life are happier requires gathering on-the-spot data about happiness levels during the first marriage (that is, doing longitudinal research), findings from the large-scale Consumers Union survey (Brecher & Consumer Reports Book Editors, 1985) support the idea that older newlyweds are indeed unusually happy. While many of the married couples in the CU survey were contented, people married less than 5 years had the highest levels of conjugal happiness. The only group that approached them in contentment were the golden anniversary couples. In other words, the joy of falling in love and marrying seems just as intense at 70 as at 25.

ADULT CHILDREN/ELDERLY PARENTS

The same uplifting tone characterizes much (but not all) of the research on that other important pioneering relationship—aging parent and adult child. Surveys consistently show that the bleak pronouncements about children neglecting aging parents are wrong. The bond between adult children and elderly parents has not weakened appreciably over the years. Closeness, caring, and a surprising amount of contact are actually the norm (see, for reviews, Aizenberg & Treas, 1985; Cicirelli, 1983).

The main blow to what gerontologists call the **myth of family uninvolvement** was struck by Ethel Shanas in a set of cross-sectional studies she did over 20 years. In 1957, 1963, and 1975, Shanas (1979a, 1979b) examined how many times per week or month large national samples of adult children and their elderly parents visited or called one another. While we would expect the frequency of contact to have markedly declined over this period spanning the Eisenhower 1950s to the liberated 1970s, there was little change. Children still lived close to their parents, over three in four within a 30-minute drive. More than half had seen each other either that day or the one before. About four in five had visited within the past week. Far from being a nation of disembodied nuclear families, the adult child/aging parent bond turned out to be very much there.

However, Shanas did discover one important change in an external aspect of the relationship between parent and child. Over this period the proportion of children and parents who actually lived together dropped dramatically. In her 1957 survey, a third of the elderly parents and their children shared households. By 1975 the figure was only 18%. Actually, though it did accelerate during the time Shanas was doing her research, this decline in the number of intergenerational households has been a continuing one. In 1900, for instance, more than 60% of all people over age 65 lived with a child (Aizenberg & Treas, 1985).

This dramatic change in living arrangements may partly explain why the myth of family uninvolvement has been so hard to dispel. People (such as Teresa Fuentes in the vignette) remember that their grandmother or grandfather used to live with the family and leap to conclude that children are less caring and committed today. But Shanas's studies also showed that this conclusion is wrong. It is the *parent* generation that wants it that way. As was true of Teresa's father, when Shanas questioned her elderly respondents, most vigorously rejected the idea of moving in with a child. Their ideal arrangement was one Shanas called **"intimacy at a distance,"** not living together but very close by.

In fact, as we will see in the next chapter, even when they are widowed and seem to be living isolated lives, older people are reluctant to move in with an adult child (Lopata, 1973, 1979). The intensity of this aversion does vary among individuals and between ethnic groups. In one Canadian study, for instance, researchers found that even after controlling for factors such as income and number of offspring, Italian widows were more likely to be living with their children than Jewish widows were (Kausar & Wister, 1984). In the decade since Shanas did her research, this aversion seems to have softened somewhat. Polls from 1973 to 1983 have shown a steady increase in the number of people of all ages who endorse the idea of multigenerational households. Still, even here the message is that the young are not those who are barring the door. The reseacher who analyzed this data (Okraku, 1987) found acceptance of sharing a household was more unqualified among younger cohorts. In any given year there was actually a strong negative relationship between endorsing the idea of living together and respondents' age.

Furthermore, as demographers Ronda Aizenberg and Judith Treas (1985) point out, there never was a rosy time when extended families lived together for decades harmoniously. In the past, intergenerational households were always fairly rare, if for no other reason than that the high mortality rates made it unlikely that the grandparent generation would live for any length of time. Moreover, when extended families did live together, their arrangement may have been dictated as much by economic necessity as by filial love. The older generation in particular simply could not afford to live separately. As we will see in the next chapter, particularly in the decades spanning Shanas's study, expanded Social Security and retirement benefits boosted the income of the elderly tremendously. The marked drop in shared households Shanas found during this period may have been due to the fact that in succeeding years more and more of her older parents had the option to live on their own.

We may be wrong to equate living together with closer relationships, too. When researchers (Cohler & Grunebaum, 1981; see also Hagestad, 1985) interviewed and tested a large sample of three-generation Chicago families (a young adult grandchild, a middle-aged father and mother, and one aged grandparent), they found that the small number of families in which the generations shared households were actually worse off. In particular, young married daughters living with middle-aged mothers were rated more unhappy and immature. While we do not know which is the chicken and which the egg (for example, the families who lived together may have chosen to do so because they were already having more trouble handling life), this research shows that rather than signifying more harmony, relationships may actually suffer when the extended family lives together.

In fact, a central message of this fascinating study is that a certain amount of distance may be good for parents and their adult children whether they live together or not. The researchers wanted to explore what the generations talked about. So they used this technique: A set of cards was shown to each person and she or he was asked "Do you and _____ talk about this?" If the answer was yes, the interviewers then asked whether the person had given or gotten advice about the topic from the other family member. They were trying to discover what issues were "hot" topics for families. In what direction did intergenerational advice giving flow?

While advising flowed in all directions, the most frequent pattern remained the same. Whether children were 20 or 55, in relation to a parent they tended to get more advice than they gave. The exception was when the parent was widowed or in bad health. Then advice giving from both sides became more equal or reversed, the role of advisor shifting to the child. So the classic complaint adult children have—"My parents treat me as a child"—seems to have a grain of truth. Unless they become frail or needy, many parents seem to hold fast to their role of teacher no matter how old they or their children are.

Interestingly, in this study, the "hot" topics for family advising differed along sex-role lines. Fathers and grandfathers gave advice about work, education and money. Mothers and grandmothers concentrated more on interpersonal concerns, such as dating, how to relate, the importance of family and friends. But it was in these very arenas that arguments were most prone to flare up. For grandfathers and fathers, the most sensitive topics for discussion were those in their advising domain. For the women, relationships were the touchy area. Here, advising had the potential to flow fast and furious and so disagreements were most intense.

Because of this, in order to preserve family harmony and good feelings, the generations reported that they had had to develop conversational "demilitarized" zones—to *not* talk to one another too much about their concerns in emotionally charged central arenas of life. Paradoxically, keeping close meant keeping a measure of separation; knowing when to be silent; allowing the other generation the autonomy to make their own mistakes.

Quantity Does Not Mean Quality

The lesson that *more* does not necessarily mean better in elderly parent/adult child relationships was forcefully brought home when gerontologists used what they thought would be a good measure to assess family closeness—the actual amount of contact between parent and child. They repeatedly found this puzzling result: There was *no* relationship between the frequency of contact between parents and children and how close the generations felt (see, for reviews, Aizenberg & Treas, 1985; Circirelli, 1983; Mancini, 1984). Some studies even showed an inverse relationship between the flow of help between the generations and feelings of intimacy (Walker & Thompson, 1983).

Just as surprising, despite the fact that older people typically say their children are the most important people in their life, studies have repeatedly shown that elderly parents who see their offspring very often are no more content or happy than those who see their children more infrequently (Houser & Berkman, 1984; Lee & Ellithorpe, 1982; Quinn, 1983). Rather than any objective measure such as how many visits or calls, a more subjective parameter is correlated with morale: a parent's satisfaction with what his or her children are giving—that is, the older person's sense of being cared for and loved.

Why is it that the frequency of contact is such a poor indicator of intergenerational solidarity, so unrelated to morale? As I suggested in the last chapter, one reason may be that the impetus for the generations to rally around arises not just out of a positive emotion, such as the desire to be close, but out of a negative one, need. As we will see in the next section, a typical example occurs after a child is going through a divorce. In response to this crisis, researchers find that the level of intergenerational contact tends to rise dramatically (Aldous, 1985; Cherlin & Furstenberg, 1985). Parents step in, babysit frequently, and offer emotional support to their needy daughters or sons. On the other generation's side, the problem that causes children to flock around tends to be illness, a mother's or father's failing health. In fact, poor health in the oldest generation sometimes pulls even far-flung parents and children close in the most basic objective way. Demographers have now identified two types of long-distance migration among the elderly: the move away from children immediately after retirement (for instance, to a sunbelt state) made by primarily healthy middle-class young-old couples; and, as we saw in the vignette, a smaller, reverse migration often decades later to be near children when, typically in the 80s, frailty strikes (Flynn, Longino, Wiseman, & Biggar, 1985; Litwak & Longino, 1987; Longino, 1984). So, more contact does not necessarily signify a family good. It can be a sign of a family in trouble, too.

Joseph Kuypers and Vern Bengtson (1983) make a similar argument, hypothesizing that adult parent/child relationships are based on unspoken rules of waning involvement. As children grow up they need less time and attention from their parents. When children marry and have children, responsibility to their family of origin takes second place to the family they create. Kuypers and Bengtson feel that relationships are most at risk when these natural rules are breached and either the parent or child generation needs an excessive level of help; for instance, when a 30- or 50-year-old child depends on his or her parents for financial or emotional support rather than establishing an independent life; when, as in the vignette, an elderly parent becomes disabled and needs the child to devote hours to caregiving.

Caring for an Ill Parent

The fact that nursing homes are such obvious features in the North American landscape masks a hidden reality. At least twice as many severely disabled older people do not live in institutions as do. As I emphasized in Chapter 4, most of the care of these very frail older people is being provided by their families, sometimes at great personal cost (Arling & McAuley, 1984; U.S. Senate Special Committee on Aging, 1987; see Figure 8-1). Nursing home placement is something many families work strenuously to avoid. When a person has living sons or daughters it often happens as a last resort, when the older person's children simply become unable to manage caregiving (Brody, 1977).

While we give lip service to the ideal that sons and daughters should share the caregiving equally, studies show the job of caring for a frail parent usually falls to a daughter, or more rarely, daughter-in-law (Brody, 1985; Lang & Brody, 1983;

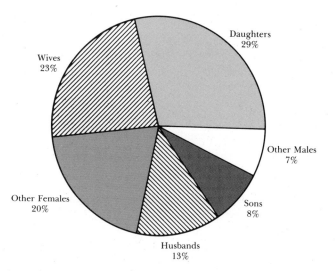

Figure 8-1. Distribution of informal caregivers by relationship
to elderly care recipient, 1982.
Source: U.S. Senate Special Committee on Aging, 1987.

Figure 8-1). These women, typically in their late 40s or 50s, face competing responsibilities. If they are late middle aged or young-old when the need for parent care arises, they may also be caring for an ill spouse. If they are in their 30s or 40s, they are likely to have children in the house. Today, with 62% of all women aged 45 to 55 and 42% aged 55 to 64 in the work force (U.S. Senate Special Committee on Aging, 1984), they are apt to have full-time jobs. Furthermore, it has been argued (Brody, 1985) that unlike any time in the past, today the job of caring for a frail parent has become a "normative event." The historic increase in the old-old coupled with declining family size has made this task one this cohort of middle-aged daughters can *expect* to assume, sometimes for years.

While it has been estimated that the fraction of women actually in this situation is way too low to deserve the word norm (Matthews, Rosenthal, & Marshall, 1986), there is no doubt that honoring the obligation to care for parents in their old age presents unusually heavy burdens for this cohort of daughters and sons. Despite the availability of services such as home and day care to lighten the load, studies agree that these formal sources of help tend to be used as adjuncts rather than substitutes (Arling & McAuley, 1984; Cantor, 1983; Johnson, C. L., & Catalano, 1983). When a parent does not have a living spouse, children, daughters in particular, continue to be the main line of defense against a nursing home.

Elaine Brody, who has devoted much of her career to exploring the pressures that these "women in the middle" face (see Box 8-2), has studied the especially heavy burdens on caregivers who work. When she and her colleagues compared employed and nonemployed daughters in this situation, they found that the women who worked provided just as much help with shopping, household tasks, and emotional support as the nonworking group, though they did hire home help more often for personal care (Brody & Schoonover, 1986). As we might imagine, particularly when a parent is severely disabled, the overload this can create may force some women to quit their jobs. Among Brody's nonrandom sample, 12% left work totally. Another 13% were conflicted, either considering leaving work or reducing their hours because of their parent's need for help (Brody, Kleban, Johnsen, Hoffman, & Schoonover, 1987). A national survey of informal caregiving done in 1982 lends Brody's findings weight. Of the more than 2.2 million family caregivers (spouses, children, and other relatives) in the United States that year, 21% of those who worked reported reducing their hours. About 9% had quit their jobs to become caregivers (U.S. Senate Special Committee on Aging, 1987).

Study after study has also documented the emotional toll that caring for an aging parent takes. Children caring for ailing parents have relatively high rates of depression and anxiety, low levels of morale (Cantor, 1983; Fischer, 1985; George & Gwyther, 1986). As Box 8-2 illustrates, they also may feel guilty, plagued by an unrealistic sense they should be feeling more loving or doing more. Moreover, rather than fostering increasing closeness, just as Kuypers and Bengtson (1983) predict, studies suggest that illness in a parent is related to poorer family relationships (Johnson, E.S., & Bursk, 1977), and increases the potential for conflict between parent and child (Cantor, 1983). Colleen Johnson and Joseph Catalano's (1983) longitudinal comparison of spouse compared to child caregivers mentioned earlier highlights this point. While the researchers found that enmeshing (that is, retreating *into* the relationship) was a common response if the caregiver was a spouse—if the caregiver was a child, the predominant reaction was a distancing one. The older person's needs and demands caused conflict, the relationship deteriorated, competing demands from family added to the friction, and the child would attempt to disengage, either separating herself from her parent emotionally by going into therapy or deciding "I've done all I can" and turning to paid sources of help.

Interventions

The research shows that while caring for an ill spouse may be somewhat less stressful, caregiving children are a group at considerable psychological risk. To ease the pressures these children in the middle face, services such as day care, home care, or respite care must be made a genuine financial option. As discussed in Chapter 4, while today formal sources of care are widely available, these services typically must be paid for out of pocket unless a person is poor enough to qualify for Medicaid. This puts children in the difficult position of either witnessing the impoverishment of a disabled parent (or of themselves!) or doing the ongoing caregiving on their own. Even if "paid for" home care or day care does not stave off institutionalization (Capitman, 1986), our discussion clearly reveals the enormous hidden price that *not* paying for this care exacts on families—in hours off of work, in emotional distress, in intergenerational discord. Society has a responsibility to explore other strategies to ease the burden

BOX 8-2
Guilt, Love, and Parent Care

Why, in spite of clear research to the contrary, does the idea that today's children are shirking their responsibility to their elderly parents remain so widespread? Elaine Brody (1985), perhaps the foremost researcher on family caregiving, argues that one reason is that, as in the vignette, people mistakenly equate the past to now. Children ignore the reality that, in the past, people didn't live on for years requiring the kind of care they do today. No matter how much they are doing for an ill mother or father, they have the nagging sense they should be doing more. Their feelings are based on a false analogy—in reality, the burden of caregiving today is much heavier than in any era before.

Not only do caregiving children feel their actions are deficient, they reproach themselves for their thoughts—berating themselves for feeling resentful, for not giving with a fully free heart. According to psychologist William Jarrett (1985) this emotion, too, is based on a mistaken idea about the good old days. Caring for elderly parents has always been a job done out of obligation as much as pure love.

In a thought-provoking article, Jarrett argues that the idea that caring for aged parents should be a labor of love is a modern one. Parent care was always an ambivalent occupation. It is only today that people are expected to feel affectionate, rarely resentful, when they assume this job. This implicit pressure to feel an emotionally "correct" way compounds the pressure today's caregiving children face. They torture themselves about not loving as much as they should because they believe in an emotional standard no one ever had.

Historical investigations support Jarrett's point. Mixed emotions about caring for elderly parents is far from a "moral deficit" peculiar to this day and age. When Teri Premo (1984–1985) analyzed writings from late 18th-century America, she found some surprisingly contemporary themes. Two centuries ago in the United States caregiving was also assumed to be the job of daughters; then, like now, women accepted this responsibility as their duty but felt considerable ambivalence. For instance, note the echoes of today's "woman in the middle" in this lament of a daughter when her aging mother developed debilitating rheumatism: "But with all the personal sacrifices I can possibly make . . . I cannot do for her as I wish to do while I have so many other cares" (p. 71). In fact, to understand that ambivalence about parent care is really an ageless emotion, we need turn no further than to *King Lear.*

□

on caregiving children, such as paid job leave for parent care; or tax relief or special tax credits for caregivers. Most important, however, the critical national need is for formal services that are genuinely financially available—so that the job of ministering to a disabled parent for years does not fall on daughters (or sons) alone.

Once formal sources of help are within the average family's economic grasp, we would then need to educate children to *immediately* take advantage of them rather than learning by experience the emotional costs of interpreting the obligation to care for aging parents as "I have to do everything myself." However, while the thorny problem of financing chronic care still eludes us, progress is occurring in offering aid along this more emotional front.

In the past decade, counseling programs to help families caring for disabled relatives have proliferated, run by human services agencies, churches, and senior citizens organizations (Brubaker & Brubaker, 1984). The most well known is the national network of support groups for family caregivers sponsored by the Alzheimer's Disease and Related Disorders Association (see Chapter 11). There are also counselors who specialize in working with caregivers. Some mental health workers have even developed unique strategies for teaching people caring for a disabled relative problem-solving skills (Zarit, Orr, & Zarit, 1985).

Programs to help caregivers tend to serve two functions. They counteract the isolation, providing families with a place to discuss problems and get social support (via a group). Most important, they help people cope with the difficult feelings being in this situation evokes (Clark & Rakowski, 1983).

Do these programs actually work? While the testimonials are enthusiastic—people report considerable benefits from attending—the few truly scientific studies of the effectiveness of these groups have had disappointing findings. For instance, when researchers (Haley, Brown, & Levine, 1987) evaluated the impact of a support group for caregivers of dementia patients, they found that while the participants rated their experience as helpful, the support group did *not* lead to improvements on objective measures of depression, life satisfaction, social support, or coping. Perhaps it is simply unrealistic to expect that any limited intervention can make a genuine impact on the shattering trauma of caring full time for a loved one with this devastating disease. (For a fuller discussion, see Chapter 10.)

GRANDPARENTS

As is true of relationships between adjoining generations, in recent years there has been an explosion of interest in grandparenthood—a new appreciation of the importance of this life role for the family and a dramatic rise in the number of studies exploring the experience of being a grandparent. In part this may be because the high divorce rate has increased the visibility and importance of this role (Aldous, 1985). And in part this may be because researchers are finally looking beyond measures of quantity (the frequency of interaction, the number of contacts per day or week) in studying family life.

While the actual amount of contact does matter somewhat (see below), even people who report seeing their grandchildren infrequently still say that being a grandparent has vital meaning in their life (Wood & Robertson, 1978). Some experts speculate that the reason is that grandparenthood is different from practically any other role in life. Normally our value is tied to our achievements, the actual content of what we do. Grandparents are loved for a quality that far outshadows the visits or the calls, just **being there** (Hagestad, 1985).

Lillian Troll captures this quality by labeling grandparents the **"family watch-dogs"** (1983). While they normally are waiting in the wings, in a time of crisis they step in and stabilize the family as a whole. At that time their crucial value is illuminated, their shrouded importance revealed. Grandparents are the family's safety net.

Troll's belief that grandparents serve as "guardians" or "watchdogs" is supported by research on grandmothers during divorce. When comparing the amount of help a sample of midwestern parents gave to their grownup children, one researcher (Aldous, 1985) found that the extent of aid and support the parent provided varied considerably depending on the child's marital status, such as single or married, divorced with or without children. While in general parents gave less help to married offspring than to those who were single, a dramatic exception occurred when a daughter with children was divorced. Then the older generation gave much more concrete help (babysitting, helping with housework) and also provided the younger generation with more ongoing emotional support. In other words, grandparents do seem to step in during times of trouble to keep the family afloat (see also Cherlin & Furstenberg, 1985).

In a recent review, Gunhild Hagestad (1985) notes that even during calmer times there are hints that the job of family stabilizer can be an important one. She cites studies implying that grandparents can help their grandchildren indirectly by helping their children become better parents. (For example, a grandmother might help her anxious new mother/daughter by the calming words, "Relax, you're doing a great job.") Grandparents can be family mediators, helping adolescent children and their parents resolve their differences. She also adds that grandparents are often the cement that keeps the extended family close; they are the focal point for family get-togethers, one reason sisters and brothers may fly in to see one another at special times such as birthdays and holidays. As Hagestad writes, their vital "being there" quality actually has many intangible meanings:

Grandparents serve—as symbols of connectedness within and between lives;
as people who can listen and have the time to do so;
as reserves of time, help, and attention;
as links to the unknown past;
as people who are sufficiently varied, flexible, and complex to defy
easy categories and clear-cut roles [p. 48].

With the understanding that far from all grandparents fulfill these idealized functions, let's look at Hagestad's last statement in more detail. What are the varied, flexible, and complex styles of being a grandparent today?

Grandparenting Styles

The classic image of the grandmother is of a white-haired woman knitting booties by the fire—elderly, disengaged, within a few years of death. Today this image is more likely to fit great- or even great-great-grandparenthood. In an age when most women become grandmothers in their late 40s or 50s, grandmother might be more realistically portrayed in a jogging suit taking her daily run or in a suit coming home from her job (Hagestad, 1985).

As Colleen Johnson (1985a) points out, this may cause confusion, trouble reconciling the outmoded image with the reality. The reality that grandparenthood now occurs in health and relative youth may also partly explain the marked difference in tone between the newest research and studies done even a mere generation ago. Earlier research minimized the centrality of grandparenthood, suggesting that this life role has "little significance" for a majority of people (Kahana & Coe, 1969). Perhaps the new studies suggesting how important this role can be are a function of the fact that today's more vital midlife grandparents have the energy and motivation to be involved in their grandchildren's lives for years in an unprecedented way.

Actually, age is an important predictor of a person's grandparenting style. Studies agree that younger grandparents are more likely to be highly active and involved; older grandparents, those over age 65, tend to be more removed and peripherally involved (Cherlin & Furstenberg, 1985; Neugarten & Weinstein, 1964; Robertson, 1977; Thomas, J. L., 1986). One reason is that younger grandparents may have the energy to be heavily involved—to be able to play basketball with an 8-year-old grandchild or keep up with a 2-year-old for hours.

In a classic study, Bernice Neugarten and Vivian Weinstein (1964) classified this relaxed, nonauthoritarian style of relating to grandchildren as "fun seeking." It was one of several ways their middle-class sample of grandparents chose to interpret their role. "Formal grandparents" (who tended to be older) behaved in a more rigid, traditional way: not as a "friend," but definitely as an authority figure. However, they were still involved, visiting much more regularly than a third type the researchers labeled "distant figures." These were grandparents who rarely saw their grandchildren, perhaps visiting for a few hours once or twice a year. At the opposite end of the spectrum were the "surrogate parents," grandparents who assumed heavy day-to-day caretaking responsibilities. While grandmothers predominated among the surrogate parents, grandfathers were overrepresented among the last grandparenting style Neugarten and Weinstein found, the "reservoir of family wisdom," grandparents who interpreted their function as being the guardian of family history, the person who imparted information about the family's roots.

In more recent studies, researchers have either devised alternative grandparenting typologies (Robertson, 1977) or discovered that certain of Neugarten's and Weinstein's grandparenting styles are notably absent. For instance, in study-ing how grandparents related with a teenaged child, Andrew Cherlin and Frank Furstenberg (1985) found that the "fun seeking" style, a mode of relating Neu-garten and Weinstein found quite common, did not appear at all. The researchers hypothesized that this is because grandparents do not act out their role rigidly, but change the way they behave as their grandchildren grow up. "It's easy and natural for grandparents to treat toddlers as sources of leisure time fun. But no matter how deep and warm the relationship remains over time, a grandmother doesn't bounce a teenaged grandchild on her knee" (p. 100).

How do grandparents act with their teenaged grandchildren? In addition to talking, joking, and advising, Cherlin and Furstenberg's national sample (com-prised of all races and socioeconomic classes) exchanged help; some even had a large role in how the teenager was being raised. To see how involved grand-parents tend to be when their grandchildren are at this stage of life, the re-searchers developed scales to measure the amount of advising and disciplining that went on and the flow of concrete services between the grandparent and the particular teenaged child.

Interestingly, they found that a high percentage of the grandparents were quite involved. About one-fourth were classified as "detached," scoring low on the measures of closeness and also seeing the grandchild infrequently, less than twice a month over the past year. A slightly larger fraction were rated as "pas-sive," scoring low on the measures of involvement but seeing the grandchild more often. However, the group the researchers classified as "active" comprised almost half of all of these grandparents. These respondents not only exchanged help and confidences but sometimes were a real force in how that given grand-child was being raised. This is particularly heartening considering these grand-children were adolescents, when we might expect the grandparent/grandchild bond to be at one of its lowest ebbs.

Problems in Categorizing Grandparents.   Cherlin and Furstenberg were examining a grandparent's relationship with one grandchild. Might their findings have been different if they had picked another child? This brings up the point that classifying grandparents according to styles or even asking for global assessments such as "how close are you to your grandchildren?" (Kivnick, 1984) may not always be meaningful or appropriate. Grandchildren are all different. It strains common sense to think they are related to in the same way.

In fact, when they questioned their respondents about their relationships with other grandchildren, Cherlin and Furstenberg found that classifying a person as just either "active," "detached," or "passive" was indeed sometimes inaccurate. A given person's involvement sometimes varied dramatically from grandchild to grandchild. At least 30% of the respondents reported having favorites, a particu-lar grandchild or grandchildren they felt closest to. Closeness also seemed to depend on physical proximity. A grandparent was more likely to take an active role in the life of a grandchild who lived around the block than one a 6-hour plane ride away. Compatibility was also involved, how appealing or responsive a particular grandchild was. Another factor was also important—the grandparent's relationship with the generation in between.

While grandparents report that loving without having the anxieties of actually bringing up the younger generation is part of what makes this life role particularly satisfying (Robertson, 1977), this freedom from responsibility has its price. Grandparents do not have the same control over their involvement the parent generation has. A prime example is the **"norm of noninterference"** researchers agree many grandparents try to live by as a kind of golden rule: "Do not meddle in how the grandchildren are being raised" (Cherlin and Furstenberg, 1985; Johnson, C. L., 1985a). People may arrive at this golden rule of grandparenting out of experience—knowing that by violating it they risk seeing the grandchildren less often.

Grandparents are vulnerable. Their access to their grandchildren depends on the parent generation. This fact was underlined not only in Cherlin and Furstenberg's research but in another study of older grandchildren. When college students completed questionnaires about their closeness to each living grandparent, the researchers (Matthews & Sprey, 1985) found that the grandparent these young adults reported feeling closest to tended to be the one they saw most often during childhood. This person in turn was the grandparent their *parents* had the closest relationship with.

Yet there was another related finding. The grandchildren were most likely to feel closest to their maternal grandmothers and least likely to feel close to their paternal grandfathers. While age may be a bit involved (maternal grandparents are likely to be younger than paternal grandfathers), the main reason seems to be that family relationships still tend to be the woman's preserve.

While not all studies agree (Thomas, J. L., 1986), most suggest that grandparenthood is especially central to women. Grandmothers tend to be more active, more emotionally involved with their grandchildren than grandfathers are (Cherlin & Furstenberg, 1985; Neugarten & Weinstein, 1964). Furthermore, American families have what sociologists call a **"matrifocal tilt."** The generations are usually more closely knit on the mother's side. Sons separate from their parents more easily. Daughters care more about staying close. Family ties are usually stronger along maternal lines (Hagestad, 1985). So maternal grandparents are at an advantage. Because of their position as the parents of the mother, their odds of being highly involved are greater than their counterparts on the paternal side. In fact, the study just discussed underlines just how vulnerable mothers of sons really are. The researchers found that while whether a mother's mother (or father) got along with her son-in-law was unimportant, this was not true of the other grandmother. In order to have a close relationship with the grandchild she had to satisfy two requirements: not only to be close to her son but also develop close ties with his wife.

The way the matrifocal tilt of the family works against paternal grandparents is heartbreakingly evident in the situation that sometimes happens after a bitter divorce. When the wife gets custody, a son's parents may be barred from seeing their grandchildren again (Wilson & DeShane, 1982).

A fascinating study shows how after a divorce mothers of sons work hard to avoid this possibility by trying to preserve their relationships with their former daughters-in-law. In studying a middle-class sample of grandmothers, Colleen Johnson and Barbara Barer (1987) found that while 36% of the paternal grandmothers continued to see former daughters-in-law at least once a week, only 9% of the maternal grandmothers saw their former sons-in-law. In other words, to preserve their access to the grandchildren, paternal grandmothers may be unable to side wholeheartedly with their sons after a divorce. They seem to make a special effort to maintain ties with the person who usually controls that access—the custodial parent, their former daughter-in-law.

There is one benefit for these women that occurs as a consequence of the divorce. While after the divorce Johnson and Barer found that the family network of maternal grandmothers was likely to shrink because these women tended to cut off relationships with their former sons-in-law, for a paternal grandmother a child's divorce and remarriage was more likely to mean an enlargement in the number of kin. Not only had many of these women preserved their relationships with their former daughter-in-law but they added another relative when their son took a new wife.

Interventions

This discussion suggests that while the grandparent/grandchild bond is indeed often quite sturdy, grandparents need help in certain situations. The best example is after a divorce. Grandparents whose children do not have custody need safeguards to preserve their access to their grandchildren, assurance that even after the most acrimonious divorce they will still be able to visit and call. However, until recently these safeguards did not exist. Daughters (or sons) with custody were perfectly free to (and sometimes did) summarily shut their former in-laws out (Wilson & DeShane, 1982).

Passing laws in this realm has pitfalls. Shouldn't parents have the final say over their children's welfare? How much should the state intrude on a parent's prerogative to determine whom his or her child sees? However, under pressure from irate grandparents who had suffered this unhappy fate, in 1982 the House of Representatives urged the National Conference of Commissioners on Uniform State Laws to develop a model act on grandparent visitation, one that ensured noncustodial grandparents at least some rights. Today most states do have statutes giving grandparents the right to petition to see their grandchildren; however, these laws are quite diverse (Robertson, Tice, & Loeb, 1985).

In addition, because the research suggests that this life role can be so important both to grandparents and the family as a whole, attempts have been made to highlight it. Congress has proclaimed a national Grandparents' Day, now celebrated annually on the first Sunday after Labor Day. One psychiatrist, Arthur Kornhaber (1985; Kornhaber & Woodward, 1981), has established a private foundation that sponsors projects to strengthen the bonds between grandparents and grandchildren.

KEY TERMS

Continuous decline and curvilinear
   models of marital quality
Vital relationship
Myth of family uninvolvement
Intimacy at a distance

Being there
Family watchdogs
Norm of noninterference
Matrifocal tilt

RECOMMENDED READINGS

Aizenberg, R., & Treas, J. (1985). The family in late life: Psychosocial and demographic considerations. In J. E. Birren & K. W. Schaie (Eds.), *Handbook of the psychology of aging* (2nd ed). New York: Van Nostrand Reinhold. Summarizes the research on marriages and family relations in later life. Particularly good for statistics on changing demographics. Not difficult.

Bengtson, V. L., & Robertson, J. (Eds.). (1985) *Grandparenthood.* Beverly Hills, CA: Sage. Excellent collection of theoretical and research articles on grandparenthood. Highly recommended. Not difficult.

Brody, E. M. (1985). Parent care as a normative family stress. *Gerontologist, 25,* 19–29. In this Donald Kent Memorial Lecture, Brody summarizes the literature on caring for a disabled parent as well as putting forth her ideas about the difficulties this generation of caregiving daughters face. Not difficult.

Brubaker, T. H. (Ed.). (1983). *Family relationships in later life.* Beverly Hills, CA: Sage. Edited volume of articles. Includes Atchley and Miller's study of later-life marriages and Troll's famous article in which she labels grandparents as the family watchdogs. Moderately difficult.

Chapter 9

□

External Changes:
Retirement and Widowhood

□

Retirement
- The Early Retirement Norm
- The Retirement Decision
- The Consequences of Retirement
- Interventions

Widowhood
- Bereavement
- Life as a Widowed Person
- Interventions

Key Terms

Recommended Readings

José Fuentes was only 64 when he died. The year before, his emphysema had gotten so bad that he had been forced to give up his job at the mill. It was simply too exhausting to do a full day's work. Besides, he had more than enough money from Social Security, his pension, and savings to retire, and—while he did love his job—José had dreamed for years of the day he would collect his gold watch and leave to devote himself to his lifelong passion, landscape painting. José's dreams of being a professional artist had once had to yield to reality—the need to support himself and his new wife. Now he yearned to translate them into action, in this third phase of life. It would also be wonderful to have time to spend with Teresa, to revel in just being together and enjoy these last precious years.

Unfortunately, José's life as a retiree was measured in months not years. And the months were punctuated by frantic phone calls to the doctor and anxious trips to the emergency room. Most days he was too ill to paint; at the end he was too sick to even talk. Teresa was forced to serve as a full-time caretaker and suffer the pain of watching her husband approach death.

Hiring a nurse was out of the question. Teresa did not even feel she could ask Rosa to help. Rosa now had a full-time job as an attorney and was still raising two children. It would just not be fair to impose. Asking her son Tomás was out of the question—nursing was woman's work. She could not turn to her friends. Problems should stay within the family. It was out of the question to burden people who were not relatives with such intimate requests.

Teresa felt the same way after José died. She had to go it alone and not burden others with her pain. When she was with friends, she tried to be cheery. Only once, with a widowed friend, did she let herself really break down. Luckily, most people avoided any discussion of José. In the end, Teresa knew she had to come to terms with her husband's loss on her own and remake her life.

At first it didn't seem possible. She had gone straight from being a schoolgirl living with her parents to being a wife. She had never lived alone, had always depended on José for so many things, from doing the taxes to taking out the garbage. How could she even go away by herself? José had always planned their trips, checked them into the hotels. How she missed him, her closest companion and best friend! Sometimes the longing was so intense she actually felt he was beside her in the room.

During the first few months her grief was almost unbearable. Even though she knew José was dead, she kept feeling he was alive some-where. She had other strange obsessions and ideas, and at times felt she must be going mad. Gradually the frightening feelings went away, though just as she thought she was getting better, something might set her off and the longing for her husband would well up again. She was only sure she was making genuine progress when Tomás's wife gave birth to their first child. Although Teresa desperately missed José at the christening, she felt a surge of love for the baby and knew she would be all right. She even applied for a part-time job near the end of the first year and was hired! Yes, she felt she was doing well, that she could cope after all. Of course, she still found herself thinking about José 50 times a day. Her new life was satisfying but it did not make up for the gap that would never be filled. Sometimes she still felt José was physically with her, especially when she was enjoying her new hobby—landscape painting.

■

If work and love are humanity's central concerns, then the most wrenching losses that can happen to people are predictable events in later life: retirement and widowhood. Any view of the elderly is impoverished then if it doesn't focus on these tremendous changes in depth. Understanding how people adapt to retirement and widowhood will enrich our knowledge of the day-to-day lives of older people. It will underline the falsity of the stereotype that older people are rigid, emotionally fragile, and unable to cope with change. And it will also help us evaluate further the theories presented earlier in this book. As psychoanalytic theory clearly implies, are these wrenching transitions likely to cause psychological problems, decrements in physical health? What about the evidence for personality consistency and the activity versus disengagement debate? Do these dramatic tears in the outer fabric of life alter people internally? Is keeping active indeed the best way of adapting to these normal disengagements of later life?

RETIREMENT

Along with this century's dramatic rise in life expectancy has come an increase in the years we devote to life's three major activities: education, work, and retirement. Children are spending more time in school; men and women in their middle years are spending more years working; and older people are spending *much* more time in retirement. The most striking change in how we spend our life has been the evolution of retirement as a third phase of life in the United States.

At the turn of the century, life was made up of school and work. Men, with a life expectancy of 46.3 years, spent on average only 1.2 years being retired. Comprising a mere 3% of the average man's life span, retirement was a comma at the end of life. But by 1980, the average man spent 13.8 years as a retiree, a full 20% of his 69.3 years. Within these brief eight decades not only has retirement evolved into a genuine life-stage, men who retire today can expect to spend more time being retired than they did in school (U.S. Senate Special Committee on Aging, 1984).

Two influences have shaped the emergence of retirement as a U.S. institution:

the lure of being able to live without collecting a paycheck, and the prod of mandatory retirement laws.

The Social Security Act of 1935 made leaving work at age 65 a financial possibility. However, retirement only became a *palatable* economic option for many older workers about 20 years ago. From 1968 to 1971 Congress raised Social Security benefits by 43% while prices increased by only 27%. In 1972 benefits were increased by another 20%. During the decade of the 1970s pension plans also proliferated. At the same time special programs and tax breaks were instituted to boost the economic status of the elderly, increasing the lure of retirement (U.S. Senate Special Committee on Aging, 1987).

However, retirement also has become a U.S. fact of life by force. As small family businesses prospered and grew into large firms, employers had to build in a way for younger workers to advance and to gracefully get rid of older ones who were too expensive or could no longer perform. Their solution was usually to institute company policies mandating compulsory retirement by age 65. (In 1978 Congress passed the Amended Age Discrimination in Employment Act, which put a stop to this practice, making most compulsory retirement before age 70 illegal.)

The fact that retirement is now a firmly entrenched life-stage does not mean, however, that we believe it's a pleasant transition. The idea still lingers that being retired is bad for people both emotionally and physically. Because, particularly for men, work is supposed to be a central, self-defining activity, retirement is still fraught with overtones of being discarded, deprived of membership in adult society. This loss of status, coupled with enforced inactivity, is thought to produce illness and hasten death. These dire predictions are not just popular stereotypes. Consider this recent professional pronouncement by the American Medical Association's Committee on Aging:

> This condition—enforced idleness—robs those affected of the will to live full, rounded lives, deprives them of opportunities for compelling physical and mental activity, and encourages atrophy and decay. It robs the worker of his initiative and independence. It narrows physical and mental horizons. Compulsory retirement on the basis of age will impair the health of many individuals whose job represents a major source of status, creative satisfaction and social relationships or self-respect [quoted in Lazarus & Lauer, 1986, p. 48].

In contrast to this belief is that of retirement as liberation, a healthful and happy reprieve from the stress of having to work. This idea of retirement as a desired and desirable event is becoming well publicized as the debate has raged over cutting Social Security benefits. Suddenly we are aware that most young and older workers look forward to retiring with joy, not dread. Now advocates for the elderly are arguing that delaying the retirement age will increase mortality!

Before exploring the truth of these competing conceptions we need to understand an important fact about this third life-stage—typically, it no longer starts at age 65.

The Early Retirement Norm

While we still think of 65 as the age at which people normally retire, over the years the average retirement age has actually been inching down. A 1978 Harris

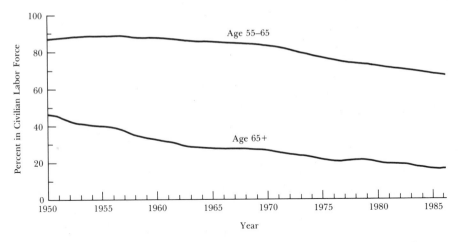

Figure 9-1. Labor force participation of older men by age, 1950–1986.
Source: U.S. Senate Special Committee on Aging, 1987.

poll underlined just how wide of the mark our traditional marker, 65, is. Almost two out of three of the retirees Harris and his associates polled had left work before this age; the *true* average U.S. retirement age turned out to be 60.6 (as reported in Foner & Schwab, 1981).

Figure 9-1 shows this downward drift in a more differentiated way. Since 1950, labor force participation rates among older male workers (aged 55–64) have declined precipitously—from 88% to 64%. Not only are more people retiring in their late 50s and early 60s, many fewer are working past age 65. For instance, in 1950 about half of all men still worked beyond the traditional retirement age; by 1970, one in four; by 1986, only about one in six. (While this trend to retire early also applies to women, because of their historic entry into the work force during the past two decades, the actual proportion of women aged 55 to 64 who worked in 1986 was much higher than it had been in 1950, 42% versus 27%.)

What is responsible for the early retirement trend? We can get answers from examining the complex influences prompting the decision to stop working.

The Retirement Decision

The most accurate information gerontologists currently have on why U.S. workers decide to retire, and the impact of that decision on their finances and physical and mental health, is from a synthesis of the results of seven of the "best" studies of U.S. retirement done within the past 25 years (Palmore, Burchett, Fillenbaum, George, & Wallman, 1985). A Duke University research team headed by Erdman Palmore carefully chose a handful from the hundreds of studies conducted on this life transition to analyze. The investigations had to satisfy a rigorous set of scientific criteria: be longitudinal; be based on large, nationally representative samples; be methodologically and statistically sound; use several

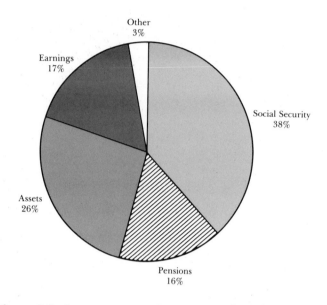

Figure 9-2. Income sources of people aged 65 and older, 1986.
Source: U.S. Senate Special Committee on Aging, 1987.

definitions of retirement; and measure this important life event in a differenti-ated way—comparing the experiences of men and women, Whites and Blacks, middle- and working-class subjects, involuntary and voluntary retirees, and people who retired early and late.

The reasons people choose to retire or keep working turn out to vary greatly. One component of the decision is financial—whether the person has enough income to live without a salary. Some people are pushed out of the job market by subtle pressures on them to retire or by mandatory retirement rules. Others leave work due to a more internal pressure, poor health. Another important aspect of the decision is psychological—how much people like their job, their commit-ment to the "work ethic," and the extent to which they have prepared for this new life-stage. As the vignette suggests, several of these influences often operate simultaneously to propel people either to leave work or stay on the job. We will examine each separately.

Financial Influences on Retirement Decisions.   The availability of Social Security provides the primary financial impetus allowing people to retire. Social Security benefits constitute the average retiree's major and sometimes sole source of income (see Figure 9-2). People pay into the Social Security system during their working years and then get benefits when they leave the work force at age 65. Over the years there has been a marked expansion in Social Security: benefit levels have risen; the categories of eligible recipients have increased; and the age for collecting partial benefits has been lowered.

Today, a person retiring at age 62 can collect 80% of the benefits he or she would get at age 65. This fact alone partially accounts for the shift to early retirement. Also, Social Security recipients between 65 and 70 who work are penalized if they earn over a certain amount. They have to forfeit some or all of their benefits depending on the amount of income they earn.

However, the Social Security system also contains incentives to discourage retirement. A person over age 70 who works can earn an unlimited amount and still collect all of his or her benefits. A worker who delays receiving benefits until after age 65 receives a bonus for each year he or she delays. And, in an effort to keep the Social Security system solvent by slowing the retirement movement, major modifications in the Social Security Act were passed in 1983. Now workers between age 65 and 70 can keep more of their benefits; the yearly bonus for retiring late has been raised from a former 3% to 8%; and the fraction of benefits awarded at age 62 will be gradually reduced from 80% to 70% by 2022. The most controversial change is a gradual increase in the age for collecting full Social Security benefits, from 65 to 67 by 2027.

Will these efforts to tinker with our nation's financial retirement cornerstone really delay retirement? Not appreciably, according to a 1983 study conducted by the National Commission for Employment Policy (U.S. Senate Special Committee on Aging, 1987). The commission calculated that delaying the age for collecting full Social Security benefits would only raise the current retirement age by about 3 months. The other incentives to keep people working described above will have the same minimal effect. Today, other influences are more important in motivating retirement than Social Security. While Social Security revved up the retirement engine, that engine now is also fueled by other sources.

One other financial fuel is the widespread availability of pensions. For example, in 1984 about one in three elderly households was receiving income from a pension (U.S. Senate Special Committee on Aging, 1984). Tax breaks favoring the elderly and government programs (such as Medicare) have also helped fuel the retirement drive by making leaving work increasingly possible economically.

That adequate finances is an important component of the decision to retire is obliquely shown by the Duke team's finding that people with dependents (that is, children under 18) are more likely to retire late. In a similar vein, having a job covered by a pension is a strong predictor of early retirement. In fact, the Duke researchers concluded that having adequate income to live without working is a central motivating force for early retirees, because they are not retiring at the "expected" age. They have to actively *decide* to leave the job.

But, why is *taking* the financial option to retire early so compelling? This brings us to another crucial influence fueling the retirement drive: attitude.

Attitudinal Influences on Retirement Decisions.　Retirement was once symbolic of the end of life. Able-bodied men collected a paycheck. Retirement was when a person was put out to pasture because he could no longer perform. As people became able to retire in relative economic comfort, the emotional connotations attached to retirement changed. The pasture began to look greener and greener. From a tragedy, retirement was transformed into the time of life people were working *for.*

For the past two decades, this new attitude has been the dominant one. As in the vignette, surveys show that the majority of U.S. workers look forward to retirement. Even people who love their jobs vote yes to the idea of eventually not having to work (Fillenbaum, 1971; Glamser, 1976). But looking forward to the idea of retiring in the future is very different than giving up an activity that has filled a person's life for all of adulthood. Why does it seem to be so easy for so many people to actually take the step early on?

One reason may be that—as in the vignette—people begin emotionally preparing for this life transition even much earlier. In a longitudinal study of 816 Boston-area men, what had been the conventional wisdom—that workers don't really plan for retirement—was stood on its head. In contrast to previous studies that measured retirement preparation by formal indexes such as attendance at company-sponsored retirement seminars, in this investigation the researchers (Evans, Ekerdt, & Bosse, 1985) focused on more informal signs: How often did a man discuss retirement with his wife, relatives, or retired friends? How often did he read articles about retirement? While the intensity of all of these types of preparation increased in a linear way as retirement time approached, the researchers found that even men who saw leaving work as a good 15 years away still did a good deal of informal planning for their retirement life.

Sociologists call this process of internal rehearsal for an impending new role **anticipatory socialization.** Not only may anticipatory socialization help postretirement adjustment, it may also explain why so many people are so willing to retire. They are primed for the step because they have been rehearsing in fantasy for retirement for years.

We might argue, though, that this cohort of male retirees in particular should react more negatively than they do when actually faced with the prospect of losing this traditionally central male role. As retirement day looms close, why aren't more of them more upset?

One explanation serves as a kind of validation of David Gutmann's beleaguered theory about midlife sex-role shifts (see Chapter 7). If men do become less interested in outer-world achievement and become more concerned with home-oriented, traditionally feminine values as they reach late middle age, the leap to retire makes emotional sense. By retirement age the thrill of the trappings of success has dimmed; work is not as important psychologically, it is no longer the bedrock of a man's identity.

A fascinating study supports this idea, though because it is cross sectional it can only suggest that there is indeed an age-related shift in the emotional importance of work for men. The researcher (Cohn, 1979) asked men of different ages about the degree of intrinsic satisfaction they got from work. He then correlated their answers with a measure of morale. While he found that as many older as younger workers enjoyed their work, only for the younger men was work satisfaction correlated with life satisfaction. For the older men the two were unrelated. In other words, though men may get just as much pleasure as ever from working as they get older, the psychological centrality of the work role does seem to decline with age; as retirement age draws nearer, being happy in work is no longer central to being a happy human being.

However, as retirement researcher David Ekerdt (1986) argues, the work ethic may not be so easily discarded; the terror of *just* relaxing persists. So, to make retirement a fully palatable option psychologically, he feels Americans have evolved a new national retirement ethic that stresses "busyness." By "keeping as busy and involved as ever," retirees prove that they have not been put out to pasture, that they are not "over the hill." In other words, Ekerdt's interesting hypothesis is that in order to fully embrace retirement, we as a nation have had to imbue leisure with the identical connotations of productivity as work. (If this fascinating observation that a **busy ethic** permeates retirement is accurate, we can also see it in a different framework, as yet another sign that personality stability strongly shapes our life. In the service of maintaining continuity, we pattern our orientation to retirement on the working years that went before.)

However, in spite of retirement becoming more desirable, far from every worker leaps to leave his or her job. Many people view this third life-stage not with longing but dread. Who are the reluctant retirees?

The Duke team found that people with more attractive jobs (that is, well-educated, self-employed professionals), were more likely to retire late. People with less desirable jobs with pensions (that is, workers in core industries) were most likely to leave work before age 65. In other words, as we might expect, liking or disliking one's job is an important factor in the retirement decision, too, particularly among people for whom retiring involves making an active decision, early or late retirees.

Health Influences on Retirement.   We might imagine that poor health would be another common reason for retiring at any age. Interestingly, however, in contrast to earlier studies, the Duke analyses showed that health problems were only an important predictor of *early* retirement. Actually, though, on deeper reflection, this finding makes sense. Influences such as poor health or a person's feelings about his or her job should be paramount in explaining retirement at a less "normal" or socially sanctioned time of life. Since at age 65, people have been conditioned to *expect* to leave work, the norm itself may explain why many workers retire at the "traditional" age. In other words, even if they are healthy and like their jobs, many people retire at 65 simply because they view leaving work at that age as the "right" or "appropriate" thing to do (see Palmore et al., 1985).

But what happens when social expectation becomes active pressure—when people are pushed out of the work force, forced to leave a job? How important is age discrimination in contributing to the retirement tide?

Age Discrimination.   Age discrimination is against the law, so its actual extent is difficult to prove. What is measurable are the variations in hiring practices when older versus younger employees are out of work.

A mid-1970s review showed that older employees are less likely to be rehired after industry layoffs. This was true not just for blue-collar workers but for people looking for high-status jobs (as reported in Sheppard, 1976). More recent statistics suggest that the situation has not changed. It typically takes older unemployed workers almost twice as long to find new jobs as those who are starting out. According to 1986 figures, while job seekers aged 20 to 24 were out of work an average of 13 weeks, the mean duration of unemployment for those aged 55 to 64 was a full 24 (U.S. Senate Special Committee on Aging, 1987).

The *official* unemployment figures for older people are low. But some experts (Robinson, Coberly, & Paul, 1985) believe that these statistics severely minimize the gravity of the problem because they measure only people actively seeking work. Many out-of-work older people may get discouraged, abandon the job search, and opt for early retirement. These reviewers estimate that unemployment may be the first step to early retirement for as many as one in five men.

While we do not have hard evidence on its extent, on-the-job age discrimination is probably not rare either. For instance, in a 1978 Harris poll, when people responsible for hiring and firing in a variety of industries were questioned, a full 87% agreed that it was prevalent (as reported in Tibbetts, 1979). Because today most mandatory retirement before age 70 is illegal, pressure on older workers to retire may typically take a more subtle form—depriving a person of an expected raise or promotion, stripping him or her of some responsibilities. When faced with these tactics, many older workers may "voluntarily" choose to retire to save their pride.

The extent of age discrimination in the work force may look more minor than it is because of the legal system, too. The money awarded for winning an age-discrimination suit is small, typically, the few years of salary that a worker would have earned by staying on the job until the normal retirement time. So malpractice lawyers tend to be reluctant to take on age-discrimination cases (Peter Strauss, personal communication, 1986). When a victim of even clear-cut discrimination consults a lawyer, she or he may be advised not to go to court. And taking the option of retiring a few years earlier versus wasting years in litigation can seem the practical course.

In summary, the decision to retire is motivated by a variety of forces—both internal and external, both positive and negative. Now let's turn to the consequences of that choice.

The Consequences of Retirement

What are the financial effects of not working? Is being retired good or bad for one's health? How do people adapt psychologically to this life change?

The Financial Impact of Retirement.   In 1960, one out of every three older Americans lived below the poverty line, a poverty rate twice that of younger adults. Today, due mainly to the improvements in retirement benefits discussed above, the poverty gap between older people and younger adults has narrowed considerably. For instance, in 1986, 12.4% of the elderly were living below official poverty levels. The comparable figure for people 18 to 64 was 10.8% (U.S. Senate Special Committee on Aging, 1987).

These statistics obscure the fact that people over 65 (the vast majority of whom are retired) continue to be *significantly* economically worse off (U.S. Senate

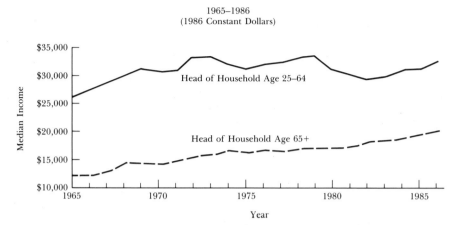

1965–1986
(1986 Constant Dollars)

Figure 9-3. Median income of older and younger families.
Source: U.S. Senate Special Committee on Aging, 1987.

Special Committee on Aging, 1987; see Figure 9-3). While boosts in Social Security have indeed helped to lift older people out of abject poverty, their income is still concentrated on the economic scale's lower rungs. For instance, in 1986 one in three elderly families had annual incomes below $15,000, compared to about one in six families headed by a 25- to 64-year-old. And the average income of an elderly family was *much* less than that of a younger family—$19,936 versus $32,368 (see Figure 9-3).

Moreover, the "encouraging" poverty comparisons are misleading because they lump together everyone over age 65. Key elderly groups—single women, minorities, the old-old—are much more likely to live below the poverty line. Also, the Census Bureau uses a lower cutoff point for determining poverty levels for older adults. In 1986, for instance, while nonelderly couples with incomes below $7,372 were considered poor, elderly couples were not defined as living in poverty unless their incomes were lower than $6,630. While (as we will see below) there is a rationale for making this distinction, this different cutoff point should be taken into account before making statements about the decline of poverty in old age.

These facts about the lower economic status of the elderly strongly imply that retiring is often a real financial blow. When they controlled for preretirement characteristcs, however, the Duke team found that this blow, while indeed significant, is much smaller than had been previously thought. After retirement, a person's income is reduced by about one-fourth.

Surveys show that this loss tends to be taken in stride. Most new retirees say their income is adequate for their needs (Foner & Schwab, 1981; Streib & Schneider, 1971). In fact, in a Harris poll conducted in 1980, people *under* retirement age reported being more bothered by not having enough income than people over 65 (Harris & Associates, 1981).

Economic reasons partly explain why retirees do not feel more financially strapped. Because of favorable tax advantages, the elderly pay a smaller portion of the income they do have in taxes than people under age 65 do. They also tend to have more assets and fewer expenses. For instance, three out of four own their own homes and 80% of these are owned "free and clear" (U.S. Senate Special Committee on Aging, 1984). Not only are the furniture, the silver, the dishes there, the *tremendous expense* of raising children is gone.

Do these advantages partially make up for losing income at retirement? One study implies that they do. Researchers (Strate & Dubnoff, 1986) analyzed the results of two community surveys in which adults varying in income, family size, and retirement status had been asked questions such as: "What would be the very smallest income you (and your family) would need to make ends meet?" "What is the highest amount of income you could have and still consider yourself poor?" In comparing how retired and nonretired people answered these questions, they found evidence that in this third life-stage we may indeed need less income. The retirees, especially retired couples, reported that they needed less money than the nonretired families of the same size to make ends meet.

Psychological factors may also explain the lack of pain. Emotionally, retirement is unlike any other economic reversal of life. The terrible jolt of being unexpectedly forced to tighten one's belt is not there. People *expect* to live on a more limited budget after they retire; plus there isn't the sense of failure that may add to the pain of earlier financial losses—being fired, investing unwisely, or having one's business fail. And, the pinch may hurt less because of another reason: the person's reference group has shifted. Many of his or her friends are in the same boat.

One study (Usui, Keil, & Durig, 1985) brings this point home, suggesting that while our wealth may indeed affect our well-being, it is wealth judged by the comparative, not the absolute, size of our pocketbook. The researchers asked 704 older people whether they felt better or worse off economically from nine people: their three closest friends, three closest neighbors, and three closest relatives. They then questioned this stratified random sample of community residents about their socioeconomic status and objective income. Finally, they related each of these indicators of wealth to a measure of morale. They discovered that even controlling for factors such as health, age, sex, and marital status, a person's financial situation was indeed correlated with life satisfaction scores—but only in a comparative way. That is, if someone reported being poorer than the people he or she was close to, that individual felt unhappy and deprived. While it certainly is possible that low morale may have colored these judgments of relative wealth, the connection may indeed go the other way—our morale is partly dependent on how rich or poor we feel vis-à-vis our family and friends.

This is not to paint the unrealistic picture that today's retirees have no problems at all (an idea often propounded to justify cutting programs such as Social Security or Medicare). Not only are the elderly on average still significantly poorer than younger adults, as I suggested, key subgroups within the older population tend to be in especially serious economic straits—women, minorities, and the old-old. Furthermore, we must remember that the growth in elderly "entitlement" programs is responsible for the economic progress that has been made. Finally, by now we should know enough to take survey data showing that retirees report that their income is "fine" with a grain of salt. This cohort of U.S. elderly has a bias against admitting pain of any kind. So, while rejoicing in the news that the financial impact of being old and retired is not as devastating as it once was, we must remember that older people are still a group at serious economic risk.

The Psychological and Physical Impact of Retirement.   The same generally encouraging picture—with some major qualifications—applies to the impact of retirement on health and morale. Contrary to the widespread fear that retirement produces depression and hastens death, the Duke team's analyses suggested that, on average, *retiring has no effect on physical or mental health!* True, the researchers did find small correlations between retirement and physical health, but their data suggested that rather than retirement causing declining health, the link probably went the other way. Declining health may have caused some workers to retire.

Considering that we spend so much of adult life working, this statistical noneffect of retirement on health and happiness seems surprising. However, these are averages. Not everyone is affected in the same way. The figures merely show that the people who are affected negatively by leaving work are canceled out by those for whom retiring *boosts* health and morale.

However, the Duke team did find that *early* retirement had negative effects. The income of early retirees dropped more sharply. In part because health problems are indeed a major reason why people leave work at this time, early retirement was also strongly associated with declining health. So, once again, the rosy statistics must be interpreted cautiously. They far from apply to all retirees. So, who does well or badly in this third life stage?

Factors Influencing Retirement Adjustment.   Being healthy and not being strapped for money seem to provide an underpinning for retirement happiness. Not unexpectedly, the Duke team found retirement smiled on people who were not sick and who had the financial resources to enjoy life. The researchers also found that people who were well educated, married, and more heavily involved in social activities tended to be happy. In fact, with the possible exception of a person's social involvement, the same factors that predict happiness as a worker seem to predict happiness as a retiree.

Another study (Reichard, Livson, & Peterson, 1962) illustrates this with regard to personality—unhappy poorly adjusted people are likely to be unhappy poorly adjusted retirees. The investigators found their sample of middle-class male retirees fit into five personality types; three were adjusting well and two were handling retirement poorly. The types were:

1. *The "mature man."* This type of man looked at the world and life realistically, was not upset about growing older, and saw life as fulfilling. His mature attitude toward living made for a happy retirement life. (Luckily, most of the retirees in this study fit into this category.)

2. *The "rocking chair man."* This type of person disliked responsibility, preferring to take a backseat. Because retirement allowed him to indulge this need,
   he, too, was happy being retired.
3. *The "armored man."* This type of person needed to be extremely busy. The
   idea of contemplating his navel—or his feelings—made him very anxious.
   Ironically, this person, too, was likely to be a happy retiree because he packed
   his leisure day frantically with activities.
4. *The "angry man."* This type of person felt he had been a failure and bitterly
   blamed the world.
5. *The "self-hating man."* This type of person was also upset about how his life
   had gone but internalized his anger, blaming himself.

With the exception of the mature men, many of whom said they had grown
emotionally as the years passed, these men reported being the same as retirees as
they had always been. The angry men and self-haters said they had been
unhappy in youth and middle age also. The armored and rocking chair men said
they had approached their working years in an identical way.

So with the *strong* caution that these findings may apply only to men and that
we can only judge the accuracy of these retrospective reports if we were to do a
longitudinal study, here, too, we see evidence that we carry ourselves with us as
we shed our work skin. Rather than retirement shaping the individual, people
seem to bend this third life era to fit who they are.

Do people find their retirement niche immediately or does it take some time to
evolve the lifestyle that emotionally fits? This brings us to a different aspect of the
retirement experience, the *process* by which people adapt.

The Adjustment Process.   More than a decade ago, Robert Atchley (1977)
offered some speculations about this shaping process, hypothesizing that retirees go through distinct stages in adjusting to this important transition of life.
Immediately after people leave work, there is a honeymoon period when everything is rosy. Retirees luxuriate in their new freedom and excitedly pack in
leisure activities. Then, a letdown sets in. Something is missing. Either the
person is doing too much and ends up exhausted or begins to feel at loose ends
without something productive to do. At this point, there is a period of reorientation, evolving realistic answers to the question: How do I want the rest of my life
to go? Finally, there is a period of stability. Retirees settle down to a predictable
routine.

These phases are idealized and theoretical, presented as a "typical progression
of processes" that may or may not fit the fluid realities of life. Interestingly, one
study using cross-sectional samples of male retirees drawn from an ongoing
longitudinal investigation, lends tantalizing support for some of their general
outlines.

David Ekerdt, Raymond Bosse, and Sue Levkoff (1985) compared the happiness, activity levels, and optimism of the men at 6-month intervals during their
first 3 retirement years. Compared to the men who were retired for less than
6 months, those who had left work 12 to 18 months previously did seem to be in

a slump: they reported fewer activities, had poorer morale, and were less optimistic about the future. As Atchley predicts, after an early euphoria, disenchantment may indeed set in. Interestingly, the researchers also found signs that Atchley may be right that people emerge from this low. While the optimism of the first months was never recaptured, among men approaching the 2-year mark after retirement, morale and activity levels were higher again. While these findings need to be confirmed by a longitudinal look at both male and female retirees, considering how difficult it is to fit human reactions into anything like predictable phases (as we will see the next section), they are fascinating indeed.

Interventions

The Ekerdt, Bosse, and Levkoff study implies that some people might benefit from preparing for retirement in a more structured way. *Realistic* preparation (instead of fantasizing) might short-circuit the letdown that people may feel at the beginning of the second retirement year. Or, bending retirement to fit a person's interests and needs might be made easier if the options open to retirees were broadened so that people could pick from a wide number of alternatives in engineering a satisfying life.

Retirement counselors or leisure counselors help fulfill this first need on an individual level, offering counseling to help people identify their interests and plan a satisfying retirement life (see Edwards, 1984). On the institutional level, many large companies now offer **preretirement programs** to their about-to-retire employees. While these company-sponsored programs can be extremely limited, offering just information about Social Security and the company's pension plan, others are more extensive. Participants are encouraged to think about and plan for all aspects of retirement.

One study (Glamser & DeJong, 1975) compared the effects of no program, a brief one, and an in-depth intervention in getting workers to really prepare for this event. Male industrial employees approaching retirement were assigned to one of three groups: eight sessions of intense discussions exploring all facets of retirement; one 30-minute session devoted to explaining retirement benefits; or no intervention. Workers in the eight-session group were stimulated to do more thinking about retirement. In contrast, the single session caused no changes. It was as ineffective as no intervention at all in getting people to systematically plan for retirement.

However, perhaps because people tend to do a good deal of planning on their own anyway and even the most ambitious company-sponsored preretirement program rarely offers more than a handful of sessions, these formal programs have not shown that they actually do enhance retirement satisfaction (Glamser, 1981). But they may serve a useful function: By offering workers realistic information about this third life-stage, they may ease their anxiety. In fact, one outcome of the study just mentioned was that workers in the eight-session group said they felt much less apprehensive about leaving work than before.

There are many efforts to broaden the kinds of opportunities available to retirees. For instance, faced with declining enrollments, many colleges are now competing for retired students, offering a variety of incentives from reductions in tuition (or no tuition) to full-blown programs for "senior citizens" or "retired professionals." Some of these programs are segregated by age: Older people who enroll take courses only with their group. Others offer a graduated entry into college life: Elderly students begin by taking special courses and then, when they feel comfortable, start taking the standard offerings at the school. In yet a third variety, older people do not take a specialized program, but are given extensive counseling and help in negotiating this unfamiliar environment (Belsky, 1988).

Opportunities for people to find fulfillment as a volunteer are also expanding, as organizations are beginning to understand what a tremendous resource our nation's legions of vital retirees are. Three of the best known volunteer programs for older people are sponsored by the federal government: The Retired Senior Volunteer program (RSVP) is by far the largest older adult volunteer program, having more than a quarter of a million participants serving on nearly 700 projects in all 50 states. People in this program can select from a variety of placements, from hospitals to prisons to schools. The Service Corps of Retired Executives (SCORE), run by the Small Business Administration, is specifically for retired businesspeople who want to use their skills helping others. Participants in this program offer assistance and guidance to small businesses in accounting, finance, advertising, marketing, taxation, and other aspects of management. Finally, the Foster Grandparent Program and the newer, less well known Senior Companion Program are *only* for low-income people. Foster grandparents serve as caring grandparents to emotionally disturbed or physically and mentally handicapped children. Senior companions serve the opposite end of the age spectrum, physically and mentally impaired older adults. Senior companions read, shop, and take walks with their clients. They may help with services such as filling out Medicaid forms or applying for food stamps.

While studies have consistently shown that older people who volunteer are healthier, more well educated, and so have higher morale, is there a relationship between volunteering itself and retirement happiness? At least among rural women, one study suggests that there is. When they related a variety of factors to life satisfaction among a large group of widowed and married rural women retirees, sociologists (Dorfman & Moffett, 1987) found that an increase in the number of volunteer activities was the most consistent social predictor of high morale.

For retirees who are not happy and want to return to the work force, there are options, too. A burgeoning number of special job-finding services and agencies specialize in placing older workers (see Belsky, 1988). Despite the evidence of age discrimination, it is not as hard to find a postretirement job as we might believe. The Duke team found that after retiring, between a quarter and a third of all people return to work, nearly half of these for at least a year and an equal percentage to full-time jobs. Rather than being forced to take lower status jobs, the researchers found another encouraging fact: Most found jobs of equal status to the ones they left!

BOX 9-1
The Working Retired

What motivates people to retire and then decide to return to work—the money, the satisfaction, the dread of leisure? What type of people are these legions of postretirement workers, the one out of three or four retirees who reenter the labor force? Here, too, the landmark Duke analyses offer clues.

When Palmore and his coworkers (1985) compared people who worked after retirement with two groups (people who hadn't retired and those who retired permanently), they found that people who return to work after retiring tend to be relatively young, drawn mainly from the ranks of early and on-time retirees. People who retire late generally retire permanently, never going back to work.

Interestingly, people who return to work after retiring also are relatively disadvantaged—having less education, lower occupational status, and more dependents to support than the two other groups. So while some people may go back to work after retiring for self-expression (the pleasure of having a paying job), the decision to take a job after retirement seems more often forced by necessity—needing the income to live.

Who specifically returns to work? The Duke team found that farm managers, farmers, and people who are self-employed are most prone to go back, probably because they are least likely to have pensions to boost their income and their jobs present the fewest barriers to rejoining the labor force.

However, in spite of this gloomy picture, there is a bright note: Compared to people who stay retired (but not the nonretired), people who work after retirement are better off economically. They also seem happy, satisfied with their activity level, satisfied with their life.

□

WIDOWHOOD

Like retiring, losing a spouse is a predictable event of later life. In contrast to retirement, however, there are no surveys proclaiming the value of this unwelcome life change or programs designed to prepare people psychologically for this traumatic event. Also, unlike retirement, the passage to being widowed is not helpfully institutionalized to occur at a particular age. Dealing with the death of a spouse, though, is predictable in one way. As in the vignette, it is most likely to happen to women because of their higher life expectancy and their tendency to marry older men.

The importance of widowhood in a woman's life is clearly shown by these statistics: Of the approximately 12 million widowed people in the United States, about 10 million are women (as reported in Silverman, 1981). Because women now outlive men by about 7 years, the difference in numbers is especially striking at the oldest ages. For instance, in 1984 a whopping two out of three women over age 70 were widows, a figure exactly reversed for the opposite sex—two out of three men still had a living wife (U.S. Senate Special Committee on Aging, 1984). Because of this extreme disproportion, most widowhood research has focused on the experience of women (Heinemann, 1983; Rubinstein, 1984). Researchers are just recently beginning to plumb this tragedy from the perspective of men.

Being widowed means mourning the painful loss of a life companion. It also means being forced to change one's life radically. Jobs that may have seemed impossible—untangling the finances, cooking the meals, shopping, fixing the faucet—suddenly fall on the new widow or widower. Even waking up takes on new meaning when it is done alone. Relationships with friends may have to be modified or broken since many friendships during marriage are based on being part of a couple (Lopata, 1973). Other ties may weaken or erode, such as relationships with the in-laws, the other side of the family. The newly widowed person must change his or her whole framework for viewing the world, remake an identity whose root may have been "married person" for all of adult life. British psychiatrist Colin Parkes, whose research on widows during the first year of bereavement is discussed in the next section, beautifully describes how a person's basic perceptions tilt after this traumatic event: "Even when words remain the same their meaning changes—the family is no longer the same object it was. Neither is home or a marriage" (1972, p. 93).

In the vignette we saw how Teresa Fuentes had to cope with these internal and external changes. Now we will see how typical her behavior is of most widows and widowers.

Unfortunately, until recently comparisons were sparse. In marked contrast to the literally hundreds of studies exploring the experience of retirees, relatively few have probed how people deal with the death of a spouse. Inquiring into such a sensitive area may have been difficult for researchers. Many may have shied away from probing into another's pain. However, people brave enough to do the early research on this topic found many of their respondents surprisingly willing to open up (Lopata, 1973). It is often a welcome comfort for widows and widowers to talk openly about this difficult experience (see Silverman, 1981).

Most widowhood studies focus on one of two areas: They either attempt to understand bereavement itself, looking at the symptoms of grief, the course and pattern mourning takes, or exploring factors that either hinder or help people come to terms with their loss. Or they examine the day-to-day lives of widows and widowers, looking at their relationships, life satisfaction, emotions, and lifestyle once they have passed the period of intense mourning. The classic studies of bereavement have been done by psychoanalytically oriented clini-

---

BOX 9-2
Chances of Remarriage for the Elderly and the Widowed

The large numbers of widows bode ill for older women who want to remarry. They should cause joy for older men who want to find a mate. But just how likely is it for older people of either sex to remarry? What are the chances of widows versus widowers of different ages being able to find a new spouse?

To answer the first question, Judith Treas and Anke Van Hilst (1976) looked at marriage statistics from 47 states for a given year (1970). They found that while marriage for people over age 65 was unlikely for either sex, it was especially improbable for women. While 17 out of every 1000 elderly men married that year, the figure for women was a mere 3 per 1000. Furthermore, these elderly grooms were not choosing wives from among their age-mates. A full 20% had brides under 55.

To answer the second question, we have a compelling study published by Duke University researchers William Cleveland and Daniel Gianturco (1976). Unfortunately for older women, it has the same theme. When they looked at marriage certificates in North Carolina from April 1970 to March 1971 and compared this data with information on widows versus widowers who rewed, the investigators found that remarriage chances are high for people of either sex who are widowed young (under age 35) and steadily decrease at older ages. But the chances of remarrying decrease much faster for women than for men. The researchers calculated that by age 64 to 74, widowers had about a .25 chance of remarrying. The remarriage probability for widows of the same age was a meager .004.

□

---

cians mainly interested in helping people cope by understanding normal and pathological mourning. As I will describe in a later section, the landmark studies of the widowed state were conducted by Helena Lopata, a sociologist interested in examining the role of the widow in the United States.

Bereavement

How do people actually feel and act in the first traumatic weeks and months after losing a loved one? Does bereavement follow a predictable course? What influences predict "normal recovery" or increase the probability of a person developing a pathological bereavement response? While the studies described below often bear on all of these questions, we'll look at each compelling topic separately.

The Early Symptoms of Bereavement.   The first genuinely scientific study of mourning grew out of a famous disaster, the Coconut Grove nightclub fire that took the lives of several hundred people in Boston in 1942. In an effort to clarify the symptoms of bereavement, psychiatrist Erich Lindemann (1944) interviewed during the following year roughly 100 people who had lost loved ones in the tragedy. He found the normal signs of any upset—for example, crying or problems eating and sleeping. He discovered some quite unexpected reactions, too. Mourners, he observed, were often troubled by intense guilt, blaming themselves for not doing enough for their loved one when he or she was alive. They felt angry at or distant from others, even people they normally cared deeply about. Perhaps most interesting, they were preoccupied by the image of the person who had died, at times so intensely that they almost hallucinated his or her presence. This last reaction in particular, we might remember, frightened Teresa Fuentes who saw it as a sign she might be breaking down.

Two and a half decades later, British psychiatrist Colin Parkes corroborated these findings in an intensive study of a group of London widows during the first year after their husband's death. Like Lindemann, Parkes found that anger, inappropriate guilt, and a sense of the lost one's actual physical presence were all common symptoms of bereavement. In addition, sometimes a widow showed an almost total sense of identification with her dead husband, feeling that he was actually part of herself. As one woman said, "My husband is in me right through and through. I can feel him in me doing everything. . . . I suppose he is guiding me all of the time" (1972, p. 89; the work was reissued in 1987). Perhaps a denial of reality this intense might be adaptive, allowing the new widow to absorb the full impact of her loss gradually and giving her the strength to carry on during the first difficult weeks after her husband's death.

Parkes's widows had other puzzling symptoms. They were frequently obsessed with the events surrounding the death itself, repeatedly going over and over their husband's final hours, his last day. Some reported trying to look for their spouse, even though they knew that what they were doing was completely irrational. Another well-known British observer of mourning, psychiatrist and ethologist John Bowlby, puts this searching behavior in a fascinating context, as a manifestation of our instinctive "attachment response" to separation—a response that unfolds in its most pure form at age 1 when the infant howls vigorously, clings to, and crawls after her or his mother as she is about to leave the room. According to Bowlby (1980), not only is this frantic drive for reunion automatically evoked when we lose our primary attachment figure at any time of life, it is far from just a human response. Consider this beautiful description by ethologist Konrad Lorenz of bereavement in the greylag goose:

> The first response to the disappearance of the partner consists in the anxious attempt to find him again. The goose moves about restlessly by day and night, flying great distances and visiting places where the partner might be found, uttering all the time the penetrating trisyllabic call. . . . The searching expeditions are extended further and further and quite often the searcher gets lost; or succumbs to an accident. . . . All the objective, observable characteristics of the goose's behavior on losing its mate are roughly identical with human grief [as quoted in Worden, 1982, p. 9].

According to these experts, the symptoms mentioned above are *characteristic* of the first few months of bereavement. They are not pathological. They are signs of a normal response. But, how typical are these reactions really? Do they regularly appear in the age group we are interested in, elderly widows and widowers? For answers we have a study that is more empirical than these early observational accounts: one sampling a large, more representative group of older widows and widowers, using a standardized test of depression and employing a nonbereaved control group.

In this study of the symptoms of early bereavement, researchers (Breckenridge, Gallagher, Thompson, & Peterson, 1986) drew on Los Angeles County Health Department records to recruit about 200 men and women over 55 who had recently lost a spouse. The volunteers, interviewed and tested in their homes approximately 2 months after the death, were mainly middle class and long married, having been wed an average 37 years. Their symptoms were compared with those of a group of nonbereaved older people drawn from senior citizen centers.

Interestingly, in this sample, at least one of the supposedly normal signs of mourning listed above, intense guilt and self-blame, while occurring a certain percentage of the time, was not a *characteristic* response. Only 25% of the widows and widows reported any feelings of guilt and most who did said these feelings were mild. Less than 10% said that they had other signs of anger directed against the self (that is, a sense of having failed or feelings of being punished). The three most frequent symptoms people did have were typical reactions to any severely upsetting experience: crying, unhappiness, and insomnia.

According to the researchers, their findings suggest not only that self-blame should not be viewed as an *expected* feature of mourning (at least among the elderly), but that its presence may indicate that normal bereavement is shading into a true emotional problem, depression. A typical symptom depressed people tend to have is excessive, irrational guilt—feeling "terrible about myself" (see Chapter 10). These emotions present to a *marked* degree in a new widow or widower suggest that mourning may not be progressing normally and that the person may be becoming depressed and may need professional help.

But what does "progressing normally" mean? This brings us to our second question, does bereavement follow a typical pattern or course?

Charting Normal Mourning.   In the original edition of his classic, Parkes (1972) argued that mourning does have a predictable course. After a brief period of numbness, he observed that most widows broke down, feeling waves of intense yearning and pining alternating with periods of depression and apathy. As time went by, these intense expressions of mourning tended to decrease in intensity and frequency, though they could always be reevoked at certain times. Eventually, most widows were able to remake a new life. Bowlby (1980) was even more specific, dividing grieving into four phases: a phase of numbness or disbelief, a phase of yearning and searching, a phase of disorganization and despair, and finally, a phase of recovery.

From a slightly different perspective, other theorists conceptualize mourning as involving a set of tasks. In order to recover from this traumatic event, the widowed person must reach certain benchmarks. For example, according to bereavement specialist William Worden (1982), these are the **tasks of mourning:**

1. *Accepting the reality of the death.* Right after the spouse dies, there is a sense that it hasn't happened. The newly widowed person may understand the facts intellectually but still feel that any moment she or he will wake up from a bad dream. The first task of mourning, which generally occurs in the first few months, is to accept the actual fact of the death.
2. *Feeling the pain.* In order to get over a loved one's death, the widowed person must also accept reality emotionally by confronting the painful feelings of loss directly—mourning deeply and openly.
3. *Adjusting to a new life.* The person must learn to function in areas his or her spouse had been responsible for, eventually constructing a stable, relatively satisfying new life.
4. *Loving again.* While it is not necessary to develop a new romantic involvement, it is important to regain the capacity to love in a broader sense. Recovering from mourning means reinvesting emotionally in the world—being able to care deeply about life and other people again.

These benchmarks are idealized and theoretical. They are used clinically to judge whether a person is getting over this terrible life trauma. Are they empirically valid?

Because it is the least intuitively correct, let's center our questions around the validity of task 2, the idea that recovering from mourning depends on intensely feeling the pain. This idea is widely accepted among bereavement counselors, people who treat widows and widowers (see, for instance, Rando, 1984; Worden, 1982). In counseling sessions and self-help groups, widowed people are often encouraged to give vent to their feelings, to confront the painful feelings of their loss directly. But what about the person whose mourning style is less emotional? Does the assumption that one style of grieving is best really do justice to the importance of individual differences, the diversity of human beings? What data support the claim that in order to rebuild a new life it is necessary to intensely mourn?

Lindemann (1944) was the first person to suggest that mourning in this way might be important to recovering. He noticed that people who broke down and let themselves experience the full impact of the death seemed to adjust best to the trauma. Those who seemed to deny, to minimize their feelings, or to react unemotionally had the most trouble adjusting to their loss. Originally, Parkes, too, proposed that becoming very upset early on was important to recovering well. His London widows who seemed relatively calm and unemotional during the first 2 months were the most disturbed and least able to function at the end of the first year. However, in a later, more extensive study of bereavement (but of widows and widowers *under* age 45), he actually found that the opposite was true—people with the most intense emotional reactions in the first few months were the most likely to recover poorly. Being totally inconsolable early on was a bad sign (Parkes & Weiss, 1983).

The truth is that even if we found a firmly documented correlation between intense grieving and good recovery, it would not suggest a causal link. A third factor, such as Costa's "openness to experience" or having an unambivalent, fully loving marriage might just as logically be independently producing these two events.

Actually, the whole idea that grieving can be fitted into defined stages has been called into question in a longitudinal study of the first 2 years of bereavement (Lund, Caserta, & Dimond, 1986). When a large sample of elderly widows and widowers was interviewed at regular intervals during this period—questioned about their symptoms, behaviors, experiences, and feelings and given standardized tests of depression and morale—researchers found that rather than progressing in a truly orderly pattern (as all stage theories imply), bereavement was really much more chaotic, with people experiencing conflicting emotions and behaviors simultaneously. A classic example occurred in the tumultuous first few months. At that time *both* depression and scores on measures of psychological strength and coping were at their peak. In other words, rather than just feeling "at their worst" during this difficult early period, people really felt a mixture of emotions, feeling both very distressed and also very proud about how they were handling things. Moreover, while it was true that improvement did gradually occur, there was little truth to the stage idea that there was a defined time when mourning could be said to be finished or "complete." At the end of 2 years people were still grieving, still actively reconstructing elements of their new life. In fact, along with signs of recovery, some even had symptoms supposedly typical of the earliest weeks—shock, disbelief, avoidance of the fact.

Pathological Mourning.   But even if it is hard to fit mourning into defined stages, we all intuitively know that the idea of charting recovery does have some validity. After some time, the person must indeed "get better"—no longer be immersed in grief, and begin to remake a new satisfying life. After a certain period, we are right to get concerned if our mother is still setting the table for our dead father, or weeping continually, or unable to find any joy in life.

But what is the timetable for our concern, the point at which experts label the widow or widower as suffering from **pathological mourning** or **chronic grief?** In Worden's opinion the tasks of mourning should be well under way by the end of the first year, though the period of bereavement often lasts 2. Another clinician, Therese Rando (1984), feels that, especially for widows, 3 years may not be too long.

While most widows and widowers cope remarkably well, there are clearly those who do not fit this timetable, having prolonged, unremitting grief reactions, becoming chronically depressed. As Table 9-1 suggests, many factors may affect the depth of bereavement and the ease of recovery. Let's amplify on some of the items in the table briefly and then explore two the table lists more in depth: age and sex.

TABLE 9-1. Hypothetical factors determining the outcome of mourning.

Antecedent Factors	Mode of Death	Concurrent Factors	Subsequent Factors
Childhood experiences (especially losses of significant persons)	Timeliness Previous warning Preparation for bereavement Need to hide feelings	Sex Age Personality Socioeconomic status Nationality Religion Cultural factors Familial factors	Social support or isolation Secondary stresses Emergent life opportunities
Later experiences (especially losses of significant persons)			
Previous mental illnesses (especially depressive illness)			
Life crises prior to the bereavement			
Relationship with the deceased: kinship, strength of attachment, security of attachment, degree of reliance, intensity of reliance, intensity of ambivalence (love/hate)			

Source: Parkes, 1972.

In addition to the probably important influence of personality (see Chapter 7), difficult life experiences may make us more vulnerable to widowhood: the loss of loved ones in childhood and later on, a past punctuated with traumatic events. Also important is the quality of our "support system" at the time of bereavement, that is, if we have other relationships to cushion the blow. The quality of our marriage seems to play a part, too. For instance, in a large-scale study of young Boston-area widows and widowers, Parkes and his co-worker Robert Weiss (1983) found that people with highly dependent or highly ambivalent relationships seemed to adjust more poorly to this life event. And a variety of studies suggest that, for younger people at least, when the death occurs without warning or "out of the blue" this trauma seems more difficult to come to terms with.

Without doubt, however, two of the most thoroughly investigated items on the table have been age and sex. Many studies suggest that older people handle the death of a spouse better. They have less intense levels of distress during the first few months (Breckenridge, Gallagher, Thompson, & Peterson, 1986) and show few (or no) differences from nonbereaved controls at the end of the year (Clayton, 1979). They may be less likely to become physically ill, too. For example, Parkes (1972) reported research showing that younger widows are hospitalized more frequently and visit their doctors with more medical complaints during the first year of bereavement. However, he could find no studies showing that older widows had increased rates of disease.

Being female is supposed to be an advantage, too. Many experts feel that older women handle the trauma of widowhood best. Of any group, they are least likely to develop emotional and physical problems after their spouse dies (Rando, 1984; Worden, 1982; see Box 9-3).

BOX 9-3
Gender and the Mortality of Bereavement

The phrase "soon after one goes, the other does," expresses the romantic idea that being widowed is a life-threatening event for the surviving spouse. How true is this widespread idea?

Interestingly, this common conception does have a grain of truth, but only for men. When Duke University epidemiologists followed several thousand people for several years after a spouse's death, they found that the women did not have a higher death rate compared to a matched group of still married middle-aged and older adults, but widowers did die with greater frequency—both during the first intensely emotional 6 months of bereavement and later on. In fact, a widower's slightly elevated risk of dying only returned to normal under one condition—if he remarried! While this fascinating finding may be due to selection—the healthier widowers having the energy and appeal to find new mates—another interpretation may be the one women have surmised: being married is good for a man's health!

☐

While there are likely to be a variety of reasons for these age and sex differences, both make sense in terms of anticipatory socialization. While we never plan for widowhood the way we plan for retirement, older people have many chances to rehearse in fantasy for their new role. They have seen friends go through this transition; they have models for how to cope. This is most true for elderly women. For them the blow is most predictable—the anticipatory socialization for widowhood has been most intense.

On the other hand, a person widowed young is thrust into this new role unprepared. Even if the death itself was predictable, its timing is not. Whom among their friends can people widowed in their 30s and 40s turn to for guidance? Fate has swooped down and singled them out for an arbitrary, unexpected blow.

But does widowhood later in life really hit men harder than women? The longitudinal investigation of the first 2 years of bereavement discussed in the last section (Lund, Caserta, & Dimond, 1986) casts doubt on this widely accepted view. When they looked for the expected gender differences in mourning, the researchers found that their male respondents did not have more intense symptoms than the widows. Both men and women also recovered at the same rate. In fact, contrary to the idea that men suffer more, this careful empirical study suggests that the bereavement reactions of elderly widows and widowers are essentially indistinguishable.

In a recent review of the literature, Margery Feinson (1986) makes the same point: The research showing that men suffer more after a spouse's death is inconsistent. While the evidence that older men suffer more negative physical effects than older women do is firmer (see Box 9-3), this generalization does not seem to hold for a large group of elderly widowers, men over age 75. In fact, in her own research, comparing the bereavement reactions of several hundred elderly men and women, Feinson also found no gender differences in mourning at all.

This controversy underlines the fact that gender is not the real issue in a person's ability to adapt to this trauma. Having the right mix of inner qualities and outerworld opportunities is the issue, having attributes such as ego strength, emotional resilience, and adaptability and an environment that fosters recovery. This becomes clear when we look at the period after the initial phase of mourning—how life as a widow is lived.

Life as a Widowed Person

Mourning is only the beginning of widowhood. It says nothing about what happens to the person when life must go on in a new way. To understand what this life is like we have the benefit of a host of studies exploring more limited aspects of widowhood, such as the person's social relationships. And we have the rich insights of two comprehensive studies conducted by sociologist Helena Lopata. While Lopata's research was done more than 15 years ago and only explores the experiences of women, I will focus mainly on her studies because they still offer the fullest, most finely etched portrait we have of widowhood in the United States.

The subjects of Lopata's first study were 301 Chicago widows over age 50. The women, selected so half were under and half over age 65, were interviewed in their homes (Lopata, 1973). Because of Chicago's uniquely insulated ethnic neighborhoods (this may be one of the few U.S. cities where people can survive for generations without knowing English), these respondents were not only ethnically and economically diverse, they also differed greatly in how Americanized (assimilated) they were. Most were well past the initial period of bereavement, having been widows an average of 11 years.

This study was mainly devoted to understanding the widows' current lives, but the women were also asked about the quality of their marriage and the events leading up to their husband's death. They were questioned about a variety of roles: wife, mother, relative, friend, and participant in the life of the community. On a special scale Lopata and her colleagues constructed, their degree of social isolation was measured as were their feelings about the way other people treated them specifically and widows in general.

The study showed that the women were actually living very independent lives. Most either lived alone or were heads of households. Widows living alone complained of being lonely but usually said that they preferred this arrangement to moving in with their adult children. Not only did they prize the freedom of living alone, they were afraid conflict would be inevitable if they were to move in

---

BOX 9-4
Do Divorcees Adjust Less Well to Being Single than Widows?

Divorce and widowhood have many of the same consequences: the need to mourn and come to terms with a loss; the need to change one's life in a radical way; the need to adjust to living as a single person. Because widowhood often means the end of a happy situation, we might assume that widows would be more bitter about the hand fate has dealt them than divorcees. Because divorce is often fraught with rancor, we might feel that divorcees would recover less well than widows. We would expect them to be more dissatisfied with themselves, more upset about how others treat them in their new, single role.

Lopata and her colleagues (Kitson, Lopata, Holmes, & Meyering, 1980) had an ideal chance to test this question. They compared the responses of widows to items on the scale mentioned in the text with those of divorcees, substituting the word *divorcee* for *widow* in the questions.

The divorcees were indeed more negative than the widows: They were more prone to feel they had lost status, were taken advantage of, and were more wary and suspicious of others. Actually this is no surprise. Divorce, unlike widowhood, is tailor-made for feeling angry and disappointed—toward oneself, toward the ex-spouse, toward the world.

□

---

with a child. This spirit of self-reliance also extended to finances. Although more than half reported that their income had dropped dramatically after their husband's death, few said they felt deprived economically. Even fewer wanted to receive help from relatives.

For many of these widows their role as wife had been central to their adult lives. Fully 20% felt that they had never really gotten over their husband's death. However, most said they did not want to remarry, mentioning among other reasons, their age, the fear they would have to take care of a sick husband (one out of six had nursed their husband at home for at least a year before his death), and their feeling that they could never find a man as good as their late spouse. This last reason for not marrying is particularly interesting because it epitomizes a fascinating psychological process Lopata calls *sanctification.* Many widows romanticized their life with their husband, enshrining his memory, idealizing their married life as total bliss.

In comparison, their current relationships, especially with their children, were more ambivalent and conflict-ridden. Although their children were very important to most of the widows, relationships with them were rarely totally close. Usually the widows felt closest to one child in particular, most often a daughter. Relationships with their other relatives seemed more peripheral. For instance, most women said they had a sister or brother but did not feel close to that person.

Friends were important mainly to the most well-educated widows. Many women reported having problems changing friendships based on being part of a couple. When their old friendships could not survive the strain of this life change, the widow had to make new friends. One reason friends may have been so important to the better educated women was that they were more able to make these adaptations; they were more likely to have the social skills to transform old relationships and build satisfying new ones.

In fact, education and social class were important factors predicting how well a widow was able to adjust. Lopata found that the least well educated, lower-class widows were the most likely to be depressed and socially isolated. She suggested that the traditional upbringing and lifestyle these women had before being widowed was partly to blame because it stressed conforming to rules, dependence, and discouraged initiative. Traditionally reared women, she argued, could only be happy when their environment remained the same. When being widowed meant having to actively construct a new life, these women had not been prepared by their training to cope. One price they paid was disengagement from others. This social isolation in turn was associated with poor morale—a finding that is one more nail in the coffin of disengagement theory.

In addition to serving as another disconfirmation of this discredited theory, this study supports the continuity point of view. The Chicago widows' ability to cope with widowhood was a function of their previous approach to life. If their married life fostered initiative, they were good at adjusting to their new single role; if they were socialized to be dependent, they did poorly in this life-stage demanding independence and flexibility.

Lopata's second study (1979) expanded on the first and gives us more insights into widows' lives. This time she and her colleagues interviewed a large group of widows selected from the ranks of Social Security recipients. Their goal was to understand what they called each widow's "support system"—who helped her, whom she helped, and how much support she got and gave to others in important areas of life.

This study, too, showed that most widows were very independent. Respondents seldom reported getting financial help from friends and relatives or help with other activities such as shopping or housework (see also Lopata, 1978a, 1978b). They cited their children as being the most important class of people providing any concrete help and the most important source of emotional support. Significantly, though, when asked to name the people they were closest to emotionally, many widows listed themselves or their dead husbands. Although the vignette shows that a woman can still feel a strong bond to her dead spouse and live a full, involved life, the limited quality of these answers suggests that many of these women were quite lonely; that is, their independence had a negative tinge—signifying isolation from others. Also, when these women were asked about their activities, over half said that they never went to places such as movie theaters; four in ten never entertained; the same fraction reported that they always ate lunch alone. While lack of money probably played a part in restricting these widows, their answers show that, for whatever reason, many were living solitary, limited lives.

While more recent studies paint a somewhat brighter picture, suggesting that widows may make up for the loss of their husband by increasing the intensity and frequency of their contacts with people in general (Kohen, 1983) and in particular cultivating deeper relationships with other relatives such as siblings and children (Anderson, T., 1984; Morgan, 1984), they still confirm that widows are more isolated—that they have fewer social contacts than their married counterparts. This sense of isolation is not confined to just women who lose a spouse. In one British study of both widows and widowers (Bowling & Cartwright, 1981), half of the respondents said that loneliness was a big problem; two-thirds said that they found it difficult to adjust to living alone.

Is the situation for elderly widowers in North America any different? An exploratory, clinical look at the lives of widowed men implies not much. Anthropologist Robert Rubinstein (1986; also 1984) intensively interviewed elderly men who had been widowed for about 5 years. He questioned them about their activities, relationships, life satisfaction, and loneliness. He estimated that more than half (14) were floundering emotionally—either clinging to the past, unable to form new satisfying relationships, or no longer finding purpose in life. These widowers had trouble finding focus or meaning for their hours; they felt they were living "day by day." While his sample was confined to 25 subjects and his study was observational, Rubinstein's case histories echo those of the widows in an uncanny way. A surprising number of older men and women may have a good deal of trouble reconstructing a satisfying new life after their life companion dies.

Interventions

I must emphasize that these findings do not apply to *all* widows or *all* widowers. In each study described above, a good proportion of the people were indeed able to remake full, happy new lives. Also remember that the subjects were confined to a particular cohort of older people. In the future widows may be less emotionally bound to just a role as wife, more prone to chance new involvements, even more willing to risk visiting restaurants and movie theaters alone. Future cohorts of widowers, too, having been socialized in the new, post-women's liberation movement relationship-oriented masculine role, may enter widowhood with more close attachments and the tools to redevelop satisfying new relationships. Still, today, life as an older widowed person can be lonely. Lopata felt society could help in a structured way. She was convinced that services set up to provide information, opportunities to meet people, individual counseling, and even concrete help might have made her widows' lives easier—offering ready-made chances to form new relationships and providing vital help in negotiating this difficult transition of life. However, clearly her widows were not getting this help. Clergy, widows support groups, or other formal services were conspicuously absent from the Chicago subjects' list of support systems.

This is unfortunate because these types of help can be effective at helping people cope. In one study (Raphael, 1977), widows under age 60 at risk for poor adaptation to bereavement were randomly assigned to treatment and no-treatment conditions in the first weeks after their husband's death. The treatment consisted of regular, 2-hour sessions during the first 3 months of bereavement in which a counselor encouraged the widow to talk about her loss. The widows who had participated in the treatment rated themselves as less depressed, reported fewer physical symptoms, had visited their doctors less often, and were generally better off at the end of the first year of bereavement than the widows who had not received help.

Luckily, in the years since Lopata's research was done, more people may indeed be getting formal help. Services to help widowed persons have proliferated, sponsored by religious and human service organizations and community groups. Unfortunately, however, all these programs depend on voluntary participation and so may miss many people most in need—widows and widowers too shy or fearful to visit, call, or participate.

An example of one of these programs is a widowed person's service begun in Boston in 1969 (McCourt, Barnett, Brennan, & Becker, 1976). This service offers social gatherings and biweekly seminars dealing with issues important to widowhood. It operates a telephone hot line staffed by widow volunteers. Widow volunteers also make weekly home visits, particularly during the first traumatic months, to people in need. These trained volunteers listen to the widow or widower, lending support.

There is a reason why this program and others draw on peer counselors, not professionals. Widowed people past the difficult period of bereavement who are coping well can serve as models in addition to being able to fully empathize with what the new widow or widower is going through. In fact, the use of widowed counselors embodies the principle of modeling in clinical practice. It is a systematic attempt to use this major type of learning in producing psychological change.

In sum, the crucible of retirement and widowhood gives us a chance to test the change versus consistency ideas about personality. A strong theme running through both the widowhood and retirement research is that our previous personality does shape how we deal with these life events. It determines the form we give to our new life. On the other hand, there are nagging doubts. Why does widowhood seem a more difficult blow than retirement for men? Why do so many men seem so willing to relinquish the work role? Mightn't this mean that Gutmann's views about male midlife sex-role changes have a grain of truth, too?

So, our look at how people cope with these transitions underlines the importance of consistency, but it also implies the existence of change. However, with regard to one aspect of personality, this chapter has a clear message. Without minimizing the importance of individual differences, many people do remarkably well in adjusting to retirement. While widowhood does seem to be a more wrenching blow, the elderly may be better able to handle this life trauma than the young. This means that when we combine this information with the studies in Chapter 7, we can happily conclude that the stereotypical image of the fragile, inflexible older person is just not true!

KEY TERMS

Anticipatory socialization
Busy ethic
Retirement counselors

Preretirement programs
Tasks of mourning
Pathological mourning or chronic grief

RECOMMENDED READINGS

Lopata, H. Z. (1973). *Widowhood in an American city.* Cambridge, MA: Schenkman.
Lopata, H. Z. (1979). *Women as widows: Support systems.* Cambridge: Schenkman. Lopata's landmark studies of widows. The first book also contains information on customs involving widows worldwide and an overview of widowhood in the United States. Not difficult.
Palmore, E. B., Burchett, B., Fillenbaum, G. G., George, L. K., & Wallman, L. M. (1985). *Retirement: Causes and consequences.* New York: Springer. The Duke analyses of retirement in the United States. Moderately difficult.
Worden, J. W. (1982). *Grief counseling and grief therapy.* New York: Springer. A clinician's point of view about mourning. Offers interventions to help people accomplish the tasks of bereavement. Not difficult.

Part 5

■

Psychopathology

Chapter 10

□

Mental Disorders 1: Description, Diagnosis, Assessment

□

Epidemiology of Later-Life Mental Disorders
- Purposes of Epidemiological Studies
- Problems in Measuring Psychological Disorders
  - Psychological Problems in Old Age

Dementia
- Symptoms of Dementia
- The Prevalence of Dementia
  - Alzheimer's Disease
  - Multi-Infarct Dementia
- Personality Changes and Dementia
- The Strains and Stresses of Caregiving
- Accurately Distinguishing Dementia from Delirium and Depression

Depression
- Symptoms and Prevalence of Depression
- Categories and Causes of Depression
- The Worst Consequence of Depression—Suicide

Assessment
- The Diagnostic Question
- Assessment Strategies for Dementia
  - Recommendations

Key Terms

Recommended Readings

Ruben Gold began to notice the distressing changes a few weeks after their move south. His wife, Sophie, had always been fastidious about her appearance and had kept an immaculate house. In Fort Lauderdale, Florida, however, she seemed to lose interest in how she looked. One week he was shocked to see her wearing the same dress 3 days in a row. Dinner or breakfast dishes were sometimes left uncleared, particularly if she was called away from the table while cleaning up. She simply forgot they were there.

There were other unsettling changes in the woman he had loved for 54 years. In Philadelphia, though Sophie had always been somewhat dependent on him, she had also been outgoing, happy, and active. She was the kind of person who relished relationships—taking care to keep in touch with her many old friends, and actively cultivating new ones. She reveled in her children and grandchildren. This all changed in Florida. She lost interest in her family; had no desire to meet new people. Activities she loved, like playing bingo, dancing, and swimming, were plentiful at the retirement community, but she refused to take advantage of them. She just sat at home and watched soap operas.

At first, Ruben was not too worried. He had to admit, he even liked having Sophie at home more. He was the one who had decided on the move. Sophie had been lukewarm. Ruben felt she just needed some time to get over her natural pain at leaving her old friends. Knowing his wife, in a few months she would have hundreds of new ones. Although her 10-pound weight loss and problems sleeping were troubling, a physical checkup showed nothing was wrong. Ruben had read that depression often caused sleepless nights, appetite loss, apathy, even the memory problems his wife was having.

He became alarmed, though, that terrible Monday a security officer at the nearby shopping center arrived at the door with his hysterical wife. She had gone out to pick up a few groceries, left her wallet at the checkout counter, and been found wandering in the parking lot, unable to remember how to get home. This was frightening because they lived only a few blocks away and she had never forgotten anything this basic before. After this trauma, Sophie was too terrified to venture out alone. Ruben forbade her to leave the house without him. What if something like this happened again? What if she did something that risked her life? But housebound, Sophie sank deeper into apathy. Finally Ruben could stand no more. If Sophie was becoming senile, better face up to the bitter truth. He decided to go to a clinic in Philadelphia his daughter had recommended, one that specialized in diagnosing this problem in older people.

Sophie spent several days at the clinic being probed and examined, tested and interviewed. She spent an hour with an internist: blood was drawn and specimens were sent to the lab. She was given a brain scan and subjected to various neurological tests. The most intensive probing, however, was done by a psychiatrist, a psychologist, and a social worker.

The psychiatrist saw Sophie first. She asked Sophie about her memory, her marriage, and her feelings about the move. She even questioned her about her parents and childhood events. Then the psychologist asked yet more questions about her memory and then had her take an extensive battery of tests. The social worker talked to Ruben for over an hour and phoned the couple's daughter and son. What did they think was their mother's problem? What might be done to help?

Both the social worker and the psychiatrist agreed that though Sophie did have some rather marked cognitive deficits, her real problem was depression. Her memory problems had not gradually appeared out of the blue, which would suggest a diagnosis of Alzheimer's disease. They had a clear external cause, the move. The social worker, noticing how overprotective and domineering Ruben was, believed that Ruben encouraged his wife's dependency and isolation, that Sophie was furious at him but too intimidated to express it. Her forgetting was a way of unconsciously getting back.

The psychologist disagreed with them. The neuropsychological examination showed deficits suggesting an early stage dementia. Sophie's reasoning was concrete and her short-term memory was impaired. He did not deny that depression could have compounded her poor test performance, but held firm that she had an organic problem.

Before telling the family the results, the team met together to hash out their disagreements. They decided on a compromise: a diagnosis of possible Alzheimer's disease with a superimposed depression. They also considered the circumstances that had to be exacerbating any organic deficit Sophie might have—the move and her husband's tendency to overprotect her—and agreed that if possible the couple should move back to Philadelphia. Being in familiar territory, surrounded by friends and family, would make negotiating life much easier for Sophie. With luck, it might even restore her to her normal self. The team also decided to recommend psychotherapy or a trial of antidepressant drugs and to honestly tell the family about their uncertainty: While Sophie might be suffering from a dementing illness, only time and careful observation could really tell. In the meantime, dealing with the emotional and situational causes of her symptoms was important. If everyone kept their fingers crossed, what looked like an early stage Alzheimer's disease might really be depression after all!

■

Because we tend to view old age so negatively, as life's era of loss and decline, most of us would probably predict that in later life emotional problems would be common. The losses older people must absorb—of health, of work, of spouse—

must lead to depression, to intense psychological distress. The ravages of aging must take their emotional toll. The elderly should be more susceptible than the young to almost every psychological problem.

However, this idea does not fit with the research on personality. According to Paul Costa's studies (see Chapter 7), the emotionally disturbed stay emotionally disturbed; their ranks do not swell in later life. Furthermore, as we saw in the last chapter, two major later-life losses we might expect to cause psychological problems—retirement and widowhood—do not have dire emotional conse-quences. At least considered by themselves, these changes seem to cause surpris-ingly few *long-term* psychological problems for most older adults. In fact, some of the studies discussed in Chapter 7 even suggest that age can bring emotional resilience. Is it possible that—with the dramatic exception of dementias such as Alzheimer's disease—people over age 65 are *less* likely to suffer from mental disorders than the young?

So we need to take a careful look at the stereotype of rampant psycho-pathology in old age. How common are emotional problems among the elderly? How does their frequency compare with problems among other age groups? What types of problems are older people most likely to have? Answers to these questions come from what are called epidemiologic studies.

EPIDEMIOLOGY OF LATER-LIFE MENTAL DISORDERS

Epidemiology is a field that deals with any issue relating to the prevalence or incidence (rate of occurrence) of illnesses in the population. For example, how common is the illness or problem in a given area? Is it found more frequently in certain geographic sections; among particular groups? Is the illness becoming more widespread or less of a threat over time?

Purposes of Epidemiological Studies

Epidemiological studies help practitioners evaluate a community's need for medical or health services (Kay & Bergmann, 1980). They can also give impor-tant insights into the causes of illnesses. For example, having done surveys of the prevalence of heart attacks in different countries, epidemiologists were among the first people to suggest that a high-fat diet might play a role in causing heart disease. They did this by detective work, discovering that one factor differentiat-ing countries where people developed higher rates of heart disease was that residents ate a diet high in saturated fats.

Problems in Measuring Psychological Disorders

Ideally, by doing the same type of cross-national epidemiological research, we might come up with similar insights about the causes of mental disorders. In countries where the elderly are given more status or where social services are more widely available, is the rate of depression or anxiety lower? If there are particular regions of the world with a very high (or low) incidence of Alzheimer's disease, does this tell us something about why this devastating illness arises? Unfortunately, though, the vital insights these studies might offer are hampered by a simple fact—accurately measuring the rate of psychological problems is not as easy as it appears. In community surveys, the residents must agree to be interviewed or tested (see Kay & Bergmann, 1980). We might expect that some of the very people most likely to have true psychological problems would refuse (for instance, older people who are paranoid or are frightened about their failing memory).

The main reason these studies are not so accurate, though, stems from a more distressing problem—difficulties with the diagnoses themselves. Even skilled diagnosticians can disagree on whether a given person should be diagnosed as having a mental disorder or what particular diagnostic category a patient fits (Gurland, Dean, Copeland, Gurland, & Golden, 1982). In an effort to combat the thorny problem of poor reliability—diagnosing the same patient differently—a decade ago the American Psychiatric Association (1980) developed a manual, the third edition of the *Diagnostic and Statistical Manual of Mental Disorders* (DSM-III), which carefully spells out explicit criteria for making a psychological diagnosis. In spite of the manual's extensive descriptions, however, and so wider agreement on *where* a person fits, *whether* to diagnose in a given way is still a question. Does the presence of symptoms X, Y, and Z really signify that a person has a distinct disease entity labeled "sexual sadism" or "attention deficit disorder"? Does a definite condition called "social phobia" or "passive aggressive personality disorder" really exist? This is the all-important question of validity.

Unfortunately, concerns about validity and reliability are especially salient in the elderly because in this age group two related influences conspire to make diagnosing emotional problems especially difficult: Older people may approach interviews and diagnostic tests differently than younger people do. In old age psychological problems and their symptoms may appear different than they do earlier on. Let's take depression as an example. As I will describe in more detail later in this chapter, in later life depression may be manifested by physical complaints or by memory problems alone. Furthermore, this cohort of older people tends to underreport negative symptoms of any kind (see Chapters 4 and 7). So when an epidemiologist probes for this problem in an interview or has an older respondent fill in a depression checklist, the findings might be "no depression" even when this emotional disorder is really there.

So surveys of the rate of mental disorders at different ages must be taken with a grain of salt. With this caveat in mind, the studies that have attempted to assess how emotional problems are distributed by age do offer fascinating insights. How common are these problems in general during adulthood? Are the elderly more prone to suffer from these disorders than the young?

Psychological Problems in Old Age

One classic survey showed that unfortunately emotional problems are surprisingly common among adults of any age—affecting as many as 25% of all people

TABLE 10-1. Examples of major classes of functional psychological disorders and representative symptoms.

Disorders	Symptoms
Schizophrenic disorders	Bizarre delusions (irrational ideas) and/or auditory hallucinations (hearing voices), incoherence, illogical thinking, blunted affect (emotional tone)
Affective disorders	Alterations of mood. In manic disorders, periods of highly elevated mood and activity including hyperactivity, sleeplessness, racing thoughts, euphoria, actions that may be reckless or self-destructive. In depressive disorders, unhappy mood, guilt feelings, slowed thinking, physical symptoms (see section on Depression)
Anxiety disorders	Intense, generalized anxiety or anxiety attached to specific irrational situations: feelings of dread, dizzyness, sweating, heart pounding, irritability
Paranoid disorders	Systematized delusions of being persecuted or delusional jealousy

in the United States (Srole, Langner, Michael, Opler, & Rennie, 1962). Estimates of the prevalence of psychological problems in older people are in the same range (see Allan & Brotman, 1981; Kay & Bergmann, 1980). Surveys show anywhere from 8% (Lowenthal & Berkman, 1967) to 30% (Kay, Beamish, & Roth, 1964) of community-dwelling over-65-year-olds have what are called **functional psychological disorders**—those types of emotional problems for which no established organic (physiological) cause has been found (see Table 10-1 for examples). In fact, some recent surveys suggest that among noninstitutionalized older people, if anything, the rate of mental disturbance may even be slightly *lower* than it is in youth or middle age. This was the surprising finding of the most advanced epidemiological study done to date conducted by researchers at the National Institute of Mental Health (Weismann et al., 1985). It was echoed by another recent epidemiological investigation of elderly New Jersey residents (Feinson & Thoits, 1986). Even the "fact" that older people suffer from higher rates of depression—put forth as holy writ in the literature (and in the first edition of this text)—has been called into question. Based on the NIMH study, a widely distributed 1984 status report on aging in America prepared by the Senate Special Committee on Aging and the American Association of Retired Persons stated that depression is *not* a major problem in old age (U.S. Senate Special Committee on Aging, 1984).

How can we make sense of this surprising new information? Perhaps people with serious emotional disorders disproportionately die before reaching later life—from neglecting their health; abusing their bodies; or succumbing to a middle-aged, stress-induced heart attack. The members of a cohort who survive to old age may be both an emotional and physical elite! Maybe life is less stressful once people are retired and their children are grown. Or, better yet, perhaps some people really may develop a kind of wisdom, a more mature way of coping with problems, as they advance in years.

However, there are serious cautions: As we know now, older people may be more reluctant to admit having emotional problems, and emotional disorders may masquerade as physical problems in old age. Furthermore, some gerontologists point out that the encouraging new NIMH findings may seriously undercount the number of elderly with psychological problems because to be labeled as having an emotional disorder in this study a person's symptoms had to satisfy unusually rigid criteria (Blazer, Hughes, & George, 1987; Kermis, 1986). Finally, the surveys are only of elderly living in the community, not the fraction of the older population physically and often mentally impaired enough to need a nursing home. If we considered the total older population, those residing in long-term care as well as those outside, the rate of mental disorders in old age might surpass that of younger adults (Kermis, 1986). Furthermore, these age comparisons do not include that terrible class of mental problems that growing old in particular brings—**dementia.**

Dementia is actually not a pathology of our emotions but a disorder of cognition—grossly impaired thinking, memory, and reasoning. It has a clear *organic* basis. The changes dementia wreaks in the brain can be clearly seen at autopsy. This is in contrast to, for example, schizophrenia or anxiety disorders that affect mainly personality rather than memory or IQ and that do not have an *observable* organic cause.

But what is dementia really like? Is this condition the inevitable price we must pay for living to a ripe old age?

DEMENTIA

Symptoms of Dementia

The term *dementia* does not refer to a single illness. It is a label applied to a set of chronic illnesses that have basically similar symptoms—a progressive decline in all intellectual functions. Problems are often first seen in a person's memory for relatively recent events. The individual has trouble remembering what occurred within the last few days, hours, or minutes. A woman may forget that she just spoke to her daughter and call her again. A man may not remember driving to the store an hour earlier and make a second trip. The vignette clearly illustrates some symptoms that may be characteristic of a dementia's beginning stage: Sophie regularly forgot she had worn the same dress the day before and sometimes left the dishes uncleared after meals.

As in the vignette, memory lapses can be hard to interpret. They may be indistinguishable from forgetting caused by depression or anxiety or being under too much stress. Strange or atypical behavior may only be seen in retrospect as the first sign of a dementing illness when, over time, the person's mental processes deteriorate further.

When researchers (Chenoweth & Spenser, 1986) interviewed 296 family members of Alzheimer's victims, many said they had interpreted changes in their relative, later diagnosed as dementia, as emotional problems. When their mother became forgetful, the children decided she was depressed or tuning them out. When a husband began behaving strangely, some wives worried that their marriage was deteriorating. A few actually went for counseling or considered a divorce.

Even if a family sensed what was happening early on, they sometimes had trouble articulating *exactly* what was peculiar or amiss and so had trouble convincing their doctor to take their anxiety seriously. Months or years might go by before the person's true problem was diagnosed. (I must emphasize that we cannot wholly blame doctors for this state of affairs. As we will see later in this chapter, there is no way of directly examining the brain to prove that the pathological changes of Alzheimer's disease exist. So this most prevalent form of dementia is very difficult to diagnose in its earliest stages. The diagnosis depends on ruling out other illnesses and is actually based on a history of deterioration over time.)

If someone is genuinely suffering from dementia, however, eventually the fact that there is something terribly wrong becomes obvious. As the illness reaches its middle stages, every aspect of the person's thinking becomes affected. Abstract reasoning becomes difficult. The individual can no longer think through options when making decisions. Judgment becomes faulty. People may act inappropriately, perhaps undressing in public, running out in traffic, yelling in the street. They may behave recklessly, be unaware of endangering their life or health. Language becomes limited. The person has trouble naming objects and is incapable of taking a listener's point of view into account. True human communication, the bridge that binds us to other people, has broken down.

As the illness progresses, the person becomes disoriented in relation to time, place, and person. A man may think this is 1943 and he is at sea talking to his commanding officer, rather than understanding he is a resident of Four Acres nursing home in 1989. Well-established memories are affected. A woman may forget her name, the name of the city where she has lived for 50 years, or that she has four children. In the last stage, people lose the ability to speak at all. At this point, they are also likely to be unable to perform the most elemental human activities—walk, go to the toilet, even swallow food well.

Psychiatrist Barry Gurland (personal communication, 1985) believes the mental losses that occur as this dreadful condition progresses are like peeling an onion. As the brain damage cuts a wider swath, each cognitive layer is stripped away in the reverse order in which it was attained. So first the mental skills—complicated abstract thought—acquired in adolescence are lost; then what was learned in elementary school—reading, the ability to add and subtract. Finally, the milestones reached at younger ages are gone—knowing one's name, walking, speaking.

However, most experts on dementia's clinical course (Reisberg, 1981; Zarit, 1980; Zarit, Orr, & Zarit, 1985) stress that not all people deteriorate in the same way. Some may be able to perform basic tasks like dressing and going to the toilet even with the most extreme impairments in memory and reasoning. Others, whose thinking is much better, may need nursing care for these basic activities of daily living.

The most heartbreaking variability, however, lies in the actual time-course of the illness. It is hard to give family members an idea of how fast the damage will progress, how long the deterioration will take. Some people get worse very rapidly, becoming unable to understand the basics of life within a few months. Others stay at relatively the same mental level for years. On average, people live about 5 years from the time their illness is diagnosed. But some die within a month or two and, with excellent care, others can live for 20 years (Zarit, Orr, & Zarit, 1985). So planning for the future becomes difficult, as the family prays either that their loved one will not get much worse or yearns for the death that will put a parent or spouse out of misery.

The Prevalence of Dementia

Epidemiological studies suggest that about 5% to 8% of the elderly living outside of institutions have cognitive impairments consonant with dementia (Kay & Bergmann, 1980). Although these figures are not high, they do translate into many older people living in the community who have marked problems dealing with the basics of daily life. Because dementia is often a reason for nursing home admission, the proportion of institutionalized older people who suffer from dementing illnesses is dramatically higher—perhaps 70% (Blazer, 1980).

Compared to other illnesses of aging, dementia strikes relatively late in life: it is very rare before age 50, gradually rises in prevalence during the next 3 decades, and jumps dramatically in frequency in advanced old age. Although only a small fraction of the young-old are affected, after the mid-80s about one in four people *living at home* suffer from moderate to severe mental loss (see Table 10-2). The fact that dementia becomes almost epidemic at life's uppermost rungs is especially distressing because of the rising number of people surviving to this age. Some experts feel dementia may be the number one health problem in the next century.

To understand these threatening diseases, it is important first to stress that *many* different brain conditions may cause progressive, irreversible intellectual decline (see Table 10-3 for some rare examples). On the other hand, two specific

TABLE 10-2. Percent of people with dementia* at different ages in selected community surveys.

Survey	Ages				
	65–69	**70–74**	**75–79**	**80–84**	**85 +**
Denmark (*N* = 978)	2.1	4.0	7.8	7.8	21.4
England (*N* = 758)	2.4	2.9	5.6	22.0	
Japan (*N* = 531)	1.9	2.7	11.3	9.9	33.3
Sweden (*N* = 443)	0.9		5.1	21.6	
Syracuse, NY (*N* = 1805)	3.7	5.4	9.3	8.8	23.7

   * Moderate or severe memory and thinking problems.

Source: Adapted from Kay & Bergmann, 1980.

TABLE 10-3. Four of the rarer dementing illnesses.

Disease	Symptoms and Description
Creutzfeldt-Jakob disease	This very rare dementing disease, usually beginning in the fifth or sixth decade of life, is of particular interest because it is transmissible: It is caused by a slow-growing virus
Huntington's chorea	The tragedy of this highly heritable illness is that the offspring of a victim have a 50/50 chance of developing it, yet it manifests itself after the person's peak childbearing years—in the mid-40s. The disease is characterized not only by progressively worsening thinking and memory but by involuntary movements that become more abnormal as the illness advances
Normal-pressure hydrocephalus	This type of dementia is caused by a buildup of fluid in the ventricles of the brain. Treatment, partially effective in about half the cases, consists of surgery to drain the fluid
Pick's disease	While it produces many of the pathological changes characteristic of the most common dementing illness, Alzheimer's disease, this illness seems to progress differently—initially attacking different sections of the brain

illnesses account for more than 90% of all later-life dementias—*Alzheimer's disease* (or *primary degenerative dementia*) and *multi-infarct dementia* (Reisberg, 1981).

Alzheimer's Disease

Actually, the disorder called **Alzheimer's disease** used to be thought to be two separate illnesses: a disease that began before age 65 and a less virulent, more slowly advancing condition involving the same pathological changes, which began in old age. Alzheimer's disease, or *presenile dementia*, was the diagnostic label that was used when a person developed the illness in middle age. *Senile dementia* was the diagnosis when the illness began after age 65. While at least one authority, psychiatrist Martin Roth (1985), believes the distinction between early and late onset should still be kept, most experts feel that there is no reason for making this differentiation. The brain disorder not only looks the same, it progresses in the same way whether it begins in middle or later life (Sloane, 1980; Tomlinson, 1984). Although Alzheimer's disease has become the label used for this illness in a person of any age, be aware that the diagnoses presenile or senile dementia, or even senile dementia of the Alzheimer's type, are also frequently applied. Adding to the confusion, the framers of DSM-III have given this illness the other name mentioned above—**primary degenerative dementia.**

About 50% to 60% of elderly people who suffer from dementia have Alzheimer's disease, making it by far the most prevalent chronic brain impairment of old age (Reisberg, 1981). Alzheimer's disease attacks our humanity at its core—destroying the neurons in the brain. The brain atrophies and there are fewer interconnections between the normal neurons. Most important, the healthy neurons are literally eaten away.

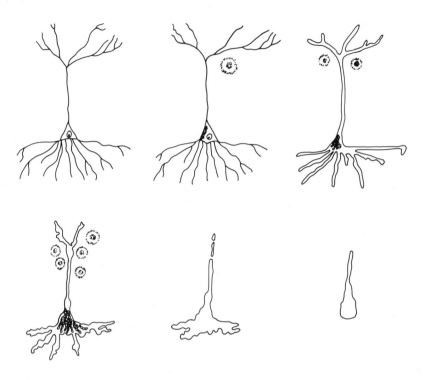

Figure 10-1. Progressive degeneration of a neuron in Alzheimer's disease.
Source: From Zarit, Orr, & Zarit, 1985.

Normally a neuron looks like a tree. When a person has Alzheimer's disease, it appears as if the tree is slowly being killed by an infection. First it loses its branches, then it swells and becomes gnarled. Finally, its trunk shrivels to a stump (I have taken this vivid description from Zarit, Orr, & Zarit, 1985; see Recommended Readings and Figure 10-1). In place of the once-normal brain tissue are wavy filaments called **neurofibrillary tangles;** thick, bulletlike bodies of protein called **senile plaques;** and other pathological signs of deterioration.

At first the destruction is limited and confined to certain areas of the brain. As the illness progresses, it gradually cuts a wider swath. More and more healthy neurons die and are replaced by these peculiar structures. The brain of a person with advanced Alzheimer's disease may be so studded with abnormal fragments that there are few normal-appearing neurons left.

In a classic study, British researchers showed that the memory and thinking problems a person has are a direct function of the amount of neural destruction that has taken place. After death, the brains of elderly people with memory losses of varying severity were autopsied. The researchers found a good correlation between the density of senile plaques and the person's intellectual abilities near the time of death (Blessed, Tomlinson, & Roth, 1968; Roth, Tomlinson, & Blessed, 1966; Tomlinson, 1977).

Unfortunately, there is also a catch—*normal* older people also have these pathological changes. They have senile plaques. They have neurofibrillary tangles and cortical atrophy as well. But the number of these abnormal structures is far less and their scope is far narrower—they tend to be confined to limited areas of the brain (Roth, 1980; Terry & Wisneiwski, 1977). Specifically, they are not likely to be present in the brain's outermost part, the neocortex. In dementia, the neocortex is involved, and the damage is much more marked and extensive (Reisberg, 1981).

The presence of these qualitatively similar changes in normal older adults illustrates that the link between normal aging and a pathological condition—in this case, dementia—is uncomfortably close. And, unfortunately, because its risk does increase so dramatically at the end of the life span, the statistics spell out another uncomfortable truth. While granted there are still many people who reach their 90s sound in mind, not infrequently dementia is indeed the price of living to the *ripest* old age. (The way abnormalities increase at older ages is clearly shown in Figure 10-2. As the decades advance, autopsies show that an increasingly greater proportion of people manifest the brain features of Alzheimer's disease.)

What causes the neural decay? While we still do not know, theories have centered around a handful of agents of destruction. In reading the following list, keep in mind that one possible cause does not exclude the others. Rather than having a unitary cause, it is just as likely that Alzheimer's disease is the final common pathway of several different types of insults to the brain (Reisberg, 1981; Roth, 1985).

Possible Causes of Alzheimer's Disease.

• *A virus:* Because a virus is known to cause a rare type of dementia, Creutzfeldt-Jakob disease, some researchers feel that a slow-acting virus, one that may take decades to incubate in the body, might be implicated in Alzheimer's disease.

• *An immune system malfunction:* Another set of speculations centers around an autoimmune response. In support of this possibility, researchers (Fillit, Kemeny, Luine, Weksler, & Zabriskie, 1987) reported finding abnormal antibodies in patients with Alzheimer's disease. They hypothesized that these antibodies, instead of functioning normally to repel outside invaders, may attack components of the blood/brain barrier, the chemical sheath that keeps injurious substances from gaining access to the brain. Once the integrity of the blood/brain barrier is breached, then a virus or other toxin might gain access to the brain and set the illness off.

• *Aluminum:* Other than a virus, a strong candidate for an Alzheimer's disease instigating toxin is aluminum, because a striking feature of the brains of Alzheimer's victims is an abnormally high concentration of this substance in particular. Does absorbing too much aluminum over a lifetime play any part in the disease? In the past, direct tests of this hypothesis yielded negative results; however, one recent epidemiological study comparing 88 counties in Wales and

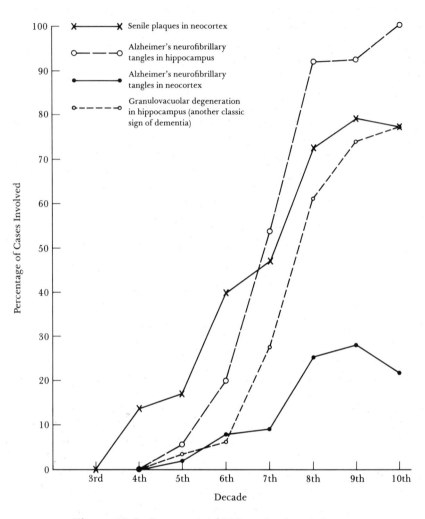

Figure 10-2. Percentage of 219 routine hospital cases
showing evidence of senile changes by decade of age.
Source: From Smith & Kinsbourne, 1977.

England does show cause for concern. The investigators found that in regions
having higher aluminum concentrations in the drinking water, residents did
indeed have a greater incidence of Alzheimer's disease (see Lubin, 1989). While
there may be other reasons than aluminum to explain these variations in Alzheimer's rates, this finding does lend more credence to the idea that aluminum
may play some role in the etiology of Alzheimer's disease.

▪ *A genetic defect:* Another new research lead involves genetics. Family studies have long implied that there may be a genetic component to Alzheimer's
disease. In 1987 researchers finally identified a specific genetic defect in a small
sample of people with an *unusually* strong family history of the illness (see

Barnes, 1987). Interestingly, the genetic marker the researchers found is located on chromosome 21—the chromosome that people suffering from the birth defect Down's syndrome have an extra copy of. For years, scientists had been intrigued by what they knew was an important connection between these two illnesses because victims of Down's syndrome almost universally develop Alzheimer's disease if they live to age 40. Now the possible reason for the link is revealed. Having an extra chromosome 21 may be giving victims of Down's syndrome a double dose of the Alzheimer's-producing genetic program.

Other research, also reported in early 1987 (see Barnes, 1987), suggests that the illness may be set off by abnormal deposits of a protein called amyloid building up in the brain. Amyloid is a core constituent of both senile plaques and neurofibrillary tangles. Do the genetic instructions "produce amyloid" trigger the disease directly by causing this toxin to accumulate? Does an Alzheimer's gene (or set of genes) act in concert with a substance such as aluminum or a virus to set the illness off? Whatever the answer, attention is now focused on elucidating what part the accumulation of this substance may play in the illness.

• *Acetylcholine deficiencies:* Another focus of research involves neurotransmitters, the chemical substances released at synapses that enable our neurons to communicate with one another. For more than a decade researchers have known that a striking deficiency of one type of neurotransmitter, acetylcholine, is a characteristic feature of the brains of Alzheimer's victims (see Roth, 1985). If Alzheimer's disease selectively attacks the acetylcholine-producing (cholinergic) neurons, stimulating the brain's production of this chemical might be an effective antidote. While so far research efforts to do this have not produced dramatic results (see Chapter 11), the search for strategies that might restore acetylcholine continues at a feverish pace (Crook, 1986; Roth, 1985).

Multi-Infarct Dementia

The second most common dementia of old age—**multi-infarct dementia** (comprising about 15% to 20% of all dementias)—is caused by the death of a significant amount of brain tissue due to many small strokes (Scheinberg, 1978). Multi-infarct dementia used to be called *arteriosclerotic dementia* (arteriosclerosis is the medical term for "hardening of the arteries"). At the time this seemed to be the right label because experts thought this type of dementia was caused by atherosclerosis and arteriosclerosis, which cause the walls of the arteries pumping blood to the brain to stiffen and harden (Hachinski, Lassen, & Marshal, 1974). Today we know that this vascular type of dementia is not caused by partially clogged arteries but by completely blocked ones. A series of small strokes (or, in medical terminology, infarcts) is what really produces the cognitive deterioration, so the new name has become multi-infarct dementia.

A stroke occurs when an artery feeding the brain becomes completely blocked, cutting off the blood supply so that the part of the brain nourished by that vessel is either damaged or dies. A large stroke produces symptoms that are difficult to miss—paralysis, impaired speech, perhaps death. The person who has multi-infarct dementia is subject to strokes so minor that they produce few

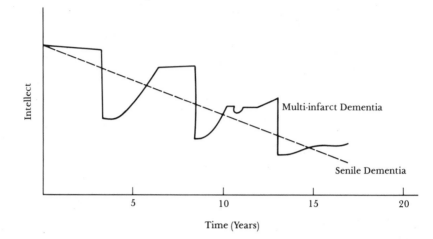

Figure 10-3. Course of intellectual deterioration in senile dementia
(Alzheimer's disease) and multi-infarct dementia.
Source: From Reisberg, 1981.

perceptible symptoms. But as their number increases and more brain tissue dies, memory and thinking gradually get worse.

Because strokes of any kind are in part precipitated by potentially treatable problems such as high blood pressure, there may be some chance of stemming the downhill course of this type of dementia by, for example, lowering blood pressure through diet and medication (Hachinski, Lassen, & Marshal, 1974; Sloane, 1980). Normally, however, as with Alzheimer's disease, the person with multi-infarct dementia usually gets worse and worse because the strokes accumulate, affecting larger segments of the brain.

While the two major dementias can only be distinguished with certainty at autopsy, and studies suggest that both illnesses are present in about 25% of people with dementia, there are signs suggesting that a person may have dementia of the multi-infarct type. The individual may be more physically ill, suffering from other symptoms of impaired circulation; more classical signs of stroke may be present, such as motor or sensory problems (or evidence of a stroke may show up on measures such as the CT scan); behavior may get worse in steps rather than deteriorating gradually (Sloane, 1980). Because the number of strokes accumulates erratically, with multi-infarct dementia there tends to be a more jerky, stepwise decline in functioning rather than the smoother, regular loss of abilities more typical of Alzheimer's disease (see Figure 10-3).

Personality Changes and Dementia

Even though changes in thinking are the hallmark of dementing illnesses, it is the emotional alterations—physical and verbal aggression, delusions, suspiciousness, uncontrollable agitation, and wandering—these devastating illnesses wreak that tend to cause families the most distress (Deimling & Bass, 1986; Niederehe & Fruge, 1984; Rabins, Mace, & Lucas, 1982). These very difficult symptoms, which most often appear when the illness is in its middle stages, may result from the loss of neurons in areas of the brain that control and modulate emotions. Or they may have an indirect cause. At this stage of the illness, the person is still partially aware of his or her condition and is struggling psychologically with this devastating perception (Reisberg, 1981). Because the most disruptive symptoms often abate as the impairment worsens and more abilities are lost, ironically, in interviewing spouse caregivers, Steve Zarit and his colleagues (Zarit, Todd, & Zarit, 1986) found that as the illness reached its final stages, caregivers reported that coping was easier because when the deterioration became profound the person became easier to control.

Not every demented person develops these upsetting symptoms. For instance, in one study when patients with Alzheimer's disease were followed, researchers (Borson, Teri, Kiyak, & Montgomery, 1986) found that severe agitation, physical abusiveness, or paranoid reactions each appeared in only about 10% to 15% of the cases. While most investigators emphasize that the behavioral changes that do occur are completely foreign, having no real relation to how a person behaved before the disease struck, a fascinating anecdotal study suggests that the new, demented behavior may not appear *totally* out of the blue.

Dianna Shomaker (1987) asked the families of nine patients to reminisce about their relative's personality before developing Alzheimer's disease and then examined the person's current actions closely for similarities. She found that while there were vast differences in the manner of presentation, there did indeed seem to be continuities. For instance, the expert cook might develop a kitchen-centered preoccupation, the compulsion to make meal after meal. A closer look at the aimless wandering of the former workaholic showed that it was his frantic effort to get to his office. Previous traits such as self-pity, generosity, or stinginess often might reappear, though in intensified, diminished, or inappropriate form. While this study suffers from the *extremely* major deficiencies of being retrospective, interpretive, qualitative, and based on far too few subjects, it does suggest that with dementia there might be more of a relationship between then and now than people realize.

In addition to the disruptive behaviors that make life so difficult for caregivers (and the person, too!), when the illness is not too far advanced people may also show signs of depression—an understandably common response to being somewhat aware of one's terrible fate. Depression, however, and the other catastrophic reactions listed above, tend to exacerbate cognitive deficits that are genuinely there (Wang, 1977). Rather than grappling with cognitive challenges they can master, people who develop these reactions give up. In the clinical vignette, by staying at home so much, Sophie ensured that when she did leave the house the outside world would be genuinely foreign, bereft of familiar markers. In fact, her reaction illustrates the way a too demanding environment may cause excess disabilities of any type. Negotiating an environment incongruent with one's abilities may produce an intolerable degree of anxiety, causing the person to retreat and abandon any attempt to function at his or her potential. The avoidance then exaggerates the problem, multiplying the deficits the person has.

Does this mean that encouraging the person with Alzheimer's disease to do as much as possible is the best strategy? Steve Zarit, who has worked extensively with victims of dementing illnesses and their families, suggests that this approach can be very dangerous. Pushing the person is tailor-made to cause frustration. Families often blame their relatives for not trying to "remember," berate them for not "controlling" themselves. Not only does this magnify everyone's pain, the idea that these people *can* behave differently is wrong. The tragedy of these illnesses is that the human ability to reflect on and control behavior is lost. People with dementia cannot help how they act (Zarit, Orr, & Zarit, 1985).

The Strains and Stresses of Caregiving

This discussion suggests that caring for a family member with dementia poses unusually intense strains. Not only may caregivers need to be "on duty" full time to protect the person, they must cope with a loved human being turned alien, where the tools used in normal human encounters no longer apply. But are people in this difficult situation really markedly worse off than others dealing just with the normal stresses of life? If these caregivers are more stressed, what aspects of the caregiving situation tend to multiply the pain?

Because the *specific* ways that caregivers are more distressed had never been fully documented, Linda George and Lisa Gwyther (1986) decided to compare a sample of people caring for a demented relative with matched controls not in this situation in four arenas: physical health, mental health, financial resources, and social participation. As we might expect, the most marked differences were present in the emotional and social realms of life. Caregivers averaged three times as many stress symptoms; they were much more prone to use tranquilizers; had lower morale; and spent much less time pursuing outside activities than the comparison group. Hobbies, visits with family and friends, and, especially, just relaxing by themselves all were casualties to the burden of dealing with this terrible disease. The one bright glimmer was that physically and financially these caregivers were holding up, were not worse off than the comparison group.

It comes as no surprise that other studies also show that caregiving is a tremendous stress (for example, see Haley, Levine, Brown, Berry, & Hughes, 1987). What is unexpected is that the severity of the person's illness itself is not the primary determinant of that strain. A growing amount of research suggests that rather than the victim's objective symptoms, other aspects of the caregiving situation make the burden feel especially overwhelming (Gwyther & George, 1986)—not feeling supported by family and friends; having had an ambivalent or poor relationship with the person before the illness struck; not using active, problem-solving strategies in coping with the illness (Haley, Levine, Brown, & Bartolucci, 1987; Zarit, Orr, & Zarit, 1985; Zarit, Todd, and Zarit, 1986). In other words, caregiving weighs much less heavily when a person feels appreciated and supported or when the job is cushioned by a legacy of love. It is the perception of feeling out of control of the situation, not the objective severity of the situation itself, which causes the most distress.

Other variables may also be related to how well caregivers cope and how overburdened they feel—factors as varied as the caregiver's age, sex, and life-stage (Fitting, Rabins, Lucas, & Eastham, 1986), the formal help the person is getting (Johnson, C. L., 1983), the number of outside activities the person has (Haley, Levine, Brown, & Bartolucci, 1987). Until we find a cure for these illnesses, perhaps our best hope for minimizing the pain lies in this immensely practical new research. What helps or hinders the second victims of dementia, the caregiving families, from doing their difficult job? What formal services are most needed? (The discussion in Chapter 4 implies, for instance, that while family members committed to ministering to an Alzheimer's victim are less likely to want ongoing services such as day care, they would benefit a good deal from the periodic help of respite services.) What is the long-term impact of caregiving on the family as whole?

Accurately Distinguishing Dementia from Delirium and Depression

Because no technological advance has enabled us to see into the brain to prove that Alzheimer's disease is conclusively there, the diagnosis of the major dementing illnesses is made by exclusion, by taking a careful history and ruling out the many problems that produce mental impairment but are at least potentially reversible (McKhann, Drachman, Folstein, Katzman, Price, & Stadlan, 1984). Unfortunately, the number of treatable conditions that can masquerade as irreversible cognitive impairment are legion—leading to the alarming estimate that from 20% to 30% of all people labeled as "senile" may actually have a treatable disease (McKhann et al., 1984). The clouding of consciousness these illnesses and conditions produce goes by another name, **delirium.**

Delirium.   Delirium, or a delirious state, refers to the marked impairment in awareness that problems as varied as cancer, toxic drug effects, or the disorientation of just hearing about a loved one's death can produce (see Table 10-4). Anyone, old or young, can become delirious. Older people, however, are particularly vulnerable to developing these symptoms of disturbed consciousness because they are not as physiologically hardy as the young. Delirium is particularly common among hospitalized older people because so many physical illnesses and medical interventions can precipitate these cognitive changes (Habot & Libow, 1980). Moreover, a person ill enough to be hospitalized is likely to be taking drugs, which can cause delirium, too. Particularly in the elderly, delirium can even be produced by lack of stimulation—lying in bed for weeks.

The clinical course of delirium is markedly different from the slow, progressive cognitive impairment that characterizes Alzheimer's disease. Delirium develops rapidly. Thinking may become grossly impaired within a few hours or days. One hour a rational human being may be in the room, the next a madman appears.

TABLE 10-4. Some causes of delirium in the elderly.

Precipitating Causes	Underlying Reasons
Accidents or assaults	Both may occur more frequently as people age; physical and emotional effects may cause delirium
Environmental changes	Death of a loved one; a major move; prolonged hospitalization
Illnesses and physical conditions	Cardiac problems including heart attack; neurological conditions such as stroke, encephalitis, tumors; metabolic disorders of all types; cancer of the pancreas; pneumonia or any illness causing fever; constipation; heat stroke
Medications	Errors in self-administration; polypharmacy (taking a number of different medications simultaneously); abuse of nonprescription drugs; side effects of drugs given appropriately; inappropriate drug dosage for the individual
Poor nutrition	Inadequate vitamin or protein intake (older people as a group are at high risk of being malnourished)
Surgery	Aftereffects of anesthesia; surgical complications

And the delirious person may indeed seem mad, perhaps hallucinating images on the wall or babbling incoherently. Periods of profound disorientation may fluctuate dramatically with lucid periods, times when the person shows no impairment at all (Sloane, 1980). For instance, when he wakes up from surgery, 84-year-old Ted Jones begins talking to his long-dead bridge partner. He is wildly psychotic, not recognizing his wife and children at all. The next morning when the chemicals clear, he is his old self again. While cognitive changes almost as marked as this may occur with dementia, too, with delirium the shifts are especially dramatic. And, as in this case, the disorientation is often linked to a clear external precipitant. So trained observers should be able to tell this problem from Alzheimer's disease.

However, because people are so primed to read senility into any old age cognitive impairment, older people such as Ted Jones are sometimes misdiagnosed as demented. An 80-year-old man who arrives in the busy emergency room confused but without pain may be diagnosed as having Alzheimer's disease even though his real problem is a heart attack (see Chapter 4); family members may assume that their 90-year-old mother's confusion is due to dementia, not remembering that it began when the doctor prescribed those heart pills a month ago. Or (as recently happened to my 80-year-old father—whose memory is excellent), while heavily sedated and terrified in the operating room awaiting heart surgery, the older person is given a mental status test and "diagnosed" as having probable Alzheimer's disease.

These misinterpretations are costly not just because they cause excess disabilities—but because, as Table 10-4 shows, the reason for the delirium may be a life-threatening condition, misdiagnosis may cost the person his or her life!

Depression.   The second type of problem that tends to be misdiagnosed as dementia, depression, may even be more difficult to distinguish because it does not produce the dramatic change in thinking that signals delirium.

On the surface, depression seems as if it should be easy to differentiate from dementia. How can an emotional disorder be mistaken for a pathology of intellect? The reason is that (as we will see in the next section) a cardinal symptom of depression is intellectual change—cloudy thinking, problems focusing, a general mental slowing up. Unfortunately these very symptoms of impaired cognition may be even more typical of depression in the elderly than in the young, sometimes making the task of differentiating between depression and an early stage dementia difficult.

Since depression is potentially treatable and dementia is generally not, it seems reasonable that diagnosticians should err on the positive side. As in the vignette, they should assume that the person's problem is the condition that can be treated (depression) until proven otherwise. Unfortunately, however, a cross-sectional study suggests that in our country professionals may actually leap to adopt the negative view. When researchers (see Copeland, 1978) compared the frequency with which psychiatrists in the United States and Great Britain assigned the diagnostic labels depression and dementia to given patients, they found that the Americans were more likely to classify people as demented. The British, looking at the same symptoms, were more likely to label the older person as depressed. Since this study was done 15 years ago, diagnosticians today may act differently. Still, the nagging question remains. How many U.S. elderly are written off as senile and ignored when they really are depressed?

Luckily, one study shows that despite the difficulty of diagnosing dementia, in the hands of *geriatrically knowledgeable* professionals, accuracy is the norm. When 200 patients evaluated in a geriatric clinic specializing in the diagnosis of dementia were followed up for a year, researchers (Larson, E. B., Reifler, Sumi, Canfield, & Chinn, 1985) found there were indeed very few diagnostic mistakes. If a person was labeled as having dementia, over time that diagnosis was almost always confirmed.

On the other hand, this study pointed up a crucial fact. Even when a person does have Alzheimer's disease, the impairment is often made worse by the presence of simultaneous treatable conditions such as overmedication or other diseases. Twenty-seven percent of these demented elderly showed improvements in cognition when the staff aggressively ferreted out and treated the reversible conditions that coexisted with the dementing illness. So the issue is not just to avoid misdiagnosis but to accurately diagnose and treat what often makes the impairment much worse: the many treatable problems that magnify the deficits caused by the irreversible brain disease.

DEPRESSION

Dementing illnesses, as just mentioned, have two distinguishing features—they primarily affect memory and intelligence and they have a clear physiological basis. Now we turn to a functional psychological problem that, even though it can produce intellectual decrements, has mainly nonintellectual effects— **depression.** Depressed people are potentially capable of doing very well on tests of memory and abstract thought, but their perceptions about the world and their emotional reactions are askew.

Why single out depression versus other emotional problems to discuss? The reason, as we will see, is that even though only a small fraction of older people qualify as depressed according to rigorous DSM-III standards, mild depressive symptoms are extremely common in later life (Blazer, Hughes, & George, 1987).

Symptoms and Prevalence of Depression

The emotional problem of depression is not the same as the sadness, frustration, and unhappiness we all feel occasionally as the price of being alive. It is a real mental disorder that can have a number of causes. Genetic and personality predispositions, early life experiences, current and past losses and failures may all produce or contribute jointly to a person's becoming depressed. Depression is also expressed by a great variety of physical and psychological complaints (Becker, 1974). Not only may depression look very different clinically in different people, in the older person, as mentioned earlier, it may take a qualitatively different form than it might in a younger adult (Gurland, 1976).

To make order out of this variety, psychiatrist Aaron Beck (1979) groups depressive symptoms into distinct categories: emotional signs, changes in cognition, motivational signs, physical signs, and, in severe cases, delusions and hallucinations.

The symptoms that Beck lists under emotional signs are the most familiar to us. The depressed person may have crying spells, look glum, and be unable to feel any joy. Surprisingly, however, not everyone who is depressed has these obvious mood changes. Depression, especially in the older person, may be "masked," expressing itself, for instance, only in exaggerated physical complaints (Epstein, 1976; Waxman, McCreary, Weinrit, & Carner, 1985). When the older person's depressive illness is only manifested by excessive tiredness, or heart pain, or some other physical symptom, diagnosing the real problem can be very difficult.

Cognitive changes characteristic of depression include thoughts of worthlessness and uselessness, irrational guilt feelings, and ideas that the world is empty and has nothing positive to offer. The older depressed person may be convinced that he or she is getting senile or is terminally ill. These symptoms are labeled as cognitive because it is the person's thoughts, or cognitions, which are unrealistically skewed.

In severe cases, the person's thinking may become psychotic. He or she may have delusions (fixed irrational ideas) or hallucinations (hear imaginary voices). Depressive delusions and hallucinations tend to be severely self-blaming. The person may be convinced that he or she has committed a horrible crime or can be tortured by voices making terrible accusations and whispering horrible warnings of doom.

The motivational changes depression causes center around an inability to act, or the desire to escape or avoid the world. As with Sophie Gold in the vignette, the depressed person may be sunk in apathy or locked into inaction by paralyzing fear. Occasionally there may be suicidal thinking; often there is a supreme indifference to life.

Depression also can produce a range of physical changes: disturbances of appetite—either indifference to food or compulsive overeating; problems with sleep—sleeplessness or, less commonly, sleeping excessively; impairments of digestion and elimination—nausea, heartburn, constipation. Fatigue, inability to concentrate, and slowed thinking and moving are also characteristic physical signs.

Unfortunately, when the older person's depression is manifested by these somatic or cognitive symptoms alone it may be misread as normal aging (Epstein, 1976; Gurland, 1976) or misinterpreted as a physical disease (Kermis, 1986). A doctor may pass off the 2 a.m. awakening that signals depression in her 80-year-old patient as normal aging. She may label the person's lack of appetite as a problem in the digestive tract. Slow thinking may be passed off as the "typical" deficit old age brings or, worse, misread as Alzheimer's disease. How often are these errors likely to be made? One study (Waxman et al., 1985) offers some unsettling clues: 127 participants in senior center lunch programs filled out a depression inventory and then a standard questionnaire of self-rated health (the Cornell Medical Health Index) in which they were asked to report on the presence of close to 200 specific symptoms and also any chronic diseases. While the respondents who scored as depressed on the inventory reported no more chronic illnesses than their nondepressed peers, they did check off a much greater number of somatic symptoms. In other words, depression in old age does tend to be accompanied by an outpouring of physical complaints. How many doctors, listening to this avalanche in a depressed older patient, are misled, missing the underlying emotional disorder this litany really signifies?

This study revealed another surprising fact. Among this random sample of community dwelling older people depression was rampant—a full 33.1% of the respondents scored in the depressed range on the inventory. This figure is not too different from the 27% statistic Duke University researchers found in a full-scale epidemiological study (Blazer, Hughes, & George, 1987). These statistics—which suggest that depression is a *widespread* problem in later life—are very discrepant from those in the NIMH survey because the researchers in these studies were counting people with mild depressive symptoms, ones that would not qualify as a real depressive disorder as defined by DSM-III. In other words, the encouraging NIMH study may only show the iceberg's most serious tip. While relatively serious depressions may indeed be uncommon, mild depression seems a distressingly frequent feature of the later years.

Findings from the Duke Longitudinal Study echo this theme (Gianturco & Busse, 1978): 20% to 25% of the Duke study elderly were diagnosed as depressed at a given round of testings. By the ninth or tenth evaluation, about 60% had been labeled as depressed at least once. And depression in the Duke volunteers was often chronic: The same people tended to be rated as depressed in successive testings.

Categories and Causes of Depression

Typically, depression is classified into two categories: **major** and **minor** (also called *dysthymic disorder* or *neurotic depression* in DSM-III). While most experts believe these distinctions are important because major and minor depressions not only have a different constellation of symptoms, they suggest which therapeutic approaches may be most fruitful to use, there is some controversy over the usefulness of this classification, too (Becker, 1974). Depression in real life does not always fit neatly into these categories; many depressed people have features of *both* a major and a minor depression simultaneously.

A person diagnosed as having a major depression has more severe symptoms. The problem is less likely to have a clear-cut external or situational cause. Specific physical changes are predominant: loss of appetite, early morning awakening (the person can get to sleep but wakes up spontaneously a few hours later), constipation, slowed or speeded up motor activity. Other family members may suffer from the illness. Medication may work especially well. Because this type of depression seems more hereditary, more tied to physical signs, less related to events, and can sometimes be helped dramatically by medical treatments alone, it seems tied in part to biochemistry—the person has a genuine physiological predisposition to become depressed.

In contrast, for minor depressions, unhappy life events—loss, rejection, failure—often play a clear-cut role. Physical symptoms are not major features; genetic correlates are not there. The major focus of treatment involves changing the depression-causing situation or modifying the person's depression-generating thoughts. While medications can also be effective, psychotherapy is the approach of choice.

As we will see in the next chapter, it is useful to attempt to make these distinctions in older depressed people. Elderly people with major depressions are more likely to respond to drug therapy, less apt to profit as much from *just* psychotherapy (Gallagher & Thompson, 1983; Thompson, Davies, Gallagher, & Krantz, 1986). However, in later life, the frequent combination of clear physical symptoms plus environmental reasons why the person might be depressed make categorizing especially difficult (Gurland, 1976; Zarit & Zarit, 1984). Depressions in old age often appear both minor and major simultaneously, with mixtures of both types of symptoms. For example, in the vignette, Sophie Gold had some somatic signs characteristic of a major depression (loss of appetite, problems sleeping), but her depression also seems minor in that it followed an upsetting event, the move.

The fact that major and minor depressions seem so different has given rise to two types of investigations: theories and research exploring the psychological mechanisms that produce depression, and studies elucidating depression's biochemistry.

The Psychology of Depression.   Losses, particularly those that are highly personally meaningful, have long been viewed as the primary cause of depression in children, young or middle-aged adults, and in the elderly (Lipton, 1976). The loss might be of a beloved parent; a lover's rejection; being fired from a job; losing one's money; or, as in the vignette, mourning the loss of home and friends. However, as we know, at least two major late-life losses—retirement and widowhood—only sometimes produce depression in older adults. The type of event that seems to have this effect most often is a loss of another kind: one's health (see Zarit & Zarit, 1984, for a review). For example, in one study, a serious illness preceded the onset of depressive symptoms in a full 18% of a random group of depressed elderly people (Roth & Kay, 1956).

Knowing that losses may cause depression, however, does not explain the psychological mechanism by which this happens. For this we turn to hypotheses, a few ideas offered by people who subscribe to the two very different world views about what causes emotional problems—behaviorism and psychoanalytic theory.

Freud (1957; translation of 1917 paper) was the first to attempt to explain depression. He wanted to understand why guilt and self-blame were such typical features of depressive thinking, why depressed people often berated themselves as if they had committed terrible crimes. He tied these symptoms to the loss of an ambivalently loved object (person) and contrasted depression with normal mourning. In mourning, he hypothesized, a person comes to terms with the loss of a loved person by identification. (We saw an example of this psychological mechanism in Chapter 9's vignette.) The bereaved person internalizes qualities of the lost loved one, and these qualities become part of the mourner's own self. Normal mourning becomes depression, Freud reasoned, when the survivor has unconscious negative feelings for the lost person. These negative feelings are also turned inward, and the person internalizes the unresolved angry feelings once reserved for the other. In Freud's view, then, after a loss of someone both loved and hated, feelings about the other person are turned inward, explaining why depressed people are so tortured by self-hate.

Freud's interpretation may apply to some depressions in old age but it seems far too limited to cover all. Not all depressions in later life appear after the loss of a loved person. As noted earlier, depressive symptoms may occur even more predictably, for instance, after an illness strikes. It is difficult to see how Freud's analysis applies to this most frequent cause of depression in later life.

In fact, other psychoanalytic writers have noted that depression in later life is more often characterized by apathy and a sense of helplessness and exhaustion than the vehement self-hate Freud's theory was attempting to explain (Cath, 1965; Gianturco & Busse, 1978). These symptoms, so common in older depressed people, of withdrawal, lack of interest in the outside world, and slowed thinking and moving suggest another cause. Depression in old age most often arises from a sense of helplessness and hopelessness in the face of unavoidable, quite real losses (Cath, 1965).

Actually, the idea that "helplessness and hopelessness" is at the root of depression has been proposed by writers in both the behavioral and psychoanalytic camps (see Becker, 1974, for review). For example, a psychoanalyst, Edward Bibring (1953) suggests that depression occurs when losses shake a person's confidence in his or her ability to get gratification. These losses also deprive the person of important ego supports necessary to maintaining self-esteem. As a result, a state of "ego helplessness" occurs. The person feels inadequate and incompetent. The depressive symptoms of apathy and low self-esteem are an outgrowth of the person's feelings of not being in control.

The idea is amazingly similar to the original precepts of an influential behavioral theory, experimental psychologist Martin Seligman's concept of **learned helplessness** (1975). Seligman's ideas about the genesis of depression stemmed from an unlikely source, his research with laboratory animals. In a series of experiments, he showed that dogs repeatedly subjected to electrical shocks they could not escape eventually developed "depressive" symptoms: They became apathetic; they seemed sad; they were unable to think or move quickly. In addition, his fascinating finding was that when the animals were later put in a situation where they could avoid the shocks, they were incapable of doing so. They had learned to be helpless—a lesson that actions were futile that interfered with any new learning and so perpetuated the depressive response.

To Seligman his studies offered an ideal model for how human depression often occurs. After a series of losses, failures, or misfortunes, people naturally develop the idea that they are helpless, unable to do anything to control their destiny. This lesson in helplessness profoundly affects their world outlook and the way they behave. They become apathetic, withdrawn, and hopeless. They become depressed.

About a decade ago, consonant with behaviorism's new cognitive emphasis, Seligman and his colleagues moved beyond a simplistic stress on helplessness-inducing events, believing that it is the attributions we make about life occurrences or life stresses (for example, "I am helpless to shape my fate") and not the objective events in themselves that are at the root of becoming depressed. (As I will describe in the next chapter, similar ideas, that people interpret the same events differently and that unrealistic negative inferences about events are what typically cause depression, underlie the most influential behavioral treatment for this emotional disorder today—Aaron Beck's 1973, 1979, cognitive behavioral approach.)

Seligman's theory of learned helplessness has had broad applications for gerontology. It underlies the rich set of control-enhancing interventions discussed in Chapter 2. As we saw in that chapter, giving deprived older people who lack control over their environment the chance to make choices not only boosts morale, it can actually extend life expectancy (see, for reviews, *Autonomy and Long-Term Care,* 1988; Rodin, 1986a, 1986b). And, because fear of being dependent (or helpless) and the need to be competent are such important concerns of older adults, Seligman's theory does indeed seem to offer a reasonable explanation of why depression is such a common emotional problem among the elderly.

The Biology of Depression.   In contrast to the psychological explanations for depression are the explorations of possible physiological causes. Researchers probing this avenue feel that some depressions may be set off by abnormalities in neurotransmitters, the chemicals that transmit impulses from neuron to neuron. A particular neurotransmitter, norepinephrine, has been the focus of most of the speculations.

Drug studies strongly suggest that low levels of norepinephrine play a central role in producing major depressions. Medications and medical procedures that decrease the amount of this chemical in the brain often produce depressive symptoms; those that increase norepinephrine levels have antidepressant effects—curing or minimizing symptoms in people suffering from major depressions. So many researchers feel that depression-prone people have a specific biochemical defect, constitutionally low levels of brain norepinephrine (Davis, J. M., Segal, & Spring, 1983; Greist & Greist, 1979). When a person's depressive symptoms seem to come out of the blue, a sudden decrease in brain norepinephrine may be responsible.

This idea is still unproven and is based on circumstantial evidence. In fact, other neurotransmitters—serotonin, acetylcholine—have been implicated in depression, too (Davis, J. M., Segal, & Spring, 1983). Actually, as may be true of Alzheimer's disease, there may be a variety of physiological causes for depression; perhaps even several different biochemical routes by which people develop this illness. Furthermore, just as having a biochemical predisposition to depression may skew our cognitions (leading us, for example, to see life's events in shades of gray), external stresses and skewed cognitions in themselves may interact to produce altered biochemistry. This brings us back to the point made at the beginning of the discussion—the complex, intertwined etiology of this multifaceted disease.

The Worst Consequence of Depression—Suicide

While only a tiny minority of depressed people attempt suicide, the reverse is true—most people who make serious suicide attempts are depressed. This is particularly true for older adults. It has been estimated that if we define depression broadly, almost 100% of the older people who attempt suicide have symptoms of depression (Stenback, 1980). Is it right to conclude, then, that since depression is a relatively common problem in later life, the suicide rate in old age is higher than at any other time of life?

The answer is a resounding yes. A full 17% of all reported suicides are committed by the 11% of the population over age 65. But, as Figure 10-4 shows, there is a wrinkle. One group is mainly responsible for this elevated rate—White men. In addition to White males committing suicide with disproportionate frequency at *every* age (except for two brief dips in late middle age and advanced old age), the suicide rate for this group also rises more dramatically as the years advance than for any other group. At its peak around age 85, White men commit suicide three times as frequently as anyone else (Manton, Blazer, & Woodbury, 1987)! Furthermore, the suicide rate sharply rises at the end of the life span for non-White males, too.

Why is later-life suicide such a male phenomenon? Do the losses of old age hit men harder because they are more used to being at the top of the social ladder (Miller, M., 1979)? Are women more resilient emotionally to the reversals that advancing years bring? Researchers speculate that because suicide is at its peak among old-old men, physical dependency may be one key (Manton, Blazer, & Woodbury, 1987). The bodily helplessness of advanced old age is more intolera-

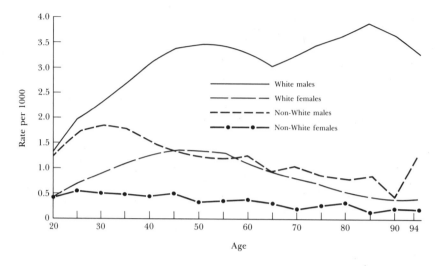

Figure 10-4. Suicide rates by age, for different groups.
Source: From Manton, Blazer, & Woodbury, 1987.

ble for men than for women because being independent and in control are so critical to masculine self-esteem.

Another important influence associated with old age suicide may also affect men more—social isolation. Isolation from meaningful relationships is frequently mentioned as a prime risk factor for suicide in the elderly (Stenback, 1980). Men may be more vulnerable to this problem in late life than women because, being less likely to have close relationships outside of marriage, they are more at risk of being totally cut off from other people when their wives die. This not only may offer one explanation for why some studies show that widowhood is more stressful for men (see Chapter 9), it also may partly account for the alarmingly high male suicide rate.

However, we also must take these sex differences with a grain of salt: The statistics may seriously undercount the number of women who commit suicide because the figures only count successful suicides, deaths in which an obviously suicidal motive could be inferred. Men, more than women, make successful suicide attempts; and because they use more violent methods (shooting, jumping), their intentions are more often clear. Women tend to use more passive methods, such as pills, when they attempt to take their lives, strategies more likely to be mislabeled as an accident or to lead to being rescued in the emergency room (see Miller, M., 1979).

The statistics leave out another fact. In contrast to adolescents and young adults, who are more likely to make a suicidal gesture to manipulate people or get attention, older people who attempt suicide are more often serious. Their efforts are more likely to be successful because they are motivated by a genuine desire to end their life (see Shneidman & Farberow, 1961). For this reason, suicidal threats are more ominous in older people. For the isolated, ill, depressed older person who threatens suicide, death is a real possibility.

ASSESSMENT

The first step in dealing with depression, dementia, or any mental disorder is to determine what the person's problem is and to understand it as completely as possible. This is the goal of the **diagnostic evaluation,** which is done in most mental health settings before any decisions are made about treatment. While the actual format may vary, the vignette illustrates how a diagnostic evaluation often takes place, as well as the sometimes wide differences of opinion about what diagnosis a patient should be given.

The diagnostic evaluation has two goals: to provide a correct diagnosis and to understand the difficulty in as much depth as possible within a relatively short time. Both giving the problem a diagnostic label and understanding it in a more detailed way are critical to effectively treating the problem.

Not every mental health professional is comfortable assigning diagnostic labels. Some people, though they may think labels in the abstract are appropriate to use, have questions about the particular diagnoses employed in the current classification system—the DSM-III. For instance, as described earlier, some feel the manual's criteria for diagnosing a certain condition (such as depression) may be too stringent, or propose that a given disorder (such as Alzheimer's disease) should be categorized in a different way. Some have strong ethical concerns, believing that labeling sets up a self-fulfilling prophecy in which everyone sees the person as 'sick' and so ensures that the individual remains in that devalued role. Others go even further. They feel that the whole idea that a person who comes for treatment has a diagnosable illness is wrong. It is the person's environment or situation—not the individual—that is pathological (see Chapter 11's discussion of family therapy).

Nevertheless, in almost all clinical settings, DSM-III diagnoses are used. This practice has considerable advantages. Diagnostic labels convey a great deal of information in a few words: they give a shorthand description of the person's symptoms, suggest possible causes of the problem, and provide the mental health worker with clues about the future. Most important, the diagnosis suggests whether treatment can help and what interventions are likely to be successful.

Earlier in this chapter we saw how the labels "Alzheimer's disease" and "depression" have profoundly different implications: Alzheimer's disease is a death sentence. The depressed person, if properly treated, can live a happy life. We also saw that distinguishing among depression, dementia, and delirium is not always easy. A death-sentence diagnosis wrongly imposed may have tragic consequences when the older person is depressed—causing needless emotional pain and impeding cure. When cognitive problems are caused by a physical illness, wrongly labeling the person as demented can be life threatening.

The second goal of the diagnostic assessment—to understand the problem in as much depth as possible—is just as important in treating the person. The label by itself is too vague to include important specifics about what can be done to help. A person with Alzheimer's disease may be able to handle life independently or need 24-hour nursing home care. The individual may be aggressive, agitated, impossible to handle at home, or have relatively few behavioral problems. The family may be very involved or absent. All these facts about the problem are very relevant to the future. By describing the person and the problem in depth— coping capacities, present and past behavior, financial options, social supports— a treatment plan can naturally unfold. The diagnostic evaluation should provide accurate information to help answer those crucial questions: What will really help? Where do we go from here?

When an older person arrives for psychological care at a hospital, a mental health clinic, or a private practitioner's office, the diagnostic procedure is likely to be indistinguishable from that used with a younger adult. However, with reason, a complete physical examination is more likely to be recommended for the older adult. Often in the elderly, a genuine physical problem may be causing symptoms that appear emotional. For example, these serious illnesses are manifested partly by depressive symptoms: hypothyroidism, Addison's disease, Cushing's disease, pernicious anemia, idiopathic parkinsonism, uremia, congestive heart failure, cancer of the pancreas, leukemia, and brain tumors (Klerman, 1983)!

Apart from the medical assessment, the evaluation is done by a mental health worker, usually either a psychiatrist, a clinical psychologist, a psychiatric social worker, or, less frequently, a psychiatric nurse (see Table 10-5). Members of all four professions, when certified, are qualified to diagnose and treat psychological problems. This person, working alone or, as in the vignette, as part of a multidisciplinary team in a hospital or clinic, may use one or more of the following general approaches to understanding older (or younger) patients: interviewing them and their families, observing their behavior, and/or giving them standard tests of personality and cognition. When the older person is too disabled physically to take certain tests or to submit to certain interviews, the mental health worker may modify the approach (for instance, writing down questions for a person with a hearing deficit, or shortening the interview because of fatigue) (Lawton, Whelihan, & Belsky, 1980). If the presence or severity of an existing dementia needs to be determined, special strategies are required. In fact, an additional element of the diagnostic procedure used with older adults is sometimes to test for the presence of dementia even if the person appears to be suffering from a purely emotional problem.

The Diagnostic Question

The actual tests, interviews, and/or observations a mental health worker uses are dictated by what is called the **diagnostic question**—the main problem that needs to be evaluated. For example, if the person seems to have no cognitive impairment but may be depressed, the diagnostician will focus mainly on

TABLE 10-5. The core mental health professions.

Title and Training	Special Additional Skills
Psychiatrist, M.D., psychiatric residency (usually 3 years in a mental health setting)	Administers drugs; diagnoses and treats medical problems; skilled in the diagnostic interview
Clinical psychologist, Ph.D. in psychology, internship in mental health setting	Administers and interprets psychological tests; does research
Psychiatric social worker, B.A. or M.S.W., supervised field experience in mental health setting	Works with social agencies, families; knowledgeable about community resources
Psychiatric nurse, RN in nursing plus specialized training in care and treatment of psychiatric patients	Gives physical care; can assess self-care skills

classifying and understanding the reasons for the patient's depression. If the person is suspected of having dementia, the mental health worker will evaluate the person's cognitive capacities in depth.

However, as we saw in the vignette, often the person's real problem cannot be clearly identified. This is why the assessment typically covers considerable ground—painting a picture of the person's life and functioning in broad strokes. The far-ranging probe is likely to cover the following topics:

1. What are the present problems? Has the person had these problems before?
2. Are there precipitating events—a recent trauma such as the death of a loved one, retirement, economic reversal, or the onset of a physical illness?
3. What are the important events in the person's life history? Family circumstances? Immigrations? Work experiences? Marriage? Children?
4. Does the person or his or her family have a history of mental problems?
5. What is the person's medical history? What medications is he or she taking? What illnesses are present?
6. What are the person's strengths, previous coping strategies?
7. What is the person's mental and emotional status? Is he or she anxious or depressed? Are there memory problems, difficulties in judgment, the quality of thinking, the person's ability to take care of himself or herself?
8. What resources exist in the community to help the person (for example, senior centers, day care centers, social services)?
9. How adequate is the person's social network? Who in the family and what friends might be counted on to help?
10. What type of intervention is appropriate for the person? Psychotherapy? Drug therapy? A change in environment?

When, as happened in the vignette, a clinical team does the evaluation, the approach used by each member of the team reflects her or his particular skills. The clinical psychologist administers psychological tests (some commonly used measures are listed in Table 10-6). The social worker interviews the family and gathers information about relevant community resources. The psychiatrist interviews the patient, using skilled observation to understand the person in depth. If a psychiatric nurse is part of the team, he or she may assess functional capacities.

TABLE 10-6. The typical psychological tests used in a traditional mental health assessment.*

Test	Description
Rorschach Test	Ten inkblots. Person is asked to say what each card looks like and to explain why the card looks that way. The psychologist uses a complicated scoring system designed to reveal the person's basic character structure and emotional conflicts plus clinical judgment in evaluating responses
Thematic Apperception Test (TAT)	Twenty pictures. Person is asked to tell a story about each (or a selected group). The psychologist usually evaluates character and conflicts from the stories
Draw-a-Person Test (DAP)	Person is asked to draw a human figure. The psychologist evaluates personality by looking at various aspects of the drawing (for example, its placement on the page, what body parts are emphasized)
Bender Gestalt Test	Nine cards, each with a different geometric shape. Person is asked to copy each form. The psychologist evaluates the adequacy of the drawings to assess the presence of brain damage as well as emotional conflicts
Minnesota Multiphasic Personality Inventory (MMPI)	Objective true/false items. Each subscale assesses different aspects of personality

* I have omitted the WAIS-R, also commonly administered, because it was described in detail in Chapter 5.

Additional health professionals (such as a physical therapist, a neurologist, or a speech therapist) may also be called in.

Assessment Strategies for Dementia

Sometimes the standard tests and interviews may not be enough—for example, when the diagnostic question involves dementia. The WAIS-R may be too difficult a cognitive challenge. Or, when the person's deficits are more subtle, it may not provide the detailed picture of functioning needed to make the difficult distinction between dementia and depression or rule out the presence of dementia versus another disease. When this happens, a referral may be made for **neuropsychological testing.** A psychologist with special training in neuropsychology (the assessment and understanding of neurological problems) will administer a battery of tests that covers various facets of behavior such as memory, learning, abstract reasoning, visual perception, reaction time, and language skills. Another important index that is essential to understanding an older adult with dementia is one that is crucial to assessing adults with any problem that impairs independent living—measures of functional capacities (see Chapter 2).

The assessment also usually includes direct measures of brain functioning such as those listed on page 285. In reading this list, keep in mind that while each of the following tests can suggest that a given person has dementia or even imply which specific dementing condition may be there, none provides the picture of individual neurons needed to prove conclusively that the person being diagnosed is suffering from the most important dementing illness of later life,

Alzheimer's disease (McKhann, Drachman, Folstein, Katzman, Price, & Stadlan, 1984):

• *CAT (Computerized Axial Tomography) scan:* The CAT scan provides a computer-generated picture of the brain's mass. It is useful in diagnosing dementia mainly because it allows the diagnostician to rule out conditions such as brain tumors and can show the presence of infarcts (strokes).

• *EEG:* The EEG of patients with Alzheimer's disease shows increased slow-wave activity that may become more pronounced as the illness advances. However, this slowing occurs in different types of dementia and also in some normal older adults, making this test also not a precise diagnostic tool.

• *Regional cerebral blood flow:* Measures of the blood flow, oxygen consumption, and metabolism of the brain may help somewhat in the differential diagnosis of multi-infarct dementia versus Alzheimer's disease.

• *PET (Positron Emission Tomography) scan:* This newest and least widely available measure of brain functioning provides the clearest picture of the brain's metabolism—showing its rate of glucose utilization and oxygen consumption in specific areas. While most patients with Alzheimer's disease have a lower-than-normal metabolic rate, and the specific deficits a person does have tend to be reflected in changes in the areas of the brain responsible for those functions (for example, speech impairments correlate with decreased activity in the brain's speech centers, and so on), unfortunately there is great variation on this test among normal subjects, too. So the PET scan is an unreliable tool for diagnosing dementia in its earliest stages.

It is also crucial that the patient's social environment be assessed. How involved are family members? Are they able to provide the care the patient needs? What formal services are available—nursing homes, home care, day care, respite care? Is the family able financially or psychologically to take advantage of these options?

Recommendations

After the diagnostic information is collected, a conference is usually held to discuss the findings and recommend treatment. As in the vignette, while there may be intense disagreements among the team members as they struggle to fit the puzzle together, some consensus emerges about what is wrong and what is most likely to help. Specific recommendations are given to the patient and the family about how to proceed.

The diagnostic recommendations may vary greatly—from a suggestion to consider immediate nursing home placement to the reassuring words "nothing is wrong." In between are a broad array of other options, treatments that are examined in the next chapter. In the vignette three interventions are suggested: environmental change, psychotherapy, and drug therapy. We will see in Chapter 11 what happens to our patient after the team makes their recommendations.

KEY TERMS

Epidemiology

Functional psychological disorders

Dementia

Alzheimer's disease

Primary degenerative dementia

Neurofibrillary tangles

Senile plaques

Multi-infarct dementia

Delirium

Depression

Major depression

Minor depression

Learned helplessness

Diagnostic evaluation

Diagnostic question

Neuropsychological testing

RECOMMENDED READINGS

Beck, A. T. (1979). *Depression: Causes and treatment (7th ed).* Philadelphia: University of Pennsylvania Press. Read Part 1 of this comprehensive book for a detailed description of the symptoms and issues in classifying the varying types of depression. Not difficult.

Breslau, L. D., & Haug, M. R. (Eds.) (1983). *Depression and aging: Causes, care, and consequences.* New York: Springer. Edited collection of articles on depression and aging covering all aspects of the problem from diagnosis, to causes, to treatments. Not difficult to moderately difficult depending on the chapter.

Freud, S. (1957). Mourning and melancholia. In *Standard edition* (Vol. 14). London: Hogarth Press. Freud's classic work on depression. Difficult.

Reisberg, B. (1981). *Brain failure: An introduction to current concepts of senility.* New York: Free Press. Extremely clear, comprehensive discussion of causes, symptoms, and characteristics of the major dementing illnesses. Highly recommended. Not difficult.

Seligman, M. E. P. (1975). *Helplessness: On depression, development and death.* San Francisco: W. H. Freeman. The theory of learned helplessness applied not just to depression but other phenomena such as anxiety and sudden death. Not difficult.

Zarit, S. H., Orr, N., & Zarit, J. (1985). *The hidden victims of Alzheimer's disease: Families under stress.* New York: New York University Press. Written for caregivers of dementia victims and also professionals in aging, this slim book is exceptionally useful for understanding the stresses caregivers face and the management problems dementia can present. It explores psychological treatments for dementia in depth. Not difficult.

Chapter 11

□

Mental Disorders 2: Treatment

□

The Older Person and the Mental Health System
- The Older Person's Contribution to Poor Care
- The Mental Health Provider's Contribution to Poor Care

Psychotherapy
- Psychoanalytic Psychotherapy
- Behavior Therapy
- Group Therapy
- Marital and Family Therapy

Chemotherapy
- Antipsychotic Drugs
- Antidepressant Drugs
- Antianxiety Drugs
- Psychotropic Drugs and the Older Person

Treatments for Dementia
- Environmental Treatments
- Biological Treatments
- Treating the Second Casualty: Families

Key Terms

Recommended Readings

Because the Golds are a close-knit family, after the evaluation they met to discuss their choices. The people at the center had suggested that Mr. and Mrs. Gold move back to Philadelphia. Their children agreed. Not only would their mother be in a familiar place where they could check in regularly and not have those long-distance worries, the center had recommended a psychologist who specialized in geriatrics.

Even though he agreed to move back, a week later Ruben changed his mind. They had just gone through the exhaustion of one move. Making another might multiply the pain. Besides, since more psychologists now have training in geriatrics, finding one in Florida would probably be easy. Moving back also seemed to mean defeat, something that Ruben had always abhorred. Couldn't Sophie really just be in the midst of that relocation trauma he'd read about in last Sunday's *Times?* Wouldn't she be back to her old self once she got used to their new home? When Sophie suggested she would rather leave Florida, Ruben brushed her timid protestations aside.

Unfortunately, rather than making things better, the extra months in Florida made them worse. Sophie clung just as tightly to home, never ventured out the door. Mentally and emotionally she seemed to just switch off. Even the way she looked changed. From January to June she seemed to have aged 10 years. Worse yet, their efforts to find psychological help stalled. When they asked their new family doctor about a referral to a psychologist, he said he doubted that a woman of 70 could change. The psychiatrist they consulted was patronizing and brushed them off. Ruben's fury at his wife being treated as a hopeless case was the final straw. He now understood the folly of staying and made plans to return to Philadelphia.

Luckily it was easy to sell their condominium and find a one-bedroom apartment near their old house. Ruben's first act after unpacking was to call the psychologist the center had recommended. Even in the first week, it was obvious this was the right decision. Sophie was much better. When her children and friends came by to visit, she perked up— her old vitality and grace reappeared. She carried on an intelligent conversation and was only somewhat abstracted when she tried to remember where she had put the coffee cups to serve her guests. However, her fear of going out did not abate a bit. When a friend who lived a few blocks away invited her over, Sophie said she was just too tired.

The psychologist saw the Golds together during the first few therapy sessions. Dr. Zaccarelli wanted to see if the marriage might be contributing to Sophie's problems. Like the social worker at the center, he observed Ruben's habit of constantly taking over. This was apparent every time Dr. Zaccarelli asked Sophie a question—Ruben had the annoying habit of answering for her!

Dr. Zaccarelli decided on a two-pronged therapeutic strategy. He would try to change the destructive marital pattern (Ruben's tendency to treat Sophie as totally incapable and so make her problems worse) and at the same time work with Sophie alone on her distressing symptoms. Rather than focusing on her depression directly, he decided to attack her phobia instead, using a technique called in vivo desensitization. He felt her terror of leaving the house was at the root of the depressive symptoms—perpetuating her terrible conviction of not being mentally capable, which caused her dark mood, her helpless and hopeless perspective on life. Moreover, the very fact of being housebound would naturally make any person apathetic and morose. Because he felt that Sophie did not have a major depression, Dr. Zaccarelli did not recommend antidepressants. He knew that giving medications to an older person was not a good idea unless the medications were absolutely needed.

Being trained in systems family therapy, Dr. Zaccarelli's first step was to restructure the marital relationship by giving the couple instructions designed to transform Sophie's role from patient to that of competent person. Even though she could not leave the house, Sophie was to be in charge of all household chores that could be done without going out, such as ordering groceries and other supplies by phone. Rather than using the washer/dryer in her apartment, she was to do the laundry in the machines in the basement of the building, a place midway to venturing outside where she might also meet some new friends. In delivering these instructions, Dr. Zaccarelli made it clear that he considered Sophie eminently capable of doing most things by herself, including taking charge of her treatment. He also asked Ruben to stay in the waiting room during subsequent sessions.

To help rid Sophie of her phobia, Dr. Zaccarelli told her to approach leaving the house in small steps. First, she should spend time in places where she was only slightly anxious, such as the yard of her building and the basement laundry room. Then, gradually, as she gained more confidence, she was to go farther and farther from home. To give her courage, Dr. Zaccarelli told her to carry a card with her address on it. He knew that this prop was mostly a good luck charm. The neighborhood was so familiar that Sophie should have little problem remembering how to get home even if her memory difficulties did have a minor organic component.

After a few months of regular practice, Sophie's phobia was almost gone. She could visit her friends and do most errands by herself. She had shaky moments from time to time, but her anxiety always subsided when she realized she had her address with her. She kept the psychologist's number with her at all times too, so she could call him in an emergency. As Dr. Zaccarelli had predicted, along with the phobia, her depressive symptoms also gradually subsided.

When she began treatment, Sophie had doubts. Not only was it embarrassing to admit she had mental problems, but this doctor looked so young! Could anyone her son's age really understand her problems or be able to advise her on how to live? As the sessions continued, though, these doubts were more than erased. Sophie looked forward to the hour she spent in therapy as the highlight of her week. She admired her therapist tremendously, felt in awe of his expertise, but also knew she had a good deal to offer him. One of the things she could give back was an understanding of what it was like to grow old. So in addition to discussing her progress at venturing out, she spent time during sessions telling Dr. Zaccarelli what the world had been like while she was grow-ing up and teaching him some of the insights about living she had acquired over the years.

Ruben at first felt ambivalent about his new, more competent wife. Because he had to give up his role of caregiver (and absolute boss), he began to get somewhat depressed himself. Dr. Zaccarelli was able to remedy this by seeing Ruben for a few sessions and encouraging him to become active in the community as he had been before Sophie had gotten ill. They have both continued to do well since ending their treatment 6 months ago.

■

As we saw in Chapter 10, experts disagree about how common psychological problems are among older people. However, we can assume that the elderly's share of these problems is far from minimal. It at least approaches the rate for people under age 65. In addition, older people may have a problem younger people do not—dementia. So we might expect that the elderly would be receiv-ing a significant amount of treatment for mental health complaints.

THE OLDER PERSON AND THE MENTAL HEALTH SYSTEM

Unfortunately, this is not happening. People over age 65, in proportion to their numbers, are getting relatively little psychological care. They visit mental health clinics and private psychotherapists much less frequently than young or middle-aged adults do. When they do come, their problems tend to be more serious. They are usually given medications, not psychotherapy, and are more likely to be seen briefly, perhaps dropping out of treatment prematurely without their prob-lems being resolved (Gallagher & Thompson, 1982; Goldstrom et al., 1987; Kahn, 1977; Lowy, 1980).

Despite a heightened interest in the mental health needs of the elderly during the past 15 years, these bleak facts have not changed. In the early 1970s, despite comprising more than 10% of the population, the elderly accounted for only 4% of the visits to community mental health centers (Redick & Taube, 1980). A decade later, an American Psychological Association survey showed an only

TABLE 11-1. Services provided and patients served in some types of mental health settings.

Setting	Services*
Outpatient	
Private therapist	Active treatment to less disturbed, higher income patients
Community mental health center or other outpatient clinic	Active treatment to less disturbed, low-income patients
Inpatient	
Private psychiatric hospital	More likely to provide active treatment to very disturbed higher income patients on a short- or long-term basis
General hospital, psychiatric unit	More likely to provide active treatment to very disturbed patients on a short-term basis
State or county mental hospital	Minimal treatment (psychotherapy) to chronic highly disturbed low-income patients

* There are many exceptions to these generalizations.

minimal increase: about 6% of these sessions took place with people over age 65 (Flemming, Buchanan, Santos, & Rickards, 1984).

The same is true of outpatient visits to private psychiatrists. Only about 4% of the caseload of private psychiatrists is composed of older adults (Schurman, Kramer, & Mitchell, 1985). Considering that the fraction of older Americans has inched toward 12% in this period, this is underrepresentation indeed.

Even under optimal conditions, when psychological services are easily accessible and primary care doctors are sensitive to their patients' mental health concerns, the same situation prevails. In one study, researchers (Goldstrom et al., 1987) examined how frequently the older people who used an innovative community health center affiliated with a teaching hospital visited the mental health specialists the center employed. While diagnosed just as frequently as patients under 65 as having mental disorders, the older patients used the center-based psychological services less often. Less than one-half labeled with an emotional disorder actually went for help, a much smaller proportion than was true of the middle-aged or younger adults. Furthermore, when the elderly did contact the mental health unit, they came for fewer sessions.

The pattern of underuse was particularly striking for people whose problems were less likely to require immediate hospitalization—those with neuroses, personality disorders, or problems with alcohol or drugs. While most of the older patients diagnosed as having an emotional disorder had a problem of this type, only one in three of these went for psychological help. However, when the problem was a psychosis, the person did tend to be seen at the mental health unit at least once. This illustrates yet another point about the mental health care of older adults. Older people who do enter the mental health system are those with the most severe disorders—problems more likely to be seen as chronic or "hopeless" and to be treated by medications not psychotherapy, conditions that are more likely to warrant inpatient not outpatient care.

Table 11-1 shows the status hierarchy in the mental health system. Older people are concentrated at its lowest rungs. While at the upper end of the hierarchy—outpatient services—the elderly are markedly underrepresented, older people make up a whopping 30% of the residents of state and county mental hospitals (Pfeiffer, 1976). State and county hospitals are places of last resort in the mental health system, serving chronic, severely disturbed, often impoverished patients. The care provided in these institutions is often **custodial.** Residents are simply housed, fed, and given medications. In the office of a private practitioner the patient tends to be vigorously treated; in these institutions, just "warehoused."

Older persons with illnesses such as dementia or schizophrenia used to be regularly sent to the many large psychiatric facilities that dotted the countryside. However, for the past 2 decades, these seriously disturbed people (along with the mentally ill and socioeconomically deprived of any age) have typically met a different fate. During the 1960s a reform movement succeeded in closing the doors of many state and county mental hospitals. A nationwide network of community mental health centers was set up in the hope that with regular outpatient care and the use of the promising new antipsychotic medications, even the severely mentally ill could live productive lives in the community. Unfortunately, however, these high hopes did not often materialize. As the droves of psychotic homeless people in our large cities bear tragic testament, many people in critical need probably got no mental health services at all. Or, if they were over age 65, they were sent to another custodial inpatient setting, the nursing home.

Nursing homes have become the (often unwilling) repository of the mentally ill elderly. The vast majority of psychologically disturbed older people who live in institutions now live in nursing homes (Sherwood & Mor, 1980). However, with a few notable exceptions, from the viewpoint of getting adequate mental health care, nursing homes may be even more malignant than the large psychiatric institutions they replaced. They combine many of the negative qualities of the old institutions—being custodial, impersonal, perhaps promoting excess disabilities—with a mission that is defined as serving the physically, not mentally, impaired. So despite emotional problems being rampant among nursing home residents—estimates range as high as 80% (Carver, 1974)—in a nursing home the odds of being regularly seen by a mental health professional are probably lower than they ever were.

Why is this situation so grim? While our first temptation may be to blame the mental health profession, older people may not get adequate services for another reason—their own reluctance to seek out treatment.

The Older Person's Contribution to Poor Care

In contrast to young and middle-aged adults, this cohort of over-65-year-olds did not grow up in an era where seeking psychological help was accepted. They were more likely to have been socialized with the idea that only people who are crazy see a psychologist (Lazarus & Weinberg, 1980). This onus against getting mental health help may change within the next decades as the baby boom cohort turns 65. However, some experts make the compelling point that it may also be *inherently* more difficult for an older person to seek treatment because taking this step is fraught with overtones of being mentally incompetent, and fears about being incompetent, of being no longer in control mentally, are terrifying worries at this life-stage (Gatz, Popkin, Pino, & VandenBos, 1985).

Part of the problem may also be embarrassment. The person being seen would most likely be years younger and it is humiliating to turn to someone a son or daughter's age for guidance about life. For instance, studies show that, in particular, low-income older people prefer to be treated by a physician close to their own age (see Gatz et al., 1985). While there has been no research on age preferences with regard to seeing a mental health worker, it is likely that here the age issue might make even more of a difference. For some elderly people the idea of going to someone decades younger for psychological help may smack of too much of a role reversal to be swallowed comfortably.

People may be deterred by the stereotypes: the idea that at their age they are too old to change; the belief that unhappiness is the price of being over 65. Unfortunately, these very ideas are most likely to be wholeheartedly embraced by the very people who might really be able to benefit from treatment the most—those who are depressed. As we saw in Chapter 10, depressed people are particularly susceptible to these nihilistic old age stereotypes because they fit in so well with their gloom and doom philosophy, their helpless and hopeless world view.

Older people with emotional problems do often visit at least one health care professional, however, their family doctor, and so he or she should be in a good position to overcome their biases (Lazarus & Weinberg, 1980). A family doctor who felt strongly about the need for mental health care could be very persuasive at getting an older patient to at least make an appointment for psychological help. And primary care doctors are typically the conduit by which people get into the mental health services system, whether they are young or old. As one expert points out, these nonpsychologically trained physicians may actually be providing the bulk of this nation's mental health care (Kiesler, 1980). Nowhere does this seem more true than for the elderly. For instance, in one study, the researchers found that while four out of five people over age 65 with a mental illness diagnosed in an office-based practice were being treated by their primary care doctor, the comparable figure for those under 65 was only two in five (Schurman, Kramer, & Mitchell, 1985).

Is the fault solely the older patients'? Are the elderly referred for treatment but unwilling to go? Or, do doctors share the blame? Either because they also believe the stereotype that older people are beyond changing or because they leap to the conclusion that any sign of confusion or agitation in a patient over 65 means dementia, primary care doctors seem less than willing to refer their older patients for help.

One study (Kucharski, White, & Schratz, 1979) does suggest that indeed the physicians may be partly to blame. A random sample of primary care doctors were mailed vignettes that described eight hypothetical patients, each with a different set of psychological symptoms. The descriptions sent to each doctor were identical except for the patients' ages. If the symptoms were severe and so *could* have been due to dementia, there was a clear age difference in the tendency to refer. If the patients were under age 65, the doctors were likely to say they would suggest treatment. Identical symptoms in an older person were less likely to be thought to warrant a mental health referral, even though they, too, might be signs of a treatable problem.

Underreferral is tied to underdiagnosis. When researchers (German et al., 1987) gave patients an inventory to assess the presence of emotional problems and compared the results with their primary care doctors' diagnoses, they found that while the doctors were quite accurate at recognizing psychological problems in their younger patients, they were more likely to miss the existence of a problem in their patients over age 65. Perhaps this is because emotional problems in later life may be inherently more difficult to diagnose (for instance, psychological problems are more likely to be expressed as symptoms that appear purely physical). Perhaps elderly patients are less likely to bring up their psychological symptoms and problems when they do visit their primary care doctor (see Chapter 4). Or perhaps some doctors really do see intense unhappiness, or overpowering anxiety, or other signs of mental distress as "normal" in old age. Whatever the reason, it is clear that elderly patients with psychological problems may not get the help they need in part because their problem goes unrecognized, their emotional distress goes unseen.

Finally, there is the all-important financial deterrent. While Medicare pays for an unlimited number of primary care visits, it only covers a small number of outpatient sessions with a psychiatrist. Furthermore, even when it does pay, its reimbursement rate per session is lower than it would be if the person were seeking help for a physical concern (Gatz et al., 1985). So, particularly because the elderly tend to have less money (see Chapter 9), many older people may logically decide it would make more economic sense to see their family doctor rather than a mental health specialist for any psychological complaints.

In an unfortunate parallel to the economic incentive to enter a nursing home, the money that Medicare actually provides for mental health may further the wrong needs. Inpatient mental health services are covered; outpatient psychotherapy is relatively ignored. So rather than catching problems before they warrant hospitalization or offering the ongoing noninstitutional care required to keep an emotionally disturbed older person functioning in the community, the system encourages *not* getting help when it might be most useful and intervening in the most radical (and expensive) way. Compounding the problem, Medicare only covers the often less costly services of psychologists under certain conditions, and does not cover the typically least expensive mental health professional, social workers, at all. Not only does this add to the financial deterrent to getting help, it discourages the older person from using a whole class of qualified professionals—perhaps the very disciplines most likely to be interested in providing sensitive, geriatrically informed care.

Ironically, while the new stress on functional disability emphasizes the importance of emotions and behavior in determining health in old age (as well as the crucial role nonphysicians such as social workers or psychologists can play in providing geriatric care), federal funding for physical-illness-oriented geriatric research and training far outstrips that for mental health. Because the development of a large cadre of geriatrically trained mental health workers is not being actively encouraged, even the older person who wants mental health help may be deterred from getting it because he or she simply cannot find someone qualified to help.

The Mental Health Provider's Contribution to Poor Care

We might argue, though, that it is not just the older person, primary care doctors, or the government that is at fault. More of the elderly would be getting the help they need if the providers of mental health services really stepped in—educating older people, primary care doctors, and the public that later-life emotional problems are treatable; agitating for funds for geriatric training; and launching a campaign to make mental health care for the elderly a genuine priority. However, until quite recently, this has not happened. One reason is not hard to guess— mental health workers may also be reluctant to treat older adults.

This aversion to treating the elderly has long and respected roots. In a classic statement, Freud himself (1924) specifically warned that treating people over age 50 posed special problems, that older people often lacked the mental flexibility to really change. While psychoanalytically oriented clinicians who do specialize in geriatrics have taken special pains to discount this well-known pronouncement (Grotjan, 1955; Meerloo, 1961; Newton, Brauer, Guttman, & Grunes, 1986; Simberg, 1985), psychoanalytic writings about old age still can be quite negative, couched in terms of irrevocable loss and decline (see Cath, 1965). Since many clinicians do subscribe to this influential theory of human behavior, these negative comments can only have a chilling effect on the profession's general willingness to reach out to older adults.

Moreover, the professional judgment that the elderly are untreatable may fall on fertile emotional ground, rationalizing a predisposition to shun the elderly anyway. Some therapists may be afraid that treating older patients will evoke painful emotions: (1) anxieties about growing old, (2) ambivalent feelings about parents and other authority figures, and (3) feelings of personal inadequacy: "How could I feel comfortable being the advisor to people who have so many more years of life experience than I do?" (Gotestam, 1980; Pfeiffer, 1976).

There may be fears of professional incompetence, too, of not having the skills to treat this age group. The principle that special training in geriatrics is needed to effectively treat older people (Swenson, 1982) may have virtues, but some experts suggest that it also has unintended negative effects—becoming another roadblock to the elderly getting mental health services and further exacerbating the aversion to treating people over 65 (Gatz et al., 1985).

Finally, mental health workers sometimes say they are reluctant to treat older people because the objective problems the old have will force them to function as case managers rather than as therapists, to spend their time arranging for concrete services (such as a homemaker) rather than doing what they have been trained to do—providing purely psychological help (U.S. Commission on Civil

Rights, 1979). And even though it may sometimes be used as a rationalization, this concern has some truth. Particularly in treating frail older people, the mental health worker's role often must expand beyond traditional lines—becoming advocate as well as therapist, helping the person negotiate the concrete details of life (see Blum & Tross, 1980).

Arranging the externals of life is not what mental health professionals generally do. They focus on changing the person—modifying the maladaptive attitudes, self-defeating behavior, and upsetting feelings that limit a full happy life. Now that we know that age does not bring more rigidity (see Chapter 7) there is no reason why there should be a magical cutoff date beyond which psychological services are ineffective, an age beyond which people are too old to change. The testimonials of clinicians who specialize in psychotherapy with the elderly echo this theme: Older people, because of their greater maturity, can be excellent candidates for therapy (Grotjan, 1955; Newton et al., 1986). Because of their greater wisdom, their truly "adult" perspective on life, it is often very gratifying to work with older adults (Cyrus-Lutz & Gaitz, 1972). Psychiatrist Eric Pfeiffer (1976) has even argued that, paradoxically, precisely because in old age the options for outer world change are more limited, mental health services can be doubly important. When our store of close relationships is eroded by the deaths of family and friends, having an ongoing relationship with a therapist may become life sustaining, whether or not our life permits much concrete change.

No one can win the argument that mental health interventions work or are ineffective with the elderly without examining the evidence. This is why, in looking at the following treatments, I will pay special attention to studies demonstrating their worth. Does a particular therapy produce genuine changes that the passage of time would not? Are some treatments more effective than others in dealing with mental disorders in later life? What older patients are likely to respond best to a given intervention? When (as is often the case) these studies of effectiveness, called **outcome studies,** are scanty or contradictory, I will resort to less scientific criteria in judging their usefulness—my own subjective appraisal of whether and under what conditions that treatment might benefit older adults.

There are mental health treatments specifically for people who have functional mental disorders and others for dementia, interventions aimed both at helping the person with this devastating disease and family members straining to cope. We will first look at the two major treatments for functional disorders: psychotherapy and chemotherapy (drug therapy).

PSYCHOTHERAPY

As everyone knows, psychotherapy attempts to cure emotional problems by verbal means, by talking, instructing, listening. Although, unfortunately, in some states anyone can call him- or herself a psychotherapist, people who do psychotherapy are usually trained in one of the core mental health professions listed in Table 10-5 in the last chapter.

While all psychotherapies are based on the idea that emotional change can take place by talking, psychotherapists vary greatly in the techniques they use and in their worldview. These different ideas are reflected in many diverse schools of therapy, of which only the most common will be discussed here.

Psychoanalytic Psychotherapy

The main principles of psychoanalytic theory are that the experiences, wishes, and events of childhood are the basis of adult personality, and that these experiences, and other thoughts and feelings in the unconscious, powerfully determine all human actions, both normal and pathological (see Chapter 1). These principles, plus the belief that gaining awareness of these unconscious feelings and thoughts is the key to mental health, form the essence of **psychoanalytic psychotherapy.**

Psychoanalytically oriented therapists view emotional problems as being caused by personality defects resulting from unfortunate childhood experiences. These experiences do not allow psychological development to proceed in a healthy way. Normally, feelings and fantasies in the id are subordinated, to a certain extent, as the young child learns to adapt to external reality (that is, as the child develops an ego) and to obey moral and societal ideas of right and wrong (that is, as the child develops a superego). However, when a person's childhood is too depriving or intensely gratifying, the normal development of an adequate ego (and superego) does not occur. Id impulses remain overly intense and there is a corresponding inadequacy of ego functioning.

Psychotic symptoms are the outcome of the most extreme deficiencies in ego formation. The hallucinations, delusions, and totally irrational ideas characteristic of these severe mental disturbances are manifestations of the id, which has overwhelmed the fragile ego. (Today, even the most diehard psychoanalyst is likely to grant, based on the overwhelming scientific evidence, that there also tends to be a strong biological predisposition to psychotic disorders.) In the less severe emotional disorders, the neuroses, the ego is strong enough to prevent the direct expression of these unconscious impulses but they are still so intense that they come out in an indirect way, through upsetting symptoms and self-defeating ways of behaving that impair living and limit the quality of life. It is these less severe disturbances—irrational fears, unexplainable bouts of depression, the ways people feel compelled to act in their own worst interest—that psychoanalytic therapy is designed to treat.

The goal of **insight-oriented psychoanalytic treatment** is to help the neurotic patient understand the unconscious origins of his or her behavior, the disguised childhood wishes, desires, and fantasies that are causing the symptoms. According to the theory, once these feelings stemming from early childhood are understood, they will no longer need to be expressed in symptoms and the patient will be cured. So the essence of the therapy lies in making conscious, or getting insight into, these unconscious experiences and thoughts.

In contrast, the treatment usually recommended for more severely disturbed people (who have a more fragile hold on reality) is called **supportive.** Here the goal is not to probe the unconscious but to help solidify the patient's more shaky hold on the real world. The therapist uses an understanding of the patient's dynamics (the unconscious forces that motivate the patient) to foster realistic thinking, performing the delicate task of bolstering the ego without risking bringing up too much painful information from the past.

Within the past decade or so there has been considerable interest in short-term insight-oriented psychodynamic techniques, treatments that would compress the years this intense exploration of the psyche tends to normally take. However, as usually practiced today, psychoanalytically oriented therapy still requires a substantial commitment, both of time and emotional effort. Patients must explore diverse aspects of their personality and dig deep into the past, even when this self-examination is painful and seems to have only the most remote connection to the actual problem that propelled getting help. As part of what is called the therapeutic alliance, the patient and therapist scrutinize all aspects of the patient's life and childhood experiences. Curing the problem that brought the patient into therapy tends to become secondary to a more overarching goal—to understand as much as possible about oneself. (Actually, this is the only goal of psychoanalysis, the most intense form of psychoanalytic therapy. Here the aim is tremendously ambitious—to fully probe the unconscious.)

This brief description gives us a framework for understanding both how older adults are treated using this type of treatment and some pitfalls in using psychoanalytic techniques with this age group. Although the literature on psychoanalytic therapy with the elderly is sparse compared to the avalanche of articles on behavioral techniques (see Gatz et al., 1985), there are a few case reports of this type of therapy being used effectively (see Newton et al., 1986, for a review). Here are two examples:

Insight-Oriented Therapy.   The following description is from an analyst who believes that older people in particular can appreciate the connections between childhood experiences and adult behavior and so are well suited for insight-oriented therapy (Meerloo, 1961). The analyst is describing how he treated a severely disturbed 70-year-old man using an insight-oriented approach. In reading the quotation, note the emphasis on childhood experiences and the unconscious, all critical to the psychoanalytic approach:

> A counselor [lawyer] develops an agitated melancholia after a gall bladder operation. He cannot sleep anymore and he cannot stop crying. . . . We started an analytically oriented form of psychotherapy. . . . He produced dreams at every session, which he started to interpret for himself without intervention. So uppermost were they in his mind that some dreams pictured direct childhood memories . . . at a later period a fear of death came into the foreground . . . [The patient reports] I was at a railroad station. . . . There was not much time. Will I be able to catch the train? The loudspeaker voice called the passengers to track 999. . . . I [the analyst] limited myself to letting the patient understand the general patterns of the dream. Track 999 was for him the last station of departure. He spontaneously interpreted the other part of the dream as his unwillingness to go [to his death]. . . . In the meantime he had been able to go back to work [Meerloo, 1961, p. 195].

BOX 11-1
Transference in the Older Person

The concept of **transference** is central to psychoanalytic thinking about how therapy works: As a natural consequence of being in treatment, the patient begins to view the therapist in a distorted way—imbuing the therapist with highly unrealistic qualities; making the therapeutic relationship the psychological center of life. These intense feelings are called transference because they are thought to be transferred or carried over from that most basic relationship, the parental one during the patient's earliest years. In transference, the patient is supposed to replay that relationship, making the analyst the focal point of all those feelings from early life.

Psychoanalysts see transference as the emotional motor that runs therapy. This intense attachment to the analyst gives the patient the motivation to continue the painful task of self-exploration. The character of the transference offers essential information about those long-distant years. Feelings from the past come alive in the present where they can be felt, understood, examined, and come to terms with. And unlike the patient's parents, the analyst represents a good father or mother, which allows the patient to get over these negative experiences.

Transference has always been viewed as the patient thrusting the therapist into the role of a parent figure. Some gerontologists (Lazarus & Weinberg, 1980) question, though, whether in older people this parental transference always evolves. Rather than representing a father or mother figure, perhaps older people sometimes come to view the therapist as a good child—particularly when the therapist is decades younger and they have intense feelings about their own children.

As the vignette suggests, coming to see the therapist as a son or daughter may even be a strategy to regain a sense of competence that old age losses have eroded. It may be that the success of Sophie Gold's treatment can be traced in part to her viewing her role in this way—as teacher to the therapist, she was able to recapture her self-confidence, her feelings of self-worth.

On the other hand, not everyone agrees that a reverse transference really exists. Martin Berezin (1983) implies that what young, inexperienced therapists label as a parent/child transference is typically *countertransference:* the therapist's own uneasy feelings at being thrust into the role of parent by someone their parents' age. Do therapists read in a reverse transference in older patients because of their own discomfort? Or, does the common perception, "My 80-year-old patient sees me as his son," often have a basis in fact? Since psychoanalytic theory deals in the realm of fantasy, both interpretations are equally likely.

□

In the quotation on p. 298 we can clearly see the psychoanalytic perspective on what causes and cures emotional problems. According to the analyst, the lawyer's unconscious fear of death, which interpreting the dream makes conscious, is the main reason the gall bladder operation provoked the symptoms. Learning about the true content of this fear by analyzing aspects of his unconscious as revealed in dreams is what cured the depression and allowed the person to resume a normal life.

Supportive Therapy.   Unlike in that case, in supportive therapy, rather than having patients delve into the unconscious, therapists utilize their understanding to support a more fragile ego and foster a firmer hold on reality.

Alvin Goldfarb, one of the first psychiatrists to specialize in treating nursing home residents, developed an unusual supportive psychoanalytic technique for this frail group. His approach was based on his analysis of the institutionalized older person's underlying problem—extreme dependency coupled with a need to feel powerful and in control (Goldfarb, 1953; Goldfarb & Turner, 1953). Rather than helping these people gain insight into this need (which might have been impossible anyway, as many were cognitively impaired), Goldfarb used the following strategy: He saw them briefly (about 15 minutes), relatively infrequently (less than once a week), and on a continuing basis. During sessions he actively attempted to increase their sense of being powerful by allowing them to feel they had somehow triumphed over him or had him in their control. In other words, he arranged the situation so they felt they had won over an authority figure, the doctor who was supposedly more powerful than they. His thought was that this greater sense of power would strengthen their ability to function and improve their self-esteem (notice how this almost 40-year-old analysis presages the current emphasis on providing autonomy and control in this very group!).

Evaluation.   These examples far from prove that psychoanalytic therapy works. As is true of any case report, improvement was defined subjectively—by the therapist's report alone. Even if the judgments of these personally involved observers were confirmed by more objective indexes, these people might have improved just as much if they had been given another therapy or no treatment at all. To complicate matters further, even if we were to do a controlled study and find that the therapy itself produced change, it might have been successful for reasons irrelevant to psychoanalytic theory itself; for example, the older person's being listened to or treated with respect by another human being.

These are only a few reasons why some studies of the effectiveness of psychoanalytic treatment with the elderly report success and others do not (see Gotestam, 1980). Because patients and therapists vary so much—and no therapy is effective with everyone—contradictory results are endemic in the outcome literature. So, as suggested earlier, we are forced to look more to logic in judging the usefulness of this type of psychotherapy specifically for the elderly: Knowing what we now know about this treatment, how successful is insight-oriented psychoanalytic therapy likely to be with the type of older patient it is aimed at—someone who has emotional problems but is not severely disturbed?

Unfortunately, I feel this therapy has the least applicability of any type of treatment for the cohort currently over age 65. My speculation has nothing to do with older people being more inflexible but with a clash of expectations—not many older adults might feel comfortable complying with the requirements of this approach.

To undergo insight-oriented therapy, a person must agree with its basic assumptions, that there is an unconscious and that focusing on one's childhood is an important thing to do. The person must also accept the far from intuitively reasonable idea that emotional problems can only be cured indirectly, through understanding oneself in a general way. Although these ideas about the unconscious, the importance of self-knowledge, and the value of discussing feelings have been part of the cultural milieu for some time, they were not so common during the first part of this century. To people who reached adulthood well before the era of self-examination in the 1960s these ideas might seem peculiar or even silly—making undergoing this form of treatment difficult or impossible.

And the unwillingness to explore feelings may be more than just a cohort phenomenon. Some of the research discussed in Chapter 7 implies that it may be intrinsic to advancing age itself—the recent finding showing that older people use coping strategies such as cutting off feelings to deal with stress; the decades old Kansas City finding that older age groups told more concrete, less feeling-laden stories on the TAT. In other words, even future cohorts of older people may not be so interested in the intense self-examination psychoanalytic treatment demands. The youthful lust to spend years examining our inner motivations may dim considerably in the latter part of life.

Psychoanalytic therapy may also violate the older person's more traditional idea of what the doctor/patient relationship is like (see Haug, 1981; and Chapter 4). Rather than telling the person what to do to get well, in insight-oriented therapy the authority figure refrains from giving any advice at all. The person is responsible for directing the treatment, for bringing up all the information necessary for a cure. Then there is the issue of length. How many older people would see spending years in therapy as productive, given the years of living they have left? How many would feel comfortable about the expense, particularly when the sessions required for cure far exceed those covered by Medicare?

These questions suggest that a variety of considerations basic to age itself may limit the appeal of the psychoanalytic approach. Not only are there problems of time and expense and the need to discuss feelings, but the fact that the person must focus attention on a far-distant past. It is one thing for a 30-year-old to see probing into what happened at age 3 as having meaning; it is quite another to convince a 70-year-old to see early childhood as the be-all and end-all of adult life.

For these reasons, most psychoanalytically oriented therapists advise that standard psychoanalytic techniques be modified when working with older patients. Therapists should be more active; focus more on down-to-earth, practical concerns; expect therapy to be shorter term; and use a more supportive approach (Blum & Tross, 1980; Pfeiffer, 1976).

And, finally, it is unlikely that traditional psychoanalytic therapy will often be employed in the future, but for another reason than lack of applicability to old age. In the past few decades this treatment method has become less popular with younger people and therapists alike. In other words, psychoanalytic therapy, too, may be a cohort phenomenon—one specific to the cohort now middle class and middle aged.

Behavior Therapy

For many people, seeing a therapist conjures up images of insight-oriented psychoanalytic treatment: talking things out to an often silent person, or perhaps lying on a couch for years. Behavioral techniques have nothing in common with these images. To use a behavioral approach you do not need patients who agree about the value of talking, or even patients able to talk at all! You do not have to confine yourself to dealing with functional psychological problems as psychoanalytical therapists do. As we saw in practically every other chapter of this book, behavioral techniques are used to change not just problems labeled as mental disorders but any problem behavior—from memory deficits to incontinence to getting a wheelchair-bound person walking again.

This wider application is due to behaviorism's different theoretical framework. To repeat the discussion in Chapter 1, behaviorists believe that all responses are learned in very simple ways—acquired directly by classical or operant conditioning or indirectly by observation. Emotional problems are not a discrete entity, separate from other types of learned behavior. They, too, are responses that have been learned in the same way. The only problem is their content. The person who has developed one of these problems has learned the wrong thing. Somehow reinforcements have been set up to favor learning pathological responses, ones limiting full living rather than promoting a happy life. Behavior therapists see their role not as doctors but as retrainers or reeducators, people skilled in using the principles of learning to extinguish maladaptive behavior and build in new, healthy responses. When the therapist and patient collaborate together in this reeducation, the treatment is called **behavior therapy.** When the treatment involves the therapist's rearranging reinforcements without collaborating with the patient (actually, behaviorists use the term *client*), the treatment is called **behavior modification.**

In past chapters, we have seen how behavioral techniques are used to treat many problems not labeled as mental disorders. Now we look at examples of treatments for two problems with these labels—phobias and depression. I have specific reasons for selecting the following treatments from the wide variety of techniques a behaviorally oriented therapist might use. The first, called **desensitization,** is one of the most widely used behavioral approaches and is the standard treatment for the many problems that have anxiety at their root. Desensitization was used in the vignette. The second, a treatment for depression, offers a prime example of how the new **cognitive behavioral approach** is used in practice. As I noted in Chapter 1, in contrast to traditional behavior therapy, which deals only with *overt* responses, cognitive behavior therapists focus on changing faulty *cognitions*—they attempt to eliminate the disturbed client's disordered ways of thinking and perceiving the world (Mahoney, 1977).

Desensitization.   Desensitization, which was used to treat Sophie Gold in the vignette, is a widely used behavioral technique not just for eradicating intense anxiety but for other undesirable emotional responses, such as inappropriate anger, disgust, or sexual arousal. Most often though, systematic desensitization is used to treat phobias—intense irrational fears. The client with a problem of this type often knows his or her fear is unreasonable but cannot avoid feeling overwhelming anxiety at even the thought of being in close proximity to the person, object, or situation that is evoking the phobic response.

Being a type of anxiety disorder, phobias may, as suggested in Chapter 10, be less prevalent among the elderly than among younger adults; however, people over age 65 have their share of this extremely common class of emotional problems, too. As in the vignette, a phobia may be present along with another psychological diagnosis, such as depression; or it may exist on its own. It may be relatively benign, limited to a single, rarely encountered object, such as snakes. Or, as was the case with Sophie Gold, it may be attached to an extremely crucial activity such as going outdoors. Phobic reactions of this latter type can be extremely incapacitating—causing intense anguish and severely curtailing normal life.

Behaviorists generally view phobias as caused by inappropriate classical conditioning. A neutral situation arouses fear because it has been associated with an inherently anxiety-provoking one (see Chapter 1). For instance, in relation to Sophie Gold, her frightening experience of her mind going blank in the supermarket would be viewed as a stimulus evoking intense anxiety. Because this anxiety-provoking event occurred when she was out by herself, fear became conditioned to the initially neutral event, being out of the house alone. Eventually, even the thought of being out alone evoked intense anxiety.

The vignette also illustrates another characteristic of a phobia, its resistance to extinction. After her traumatic experience, just the idea of leaving the house was fraught with so much anxiety that Sophie no longer went out alone. This inability to encounter the feared situation after the event that caused the phobia is common. However, it only perpetuates the problem. Because the person no longer comes in contact with the really neutral situation, there is no chance to unlearn the fear. Put more technically, extinction cannot occur because there is no exposure to the conditioned stimulus without its being connected to the unconditioned one. For extinction to take place, the person would have to be repeatedly exposed to the phobic situation without its being linked with the inherently anxiety-provoking one. Or, to get over the phobia, Sophie would need to leave the house alone, probably a number of times, without her mind going blank. But, as is typical, her anxiety has become way too high for her to even think of approaching the door. This is where systematic desensitization comes in—it is a strategy designed to make the anxiety manageable enough so that the phobic person can approach and stay in the situation long enough for extinction to occur. Desensitization typically involves two facets: training in relaxation and approaching the feared situation in graded steps (see Wolpe, 1973). (This procedure can also be carried out in fantasy. That is, rather than physically encountering the feared situation, the client imagines confronting it in graduated steps. Typically, however, desensitization occurs in vivo, or real life, as in the vignette.)

The standard way of teaching relaxation is to tape soothing instructions, and have the client listen and practice daily using the tape. After mastering the art of being relaxed under nonanxiety-provoking conditions, the client is ready for the second step—encountering the situation.

To do this, the therapist and client construct what is called a *fear hierarchy*—a list of phobia-related situations that vary in their capacity to produce full-blown fear. The client arranges these situations on a scale from 1 to 100. For instance, in the vignette, the item "going out alone in the yard of my building" might be relatively low on Sophie's hierarchy. The item highest on her scale might be "go shopping alone in an unfamiliar place." The purpose of the list is to get the phobic person to encounter the fear in measured dollops. As in the vignette, situations at the low end of the scale are often able to be confronted right away, as they cause some tension but not an intolerable amount. When the client encounters these low-level tension-producing situations without the fear being reinforced, the anxiety attached to them is extinguished. This loss generalizes to the more feared situations, making them in turn somewhat less anxiety provoking. Now that they evoke a tolerable level of anxiety, the client can enter these higher fear situations, allowing extinction to occur. When the top-ranking item on the scale is encountered and the anxiety attached to it is finally dissipated, the phobia is completely cured.

While the therapist in the vignette did not use relaxation, when it is utilized, the client is told to use what he or she has learned in listening to the tape at home in proceeding from item to item. Being able to relax even a bit lessens the fear attached to each situation, accelerating extinction.

Cognitive Behavior Therapy for Depression.

This common behavioral treatment for depression epitomizes the cognitive behavioral point of view: The prime cause of the client's symptoms are irrational, unrealistically negative thoughts. It is these faulty cognitions that are producing all the other signs of the disorder—the gloomy mood, the inability to act, the slowed thinking, even the physical hallmarks of depression. Therefore the goal of treatment lies in getting the depressed client to identify and then change these malignant, depression-generating thoughts (Beck, 1973; Rush, Khatami, & Beck, 1975).

As a first step toward this goal, therapist and client work together to identify the actual content of these cognitions and the concrete situations that set them off. Because the negative thoughts that are causing the depression tend to have an automatic quality that the client isn't aware of, this is not as easy as it might appear (Gallagher & Thompson, 1983). The client may "know" when he or she is depressed but not be able to spell out why. All that is experienced is the unpleasant symptoms, not the chain of reasoning that is their causal link.

TABLE 11-2. A partially completed dysfunctional thought record and the realistic responses that might be substituted.

Situation	At home, reading—waiting for my son to call
Emotions	Sad, miserable, abandoned, lonely
Automatic thoughts	Why didn't he call? Why is he rejecting me? I feel so miserable. I don't know what to do. Why does this always happen to me? I just can't go on like this! What did I do wrong?
More rational thoughts	(1) Just because he didn't call doesn't mean he's rejecting me. I have no proof of rejection. In fact, he visited me 2 weeks ago. (2) It's not true that this always happens to me. Sometimes I don't call him when I say I will and he doesn't think it's the end of the world. (3) Besides, why should I think his not calling is my fault. He may be working late again. (4) Even if he is upset with me for some reason, it doesn't mean he will never speak to me again. (5) Suppose he is angry with me. I've survived problems with him before. All relationships have ups and downs. I'll try first to find out if anything is wrong before I give up on myself!

Source: Adapted from Gallagher & Thompson, 1983, p. 172.

According to psychiatrist Aaron Beck, the architect of this innovative approach, depression-generating thoughts have certain attributes: They magnify the unhappy significance of a single event. They usually involve overgeneralization (based on one negative experience, a globally catastrophic conclusion is reached). They may selectively abstract an unwarranted conclusion from what has happened—arbitrarily inferring something negative from a really neutral event.

After identifying these thoughts, the client is taught to monitor them, to become aware of their illogic, and to substitute more rational thoughts, learning to think, for instance, "I'm exaggerating," "I'm taking this out of context," or "I'm jumping to conclusions" when an idea of gloom and doom arises (see Table 11-2 for examples). The therapist encourages this active effort at self-control by continually challenging the logic behind each thought. The hope is that eventually the depression-prone client will have the skills to view *any* unrealistic thought objectively and to be able to replace it with a nondepression-generating idea.

Here is an example of this therapy with an 83-year-old widower:

At about eighty, Mr. D began to have difficulty with hearing and vision and by the middle of his eighty-second year was showing signs of forgetfulness . . . it was decided that he would move into his son and daughter-in-law's spare room. Shortly after this he became depressed and anxious. . . . at the family's request he agreed to seek help. . . . Therapy began by discussing Mr. D's current complaints and then targeting several for him to work on. . . . First, to reduce his awful feeling of hopelessness about himself; second to help him learn to control his feelings of being overwhelmed; and finally to help him stop feeling like a failure. . . . When the cognitive therapy model was presented, Mr. D seemed disappointed and confused because he was expecting to be given something that would solve his problems. . . . However, after three sessions had been devoted to discussing the model and its potential application to his problems . . . he agreed to note the kinds of thoughts that occurred to him at times he felt blue and anxious. Virtually all of the thoughts centered around feelings of being worthless . . . his life no longer had any meaning or purpose and it was only a matter of time before he would be placed in a home for worthless persons. . . . Two approaches were used to help Mr. D deal with this pessimistic view. The first built on the fact that his friends came to visit him. The therapist encouraged him to entertain the idea that they might be coming because they enjoyed being with him. . . . He fostered an investigative effort on his part to learn the ways in which the friends benefited from their time with him. . . . The second approach focused on helping Mr. D view himself as a model to help others cope with problems they might encounter as they grow older. . . . This seemed a pivotal point in therapy, as Mr. D accepted the idea that his life still had purpose as a teacher and role model to others. . . . The last three sessions . . . were used to review the specific skills he had learned in identifying and checking his dysfunctional thoughts and to prepare for potentially depressogenic situations in the future [Thompson, Davies, Gallagher, & Krantz, pp. 262–265].

This case illustrates the essentials of cognitive behavior therapy. The unrealistic thoughts are identified, their illogical basis is pointed out, and the client learns to substitute more realistic thoughts. By repeatedly practicing, the client eventually becomes skilled at substituting nonillness-generating thoughts every time a depressive idea arises. Furthermore, rather than taking a passive approach to the nihilistic feelings an older depressed client might bring to therapy, the cognitive behavior therapist takes pains to eradicate any doubts early on. Socializing the client into treatment—carefully addressing negative feelings and explaining the therapy itself—is viewed as an essential first step necessary to success (Gallagher & Thompson, 1983).

This particular treatment is also uniquely suited to overcoming age-related doubts about therapy. When an older person doubtfully says, "Treatment can't work with me because I'm too old to change," the response might be, "But, is it possible for you to learn?" The therapist would then describe the educational focus of the behavioral approach: "My goal is not to change your personality, but to teach you new skills to prevent and control your depression" (Gallagher & Thompson, 1983).

Evaluation.   Practically every attribute of behavior therapy suggests that it is better suited than psychoanalytic techniques to help older adults. Behavior therapy is problem oriented and short term. Ironically, while less likely to couch the treatment in medical-model-oriented terminology, behavior therapists act more like traditional doctors than their psychoanalytic counterparts: giving instructions, and telling the client what to do. Behavior therapists meet the older person's resistances head on; they take careful pains to bend their techniques to the client's needs. For instance, in the case just described, the therapist went very slowly in teaching the new way of thinking, taking care to account for Mr. D's lessened learning abilities. Rather than abruptly terminating treatment, he gradually tapered off, allowing Mr. D to independently practice his new skills and still "touch base" for several refresher sessions. While psychoanalytically oriented therapists do modify their techniques occasionally, only among behavior therapists do we see this fully flexible tailoring of treatment to embrace the needs and capacities of older adults.

It is no wonder then that in the few carefully controlled outcome studies comparing the two treatments with the elderly, the results have tended to favor behavior therapy (Gallagher & Thompson, 1983; Steuer et al., 1984; Thompson et al., 1986). For instance, in a typical example, depressed older people were randomly assigned to one of the following treatments: cognitive behavior therapy, the same number of sessions of another type of behavior therapy, psychoanalytically oriented treatment. While all three treatments were equally effective at reducing symptoms at the end of the 16 sessions of therapy, the behavioral approaches were found to be clearly superior at follow-ups: 6 weeks, 3 months, and 6 months after therapy, people assigned to these treatments were less likely to have relapsed, more likely to have remained symptom free (Gallagher & Thompson, 1983; Thompson et al., 1986).

However, this study also illustrates the limitations of behavior therapy (and I might add of *any* other psychotherapeutic technique). The behavioral approaches were more effective with the older people with minor depressions. They were less helpful for those whose depressions were classified as major. In other words, while people with major depressions can clearly benefit from psychotherapy plus drug therapy, it is problems in living, not more biological disorders, which cognitive behavior therapy *alone* is most well suited to treat.

Group Therapy

Group therapy for treating psychological problems evolved during World War Two as a solution to the many people needing psychological help and the scarcity of trained mental health workers. Today this type of treatment is quite popular. It even has expanded to people who define themselves as "normal," as not emotionally disturbed. Encounter groups, for instance, are designed to promote greater self-understanding among people who (at least in theory) are already well adjusted. And, as we saw in previous chapters, there are groups to help "average" people cope with stressful life events such as caring for disabled family members or negotiating the transitions of retirement or widowhood. In fact, many groups for the elderly are not problem oriented at all. Their goal is educational and social, to share information, to meet people (Zarit, 1980).

In contrast to those types of groups, the explicit goal of a psychotherapy group is to help people with emotional problems resolve their difficulties. What promise does this treatment method have for older adults? Clues come from examining what groups can offer people of any age.

In a classic textbook on group psychotherapy, Irving Yalom (1975) spells out the varied curative influences he feels underlie psychotherapy groups. Yalom believes that these influences are common to all successful groups regardless of their marked differences in outer form (in, for example, their membership, the frequency with which they meet, and in their theoretical orientation).

Groups, according to Yalom, facilitate interpersonal learning and allow their members to develop socializing techniques. They offer a forum for people to learn how others see their actions, including their strengths and weaknesses. Honest responses from other group members teach participants what they are doing wrong and how to relate in better ways. Groups also offer solidarity. With the group behind them, individual participants have the comfort of knowing that they aren't struggling with their problems alone. Groups promote hope and a sense of "universality," allowing members to see other people with similar problems who may be coping more successfully. This makes the individual person's struggles seem less unique and insurmountable. Related to these benefits is another curative influence: groups foster modeling. By observing how other group members deal with difficulties, participants learn new strategies for coping with their own.

And finally, in contrast to individual therapy, groups allow people to be "altruistic," to advise and help other group members. We might expect this experience of being elevated from a dependent position to one of giving help to be particularly helpful in building self-esteem among older people who may feel useless because they no longer have the chance to give to others.

All of these potential benefits (some of which may also occur in individual treatment) suggest that group therapy may be very helpful for the elderly. In fact, the literature on the use of psychotherapy groups with older people is quite extensive (Gatz et al., 1985), suggesting that many (or even most) older people who do get psychotherapeutic help are indeed treated in groups. As these two very different examples show, the types of older people treated in groups are diverse indeed.

> Mrs. L, an 86-year-old woman . . . returned home from a stay at the hospital. She was quite withdrawn and disoriented. . . . She refused to communicate with her spouse and her daughters and for the most part sat slumped over, her eyes fixed on the floor. The family members and elderly friends recognized her as being a highly functioning alert person and were unwilling to believe that Mrs. L had an irreversible condition. They asked a therapist . . . to intervene and . . . a group of elderly friends, neighbors, and relatives was formed.
>
> The therapist . . . began by asking her questions about herself. The group, taking his lead, did the same. . . . Within a half hour Mrs. L was sitting up in her chair attending to the German conversation of an elderly cousin. In the third group session she was able to talk about her recent surgery and her long stay in the hospital. Mrs. L returned to functioning quite well [Fry, 1986, p. 371].

In contrast, Robert Butler and Myrna Lewis (1973) used this treatment method in a radically different way, setting up several age-integrated psychotherapy groups whose members ranged from 15 to over 80. Their goal was both to promote personality change and counteract age segregation. Butler and Lewis felt that different generations could be very helpful to one another as they shared experiences characteristic of different life-stages.

Unlike Mrs. L, members of these groups, though upset and having problems, were not severely disturbed or intellectually impaired. The groups met weekly over a long period; the average participant attended for about 2 years. Older members had unique contributions to make, which, in turn, helped them by enhancing their sense of self-worth. They brought their wisdom and breadth of experience to the group. They served as models of growing older for the younger participants.

Evaluation.   Like all outcome research, while some studies evaluating group therapy have shown success, others have had disappointing results (see Gatz et al., 1985; Gotestam, 1980). So once again we must turn to conjecture in evaluating the merits of this approach. What older people might this type of treatment be likely to benefit? What pitfalls could there be in using groups with older adults?

Groups seem to have special promise for helping lonely, isolated older people who can benefit from the unique supportive functions just described. The fact that sharing experiences may be at the heart of the curative effect of this type of treatment also suggests that groups in which older participants are dealing with similar life concerns (for example, retirement or widowhood) might be particularly helpful.

However, as in psychoanalytic treatment, some older adults may have trouble discussing personal problems in a group. Being open in a group may even be more difficult for many older people than being open with an individual therapist. Perhaps this is why therapist Judith Altolz (1978) states that in her experience older people are slower to become comfortable in groups and are much more likely to shy away from discussing personal issues than younger adults.

Other cautions about using this type of therapy with the elderly also apply to people of any age: Groups can intensify isolation if the older adult is rejected or criticized by fellow group members (Hartford, 1980). Groups should also not be billed as being for discussion when their covert aim is to provide psychotherapy. It has been suggested that this problem may be especially common in the elderly because of the diversity of groups used with the aged. For example, in senior citizen centers, groups are often set up for socialization. When, as often happens, these groups led by nonprofessionals have a hidden agenda to provide psychotherapy (Zarit, 1980), the risk of "casualties" or negative psychological reactions multiplies. (For instance, there have been cases of people becoming suicidal or having to be hospitalized after a group probed their problems too deeply or unfeelingly offered "insights" into unacceptable truths.)

Marital and Family Therapy

In **marital and family therapy** a therapist usually sees a couple or a family together regularly. This technique evolved in response to the common observation that when a patient improved in individual treatment, something peculiar often occurred. Either the spouse or another family member developed problems, or the family somehow sabotaged the patient's progress. In other words, problems that seemed confined to the patient were actually localized more broadly in the family as a whole. It was a disturbed family unit that needed treatment, not a disturbed individual (Glick & Kessler, 1980; Satir, 1967).

Family and couple therapy is based on the idea that emotional problems are really caused by pathological relationships and that only by addressing these disturbed relationships can the individual's problems be cured. Although all therapists who work with families agree with this basic premise, as with group therapy, there are various schools of family therapy, such as psychoanalytically oriented treatment and behavioral family therapy. In addition, family therapists have developed a type of treatment that is uniquely theirs—the **systems approach** (see Haley, J., 1971). This radically different view of what causes psychopathology evolved in reaction to orthodox ways of viewing psychological problems. One impetus for its development was the often poor cure rate of traditional, particularly psychoanalytic, therapy.

Psychoanalytic therapists see problems as localized in the person and due to early childhood experiences. Systems family therapists turn this point of view on its head. They believe psychological problems are rooted in the person's current situation and see the *situation* as pathological, not the individual. In their view, disturbed behavior is an adaptive, appropriate response to a pathological, present environment.

This perspective dictates a very different treatment strategy. Rather than remaining passive and allowing childhood feelings and fantasies to emerge, the therapist intervenes actively to change the disturbed family interactions. For instance, in the vignette, Dr. Zaccarelli tried to stop Ruben Gold from overprotecting his wife by redefining her as a capable person, believing that engineering this change would make his patient less fearful. He also gave the couple homework—instructions to follow between sessions—to repair their faulty relationship.

Another interesting family systems technique is called "prescribing the symptom." The therapist instructs family members to do the very thing that bothers them on a regular basis at home. The couple that cannot stop arguing is told they must have a fight every evening; the patient with uncontrollable anxiety attacks must have an anxiety attack at 8 each night. The idea is that when the symptom loses its involuntary quality it loses its emotional meaning. Once the patient controls the illness rather than being its dreaded captive, symptoms will naturally dissipate.

Here is an example of a family therapy intervention developed for the elderly, a technique combining elements of insight-oriented and systems family therapy. First, the family interactions are actively restructured by separating the patient physically from the situation. Once out of his home, the patient improves, as we would expect if a pathological situation is indeed causing the problem. At this point the family is able to engage in insight-oriented family therapy. In this second phase of treatment, the family meets together to gain insight into their destructive ways of relating and substitute more positive actions and emotions.

Mr. H, aged 82, was tall, good looking, and appeared younger than his age. His wife, twenty years his junior, was an attractive woman whom people often mistook for his daughter. Two years before admission, Mr. H gave up his factory job. His wife operated a beauty shop and provided for both. Shortly before admission, Mr. H stopped helping his wife with the housework which had become one of his chores after retirement. The couple was in constant conflict. Mrs. H could not stand her husband's aging. He acted out by becoming more regressed and childish. . . . Without telling his wife, he manipulated his married daughters to help him with the housework. He tried to get his daughters to side with him against his demanding wife. By admitting Mr. H to the day hospital, we accomplished phase 1. There was no reason for his daughters to sneak into the house to help their father with his chores and he no longer annoyed his wife at her work. He was able to establish a more positive and less destructive role for himself in the family. . . . Although hostile toward each other, husband and wife communicated well and took sole responsibility for their behavior. Phase 2 was achieved. Mr. H reestablished his own self-respect in the family. We also helped the family to accept the father and husband in a new role. . . . Mr. H was discharged, improved from the hospital [Grauer, Betts, & Birnbom, 1973, p. 24].

Evaluation.   Marital and family therapy seems particularly well suited to classic situations that an aging couple or family with aged parents face—for example, adapting to role shifts such as illness or retirement.

While many people are able to cope surprisingly well when their spouse becomes physically (or mentally) infirm (see Chapter 8), this age-related event does have its casualties: as in the vignette, there are couples whose relationships do deteriorate under the impact of this tremendous stress. Retirement is another later-life stress that, while not typically causing problems, does affect some marriages negatively (Keating & Cole, 1980). When these changes produce marital discord, couple therapy seems to be a logical approach.

Family therapy may also be ideally suited to help children coping with a disabled parent. As we saw in Chapter 8, here troubled relationships are much more predictable—anger and distance between parent and caregiving child (Cantor, 1983) and conflicts among brothers and sisters as they struggle to handle the burden of caregiving equitably (Johnson, E. S., & Bursk, 1977). In these situations, provided the family as a whole is motivated to see a therapist (Blazer, 1982), family therapy may be the intervention of choice.

CHEMOTHERAPY

In the first half of this century, people dreamed of the day there might be a pill that could cure mental disorders. In the late 1950s this dream was partly realized when medications were developed that sometimes did have this dramatic effect. These medicines, called **psychotropic** (changing the psyche) agents, work neurologically, altering feelings, thought processes, and behavior and easing the tormenting symptoms functional psychological disorders produce.

There are three types of psychotropic medicines: **antipsychotic drugs** combat schizophrenia and other psychotic disorders. **Antidepressant drugs** are for major depressions. **Antianxiety drugs** calm people suffering from anxiety disorders. (Lithium carbonate, a salt rather than a synthetic chemical, is used in the treatment of manic-depressive disorders.)

Psychotropic medications are among our nation's most frequently prescribed drugs for adults of any age. And, in addition to being more prone to use medications in general, older people are also more frequent users of psychotropic drugs. Experts estimate that as many as one out of every three people over age 65 takes a psychotropic drug at some point in a given year (Fry, 1986; Walker,

J. I., & Brodie, 1980). In nursing homes, where serious psychopathology is rampant, the percentages are much higher: three out of every four residents may have some type of mood-altering medication prescribed for them at a given time (Baldessarini, 1977). These statistics show how imperative it is to examine the drawbacks and benefits of these drugs for the elderly.

Antipsychotic Drugs

Antipsychotic medications have revolutionized the treatment of schizophrenia. They are largely responsible for the reform movement that allowed many of the large psychiatric institutions housing the chronically mentally ill to close their doors. These drugs can have dramatic effects on the most extreme schizophrenic symptoms—they clear up the delusions, hallucinations, and other bizarre symptoms of this devastating disease. Anyone who works on an inpatient psychiatric unit cannot fail to be impressed by their power. Within hours after being given one of these drugs, an incoherent, wildly psychotic patient can be transformed into someone who can be reasoned with, talked to, and eventually discharged to live a relatively normal life outside the hospital.

But antipsychotic drugs are not panaceas. They only work to a limited extent with some people and not at all with others. They have side effects. While many of these adverse reactions are merely troublesome, others can be serious, cause permanent neurological damage, or even, in rare cases, be fatal. They do not cure schizophrenia itself but only suppress its symptoms while the person is taking the drug. Because of the inconvenience of taking pills every day and the side effects, many schizophrenics stop their medication—a decision that can lead to relapse, another psychotic episode, and readmission to the hospital.

Even though, as I noted in the last chapter, there may be fewer people over age 65 who suffer from schizophrenia, antipsychotic medications are prescribed in relative abundance for older adults. This is particularly true in nursing homes (Baldessarini, 1977; Norman & Bùrrows, 1984). In many instances the drugs may be given appropriately even if the person's primary problem is not schizophrenia. For example, severe agitation and delusions and hallucinations are fairly common accompaniments of dementia (Zarit, Orr, & Zarit, 1985; see Chapter 10). Antipsychotic drugs may be quite helpful in treating these intensely distressing secondary symptoms of Alzheimer's disease (Baldessarini, 1977).

Unfortunately, though, as is true not just for the elderly but for deprived, institutionalized people of any age, antipsychotic drugs are sometimes used for institutional rather than individual needs—to sedate people that the nursing staff finds difficult to handle (Norman & Burrows, 1984; Peabody, Warner, Whiteford, & Hollister, 1987; Zarit, Orr, & Zarit, 1985). For instance, in one survey of 12 Veterans Administration hospitals, 23% of the elderly patients taking psychotropic drugs turned out to have no mental disorder at all (Walker, J. I., & Brodie, 1980).

It is easy to imagine the powerful temptation to overmedicate residents in nursing homes. Because of poorly trained staff (and, as we saw in Chapter 4, poor staff morale) there may be little way to deal with demanding patients other

TABLE 11-3. A partial list of psychotropic drugs.

Major Classes and Chemical Types	Trade Names
Antipsychotic drugs	
Phenothiazines	Thorazine, Mellaril, Prolixin, Stelazine
Thioxanthenes	Taractan, Navane
Butyrophenones	Haldol
Antidepressant drugs	
Trycyclics	Elavil, Sinequan, Tofranil
MAO inhibitors	Marplan, Nardil, Parnate
Antianxiety drugs	
Benziodiazepines	Librium, Valium, Dalmane, Tranxene, Serax
Barbiturates	Nembutal, Seconal
Antihistamines	Benadryl, Atarax, Vistaril
Propanediols	Miltown, Tybatran

than sedation. Furthermore, nursing homes may only employ one consulting psychiatrist, or more typically have no psychiatric consultant at all. When a primary care doctor is pressured by the harried nursing staff to "do something" to quiet a difficult patient, even the most conscientious person may succumb to the pressure to dispense drugs quickly, without the thorough evaluation that is required (see the list of guidelines at the end of this section).

However, as we also saw earlier in this book, this is risky for older patients because of their greater chance of developing toxic reactions to drugs. Not only may the careless use of antipsychotic medicines needlessly create excess disabilities, it may even be life threatening.

Antidepressant Drugs

Because this class of medications does not quiet wildly disturbing behavior, antidepressants may not be so indiscriminately prescribed. Here the problem lies more in the side effects this second class of psychotropic drug can have even when prescribed appropriately.

Like antipsychotic drugs, antidepressants can work wonders for some depressed people. They work best when a person has the classic symptoms of a major depression (see Chapter 10). They work less well or not at all with minor depressions. They also take from 1 to 3 weeks to begin to be effective and so may discourage some people from taking them for the required time. They have side effects that may be unpleasant, or, particularly in the case of the elderly, even life threatening. Paradoxically, because they are especially lethal taken in large doses, they are very risky to use with depressed people who are also suicidal.

Antianxiety Drugs

Antianxiety drugs are also called minor tranquilizers because they are used for less severe emotional disorders, for problems involving intense anxiety. They calm, sedate, and relax. They may cause drowsiness and so are also used to combat insomnia (Stotsky, 1975).

Despite their popularity, however, the use of this class of medicines to treat simple anxiety has been severely criticized because of their tremendous potential for abuse. People—old and young—can easily become addicted to these drugs. The elderly may have inappropriate reasons for taking these drugs (such as to combat a perhaps normal age-related lessening of the number of hours needed for sleep). The problem with prescribing these medications for older people lies not just in their addictive quality, but in the desired effect itself. Is the calming benefit worth the risk of the older person falling because of drowsiness? Won't the decrease in mental alertness exacerbate any cognitive problems the older user may have? A poignant study amply demonstrates that this danger is real. When researchers gave cognitively intact older people 10 milligrams of Valium (a dose that, though large, is within the range a doctor might prescribe), their subjects had deficits on a memory test almost identical to those of a comparison group with Alzheimer's disease (Block, R. I., De Voe, Stanley, Stanley, & Pomara, 1985)!

Psychotropic Drugs and the Older Person

As is true of most medications, the elderly tolerate psychotropic drugs less well than younger adults do. A dose well within the range a 30-year-old can handle is likely to be excessive for someone in his or her 70s. Because the older person metabolizes and excretes medicines less efficiently, they remain in the body longer. In addition, common side effects of psychotropic drugs can exacerbate physical difficulties older people are more likely to have. For example, the tricyclic antidepressants are used very cautiously in people with cardiac problems because they can cause heartbeat irregularities and so perhaps even precipitate a heart attack (Baldessarini, 1977; Hollister, 1983).

Toxic effects from psychotropic drugs include delirium as well as a variety of specific reactions—adverse effects ranging in severity from a dry mouth to the life-threatening cardiac crisis just described. While most are not fatal, many negatively affect functional capacities or the way a person feels. The risk of negative side effects multiply if the person is concurrently taking other drugs, as is common in old age. Medications are likely to interact, sometimes in unknown ways, with the psychotropic drug (Fry, 1986; Peabody et al., 1987; Simonson, 1984). The risk of adverse reactions in the elderly is also higher because cognitive, emotional, and even vision problems also make it more likely that the drug will not be taken as prescribed.

These cautions suggest that in older people psychotropic medications should be prescribed more sparingly and in lower doses. Their use should also be carefully supervised. A major goal of a new field called **geriatric psychopharmacology** is to develop guidelines for this use. Some of these guidelines (see Fry, 1986, p. 411) are listed below:

1. Establish a drug-free baseline by discontinuing all nonessential psychotropic medicines.
2. Evaluate the elderly person's drug history for different medical ailments and functional psychological disorders.
3. Evaluate the person's blood pressure and blood count, total protein albumin ratios, urinalysis, and cardiac and respiratory conditions.
4. Evaluate drug intake and its adverse or positive effects on the elderly person.
5. Starting doses and maintenance doses of drugs for elderly persons should be one-third to one-half that for younger persons.
6. Administration of the medication to the person should be the responsibility of an adult who lives with the person and can monitor adverse effects.
7. Elderly patients on psychotropic drugs should be observed regularly by caregivers—monitored for signs of fatigue, withdrawal, cognitive confusion. Close vigilance is essential.
8. Elderly patients on drugs should be reviewed regularly by their physicians in order to avoid the risk of progressive and perhaps dangerous side effects.

TREATMENTS FOR DEMENTIA

Methods of treating dementia fall into the same two categories as those used for functional psychological problems: attempts to improve thinking using non-biological means (either by talking to the person or by restructuring the environment) and efforts to treat the person by chemical means (typically through experimental memory-enhancing drugs). Furthermore, because dementia continues to be incurable, within the past decade there has been increasing attention paid to helping the other casualty of these devastating diseases—the family.

Environmental Treatments

The outside world can be restructured in a variety of ways to help a person with dementia. For instance, any intervention that promotes physical independence may also enhance cognitive functioning. Other environmental treatments for dementia include the formal services described in Chapter 4: day hospitals and nursing homes with special units for residents suffering from dementing illnesses. There are also external devices to enhance remembering and protect the person. Some of these helpful aids are listed below (O'Quinn, personal communication, 1986):

For memory

- Bulletin board for daily plans and messages
- Kitchen timer and alarm watch to remind the person to do things

For independent living

- Clothes and shoes with Velcro closures
- Gripping aids for toothbrushes, eating utensils, pens and pencils

- Controlled-flow drinking cups
- Door knob extensions and handle restraints

For safety

- Tap water overflow alarm (alarm sounds if tap runs over)
- Automatic shut-off kettle or teapot; automatic shut-off iron; automatic shut-off stove
- Childproof cabinet and door locks
- Grab-bars around toilet and bathtub
- Appliance and light timers

And there is the treatment described next, *reality orientation*.

Reality Orientation.   **Reality orientation,** typically used in institutions with severely confused residents, is based on the principle that disorientation can be combated by increasing the amount of exposure that confused patients get to basic facts about themselves and their external situation. In other words, turning up the volume of external input about reality may partly compensate for the inner losses (Kohut, Kohut, & Fleishman, 1979). A reality orientation program typically requires the total commitment of the nursing home's staff.

First, the staff is instructed to never listen to delusional talk without informing the person about reality. When Mr. Chin says that he is in a hotel, the staff must correct him, saying, "No, you are in Four Acres nursing home." In addition, Mr. Chin's family is given the same instructions: "Never play along with your father's delusions." Then, at each encounter, the person is told basic facts—about who he is talking to, about where he is. These attempts to anchor the person in reality occur each time a staff member interacts with the confused person. In addition, the nursing home may offer reality orientation groups or classes that give residents the same input in a more structured way.

Here is what a staff member practicing reality orientation might say when giving a resident a meal. The italicized words are the cues that orient the person to his surroundings:

"Good *morning, Mr. Y.* How are you today? (Wait for reply.) It's a beautiful *fall day* and it's such a clear, crisp *morning.* Are you ready for *breakfast?* (Wait for reply.) Here's your *breakfast tray.* It's 8 o'clock in the *morning* and your *breakfast* is here. These pancakes look delicious, *Mr. Y* [adapted from Kohut, Kohut, & Fleishman, 1979, p. 68].

Although this conversation may seem artificial, it has an important aim: to anchor this man in the real world by reminding him of the time of day, the season, the weather, and what he is expected to do (to eat breakfast). When a nursing home commits itself to a full-blown reality orientation program, the staff uses this approach at every opportunity.

In addition, reality orientation often includes the use of environmental props—large calendars and clocks put in eye-catching places, an object called a reality orientation board (see Figure 11-1). Prominently displayed throughout the nursing home, these physical reminders of reality are also supposed to help decrease disorientation.

TODAY IS FRIDAY

THE DATE IS SEPTEMBER 18, 1988

THE WEATHER IS SUNNY

THE NEXT HOLIDAY IS HALLOWEEN

THE NEXT MEAL IS DINNER

TOMORROW IS SATURDAY

Figure 11-1. The reality orientation board.

Loudspeakers at the home may also announce basic facts, such as the time and date, at regular times during the day. Residents may be encouraged to personalize their rooms (for example, to keep pictures of their family and familiar objects by their beds). As simple an object as a mirror may also be a reality orientation tool. Here the thought is that it also combats disorientation by reminding the person of an essential life fact: how he or she looks.

Evaluation.   While today features of reality orientation such as the reality orientation board are standard fixtures at most nursing homes, interest in this technique has waned considerably. The basic premise of reality orientation is far from an unquestioned truth—that somehow just being reminded of reality is going to improve the confused person's life. Is the man with multi-infarct dementia really better off knowing the grim truth that he is in a nursing home and that his wife is dead, rather than feeling that he is on his honeymoon in Spain? Even more discouraging, the few studies evaluating whether reality orientation is effective have had disappointing conclusions (see, for review, Zarit, 1980).

One, which showed that the procedure was helpful, gives clues about the specific conditions that might be important for success (Brook, Degun, & Mather, 1975). The researchers put a group of patients in a room containing newspapers, a reality orientation board, and interesting objects. Another group was put in the same room with a staff member who discussed the materials and pointed out the items on the reality orientation board. Only the second group improved, suggesting that if reality orientation is at all helpful, interpersonal stimulation is required—merely being exposed to external reminders of reality has no effect. In addition, the intervention only improved cognition among patients who were not severely impaired to begin with. So a second precondition for reality orientation to be effective may be good patient selection. The technique should only be used with moderately demented older adults.

As we will see, issues of patient selection loom large in that area where success would really be earth shattering: finding an effective biological treatment for the major dementing illnesses of later life.

Biological Treatments

Discovering a medication or substance that would cure dementia is our late-twentieth-century dream, a fantasy shared not only by every person over age 65 but by anyone of any age whose life has been impoverished by witnessing (or caring for) a loved one with this terrible disease. While researchers are pursuing this dream feverishly, so far no treatment has been able to prevent, reverse, or even really slow the inexorable downward course of the most common dementing illness, Alzheimer's disease; though preventative measures such as lowering blood pressure or reducing cholesterol may have some effect in reducing the frequency of the small strokes characteristic of the second major type of dementing illness, multi-infarct dementia (see Zarit, Orr, & Zarit, 1985).

The primary approach to treating Alzheimer's disease biologically is eminently logical. Determine what substances its victims are lacking and then supply them via drugs, diet, or another treatment (see, for reviews, Cole & Liptzin, 1984; Crook, 1986). For instance, since researchers now know that a striking deficiency in the neurotransmitter acetylcholine is characteristic of the brains of Alzheimer's victims, considerable research has been devoted to trying to bolster this chemical in particular. One approach has been to have Alzheimer's victims ingest a precursor substance in its production, such as the chemical choline; another strategy has been to try to decrease the destruction of acetylcholine, primarily by having people take drugs that seem to have this effect. Other treatments for dementia include the use of vasodilating drugs (which improve cerebral blood flow), the use of stimulants that may have a memory-enhancing effect, and attempts to chemically bolster other systems that researchers theorize are also involved in Alzheimer's disease. While many of the investigators who have used these various procedures report some improvement in some patients, so far no treatment has had the kind of success that would qualify it as a real breakthrough in attacking this most feared scourge of later life.

The difficulty of doing research in this area is illustrated by some hypotheses about why one initially promising lead—the use of vasodilators to treat multi-infarct dementia—was in fact a blind alley (see Sathananthan & Gershon, 1975): (1) The drugs may not have worked because impaired cerebral blood flow may not cause this type of dementia. (2) The drugs may have been ineffective because they dilated only healthy blood vessels not, as needed, diseased ones. (3) Even if the drugs did increase blood flow within the brain, the intervention may not have been effective because too much brain tissue had already died.

This final possibility brings up a general problem that has hampered progress in finding *any* biological treatment or cure for dementia—problems in early, accurate diagnosis. Not only can establishing the presence of Alzheimer's disease (or, as above, multi-infarct dementia) be inherently difficult, dementia is particularly hard to diagnose at the very time any drug or other treatment might have the most chance of being effective: when the disease is in its earliest stages and the neural devastation is not too far advanced. This is why early diagnosis is so important even in the absence of our having an effective treatment for Alzheimer's disease or multi-infarct dementia. Finding a treatment may *depend* on developing a reliable early marker of the diseases.

Treating the Second Casualty: Families

Because a cure has eluded us, strengthening the coping capacities of dementia's "hidden victims" (see Zarit, Orr, & Zarit, 1985)—families—has become an imperative priority. Thanks to the extensive research on caregiving, we now know a good deal about the intense pressures family members coping with a loved one with this devastating disease face (see Chapters 8 and 10). We also have some idea of the concrete services these frontline caregivers so desperately need (see Chapter 4). Now we turn to an organization, begun by people caring for a relative with a dementing illness, which has led the effort to provide caregivers with that other crucial necessity, that of psychological support: the Alzheimer's Disease and Related Disorders Association (ADRDA).

While it also funds and furthers research, the main goal of ADRDA is to help families. It maintains a 24-hour toll-free hot line, serving as a clearinghouse for information about where to go and what to do. It also sponsors a nationwide network of Alzheimer's disease support groups.

While there are counselors who specialize in helping people deal with this difficult disease, the most widespread alternative for caregivers who need help coping is joining one of these Alzheimer's support groups where caregivers meet regularly with other caregivers to share information, offer one another emotional support, and help solve problems. Here is an example of the kind of insights this type of group can provide:

> Dave (who usually cared for his wife with dementia) had gone out of town the previous week and left his wife with their daughter. After (they went) to a restaurant. . . . Dave's wife refused to get in the car to go back home. . . . She began accusing her daughter of trying to hurt her and insisted on seeing Dave. They argued for some time but nothing calmed her down. Instead she got more and more agitated until she collapsed and the paramedics were called. . . . When Dave arrived home, she continued making accusations against their daughter. Dave tried to reason with her but reported to the group that he had no success. . . . Matt tried to put the incident in a different perspective for Dave. He suggested that the behavior was his wife's way of saying that she was very upset over his leaving. Matt further suggested that Dave should acknowledge that she was upset, rather than arguing with her about whether she was at fault. . . . Dave remained concerned about causes. . . . Several possible antecedents for the wife's behavior were explored. . . . When Dave began talking about the incident he expressed feelings of hopelessness. . . . The result was that he gradually felt less overwhelmed and more optimistic [Zarit, Orr, & Zarit, 1985, p. 165].

As this example suggests, people who join these groups report that they do enhance coping and reduce depression. But enthusiastic testimonials aside, are they really effective at reducing the stress and unhappiness family members feel? To answer this question, researchers (Haley, W., Brown, & Levine, 1987) did a genuine outcome study: randomly assigning caregivers to either one of two types of support group or a control waiting list and assessing levels of depression, life satisfaction, and coping before and after the ten-session intervention (see also Chapter 8). Unfortunately, though the people who participated in the groups rated them as very helpful, they had no effect on the more objective indexes of improvement. Scores on measures of depression, coping, and life satisfaction were essentially the same whether or not a person had been in a group. Perhaps ten sessions is too short a time to see genuine improvements. Perhaps the enormity of the problems caregivers face are simply too overwhelming to be "cured" or even markedly improved by any intervention of this type. On the other hand, perhaps just the fact that caregivers report feeling helped is endorsement enough of the value of support groups. The frontline heroes dealing on a daily basis with these terrible diseases need all the positive feelings they can get!

In sum, despite the progress that has been made, this chapter shows that our nation is falling far short of addressing the mental health needs of older adults. Too often older people with emotional problems are left to languish—their needs go unrecognized; they are casualties of the attitude that treatment cannot help "at their age"; or services are simply too expensive. The same neglect applies to caregivers—a group desperately in need of both concrete services and emotional support. Armed with our knowledge that (with modifications) the same treatments used for the young can be effective for the old, the agenda is clear: Make quality mental health care for our older citizens as important a priority as addressing their physical health needs.

KEY TERMS

Custodial care
Outcome studies
Psychoanalytic psychotherapy
Insight-oriented psychoanalytic treatment
Supportive psychoanalytic therapy
Transference
Behavior therapy
Behavior modification
Desensitization
Cognitive behavioral approach

Group therapy
Marital and family therapy
Systems approach
Psychotropic drugs
Antipsychotic drugs
Antidepressant drugs
Antianxiety drugs
Geriatric psychopharmacology
Reality orientation

RECOMMENDED READINGS

Baldessarini, R. J. (1977). *Chemotherapy in psychiatry.* Cambridge, MA: Harvard University Press. Comprehensive discussion of psychotropic drugs, their uses and their side effects. Includes a section on geriatric psychopharmacology. Moderately difficult.

Beck, A. T. (1979). *Depression: Causes and treatment* (7th ed.). Philadelphia: University of Pennsylvania Press. Beck's cognitive behavior therapy for depression. Not difficult.

Clinical Gerontologist. (1986). 5(3/4). Whole issue is devoted to different forms of psychotherapy with the elderly. Includes articles on psychodynamic therapy, behavior therapy, and other types of treatment. Not difficult.

Haley, J. (1971). Family therapy: A radical change. In J. Haley (Ed.), *Changing families: A family therapy reader.* New York: Grune & Stratton. Article explaining systems family therapy. Not difficult.

Wolpe, J. (1973). *The practice of behavior therapy* (2nd ed.). New York, NY: Pergamon Press. Systematic desensitization explained by its originator. Not difficult.

Yalom, I. (1975). *The theory and practice of group psychotherapy* (2nd ed.). New York: Basic Books. Each chapter of this widely used reference discusses a different curative influence of groups. Not difficult.

■

Part 6

Death and Dying

Chapter 12

□

At the End of Life

□

Death as an Abstract Idea
- The Thought of Death
- The Fear of Death
- Illness and Ego Integrity: Two Factors that May Influence the Intensity of Death Anxiety

The Experience of Dying
- The Person's Experience
- The Health Care System

Interventions
- Hospice Care
- Humanizing Hospital Care
- Helping the Dying Person by Psychotherapy

Key Terms

Recommended Readings

When Barbara Morgan learned that she had inoperable cancer, she was already a veteran at dealing with death. There had been the traumatic experience, almost 20 years before, of caring for her husband, David, during his final days. David, a childhood diabetic, had his first stroke at age 40. Barbara alone, everyone said, kept him alive and reasonably healthy for those additional 15 years. Then, a decade later, came Amy's mercifully short 6-month bout with cancer. Once again everyone had praised Barbara when she moved in to take over the nursing rather than forcing her sister to spend her last days in a nursing home. And there was that surprisingly still frequent dull ache from a more remote past, the horror of losing her first son at the brink of manhood to Hodgkin's disease.

So now it was her turn to join them. When she overheard the doctor saying "The cancer has metastasized to the liver," she felt accepting, even peaceful. This was amazing because she had always been terrified of death. There was her lifelong fear of flying that had robbed her of many an enjoyable vacation; her intense anxiety before every checkup at the doctor's; her silly quirk about taking the service road rather than risk highway driving. These death phobias were a family joke. They were so incongruous with her other qualities. She was so fearless, so competent, so full of joy at experiencing and confronting almost any other challenge of life.

Perhaps this was why, Barbara mused, that now that death was really near, she was not afraid. She was 75. She had no regrets about things not accomplished, dreams unfulfilled. Unlike her sister Amy who had never married, she had had those precious decades with David, her children, and her grandchildren, the light of her life. True, it might have been nice to have grown up in an era when women were not discouraged from having a career. She knew she was a born manager and had had fantasies of starting her own business. All in all, though, the years had been rich and full. Besides (she had to admit) her surprising courage had a more prosaic source. Even with this diagnosis someone her age could live for years.

As she also was well aware, however, cancer is a debilitating disease. So, though not fearing the actual end, she did fear dying: the wearying, intractable pain she remembered so well from nursing Amy. Even worse, the dependency, the need to have help with the most intimate bodily acts. Like her sister, she dreaded the idea of dying among strangers in a hospital. She still regretted letting David spend his last days hooked up to machines—swayed by the doctors' argument that the intensive care unit would prolong his life. She wanted to end her life at home comforted by familiar surroundings, the precious reminders of her past. Living the extra few days medical science might permit paled in importance compared with that.

But she could not afford a private nurse and it was out of the question to have her relatives take on the burden of her care. She knew very well the toll that caring for a dying loved one could take. She remembered how angry and yet understanding she had been of her children when Amy and David were very sick. Toward the end, the children would quickly drop in and be gone. They could not bear witnessing the pain, the suffering they knew could not be assuaged. They also were terrified of being in the room at the moment of death. Better to have people more familiar with and less frightened by dying to help her in her final days. At the same time, these caretakers should be as much like family as possible, sensitive, caring, concerned with her psychological and physical needs.

So, in the same way that she had approached any other important life event, Barbara set about competently arranging her death. Being widely read, she knew about the hospice movement. Hospice care seemed to embody what she wanted—trained caregivers psychologically sensitive and skilled at minimizing physical pain; the chance to spend her last days at home; the freedom from worrying too much about her family after she was gone. Counseling was provided to bereaved relatives. Medicare would cover much of the cost. She felt real relief and a new sense of security when she discovered that the geriatric center a few miles away operated a hospice program. Still, she was far from ready to call. After all, her time on earth was still measured in years, not months!

■

On any list of human concerns, death, the inevitable end of old age, ranks high. However, despite its importance to the living, behavioral scientists only really began to scientifically study death and dying about 20 years ago. It took the late 1960s revolt against traditional health care to bring death out of the shadows (Kastenbaum & Costa, 1977). During this turbulent era, the psychology of death arrived.

By the early 1970s death and dying had become the new "in" topic in psychology. It was the focus of heavily attended college courses and of numerous research projects; it even became an activist cause. This intense interest in the psychology of death subsided to a trickle as the more conservative 1980s arrived. (Note that many of the studies described in this chapter are at least 10 years old.) Yet the legacy of this outpouring endures—in a greater appreciation of the psychological needs of people who are dying and in more humane care of the terminally ill.

Because death transcends old age, psychological research in this area has focused on children, adolescents, adults, and the elderly (see Kastenbaum & Costa, 1977, for a general review). However, consonant with our orientation, this chapter pays special attention to studies examining the end of life at the end of the life span.

Research on death and dying falls into two general categories: studies probing emotions surrounding death in the abstract (How salient a concern is death to the average person? Who specifically is most fearful of death?) and investigations exploring the experience of dying itself (What does the person approaching death feel? How does society treat people who are terminally ill?). Now we turn to the insights each type of research offers for old age.

DEATH AS AN ABSTRACT IDEA

The Thought of Death

The elderly, as in the vignette, often have extensive personal experiences dealing with death. And one's own death is close at this time of life. So we would assume that older people *must* think more about death and dying than any other age group.

Not necessarily so, as researchers (Cameron, Stewart, & Biber, 1973) discovered when they interrupted 4420 people and asked them what they had been thinking about within the past 5 minutes. In this study, because the researchers wanted to see how frequently death was a focal concern and how often a fleeting thought, they questioned their subjects (ranging in age from 8 to 99) directly about death, too. Even if not a primary concern, had the thought crossed their mind at all? Also, to see whether people are more prone to think of death in certain situations, the researchers approached their subjects at varying times of day and in different places (for example, in school or at home). They also asked them to rate their mood.

There was no variation in time or place in the frequency of death thoughts. Also, surprisingly, thoughts of death did not occur just when people were feeling gloomy. They were equally likely to arise in conjunction with a variety of moods. There were sex and age differences, but only in the percentage of people reporting that the idea of death had fleetingly crossed their minds. Women had these momentary thoughts more often than men; early adolescents, young adults, and the elderly more often than people of other ages. And interestingly, fleeting thoughts about death were astonishingly common among these random people. Although only 3% to 4% of the respondents reported being focally concerned with death, a full 17% of the men and 23% of the women said the thought had crossed their minds at least once during this 5-minute period.

Perhaps by specifically probing for its presence, the researchers may have prompted some people to "remember" thinking about death even when they hadn't. And, since the researchers did not ask what specifically about death people were thinking, it is possible that over-age-65 people may think more often about their own death than people at other ages. Still, this study does make us question the stereotype that death is a more absorbing concern in old age. Everyone seems to think about death surprisingly often—the elderly no more than anyone else did.

Another puzzling finding of this study is that death preoccupations were associated with positive as well as negative moods. Shouldn't people mainly think about this topic when they're feeling gloomy, angry, or depressed? In fact, in one of the earliest investigations probing death perceptions (Kogan & Wallach, 1961), the researchers found that adults of all ages ranked death as the most aversive of a wide range of concepts. In this study, though, there were distinct age differences: Even though everyone evaluated death negatively, the elderly rated it more positively than anyone else did.

So it may be in the emotional realm where age changes our orientation to death. As we grow old, the thought of death may become less terrifying and more acceptable because dying is normal and appropriate after living a full life.

The Fear of Death

The commonsense idea that death is most terrifying for the young and that having lived our fair share of life eases our anxiety about dying is clearly implied in this quote taken from a handbook on caring for the terminally ill:

> The dying young adult is filled with rage and anger for the interruption of her life at the moment of its fulfillment. . . . There is frustration, rage, and a sense of unfairness and of being cheated. . . . The patient holds onto life more tenaciously than at any other age. The losses are now especially acute, as the patient will never see the promise for self and significant others [especially children] fulfilled [Rando, 1984, p. 246].

This idea also forms the basis of Erik Erikson's writings. In his original theory, Erikson (1963) strongly implies that people are only genuinely able to come to terms with and fully accept the fact of their own death at the end of the life cycle, in old age. However, according to Erikson, years living are not enough. Only people who have reached the developmental pinnacle of integrity, those *satisfied* with how their years have been spent, are truly unafraid to die. Older people who feel that they have squandered their life, those full of regrets about their past, are perhaps even more fearful of dying than anyone else.

Is it true that older people as a group are less frightened of death? Studies unanimously agree that the elderly report less fear than younger adults (see, for reviews, Gesser, Wong, & Reker, 1987–1988; Kastenbaum & Costa, 1977). In fact, in the Duke Longitudinal Study, when the volunteers were asked "Are you afraid to die?" only a small minority, 10%, said yes. Another 55% were ambivalent, saying, "No, but I want to live as long as possible" or, "No, but I don't want to be sick or dependent for a long time." The remaining large group answered a resounding no (Jeffers & Verwoerdt, 1977).

But can we really trust these studies probing death in the abstract, exploring the feelings of older people who are far from confronting the prospect of imminent demise? The perceptive remark of one Duke study volunteer may give us pause: "No, I'm not afraid to die—it seems to be a perfectly normal process. But you never know how you will feel when it comes to a showdown. I might get panicky" (Jeffers & Verwoerdt, 1977, p. 148).

Furthermore, as with that other taboo topic, sexuality, expressing fear of death to a stranger may not be easy for many older adults. As I have repeatedly stressed throughout this book, cross-sectional studies involving self-reports tend to be misleading. This cohort of older people may be unwilling to admit having negative emotions of any kind. Some older adults may be reluctant to say "I am frightened" in interviews because they think it is not socially acceptable to be afraid of dying at their age. This implies that direct questions may not be a good way of eliciting a person's real feelings about this emotional topic.

It may be equally difficult to admit being afraid to oneself. A person who says he or she has absolutely no fear of death may really be too anxious to even approach the subject. If we assume, as many philosophers and psychologists do, that death is a fundamental anxiety for all of us, then denying *any* anxiety at all might even be a sign of the most intense inner turmoil.

So it is difficult to know how older people genuinely feel about death. It is not socially desirable to admit to being afraid. Besides, from the psychoanalytic point of view, a superficial yes or no is an inadequate indication of someone's real concern.

Studies in which death anxiety is measured in a less direct way suggest that the psychoanalysts have a valid point. When subjects are given self-report scales and tests that probe for death anxiety in a more indirect way, the correlations between these measures are disappointingly small. People who say they are terrified of death do not necessarily show high levels of anxiety on projective tests. Those who report no fear sometimes are revealed as the most terrified when death anxiety is probed in a less overt, on-the-surface way (Handal, Peal, Napoli, & Austrin, 1984–1985; Hayslip & Stewart-Bussey, 1986–1987).

Fear seems to be more common than people admit. When researchers (Feifel & Branscomb, 1973) gave three measures of death anxiety to a group of adults, tests varying on a continuum from tapping conscious fear to progressively less conscious levels of awareness, each revealed more anxiety. When asked directly, most subjects denied that they were afraid of death. When instructed to fantasize about it, their imagery showed mainly ambivalence. On the final scale, a word-association test, their answers betrayed frank fear. Furthermore, while on the tests of more conscious anxiety, the elderly scored as less fearful than people of other ages, at this deepest, least conscious level, older subjects were ranked as being just as afraid of death as anyone else. So the elderly may be much more apprehensive about death than they admit.

These studies highlight the difficulty of assessing death anxiety. Different ways of measuring the concept uncover different degrees of fear. Not only may death anxiety have unconscious and conscious aspects, it seems to have different facets or components, too (Gesser, Wong, & Reker, 1987–1988). For instance, while some people may fear being dead, others may be terrified of dying itself—of suffering intense pain, as in the vignette, of having the humiliation of depending on others. One expert, Therese Rando (1984), hypothesizes that while anxiety about being dead may indeed be at a lower ebb in old age, the fear of dying becomes more intense at this time of life. As was true of Barbara Morgan, the anxiety centers not on afterward but before: "Who will take care of me in my final days?" "Will I suffer greatly, be in unbearable pain, be a burden to those I love?"

The type of fear may also differ depending on the disease the older person has. When Linda Viney (1984–1985) asked seriously ill people to freely talk about their life at the moment and then had these narratives transcribed and analyzed, she discovered that respondents in the midst of acute medical crises (in a hospital, scheduled for surgery) tended to be fearful of death itself; people seriously ill with chronic conditions but not immediately facing death had a different concern, what she labeled "the loss of bodily integrity," damage to their physical self.

Interestingly, while the first type of person was in more grave danger of actually dying, the second was worse off emotionally. Subjects in an acute physical crisis, while angry and upset, were also actively engaged in living—feeling their love and expressing their feelings to loved ones and determined to triumph over death. Those wrestling with fears about losing their bodily integrity were more depressed, hopeless, and dispirited:

> Rob G was . . . fearing physical loss when he was interviewed. He was a forty-six-year-old railway guard who had just learned that he probably had lesions on one kidney and should have further tests. . . . His greatest concern was about the loss of his kidney. . . . His experience about the loss of bodily integrity was expressed in this way: "The doctor says I'll lose the kidney. . . . It's terrible! I'm really scared. . . . I don't know what to do!" Reassurance about his second kidney did not help bring him back from the panic he was experiencing. He continued to describe passively and anxiously what might happen to him [Viney, 1984–1985, p. 208].

However, both groups were more anxious about dying than a comparison sample of healthy people Viney interviewed. So the Duke study volunteer's insight about his feelings in the abstract seems to have a large grain of truth. As death really draws near, even the calmest older person may get more panicky.

Does serious illness heighten our fear of death? Is Erikson right that people who have reached the developmental pinnacle of ego integrity are not afraid to die?

Illness and Ego Integrity: Two Factors that May Influence the Intensity of Death Anxiety

While we would expect being ill to make death a more salient fear, the intractable pain a terminal illness can bring might transform death from a hated to a welcomed event.

Clinical observations support the fact that not all older people who are about to die are terrified. Psychologists have noted (Kastenbaum & Aizenberg, 1972) that *imminently* terminal elderly patients rarely seem to fear death. However, if we look at the type of person described in the vignette, one who may actually feel well but has a terminal diagnosis, a different picture emerges. In a fascinating exploratory study, researchers (Coolidge & Fish, 1983–1984) compared the dreams of 14 terminally ill cancer patients and 42 healthy older adults. While several of the terminally ill people were within a few months of dying, most, despite having a fatal illness, were not very near death. The average interval between the time a person died and when this study was done was close to 3 years.

The dreams of the ill people had many more death-related themes than those of the healthy older adults. However, while many of these dreams concerned death, only one person dreamt directly about his or her own death. Respondents would dream that someone else was dead or dying; sometimes they tried to search for that person's identity. From a 27-year-old woman 1 year before she died:

> I went to an outside all-night movie and I was standing in the middle of the street when this car pulled up and dumped out a young pregnant dead woman. . . . I ran over when it was over and I was looking at me on the floor but the girl really didn't look like me [Coolidge & Fish, 1983–1984, p. 3].

According to the researchers, this type of dream betrays both anxiety and uncertainty. The dreamer's own death, while the central concern, is too horrifying to be dreamed about directly. The person also is wrestling with that crucial question: "Am I really going to die?" Interestingly, (as in this dream), compared to the control group, the terminally ill respondents not only dreamed about death more often but also of its opposite—of pregnancy, birth, or babies—as if in their dream life they fashioned themes of rebirth to compensate for the terror of dying that haunted their waking hours. From a woman in her 40s a month from death:

> I saw a woman who was very happy. The dream took place in a department store. The woman had a lovely dress and shoes. She was carrying a baby in her arms. She loved the baby very much. When I woke up I felt very happy and safe. As I was writing down the dream this fear started all over again [p. 6].

Because these subjects were mainly young and middle aged, we might question whether elderly people in this situation would also have dreams betraying an intense preoccupation with death. But it does make sense that fears about dying become intense at any age when death looms on the horizon—transformed from an abstract possibility to a present threat.

Unfortunately, the relationship between death anxiety and ego integrity is not nearly as clear-cut. While research (albeit with adults of all ages) suggests that low death anxiety is associated with personality traits similar to Erikson's concepts of ego integrity, self-actualization, competence, and self-esteem (see, for reviews, Gesser, Wong, & Reker, 1987–1988; Kastenbaum & Costa, 1977), the one direct test of Erikson's theory had disappointing results when researchers (Nehrke, Bellucci, & Gabriel, 1977–1978) explored the relationship between death anxiety and ego integrity in three groups of older adults (people living in their own homes, in public housing, and in nursing homes). Because this study was one of the few to empirically test Erikson's theory, the researchers had the difficult task of measuring the amorphous concept of ego integrity. They decided to use two different scales. The first was a test tapping the personality trait "locus of control"—the extent to which people see their own actions, not fate or forces outside their control, as responsible for what happens to them in life. The other was a well-known measure of morale. The researchers chose these tests in particular (along with two death anxiety scales) because being satisfied with life and having a sense of one's own responsibility in living seemed the dual hallmarks of the Eriksonian ideal.

Unfortunately, only among one group, the older people living in public housing, was ego integrity related to low death anxiety. Since Erikson implies that reaching this emotional pinnacle is a requirement for not fearing death, this study makes us question the validity of his theory. Is Erikson wrong or is the way the researchers decided to measure ego integrity (or death anxiety) flawed? We do not know. However, the fact that for the two other groups, internal control was actually correlated with heightened death anxiety is not that unreasonable either. Shouldn't people to whom personal mastery and control are centrally important be most frightened by death because it is the ultimate threat to their belief they hold their fate in their own hands?

When Bert Hayslip and Duke Stewart-Bussey (1986–1987) tested this question more thoroughly, correlating measures of internal control with a variety of death anxiety scales, they found even more bewildering complexity. While people high in internal control reported fearing death less, they showed just as much unconscious anxiety! Perhaps death is so threatening to people who need to feel in control of their life that they must deny having any anxiety. Perhaps this type of person has no overt fear because he or she is convinced of having some control over this terrible event (for example, by exercising, or by eating right). Whatever the answer, it is clear that the relationship between death anxiety and various aspects of personality is far from straightforward.

Unfortunately, when we turn to the second major category of research on death—the actual experience of the terminally ill—we see the same clash between a famous theory and the more ambiguous realities of life.

THE EXPERIENCE OF DYING

The Person's Experience

The most well known theory in the field of death and dying is Elisabeth Kübler-Ross's (1969) widely quoted idea that terminally ill patients go through a specific sequence of stages in coming to terms with the idea of impending death. Kübler-Ross's theory was an outgrowth of her work as a consulting psychiatrist in the teaching hospital of the University of Chicago. In dealing regularly with fatally ill people, she became convinced that, while adequately attending to the physical needs of the terminally ill, the hospital staff was neglecting that crucial other dimension, the emotional needs of this group. She decided to take the unheard-of step of actually talking to people about that taboo topic, death.

As part of an ongoing seminar for medical students, she got permission to interview dying patients. While the hospital staff was resistant and hostile, the subjects of the interviews had a different response. Many were relieved to talk openly about what was happening to them, a chance they had been denied before. To everyone's surprise, many knew their "true" diagnosis, even though an effort had typically been made to conceal the facts. Kübler-Ross published her discovery that open communication was important to dying people in *On Death and Dying* (1969). This slim seminal bestseller ushered in a revolution on how the terminally ill are approached.

The Stages of Dying.   In her book, Kübler-Ross hypothesized that terminally ill people progress through five fixed stages: *denial, anger, bargaining, depression,* and *acceptance.*

When the person first hears the diagnosis, the response is to think "There must be a mistake." Denial is often accompanied by a frantic quest for disconfirming evidence (for example, visits to doctor after doctor searching for a different diagnosis, a new, more positive set of tests). When these efforts fail, the truth begins to sink in, and denial gives way to anger.

In this stage, the person lashes out—bemoaning the injustice of fate, railing at loved ones. Doctors are castigated as uncaring and insensitive. The idea that "I" and not someone else is dying evokes intense rage. Eventually this emotion yields to a more calculating one—bargaining.

In the bargaining stage, the person pleads for more time, promising to be good if death can simply be put off until after a next (yet ever present) important event. Kübler-Ross illustrates this stage with the poignant example of a woman who begged God to let her live long enough to attend the marriage of her oldest son:

> The day preceding the wedding she left the hospital as an elegant lady. Nobody would have believed her real condition. She. . .looked radiant. I wondered what her reaction would be when the time was up for which she had bargained. . . . I will never forget the moment she returned to the hospital. She looked tired and somewhat exhausted and before I could say hello—said, "Now don't forget I have another son" [1969, p. 83].

When this reaction cannot continue, it is replaced by a deep sadness, the fourth stage, depression. Then, usually just before death, this response gives way to the fifth and final one, acceptance. Now the patient, who is quite weak, is not upset, angry, or wracked with grief. He or she calmly awaits death, even looks forward to it expectantly.

Kübler-Ross never envisioned these stages as a straitjacket, a procrustean bed for the "right way" to approach death. Unfortunately her theory was sometimes uncritically applied in just this way. Patients were labeled as abnormal if their responses did not fit into the five-stage sequence. Attempts were even made to hurry terminally ill people from stage to stage. However, as we should know by now, the idea that *all* human beings react in a uniform, rigid way to any life stress is wrong. It also is dangerous because it justifies our distancing ourselves from the person and negating the validity of his or her feelings. Rather than understanding, for instance, that depression in a person facing death is appropriate and natural, seeing it as "a phase" encourages us to view this emotion as somehow not real. An ill person's legitimate complaints about doctors, family, or friends can be discounted, passed off as "predictable" signs of the anger stage. So this groundbreaking effort to look at the emotions of dying patients was both good and bad. It focused attention on a crucial neglected topic but it was also inappropriately elevated into a universal truth.

Actually, though terminally ill people do experience a variety of emotions there is little empirical evidence that these feelings fall into a sequence of stages. Moreover, patients do not seem to progress in a fixed way from one feeling to another (Dubois, 1980; Kastenbaum, 1981). For instance, in one exploratory study, Anne Metzger (1979–1980) devised a scale made up of statements tailored to fit each of Kübler-Ross's stages and then administered it several times to two couples. In each case, the woman was suffering from potentially fatal breast cancer and had been aware of her illness for some time. Husbands and wives were separately asked which items seemed to best apply to the patient's feelings currently and at four points since the initial diagnosis.

Contrary to the theory, *hope* was the main emotion described at each time. This positive feeling may have been particular to the couples being studied. The sample (two cases) is much too small and may be unrepresentative in another critical way, because the women may not genuinely have been *terminally* ill. Furthermore, the husbands and wives were giving retrospective reports, so the present might have colored their memory of past feelings and experiences. However, it makes good sense that hope would be a person's primary emotion in this terrible situation. The vignette shows just how psychologically reasonable this so human reaction can be.

A more recent study without these deficiencies, a longitudinal investigation involving a large sample of genuinely terminally ill people, offers even more conclusive evidence rebutting the stage theory. Steven Antonoff and Bernard Spilka (1984–1985) used the interesting strategy of videotaping their subjects at random points during the early, middle, and late phases of their disease. Based on Kübler-Ross's theory, the researchers hypothesized that facial expressions would tend to change in a predictable way as the illness progressed—showing mainly anger, then sadness, then acceptance as the disease advanced from phase to phase. Not so! Expressions of sadness increased in a linear way as death approached. Anger and acceptance (which they measured by happy facial expressions) showed no pattern at all. Contrary to the theory, people were just as likely to look angry at the end as early on; just as prone to look happy (accepting) right after their diagnosis as in their final days or weeks.

Actually, the following description seems to best fit the emotions of people coping with this terrible truth: "a complicated clustering of intellectual and affective states, some fleeting, lasting for a moment, or a day" Shneidman, 1976, p. 6). Not only does it seem impossible to encapsulate these complex, chaotic feelings into fixed stages, the idea "I am destined to die" may not really penetrate in an all-or-none way. Even when people know they have a terminal diagnosis, they seem to cycle between awareness and denial at different times. Denial and awareness can even be present simultaneously.

Psychiatrist Avery Weisman (1976) uses the evocative phrase **middle knowledge** to illustrate this suspension between knowing and not knowing, a psychological state he has observed frequently in working with the terminally ill. Weisman believes that middle knowledge is most likely to be manifested at transition points during the illness; for example, when after a relapse the emotional climate shifts and loved ones turn less optimistic; when the doctor starts averting her eyes when questions about recovery arise. According to Weisman, middle knowledge

> is marked by unpredictable shifts in the margin between what is observed and inferred. Patients seem to know and want to know, yet they often talk as if they did not know and did not want to be reminded of what they have been told. Many patients rebuke their doctors for not having warned them about complications in treatment or the course of an illness even though the doctor may have been scrupulous about keeping them informed. These instances of seeming denial are usually examples of middle knowledge [1976, p. 459].

We can see an example of this understandable feeling in the vignette. While on one level Barbara Morgan genuinely knows she is going to die soon, she also denies the reality of impending death—putting the event into the remote future, telling herself she will not need the hospice program for some time. But though it does not fit into a fixed sequence of stages, the way she reacts to her diagnosis is predictable in another way—it is a function of her personality, an extension of the way she has always dealt with stressful events. This brings us to a discussion of that important influence, personality, on how people respond. Are we likely to face this final crisis of living in the same way as we faced life crises before?

Personality: An Important Determinant of How People React to Approaching Death.

When John Hinton (1975–1976) asked husbands and wives of terminally ill cancer patients to describe what their spouse was like before becoming sick and then related these characterizations to ratings by the patient, nurses, and the spouse of the person's current emotional state, he found a good deal of continuity between then and now. People described as having coped well in the past were rated as less depressed, irritable, and withdrawn than other patients. Those pictured as directly facing problems earlier on were more likely to accept the fact that they had a fatal disease. Once again, this study was not longitudinal, so these perceptions of the past may have been skewed by the way the person was acting currently. However, because stability is such a dominant theme in personality research, it seems reasonable to expect continuity here, too.

However, there were also heartening signs of discontinuity. People rated as neurotic and unstable in the past were just as able to cope as anyone else. They were not more anxious, no more likely to deny the fact of their disease. So here, too, we see evidence of the other major theme in personality research—change. Some of the most unlikely people seem to marshal unexpected courage when facing this final showdown of life.

The way people react is important because it determines the quality of their remaining days, whether they are able to use the time they have left productively or fritter it away, immobilized by depression and fear. As the following study suggests, the way a person copes may even influence the actual *length* of his or her remaining time.

In following a group of terminally ill cancer patients, Avery Weisman and William Worden (1975–1976) discovered that people who lived longer than expected on the basis of the severity of their illness tended to maintain good, responsive relationships with others, especially in the final phase of their disease. They were also more assertive, showing more "fighting spirit" than those who died earlier on. A more recent study echoes these findings. Compared to a matched group of survivors, seriously ill people who died had a characteristic pattern of traits: little directly expressed anger but much self-criticism, guilt, depression, fear of bodily harm. The nonsurvivors were also less involved in reciprocal social relationships (Viney & Westbrook, 1986–1987).

Do people stop fighting and become depressed and disengage from others because their bodies are giving off signals that death is near? Or does assertiveness and good social relationships actually *promote* survival—perhaps because having these traits enables people to receive the high-quality care that prolongs their lives? We may be able to get some clues from looking at the other side of the equation, how the primary caregivers of the dying, health care professionals, treat the terminally ill.

The Health Care System

The vignette illustrates a typical reaction many people have when visiting a dying person, even one they love—fear coupled with the desire to get away. Not only is it difficult to see a loved one in pain, there is the terror of being there to witness the moment of death. This instinctive desire to flee is common, present even when people are asked to think about terminal illness in the abstract (Epley & McCaghy, 1977–1978) and when they visit relatives in an intensive care unit (Sherizen & Paul, 1977–1978). However, we might expect a very different response from those whose work involves daily dealings with death. How do doctors and nurses feel about death and dying? How do they treat the dying patients in their care? These questions have been examined through two methods: indirectly, by questionnaires probing attitudes and anxieties, and directly, by actually observing how hospital staff members act with dying patients.

Indirect Assessments of How Health Care Professionals Treat the Dying.   Do doctors tend to withdraw once they know their interventions will not stave off death, do they give shorter shrift to their terminally ill patients? An early survey (Caldwell & Mishara, 1972–1973) supports the common prejudice that they do. When 73 doctors were asked to fill out a questionnaire about how they treated dying patients, only 13 complied. Most refused when the nature of the topic was revealed.

On the other hand, in a more recent study, the medical profession was revealed as anxious, but also caring, committed, and very emotionally involved (Rea, Greenspoon, & Spilka, 1975). Of the 174 physicians solicited for this investigation, only 11 refused. Most seemed deeply affected by the topic being addressed, taking time to respond to the long questionnaire, often elaborating on their answers by extensive remarks. The researchers were touched by the deep humanity and concern for the terminally ill that shone through—empathy illustrated by this response from a pathologist who said he "often felt like crying after a day of doing diagnostic sections in connection with surgery . . . 'It upsets me to think of the devastating effect my diagnosis will have on patients and families'" [p. 300].

A closer look at these incompatible studies shows a common underlying theme. Doctors are deeply affected by the plight of the fatally ill. Avoidance and its direct opposite are two ways of handling the intense feeling this topic evokes.

The actual quality of those feelings, however, seems to differ in part as a function of such variables as age, experience, and perhaps health care discipline. When researchers (Kane & Hogan, 1985–1986) explored death anxiety among internists, surgeons, and psychiatrists varying in age and years in practice, they found that while being in a medical specialty where one was likely to be highly involved with dying patients and their families did not make for less anxiety, being young and inexperienced did. Young doctors in any field, especially those just starting out, were most terrorized by death. A study comparing residents and nurses had a similar theme. The more experienced nurses were likely to view death in positive terms as peace or liberation. The young doctors tended to see it as a total disaster, a terrible and terrifying event (Campbell, Abernethy, & Waterhouse, 1983).

From the patient's point of view these contrasting feelings may make a great difference. Anxiety, abhorrence, or acceptance should translate into very different patient care. However, to really understand how the dying are treated we need to study *actions* not thoughts. This brings us to the second approach researchers have used—entering health care settings and observing, recording, and charting how the staff actually behave with the terminally ill.

Direct Observations of Health Care Professionals.   In a classic study, sociologists Bernard Glaser and Anselem Strauss (1968) used this naturalistic approach—unobtrusively observing nurses, doctors, and aides on different hospital wards over several months. Their focus for interpreting what they were seeing was unusual: caring for the dying was a job, and it was important to understand the principles by which that job was being organized.

The work of treating the dying did seem structured in a clear, though not explicitly spelled-out way according to the course the patient's illness was likely to take. Based on the person's diagnosis and physical state at admission, an expectation was set up about how that individual's pattern of dying would likely proceed. This projected "dying schedule" then governed how the hospital staff acted. Glaser and Strauss used an evocative phrase to refer to this dying pattern or schedule—the person's **dying trajectory.**

They pinpointed and labeled a variety of different dying trajectories. For instance, one frequently found in emergency rooms was "expected swift death"—someone whose death was imminent (perhaps from an accident or heart attack), who had no chance of surviving. "Expected lingering while dying" was another common trajectory—one typical for progressive, slowly fatal chronic diseases such as cancer. Or with an illness of this type, the trajectory could be "entry–reentry"—the person would return home several times in between hospital stays. Another trajectory might be "suspended sentence"— discharge for an unknown length of time before readmission in the final crisis before death.

Unfortunately, trajectories could not always be accurately predicted. They often changed markedly during a person's stay. "Expected swift death" could turn into "lingering while dying" or even into "expected to recover" if the patient rallied. "Expected to recover" might become "expected swift death" if the individual suddenly took a turn for the worse.

These unplanned deviations, however, impaired the smooth functioning of the work. The scenario became outmoded. Care had to suddenly be changed. The paradox was that if it was "off schedule," sometimes living itself might be transformed from a good to bad event.

> One patient who was expected to die within four hours had no money, but needed a special machine in order to last longer. A private hospital at which he had been a frequent paying patient for thirty years agreed to receive him as a charity patient. He did not die immediately but started to linger indefinitely, even to the point where there was some hope he might live. The money problem, however, created much concern among both family members and the hospital administrators . . . the doctor continually had to reassure both parties that the patient (who lived for six weeks) would soon die; that is, to try to change their expectations back to "certain to die on time" [Glaser & Strauss, 1968, pp. 11–12].

Another miscalculation had the same paradoxical effect, one in which the patient vacillated between "certain to die on time" and "lingering." In this pattern, loved ones would sadly say goodbye and then find that the person had begun to improve. Family members, nurses, and doctors sometimes went through this cycle repeatedly. The chaplain might also be involved. Here, too, everyone ended up breathing a sigh of relief when at last the end was really near. (This is not to say that the hospital workers were always wishing for death. The opposite type of mistake, a patient expected to recover who then died, was also terribly upsetting.)

Miscalculated trajectories not only upset the staff but injured the patient. If someone was "vacillating" or "lingering too long," nurses and doctors, in their frustration, might get annoyed at the dying person. They could become less responsive, give more perfunctory care, and so possibly hasten death. Another type of mistake also might speed up death: assigning the individual to a unit unfit for his or her trajectory. For instance, sometimes a patient needing constant care was put on a ward where only periodic checks were provided and died between observations.

To Glaser and Strauss, their analyses clearly suggested that hospitals' whole mode of approaching the terminally ill was flawed. The goal was smooth, efficient work, providing care with a minimum of extra or wasted steps. This focus on efficiency, when it clashed with the reality that dying is inherently unpredictable, was tailor-made for producing staff frustration and poor patient care.

This compelling indictment of terminal care, published at about the same time as Kübler-Ross's book, forcefully brought home the fact that traditional ways of caring for the dying were inadequate. A study a few years later at a different health care setting, a nursing home, added fuel to the reformist fire. This research was also done by two sociologists (Watson & Maxwell, 1977) using an innovative naturalistic approach—measuring the actual physical proximity of the nursing staff to residents near death.

In their first set of observations, the researchers drew maps of the floors where the residents lived and subdivided each map into rectangles of approximately equal size, noting the location of the nursing station. Selecting a random hour each day for 6 weeks, they then observed the floor, noting each entry by a nurse or other worker into a particular area and keeping track of the movements of residents with differing degrees of disability. Figure 12-1 shows the results for the nurses. In the unit housing the most severely impaired residents, the highest status personnel on duty, the registered nurses (RNs), spent considerably more time in the nursing station than their counterparts working on a unit where the residents were less likely to be terminally ill. Also, the more seriously ill patients were usually placed far from the nursing station where the nurses spent most of their time; those not as near death were in closer proximity, appearing in all areas of the grid, often near the nursing station.

A second study of proximity had the same discouraging theme. This time the researchers looked just at the ward housing the most disabled people and noted where the residents closest to death slept, using a person's score on a mental status exam to code for nearness to death. As they predicted, the most confused residents (those presumably nearest death) tended to have beds in the dormitory area as far away as possible from the nursing station and the medical service offices. Furthermore, a follow-up revealed that the dormitory residents were indeed more likely to be near death. While on the floor as a whole, 20 (45%) of the residents died within a 15-month period; of those deaths, 18 (90%) occurred among residents in the dormitory.

Taken together, these observations make the same disheartening point: At a time when people need the most intense ongoing care—that is, when they are most ill—they actually get the *least* attention from the nursing staff.

Fortunately, though, this conclusion may not be warranted. The RNs in the unit housing the disabled might have to do more charting and report writing than they would if they were dealing with a less ill group, explaining their excessive time spent in the nursing station. Residents near death might be found farther from the nursing station merely because they were less mobile or were confined to bed. Even the study showing that people near death were housed in the dormitory does not prove that the staff was actually avoiding these residents. To make this conclusion, we would need to chart the time the doctors and nurses actually spent in this section, as opposed to other areas of the ward.

INTERVENTIONS

Still, this study, published in the early 1970s, helped encourage what was rapidly becoming a growing national movement to humanize the health care of the terminally ill.

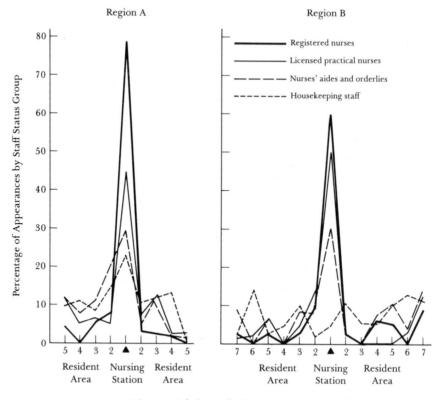

Figure 12-1. Variations in appearances of direct care staff in nursing station areas in the regions of extremely disabled patients (A) and nondisabled patients (B). *Source: From Watson & Maxwell, 1977.*

Hospice Care

The most visible outgrowth of the movement to change the way the dying are treated has been the development of that well-known alternative to traditional hospital and nursing home care of the terminally ill—the **hospice.** Hospices minister to the needs of people for whom death is certain, but who may have as much as 6 months to live. The philosophy underlying hospice care is very different from that found in traditional health care settings where the goal is to cure. The hospice's goal is to provide the best palliative care possible. Hospice personnel are skilled in techniques to minimize physical discomfort. They are trained in providing a supportive psychological environment, one that assures patients and family members that they will not be abandoned in the face of approaching death (Cohen, 1979). Here is a description of how the first secular U.S. hospice, the New Haven–Branford Hospice, came to be (Rossman, 1977). The catalyst for the hospice was the presence at Yale University in the

BOX 12-1
The Social Loss of the Aged Dying

It is only reasonable that hospital personnel would have different reactions to deaths of patients of different ages. Death in a geriatric patient is expected. The person has no future; he or she has lived a full life. The death of a child is very upsetting. The child who dies is being robbed of everything—the potential to grow, develop, and become a fulfilled, contributing adult. The person who dies in young adulthood or midlife is in his or her prime. The loss will be keenly felt by others: The dying person is often the focal center on which a family depends.

As part of his observations of dying trajectories, Bernard Glaser (1966) coined the term *social loss* to account for these different orientations. When someone of high social loss—such as a young adult—died, the nursing staff would be devastated. In contrast, when an elderly person died, it was sometimes the occasion for an emotion of a very different kind.

Glaser noticed that patients on the geriatric wards of the hospital were given less time and attention. Their care was more perfunctory; the staff was not as involved. Many of these patients, though biologically alive, seemed socially dead. In fact, when one of these patients finally died, death might be viewed with relief—as a social gain. No longer would precious time, attention, and resources have to be devoted to caring for someone whose fair share of living was already long done.

However, this astute observer also catalogued fascinating exceptions to this age hierarchy in regard to death. If the older person was a highly accomplished professional and had continued to make contributions in his or her field up until becoming ill, the death was more of a social loss. If the person was socially prominent or had a family that was very involved, the nurses might become more upset. Personality traits and the length of time on the unit might affect their feelings, too. The longer the person was in the hospital, the greater the chance of becoming attached, particularly if the patient was pleasant or cooperative. When this happened, nurses felt sad, regretful, or even shed a tear when death in old age finally arrived.

☐

mid-1960s of two of the leaders in the movement to change terminal care, Dr. Elisabeth Kübler-Ross and Dr. Cecily Saunders, the British physician who organized the first modern hospice, St. Christopher's. Their lectures inspired the chaplain at Yale–New Haven Hospital to visit England to study the fledgling hospice movement there and then to form a group determined to establish the first hospice on U.S. soil.

The group faced a continuing struggle to avoid having their proposed hospice labeled as just a hospital. They had problems getting support because their proposal was really an indictment of how the traditional health care system handled terminal care. However, funds and support were found, and the hospice was incorporated in the early 1970s.

In observing the British programs, the chaplain noted that hiring the right staff was crucial. Special people were needed—a health care team that would be competent, compassionate, and not afraid to take on an emotionally arduous job. There were particular obstacles in recruiting physicians because the hospice philosophy requires abandoning the goal doctors have been trained for, cure (see Chapter 4).

Another difficulty involved reconciling the staff's idealistic desire to do away with the traditional hospital hierarchy with the practical reality that in order to function smoothly the program needed to have a chain of command. There were problems in finding a site for the inpatient facility. People living near some proposed locations opposed the building because they imagined dying people wandering about the neighborhood spreading disease and gloom. Still, a site was found and an architectural plan approved.

The 44-bed hospice that stands today is designed to emphasize the joy of life even in the face of death. As people enter, they approach transition spaces that help relieve their anxiety, the staff dining room and a day care center for the children of employees. The rooms have greenhouse windows full of flowering plants. Furnishings are homey; halls spacious and warmly lit. Every convenience is provided for patients and families. The feeling is that this is a home.

Pain control—reducing the intense physical suffering of the dying—is fundamental to the hospice philosophy. The goal is to decrease pain, but at the same time to keep the patient as alert and independent as possible. In addition to using drugs, the hospice team may employ psychological techniques to achieve this goal, teaching the person to mentally shift focus from the discomfort, emphasizing pleasurable activities, training families to avoid expressions of anxiety and fear that might intensify the actual pain experience itself.

> One woman, for example, was in great misery because she wanted to live to see a grandchild about to be born, but knew it was impossible. The controlling of her pain, however, made it possible for her to recover enough strength to knit a gift for the child she would never see, thus helping brighten her last days. Another hospice patient had been lying all of the time in a fetal position with a hot water bottle clutched to his chest, staring into space, moaning in his private hell which he said was compounded by pain that was like fire . . . but when the hospice team showed him they could control his pain he became a different person, able to live rather than vegetate during his last days [Rossman, 1977, p. 126].

The hospice programs that dot the country today utilize the same principles. The crucial difference is that the current thrust of the hospice movement is toward outpatient care, providing the services and support that allow people to die with dignity at home. As was true of Barbara Morgan in the vignette, most people prefer to spend their last days at home rather than in any institution no matter how humane (see Hine, 1979–1980). Multidisciplinary hospice teams (made up of professionals and volunteers) go into the person's home, providing care on a part-time, scheduled, or around-the-clock basis; they offer 24-hour help in a crisis, and provide family caregivers with the moral support and concrete assistance they need to keep their relative from having to die in a hospital or nursing home. Their commitment does not end after the person dies. An important facet of hospice care is bereavement counseling for family members (Rando, 1984).

Hospices are not appropriate for everyone. To utilize this type of care requires a daunting set of decisions. A person must agree to abandon curative treatments, leave his or her current doctor, and be judged by a physician as being no more than 6 months from death. Often participants have to have family members committed to the physically and emotionally draining task of doing much of the day-to-day caregiving.

A study (Bass, Garland, & Otto, 1985–1986) assessing selected characteristics of 146 patients in a home-based hospice program provides an overview of the type of person who does enroll. Ninety-five percent of the people who utilized this program had cancer. They tended to be relatively young (on average in their early 60s) and White. Most often they were "ambulatory with assistance" or "bedridden." They were usually being taken care of by a spouse. The average time spent in the program was 3 weeks to a month. Another study (Labus & Dambrot, 1985–1986) painted a similar portrait. Compared to terminally ill hospitalized patients, hospice patients were younger and had more people living in the home.

Hospices only serve a tiny fraction of the terminally ill. The studies above suggest that, at least today, this alternative is more often used by Whites under age 65. This means that hospitals and nursing homes are the places where almost all older adults spend their last days. Luckily, efforts have been made to make these traditional medical settings more responsive, too.

Humanizing Hospital Care

In the late 1970s an international task force urged hospitals to spell out specific standards for terminal care, offering the following guidelines for administrators to use in developing these rules (this list is adapted from Kastenbaum, 1976–1977; and Rando, 1984):

1. Because family members, staff, and the community, as well as the patients, all have interests, each group's needs should be taken into account. This will avoid the common pretense that what is being done is just for the welfare of the patient alone. Honest communication will be improved and the terminally ill person will be getting better care. The standards a given hospital devises should be flexible—reflecting the individual patient's values and preferences as well as the outlook of the community that the institution serves.

2. Since patients and their families have a wide variety of concerns—psycho-logical, legal, spiritual, economic—adequate care of the dying requires an inte-grated team approach. Many disciplines should collaborate. Professionals should be specifically trained in providing terminal care. Links should be estab-lished between the hospital personnel and health care professionals in the community.

3. Efforts should be made to counteract the tendency to isolate or withdraw from the dying person. Involvement without loss of professional objectivity should be fostered in the hospital staff. Family and friends should be encouraged to become highly involved. The patient should be allowed ample contact with loved ones, and as much time as possible to be with them alone.

4. The preferences of the ill person for pain control, for information, for privacy, should be listened to. The individual should be allowed as much free-dom as possible to determine the course of his or her care.

5. The goal of fostering security and maximum decision making applies to families, too. Family members should have the chance to discuss all aspects of death and dying with the staff. Ideally, they should be offered counseling, not just during the final illness, but to ease the pain of bereavement, after the person's death.

Even the most humane guidelines must fall flat without that crucial underpin-ning—an educated hospital staff. Because they are at the top of the health care hierarchy and (as some of the previous studies suggest) may have the most trouble dealing with death, physicians are an especially important group to educate. Here is one example of a medical school course that attempts to change the perspective doctors have on death and dying (Davis & Jessen, 1980–1981): In addition to attending a regular seminar, students who enroll in this elective course spend one full night (from 5:30 P.M. to 8:00 A.M.) "on call" with the chaplain at a community hospital. The on-call chaplain visits the emergency room and the intensive care and coronary care units, consulting with the staff and comforting dying patients and their families. When they accompany the chaplain on these rounds, students are encouraged to discuss the ethical and psychological issues that arise during this intense experiential introduction to death. They then write an essay about what they have learned.

> It was perhaps most meaningful that we ended our night with a cesarean section and a live healthy baby! Once again however life was taken for granted and really not much attention was given to it. Procedure was high priority. . . . Doctors examine noses, anuses—in essence every projection or hole in the human body—and yet the very thing that holds these examined parts together—life—is not examined seemingly or fully. . . . It seemed ironic to end our "death" call with a birth—maybe we peeked into the meaning of death [Davis & Jessen, 1980–1981, p. 163].

Even though this essay shows the immediate impact can be profound, can any single experience really produce a lasting change in how students think? A one-shot glimpse of death from a humanistic perspective can be so easily eclipsed amid the avalanche of the technical-care-oriented courses of medical school.

To determine whether psychologically oriented death education has any lasting value, two researchers (Dickinson & Pearson, 1980–1981) polled recent graduates to find out whether attitudes toward dying patients differed as a function of having taken this type of course. The 20% who had a medical school course on death and dying were less likely to rigidly think it essential that every dying patient be told his or her diagnosis and were more prone to report being comfortable with the terminally ill. Perhaps these differences were due to the fact that these students were more psychologically sensitive to begin with since they had chosen to take what was an optional course. However, perhaps death education really helps!

Helping the Dying Person by Psychotherapy

The reasons for mental health care workers to avoid the dying mirror those for shunning older adults: Treatment is not a good investment. The person has no future to enjoy the fruits of therapy. Dealing with this type of person may evoke powerful negative emotions. It is tailor-made to bring up thoughts of one's own mortality. However, today there is a group of mental health workers who do specialize in counseling people who are terminally ill (see Rando, 1984).

For instance, more than 35 years ago, a psychoanalyst (Eissler, 1955) suggested two different supportive techniques a therapist should employ in treating a terminally ill patient, depending on whether the person denies or acknowledges reality. If the person denies the truth, the therapist should offer support but not convey a sense of despair. Rather than getting the patient to confront reality, the therapist should go along with the fantasy, even conveying the false impression that the dying person will survive, in the interest of bolstering courage and psychic energy.

If the person accepts the truth, however, the task of treatment involves less dissembling. Then the therapist should try as much as possible to demonstrate to the person that he or she is not alone, to get the person to view the analyst as a companion to ease the loneliness of the journey from life.

The psychoanalytic approach seems to have intrinsically more appeal for helping dying patients than behavioral techniques. As George Rebok and William Hoyer (1979–1980) note, there may be an aversion to using behaviorism's more mechanical approach. However, according to Rebok and Hoyer, behavior therapy need not be incompatible with humanistic goals. Here is a treatment they outline to lessen the intense anxiety that often haunts people living under the shadow of death: The terminally ill person is asked to define the crux of the fear. "What exactly is so terrifying about death?" If, for example, fears of being dependent and out of control are paramount, then modifying this anxiety becomes the focus of the therapeutic work. The individual would be asked to keep a log of when the anxiety is most intense. Careful attention would be paid to specifying which antecedent events seem to be eliciting the response. For instance, a man might pinpoint intense fear as arising at any sign that the medical staff is discounting his wishes or treating him as if he did not exist. The intervention would focus on preventing this from happening. The person would be taught techniques to change the behavior of his doctors and nurses; or the chance of moving to a more supportive environment such as a hospice would be explored; or he would be trained to substitute more positive thoughts, such as "I am really the one in control."

Rebok and Hoyer stress that any intervention must be employed judiciously and cautiously, as sometimes no treatment may be best. They also emphasize that standard behavioral principles must be used flexibly with this quite special group. For instance, rather than blindly applying any specific strategy, the therapist may need to spend a good deal of time listening to and empathizing with the ill person. In spite of these cautions, though, it is interesting that in this last event of aging, as in so many others, a simple behavioral approach may produce results.

KEY TERMS

Middle knowledge   Hospice
Dying trajectory

RECOMMENDED READINGS

Glaser, B., & Strauss, A. L. (1968). *A time for dying.* Chicago: Aldine. Dying trajectories explained. Very interesting and well written. Not difficult.
Kübler-Ross, E. (1969). *On death and dying.* New York: Macmillan. The most widely known book on death and dying. The five stages are enriched by many interesting clinical examples. Not difficult.

References

□

Abrahams, J. P., & Birren, J. E. (1973). Reaction time as a function of age and behavioral predisposition to coronary heart disease. *Journal of Gerontology, 28,* 471–478.

Adams, G. (1977). *Essentials of geriatric medicine.* New York: Oxford University Press.

Adelman, R., Marron, K., Libow, L. S., & Neufeld, R (1987). A community-oriented geriatric rehabilitation unit in a nursing home. *Gerontologist, 27,* 143–146.

Ade-Ridder, L., & Brubaker, T. H. (1983). The quality of long-term marriages. In T. H. Brubaker (Ed.), *Family relationshps in later life.* Beverly Hills, CA.: Sage.

Aizenberg, R., & Treas, J. (1985). The family in late life: Psychosocial and demographic considerations. In J. E. Birren & K. W. Schaie (Eds.), *Handbook of the psychology of aging* (2nd ed.). New York: Van Nostrand Reinhold.

Aldous, J. (1985). Parent-adult child relations as affected by the grandparent status. In V. L. Bengtson & J. F. Robertson (Eds.), *Grandparenthood.* Beverly Hills, CA: Sage.

Aldrich, C. K., & Mendkoff, E. (1963). Relocation of the aged and disabled: A mortality study. *Journal of the American Geriatrics Society, 11,* 185–194.

Allan, C., & Brotman, H. (1981). *Chartbook on aging in America.* Washington, DC: 1981 White House Conference on Aging.

Allison, P., & Stewart, J. (1974). Productivity differences among scientists: Evidence for accumulative advantage. *American Sociological Review, 39,* 596–606.

Altolz, J. A. S. (1978). Group psychotherapy with the elderly. In I. M. Burnside (Ed.), *Working with the elderly: Group process and techniques.* North Scituate, MA: Duxbury Press.

Ambrogli, D. M., & Lenard, F. (1988). The impact of nursing home admission agreements on resident autonomy. *Gerontologist, 28,* 82–89.

American Association of Retired Persons (1984). *Data gram: Housing satisfaction in older Americans.* Washington, DC: Author.

American Psychiatric Association, (1980). *Diagnostic and statistical manual of mental disorders* (3rd ed.). Washington, DC: Author.

Anderson, B., & Palmore, E. B. (1974). Longitudinal evaluation of ocular function. In E. Palmore (Ed.), *Normal aging II.* Durham, NC: Duke University Press.

Anderson, T. (1984). Widowhood as a life transition: Its impact on kinship ties. *Journal of Marriage and the Family, 46,* 105–114.

Andres, R. (1979). *The normality of aging: The Baltimore longitudinal study.* (NIH Publication No. 79-1410). Washington, DC: National Institute on Aging Science Writer Seminar Series. U.S. Public Health Service.

Antonoff, S. R., & Spilka, B. (1984–1985). Patterning of facial expressions among terminal cancer patients. *Omega, 15,* 101–108.

Arenberg, D. (1980). Comments on the processes that account for memory declines with age. In L. W. Poon, J. L. Fozard, L. S. Cermak, D. Arenberg & L. W. Thompson (Eds.), *New directions in memory and aging.* Hillsdale, NJ: Erlbaum.

Arling, G., & McAuley, W. J. (1984). The family, public policy, and long-term care. In W. H. Quinn & G. A. Hughston (Eds.), *Independent aging: Family and social systems perspectives.* Rockville, MD: Aspen.

Atchley, R. C. (1977). *The social forces in later life* (2nd ed.). Belmont, CA: Wadsworth.

Atchley, R. C., & Miller, S. J. (1983). Types of elderly couples. In T. H. Brubaker (Ed.), *Family relationships in later life.* Beverly Hills, CA: Sage.

Autonomy and long term care. (1988, June). [Supplementary issue]. *Gerontologist, 28.*

Avolio, B. J., & Barrett, G. V. (1987). Effects of age stereotyping in a simulated interview. *Psychology and Aging, 2,* 56–63.

Baldessarini, R. J. (1977). *Chemotherapy in psychiatry.* Cambridge, MA: Harvard University Press.

Baltes, P. B., Cornelius, S. W., Spiro, A., Nesselroade, J. R., & Willis, S. L. (1980). Integration versus differentiation of fluid/crystallized intelligence in old age. *Developmental Psychology, 16,* 625–635.

Baltes, P. B., & Labouvie, G. V. (1973). Adult development of intellectual performance: Description, explanation, and modification. In C. Eisdorfer & M. P. Lawton (Eds.), *The psychology of adult development and aging.* Washington, DC: American Psychological Association.

Baltes, P. B., Reese, H. W., & Lipsett, L. P. (1980). Lifespan developmental psychology. *Annual Review of Psychology, 31,* 65–110.

Baltes, P. B., & Schaie, K. W. (1974, 5 March). The myth of the twilight years. *Psychology Today,* pp. 35–40.

Baltes, P. B., & Schaie, K. W. (1976). On the plasticity of intelligence in adulthood and old age: Where Horn and Donaldson fail. *American Psychologist, 31,* 720–725.

Baltes, P. B., & Willis, S. L. (1977). Toward psychological theories of aging and development. In J. E. Birren & K. W. Schaie (Eds.), *Handbook of the psychology of aging.* New York: Van Nostrand Reinhold.

Barnes, D. (1987). Defect in Alzheimer's is on chromosome 21. *Science, 235,* 846–847.

Barney, J. (1974) Community presence as a key to quality of life in nursing homes. *American Journal of Public Health, 64,* 265–268.

Barney, J. (1987). Community presence in nursing homes. *Gerontologist, 27,* 367–369.

Bass, D. M., Garland, T. N., & Otto, M. E. (1985–1986). Characteristics of hospice patients and their caregivers. *Omega, 16,* 51–68.

Baum, S. A., & Rubenstein, L. Z. (1987). Old people in the emergency room: Age-related differences in emergency department use and care. *Journal of the American Geriatrics Society, 35,* 398–404.

Beck, A. T. (1973). *The diagnosis and management of depression.* Philadelphia: University of Pennsylvania Press.

Beck, A. T. (1979). *Depression: Causes and treatment.* (7th ed.). Philadelphia: University of Pennsylvania Press.

Becker, J. (1974). *Depression: Theory and research.* Washington, DC: V. H. Winston.

Béland, F. (1986). The clientele of comprehensive and traditional home care programs. *Gerontologist, 26,* 382–388.

Belsky, J. K. (1988). *Here tomorrow: Making the most of life after fifty.* Baltimore: Johns Hopkins Press.

Benet, S. (1977). Why they live to be 100 or even older in Abkhasia. In S. H. Zarit (Ed.), *Readings in aging and death: Contemporary perspectives.* New York: Harper & Row.

Bengtson, V. L., Reedy, M. N., & Gordon, C. (1985). Aging and self-conceptions: Personality processes and social contexts. In J. E. Birren & K. W. Schaie (Eds.), *Handbook of the psychology of aging* (2nd ed.). New York: Van Nostrand Reinhold.

Bennett, R., & Eckman, J. (1973). Attitudes towards aging: A critical examination of recent literature and implications for future research. In C. Eisdorfer & M. P. Lawton (Eds.), *The psychology of adult development and aging.* Washington, DC: American Psychological Association.

Berezin, M. A. (1972). Psychodynamic considerations of aging and the aged: An overview. *American Journal of Psychiatry, 128,* 1483–1491.

Berezin, M. A. (1983). Psychotherapy in the elderly. In L. D. Breslau & M. R. Haug (Eds.), *Depression and aging: Causes, care, and consequences.* New York: Springer.

Bergner, M., Robb, H., Carter, R. B., & Gilson, B. S. (1981). The sickness impact profile: Development and final revision of a health status measure. *Medical Care, 19,* 787–805.

Bergner, M., & Rothman, M. L. (1987). Health status measures: An overview and guide for selection. *Annual Review of Public Health, 8,* 191–210.

Bersoff, D. N. (1973). Silk purses into sow's ears: The decline of psychological testing and a suggestion for its redemption. *American Psychologist, 28,* 892–899.

Bibring, E. (1953). The mechanism of depression. In P. E. Greenacre (Ed.), *Affective disorders.* New York: International Universities Press.

Birkhill, W. R., & Schaie, K. W. (1975). The effect of differential reinforcement of cautiousness in intellectual performance among the elderly. *Journal of Gerontology, 30,* 578–583.

Birren, J. E. (1973). A summary: Prospects and problems of research on the longitudinal development of man's intellectual capacities throughout life. In L. F. Jarvik, C. Eisdorfer & J. E. Blum (Eds.), *Intellectual functioning in adults.* New York: Springer.

Birren, J. E. (1974). Translations in gerontology–from lab to life, psychophysiology and speed of response. *American Psychologist, 29,* 808–815.

Birren, J. E., Butler, R. N., Greenhouse, S. W., Sokoloff, L., & Yarrow, M. R. (1963). *Human aging: A biological and behavioral study.* Washington, DC: U.S. Public Health Service.

Birren, J. E., Casperson, R.C., & Botwinick, J. (1950). Age changes in pupil size. *Journal of Gerontology, 5,* 216–221.

Birren, J. E., & Renner, V. J. (1977). Research on the psychology of aging: Principles and experimentation. In J. E. Birren & K. W. Schaie (Eds.), *Handbook of the psychology of aging.* New York: Van Nostrand Reinhold.

Birren, J. E., & Schaie, K. W. (Eds.). (1977). *Handbook of the psychology of aging.* New York: Van Nostrand Reinhold.

Blackburn, J. A., Papalia-Finlay, D., Foye, B. F., & Serlin, R. C. (1988). Modifiability of figural relations performance among elderly adults. *Journal of Gerontology, 43,* 87–89.

Blazer, D. (1980). The epidemiology of mental illness in later life. In E. W. Busse & D. G. Blazer (Eds.), *Handbook of geriatric psychiatry.* New York: Van Nostrand Reinhold.

Blazer, D. (1982). *Depression in late life.* St. Louis: C. V. Mosby.

Blazer, D., Hughes, D. C., & George, L. K. (1987). The epidemiology of depression in an elderly community population. *Gerontologist, 27,* 281–287.

Blessed, G., Tomlinson, B. E., & Roth, M. (1968). The association between quantitative measures of dementia and of senile changes in the cerebral grey matter of elderly subjects. *British Journal of Psychiatry, 114,* 797–811.

Bloch, A., Maeder, J., & Haissly, J. (1975). Sexual problems after myocardial infarction. *American Heart Journal, 90,* 536–537.

Block, M. R., Davidson, J. L., & Grambs, J. D. (1981). *Women over forty: Visions and realities.* New York: Springer.

Block, R. I., De Voe, M., Stanley, B., Stanley, M., & Pomara, N. (1985). Memory performance in individuals with primary degenerative dementia: Its similarity to diazepam-induced impairments. *Experimental Aging Research, 11,* 151–155.

Blood, R. O., & Wolfe, D. M. (1960). *Husbands and wives.* New York: Macmillan.

Blum, J. E., Clark, E. T., & Jarvik, L. F. (1973). The New York State Psychiatric Institute study of aging twins. In L. F. Jarvik, C. Eisdorfer, & J. E. Blum (Eds.), *Intellectual functioning in adults.* New York: Springer.

Blum, J.E., & Tross, S. (1980). Psychodynamic treatment of the elderly: A review of issues in theory and practice. In C. Eisdorfer (Ed.), *Annual Review of Gerontology and Geriatrics* (Vol. 1). New York: Springer.

Blumenthal, M. (1980, April). Depressive illness in old age: Getting behind the mask. *Geriatrics,* pp. 34–43.

Borson, S., Teri, L., Kiyak, A., & Montgomery, R. (1986, November). *Behavioral syndromes in Alzheimer's disease: Relationship to cognitive and functional impairments.* Paper presented at the 39th annual meeting of the Gerontological Society of America, Chicago.

Botwinick, J. (1966). Cautiousness in advanced age. *Journal of Gerontology, 21,* 347–353.

Botwinick, J. (1967). *Cognitive processes in maturity and old age.* New York: Springer.

Botwinick, J. (1977). Intellectual abilities. In J. E. Birren & K. W. Schaie (Eds.), *Handbook of the psychology of aging.* New York: Van Nostrand Reinhold.

Botwinick, J. (1978). *Aging and behavior* (2nd ed.). New York: Springer.

Botwinick, J., & Birren, J. E. (1963). Mental abilities and psychomotor responses in healthy aged men. In J. E. Birren, R. N. Butler, S. W. Greenhouse, L. Sokoloff, & M. R. Yarrow (Eds.), *Human aging: A biological and behavioral study.* Washington, DC: U.S. Public Health Service.

Botwinick, J., & Storandt, M. (1974). Cardiovascular status, depressive affect and other factors in reaction time. *Journal of Gerontology, 29,* 543–548.

Botwinick, J., & Thompson, L.W. (1968). Age difference in reaction time: An artifact? *Gerontologist, 8,* 25–28.

Bowlby, J. (1980). *Loss.* New York: Basic Books.

Bowling, A., & Cartwright, A. (1981). *Life after a death.* New York: Tavistock.

Bozian, M. W., & Clark, H. M. (1980). Counteracting sensory changes in the aging. *American Journal of Nursing, 80,* 473–476.

Branch, L. (1987). Continuing care retirement communities: Self-insuring for long-term care, *Gerontologist, 27,* 4–8.

Brash, D. E., & Hart, R. W. (1978). Molecular biology of aging. In J. A. Behnke, C. E. Finch, & G. B. Moment (Eds.), *The biology of aging.* New York: Plenum.

Braun, K. L., & Rose, C. L. (1987). Geriatric patient outcomes and costs in three settings: Nursing home, foster family, and own home. *Journal of the American Geriatrics Society, 35,* 387–397.

Brecher, E. M., & Consumer Reports Book Editors. (1985). *Love, sex, and aging.* Boston: Little, Brown.

Breckenridge, J.N., Gallagher, D., Thompson, L. W., & Peterson, J. (1986). Characteristic depressive symptoms of bereaved elders. *Journal of Gerontology, 41,* 163–168.

Brody, E. M. (1977). *Long-term care of older people.* New York: Human Sciences Press.

Brody, E. M. (1985). Parent care as a normative family stress. *Gerontologist, 25,* 19–29.

Brody, E. M., Kleban, M. H., Johnsen, P. T., Hoffman, C., & Schoonover, C. B. (1987). Work status and parent care: A comparison of four groups of women. *Gerontologist, 27,* 201–208.

Brody, E. M., & Schoonover, C. B. (1986). Patterns of parent-care when adult daughters work and when they do not. *Gerontologist, 26,* 372–381.

Brook, P., Degun, G., & Mather, M. (1975). Reality orientation, a therapy for psychogeriatric patients: A controlled study. *British Journal of Psychiatry, 127,* 42–45.

Brubaker, T. (1985). Responsibility for household tasks: A look at golden anniversary couples aged 75 years and older. In W. A. Peterson & J. Quadango (Eds.), *Social bonds in later life: Aging and interdependence.* Beverly Hills, CA: Sage.

Brubaker, T., & Brubaker, E. (1984). Family support of older persons in the long-term care setting: Recommendations for practice. In W. H. Quinn & G. A. Hughston (Eds.), *Independent aging: Family and social systems perspectives.* New York: Aspen.

Buell, S. J., & Coleman, P. D. (1979). Dendritic growth in the human aged brain and failure of growth in senile dementia, *Science, 206,* 854–856.

Bulcroft, K., & O'Conner-Roden, M. (1986, June). Never too late. *Psychology Today,* pp. 66–70.

Bultena, G. L., & Powers, E. A. (1978). Denial of aging: Age identification and reference group orientations. *Journal of Gerontology, 33,* 748–754.

Busse, E. W. (1970). A physiological, psychological and sociological study of aging. In E. Palmore (Ed.), *Normal aging.* Durham, NC: Duke University Press.

Busse, E. W. (1977). Theories of aging. In E. W. Busse & E. Pfeiffer (Eds.), *Behavior and adaption in late life* (2nd ed.). Boston: Little, Brown.

Busse, E. W., & Blazer, D. (1980). The theories and processes of aging. In E. W. Busse & D. Blazer (Eds.), *Handbook of geriatric psychiatry.* New York: Van Nostrand Reinhold.

Butler, R. N. (1974). Successful aging and the role of the life review. *Journal of the American Geriatrics Society, 22,* 529–535.

Butler, R. N. (1978). *Thoughts on geriatric medicine.* (NIH Publication No. 78-1406). Washington, DC: National Institute on Aging Science Writer Seminar Series. U.S. Public Health Service.

Butler, R. N. (1980). Ageism: A forward. *Journal of Social Issues, 36,* 8–11.

Butler, R. N., & Lewis, M. I. (1973). *Aging and mental health.* St. Louis: C. V. Mosby.

Caldwell, D., & Mishara, B. L. (1972–1973). Research on attitudes of medical doctors towards the dying patient: A methodological problem. *Omega, 3,* 341–346.

Cameron, P., Stewart, L., & Biber, H. (1973). Consciousness of death across the life-span. *Journal of Gerontology, 28,* 92–95.

Campbell, D., & Fiske, D. (1959). Convergent and discriminant validation by the multitrait-multimethod matrix. *Psychological Bulletin, 56,* 81–105.

Campbell, T. W., Abernethy, V., & Waterhouse, G. L. (1983–1984). Do death attitudes of nurses and physicians differ? *Omega, 14,* 43–49.

Canestrari, R. E. (1963). Paced and self-paced learning in young and elderly adults. *Journal of Gerontology, 18,* 165–168.

Cantor, M. H. (1983). Strain among caregivers: A study of the experience in the United States. *Gerontologist, 23,* 597–604.

Capitman, J. A. (1986). Community-based long-term care models, target groups, and impacts on service use. *Gerontologist, 26,* 389–397.

Carp, F. M. (1968). Some components of disengagement. *Journal of Gerontology, 23,* 382–386.

Carp, F. M. (1974). Short-term and long-term prediction of adjustment to a new environment. *Journal of Gerontology, 29,* 444–453.

Carver, E. J. (1974). Geropsychiatric treatment: Where, why, how. In W. E. Fann & G. L. Maddox (Eds.), *Drug issues in geropsychiatry.* Baltimore: Williams & Wilkins.

Caserta, M. S., Lund, D. A., Wright, S. D., & Redburn, D. E. (1987). Caregivers to dementia patients: The utilization of community services. *Gerontologist, 27,* 209–214.

Cath, S. H. (1965). Some dynamics of middle and later years: A study in depletion and restitution. In M. A. Berezin & S. H. Cath (Eds.), *Geriatric psychiatry: Grief, loss, and emotional disorders in the aging process.* New York: International Universities Press.

Cath, S. H. (1979). The orchestration of disengagement. In A. Monk (Ed.), *The age of aging: A reader in social gerontology.* Buffalo, NY: Prometheus Press.

Cattell, R. B. (1963). Theory of fluid and crystallized intelligence: A critical experiment. *Journal of Educational Psychology, 54,* 1–22.

Charles, D. C. (1973). Explaining intelligence in adulthood: The role of the life history. *Gerontologist, 13,* 483–487.

Chenoweth, B., & Spenser, B. (1986). Dementia: The experience of family caregivers. *Gerontologist, 26,* 266–271.

Cherlin, A., & Furstenberg, F. (1985). Styles and strategies of grandparenting. In V. L. Bengtson & J. F. Robertson (Eds.), *Grandparenthood,* Beverly Hills, CA: Sage.

Chirikos, T. N., & Nestel, G. (1985). Longitudinal analysis of functional disabilities in older men. *Journal of Gerontology, 40,* 426–433.

Christenson, C. V., & Gagnon, J. H. (1965). Sexual behavior in a group of older women. *Journal of Gerontology, 20,* 351–356.

Cicirelli, V. (1983). Adult children and their elderly parents. In T. H. Brubaker (Ed.), *Family relationships in later life,* Beverly Hills, CA: Sage.

Clark, N. M., & Rakowski, W. (1983). Family caregivers of older adults: improving helping skills. *Gerontologist, 23,* 637–642.

Clayton, P. J. (1979). The sequelae and nonsequelae of conjugal bereavement. *American Journal of Psychiatry, 136,* 1530–1534.

Cleveland, W., & Gianturco, D. (1976). Remarriage probability after widowhood: A retrospective method. *Journal of Gerontology, 31,* 99–103.

Cogan, D. (1979). Summary and conclusions. In S. S. Han & D. H. Coons (Eds.), *Special senses and aging.* Ann Arbor: University of Michigan.

Cohen, K. P. (1979). *Hospice: Prescription for terminal care.* Rockville, MD: Aspen.

Cohler, B. J., & Grunebaum, H. V. (1981). *Mothers, grandmothers and daughters: Personality and childcare in three-generation families.* New York: Wiley.

Cohn, R. M. (1979). Age and the satisfactions from work. *Journal of Gerontology, 34,* 264–272.

Colavita, F. (1978). *Sensory changes in the elderly.* Springfield, IL: Charles C. Thomas.

Cole, C. L. (1984). Marital quality in later life. In W. H. Quinn & G. A. Hughston, (Eds.), *Independent aging: Family and social systems perspectives.* Rockville, MD: Aspen.

Cole, J. O., & Liptzin, B. (1980). Drug treatment of dementia in the elderly. In D. R. Kay & G. D. Burrows (Eds.), *Handbook of studies on psychiatry and old age.* Netherlands: Elsevier.

Cole, S. (1979). Age and scientific performance. *American Journal of Sociology, 84,* 264–272.

Coleman, P. D. (1986, August). Regulation of dendritic extent: Human aging brain and Alzheimer's disease. Paper presented at the 94th annual meeting of the American Psychological Association, Washington, DC.

Comfort, A. (1979). *The biology of senescence* (3rd ed.). New York: Elsevier/North Holland.

Coolidge, F. L., & Fish, C. E. (1983–1984). Dreams of the dying, *Omega, 14,* 1–7.

Cooney, T. M., Schaie, K. W., & Willis, S. L. (1988). The relationship between prior functioning on cognitive and personality dimensions and subject attrition in longitudinal research. *Journal of Gerontology, 43,* 12–17.

Cooper, A. F., & Curry, A. R. (1976). The pathology of deafness in the paranoid and affective psychoses of later life. *Journal of Psychosomatic Research, 20,* 97–105.

Cooper, K. L., & Gutmann, D. L. (1987). Gender identity and ego mastery style in middle-aged, pre- and post-empty nest women. *Gerontologist, 27,* 347-352.

Copeland, J. R. M. (1978). Evaluation of diagnostic methods: An international comparison. In A. D. Issacs & F. Post (Eds.), *Studies in geriatric psychiatry.* New York: Wiley.

Corby, N., & Solnick, R. L. (1980). Psychosocial and physiological influences on sexuality in the older adult. In J. E. Birren & R. B. Sloane (Eds.), *Handbook of mental health and aging.* Englewood Cliffs, NJ: Prentice-Hall.

Corso, J. F. (1977). Auditory perception and communication. In J. E. Birren & K. W. Schaie (Eds.), *Handbook of the psychology of aging.* New York: Van Nostrand Reinhold.

Costa, P. T., & McCrae, R. R. (1980). Influence of extraversion and neuroticism on subjective well-being: Happy and unhappy people. *Journal of Personality and Social Psychology, 38,* 668–678.

Costa, P. T., & McCrae, R. R. (1984). Personality as a lifelong determinant of well-being. In C. Malatesta & C. Izard (Eds.), *Affective processes in adult development and aging.* Beverly Hills, CA: Sage.

Costa, P. T., & McCrae, R. R. (1986). Cross-sectional studies of personality in a national sample: 1. Development and validation of survey measures. *Psychology and Aging, 1,* 140–143.

Costa, P. T., McCrae, R. R., & Arenberg, D. (1980). Enduring dispositions in adult males. *Journal of Personality and Social Psychology, 38,* 793-800.

Costa, P. T., McCrae, R. R., & Arenberg, D. (1983). Recent longitudinal research on personality and aging. In K. W. Schaie (Ed.), *Longitudinal studies of adult psychological development.* New York: Guilford.

Costa, P. T., McCrae, R. R., Zonderman, A. B., Barabano, H. E., Lebowitz, B., & Larson, D. M. (1986). Cross-sectional studies of personality in a national sample: 2. Stability in neuroticism, extraversion and openness. *Psychology and Aging, 1,* 144–149.

Costa, P. T., & Shock, N. W. (1984). New longitudinal data on the question whether hypertension influences intellectual change. In N.W. Shock, R. C. Greulich, R. Andres, D. Arenberg, P. T. Costa, E. G. Lakatta, & J. D. Tobin (Eds.), *Normal human aging: The Baltimore longitudinal study of aging.* (NIH Publication No. 84-2450). Washington, DC: U.S. Public Health Service.

Costa, P. T., Zonderman, A. B., McCrae, R. R., Cornoni-Huntley, J., Locke, B. Z., & Barabano, H. E. (1987). Longitudinal analysis of psychological well-being in a national sample: Stability of mean levels. *Journal of Gerontology, 42,* 50–55.

Craik, F. I. M. (1977). Age differences in human memory. In J. E. Birren & K. W. Schaie (Eds.), *Handbook of the psychology of aging.* New York: Van Nostrand Reinhold.

Crook, T. (1986). Drug effects in Alzheimer's disease. *Clinical Gerontologist, 5,* 489–501.

Cuber, J., & Harroff, P. (1965). *Sex and significant Americans.* New York: Appelton-Century-Crofts.

Cumming, E., & Henry, W. (1961). *Growing old.* New York: Basic Books.

Cunningham, D. A., Rechnitzer, P. A., Howard, J. H., & Donner, A. P. (1987). Exercise training of men at retirement: A clinical trial. *Journal of Gerontology, 42,* 17–23.

Cyrus-Lutz, C., & Gaitz, C. M. (1972). Psychiatrists' attitudes towards the aged and aging. *Gerontologist, 12,* 163–167.

Davidson, P. O., & Davidson, S. M. (1980). *Behavioral medicine: Changing health lifestyles.* New York: Brunner/Mazel.

Davis, G., & Jessen, A. (1980–1981). An experiment in death education in the medical curriculum: Medical students and clergy "on call" together. *Omega, 11,* 157–166.

Davis, J. M., Segal, N. L., & Spring, G. K. (1983). Biological and genetic aspects of depression in the elderly. In M.R. Haug & L. D. Breslau (Eds.), *Depression and aging: Causes, care, and consequences.* New York: Springer.

De Beauvoir, S. (1972). *The coming of age.* New York: Putnam.

Deimling, G. T., & Bass, D. M. (1986). Symptoms of mental impairment among elderly adults and their effects on family caregivers. *Journal of Gerontology, 41,* 778–784.

Dembroski, T. (Ed.). (1977). *Proceedings of the forum on coronary prone behavior.* (NIH Publication No. 78-1451). Washington, DC: U.S. Public Health Service.

Dennis, W. (1956). Age and achievement: A critique. *Journal of Gerontology, 11,* 331–337.

Dennis, W. (1958). The age decrement in outstanding scientific contributions: Fact or artifact? *American Psychologist, 13,* 457–460.

Dennis, W. (1966). Creative productivity between the ages of 20 and 80 years. *Journal of Gerontology, 21,* 1–8.

Depner, C. E., & Ingersol-Dayton, B. (1985). Conjugal social support: Patterns in later life. *Journal of Gerontology, 40,* 761–766.

Dickinson, G. E., & Pearson, A. A. (1980–1981). Death education and physicians' attitudes towards dying patients. *Omega, 11,* 167–174.

Doppelt, J. E., & Wallace, W. L. (1955). Standardization of the Wechsler Adult Intelligence Scale for older persons. *Journal of Abnormal and Social Psychology, 51,* 312–330.

Dorfman, L., & Moffett, M. (1987). Retirement satisfaction in married and widowed rural women. *Gerontologist, 27,* 215–221.

Dubois, P. M. (1980). *The hospice way of death.* New York: Human Sciences Press.

Edwards, P. B. (1984). Leisure counseling. In H. Dennis (Ed.), *Retirement preparation.* Lexington, MA: Lexington Books.

Eichorn, G. L. (1979). *Aging: Genetics and the environment.* (NIH Publication No. 79-1450). Washington, DC: National Institute on Aging Science Writer Seminar Series. U.S. Public Health Service.

Eisdorfer, C. (1970a). Developmental level and sensory impairment in the aged. In E. Palmore (Ed.), *Normal aging.* Durham, NC: Duke University Press.

Eisdorfer, C. (1970b). Rorschach rigidity and sensory decrement in a senescent population. In E. Palmore (Ed.), *Normal aging.* Durham, NC: Duke University Press.

Eisdorfer, C. (1977). Stress, disease, and cognitive change in the aged. In C. Eisdorfer & R. O. Friedel (Eds.), *Cognitive and emotional disturbance in the elderly.* Chicago: Yearbook Medical Publishers.

Eisdorfer, C., & Wilkie, F. (1973). Intellectual changes with advancing age. In L. F. Jarvik, C. Eisdorfer, & J. E. Blum (Eds.), *Intellectual functioning in adults.* New York: Springer.

Eissler, K. R. (1955). *The psychiatrist and the dying patient.* New York: International Universities Press.

Ekerdt, D. J. (1986). The busy ethic: Moral continuity between work and retirement. *Gerontologist, 26,* 239–244.

Ekerdt, D. J., Bosse, R., & Levkoff, S. (1985). An empirical test for phases of retirement: Findings from the normative aging study. *Journal of Gerontology, 40,* 95–101.

Ell, K., Mantell, J., & Hamovich, M. (1986, November). *Adaptation to cancer among different age cohorts.* Paper presented at the 39th annual meeting of the Gerontological Society of America, Chicago.

Engen, T. (1977). Taste and smell. In J.E. Birren & K. W. Schaie (Eds.), *Handbook of the psychology of aging.* New York: Van Nostrand Reinhold.

Epley, R. J., & McCaghy, C. H. (1977–1978). The stigma of dying: Attitudes towards the terminally ill. *Omega, 8,* 379–393.

Epstein, L. J. (1976). Depression in the elderly. *Journal of Gerontology, 31,* 278–282.

Erikson, E. (1963). *Childhood and society.* New York: Norton.

Erickson, R. C. (1978). Problems in the clinical assessment of memory. *Experimental Aging Research, 4,* 255–272.

Erikson, R. C., Poon, L. W., & Walsh-Sweeney, L. (1980). Clinical memory testing of the elderly. In L. W. Poon, J. L. Fozard, L. S. Cermak, D. Arenberg, & L. W. Thompson (Eds.), *New directions in memory and aging.* Hillsdale, NJ: Erlbaum.

Evans, L., Ekerdt, D. J., & Bosse, R. (1985). Proximity to retirement and anticipatory involvement: Findings from the normative aging study. *Journal of Gerontology, 40,* 368–374.

Feifel, H., & Branscomb, A. B. (1973). Who's afraid of death? *Journal of Abnormal Psychology, 81,* 282–288.

Feinson, M. C. (1986). Aging widows and widowers: Are there mental health differences? *International Journal of Aging and Human Development, 23,* 241–255.

Feinson, M. C., & Thoits, P. A. (1986). The distribution of distress among elders. *Journal of Gerontology, 41,* 225–233.

Feldman, S. S., Biringen, Z. C., & Nash, S. C. (1981). Fluctuations of sex-related self-attributions as a function of stage of family life cycle. *Developmental Psychology, 17,* 24-35.

Felton, B. J., & Revenson, T. A. (1987). Age differences in coping with chronic illness. *Psychology and Aging, 2,* 164–170.

Fengler, A. P., & Goodrich, N. (1979). Wives of elderly disabled men: The hidden patients. *Gerontologist, 19,* 175–183.

Field, D., Schaie, K. W., & Leino, E. V. (1988). Continuity in intellectual functioning: The role of self-reported health. *Psychology and Aging, 3,* 385–392.

Fillenbaum, G. G. (1971). On the relation between attitude to work and attitude to retirement. *Journal of Gerontology, 26,* 244–248.

Fillit, H. M., Kemeny, E., Luine, V., Weksler, M., & Zabriskie, J. B. (1987). Antivascular antibodies in the sera of patients with senile dementia of the Alzheimer's type. *Journal of Gerontology, 42,* 180–184.

Fischer, L. R. (1985). Elderly parents and the caregiving role: An asymmetrical transition. In W. A. Peterson & J. Quadango (Eds.), *Social bonds in later life: Aging and interdependence.* Beverly Hills, CA: Sage.

Fiske, D. (1971). *Measuring the concepts of personality.* Chicago: Aldine-Atherton.

Fitting, M., Rabins, P., Lucas, M. J., & Eastham, J. (1986). Caregivers for dementia patients: A comparison of husbands and wives. *Gerontologist, 26,* 248–252.

Flemming, A. S., Buchanan, J. G., Santos, J. F., & Rickards, L. D. (1984). *Mental health services for the elderly: Report on a survey of mental health centers.* Washington, DC: White House Conference on the Aging.

Flint, M. L. (1982). *A consumer guide to nursing home care in New York State.* New York: Friends and Relatives of the Institutionalized Aged.

Flynn, C. B., Longino, C. F., Wiseman, R. F., & Biggar, J. C. (1985). The redistribution of America's older population: Major national migration patterns for three census decades, 1960–1980. *Gerontologist, 25,* 292–296.

Foley, J. M., & Murphy, D. M. (1977, November). *Sex role identity in the aged.* Paper presented at the 30th annual meeting of the Gerontological Society of America, San Francisco.

Folkman, S., Lazarus, R. S., Pimley, S., & Novacek, J. (1987). Age differences in stress and coping processes. *Psychology and Aging, 2,* 171–184.

Foner, A., & Schwab, K. (1981). *Aging and retirement.* Monterey, CA: Brooks/Cole.

Fozard, J. L., & Popkin, S. J. (1978). Optimizing adult development: Ends and means of an applied psychology of aging. *American Psychologist, 33,* 975–989.

Fozard, J. L., Wolf, E., Bell, B., McFarland, R. A., & Podolsky, S. (1977). Visual perception and communication. In J. E. Birren & K. W. Schaie (Eds.), *Handbook of the psychology of aging.* New York: Von Nostrand Reinhold.

Freud, S. (1957). Mourning and melancholia. *Standard edition* (Vol. 14). London: Hogarth.

Freud, S. (1924). On psychotherapy. *Collected papers* (Vol. 1). London: Hogarth.

Friedman, M., & Rosenman, R. H. (1974). *Type A behavior and your heart.* Greenwich, CT: Fawcett.

Fries, J. F. (1986). The biological constraints on human aging: Implications for health policy. In Gainor-Andreoli, K., Musser, L. A., & Reiser, S. J. (Eds.), *Health care for the elderly: Regional responses to national policy issues.* Binghamton, NY: Haworth Press.

Fry, P. S. (1986). *Depression, stress, and adaptations in the elderly: Psychological assessment and treatment.* Rockville, MD: Aspen.

Furry, C. A., & Baltes, P. B. (1973). The effect of age differences in ability-extraneous performance variables on the assessment of intelligence in children, adults, and the elderly. *Journal of Gerontology, 28,* 73–80.

Gallagher, D., & Thompson, L. W. (1982, August). *Elders' maintenance of treatment benefits following individual psychotherapy for depression: Results of a pilot study and preliminary data from an ongoing replication study.* Paper presented at the 90th annual meeting of the American Psychological Association, Washington, DC.

Gallagher, D., & Thompson, L. W. (1983). Cognitive therapy for depression in the elderly: A promising model for treatment and research. In L. D. Breslau & M. R. Haug (Eds.), *Depression and aging: Causes, care, and consequences.* New York: Springer.

Gambria, L. M. (1979–1980). Sex differences in daydreaming and related mental activity from the late teens to the early nineties. *International Journal of Aging and Human Development, 10,* 1-34.

Gatz, M., Popkin, S. J., Pino, C. D., & VandenBos, G. R. (1985). Psychological interventions with older adults. In J. E. Birren & K. W. Schaie (Eds.), *Handbook of the psychology of aging* (2nd ed.). New York: Van Nostrand Reinhold.

Gelfand, D. E., & Olsen, J. K. (1979). *The aging network: Programs and services.* New York: Springer.

George, L., & Gwyther, L. (1986). Caregiver well-being: A multidimensional examination of family caregivers of demented adults. *Gerontologist, 26,* 253–259.

German, P. S., Shapiro, S., Skinner, E. A., Von Korff, M., Klein, L., Turner, R. W., Teitelbaum, M. L., Burke, J., & Burns, B. J. (1987). Detection and management of mental health problems of older patients by primary care providers. *Journal of the American Medical Association, 257,* 489–493.

Gesser, G., Wong, P. T., & Reker, G. T. (1987–1988). Death attitudes across the life-span: The development and validation of the death attitude profile (DAP). *Omega, 18,* 113–128.

Gianturco, D. T., & Busse, E. W. (1978). Psychiatric problems encountered during a long-term study of normal aging volunteers. In A. D. Issacs & F. Post (Eds.), *Studies in geriatric psychiatry.* New York: Wiley.

Glamser, F. D. (1976). Determinants of a positive attitude towards retirement. *Journal of Gerontology, 31,* 104–107.

Glamser, F. D. (1981). The impact of pre-retirement programs on the retirement experience. *Journal of Gerontology, 36,* 244–250.

Glamser, F. D., & DeJong, G. F. (1975). The efficacy of pre-retirement preparation programs for industrial workers. *Journal of Gerontology, 30,* 595–600.

Glaser, B. (1966). The social loss of aged dying patients. *Gerontologist, 6,* 77–80.

Glaser, B., & Strauss, A. L. (1968). *A time for dying.* Chicago: Aldine.

Glick, I. D., & Kessler, D. R. (1980). *Marital and family therapy* (2nd ed.). New York: Grune & Stratton.

Goldfarb, A. I. (1953). Recommendations for psychiatric care in a home for the aged. *Journal of Gerontology, 8,* 343–347.

Goldfarb, A. I., & Turner, H. (1953). Psychotherapy of aged persons. *American Journal of Psychiatry, 109,* 916–921.

Goldstrom, I. D., Burns, B. J., Kessler, L. G., Feuerberg, M. A., Larson, D. B., Miller, N. E., & Cromer, W. J. (1987). Mental health services use by elderly adults in a primary care setting. *Journal of Gerontology, 42,* 147–153.

Gotestam, K. G. (1980). Behavioral and dynamic psychotherapy with the elderly. In J. E. Birren & R. B. Sloane (Eds.), *Handbook of mental health and aging.* Englewood Cliffs, NJ: Prentice-Hall.

Gottesman, L. E., & Bourestom, N. C. (1974). Why nursing homes do what they do. *Gerontologist, 14,* 501-506.

Gould, S. J. (1981). *The mismeasure of man.* New York: Norton.

Granick, S., & Friedman, A. S. (1973). Educational experience and the maintenance of intellectual functioning by the aged: An overview. In L. F. Jarvik, C. Eisdorfer, & J. E. Blum (Eds.), *Intellectual functioning in adults.* New York: Springer.

Granick, S., Kleban, M. H., & Weiss, A. D. (1976). Relationships between hearing loss and cognition in normally hearing aged persons. *Journal of Gerontology, 31,* 438–440.

Grauer, H., Betts, D., & Birnbom, F. (1973). Welfare emotions and family therapy in geriatrics. *Journal of the American Geriatrics Society, 21,* 21–24.

Greene, M. G., Hoffman, S., Charon, R., & Adelman, R. (1987). Psychosocial concerns in the medical encounter: A comparison of the interactions of doctors with their young and old patients. *Gerontologist, 27,* 164–168.

Greist, J. H., & Greist, T. H. (1979). *Antidepressant treatment: The essentials.* Baltimore: Williams & Wilkins.

Grotjan, M. (1955). Analytic psychotherapy with the elderly. *Psychoanalytic Review, 42,* 419–427.

Gurland, B. J. (1976). The comparative frequency of depression in various adult age groups. *Journal of Gerontology, 31,* 283–292.

Gurland, B. J., Dean, L. L., Copeland, J., Gurland, R., & Golden, R. (1982). Criteria for the diagnosis of dementia in the community elderly. *Gerontologist, 22,* 180–186.

Gutmann, D. L. (1964). An exploration of ego configurations in middle and later life. In B. L. Neugarten & Associates (Eds.), *Personality in middle and late life.* New York: Atherton.

Gutmann, D. L. (1969). *The country of old men: Cultural studies in the psychology of later life.* Ann Arbor: University of Michigan/Wayne State University, Institute of Gerontology.

Gutmann, D. L. (1977). The cross-cultural perspective: Notes towards a comparative psychology of aging. In J. E. Birren & K. W. Schaie (Eds.), *Handbook of the psychology of aging.* New York: Van Nostrand Reinhold.

Gutmann, D. L. (1980). Psychoanalysis and aging: A developmental view. In S. L. Greenspan & G. H. Polock (Eds.), *The course of life: Psychoanalytic contributions towards understanding personality development* (Vol. 2). Rockville, MD: National Institute of Mental Health.

Gutmann, D. L. (1985). The parental imperative revisited. In J. Meacham (Ed.), *Family and individual development.* Basel: Karger.

Gwyther, L. P., & George, L. K. (1986). Caregivers for dementia patients: Complex determinants of well-being and burden. *Gerontologist, 26,* 245–247.

Haan, N., Millsap, R., & Hartka, E. (1986). As time goes by: Change and stability in personality over fifty years, *Psychology and Aging, 1,* 220–232.

Habot, B., & Libow, L. S. (1980). The interrelationship of mental and physical status and its assessment in the older adult: Mind-body interaction. In J. E. Birren & R. B. Sloane (Eds.), *Handbook of mental health and aging.* Englewood Cliffs, NJ: Prentice-Hall.

Hachinski, V. C., Lassen, N. A., & Marshal, J. (1974). Multi-infarct dementia. *Lancet, 2,* 207–209.

Hagestad, G. (1985). Continuity and connectedness. In V. L. Bengtson & J. Robertson (Eds.), *Grandparenthood.* Beverly Hills, CA: Sage.

Hale, S., Myerson, J., & Wagstaff, D. (1987). General slowing of nonverbal information processing: Evidence for a power law. *Journal of Gerontology, 42,* 131–136.

Haley, J. (1971). Family therapy: A radical change. In J. Haley (Ed.), *Changing families: A family therapy reader.* New York: Grune & Stratton.

Haley, W. E., Brown, S. L., & Levine, E. G. (1987). Experimental evaluation of the effectiveness of group intervention for dementia caregivers. *Gerontologist, 27,* 376–382.

Haley, W. E., Levine, E. G., Brown, S. L., & Bartolucci, A. A. (1987). Stress, appraisal, coping and social support as predictors of adaptational outcome among dementia caregivers. *Psychology and Aging, 2,* 323–330.

Haley, W. E., Levine, E. G., Brown, S. L., Berry, J. W., & Hughes, G. H. (1987). Psychological, social and health consequences of caring for a relative with dementia. *Journal of the American Geriatrics Society, 35,* 405–411.

Hall, D. A. (1976). *The ageing of connective tissue.* London: Academic Press.

Han, S. S., & Geha-Mitzel, M. (1979). Coping with sensory losses in aging. In J. M. Ordy & K. R. Brizzee (Eds.), *Aging: Vol. 10. Sensory systems and communication in the elderly.* New York: Raven.

Handal, P. J., Peal, R. L., Napoli, J. G., & Austrin, H. R. (1984–1985). The relationship between direct and indirect measures of death anxiety. *Omega, 15,* 245–262.

Harkins, S. W., Chapman, C. R., & Eisdorfer, C. (1979). Memory loss and response bias in senescence. *Journal of Gerontology, 34,* 66–72.

Harris, L., & Associates. (1975). *The myth and reality of aging in America.* Washington, DC: National Council on the Aging.

Harris, L., & Associates. (1981). *Aging in the eighties: America in transition.* Washington, DC: National Council on the Aging.

Hartford, M. E. (1980). The use of group methods for work with the aged. In J. E. Birren & R. B. Sloane (Eds.), *Handbook of mental health and aging.* Englewood Cliffs, NJ: Prentice-Hall.

Hartley, J. T., Harker, J. O., & Walsh, D. A. (1980). Contemporary issues and new directions in adult development in learning and memory. In L. Poon (Ed.), *Aging in the 1980's: Psychological issues.* Washington, DC: American Psychological Association.

Haug, M. (Ed.). (1981). *Elderly patients and their doctors.* New York: Springer.

Hayflick, L. (1987). The human life span. In G. Lesnoff-Caravaglia (Ed.), *Realistic expectations for long life.* New York: Human Sciences Press.

Hayslip, B., & Stewart-Bussey, D. (1986–1987). Locus of control—levels of death anxiety relationships. *Omega, 17,* 41–48.

Hegeman, C., & Tobin, S. (1988). Enhancing the autonomy of mentally impaired nursing home residents. *Gerontologist, 28,* 71–75.

Heinemann, G. D. (1983). Family involvement and support for widowed persons. In T. H. Brubaker (Ed.), *Family relationships in later life.* Beverly Hills, CA: Sage.

Hertzog, C., & Schaie, K. W. (1988). Stability and change in adult intelligence: 2. Simultaneous analysis of longitudinal means and covariance structures. *Psychology and Aging, 3,* 122–130.

Heyman, D. K., & Jeffers, F. C. (1963). Effect of time lapse on consistency of self-health and medical evaluations of elderly persons. *Journal of Gerontology, 18,* 160–164.

Hicks, L. H., & Birren, J. E. (1970). Aging, brain damage, and psychomotor slowing. *Psychological Bulletin, 74,* 377–396.

Hine, V. H. (1979-1980). Dying at home. Can families cope? *Omega, 10,* 175–187.

Hinton, J. (1975–1976). The influence of previous personality on reactions to having terminal cancer. *Omega, 6,* 95–111.

Hodgson, J. H., & Quinn, J. L. (1980). The impact of the triage health care delivery system upon client morale, independent living and the cost of care. *Gerontologist, 20,* 364–371.

Hofland, B. (1988). Autonomy in long term care: Background issues and a programmatic response. *Gerontologist, 28,* 3–9.

Hollister, L. E. (1983). Pharmacological treatment of depression in aged persons. In L. D. Breslau & M. R. Haug (Eds.), *Depression and aging: Causes, care, and consequences.* New York: Springer.

Holmes, T., & Rahe, R. (1967). The Social Readjustment Rating Scale. *Journal of Psychosomatic Research, 11,* 213–218.

Horn, J. L. (1970). Organization of data on life-span development of human abilities. In L. R. Goulet & P. B. Baltes (Eds.), *Life-span developmental psychology: Research and theory.* New York: Academic Press.

Horn, J. L., & Donaldson, G. (1976). On the myth of intellectual decline in adulthood. *American Psychologist, 31,* 701–719.

Horn, J. L., & Donaldson, G. (1977). Faith is not enough: A response to the Baltes-Schaie claim that intelligence does not wane. *American Psychologist, 32,* 369-373.

Horner, K. L., Rushton, J. P., & Vernon, P. A. (1986). Relation between aging and research productivity of academic psychologists. *Psychology and Aging, 1,* 319–324.

Houser, B. B., & Berkman, S. L. (1984). Aging parent/mature child relationships. *Journal of Marriage and the Family, 46,* 294–299.

Hoyer, W. J. (1973). Application of operant techniques to the modification of elderly behavior. *Gerontologist, 13,* 18–22.

Hulicka, I. M. (1967). Age differences in retention as a function of interference. *Journal of Gerontology, 22,* 180-184.

Hulicka, I. M., & Grossman, J. L. (1967). Age group comparisons for the use of mediators in paired associate learning. *Journal of Gerontology, 22,* 46–51.

Hultsch, D. F. (1974). Learning to learn in adulthood. *Journal of Gerontology, 29,* 302–308.

Hunt, E. (1986). Experimental perspectives: Theoretical memory models. In L. W. Poon, (Ed.), *Handbook for clinical memory assessment of older adults.* Washington, DC: American Psychological Association.

Hussian, R. (1981). *Geriatric psychology: A behavioral perspective.* New York: Van Nostrand Reinhold.

Huttman, E. D. (1977). *Housing and social services for the elderly: Social policy trends.* New York: Praeger.

Introduction: The age of the aging, congregate living. (1981, August). *Progressive Architecture,* pp. 64–68.

Irion, J. C., & Blanchard-Fields, F. (1987). A cross-sectional comparison of adaptive coping in adulthood. *Journal of Gerontology, 42,* 502–504.

Jacewicz, M. M., & Hartley, A. A. (1987). Age differences in the speed of cognitive operations: Resolution of inconsistent findings. *Journal of Gerontology, 42,* 86–88.

Jackson, J. (1985). Race, national origin, ethnicity and aging. In R. H. Binstock & E. Shanas (Eds.), *Handbook of aging and the social sciences* (2nd ed.). New York: Van Nostrand Reinhold.

Janowsky, D., Davis, J. M., & El-Yousef, M. K. (1974). Side effects associated with psychotropic drugs. In W. E. Fann & G. L. Maddox (Eds.), *Drug issues in geropsychiatry.* Baltimore: Williams & Wilkins.

Janson, P., & Ryder, L. K. (1983). Crime and the elderly: The relationship between risk and fear. *Gerontologist, 23,* 207–212.

Jantz, R. K., Seefeldt, C., Galper, A., & Serock, K. (1976). *Children's attitudes towards the elderly: Final report.* College Park: University of Maryland.

Jarrett, W. H. (1985). Caregiving within kinship systems: Is affection really necessary? *Gerontologist, 25,* 5–10.

Jarvik, L. F. (1973). Discussion: Patterns of intellectual functioning in the later years. In L. F. Jarvik, C. Eisdorfer, & J. E. Blum (Eds.), *Intellectual functioning in adults.* New York: Springer.

Jarvik, L. F. (1975). The aging central nervous system: Clinical aspects. In H. Brody, D. Harman, & J. M. Ordy (Eds.), *Aging: Vol. 1. Clinical, morphologic and neurochemical aspects of the aging central nervous system.* New York: Raven.

Jarvik, L. F. (1987, November). *Aging of the brain. How can we prevent it?* Paper presented at the 40th annual meeting of the Gerontological Society of America, Washington, DC.

Jarvik, L. F., & Falik, A. (1963). Intellectual stability and survival in the aged. *Journal of Gerontology, 18,* 173–176.

Jeffers, F. C., & Verwoerdt, A. (1977). How the old face death. In E. W. Busse & E. Pfeiffer (Eds.), *Behavior and adaptation in late life.* Boston: Little, Brown.

Johnson, C. L. (1983). Dyadic family relationships and family supports. *Gerontologist, 23,* 377–383.

Johnson, C. L. (1985a). Grandparenting options in divorcing families: An anthropological perspective. In V. L. Bengtson & J. Robertson (Eds.), *Grandparenthood.* Beverly Hills, CA: Sage.

Johnson, C. L. (1985b). The impact of illness on late-life marriages. *Journal of Marriage and the Family, 47,* 165–172.

Johnson, C. L., & Barer, B. M. (1987). Marital instability and the changing kinship networks of grandparents. *Gerontologist, 27,* 330–335.

Johnson, C. L., & Catalano, D. (1983). A longitudinal study of family supports to impaired elderly. *Gerontologist, 23,* 612–618.

Johnson, E. S., & Bursk, B. J. (1977). Relationships between the elderly and their adult children. *Gerontologist, 17,* 90–96.

Johnson, H. A. (1985). Is aging physiological or pathological? In H. A. Johnson (Ed.), *Relations between normal aging and disease.* New York: Raven.

Kahana, E. A. (1975). A congruence model of person-environment interaction. In P. G. Windley & G. Ernst (Eds.), *Theory development in environment and aging.* Washington, DC: Gerontological Society.

Kahana, E. A., & Coe, R. M. (1969). Perceptions of grandparenthood by community and institutionalized aged. *Proceedings of the 77th Annual Convention of the American Psychological Association, 4,* 736–737.

Kahn, R. L. (1977). The mental health system and the future aged. In S. H. Zarit (Ed.), *Readings in aging and death: Contemporary perspectives.* New York: Harper & Row.

Kahn, R. L., & Miller, N. E. (1978). Adaptational factors in memory function in the aged. *Experimental Aging Research, 4,* 273–289.

Kahn, R. L., Zarit, S. H., Hilbert, N. M., & Niederehe, G. (1975). Memory complaint and impairment in the aged; the effect of depression and altered brain function. *Archives of General Psychiatry, 32,* 1569–1573.

Kane, A. C., & Hogan, J. D. (1985–1986). Death anxiety in physicians: Defensive style, medical specialty, and exposure to death. *Omega, 16,* 11–22.

Kane, R. L., Solomon, D. H., Beck, J. C., Keeler, E., & Kane, R. A. (1981). *Geriatrics in the United States: Manpower projections and training considerations.* Lexington, MA: Heath.

Kaplan, G. (1986, August). *Aging, health, and behavior: Evidence from the Alameda County study.* Paper presented at the 94th annual meeting of the American Psychological Association, Washington, DC.

Karasu, T. B., & Murkofsky, C. M. (1976). Psychopharmacology of the elderly. In L. Bellack & T. B. Karasu (Eds.), *Geriatric psychiatry: A handbook for psychiatrists and primary care physicians.* New York: Grune & Stratton.

Kart, C. S., & Manard, B. B. (1976). Quality of care in old age institutions. *Gerontologist, 16,* 250–256.

Kart, C. S., Metress, E. S., & Metress, J. F. (1978). *Aging and health: Biologic and social perspectives.* Menlo Park, CA: Addison-Wesley.

Kastenbaum, R. (1976–1977). Toward standards of care for the terminally ill: Part III. A few guiding principles. *Omega, 7,* 191–193.

Kastenbaum, R. (1981). *Death, society, and human experience* (2nd ed.). St. Louis: C. V. Mosby.

Kastenbaum, R., & Candy, S. E. (1973). The 4% fallacy: A methodological and empirical critique of extended care facility population statistics. *International Journal of Aging and Human Development, 4,* 15–21.

Kastenbaum, R., & Aizenberg, R. (1972). *The Psychology of Death.* New York: Springer.

Kastenbaum, R., & Costa, P. (1977). Psychological perspectives on death. *Annual Review of Psychology, 28,* 225–249.

Katz, S., Ford, A. B., Moskowitz, R. W., Jackson, B. A., & Jaffee, M. W. (1963). Studies of illness in the aged: The index of ADL—a standardized measure of biological and psychosocial function. *Journal of the American Medical Association, 185,* 914–919.

Kausar, T., & Wister, A. (1984). Living arrangements of older women: The ethnic dimension. *Journal of Marriage and the Family, 46,* 301–311.

Kay, D. W. K., Beamish, P., & Roth, M. (1964). Old age mental disorders in Newcastle-upon-Tyne: Part 1. A study of prevalence. *British Journal of Psychiatry, 110,* 146–158.

Kay, D. W. K., & Bergmann, K. (1980). Epidemiology of mental disorders among the aged in the community. In J. E. Birren & R. B. Sloane (Eds.), *Handbook of mental health and aging.* Englewood Cliffs, NJ: Prentice-Hall.

Keating, N. C., & Cole, P. (1980). What do I do with him 24 hours a day? Changes in the housewife role after retirement. *Gerontologist, 20,* 84–89.

Kelly, E. L., & Conley, J. J. (1987). Personality and compatibility: A prospective analysis of marital stability and marital satisfaction. *Journal of Personality and Social Psychology, 52,* 27–40.

Kermis, M. D. (1986). The epidemiology of mental disorder in the elderly: A response to the Senate/AARP report. *Gerontologist, 26,* 482–487.

Kerski, D., Drinka, T., Carnes, M., Golob, K., & Craig, W. A. (1987). Post-geriatric evaluation unit follow-up: Team versus nonteam. *Journal of Gerontology, 42,* 191–195.

Kitson, G. C., Lopata, H. Z., Holmes, W. M., & Meyering, S. M. (1980). Divorcees and widows: Similarities and differences. *American Journal of Orthopsychiatry, 50,* 291–301.

Kiesler, C. A. (1980). Mental health policy as a field of inquiry for psychology. *American Psychologist, 35,* 1066–1080.

Kivnick, H. Q. (1984). Grandparents and family relations. In W. H. Quinn & G. A. Hughston, (Eds.), *Independent aging: Family and social systems perspectives.* Rockville, MD: Aspen.

Klerman, G. L. (1983). Problems in the definition and diagnosis of depression in the elderly. In M. R. Haug & L. E. Breslau (Eds.), *Depression and aging: Causes, care, and consequences.* New York: Springer.

Kline, D. W., & Schieber, F. (1985). Vision and aging. In J. E. Birren & K. W. Schaie (Eds.), *Handbook of the psychology of aging* (2nd ed.). New York: Van Nostrand Reinhold.

Knight, B. (1983). An evaluation of a mobile geriatric outreach team. In M. A. Smyer & M. Gatz (Eds.), *Mental health and aging: Programs and evaluations.* Beverly Hills, CA: Sage.

Kogan, N., & Wallach, M. A. (1961). Age changes in values and attitudes. *Journal of Gerontology, 16,* 272–280.

Kohen, J. A. (1983). Old but not alone: Informal social supports among the elderly by marital status and sex. *Gerontologist, 23,* 57–63.

Kohn, R. (1978). *Principles of mammalian aging* (2nd ed.). Englewood Cliffs, NJ: Prentice-Hall.

Kohn, R. (1985). Aging and age-related diseases: Normal processes. In H. A. Johnson (Ed.), *Relations between aging and disease.* New York: Raven.

Kohut, S. J., Kohut, J. J., & Fleishman, J. J. (1979). *Reality orientation in the elderly.* Oradell, NJ: Medical Economics Company.

Kornhaber, A. (1985). Grandparenthood and the "new social contract." In V. L. Bengtson & J. F. Robertson (Eds.), *Grandparenthood.* Beverly Hills, CA: Sage.

Kornhaber, A., & Woodward, K. L. (1981). *Grandparents/grandchild: The vital connection.* Garden City, NY: Anchor Books.

Kosberg, J. I. (1973). Differences in proprietary institutions caring for affluent and nonaffluent elderly. *Gerontologist, 13,* 299–304.

Kosberg, J. I. (1974). Making institutions accountable: Research and policy issues. *Gerontologist, 14,* 510–516.

Kübler-Ross, E. (1969). *On death and dying.* New York: Macmillan.

Kucharski, L. T., White, R. M., & Schratz, M. (1979). Age bias, referral for psychological assistance, and the private physician. *Journal of Gerontology, 34,* 423–428.

Kuypers, J. H., & Bengtson, V. L. (1983). Toward competence in the older family. In T. H. Brubaker (Ed.), *Family relations in late life.* Beverly Hills, CA: Sage.

Labouvie, G. V. (1973). Implications of geropsychological theories for intervention: The challenge for the 70s. *Gerontologist, 13,* 10–14.

Labouvie-Vief, G. V. (1985). Intelligence and cognition. In J. E. Birren & K. W. Schaie (Eds.), *Handbook of the psychology of aging* (2nd ed.). New York: Van Nostrand Reinhold.

Labouvie-Vief, G. V., & Blanchard-Fields, F. (1986a, August). *Modes of knowing and lifespan cognition.* Paper presented at the 94th annual meeting of the American Psychological Association, Washington, DC.

Labouvie-Vief, G. V., & Blanchard-Fields, F. (1986b, August). *Self and other and progressions in adult cognition.* Paper presented at the 94th annual meeting of the American Psychological Association, Washington, DC.

Labouvie-Vief, G. V., & Gonda, J. N. (1976). Cognitive strategy training and intellectual performance in the elderly. *Journal of Gerontology, 31,* 327–332.

Labouvie-Vief, G. V., Hoyer, W. J., Baltes, N. N., & Baltes, P. B. (1974). Operant analysis of intellectual behavior in old age. *Human Development, 17,* 259–273.

Labus, J. G., & Dambrot, F. H. (1985–1986). A comparative study of terminally ill hospice and hospital patients. *Omega, 16,* 225–233.

Lachman, M. E., & McArthur, L. Z. (1986). Adult age differences in causal attributions for cognitive, physical and social performance. *Psychology and Aging, 1,* 127–132.

Lang, A., & Brody, E. M. (1983). Characteristics of middle-aged daughters and help to their elderly mothers. *Journal of Marriage and the Family, 45,* 193–202.

Langer, E., Rodin, J., Beck, P., Weinman, C., & Spitzer, L. (1979). Environmental determinants of memory improvement in late adulthood. *Journal of Personality and Social Psychology, 37,* 2003–2013.

Larson, E. B., Reifler, B. V., Sumi, S. M., Canfield, C. G., & Chinn, N. M. (1985). Diagnostic evaluation of 200 elderly outpatients with suspected dementia. *Journal of Gerontology, 40,* 536–543.

Larson, R. (1978). Thirty years of research on the subjective well-being of older Americans. *Journal of Gerontology, 33,* 109–129.

LaRue, A., Bank, L., Jarvik, L., & Hetland, M. (1979). Health in old age: How do physicians' ratings and self-ratings compare? *Journal of Gerontology, 34,* 687–691.

Lawton, M. P. (1970). Assessment, integration, and environments for the elderly. *Gerontologist, 10,* 38–46.

Lawton, M. P. (1975). *Planning and managing housing for the elderly.* New York: Wiley.

Lawton, M. P. (1980). Environmental change: The older person as initiator and responder. In N. Datan & N. Lohmann (Eds.), *Transitions of aging.* New York: Academic Press.

Lawton, M. P. (1985). Housing and living environments of older people. In R. H. Binstock & E. Shanas (Eds.), *Handbook of aging and the social sciences* (2nd ed.). New York: Van Nostrand Reinhold.

Lawton, M. P., Greenbaum, M., & Liebowitz, B. (1980). The lifespan of housing environments for the aging. *Gerontologist, 20,* 56–64.

Lawton, M. P., Whelihan, W. M., & Belsky, J. K. (1980). Personality tests and their uses with older adults. In J. E. Birren & R. B. Sloane (Eds.), *Handbook of mental health and aging.* Englewood Cliffs, NJ: Prentice-Hall.

Lazarus, L., & Weinberg, J. (1980). Treatment in the ambulatory care setting. In E. W. Busse & D. G. Blazer (Eds.), *Handbook of geriatric psychiatry.* New York: Van Nostrand Reinhold.

Lazarus, M., & Lauer, H. (1986). Working past retirement: Practical and motivational issues. In R. Butler & H. Gleason (Eds.), *Productive aging: Enhancing vitality in later life.* New York: Springer.

Leary, W. E. (1988, February 25). The new hearing aids: Nearly invisible devices filter distracting sounds. *The New York Times,* p. B6.

Lee, G. R., & Ellithorpe, E. (1982). Intergenerational exchange and subjective well-being among the elderly. *Journal of Marriage and the Family, 44,* 217–224.

Lehman, H. C. (1953). *Age and achievement.* Philadelphia: American Philosophical Society.

Lehman, H. C. (1960). The age decrement in outstanding scientific creativity. *American Psychologist, 15,* 128–134.

Leiderman, D. B., & Grisso, J. (1985). The gomer phenomenon. *Journal of Health and Social Behavior, 26,* 222–232.

Lemke, S., & Moos, R. H. (1986). Quality of residential settings for elderly adults. *Journal of Gerontology, 41,* 268–276.

Lemon, B. W., Bengtson, V. L., & Peterson, J. A. (1972). An exploration of the activity theory of aging: Activity types and life satisfaction among in-movers to a retirement community. *Journal of Gerontology, 27,* 511–523.

Lesnoff-Caravaglia, G., & Klys, M. (1987). Lifestyle and longevity. In G. Lesnoff-Caravaglia (Ed.), *Realistic expectations for long life.* New York: Human Sciences Press.

Lezak, M. D. (1986). Neuropsychological assessment. In L. Teri & P. Lewinsohn (Eds.), *Geropsychological assessment and treatment.* New York: Springer.

Libow, L. S. (1982). Geriatric medicine and the nursing home: A mechanism for mutual excellence. *Gerontologist, 22,* 134–141.

Lieberman, M., & Tobin, S. S. (1983). *The experience of old age.* New York: Basic Books.

Liem, P. H., Chernoff, R., & Carter, W. J. (1986). Geriatric rehabilitation unit: A three-year outcome evaluation. *Journal of Gerontology, 41,* 44–50.

Lindemann, E. (1944). Symptomatology and management of acute grief. *American Journal of Psychiatry, 101,* 141–148.

Lindsley, O. R. (1964). Geratric behavioral prosthetics. In R. Kastenbaum (Ed.), *New thoughts on old age.* New York: Springer.

Lipton, M. A. (1976). Age differentiation in depression: Biochemical aspects. *Journal of Gerontology, 31,* 293–299.

Litwak, E., & Longino, C. F. (1987). Migration patterns among the elderly: A developmental perspective. *Gerontologist, 27,* 266–272.

Longino, C. F. (1984). Migration winners and losers. *American Demographics, 6,* 27–29.

Lopata, H. (1973). *Widowhood in an American city.* Cambridge, MA: Schenkman.

Lopata, H. (1978a). The absence of community resources in support systems of urban widows. *Family Coordinator, 27,* 383–388.

Lopata, H. (1978b). Contributions of extended families to the support systems of metropolitan area widows: Limitations of the modified kin network. *Journal of Marriage and the Family, 40,* 355–364.

Lopata, H. (1979). *Women as widows: Support systems.* Cambridge, MA: Schenkman.

Lowenthal, M. F., & Berkman, P. L. (1967). *Aging and mental disorder in San Francisco: A social psychiatric study.* San Francisco: Jossey-Bass.

Lowenthal, M. F., Thurnher, M., & Chiriboga, D. (1975). *Four stages of life: A comparative study of women and men facing transitions.* San Francisco: Jossey-Bass.

Lowy, L. (1980). Mental health services in the community. In J. E. Birren & R. B. Sloane (Eds.), *Handbook of mental health and aging.* Englewood Cliffs, NJ: Prentice-Hall.

Lubin, J. S. (1989, January 13). Alzheimer's linked to aluminum in water. *The Wall Street Journal,* pp. B2, 3.

Lund, D. A., Caserta, M. S., & Dimond, M. F. (1986). Gender differences through two years of bereavement among the elderly. *Gerontologist, 26,* 314–320.

Maas, H. S., & Kuypers, J. A. (1975). *From thirty to seventy: A forty-year study of adult life styles and personality.* San Francisco: Jossey-Bass.

MacDonald, L. M., & Butler, A. K. (1974). Reversal of helplessness: Producing walking behavior in nursing home wheelchair residents using behavior modification procedures. *Journal of Gerontology, 29,* 97–101.

Mace, N., & Rabins, P. (1984). Day care and dementia. *Generations, 9,* 41–45.

Maddox, G. L., & Douglass, E. B. (1973). Self-assessment of health: A longitudinal study of elderly subjects. *Journal of Health and Social Behavior, 14,* 87–93.

Mahoney, M. J. (1977). Reflections on the cognitive-learning trend in psychotherapy. *American Psychologist, 32,* 5–13.

Mancini, J. A. (1984). Research on family life in old age: Exploring the frontiers. In W. H. Quinn & G. A. Hughston (Eds.), *Independent aging: Family and social systems perspectives.* Rockville, MD: Aspen.

Manton, K. G., Blazer, D. G., & Woodbury, M. A. (1987). Suicide in middle age and later life: Sex and race specific life-table and cohort analyses. *Journal of Gerontology, 42,* 219–227.

Manton, K. G., Liu, K., & Cornelius, E. S. (1985). An analysis of the heterogeneity of U.S. nursing home patients. *Journal of Gerontology, 40,* 34–46.

Martin, C. E. (1981). Factors affecting sexual functioning in 60–79-year-old married males. *Archives of Sexual Behavior, 10,* 399–420.

Martin, G. (1985). Current views on the biology of aging. In R. N. Butler & A. G. Bearn (Eds.), *The aging process: Therapeutic implications.* New York: Raven.

Marx, J. L. (1974a). Aging research: (I). Cellular theories of senescence. *Science, 186,* 1105–1107.

Marx, J. L. (1974b). Aging research: (II). Pacemakers for aging? *Science, 186,* 1196–1197.

Masters, W. H., & Johnson, V. E. (1966). *Human sexual response.* Boston: Little, Brown.

Matthews, S. H., Rosenthal, C. J., & Marshall, V. W. (1986, November). *The incidence and prevalence of "women in the middle."* Paper presented at the 39th annual meeting of the Gerontological Society of America, Chicago.

Matthews, S. H., & Sprey, J. (1985). Adolescents' relationships with grandparents: An empirical contribution to conceptual clarification. *Journal of Gerontology, 40,* 621–626.

Mattoon, M. A. (1981). *Jungian psychology in perspective.* New York: Free Press.

Maurer, J. F., & Rupp, R. R. (1979). *Hearing and aging.* New York: Grune & Stratton.

Mazess, R. B., & Forman, S. H. (1979). Longevity and age exaggeration in Vilcabamba, Ecuador. *Journal of Gerontology, 34,* 94–98.

McClannahan, L. E. (1973). Therapeutic and prosthetic living environments for nursing home residents. *Gerontologist, 13,* 424–429.

McClelland, D. C. (1973). Testing for competence rather than for "intelligence." *American Psychologist, 28,* 1–14.

McCourt, W. F., Barnett, R. D., Brennan, J., & Becker, A. (1976). We help each other: Primary prevention for the widowed. *American Journal of Psychiatry, 140,* 98–100.

McCrae, R. R. (1982). Age differences in the use of coping machanisms. *Journal of Gerontology, 37,* 454–460.

McCrae, R. R., & Costa, P. T. (1984). *Emerging lives, enduring dispositions: Personality in adulthood.* Boston: Little, Brown.

McFarland, R. A., Tune, G. S., & Welford, A. T. (1964). On the driving of automobiles by older people. *Journal of Gerontology, 19,* 190–197.

McKhann, G., Drachman, D., Folstein, M., Katzman, R., Price, D., & Stadlan, E. M. (1984). Clinical diagnosis of Alzheimer's disease: Report of the NINCDS-ADRDA work group under the auspices of the Department of Health and Human Services task force on Alzheimer's disease. *Neurology, 34,* 939–944.

Medvedev, Z. A. (1974). Caucasus and Altay longevity: A biologic or social problem? *Gerontologist, 14,* 381–387.

Meerloo, J. A. (1961). Geriatric psychotherapy. *Acta Psychotherapeutica, 9,* 169–182.

Metzger, A. M. (1979-1980). A Q-methodological study of the Kübler-Ross stage theory. *Omega, 10,* 291–301.

Miller, B. C. (1976). A multivariate developmental model of marital satisfaction. *Journal of Marriage and the Family, 38,* 643–657.

Miller, M. (1979). *Suicide after sixty: The final alternative.* New York: Springer.

Miller, S., Blalock, J., & Ginsberg, H. (1984-1985). Children and the aged: Attitudes, contact, and discriminative ability. *International Journal of Aging and Human Development, 19,* 47–53.

Milligan, W. L., Powell, D. A., Harley, C., & Furchtgott, E. (1985). Physical health correlates of attitudes towards aging in the elderly. *Experimental Aging Research, 11,* 75–80.

Milne, J. S. (1976). Prevalence of incontinence in the elderly age groups. In F. L. Willington (Ed.), *Incontinence in the elderly.* New York: Academic Press.

Mitteness, L. (1987). The management of urinary incontinence by community-living elderly. *Gerontologist, 27,* 185–193.

Monea, H. E. (1978). The experiential approach in learning about sexuality in the aged. In R. L. Solnick (Ed.), *Sexuality and aging.* Los Angeles: University of Southern California Press.

Monk, A., & Kaye, L. (1982). The ombudsman volunteer in the nursing home: Differential role perceptions of patient representatives for the institutionalized aged. *Gerontologist, 22,* 194–199.

Moos, R., & Lemke, S. (1985). Specialized living environments for older people. In J. E. Birren & K. W. Schaie (Eds.), *Handbook of the psychology of aging* (2nd ed.). New York: Van Nostrand Reinhold.

Morgan, L. (1984). Changes in family interaction following widowhood. *Journal of Marriage and the Family, 49,* 323–331.

Murphy, C. (1985). Cognitive and chemosensory influences on age-related changes in the ability to identify blended foods. *Journal of Gerontology, 40,* 47–52.

Myers, G. C., & Manton, K. G. (1984). Compression of mortality: Myth or reality? *Gerontologist, 24,* 346–353.

National Home Caring Council. (1981). *All about home care.* New York: Author.

National Institute on Aging. (1983). *Medicine for the layman: The brain in aging and dementia* (NIH Publication No. 83-2625). Rockville, MD: Author.

Nehrke, M. F., Bellucci, G., & Gabriel, S. J. (1977-1978). Death anxiety, locus of control, and life-satisfaction in the elderly: Toward a definition of ego-integrity. *Omega, 8,* 359-368.

Netting, F. E., & Wilson, C. C. (1987). Current legislation concerning life care and continuing care contracts. *Gerontologist, 27,* 645-651.

Neugarten, B. L. (1964). Summary and implications. In B. L. Neugarten & Associates (Eds.), *Personality in middle and late life.* New York: Atherton.

Neugarten, B. L. (1977). Personality and aging. In J. E. Birren & K. W. Schaie (Eds.), *Handbook of the psychology of aging.* New York: Van Nostrand Reinhold.

Neugarten, B. L., & Associates (Eds.). (1964). *Personality in middle and late life.* New York: Atherton.

Neugarten, B. L., & Datan, N. (1975). Sociological perspectives on the life-cycle. In P. B. Baltes & K. W. Schaie (Eds.), *Lifespan developmental psychology: Personality and socialization.* New York: Academic Press.

Neugarten, B. L., & Gutmann, D. L. (1964). Age-sex roles and personality in middle age: A thematic apperception study. In B. L. Neugarten & Associates (Eds.), *Personality in middle and late life.* New York: Atherton.

Neugarten, B. L., Havinghurst, R. J., & Tobin, S. S. (1968). Personality and patterns of aging. In B. L. Neugarten (Ed.), *Middle age and aging: A reader in social psychology.* Chicago: University of Chicago Press.

Neugarten, B. L., & Weinstein, K. K. (1964). The changing American grandparent. *Journal of Marriage and the Family, 26,* 199–204.

Newman, G., & Nichols, C. R. (1960). Sexual activities and attitudes in older persons. *Journal of the American Medical Association, 173,* 33–35.

Newton, N. A., Brauer, D., Guttmann, D. L., & Grunes, J. (1986). Psychodynamic therapy with the aged: A review. *Clinical Gerontologist, 5,* 205–230.

Niederehe, G. (1986, November). *Depression and memory dysfunction in the aged.* Paper presented at the 39th annual meeting of the Gerontological Society of America, Chicago.

Niederehe, G., & Fruge, E. (1984). Dementia and family dynamics: Clinical research issues. *Journal of Geriatric Psychiatry, 17,* 21–55.

Noelker, L. S. (1987). Incontinence in elderly cared for by family. *Gerontologist, 27,* 194–200.

Noelker, L. S., & Poulshock, S. W. (1984). Intimacy: Factors affecting its development among members of a home for the aged. *International Journal of Aging and Human Development, 19,* 177–190.

Norman, T. R., & Burrows, G. D. (1984). Psychotropic drugs in the elderly. In D. W. Kay & G. D. Burrows (Eds.), *Handbook of studies on psychiatry and old age.* Netherlands: Elsevier Science Publishers.

Ogilvie, D. M. (1987). Life satisfaction and identity structure in late-middle-aged men and women. *Psychology and Aging, 2,* 217–224.

O'Hara, M. W., Hinrichs, J. V., Kohout, F. J., Wallace, R. B., & Lemke, J. H. (1986). Memory complaint and performance in the depressed elderly. *Psychology and Aging, 1,* 208–214.

Okraku, I. (1987). Age and attitudes toward multigenerational residence, 1973 to 1983. *Journal of Gerontology, 42,* 280–287.

Olsho, L. W., Harkins, S. W., & Lenhardt, M. L. (1985). Aging and the auditory system. In J. E. Birren & K. W. Schaie (Eds.), *Handbook of the psychology of aging* (2nd ed.), New York: Van Nostrand Reinhold.

Ordy, J. M., & Brizzee, K. R. (1979). Functional and structural age differences in the visual system of man and nonhuman primate models. In J. M. Ordy & K. R. Brizzee (Eds.), *Aging: Vol. 10. Sensory systems and communication in the elderly.* New York: Raven.

Ordy, J. M., Brizzee, K. R., Beavers, T., & Medart, P. (1979). Age differences in the functional and structural organization of the auditory system in man. In J. M. Ordy & K. R. Brizzee (Eds.), *Aging: Vol. 10. Sensory systems and communication in the elderly.* New York: Raven.

Osberg, J. S., McGinnis, G. E., DeJong, G., & Seward, M. (1987). Life satisfaction and quality of life among disabled elderly adults. *Journal of Gerontology, 42,* 228-230.

Ostfeld, A. M. (1975). Conference summary. In A. M. Ostfeld & C. P. Donnelly (Eds.), *Epidemiology of aging* (NIH Publication No. 75-711). Rockville, MD: U.S. Public Health Service.

Oyer, H. J., Kapur, Y. P., & Deal, L. V. (1976). Hearing disorders in the aging: Effects upon communication. In H. J. Oyer & E. J. Oyer (Eds.), *Aging and communication.* Baltimore: University Park Press.

Palmore, E. B. (1971a). Attitudes towards aging as shown by humor. *Gerontologist, 11,* 181–186.

Palmore, E. B. (1971b). The promise and problems of longevity studies. In E. B. Palmore & F. C. Jeffers (Eds.), *Prediction of the lifespan.* Lexington, MA: Heath.

Palmore, E. B, Burchett, B., Fillenbaum, G. G., George, L. K., & Wallman, L. M. (1985). *Retirement: Causes and consequences.* New York: Springer.

Palmore, E. B., & Cleveland, W. P. (1976). Aging, terminal decline, and terminal drop. *Journal of Gerontology, 31,* 76–81.

Palmore, E. B., Cleveland, W. P., Nowlin, J. B., Ramm, D., & Siegler, I. C. (1979). Stress and adaptation in later life. *Journal of Gerontology, 34,* 841–851.

Palmore, E. B., Nowlin, J. B., & Wang, H. S. (1985). Predictors of function among the old-old: A 10-year follow-up. *Journal of Gerontology, 40,* 244–250.

Parkes, C. (1972). *Bereavement: Studies of grief in adult life.* New York: International Universities Press.

Parkes, C. M., & Weiss, R. S. (1983). *Recovery from bereavement.* New York: Basic Books.

Peabody, C. A., Warner, D., Whiteford, H. A., & Hollister, L. E. (1987). Neuroleptics and the elderly. *Journal of the American Geriatrics Society, 35,* 233–238.

Pearlin, L. I., & Schooler, C. (1978). The structure of coping. *Journal of Health and Social Behavior, 19,* 2–21.

Pfeiffer, E. (1976). Psychotherapy with elderly patients. In L. Bellack & T. B. Karasu (Eds.), *Geriatric psychiatry: A handbook for psychiatrists and primary care physicians.* New York: Grune & Stratton.

Pfeiffer, E., & Davis, G. C. (1972). Determinants of sexual behavior in middle and old age. *Journal of the American Geriatrics Society, 20,* 151–158.

Pfeiffer, E., Verwoerdt, A., & Davis, G. C. (1972). Sexual behavior in middle life. *American Journal of Psychiatry, 128,* 1262–1267.

Pfeiffer, E., Verwoerdt, A., & Wang, H. S. (1968). Sexual behavior in aged men and women: 1. Observations on 254 community volunteers. *Archives of General Psychiatry, 19,* 753–758.

Pickett, J. M., Bergman, M., & Levitt, H. (1979). Aging and speech understanding. In J. M. Ordy & K. R. Brizzee (Eds.), *Aging: Vol. 10. Sensory systems and communication in the elderly.* New York: Raven.

Pieper, H. G., Petkovsek, L., & East, M. (1986, November). *Marriage among the elderly.* Paper delivered at the 39th annual meeting of the Gerontological Society of America, Chicago.

Pineo, P. (1969). Development patterns in marriage. *Family Coordinator, 18,* 135–140.

Planek, T. W., & Fowler, R. C. (1971). Traffic accident problems and exposure characteristics of the aging driver. *Journal of Gerontology, 26,* 224–230.

Plemons, J. K., Willis, S. L., & Baltes, P. B. (1978). Modifiability of fluid intelligence in aging: A short-term longitudinal training approach. *Journal of Gerontology, 33,* 224–231.

Poon, L. W. (1985). Differences in human memory with aging: Nature, causes and clinical implications. In J. E. Birren & K. W. Schaie (Eds.), *Handbook of the psychology of aging* (2nd ed.). New York: Van Nostrand Reinhold.

Poon, L. W., Fozard, J. L., Cermak, L. S., Arenberg, D., & Thompson, L. W. (Eds.). (1980). *New directions in memory and aging.* Hillside, NJ: Erlbaum.

Poon, L. W., Fozard, J. L., & Treat, N. J., (1978). From clinical and research findings on memory to intervention programs. *Experimental Aging Research, 4,* 235–253.

Poon, L. W., Gurland, B., Eisdorfer, C., Crook, T., Thompson, L. W., Kazniak, A. W., & Davis, K. L. (1986). Integration of experimental and clinical precepts in memory assessment: A tribute to George Talland. In L. W.

Poon (Ed.), *Handbook for clinical memory assessment of older adults*. Washington, DC: American Psychological Association.

Poon, L. W., Walsh-Sweeney, L., & Fozard, J. L. (1980). Memory skill training for the elderly: Salient issues on the use of imagery mnemonics. In L. W. Poon, J. L. Fozard, L. S. Cermak, D. Arenberg, & L. W. Thompson (Eds.), *New directions in memory and aging*. Hillsdale, NJ: Erlbaum.

Premo, T. (1984–1985). "A blessing to our declining years": Feminine response to filial duty in the new republic. *International Journal of Aging and Human Development, 20,* 69–74.

Proppe, H. (1968). Housing for the retired and the aged in southern California: An architectural commentary. *Gerontologist, 8,* 176–179.

Quinn, T. (1983). Personal and family adjustment in later life. *Journal of Marriage and the Family, 45,* 57–73.

Rabin, D. L., & Stockton, P. (1987). *Long-term care for the elderly: A factbook*. Oxford: Oxford University Press.

Rabins, P. V., Mace, H. L., & Lucas, M. J. (1982). The impact of dementia on the family. *Journal of the American Medical Association, 248,* 333-335.

Rahe, R. H. (1974). Life change and subsequent illness reports. In E. K. Gunderson & R. H. Rahe (Eds.), *Life stress and illness*. Springfield, IL: Charles C. Thomas.

Rando, T. A. (1984). *Grief, dying, and death: Clinical interventions for caregivers*. Champaign, IL: Research Press.

Raphael, B. (1977). Preventative intervention with the recently bereaved. *Archives of General Psychiatry, 34,* 1450–1454.

Rathbone-McCuan, E., & Coward, R. T. (1986). Respite and adult day-care services. In A. Monk (Ed.), *Handbook of gerontological services*. New York: Van Nostrand Reinhold.

Rea, M. P., Greenspoon, S., & Spilka, B. (1975–1976). Physicians and the terminal patient: Some selected attitudes and behavior. *Omega, 6,* 291–302.

Rebok, G., & Hoyer, W. J. (1977). The functional context of elderly behavior. *Gerontologist, 17,* 27–34.

Rebok, G. W., & Hoyer, W. J. Clients nearing death: Behavioral treatment perspectives. *Omega, 1979–1980, 10,* 191–201.

Redick, R., & Taube, C. (1980). Demography and mental health care of the aged. In J. E. Birren & R. B. Sloane (Eds.), *Handbook of mental health and aging*. Englewood Cliffs, NJ: Prentice-Hall.

Reichard, S., Livson, F., & Peterson, P. (1962). *Aging and personality*. New York: Wiley.

Reif, F., & Strauss, A. (1965). The impact of rapid discovery upon the scientist's career. *Social Problems, 12,* 299–311.

Reisberg, B. (1981). *Brain failure: An introduction to current concepts of senility*. New York: Free Press.

Retsinas, J., & Garrity, P. (1986). Going home: Analysis of nursing home discharges. *Gerontologist, 26,* 431-436.

Riegel, K. F. (1977). History of psychological gerontology. In J. E. Birren & K. W. Schaie (Eds.), *Handbook of the psychology of aging*. New York: Van Nostrand Reinhold.

Riegel, K. F., & Riegel, R. M. (1972). Development, drop, and death. *Developmental Psychology, 6,* 306–319.

Riegel, K. F., Riegel, R. M., & Meyer, G. (1967). A study of the dropout rates in longitudinal research on aging and the prediction of death. *Journal of Personality and Social Psychology, 5,* 342–348.

Riley, M., & Foner, A. (1968). *Aging and society: Vol. 1. An inventory of research findings*. New York: Russell Sage Foundation.

Robertson, J. F. (1977). Grandmotherhood: A study of role conceptions. *Journal of Marriage and the Family, 39,* 165–174.

Robertson, J. F., Tice, C. H., & Loeb, L. L. (1985). Grandparenthood: From knowledge to programs and policy. In V. L. Bengtson & J. F. Robertson (Eds.), *Grandparenthood*. Beverly Hills, CA: Sage.

Robinson, P., Coberly, S., & Paul, C. (1985). Work and retirement. In R. H. Binstock & E. Shanas (Eds.), *Handbook of aging and the social sciences* (2nd ed.). New York: Van Nostrand Reinhold.

Rodin, J. (1986a). Aging and health: Effects of the sense of control. *Science, 233,* 1271–1276.

Rodin, J. (1986b). Health, control, and aging. In M. M. Baltes & P. B. Baltes (Eds.), *The psychology of control and aging*. Hillsdale, NJ: Erlbaum.

Rodin, J., & Langer, E. (1977). Long-term effects of a control-relevant intervention with the institutionalized aged. *Journal of Personality and Social Psychology, 35,* 897–902.

Rodin, J., & Langer, E. (1980). Aging labels: The decline of control and the fall of self-esteem. *Journal of Social Issues, 36,* 12–29.

Rose, C. L., & Bell, B. (1971). *Predicting longevity: Methodology and critique*. Lexington, MA: Heath.

Rosen, J. L., & Neugarten, B. L. (1964). Ego functions in the middle and later years: A thematic apperception study. In B. L. Neugarten & Associates (Eds.), *Personality in middle and late life*. New York: Atherton.

Rosenthal, R. (1978). *The hearing loss handbook*. New York: Schocken Books.

Rosenwaike, I., & Dolinsky, A. (1987). The changing demographic determinants for the growth of the extreme aged. *Gerontologist, 27,* 275–280.

Roskies, E. (1980). Considerations in developing a treatment program for the coronary-prone (Type A) behavior pattern. In P. O. Davidson & S. M. Davidson (Eds.), *Behavioral medicine: Changing health lifestyles*. New York: Brunner/Mazel.

Rossman, I. (1977). Anatomic and body composition changes with aging. In C. E. Finch & L. Hayflick (Eds.), *Handbook of the biology of aging*. New York: Van Nostrand Reinhold.

Rossman, I. (1978). Clinical assessment in geriatrics. In G. L. Maddox (Conf. Chairman), *Assessment and evaluation strategies in aging: People, populations and programs*. Durham, NC: Duke University, Center for the Study of Aging and Human Development.

Rossman, P. (1977). *Hospice*. New York: Fawcett Columbine.

Roth, M. (1980). Aging of the brain and dementia: An overview. In L. Amaducci, A. N. Davison, & P. Antuono (Eds.), *Aging: Vol. 13. Aging of the brain and dementia*. New York: Raven.

Roth, M. (1985). Evidence on the possible heterogeneity of Alzheimer's disease and its bearing on future inquiries into etiology and treatment. In R. N. Butler & A. G. Bearn (Eds.), *The aging process: Therapeutic implications*. New York: Raven.

Roth, M., & Kay, D. W. K. (1956). Affective disorder arising in the senium: II. Physical disability as an aetiological factor. *Journal of Mental Science, 102*, 141–150.

Roth, M., Tomlinson, B. E., & Blessed, G. (1966). Correlation between scores for dementia and counts of "senile plaques" in cerebral grey matter of elderly subjects. *Nature, 209*, 109–110.

Rubenstein, L. A., Josephson, K. R., Weiland, G. D, English, P. A., Sayre, J. A., & Kane, R. L. (1984). Effectiveness of a geriatric evaluation unit: A randomized trial. *New England Journal of Medicine, 331*, 1664–1670.

Rubinstein, R. (1984). Old men living alone: Social networks and informal supports. In W. H. Quinn & G. A. Hughston (Eds.), *Independent aging: Family and social systems perspectives*. Rockville, MD: Aspen.

Rubinstein, R. (1986). The construction of a day by elderly widowers. *International Journal of Aging and Human Development, 23*, 161–173.

Rush, A. J., Khatami, M., & Beck, A. T. (1975). Cognitive and behavior therapy in chronic depression. *Behavior Therapy, 6*, 398–404.

Salthouse, T. A. (1980). Age and memory: Strategies for localizing the loss. In L. W. Poon, J. L. Fozard, L. S. Cermak, D. Arenberg, & L. Thompson (Eds.), *New directions in memory and aging*. Hillsdale, NJ: Erlbaum.

Salthouse, T. A. (1985). Speed of behavior and its implications for cognition. In J. E. Birren & K. W. Schaie (Eds.), *Handbook of the psychology of aging* (2nd ed.). New York: Van Nostrand Reinhold.

Salthouse, T. A., & Somberg, B. L. (1982). Skilled performance: The effects of adult age and experience on elementary processes. *Journal of Experimental Psychology: General, 111*, 176–207.

Sathananthan, G. L., & Gershon, S. (1975). Cerebral vasodilators: A review. In S. Gershon & A. Raskin (Eds.), *Aging: Vol. 2. Genesis and treatment of psychologic disorders in the elderly*. New York: Raven.

Satir, V. M. (1967). *Conjoint family therapy: A guide to theory and technique* (Rev. ed.). Palo Alto, CA: Science and Behavior Books.

Saxon, M. J., & Etten, S. V. (1978). *Physical change and aging: A guide for the helping professions*. New York: Tiresias Press.

Schaie, K. W. (1965). A general model for the study of developmental problems. *Psychological Bulletin, 64*, 92–107.

Schaie, K. W. (1974). Translations in gerontology—from lab to life: Intellectual functioning. *American Psychologist, 29*, 802–807.

Schaie, K. W. (1977–1978). Towards a stage theory of adult cognitive development. *International Journal of Aging and Human Development, 8*, 129–138.

Schaie, K. W., (1978). External validity in the assessment of intellectual development in adulthood. *Journal of Gerontology, 33*, 695–701.

Schaie, K. W. (1980). Intelligence and problem solving. In J. E. Birren & R. B. Sloane (Eds.), *Handbook of mental health and aging*. Englewood Cliffs, NJ: Prentice-Hall.

Schaie, K. W., & Baltes, P. B. (1977). Some faith helps to see the forest: A final comment on the Horn and Donaldson myth of the Baltes-Schaie position on adult intelligence. *American Psychologist, 32*, 1118–1120.

Scheidt, B. J., & Schaie, K. W. (1978). A taxonomy of situations for an elderly population: Generating situational criteria. *Journal of Gerontology, 33*, 848–857.

Scheinberg, P. (1978). Multi-infarct dementia. In R. Katzman, R. D. Terry, & K. Bick (Eds.), *Aging: Vol. 7. Alzheimer's disease: Senile dementia and related disorders*. New York: Raven.

Schiffman, S. (1977). Food recognition by the elderly. *Journal of Gerontology, 32*, 586–592.

Schiffman, S. (1979). Changes in taste and smell with age: Psychophysiological aspects. In J. M. Ordy & K. R. Brizzee (Eds.), *Aging: Vol. 10. Sensory systems and communication in the elderly*. New York: Raven.

Schiffman, S., & Pasternak, M. (1979). Decreased discrimination of food odors in the elderly. *Journal of Gerontology, 34*, 73–79.

Schmidt, D., & Boland, S. (1986). Structure of perceptions of older adults: Evidence for multiple stereotypes. *Psychology and Aging, I*, 255–260.

Schneider, E. L., & Reed, D. (1985). Modulations of aging processes. In C. E. Finch & E. L. Schneider (Eds.), *Handbook of the biology of aging* (2nd ed.). New York: Van Nostrand Reinhold.

Schram, R. (1979). Marital satisfaction over the family life cycle: A critique and a proposal. *Journal of Marriage and the Family, 41,* 7–12.

Schultz, R. (1985). Emotion and affect. In J. E. Birren & K. W. Schaie (Eds.), *Handbook of the psychology of aging* (2nd ed.). New York: Van Nostrand Reinhold.

Schurman, R. A., Kramer, P. D., & Mitchell, J. B. (1985). The hidden mental health network. *Archives of General Psychiatry, 42,* 89–94.

Schwartz, A. N. (1975). Planning micro-environments for the aged. In D. S. Woodruff & J. E. Birren (Eds.). *Aging: Scientific perspectives and social issues.* New York: D. Van Nostrand.

Schwartz, G. E., & Weiss, S. M. (1977). What is behavioral medicine? *Psychosomatic Medicine, 39,* 377–381.

Seligman, M. E. P. (1975). *Helplessness: On depression, development and death.* San Francisco: W. H. Freeman.

Selmanowitz, V. J., Rizer, R. L., & Orentreich, N. (1977). Aging of the skin and its appendages. In C. E. Finch & L. Hayflick (Eds.), *Handbook of the biology of aging.* New York: Van Nostrand Reinhold.

Shanas, E. (1962). *The health of older people: A social survey.* Cambridge, MA: Harvard University Press.

Shanas, E. (1979a). The family as a social support system in old age. *Gerontologist, 19,* 169–174.

Shanas, E. (1979b). Social myth as hypothesis: The case of the family relations of old people. *Gerontologist, 19,* 3–9.

Shanas, E. (1980). Older people and their families: The new pioneers. *Journal of Marriage and the Family, 42,* 9–15.

Shanas, E. (1984). Old parents and middle-aged children: The four- and five-generation family. *Journal of Geriatric Psychiatry, 17,* 7–19.

Shanas, E., & Maddox, G. L. (1985). Health, health resources and the utilization of care. In R. H. Binstock & E. Shanas (Eds.), *Handbook of aging and the social sciences* (2nd ed.). New York: Van Nostrand Reinhold.

Sharps, M. J., & Gollin, E. S. (1988). Aging and free recall for objects located in space. *Journal of Gerontology, 43,* 8–11.

Shenfeld, M. E. (1984–1985). The developmental course of defense mechanisms in later life. *International Journal of Aging and Human Development, 19,* 55–71.

Sheppard, H. L. (1976). Work and retirement. In E. Shanas & R. H. Binstock (Eds.), *Handbook of aging and the social sciences.* New York: Van Nostrand Reinhold.

Sherizen, S., & Paul, L. (1977–1978). Dying in a hospital intensive care unit: The social significance for the family of the patient. *Omega, 8,* 29–40.

Sherwood, S., Glassman, J., Sherwood, C., & Morris, J. N. (1974). Preinstitutionalization factors as predictors of adjustment to a long-term care facility. *International Journal of Aging and Human Development, 5,* 95–105.

Sherwood, S., & Mor, V. (1980). Mental health institutions and the elderly. In J. E. Birren & R. B. Sloane (Eds.), *Handbook of mental health and aging.* Englewood Cliffs, NJ: Prentice-Hall.

Shin, K. E., & Putnam, R. H. (1982). Age and academic-professional honors. *Journal of Gerontology, 37,* 220–227.

Shneidman, E. S. (1976). Death work and stages of dying. In E. Shneidman (Ed.), *Death: Current perspectives.* Palo Alto, CA: Mayfield.

Shneidman, E. S., & Farberow, N. L. (1961). Statistical comparisons between attempted and committed suicides. In N. L. Farberow & E. S. Shneidman (Eds.), *The cry for help.* New York: McGraw-Hill.

Shock, N. W. (1977). Biological theories of aging. In J. E. Birren & K. W. Schaie (Eds.), *Handbook of the psychology of aging.* New York: Van Nostrand Reinhold.

Shock, N. W., Greulich, R. C., Andres, R., Arenberg, D., Costa, P. T., Lakatta, E. G., & Tobin, J. D. (Eds.). (1984). *Normal human aging: The Baltimore longitudinal study of aging* (NIH Publication No. 84–2450). Washington, DC: U.S. Public Health Service.

Shomaker, D. (1987). Problematic behavior and the Alzheimer patient: Retrospection as a method of understanding and counseling. *Gerontologist, 27,* 370–375.

Shultz, R. (1985). Emotion and affect. In J. E. Birren & K. W. Schaie (Eds.), *Handbook of the psychology of aging* (2nd ed.). New York: Van Nostrand Reinhold.

Siegler, I. C., & Costa, P. T. (1985). Health behavior relationships. In J. E. Birren & K. W. Schaie (Eds.), *Handbook of the psychology of aging* (2nd ed.). New York: Van Nostrand Reinhold.

Silverman, P. (1981). *Helping women cope with grief.* Beverly Hills, CA: Sage.

Simberg, E. J. (1985). Psychoanalysis of the older patient. *Journal of the American Psychoanalytic Association, 33,* 117–132.

Simonson, W. (1984). *Medications and the elderly: A guide for promoting proper use.* Rockville, MD: Aspen.

Simonton, D. K. (1975a). Age and literary creativity: A cross-cultural and transhistorical survey. *Journal of Cross-Cultural Psychology, 6,* 259–277.

Simonton, D. K. (1975b). The sociocultural context of individual creativity: A transhistorical time series analysis. *Journal of Personality and Social Psychology, 32,* 1119–1133.

Simonton, D. K. (1977a). Creative productivity, age, and stress: A biographical time series analysis of 10 classical composers. *Journal of Personality and Social Psychology, 35,* 791–804.

Simonton, D. K. (1977b). Eminence, creativity, and geographic marginality: A recursive structural equation model. *Journal of Personality and Social Psychology, 35,* 805–816.

Sinnott, J. D. (1986). Prospective/intentional and incidental everyday memory: Effects of age and passage of time. *Psychology and Aging, 1,* 110–116.

Sloane, R. B. (1980). Organic brain syndrome. In J. E. Birren & R. B. Sloane (Eds.), *Handbook of mental health and aging.* Englewood Cliffs, NJ: Prentice-Hall.

Smith, A. D. (1980). Age differences in encoding, storage and retrieval. In L. W. Poon, J. L. Fozard, L. S. Cermak, D. Arenberg, & L. Thompson (Eds.), *New directions in memory and aging.* Hillsdale, NJ: Erlbaum.

Smith, W. L., & Kinsbourne, M. (Eds.). *Aging and dementia.* Jamaica, NY: Spectrum.

Snyder, L. H., Pyrek, J., & Smith, K. C. (1976). Vision and mental function of the elderly. *Gerontologist, 16,* 491–495.

Solnick, R. L. (1978). Sexual responsiveness, age, and change: Facts and potential. In R. L. Solnick (Ed.), *Sexuality and aging.* Los Angeles: University of California Press.

Solomon, K., & Vickers, R. (1979). Attitudes of health workers towards old people. *Journal of the American Geriatrics Society, 27,* 186–191.

Spirduso, W. W. (1975). Reaction and movement time as a function of age and physical activity level. *Journal of Gerontology, 30,* 435–440.

Srole, L., Langner, T. S., Michael, S. T., Opler, M. K., & Rennie, T. A. C. (1962). *Mental health in the metropolis: The midtown Manhattan study* (Vol. 1). New York: McGraw-Hill.

Stankov, L. (1988). Aging, attention, and intelligence. *Psychology and Aging, 3,* 59–74.

Stenback, A. (1980). Depression and suicidal behavior in old age. In J. E. Birren & R. B. Sloane (Eds.), *Handbook of mental health and aging.* Englewood Cliffs, NJ: Prentice-Hall.

Steuer, J. L., Mintz, J., Hammen, C. L., Hill, M., Jarvik, L. F., McCarley, T., Motoike, P., & Rosen, R. (1984). Cognitive-behavioral and psychodynamic group psychotherapy in treatment of geriatric depression. *Journal of Consulting and Clinical Psychology, 52,* 180–189.

Stine, E. L., & Wingfield, A. (1988). Memorability functions as an indicator of qualitative age differences in text recall. *Psychology and Aging, 3,* 179–183.

Stoller, E. P. (1983). Parental caregiving by adult children. *Journal of Marriage and the Family, 45,* 851–858.

Stotsky, B. (1975). Psychoactive drugs for geriatric patients with psychiatric disorders. In S. Gershon & A. Raskin (Eds.), *Aging: Vol. 2. Genesis and treatment of psychologic disorders in the elderly.* New York: Raven.

Strate, J. M., & Dubnoff, S. J. (1986). How much income is enough? Measuring the income adequacy of retired persons using a survey based approach. *Journal of Gerontology, 41,* 393–400.

Strehler, B. (1962). *Time, cells, and aging.* New York: Academic Press.

Streib, G., & Schneider, C. J. (1971). *Retirement in American society: Impact and process.* Ithaca, NY: Cornell University Press.

Summers, M. N., Haley, W. E., Reveile, D. J., & Alarcon, G. S. (1988). Radiographic assessment and psychologic variables as predictors of pain and functional impairment in osteoarthritis of the knee or hip. *Arthritis and Rheumatism, 31,* 204–209.

Sward, K. (1945). Age and mental ability in superior men. *American Journal of Psychology, 58,* 443–479.

Swenson, C. (1982). A curriculum for training psychologists for work with the aging. In J. F. Santos & G. R. Vandenbos (Eds.), *Psychology and the older adult: Challenges for training in the 1980s.* Washington, DC: American Psychological Association.

Swenson, C. H., & Trahaug, G. (1985). Commitment and the long-term marriage relationship. *Journal of Marriage and the Family, 47,* 939–944.

Terry, R. D., & Wisneiwski, H. (1977). Structural aspects of aging of the brain. In C. Eisdorfer & R. O. Freidel (Eds.), *Cognitive and emotional disturbance in the elderly.* Chicago: Yearbook Medical Publishers.

Thomas, J. L. (1986). Age and sex differences in perceptions of grandparenting. *Journal of Gerontology, 41,* 417–423.

Thomas, P. D., Hunt, W. C., Garry, P. J., Hood, R. B., Goodwin, J. M., & Goodwin, J. S. (1983). Hearing acuity in a healthy elderly population: Effects on emotional, cognitive, and social status. *Journal of Gerontology, 38,* 321–325.

Thompson, L. W., Davies, R., Gallagher, D., & Krantz, S. (1986). Cognitive therapy with older adults. *Clinical Gerontologist, 5,* 245–280.

Thompson, L. W., Eisdorfer, C., & Estes, E. H. (1970). Cardiovascular disease and behavioral changes in the elderly. In E. B. Palmore (Ed.), *Normal aging.* Durham, NC: Duke University Press.

Tibbetts, C. (1979). Can we invalidate negative stereotypes of aging? *Gerontologist, 19,* 10–20.

Tissue, T. (1972). Another look at self-rated health among the elderly. *Journal of Gerontology, 27,* 91–94.

Tobin, J. D. (1977). Normal aging—the inevitability syndrome. In S. H. Zarit (Ed.), *Readings in aging and death: Contemporary perspectives.* New York: Harper & Row.

Tobin, J. D., & Andres, R. (1979). *Diabetes and aging.* (NIH Publication No. 79-1408). Washington, DC: National Institute on Aging Science Writer Seminar Series. U.S. Public Health Service.

Tobin, S. S. (1980). Institutionalization of the aged. In N. Datan & N. Lohmann (Eds.), *Transitions of aging.* New York: Academic Press.

Tomlinson, B. (1977). Morphological changes and dementia in old age. In W. L. Smith & M. Kinsbourne (Eds.), *Aging and dementia.* Jamaica, New York: Spectrum.

Tomlinson, B. (1984). The pathology of Alzheimer's disease and senile dementia of Alzheimer type. In D. W. Kay & G. D. Burrows (Eds.), *Handbook of studies on psychiatry and old age.* Netherlands: Elsevier.

Traupmann, J., & Hatfield, E. (1981). Love and its effect on mental and physical health. In R. Fogel, S. Kiesler, & J. March (Eds.), *Aging: Stability and change in the family.* New York: Academic Press.

Treas, J., & Van Hilst, A. (1976). Marriage and remarriage rates among older Americans. *Gerontologist, 16,* 132–136.

Treat, N. J., Poon, L. W., Fozard, J. L., & Popkin, S. J. (1978). Toward applying cognitive skill training to memory problems. *Experimental Aging Research, 4,* 305–319.

Treat, N. J., & Reese, H. W. (1976). Age, pacing, and imagery in paired associate learning. *Developmental Psychology, 12,* 119–124.

Troll, L. E. (1971). The family of later life: A decade review. *Journal of Marriage and the Family, 33,* 263–290.

Troll, L. E. (1983). Grandparents: The family watchdogs. In T. Brubaker (Ed.), *Family relationships in later life.* Beverly Hills, CA: Sage.

Turner, B. F., Tobin, S. S., & Lieberman, M. A. (1972). Personality traits as predictors of institutional adaptation among the aged. *Journal of Gerontology, 27,* 61–68.

U.S. Commission on Civil Rights. (1979). *The age discrimination study: A report of the U.S. Commission on Civil Rights.* (Part II). Washington, DC: U.S. Government Printing Office.

U.S. Senate Special Committee on Aging. (1984). *Aging America: Trends and projections* (1985–1986 ed.). Washington, DC: U.S. Department of Health and Human Services.

U.S. Senate Special Committee on Aging. (1987). *Aging America: Trends and projections* (1987–1988 ed.). Washington, DC: U.S. Department of Health and Human Services.

Usui, W., Keil, T. J., & Durig, K. R. (1985). Socioeconomic comparisons and life satisfaction of elderly adults. *Journal of Gerontology, 40,* 110–114.

Vaughan, W. J., Schmitz, P., & Fatt, I. (1979). The human lens—a model system for the study of aging. In J. M. Ordy & K. R. Brizzee (Eds.), *Aging: Vol. 10. Sensory systems and communication in the elderly.* New York: Raven.

Verwoerdt, A., Pfeiffer, E., & Wang, H. S. (1969, February). Sexual behavior in senescence: 2. Patterns of sexual activity and interest. *Geriatrics,* pp. 137–154.

Vincente, L., Wiley, J., & Carrington, A. (1979). The risk of institutionalization before death. *Gerontologist, 19,* 361–367.

Viney, L. L. (1984–1985). Loss of life and loss of bodily integrity: Two different sources of threat for people who are ill. *Omega, 15,* 207–220.

Viney, L. L., & Westbrook, M. (1986–1987). Is there a pattern of psychological reactions to chronic illness which is associated with death? *Omega, 17,* 169–180.

Walford, R. L. (1969). *The immunologic theory of aging.* Baltimore: Williams & Wilkins.

Walford, R. L. (1983). *Maximum lifespan.* New York: Avon.

Walker, A. J., & Thompson, L. (1983). Intimacy and intergenerational aid and contact among mothers and daughters. *Journal of Marriage and the Family, 45,* 841–848.

Walker, J. I., & Brodie, K. H. (1980). Neuropharmacology of aging. In E. W. Busse & D. G. Blazer (Eds.), *Handbook of geriatric psychiatry.* New York: Van Nostrand Reinhold.

Wang, H. S. (1977). Dementia of old age. In W. L. Smith & M. Kinsbourne (Eds.), *Aging and dementia.* Jamaica, New York: Spectrum.

Wasow, M., & Loeb, M. B. (1978). Sexuality in nursing homes. In R. L. Solnick (Ed.), *Sexuality and aging.* Los Angeles: University of California Press.

Watson, W. H., & Maxwell, R. J. (1977). *Human aging and dying.* New York: St. Martin's Press.

Waxman, H. M., McCreary, G., Weinrit, R. M., & Carner, E. A. (1985). A comparison of somatic complaints among depressed and non-depressed older persons. *Gerontologist, 25,* 501–507.

Wechsler, D. (1955). *Manual for the Wechsler Adult Intelligence Scale.* New York: Psychological Corporation.

Wechsler, D. (1981). *WAIS-R manual.* New York: Psychological Corporation.

Weinberger, M., Darnell, J. C., Martz, B. L., Hiner, S. L., Neill, P. C., & Tierney, W. M. (1986). The effects of positive and negative life changes on the self-reported health status of elderly adults. *Journal of Gerontology, 41,* 114–119.

Weiner, J. M., Ehrenworth, D. A., & Spense, D. A. (1987). Private long-term care insurance: Cost, coverage, and restrictions. *Gerontologist, 27,* 487–493.

Weisman, A. D. (1976). Denial and middle knowledge. In E. Shneidman (Ed.), *Death: Current perspectives.* Palo Alto, CA: Mayfield.

Weisman, A. D., & Worden, J. W. (1975–1976). Psychosocial analysis of cancer deaths. *Omega, 6,* 61–75.

Weismann, M. M., Myers, J. K., Tischler, G. L., Holtzer, C. E., III, Leaf, P. J., Orvascel, H., & Brody, J. A. (1985). Psychiatric disorders (DSM-III) and cognitive impairment among the elderly in a U.S. urban community. *Acta Psychiatrica Scandinavica, 71,* 366–379.

Welford, A. T. (1969). Age and skill: Motor, intellectual, and social. In A. T. Welford (Ed.), *Interdisciplinary topics in gerontology: (4). Decision making and age.* Basel: Karger.

Welford, A. T. (1977). Motor performance. In J. E. Birren & K. W. Schaie (Eds.), *Handbook of the psychology of aging.* New York: Van Nostrand Reinhold.

Welford, A. T. (1984). Between bodily changes and performance: Some possible reasons for slowing with age. *Experimental Aging Research, 10,* 73–88.

West, R. (1985). *Memory fitness after forty.* Gainesville, FL: Triad Press.

Whitbourne, S. (1976). Test anxiety in elderly and young adults. *International Journal of Aging and Human Development, 7,* 201–210.

Whitbourne, S. (1985). *The aging body: Physiological changes and psychological consequences.* New York: Springer-Verlag.

Wilkie, F., & Eisdorfer, C. (1973). Systemic disease and behavioral correlates. In L. F. Jarvik, C. Eisdorfer, & J. E. Blum (Eds.), *Intellectual functioning in adults.* New York: Springer.

Williams, T. F. (1986). Geriatrics: The fruition of the clinician reconsidered. *Gerontologist, 26,* 345–349.

Willis, S. L., & Baltes, P. B. (1980). Intelligence in adulthood and aging: Contemporary issues. In L. W. Poon (Ed.), *Aging in the 1980s.* Washington, DC: American Psychological Association.

Wilson, K. B., & DeShane, M. R. (1982). Legal rights of grandparents: A preliminary discussion. *Gerontologist 22,* 67–71.

Wolpe, J. (1973). *The practice of behavior therapy* (2nd ed.). New York: Pergamon Press.

Wood, V., & Robertson, J. F. (1978). Friendship and kinship interaction: Differential effect on the morale of the elderly. *Journal of Marriage and the Family, 40,* 367–375.

Woodruff, D. S., & Walsh, D. A. (1975). Research in adult learning: The individual. *Gerontologist, 15,* 424–430.

Worden, J. W. (1982). *Grief counseling and grief therapy.* New York: Springer.

Yalom, I. D. (1975). *The theory and practice of group psychotherapy* (2nd ed.). New York: Basic Books.

Yeo, G., Ingram, L., Skurnick, J., & Crapo, L. (1987). Effects of a geriatric clinic on functional health and well-being of elders. *Journal of Gerontology, 42,* 252–258.

Zarit, S. H. (1980). *Aging and mental disorders: Psychological approaches to assessment and treatment.* New York: Free Press.

Zarit, S. H., Cole, K. D., & Guider, R. L. (1981). Memory training strategies and subjective complaints of memory in the aged. *Gerontologist, 21,* 158–164.

Zarit, S. H., Orr, N., & Zarit, J. (1985). *The hidden victims of Alzheimer's disease: Families under stress.* New York: New York University Press.

Zarit, S. H., Todd, P. A., & Zarit, J. M. (1986). Subjective burden of husbands and wives as caregivers: A longitudinal study. *Gerontologist, 26,* 260–266.

Zarit, S. H., & Zarit, J. M. (1984). Depression in later life: Theory and assessment. In J. P. Abrahams & V. Crooks (Eds.), *Geriatric mental health.* New York: Grune & Stratton.

Zelinski, E. M., & Miura, S. A. (1988). Effects of thematic information on script memory in young and old adults. *Psychology and Aging, 3,* 292–299.

Zimmer, J. G., Groth-Juncker, A., & McCusker, J. (1985). A randomized controlled study of a home health care team. *American Journal of Public Health, 75,* 134–141.

Zuckerman, H., & Merton, R. K. (1972). Age, aging, and age structure in science. In M. Riley, M. Johnson, & A. Foner (Eds.), *Aging and society: Vol. 3. A sociology of age stratification.* New York: Russell Sage Foundation.

Name Index

□

Abernethy, V., 337
Abrahams, J. P., 86
Adams, G., 50, 62, 96, 99
Ade-Ridder, L., 199
Adelman, R., 97, 114
Aizenberg, R., 198, 199, 201, 207, 208, 209, 330
Alarcon, G. S., 53
Aldous, J., 210, 214, 215
Aldrich, C. K., 58
Allison, P., 165
Allan, C., 259
Altolz, J., 309
Ambrogli, D. M., 108
American Association of Retired Persons (AARP), 89
American Psychiatric Association, 258
Anderson, B., 68, 69, 74
Anderson, T., 249
Andres, R., 46, 47, 135, 179, 184
Antonoff, S., 334
Arenberg, D., 47, 135, 146, 148, 179, 181, 184
Arling, G., 210, 211
Atchley, R. C., 201, 203, 234
Austrin, H. R., 329
Avolio, B. J., 3

Baldessarini, R. J., 312, 314
Baltes, N. N., 140
Baltes, P. B., 24, 126, 127, 130, 136, 138, 139, 140
Bank, L., 98
Barabano, H. E., 179
Barer, B. M., 219
Barnes, D., 267
Barnett, R. D., 250
Barney, J., 108, 112
Barrett, G. V., 3
Bartolucci, A. A., 270, 271
Bass, D. M., 269, 343
Baum, S. A., 98
Beamish, P., 259
Beavers, T., 75, 78
Beck, A. T., 274, 278, 304
Beck, J. C., 96, 97
Beck, P., 155
Becker, A., 250
Becker, J., 274, 276, 277
Béland, 102
Bell, B., 55, 71
Bellucci, G., 331
Belsky, J. K., 103, 154, 202, 236, 282
Benet, S., 41

Bengtson, V., 210
Bengtson, V. L., 175, 176, 181, 199, 212
Bennett, R., 3
Berezin, M. A., 20, 299
Bergman, M., 76
Bergmann, K., 257, 258, 259, 262
Bergner, M., 52, 54
Berkman, P. L., 209, 259
Berry, J. W., 270
Bersoff, D. N., 135
Betts, D., 311
Biber, H., 327
Bibring, E., 277
Biggar, J. C., 210
Biringen, Z. C., 175
Birkhill, W. R., 130
Birnbom, F., 311
Birren, J. E., 70, 71, 82, 83, 85, 86, 132, 135
Blackburn, J. A., 140
Blalock, J., 4
Blanchard-Fields, F., 136, 137, 183
Blazer, D. G., 42, 260, 262, 274, 275, 279, 280, 311
Blessed, G., 264
Bloch, A., 193
Block, M. R., 192
Block, R. I., 314
Blood, R. O., 200
Blum, J. E., 134, 296, 302
Boland, S., 5
Borson, S., 269
Bosse, R., 228, 234
Botwinick, J., 67, 68, 69, 70, 71, 86, 122, 123, 124, 125, 132, 189
Bourestom, N. C., 108, 109
Bowlby, J., 240, 241
Bozian, M. W., 89
Branch, L., 104
Branscomb, A. B., 329
Brash, D. E., 42
Brauer, D., 295, 296, 298
Braun, K. L., 99
Brecher, E. M., 190, 192, 207
Breckinridge, J. N., 241, 244
Brennan, J., 250
Brizzee, K. R., 70, 71, 75, 78
Brodie, K. H., 312
Brody, E. M., 110, 198, 210, 211, 212, 213
Brody, J. A., 259
Brook, P., 317
Brotman, H., 259

Brown, S. L., 214, 270, 271, 320
Brubaker, E., 214
Brubaker, T. H., 199, 205, 214
Buchanan, J. G., 291
Buell, S. J., 126
Bulcroft, K., 205
Bultena, G. L., 4
Burchett, B., 225, 229, 237
Burke, B., 294
Burns, B. J., 290, 291
Burrows, G. D., 312
Bursk, B. J., 212, 311
Busse, E. W., 29, 31, 40, 42, 275, 277
Butler, A. K., 18
Butler, R. N., 3, 96, 132, 193, 308

Caldwell, D., 336
Cameron, P., 327
Campbell, D., 174, 181
Campbell, T. W., 337
Candy, S., 105
Canestrari, R., 149
Canfield, C. G., 273
Cantor, M. H., 203, 211, 212, 311
Capitman, J. A., 102, 212
Carner, E. A., 274, 275
Carnes, M., 97
Carp, F. M., 58, 176
Carrington, A., 106
Carter, R. B., 52, 54
Carter, W. J., 94
Carver, E. J., 292
Caserta, M. S., 105, 243, 245
Casperson, R. C., 71
Catalano, D., 203, 211, 212
Cath, S. H., 176, 295
Cattell, R. B., 124
Cermak, L. S., 146
Chapman, C. R., 148
Charles, D. C., 135
Charon, R., 97
Chenoweth, B., 260
Cherlin, A., 210, 215, 216, 217, 218
Chernoff, R., 94
Chinn, N. M., 273
Chiriboga, D., 174
Chirikos, T., 94
Christenson, C. V., 192
Cicirelli, V., 199, 207, 209
Clark, E. T., 134
Clark, H. M., 89
Clark, N. M., 214
Clayton, P. J., 244
Cleveland, W. P., 134, 239
Coberly, S., 230
Coe, R. M., 216
Cogan, D., 68
Cohen, K. P., 340
Cohler, B. J., 208
Cohn, R. M., 228
Colavita, F., 69, 71

Cole, C. L., 199
Cole, J. O., 318
Cole, K., 155
Cole, P., 311
Cole, S., 164
Coleman, P. D., 126
Comfort, A., 40, 42, 44
Conley, J. J., 204
Consumer Reports Book Editors, 190, 192, 200, 207
Coolidge, F. L., 330, 331
Cooney, T. M., 134
Cooper, A. F., 79
Cooper, K. L., 175
Copeland, J. R. M., 273
Copeland, R., 258
Corby, N., 189, 193
Cornelius, E. S., 109
Cornelius, S. W., 126
Cornoni-Huntley, J., 179
Corso, J. F., 74
Costa, P. T., 47, 58, 133, 135, 174, 179, 180, 181, 184, 326, 331
Coward, R. T., 103
Craig, W. A., 97
Craik, F. I. M., 146, 147
Crapo, L., 97
Cromer, W. J., 290, 291
Crook, T., 151, 153, 267, 318
Cuber, J., 202
Cumming, E. W., 171, 176, 187
Cunningham, D. A., 56
Curry, A. R., 79
Cyrus-Lutz, C., 296

Dambrot, F. H., 343
Darnell, J. C., 58
Datan, N., 182
Davidson, J. L., 192
Davidson, P. O., 60
Davidson, S. M., 60
Davies, R., 276, 306, 307
Davis, G. C., 191, 344
Davis, J. M., 279
Davis, K. L., 151, 153
Deal, L. V., 76, 79
Dean, L. L., 258
de Beauvoir, S., 48
Degun, G., 317
Deimling, G. T., 269
DeJong, G. F., 93, 235
Dembrowski, T., 61
Dennis, W., 158, 159, 160, 161
Depner, C. E., 202
DeShane, M. R., 218, 219
De Voe, M., 314
Dickinson, G. E., 345
Dimond, M. F., 243, 245
Dolinsky, A., 8, 198
Donaldson, G., 138, 139
Donner, A. D., 56
Doppelt, J. E., 122

Dorfman, L., 236
Douglas, E. B., 98
Drachman, D., 271, 284
Drinka, T., 97
Dubnoff, 232
Dubois, P. M., 334
Durig, K. R., 232

East, M., 206
Eastham, J., 203, 271
Eckman, J., 3
Edwards, P. B., 235
Ehrenworth, D. A., 100
Eichorn, G. L., 40
Eisdorfer, C., 73, 123, 133, 148, 151, 153
Eissler, K. R., 345
Ekerdt, D., 228, 229, 234
Ell, K., 182
Ellithorpe, E., 209
Engen, T., 80
English, P. A., 97
Epley, R. J., 336
Epstein, L. J., 274, 275
Erikson, E., 23, 24, 328
Erikson, R. C., 150, 151, 152, 153
Estes, E. H., 133
Etten, S. V., 72, 74
Evans, L., 228

Falik, A., 134
Farberow, N. L., 280
Fatt, I., 69
Feifel, H., 329
Feinson, M. C., 245, 259
Feldman, S. S., 175
Felton, B. J., 183
Fengler, A. P., 204
Feuerberg, M. A., 290, 292
Field, D., 133
Fillenbaum, G. G., 225, 228, 229, 237
Fillit, H. M., 265
Fischer, L. R., 212
Fish, C. E., 330, 331
Fiske, D., 174, 181
Fitting, M., 203, 271
Fleishman, J. J., 316
Flemming, A. S., 291
Flint, M. L., 99, 107
Flynn, C. B., 210
Foley, J. M., 174
Folkman, S., 183
Folstein, M., 271, 284
Foner, A., 159, 225, 231
Ford, A. B., 52
Forman, S. H., 41
Fowler, R., 85
Foye, B. F., 140
Fozard, J. L., 71, 146, 150, 153, 154
Freud, S., 277, 295
Friedman, A. S., 127
Friedman, M., 61

Fries, J. F., 40
Fruge, E., 269
Fry, P. S., 308, 311, 314
Furchtgott, E., 4
Furry, C., 130
Furstenberg, F., 210, 215, 216, 217, 218

Gabriel, S. J., 331
Gagnon, J. H., 192
Gaitz, C. M., 296
Gallagher, D., 241, 244, 276, 290, 304, 305, 306, 307
Galper, A., 4
Gambria, L. M., 174
Garland, T. N., 343
Garrity, P., 100
Garry, P. J., 80
Gatz, M., 293, 294, 295, 298, 308, 309
Geha-Mitzel, M., 74
Gelfand, D. E., 110
George, L. K., 225, 229, 237, 260, 270, 274, 275
German, P. S., 294
Gerontologist, The, 59
Gershon, S., 318
Gesser, G., 328, 329, 331
Gianturco, D. T., 239, 275, 277
Gilson, B. S., 52, 54
Ginsberg, H., 4
Glamser, F. D., 228, 235
Glaser, B., 337, 338, 341
Glassman, J., 111
Glick, I. D., 309
Golden, R., 258
Goldfarb, A. I., 300
Goldstrom, I. D., 290, 291
Gollin, E. S., 151
Golob, K., 97
Gonda, J. N., 140
Goodrich, N., 204
Goodwin, J. M., 80
Goodwin, J. S., 80
Gordon, C., 175, 181
Gotestam, K. G., 295, 300, 309
Gottesman, L. E., 108, 109
Gould, S. J., 127
Grambs, J. D., 192
Granick, S., 80, 127
Grauer, H., 311
Greenbaum, M., 88
Greene, M. G., 97
Greenhouse, S. W., 132
Greenspoon, S., 336
Greist, J. H., 279
Greist, T. H., 279
Greulich, R. C., 47, 135, 179, 184
Grisso, J., 3
Grossman, J. L., 146, 149
Groth-Juncker, A., 97
Grotjan, M., 295, 296
Grunebaum, H. V., 208
Grunes, J., 295, 296, 298
Guider, R., 155

Gurland, B. J., 151, 153, 258, 261, 274, 275, 276
Gurland, R., 258
Gutmann, D. L., 171, 172, 173, 174, 175, 295, 296, 298
Gwyther, L., 270

Haan, N., 181, 184
Habot, B., 271
Hachinski, V. C., 267, 268
Hagestad, G., 198, 208, 215, 216, 218
Haissly, J., 193
Hale, S., 82
Haley, J., 310
Haley, W. E., 53, 214, 270, 271, 320
Hall, D. A., 42, 44
Hammen, C. L., 307
Hamovich, M., 182
Han, S. S., 74
Handal, P. J., 329
Harker, J. O., 151
Harkins, S. W., 67, 74, 148
Harley, C., 4
Harris, L., 10, 12, 231
Harroff, D., 202
Hart, R. W., 42
Hartford, M. E., 309
Hartka, E., 181, 184
Hartley, A. A., 85
Hartley, J. T., 151
Hatfield, E., 200
Haug, M., 98, 301
Havinghurst, R., 177
Hayflick, L., 40, 44
Hayslip, B., 329, 332
Hegeman, C., 113
Heinemann, G. D., 238
Henry, W., 171, 176, 187
Hertzog, C., 139
Hetland, M., 98
Heyman, D. K., 98
Hicks, L. H., 83, 86
Hilbert, N. M., 153
Hill, M., 307
Hine, V. H., 343
Hiner, S. L., 58
Hinrichs, J. V., 153
Hinton, J., 335
Hodgson, J. H., 99
Hoffman, C., 212
Hoffman, S., 97
Hofland, B., 59
Hogan, J. D., 337
Hollister, L. E., 312, 314
Holmes, T., 57
Holmes, W. M., 247
Holtzer, 259
Hood, R. B., 80
Horn, J. L., 124, 125, 128, 138, 139
Horner, K. L., 166
Houser, B. B., 209
Howard, J. H., 56
Hoyer, W. J., 21, 140, 345

Hughes, D. C., 260, 274, 275
Hughes, G. H., 270
Hulicka, I. M., 146, 149, 151
Hultsch, D., 153
Hunt, E., 151, 152
Hunt, W. C., 80
Hussian, R., 62
Huttman, E. D., 88, 89, 90

Ingersol-Dayton, B., 202
Ingram, L., 97
"Introduction: The Age of the Aging, Congregate
  Living," 88
Irion, J. C., 183

Jacewicz, M. M., 85
Jackson, B. A., 52
Jackson, J., 10
Jaffee, M. W., 52
Janson, P., 11
Jantz, R. K., 4
Jarrett, W., 213
Jarvik, L. F., 98, 121, 124, 134, 307
Jeffers, F. C., 98, 328
Jessen, A., 344
Johnsen, P. T., 212
Johnson, C. L., 201, 203, 211, 212, 216, 218, 219,
  271
Johnson, E. S., 212, 311
Johnson, H. A., 40, 48, 51
Johnson, V. E., 187, 188
Josephson, K. R., 97

Kahana, E. A., 87, 216
Kahn, R. L., 153, 154, 290
Kane, A. C., 337
Kane, R. A., 96, 97
Kane, R. L., 96, 97
Kaplan, G., 55
Kapur, T. P., 79
Kaput, Y. P., 76
Kart, C. S., 50, 51, 76, 95, 108
Kastenbaum, R., 105, 326, 330, 331, 334, 343
Katz, S., 52
Katzman, R., 271, 284
Kauser, T., 208
Kay, D. W. K., 257, 258, 259, 262, 277
Kaye, L., 112
Kazniak, A. W., 151, 153
Keating, N. C., 311
Keeler, E., 96, 97
Keil, T. J., 232
Kelly, E. L., 204
Kemeny, E., 265
Kermis, M. D., 260, 275
Kerski, D., 97
Kessler, D. R., 309
Kessler, L. G., 290, 291
Khatami, M., 304
Kiesler, C. A., 293

Kinsbourne, M., 266
Kitson, G. C., 247
Kivnick, H. Q., 217
Kiyak, A., 269
Kleban, M., 80
Kleban, M. H., 212
Klein, L., 294
Klerman, G. L., 282
Kline, D. W., 68, 71, 73
Klys, M., 55, 56
Kogan, N., 328
Kohen, J. A., 249
Kohn, R., 43
Kohout, F. J., 153
Kohut, J. J., 316
Kohut, S. J., 316
Kornhaber, A., 219
Kosberg, J. I., 108
Kramer, P. D., 291, 293
Krantz, S., 276, 306, 307
Kübler-Ross, E., 332, 333, 341
Kucharski, L. T., 293
Kuypers, J. A., 184, 185
Kuypers, J. H., 199, 210, 212

Labouvie, G. V., 21
Labouvie-Vief, G. V., 123, 124, 125, 136, 137, 140, 141
Labus, J. G., 343
Lachman, M. E., 3, 4
Lakatta, E. G., 47, 135, 179, 184
Lang, A., 210
Langer, E., 3, 4, 59, 145, 155
Langner, T. S., 259
Larson, D. B., 290, 291
Larson, D. M., 179
Larson, E. B., 273
Larson, R., 11, 177, 178, 203
LaRue, A., 98
Lassen, N. A., 267, 268
Lauer, H., 224
Lawton, M. P., 87, 88, 89, 282
Lazarus, L., 292, 293, 299
Lazarus, M., 224
Lazarus, R. S., 183
Leaf, 259
Leary, W. E., 79
Lebowitz, B., 179
Lee, G. R., 209
Lehman, H. C., 157, 158
Leiderman, D. B., 3
Leino, E. V., 133
Lemke, J. H., 153
Lemke, S., 58, 108
Lemon, B. W., 176
Lenard, F., 108
Lenhardt, M. L., 67, 74
Lesnoff-Caravaglia, G., 55, 56
Levine, E. G., 214, 270, 271, 320
Levitt, H., 76
Levkoff, S., 234

Lewis, M. I., 193, 308
Libow, L. S., 96, 114, 271
Lieberman, M. A., 111
Liebowitz, B., 88
Liem, P. H., 94
Lindemann, E., 240, 242
Lindsley, O. R., 87
Lipsett, L. P., 24
Lipton, M. A., 276
Liptzin, B., 318
Litwak, E., 210
Liu, K., 109
Livson, F., 233
Locke, B. Z., 179
Loeb, L. L., 219
Loeb, M. B., 195
Longino, C. F., 210
Lopata, H. Z., 208, 238, 246, 247, 248
Lowenthal, M. F., 174, 259
Lowy, L., 290
Lubin, J. S., 266
Lucas, M. J., 203, 269, 271
Luine, V., 265
Lund, D. A., 105, 243, 245

Maas, H. S., 184, 185
MacDonald, L. M., 18
Mace, H. L., 269
Mace, N., 103
Maddox, G. L., 98
Maeder, J., 193
Mahoney, M. J., 15, 303
Manard, B. B., 108
Mancini, J. A., 199, 209
Mantell, J., 182
Manton, K. G., 40, 109, 279, 280
Marron, K., 114
Marshal, J., 267, 268
Marshall, V. W., 211
Martin, C. E., 190, 191
Martin, G., 42
Martz, B. L., 58
Marx, J. L., 43
Masters, W. H., 187, 188
Mather, M., 317
Matthews, S. H., 211, 218
Mattoon, M. A., 22
Maurer, J. F., 74
Maxwell, R. J., 339, 340
Mazess, R. B., 41
McArthur, L. Z., 3, 4
McAuley, W. J., 210, 211
McCaghy, C. H., 336
McCarley, T., 307
McClannahan, L. E., 87, 90
McClelland, D. C., 135
McCourt, W. F., 250
McCrae, R. R., 174, 179, 180, 181, 183
McCreary, G., 274, 275
McCusker, J., 97
McFarland, R. A., 71, 85

McGinnis, G. E., 93
McKhann, G., 271, 284
Medart, P., 75, 78
Medvedev, Z. A., 41
Meerloo, J. A., 295, 298
Mendkoff, E., 58
Merton, R. K., 157, 163
Metress, E. S., 50, 51, 76, 95
Metress, J. F., 50, 51, 76, 95
Metzger, A., 334
Meyer, G., 134
Meyering, S. M., 247
Michael, S. T., 259
Miller, B. C., 200
Miller, M., 279, 280
Miller, N. E., 154, 290, 291
Miller, S., 4, 201, 203
Milligan, W. L., 4
Millsap, R., 181, 184
Milne, J. S., 62
Mintz, J., 307
Mishara, B. L., 336
Mitchell, J. B., 291, 293
Mitteness, L., 62
Miura, S. A., 151
Moffett, M., 236
Monea, H. E., 195
Monk, A., 112
Montgomery, R., 269
Moos, R. H., 58, 108
Mor, V., 292
Morgan, L., 249
Morris, J. N., 111
Moskowitz, R. W., 52
Motoike, P., 307
Murphy, C., 80, 81
Murphy, D. M., 174
Myers, G. C., 40
Myers, J. K., 259
Myerson, J., 82

Napoli, J. G., 329
Nash, S. C., 175
National Home Caring Council, 102
National Institute on Aging, 126
Nehrke, M. F., 331
Neill, P., 58
Nesselroade, J. R., 126
Nestel, G., 94
Netting, F. E., 104
Neufeld, R., 114
Neugarten, B. L., 171, 172, 173, 174, 177, 181, 182, 216, 219
Newman, G., 190, 192
Newton, N. A., 295, 296, 298
Nichols, C. R., 190, 192
Niederehe, G., 153, 269
Noelker, L. S., 62, 109
Norman, T. R., 312
Novacek, J., 183
Nowlin, J. B., 94

O'Conner-Roden, M., 205
Ogilvie, D., 177
O'Hara, M. W., 153
Okraku, I., 208
Olsen, J. K., 110
Olsho, L. W., 67, 74
Opler, M. K., 259
O'Quinn, 315
Ordy, J. M., 70, 71, 75, 78
Orentreich, N., 49
Orr, N., 214, 261, 262, 264, 270, 312, 318, 319
Orvascel, H., 259
Osberg, J. S., 93
Ostfeld, A. M., 39, 51
Otto, M. E., 343
Oyer, H. J., 76, 79

Palmore, E. B., 55, 68, 69, 74, 94, 134, 186, 225, 229, 237
Papalia-Finlay, D., 140
Parkes, C., 238, 240, 241, 242, 244
Parkes, C. M., 243
Pasternak, M., 80, 81
Paul, C., 230
Paul, L., 336
Peabody, C. A., 312, 314
Peal, R. L., 329
Pearlin, L. I., 183
Pearson, A. A., 345
Peterson, J. A., 176, 241, 244
Peterson, P., 233
Petkovsek, L., 206
Pfeiffer, E., 190, 191, 192, 292, 295, 296, 302
Pickett, J. M., 76
Pieper, H. G., 206
Pimley, S., 183
Pineo, S. P., 200
Pino, C. D., 293, 294, 295, 298, 308, 309
Planek, T., 85
Plemons, J. K., 140
Podolsky, S., 71
Pomara, N., 314
Poon, L. W., 144, 146, 147, 148, 149, 150, 151, 152, 153, 154
Popkin, S. J., 150, 153, 154, 293, 294, 295, 298, 308, 309
Poulshock, W., 109
Powell, D. A., 4
Powers, E. A., 4
Premo, T., 213
Price, D., 271, 284
Proppe, H., 89
Putnam, R. H., 163
Pyrek, J., 74

Quinn, J. L., 99
Quinn, T., 209

Rabin, D. L., 100, 106, 110
Rabins, P. V., 103, 203, 269, 271
Rahe, R., 57

Rakowski, W., 214
Rando, T. A., 242, 243, 244, 328, 329, 343, 345
Raphael, B., 250
Rathbone-McCuan, E., 103
Rea, M. P., 336
Rebok, G., 345
Rechnitzer, P. A., 56
Redburn, D. E., 105
Redick, R., 290
Reed, D., 46
Reedy, M. N., 175, 181
Reese, H. W., 24, 154
Reichard, S., 233
Reif, F., 162
Reifler, B. V., 273
Reisberg, B., 261, 263, 265, 268, 269
Reker, G. T., 328, 329, 331
Renner, V. J., 82, 83, 86
Rennie, T. A. C., 259
Retsinas, J., 100
Reveile, D. J., 53
Revenson, T. A., 183
Rickards, L. D., 291
Riegel, K. F., 12, 13, 134
Riegel, R. M., 134
Riley, M., 159
Rizer, R. L., 49
Robb, H., 52, 54
Robertson, J. F., 215, 216, 218, 219
Robinson, P., 230
Rodin, J., 3, 4, 59, 145, 155, 278
Rose, C. L., 55, 99
Rosen, J. L., 172
Rosen, R., 307
Rosenman, R., 61
Rosenthal, C. J., 211
Rosenthal, R., 76
Rosenwaike, I., 8, 198
Roskies, E., 61
Rossman, I., 49, 52
Rossman, P., 340, 342
Roth, M., 259, 263, 264, 265, 267, 277
Rothmen, M. L., 52
Rubenstein, L. A., 97
Rubenstein, L. Z., 98
Rubinstein, R., 238, 249
Rupp, R.R., 74
Rush, A. J., 304
Rushton, J. P., 166
Ryder, L. K., 11

Salthouse, T. A., 82, 83, 85, 86, 150
Santos, J. F., 291
Sathananthan, G. L., 318
Satir, V. M., 309
Saunders, C., 341
Saxon, M. J., 72, 74
Sayre, J. A., 97
Schaie, K. W., 29, 70, 127, 130, 133, 134, 135, 136, 137, 138, 139
Scheidt, B. J., 137

Scheinberg, P., 267
Schieber, F., 68, 71, 73
Schiffman, S., 80, 81
Schmidt, D., 5
Schmitz, P., 69
Schneider, C. J., 231
Schneider, E. L., 46
Schooler, C., 183
Schoonover, C. B., 212
Schram, R., 201
Schratz, M., 293
Schultz, R., 183
Schurman, R. A., 291, 293
Schwab, K., 225, 231
Schwartz, A. N., 89
Schwartz, G. E., 57
Seefeldt, C., 4
Segal, N. L., 279
Seligman, M., 278
Selmanowitz, J., 49
Serlin, R. C., 140
Serock, K., 4
Seward, M., 93
Shanas, E., 4, 98, 99, 198, 199, 207
Shapiro, S., 294
Sharps, M. J., 151
Shenfeld, M. E., 183
Sheppard, H. L., 229
Sherizen, S., 336
Sherwood, C., 111
Sherwood, S., 111, 292
Shin, K. E., 163
Shneidman, E. S., 280, 334
Shock, N. W., 42, 47, 133, 135, 179, 184
Shomaker, D., 269
Siegler, I. C., 58
Silverman, P., 238
Simberg, E. J., 295
Simonson, W., 314
Simonton, D. K., 159, 160, 161, 162
Sinnott, J. D., 150, 151
Skinner, E. A., 294
Skurnick, J., 97
Sloane, R. B., 263, 268, 272
Smith, A. D., 146, 148
Smith, K. C., 74
Smith, W. L., 266
Snyder, L. H., 74
Sokoloff, L., 132
Solnick, R. L., 188, 189, 193, 194
Solomon, D. H., 96, 97
Solomon, K., 3
Somberg, B. L., 86
Spense, D. A., 100
Spenser, B., 260
Spilka, B., 334, 336
Spirduso, W. W., 86
Spiro, A., 126
Spitzer, L., 155
Sprey, J., 218
Spring, G. K., 279

Srole, L., 259
Stadlan, E. M., 271, 284
Stankov, L., 131
Stanley, B., 314
Stanley, M., 314
Stenback, A., 279, 280
Steuer, J. L., 307
Stewart, J., 165
Stewart, L., 327
Stewart-Busse, D., 329, 332
Stine, E. L., 151
Stockton, P., 100, 106, 110
Stoller, 203
Storandt, 86
Stotsky, B., 314
Strate, J. M., 232
Strauss, A., 162, 337, 338
Strauss, P., 230
Strehler, B., 39
Streib, G., 231
Sumi, S. M., 273
Summers, M. N., 53
Sward, K., 128
Swenson, C. H., 202, 295

Taube, C., 290
Teitelbaum, M. L., 294
Teri, L., 269
Terry, R. D., 265
Thoits, P. A., 259
Thomas, J. L., 216, 218
Thomas, P. D., 80
Thompson, L. W., 86, 133, 146, 151, 153, 209, 241,
    244, 276, 290, 304, 305, 306, 307
Thurnher, M., 174
Tibbetts, C., 230
Tice, C. H., 219
Tierney, W. M., 58
Tischler, G. L., 259
Tissue, T., 98
Tobin, J. D., 39, 46, 47, 135, 179, 184
Tobin, S. S., 111, 113, 177
Todd, P. A., 203, 269, 270
Tomlinson, B., 263, 264
Trahaug, G., 202
Traupmann, J., 200
Treas, J., 198–199, 201, 207, 208, 209, 239
Treat, N. J., 153, 154
Troll, L. E., 198, 215
Tross, S., 296, 302
Tune, G. S., 85
Turner, B. F., 111
Turner, H., 300
Turner, R. W., 294

U.S. Commission on Civil Rights, 295, 296
U.S. Senate Special Committee on Aging, 5, 6, 7, 9, 50,
    52, 75, 93, 94, 95, 96, 100, 106, 110, 199, 210, 211,
    212, 223, 224, 225, 226, 227, 230, 231, 232, 238, 259
Usui, W., 232

VandenBos, G. R., 293, 294, 295, 298, 308, 309
Van Hilst, A., 239
Van Korff, M., 294
Vaughan, W. J., 69
Vernon, P. A., 166
Verwoerdt, A., 190, 192, 328
Vickers, R., 3
Vincente, L., 106
Viney, L. L., 330, 336

Wagstaff, D., 82
Walford, R. L., 45
Walker, A. J., 209
Walker, J. I., 311, 312
Wallace, R. B., 153
Wallace, W. L., 122
Wallach, M. A., 328
Wallman, L. M., 225, 229, 237
Walsh, D. A., 150, 151
Walsh-Sweeney, L., 150, 151, 152, 153, 154
Wang, H. S., 94, 190, 192, 269
Warner, D., 312, 314
Wasow, M., 195
Waterhouse, G. L., 337
Watson, W. H., 339, 340
Waxman, H. M., 274, 275
Wechsler, D., 119, 120, 121
Weiland, G. D., 97
Weinberg, J., 292, 293, 299
Weinberger, M., 58
Weiner, J. M., 100
Weinman, C., 155
Weinrit, R. M., 274, 275
Weinstein, K. K., 216, 218
Weisman, A., 334, 335, 336
Weismann, M. M., 259
Weiss, A., 80
Weiss, R. S., 243, 244
Weiss, S. M., 57
Weksler, M., 265
Welford, A. T., 67, 82, 83, 84, 85, 86
West, R., 154
Westbrook, M., 336
Whelihan, W. M., 282
Whitbourne, S., 48, 49, 50, 56, 73, 80, 128, 129
White, R. M., 293
White House Conference on Aging, 7
Whiteford, H. A., 312, 314
Wiley, J., 106
Wilkie, F., 123, 133
Williams, T. F., 96
Willis, S. L., 24, 126, 134, 136, 140
Wilson, C. C., 104
Wilson, K. B., 218, 219
Wingfield, A., 151
Wiseman, R. F., 210
Wisneiwski, H., 265
Wister, A., 208
Wolf, E., 71
Wolfe, D. M., 200
Wolpe, J., 304

Wong, P. T., 328, 329, 331
Wood, V., 215
Woodbury, M. A., 279, 280
Woodruff, D. S., 150
Woodward, K. L., 219
Worden, J. W., 240, 242, 244, 336
Wright, S. D., 105

Yalom, I., 307
Yarrow, M. R., 132
Yeo, G., 97

Zabriskie, J. B., 265
Zarit, J., 214, 261, 262, 264, 312, 318, 319
Zarit, J. M., 203, 269, 270, 276, 277
Zarit, S. H., 153, 155, 203, 214, 261, 262, 264,
    269, 270, 276, 277, 307, 309, 312, 317, 318,
    319
Zelinski, E. M., 151
Zimmer, J. G., 97
Zonderman, A. B., 179, 180
Zuckerman, H., 157, 163

Subject Index

☐

Acceptance stage, of dying, 333
Activity:
  busy ethic and retirement, 229
  theory, 176–178
Acuity, visual, 68–69
Adjustment:
  coping and age, 182–184
  to nursing home, 111, 113
  to retirement, 233–235
  to widowhood, 246–248
Adult children of elderly parents:
  advice giving and, 209
  care of ill parents, 210–214
  family uninvolvement, myth of, 207
  frequency of contact and closeness, 209–210
  intergenerational households, 207, 208
  intimacy at a distance, concept of, 207
  psychological risk factors, 212–214
Advocacy group, for nursing home residents, 112
Age discrimination, retirement and, 229–230
Ageism, 4
Aging, physical process of (*see also individual topics*):
  Baltimore Longitudinal Study findings, 46–47
  biological theories of, 40–45
  cellular changes, 42–43
  graying of hair, 48, 49
  lifestyle and, 53–60
  musculoskeletal changes, 49–50
  normal, 46–50
  patterns of, 47
  physical changes, 39–40
  reserve capacity concept, 48
  skin changes, 49
  variability and aging, 47
Aging, psychological denial of, 3–5
Aging pattern, 123, 127
Aging population, demographic view of, 5–11 (*see also* Older adults)
Alzheimer's disease, 263–267
  acetylcholine deficiencies, 267
  caregiver support groups, 319–320
  early diagnosis of, 318–319
  neural deterioration in, 263–265
  personality changes, 269–270
  possible causes of, 265–267
  primary degenerative dementia as, 263
  reaction time and, 86
  treatment of, 318
Amplified foods, 81

Anticipatory socialization:
  bereavement, 245
  retirement, 228
Anxiety:
  about death, 330–332
  drugs to relieve, 311, 313–314
  testing situation and, 129–130, 149, 150
Attachment response, and bereavement, 240
Autonomy:
  effects of, 58–60
  and life in nursing homes, 108–109

Baltimore Longitudinal Study:
  method and outcome, 32
  personality research, 178–182
  physiology and aging, 46–47
  sexual interest and activity, 191, 194
Bargaining stage, of dying, 333
Behaviorism, concepts of, 14–19
  and aging, 16, 17, 19, 21
Behavior modification:
  incontinence, 62–63
  memory training, 154–156
  phobias, 303–304
  sexual response, 194
Behavior therapy, 302–307
  for depression, 304–306
Bereavement:
  early symptoms of, 240–241
  guilt in, 240, 241
  normal mourning, 241–243
  pathological mourning, 243–245
  pioneering study of, 240
  sex differences in, 244–245, 246
Biological theories, 43–45 (*see also* Aging, physical process of)
Blood pressure, cognitive functioning and, 133
Bones, in aging body, 49–51
Brain, deterioration in Alzheimer's disease, 263–265

Caregiving, strains and stresses of, 270–271
Cataracts, 72
CAT scan, for assessment of dementia, 284–285
Cellular changes, in aging, 42–43
Central nervous system (CNS), 83
Children, *see* Adult children of elderly parents
Chronic diseases, 51–53
Classical conditioning, 14
Codification hypothesis, 164
Cognitive behavior therapy, for depression, 304–306

Cognitive learning theory, 14, 15, 21
Cognitive skill training, 154, 155
Cohort, 27
Color vision, 72
Conductive hearing loss, 78
Congregate-care housing, 88–89
Consumer Union survey, 189–190
Continuing care retirement community, 104
Continuum of care, 88
Coping, and age, 182–184
Correlational approach, 30
Counseling, retirement, 235
Creativity, and age, 126, 156–166
    in the arts, 159–162
    and fluid intelligence, 157
    pioneering study of, 157–159
    in the sciences, 162–166
Crime, fear of, 10–11
Cross-sectional studies, 26–27
Crystallized intelligence, 157
    age and, 124–127
Custodial care, 292

Dark adaptation, 73
Dating, among the elderly, 205–206
Day programs, 103
Death and dying:
    anxiety about, 330–332
    Erikson's view of, 24, 328
    fear of, 328–330
    health care professionals' treatment of, 336–339
    hospice care, 340–343
    humanizing hospital care, 343–345
    Jung's view of, 23
    personality and, 335–336
    psychotherapy, 345–346
    research, focus of, 327
    stages of dying, 333–335
    terminal-drop phenomenon, 133–135
    thoughts about, 327–328
Decision-making powers, effects of, 59–60
Delirium, 271–272
Dementia, 260–271
    Alzheimer's disease, 263–267
    assessment of, 284–285
    biological treatments of, 318–319
    environmental treatments, 315–318
    group therapy, 307–309
    multi-infarct , 263, 267–268
    personality changes and, 268–270
    prevalence of, 262–263
    psychotherapy, 296–307
    stress of caregiving and, 270–271
    symptoms of, 260–262
    time factors in, 261–262
Demographics of aging, 5–11
Denial stage, of dying, 333
Depression, 272–281
    in Alzheimer's disease, 269–270
    antidepressant drugs for, 311, 313
    biological aspects of, 278–279

    causes of, 276–278
    versus dementia, 272–273
    diagnosis, 273–283
    and dying, 333
    major, 275–276
    minor, 276
    prevalence of, 275
    psychological aspects of, 277–278
    suicide and, 279–281
    symptoms of, 274–275
    treatment of, 276, 278, 279, 304–306
Desensitization, 303–304
Diabetic retinopathy, 72
Diet and nutrition, 45–46
Disabilities:
    ecological approach to, 87–90
    excess, 53
    functional impairment, 51–53
    nondisease factors, 54
    trajectory of, 93–95
Disabled elderly, care of:
    continuing care retirement community, 104
    day programs, 103
    home care, 101–103
    nursing homes, 99–101, 105–113
    respite care, 103, 105
    specialized services, 105
Disease, 40, 51
Disengagement theory, 173, 176–177
Divorce:
    effects of on grandparents, 218–219
    versus widowhood, 247
DNA, in theory of aging, 43–44
Double jeopardy, 10
Driving, 85
Duke Longitudinal Study:
    method and outcome, 31–32
    sexual interest and activity in, 190, 191, 192

Ecological approach to disabilities, 87
Economic factors, see Financial aspects of aging
Educational programs, for retirees, 236
EEG, use of, in assessment of dementia, 285
Ego energy, 172
Ego integrity:
    and death anxiety, 331–332
    versus despair, 23–24
Empty nest, 199
Encoding, memory, 147, 148, 149
Environmental influences, 56–60
Epidemiology, of later-life mental disorders, 257–260
Erection, penile:
    changes with aging, 188–189
    erectile dysfunction, 193
    penile implants, 194
Erikson's theory, 23–24
    approach to death and dying, 328
Estrogen, 188
Excess disabilities, 53
Exercise:
    rate of aging and, 56

Exercise (*continued*)
   response speed and, 86–87
   and skeletal system, 50
Extinction, 16
Extroversion, 179
Eye, *see* Vision

Familiarity, as memory aid, 149
Family uninvolvement, myth of, 207
Fear of death, 328–330
Fears, *see* Phobias
Fiction writing, and age, 161
Financial aspects of aging, 10, 226–227, 230–237, 294
Fluid intelligence, 124–127, 157
Foods, amplified, 81
Free will, effects of, 58–60
Freud's theory, about depression, 277
Functional impairment, 51–53

Generalization, 14, 16
Genetic defect, in Alzheimer's disease, 266–267
Geriatric medicine, 96–98
Glaucoma, 72
Grandparents:
   divorce, effects of, 218–219
   as family stabilizers, 215
   interactions with teenagers, 217
   matrifocal tilt and, 218–219
   meaningful role of, 215
   norm of noninterference, 218
   styles of grandparenting, 216–217
   watchdog role, 215
Graying of hair, 48, 49
Group therapy, 307–309
Guilt and bereavement, 240, 241

Hair cells, atrophy of, 78
Health, 11
Health habits, impact of, 55–56
Hearing, 74–80
   age-related changes, 78
   aids for, 79
   loss, 79–80
   steps involved in, 76–78
Heart attacks, sexuality and, 193
Heart disease, reaction time and, 86
Helplessness:
   feeling of, in depression, 277–278
   operant techniques and, 18
Home-based adaptations, 89–90
Home care, 101–103
   costs of, 101–102
   hospice teams, 343
   types of services, 101, 102
Hospice care, 340–343
Housing design, 87–89
   adapting private homes, 89–90
   congregate-care housing, 88–89
Hypothalamus, 44

Illness:
   adult children as caregivers, 210–212
   and IQ testing, 131–133
   marital quality and, 202–204
   retirement and, 229
   sexuality and, 193
   terminal, 330–331, 334–335
Immune system, 44–45
Incontinence, 62–63
Insight-oriented therapy, 298, 300, 301
Insurance, nursing home, 100
Intelligence:
   blood pressure and, 133
   fluid vs. crystallized, 124–127, 134–135
   two-factor theory, 124–127
Intelligence tests (*see also* Wechsler Adult Intelligence Scale):
   age-relevant, 136–140
   factors affecting scores on, 127–131
   improving performance on, 140–141
   IQ losses, debates about, 138–139
   terminal-drop phenomenon, 133–135
   validity of, 135–136
   Wechsler Adult Intelligence Scale (WAIS), 119–123
Interiority, 171–172
Intimacy at a distance, 207
"Intrinsic" changes, 39
Isolation:
   and suicide, 280
   of widows, 248–249

Joints, changes in, 49–50
Jung's theory, 22–23
   research as support for, 173

Kansas City Studies of Adult Life, 171–174

Laboratory tests, age norms and, 46
Learning theory (*see also* Behaviorism)
   cognitive, 14, 15, 21
Life events:
   and illness, 57–59
   on-time versus off-time events, 183
   relocation effect, 58
Life expectancy:
   demographic view of, 6–7
   disease control factors, 8
   historical and geographical differences, 42
   and life style, 55
   minority populations, 9–10
   Soviet Georgians, 41
Life satisfaction, 11–12
   and meaningful activities, 177–178
   and personality, 180
Life span:
   average, 40
   extending, 45–46
   maximum, 40, 45–46
   of related versus unrelated persons, 55

Life-span developmental approach, 24–34
  basis of, 25
  research methods, 25–32
Lifestyle:
  effects of, on aging, 53–60
  interventions, 60–63
Literature, written output and age, 161
Longitudinal studies, 28–29, 31–32
  Baltimore Longitudinal Study, 32
  Duke Longitudinal Study, 31–32
  limitations of, 28–29
  method of, 28
  of scientific creativity and age, 164–166
  time-of-measurement effects, 29

Marriage:
  division of labor and marital quality, 205
  empty nest period, 199
  and family therapy, 309–311
  golden anniversary marriages, profile of, 205
  illness and, 202–204
  lasting, factors in, 204
  marital-quality studies, 199–204
  newly married elderly, 205–207
  remarriage and widowhood, 239, 247
  sexuality and, 191–192
  as vital relationship, 202
Mastery styles, 172–173, 182
Matrifocal tilt, and grandparents, 218–219
Maximum life span, 40
Mediators, as memory aid, 149, 154
Medicaid, and nursing homes, 106
Medical profession:
  approach to disabilities, 96
  attitudes toward elderly, 97–98
  elderly's attitudes toward, 98–99
  ongoing patient management, 95–96
  time spent with elderly patients, 98–99
Medicare, 100–102
Memory, 145–146
  age changes in, 147–150
  aids to, 149–150
  interventions for, 153–156
  laboratory investigations of, 145–146
  naturalistic research trends, 151–152
  processes in, 146–147
  research problems, 150–153
  senile plaques and brain, 264–265
  time pressure as hindrance, 149, 150
Memory training, 153–156
  behavior modification, 154–156
  cognitive skill training, 154, 155
  simple practice, 153–154, 156
Men:
  sex-role shifts and aging, 173–175
  sexual response, 188–189
  successful marriage and personality, 204
  suicide and, 279–280
Mental disorders (see also specific disorders):
  delirium, 271–272
  dementia, 260–271

depression, 272–281
  diagnostic evaluation of, 281–285
  epidemiological studies, 257–258
Mental health professionals, types of, 283
Mental health system:
  aversion to treating elderly, 295–296
  behavior therapy, 302–307
  custodial care, 292
  effectiveness of, 296
  group therapy, 307–309
  hierarchy of services, 291, 292
  lack of use by elderly, 292–295
  marriage and family therapy, 309–311
  nursing homes and mentally ill, 292
  psychotherapy, 296–302
  psychotropic drug treatment, 311–315
Mental status, of nursing home patients, 110–111
Midlife crisis, 22
Minorities:
  double jeopardy, 10
  life expectancy, 9–10
Modeling, 17
Motor performance, see Response speed
Mourning, see Bereavement
Movement time, 83
Moving, relocation effect of, 58
Multi-infarct dementia, 263, 267–268, 318
Musculoskeletal changes, 49–50

Neuroticism, 179
Neurotransmitters:
  abnormalities in depression, 278–279
  alterations in treatment for dementia, 318
Norepinephrine, 278–279
Nursing homes, 99–101, 105–113
  abuses in, 106–107, 113
  admission contracts, 108–109
  costs, 100, 106
  crisis decision making and, 99
  improvement efforts, 112
  Jewish Institute for Geriatric Care, 113–114
  mentally ill patients, 292
  neglect of patients, 109
  projections of population, 106
  quality of, 107–109
  reasons for admission, 110
  residents, 109–113
  return to community and, 99, 101
  types of, 107

Older adults:
  categories of, 8
  economic concerns, 10
  median income, 9
  satisfaction/happiness, 11–12
  survey on aging and results, 10–11
Ombudsman program, for nursing home residents, 112
Openness to experience, 179
Operant conditioning, 15, 16
Orgasm, changes and aging, 188–189

Osteoarthritis, 50, 51
Osteoporosis, 50, 51

Pain control, in hospices, 342
Parental imperative, 174–175
Pathological mourning, 243–245
Patterns of aging, 47
Pensions and retirement, 227
Performance subtests (WAIS), 120, 121, 123
Personality:
    activity theory, 176–178
    adjustment to retirement and, 233–235
    changes of, in dementia, 268–270
    coping, 182–184
    death reactions and, 335–336
    disengagement theory, 173, 176–177
    ego energy, 172
    extraversion, 179
    happiness and, 180
    interiority, 171–172
    mastery styles, 172–173, 182
    neuroticism, 179
    openness to experience, 179
    stability, 178–179, 184–186
Personality research:
    Baltimore Longitudinal Study, 178–182
    Jung's theory and, 173
    Kansas City Studies of Adult Life, 171–174
    sex-differences investigation, 173–175, 184–185
    Thematic Apperception Test (TAT), 171–173, 174
Person/environment congruence, 87–90
Phobias, 303–304
Physicians, see Medical profession
Pluralism, psychological theories and, 25
Poetry writing, and age, 161
Positron Emission Tomography (PET) scan, 285
Prejudice about age, 162–163
Presbycusis, 76
Presbyopia, 69
Primary memory, 147
Programmed-aging theories, 44–45
Prospective studies, 55
Prosthetic environments, 87
    home-based adaptations, 89–90
    housing design, 87–89
Psychoanalytic theory, 19–21
    of depression, 277
    id/ego/superego, 19
    implications for the aged, 20–21, 22
    parental influences, 19–20
    personality development, 19–20
Psychological disorders, 259 (See also Mental disorders)
Psychological effects, of retirement, 233–235
Psychological tests, 284
Psychological theories:
    behaviorism, 14–19
    Erikson's theory, 23–24
    Jung's theory, 22–23
    life-span developmental approach, 24–34

pluralism, 25
psychoanalytic theory, 19–21
Psychomotor performance, 82 (see also Response speed)
    central nervous system (CNS), 83
    movement time, 83
    reaction-time experiments, 82
    responding, phases of, 82–83
Psychotherapy, 296–311
    behavior therapy, 302–307
    for the dying, 345–346
    effectiveness of, 300–302
    group, 307–309
    marital and family, 309–311
    psychoanalytic, 297–302
    therapeutic alliance in, 298
Psychotropic drug treatment, 311–315
    antianxiety drugs, 313–314
    antidepressant drugs, 313
    antipsychotic drugs, 312–313
    guidelines for use, 314
    toxic effects, 314
    tradenames, 313

Random-damage theories of aging, 43–44
Reaction-time experiments, 82
Reality orientation, 316–317
Recruitment, 76
Reinforcement, 15–16, 18
    schedules of, 16–17
    scientific creativity and, 165
Relaxation methods, 61
Research methods:
    cohort factors and, 27, 28, 29
    correlational approach, 30
    cross-sectional studies, 26–27
    experiments, 30
    longitudinal studies, 28–29, 31–32
    outcome studies, 296
    prospective studies, 55
    reaction time experiments, 82
    retrospective reports, 57
    sequential strategies, 29
Reserve capacity, 48
Respite care, 103, 105
Response speed:
    age-related changes, 82–86
    diseases and, 86
    effects of changes, 86
    elderly drivers, 85
    individual differences, 86
Retinal detachment, 72
Retirement:
    adjustment to, 234–235
    busy ethic and, 229
    consequences of, 230–233
    decision making about, 225–230
    early-retirement trend, 224–225
    early versus late retirees, 229, 233
    legal factors, 224
    personality and, 233–235

Retirement (*continued*)
  postretirement, 235–237
  Social Security and, 227
  working retirees, 236–237
Retirement communities, 104
Retrieval, memory, 147, 148
Retrospective reports, 57
Role changes, anticipatory socialization, 228

Satisfaction, *see* Life satisfaction
Schedules of reinforcement, 16–17
Sciences, creativity in, 162–166
Secondary memory, 147
Senile macular degeneration, 72
Senility, delirium, 271–272
Senses:
  ecological approach to disabilities, 87–90
  hearing, 74–80
  response speed, 82–86
  sensorimotor system, 84
  sensory store, 146–147
  taste and smell, 80–81
  testing bias, 67
  vision, 68–74
Sequential strategies, 29
Sex differences:
  in bereavement, 244–245, 246
  and suicide, 279–280
Sex-role shifts, and aging, 173–175, 184–185
Sexuality:
  dating couples, 206
  erectile dysfunction, 193
  factors influencing, 191–193
  illness and, 193
  interventions for dysfunction, 194–195
  marital status and, 191–192
  physical changes, 188
  sexual interest and activity, 189–191
  sexual response, 187–189
  stereotypes about aging, 186–187
Sight, *see* Vision
Skin changes, 49
Social day centers, 103
Social life, widows, 246–248
Social Security, and retirement, 227
Specialized services, 105
Storage, memory, 147
Stress:
  caregivers of Alzheimer's victim, 270–271
  coping and age, 182–184
  effects of, 56–57
  relaxation methods, 61
  relocation effect, 58
  Type A behavior, 61–62
Strokes:
  multi-infarct dementia, 267–268
  reaction time and, 86
Suicide, 279–281
  isolation and, 280
  rates by age, 280
  sex differences, 279–280
Supportive therapy, 300

Tasks of mourning, 242, 243
Taste and smell:
  and amplified foods, 81
  studies on, 80–81
Terminal-drop phenomenon, 133–135
Terminally ill, imminent death and, 330–331,
  334–335, 336
Testosterone, 188
Time-of-measurement effects, longitudinal studies, 29
Traffic accidents, elderly drivers, 85
Transference, 299
Two-factor theory, intelligence, 124–127
Type A behavior:
  modification of, 61–62
  reaction time and, 86
  underlying problem, 61

Validity, IQ tests, 135–136
Vasodilating drugs, treatment for dementia, 318
Verbal subtests, WAIS, 120, 123
Virus, Alzheimer's disease, 265
Vision, 68–74
  age-related changes, 70–73
  cataracts, 72
  color vision, 72
  dark adaptation, 73
  diabetic retinopathy, 72
  effects of visual impairments, 73–74
  glaucoma, 72
  presbyopia, 69
  retinal detachment, 72
  senile macular degeneration, 72
  steps involved in, 69–71
  visual-acuity impairments, 68–69
Volunteer programs, for retirees, 236

Wechsler Adult Intelligence Scale (WAIS):
  age group and IQ, 121
  age-related changes, 121–123
  aging pattern, 123, 127
  IQ, formulation of, 120–121
  longitudinal study of, 123
  performance subtests, 120, 121, 123
  as predictor of death, 134–135
  verbal subtests, 120, 123
Widowhood, 237–251 (*see also* Bereavement)
  bereavement, 239–245
  changes related to, 238
  counseling services, 250
  emotional life in, 249
  isolation in, 248–249
  lifestyles, 246–248
  remarriage and, 239
  sanctification of dead spouse, 247–248
  statistical information about, 238
  studies, focus of, 238–239
Women (*see also* Widowhood):
  care of elderly parent, 210–212
  sex-role shifts and aging, 173–175
  sexual response, 187–189
Wrinkling of skin, 49

CREDITS

These pages represent an extension of the copyright page.

PART-OPENING PHOTOS. **1,** Courtesy of David S. Strickler, © Atoz Images. **35,** Courtesy of Alex Webb, © Magnum. **115,** Courtesy of Alex Webb, © Magnum. **167,** Courtesy of Marianne Gontarz. **253,** Courtesy of Alex Webb, © Magnum. **323,** Courtesy of Freda Leinwand, Monkmeyer Press Photo Service.

CHAPTER 1. **12, Table 1-1:** From *Aging in the Eighties: America in Transition,* 1981, published by the National Council on the Aging, Inc. **13, Figure 1-5:** From "The History of Psychological Gerontology," by K. Riegel. In J. E. Birren and K. W. Schaie (Eds.), *Handbook of the Psychology of Aging.* Copyright © 1977 by Van Nostrand Reinhold Company. Reprinted by permission of the publisher. **29, Table 1-2:** From "A Physiological, Psychological, and Sociological Study of Aging," by E. Busse. In E. Palmore (Ed.), *Normal Aging.* Copyright © 1970 by Duke University Press. Reprinted by permission.

CHAPTER 2. **42, Figure 2-1:** From *The Biology of Senescence,* by A. Comfort. Copyright © 1979 by Alex Comfort. Reprinted by permission of Elsevier Science Publishing Company and the author. **54, Table 2-1:** From "The Sickness Impact Profile: Development and Final Revision of a Health Status Measure," by Bergner et al., *Medical Care, 19,* 787–805. Reprinted by permission.

CHAPTER 3. **70, Figure 3-1:** From *Handbook of the Psychology of Aging,* by J. E. Birren and K. W. Schaie. Copyright © 1977 by Van Nostrand Reinhold Company. Slides prepared by Dr. Leon Pastalan. Reprinted by permission of the publisher. **84, Figure 3-5:** From "Motor Performance," by A. T. Welford. In J. E. Birren and K. W. Schaie (Eds.), *Handbook of the Psychology of Aging.* Copyright © 1977 by Van Nostrand Reinhold Company. Reprinted by permission of the publisher. **88, Figure 3-6:** From "Introduction: The Age of the Aging: Congregate Living," *Progressive Architecture,* August 1981, pp. 64–68. A team project of: Donham and Sweeney—Architects of record; Korobkin Jahan Associates—Design Architects; Building Diagnostics, Inc.—Design and Research Coordination. Photo by Steve Rosenthal. Reprinted by permission.

CHAPTER 4. **102, Table 4-3:** Adapted from *All About Home Care: A Consumer's Guide,* National Home Caring Council, New York, NY, 1981.

CHAPTER 5. **120, Table 5-1:** Adapted and reproduced by permission from the *Wechsler Adult Intelligence Scale Manual.* Copyright © 1955 by The Psychological Corporation. All rights reserved. Similar questions from the Wechsler Scales courtesy of The Psychological Corporation. **121, Table 5-2:** Adapted and reproduced by permission from the *Wechsler Adult Intelligence Scale Manual.* Copyright © 1955 by The Psychological Corporation. All rights reserved. **122, Figure 5-1:** Adapted from "Standardization of the Wechsler Adult Intelligence Scale for Older Persons," by J. E. Doppelt and W. L. Wallace, *Journal of Abnormal and Social Psychology,* 1955, *51,* 312–330. Reprinted by permission. **125, Figure 5-2:** From "Intellectual Abilities," by J. Botwinick. In J. E. Birren and K. W. Schaie (Eds.), *Handbook of the Psychology of Aging.* Copyright © 1977 by Van Nostrand Reinhold Company. Reprinted by permission of the publisher. **126, Figure 5-3:** From *Medicine for the Layman: The Brain in Aging and Dementia,* NIH Publication 83-2625. **129, Table 5-3:** From "Test Anxiety in Elderly and Young Adults," by S. K. Whitbourne. In *International Journal of Aging and Human Development,* 1976, 7, 201–210. Copyright © 1976 by Baywood Publishing Company. Reprinted by permission. **137, Figure 5-4:** From "Toward a Stage Theory of Adult Cognitive Development," by K. W. Schaie. In *The International Journal of Aging and Human Development,* 1977–78, *8,* 129–138. Reprinted by permission.

CHAPTER 6. **146, Table 6-1:** Adapted from "Age Group Comparisons for the Use of Mediators in Paired Associate Learning," by I. M. Hulicka and J. L. Grossman, *Journal of Gerontology,* 1967, *22,* 46–51. **159, Table 6-2:** Adapted from "The Age Decrement in Outstanding Scientific Contributions: Fact or Artifact," by W. Dennis. In *American Psychologist,* 1958, *13,* 457–460. Copyright © 1958 by the American Psychological Association. Reprinted by permission of the publisher. **160, Table 6-3:** Adapted from "Creative Productivity between the Ages of 20 and 80," by W. Dennis. In *Journal of Gerontology*, 1966, *21*, 1–18. Copyright © 1966 by The Gerontological Society. Reprinted by permission.

CHAPTER 7.   172, Table 7-1: Adapted from *The Country of Old Men: Cultural Studies in the Psychology of Later Life,* by D. L. Gutmann. Copyright © 1969 by the Institute of Gerontology, University of Michigan–Wayne State University. Reprinted by permission. **185, Table 7-2:** Adapted from *From Thirty to Seventy*, by H. S. Maas and J. Kuypers. Copyright © 1975 by Jossey-Bass, Inc. Reprinted by permission.

CHAPTER 9.   244, Table 9-1: From *Bereavement: Studies of Grief in Adult Life,* by C. M. Parkes. Copyright © 1972 by International Universities Press. Reprinted by permission.

CHAPTER 10.   262, Table 10-2: Adapted from "The Epidemiology of Mental Disorders Among the Aged in the Community," by D. W. Kay and K. Bergmann. In J. Birren and R. B. Sloane (Eds.), *Handbook of Mental Health and Aging.* Copyright © 1980 by Prentice-Hall, Inc. Reprinted by permission. **264, Figure 10-1:** From *The Hidden Victims of Alzheimer's Disease: Families Under Stress,* by S. H. Zarit, N. Orr, and J. Zarit. Copyright © 1985 by New York University Press. Reprinted by permission. **266, Figure 10-2:** From *Aging and Dementia,* by W. L. Smith and M. Kinsbourne (Eds.). Copyright © 1977 by Spectrum Publications, Inc. Reprinted by permission. **268, Figure 10-3:** From *Brain Failure: An Introduction to Current Concepts of Senility,* by B. Reisberg. Copyright © 1981 by Barry Reisberg, M.D. Reprinted by permission. **280, Figure 10-4:** From *Suicide in Middle Age and Later Life: Sex and Race Specific Life-Table and Cohort Analysis,* by K. Manton, D. Blazer, and M. Woodbury. Copyright © 1987 by Kenneth Manton, Dan Blazer, and Max Woodbury. Reprinted by permission.

CHAPTER 11.   305, Table 11-2: From "Cognitive Therapy for Depression in the Elderly: A Promising Model for Treatment and Research," by D. Gallagher and L. W. Thompson. In L. D. Breslau and M. R. Haug (Eds.), *Depression and Aging: Causes, Care, and Consequences.* Copyright © 1983 by Springer Publishing Company. Reprinted by permission. **305–306, excerpt:** From "Cognitive Therapy with Older Adults," by L. W. Thompson, R. Davies, D. Gallagher, and S. Krantz, *Clinical Gerontologist, 5,* 245–280. Reprinted by permission. **308, 315, excerpts:** From *Depression, Stress, and Adaptations in the Elderly: Psychological Assessment and Treatment,* by P. S. Fry. Copyright © 1986 by Aspen Publishing Company. **310–311, excerpt:** From "Welfare Emotions and Family Therapy in Geriatrics," by H. Grauer, D. Betts, and F. Birnbom, *Journal of the American Geriatrics Society,* 1973, *21,* 21–24. Reprinted by permission. **319, excerpt:** *The Hidden Victims of Alzheimer's Disease: Families Under Stress,* by S. H. Zarit, N. Orr, and J. Zarit. Copyright © 1985 by New York University Press. Reprinted by permission.

CHAPTER 12.   340, Figure 12-1: From *Human Aging and Dying,* by W. H. Watson and R. J. Maxwell. © 1977 by St. Martin's Press.